This study brings recent scholarly debates on oral cultures and literate societies to bear on the earliest recorded literature in German (800–1300). It considers the criteria for assessing what works were destined for listeners, what examples anticipated readers, and how far both modes of reception could apply to one work, exploring the possible interplay between them.

The opening two chapters review previous scholarship and the introduction of writing into preliterate Germany. The core of the book presents lexical and non-lexical evidence for the different modes of reception, taken from the whole spectrum of genres, from dance songs to liturgy, from drama and heroic literature to the court narrative and lyric poetry. The social contexts of reception and the physical process of reading books are also considered. Two concluding chapters explore the literary and historical implications of the slow interpenetration of orality and literacy. There is a comprehensive bibliographical index of primary sources.

Medieval Listening and Reading

Medieval Listening and Reading
The primary reception of German literature 800–1300

D. H. GREEN
Trinity College, Cambridge

Published by the Press Syndicate of the University of Cambridge
The Pitt Building, Trumpington Street, Cambridge CB2 1RP
40 West 20th Street, New York, NY 10011–4211, USA
10 Stamford Road, Oakleigh, Melbourne 3166, Australia

© Cambridge University Press 1994

First published 1994

Printed in Great Britain at the University Press, Cambridge

A catalogue record for this book is available from the British Library

Library of Congress cataloguing in publication data
Green, Dennis Howard, 1922–
Medieval Listening and Reading: the primary reception of German literature 800–1300 / D. H. Green.
p. cm.
Includes bibliographical references and index.
ISBN 0 521 44493 4
1. German literature – Old High German, 750–1050 – History and criticism.
2. German literature – Middle High German, 1050–1500 – History and criticism.
3. Oral tradition – Germany. I. Title.
PT183.G67 1994
830.9'001 – dc20 93-33626 CIP

ISBN 0 521 44493 4 hardback

CE

Contents

Preface   *page* xi
List of abbreviations   xiii

PART I: Preliminary problems

1 Orality and writing   3
   a. Recent work 4; b. The oral-formulaic theory 5; c. The introduction of writing 7; d. Medieval literacy and illiteracy 8; e. Hearing and reading 10; f. The introduction of printing 12; g. Avoiding anachronisms 15; h. Guidelines 17

2 The historical background   20
   a. Native orality 21; b. Written tradition 26; c. Orality within the written tradition 30; d. Writing in an oral society 35; e. Obstacles to the written tradition 40; f. The Carolingian renaissance of literacy 43; g. The transition of Old High German to a written tradition 47; h. The course of Old High German as a written tradition 50

PART II: Three modes of reception

Introduction   57

3 Criteria for reception by hearing   61
   a. Collective function and reception 63
   Non-lexical evidence 65
   b. Singing 65; c. Musical evidence 67; d. Dance song 69; e. Processional song 70; f. Court entertainment 71; g. Collective audience 73; h. Request for attention 77; i. *Tu autem, domine, miserere nobis* 78; j. Memorisation 79
   Lexical evidence 79
   k. *Hoeren* 79; l. *Sprechen, sagen, singen* 82; m. *Lesen* 84; n. *Lesen oder hoeren* 93

4 Survey of reception by hearing   95
   a. Functional literature 95; b. Literature of religious worship and instruction 96; c. Legal literature 99; d. Historiography 101; e. Biblical literature 102; f. Legends 103; g. Drama 105; h. Heroic literature 105; i. Court narrative literature 107; j. Lyric poetry 110

5 Criteria for reception by reading   113
   Ambiguous criteria   115
   a. *Wir lesen; man liset*   115; b. *Schrîben* + dative   117; c. *Hie stân*   118; d. *Suochen; vinden*   119; e. *Obene; dort vorne*   121; f. Recommendations to collate, copy or skip the text   123; g. Recommendations to consult the source or further texts   124; h. Text and illustration   126; i. The book or story in the first person   128

   Less ambiguous criteria   130
   j. Recommendations to correct the text   130; k. Acrostics and anagrams   131; l. Physical contact with the book   134

   Lexical evidence   135
   m. *Lesen* + reflexive dative   136; n. *Lesen* + *selber*   137; o. *Lesen, sehen, schouwen*   139; p. *Lesen oder hoeren*   141; q. The individual reader   142; r. Oral aspects of reading   147

6 Survey of reception by reading   150
   a. Functional literature   150; b. Literature of religious worship and instruction   152; c. Legal literature   154; d. Historiography   156; e. Biblical literature   157; f. Legends   159; g. Drama   160; h. Heroic literature   161; i. Court narrative literature   163; j. Lyric poetry   166

7 Criteria for the intermediate mode of reception   169
   a. Diagonal channels of communication   170; b. Criteria for recognition   172; c. Latin examples   177; d. Otfrid von Weissenburg   179; e. Notker the German   183; f. Hartmann von Aue   186; g. Wolfram von Eschenbach, *Parzival*   190; h. Gottfried von Strassburg   194; i. Brun von Schönebeck, *Das Hohe Lied*   198

8 Survey of the intermediate mode of reception   203
   Genres   203
   a. Functional literature   204; b. Literature of religious worship and instruction   204; c. Legal literature   205; d. Historiography   205; e. Biblical literature   206; f. Legends   207; g. Drama   208; h. Heroic literature   208; i. Court narrative literature   208; j. Lyric poetry   210

   Context of reception   210
   k. Court of the secular aristocracy   211; l. Monastery   215; m. Town   219; n. Religious lay community   222; o. Episcopal court   223

   The double formula   225
   p. *Hoeren oder lesen*   225

   Conclusions for Part II   231

PART III: Conclusions

9 Literacy, history and fiction   237
   History and literacy or orality   237
   a. The Latin conception of written history   237; b. Oral history   239; c. Written and oral history   242; d. Written history in the vernacular   244

Fiction and literacy or orality 249

e. History and fiction in Arthurian material 249; f. Examples of fiction in the romance 254

The return to history 265

g. Thirteenth-century developments 265; h. The Grail romance 267

10 Recital and reading in their historical context   270

a. Historical factors in the rise of vernacular written literature 270; b. Education and literacy 279; c. Vernacular literacy 284; d. Dating of the intermediate mode of reception 299; e. Individual reading 303; f. Cleric and layman, Latin and vernacular 310

Appendix   Middle High German 'lesen' = 'to narrate, recount, tell' 316

Notes	324
Bibliographical index	427
Index of names	477

Preface

This book has been a long time in the making. It goes back to 1978, when I published an essay on oral poetry and written composition, and 1979, when in a book on medieval irony I touched on oral and written composition in the context of the narrator. Looking back on these attempts I see now that the first suffered from a too ready equation of verbs like *hoeren* and *sagen* with orality and the second from an uncritical acceptance of the oral-formulaic theory. In other words, they suffered the disadvantage of being written at that time. In German literature the pioneer is M. G. Scholz and it is a pleasant duty to record my debt to his work. My own would have been unthinkable without his preliminary labours and the courtesy he has shown in prolonged correspondence. We stand closer together than often appears.

On beginning work in 1980 I held the tentative view that it might yield one or two articles. Twelve years and hundreds of pages later I can only marvel at this naïvety. The work has been long and enjoyable, but writing could only be done in retirement (our political masters do not make it easy for academics to write books before this). Writing in retirement imposes its own urgency, for one is aware of the passing of time. This is mentioned only to explain why aspects of my problem are not touched on in these pages, so that work enough remains to be done.

It is a pleasure to record debts of gratitude incurred in working on this book. I have made many calls on the time of staff at the University Library at Cambridge, the Herzog August Bibliothek at Wolfenbüttel, the Bayerische Staatsbibliothek at Munich, the Arbeitsstelle des Mittellateinischen Wörterbuchs at Munich and the German seminar libraries at the Universities of Munich and Freiburg. I have also received financial support and research scholarships, allowing me to work for long periods in Germany, both from this country (my University and my College, the British Academy and the Leverhulme Trust) and from Germany (the Deutsche Akademische Austauschdienst and the Herzog August Bibliothek). Thanks are also due to my College for financial support in publishing this book.

Encouragement has also been given by invitations to lecture on this topic and by ensuing discussion and correspondence. The occasions have been in this country, the USA, Canada, Germany, Switzerland and Italy. I am particularly indebted to the Sonderforschungsbereich 'Übergänge und Spannungsfelder zwischen Mündlichkeit und Schriftlichkeit' at Freiburg for inviting me to lecture there so often and to teach in the summer term 1990. For stimulus and suggestions I thank the members of my seminars at Cambridge and at Freiburg, but also those colleagues, too many to list, who have exchanged offprints and found time for correspondence on shared problems.

Finally, my thanks are due to Laura Pieters Cordy for her skill with the computer, her willingness to instruct my wife and myself in its mysteries and the high standards which she set. My gratitude to my wife Margaret, for her readiness to venture on to this terrain, as for so much else, is expressed by my dedicating this book to her.

Abbreviations

AfB	Archiv für Begriffsgeschichte
AfD	Archiv für Diplomatik
AfdA	Anzeiger für deutsches Altertum
AfK	Archiv für Kulturgeschichte
AH	Art History
AHR	American Historical Review
AJPh	American Journal of Philology
AS	The American Scholar
ASE	Anglo-Saxon England
BBSIA	Bulletin Bibliographique de la Société Internationale Arthurienne
BEC	Bibliothèque de l'Ecole des Chartes
BuW	Buch und Wissen
CCM	Cahiers de Civilisation Médiévale
CetM	Classica et Mediaevalia
ChR	Chaucer Review
CJ	Classical Journal
CL	Comparative Literature
CR	Classical Review
CSEL	Corpus Scriptorum Ecclesiasticorum Latinorum
DA	Deutsches Archiv für Erforschung des Mittelalters
DU	Deutschunterricht
DVjs	Deutsche Vierteljahrsschrift
EG	Etudes Germaniques
EMH	Early Music History
FMLS	Forum for Modern Language Studies
FMS	Frühmittelalterliche Studien
FS	Festschrift
GL	Germanistische Linguistik
GLL	German Life and Letters
GRBS	Greek, Roman and Byzantine Studies
GRM	Germanisch-Romanische Monatsschrift
HJb	Historisches Jahrbuch
HJbb	Heidelberger Jahrbücher
HZ	Historische Zeitschrift
IASL	Internationales Archiv für Sozialgeschichte der Literatur
JAMS	Journal of the American Musicological Society
JbfrL	Jahrbuch für fränkische Landesforschung
JEGPh	Journal of English and Germanic Philology
KDL	C. von Kraus, Deutsche Liederdichter des 13. Jahrhunderts, Tübingen 1951ff.
LiLi	Zeitschrift für Literaturwissenschaft und Linguistik

LIST OF ABBREVIATIONS

LwJb	*Literaturwissenschaftliches Jahrbuch*
MF	*Minnesangs Frühling*
MGH	Monumenta Germaniae Historica
AA	Auctores Antiquissimi
Cap.	Capitularia
Const.	Constitutiones
Epp.	Epistulae
Leg.	Leges
Leg.Germ.	Leges nationum Germanicarum
SS	Scriptores
SS r.M.	Scriptores rerum Merovingicarum
MHG	Middle High German
MIÖG	*Mitteilungen des Instituts für österreichische Geschichtsforschung*
MLG	Middle Low German
MlJb	*Mittellateinisches Jahrbuch*
MLR	*Modern Language Review*
MM	*Miscellanea Mediaevalia*
MÖIG	*Mitteilungen des österreichischen Instituts für Geschichtsforschung*
MQ	*Musical Quarterly*
MSD	K. Müllenhoff and W. Scherer, *Denkmäler deutscher Poesie und Prosa aus dem 8.–12. Jahrhundert*, Berlin 1892
MSt	*Mediaeval Studies*
MuA	*Musik und Altar*
NdJb	*Niederdeutsches Jahrbuch*
NLH	*New Literary History*
NM	*Neuphilologische Mitteilungen*
ÖAK	*Österreichisches Archiv für Kirchenrecht*
OE	Old English
OHG	Old High German
ON	Old Norse
OS	Old Saxon
OT	Oral Tradition
PBA	*Proceedings of the British Academy*
PBB	*Paul und Braunes Beiträge*
PG	J. P. Migne, *Patrologiae cursus completus. Series Graeca*
PL	J. P. Migne, *Patrologiae cursus completus. Series Latina*
PMLA	*Publications of the Modern Language Association*
RAALBA	*Rendiconti della Accademia di Archeologia, Lettere e Belle Arti*
REL	*Revue des Etudes Latines*
RF	*Romanische Forschungen*
RFHL	*Revue française d'histoire du livre*
RG	*Romanica Gandensia*
RhVj	*Rheinische Vierteljahrsblätter*
RhM	*Rheinisches Museum*
RPL	*Res Publica Litterarum*
RR	*Romanic Review*
SE	*Sacris Erudiri*
SMV	*Studi Mediolatini e Volgari*
TRHS	*Transactions of the Royal Historical Society*
UR	*U.R. Schriftenreihe der Universität Regensburg*
UTQ	*University of Toronto Quarterly*
VB	*Vestigia Bibliae*

LIST OF ABBREVIATIONS

VfL	K. Ruh (ed.), *Die deutsche Literatur des Mittelalters. Verfasserlexikon*, Berlin 1978ff.
VR	*Vox Romanica*
WA	*Wiener Arbeiten zur germanischen Altertumskunde und Philologie*
WaG	*Welt als Geschichte*
WW	*Wirkendes Wort*
YFS	*Yale French Studies*
ZfbLg	*Zeitschrift für bayerische Landesgeschichte*
ZfdA	*Zeitschrift für deutsches Altertum*
ZfdPh	*Zeitschrift für deutsche Philologie*
ZfSL	*Zeitschrift für französische Sprache und Literatur*
ZHF	*Zeitschrift für Historische Forschung*
ZRG(GA)	*Zeitschrift für Rechtsgeschichte (Germanistische Abteilung)*
ZVLGA	*Zeitschrift des Vereins für Lübeckische Geschichte und Altertumskunde*

PART I

Preliminary problems

I

Orality and writing

When Guillaume Fichet, a member of the Sorbonne, looked back in 1471 on the history of what we today should term communications technology he divided it into three periods: classical antiquity (which employed the *calamus* or reed pen), followed by a period which for us is the Middle Ages (which used the *penna* or quill pen), and then a period which had only just begun (characterised by *aereae litterae* or movable type).[1] Just over 500 years later an American scholar, Ong, divided a historical span longer than with Fichet into orality, writing, printing, and electronic communications.[2] However much these two may differ over details, the position they occupy is comparable: each stands near the start of a communications shift which has alerted him to other changes in the past. Literacy has attracted scholarly attention at a point when its ascendancy seems threatened by modes of communication which also depend on a 'secondary orality',[3] whilst Ong has claimed explicitly that 'contrasts between electronic media and print have sensitized us to the earlier contrast between writing and orality'.[4] We need not go as far as Havelock, who proposed that our new alertness can be dated by a number of publications in the *annus mirabilis* 1962–3 (including, unsurprisingly, one of his own), in order to agree with the point that recent work has been stimulated by recent technology.[5]

Such developments might seem to bypass the Middle Ages, especially in the light of Goody's view that intellectual revolutions followed revolutions in the modes of communication (in Babylonia with writing, in Greece with the alphabet, in Europe with printing)[6] or Havelock's conviction that the Middle Ages are a cultural trough in the historical development of literacy.[7] We can, however, rescue the Middle Ages as a fit object of study for these new concerns. It is justifiable to see the medieval period as one in which literacy gradually expands, encroaching upon the hitherto oral area of Northern Europe, so that the period is characterised by the clash and interpenetration of orality and writing.[8] It is a sign of these new concerns that two recent histories of medieval German literature conceive their task as tracing the development of vernacular writing alongside the persistence of oral forms.[9] To take this view seriously means following Schmidt's suggestion that the gradual spread of lay literacy from the twelfth century was a precondition for the success of the invention of printing, that the emergence of a visual alongside an oral reception occupied these centuries before Gutenberg, and that in this respect it makes little difference whether the texts read were *codices manuscripti* or *codices impressi*.[10] It also means accepting the force of Clanchy's observation that Gutenberg's invention can be overdramatised, that printing has a prehistory, one of whose constituents is the literate culture of the Middle Ages.[11] The study of this literate culture, alongside its oral rival, belongs firmly to the medievalist's field; it is no mere appendage coming at the end of his period. That certainly is the view which has been taken over the last years by medievalists working in a number of distinct disciplines.

(a) Recent work

The medievalist cannot dispense with help provided by the history of religion in this field. The relationship between scripture and tradition, the written and the oral Torah, concerned Judaism, but was reflected in the problem of oral tradition and written transmission in the Christian gospels.[12] In a much wider context Graham argues the orality of scripture (when recited, read aloud or chanted) as an interpenetration of the written and the spoken word.[13]

Medieval historians have long seen the implications of orality and writing for their discipline.[14] Vollrath classifies the Middle Ages as an oral society in transition to writing, and Richter has studied communication problems in the Middle Ages in terms of the contrasts 'vernacular–Latin' and 'oral–written'.[15] In a book devoted to a short span of English history Clanchy discusses much wider problems: the technology of writing, literacy and illiteracy, hearing and seeing.[16]

In linguistics it has been argued, against Bloomfield's assertion of the primacy of the spoken word, that the visual representation of speech, in isolating units of speech, performs an act of linguistic analysis and makes linguistic consciousness possible.[17] The fact that a language is written cannot be without consequences for that language, which must be seen in its oral function, but also in connection with literacy.[18]

In musicology Hucke and Treitler have been concerned with the transition from oral to written transmission in our period, the latter in particular with the fact that music writing was introduced into an oral tradition and was used initially to support that tradition, not at first displacing it, but assuming a role within it.[19]

The possibility of linking orality and writing to the visual arts has arisen from two considerations: a general one (medieval bookpainting was largely conceived with an eye to the symbiosis of word and picture) and a particular one (Gregory the Great's claim that, whereas literate clerics acquired knowledge from writing, pictures were the books of the illiterate).[20] This situation has been explored for pictures by Camille and for stained glass windows by Kemp.[21]

Over a wide range of disciplines our problem has thus attracted attention of late, more precisely with regard to the position in Germany. In law Schmidt-Wiegand has discussed the tension between oral law and written codification, whilst Heck combines this with the relationship between vernacular and Latin.[22] In history the same tension between orality and writing has been applied to the transmission of vernacular works in the Carolingian period by Geuenich and to the linguistic policy of Charles the Great by Richter.[23] McKitterick begins her study of the Carolingians' attitude to writing with a consideration of the spoken and written word.[24] In linguistics Feldbusch has used her findings on the written language to explain the development of writing in OHG in the Carolingian period.[25] Treitler, too, ties the first use of musical notation to the Carolingian renaissance and its cultivation of writing, but also reminds the Germanist that one of the earliest examples of neumes is the Heidelberg MS of Otfrid's *Evangelienbuch*.[26] Finally, in an article which adds to the double formula 'hearing and reading' the dimension of 'seeing' Curschmann argues that preoccupation with a text also included preoccupation with a picture, and that the genesis of illustrations for secular texts must be seen in connection with the rise of writing in the lay culture of the medieval German court.[27]

In this highly selective survey of a flood of work in various disciplines I have largely avoided touching upon work on vernacular literature, mainly because, whereas in these other disciplines the emphasis was on the two dimensions of orality and writing, work on vernacular literature has been slower to reach this position. If this is because the stimulus given by the oral-formulaic theory of Parry and Lord has led to a concentration on oral composition at the cost of other aspects,[28] this is now beginning to change. Bäuml, to whom we owe the first application of this theory to medieval German, now stresses more the interrelationship of orality and literacy.[29] Curschmann, always critical of the theory, now sees the dimension of hearing alongside reading and seeing.[30] Finnegan, never a disciple, once wrote on oral poetry alone, but more recently on literacy and orality.[31] This shift of emphasis has even affected those who remain within the oral-formulaic camp. Lord has recently acknowledged the conjunction of oral tradition and literacy in the Middle Ages, and Renoir has conceded the slow transition from a preliterate to a literate culture, hence the opportunity for interaction between them.[32] Haymes, who once saw the *Nibelungenlied* in terms of the oral-formulaic theory, now situates it between oral and written composition.[33]

(b) The oral-formulaic theory

Any survey must therefore proceed from Lord's classic presentation of the theory.[34] Its impact has been considerable: to it we owe the first clear statement of the nature of an oral poetics as distinct from a written one. How revolutionary this recognition of an oral tradition has been is conveyed by Ong's remark that literary history is no longer exclusively literary, that oral forms preceded, in part predetermined and survived alongside the written works which make up literature as traditionally known.[35] Lord was also the first to apply the theory tentatively to medieval literature,[36] but the practice has spread far beyond this. Foley has pointed to its appeal to classical Greek, early Chinese, Vedic Sanskrit and the folk-preaching of the American rural south, whilst Finnegan, more critically, has listed further fields.[37] Any serious concern with oral tradition stems from the theory,[38] so that if we talk of an interplay between oral and written this is because Lord drew our attention to the importance of one pole. For all our debt, reservations are called for.

The first concerns the role of analogy in the argument. In applying findings from oral singing in the Balkans to Homeric texts the theory claims that the latter, showing similar features, were likewise orally composed – a claim which rests on no more than analogy.[39] This is equally true of the extension from the Balkan singer to the medieval oral poet, for it is uncritical to apply a method devised for a living oral tradition to a medieval text which has reached us only in written form.[40] In criticising Magoun's application of the Parry–Lord theory to Anglo-Saxon poetry (based on the assumption that Parry's definition of the oral poet held good for all oral poets) Opland objects that it is unsound to base a general definition on one tradition alone and then to force it on others.[41]

From this it is a short step to questioning whether the practice described by the theory (the poet composes his work orally, by means of formulas, in the act of performing) can be equated with oral practice at large.[42] Finnegan reminds us that composition-in-performance is not the only kind of oral composition, that there are recorded instances of oral composition preceding and separate from performance: by the criterion of composition these examples are oral, but by the criterion of performance they are not oral-formulaic.[43] In addition, there is the common medieval situation of works composed in writing, but delivered orally, so that by the criterion of performance they must be termed oral.[44] She argues that accepting Lord's view that what counts is 'the composition *during* oral performance' would blind us to different ways in which composition, memorisation and performance may be in play in or before the delivery of an oral poem.[45]

Lord is quite explicit in rejecting memorising as a possible basis of some oral performances (as opposed to extemporising composition-in-performance). He distinguishes between unconscious remembering (formulas are recalled from a traditional fund, like phrases in everyday speech) and conscious memorising (learning a poem by heart in a fixed form): for him oral-formulaic poetry involves remembering, not memorising.[46] This leaves him occupying a dubious position when confronted by evidence of oral composition preceding performance, with memorising as a bridge, for he has recourse to forced phrasing in saying of such cases that they 'may not be oral composition, but rather *written composition without writing*'.[47] Elsewhere he says that poems of this type are oral only in the most literal sense and that their method of composition is the same as written poetry, so that they should be considered as such.[48] To equate composition without writing with written poetry is another attempt to save the appearances of the theory by dismissing what does not conform to it, and suggests that the theory cannot accommodate all the facts. It must also be stressed that most proponents of memorisation in oral poetry do not exclude the further possibility of (oral-formulaic) improvisation, an openness to both possibilities which is in marked contrast to the theory's exclusion of memorisation.[49]

That the theory's restriction of oral poetry at large to 'poetry composed in oral performance'[50] is only part of the picture has been shown by evidence from outside Europe. This includes the Hindu Veda, transmitted orally with a meticulous accuracy achieved by memorising it in various modes of recitation requiring a complex manipulation of the base text, but also literature of the Pacific Islands, composed orally before performance and then memorised.[51] Such awkward evidence might be dismissed as irrelevant because of its geographical remoteness (although that sits uneasily with the theory's universalist pretensions). Against this, however, memorisation has been suggested repeatedly for Germanic oral tradition: the heroic lay and praise-song, the Eddic lay, and skaldic verse.[52] These examples suggest that memorisation may not be so remote from our field of study as the Pacific evidence was geographically. Moreover, in applying Lord's findings to Anglo-Saxon Magoun gave an oral-formulaic analysis of *Caedmon's Hymn*, with support from Bede,[53] but recent work sees this hymn rather in terms of memorisation. Renoir stresses that Caedmon, asked to make a poem of a story recounted to him, would go away and return the next morning, having spent the time ruminating on his material like an animal chewing the cud.[54] Since he was illiterate, this suggests preparation ahead of performance. Fry points out that, according to Bede, Caedmon improvised only once (in his dream), and that otherwise his poetic activity was confined to memorial transmission.[55] Conscious memorising outweighed unconscious remembering here, and there was in any case a time-lag between composition and performance.

From the demonstration of the high formulaic content of Anglo-Saxon texts known to have been composed in writing it follows that poems could be both formulaic and literary, literate poets could write formulaic verse.[56] If we accept that there was a lettered tradition which had assimilated the formulaic style to its own purposes, the theory faces the difficulty of telling us when a formulaic text is still oral and when it is already literate. Applying this to the theme of this book we have to acknowledge that, confronted with works which have reached us in written form, the oral-formulaic school has at the most suggested oral predecessors, telling us something about oral transmission, but unable to point to specific examples.[57]

(c) The introduction of writing

The classicist Havelock and the anthropologist Goody have discussed the discovery of writing and its penetration into an oral society. By dwelling on the interplay between these two means of communication they avoid the onesidedness of the Parry–Lord concentration on orality alone.[58] Havelock treats the educational role of orality in Greek society, the nature of a preliterate culture, the problem of cultural storage and the role of memory,[59] but at the other pole he also discusses 'democratised literacy' and the need to see a literate society as resting on readers rather than writers.[60] Goody is concerned with what he terms the 'technology of the intellect': with regard to orality he writes on cultural tradition in non-literate societies,[61] whilst under literacy he treats of the nature of an alphabetic culture, the social effects of writing and restrictions on literacy.[62] He also explicitly compares these two modes of communication and sees them in their interplay.[63]

What these two scholars achieve is to shift the ground of the debate from the merely oral to the relationship between oral and written.[64] Within this overall shift they also, first, widen the debate on orality itself by passing beyond the technique of composition-in-performance to the general function of oral poetry within a preliterate society (cultural storage, acting as a 'tribal encyclopaedia').[65] Secondly, they consider the nature and function of writing and the ways in which its storage of information differs from what is available to a preliterate society.[66] Thirdly, they also detail the losses and gains resulting from a communications shift from orality to literacy. On the debit side belong the impoverishments brought about by writing, but also, less drastically, its initial subordination to oral purposes and failure to realise its full potential.[67] On the positive side, however, they point to emancipatory possibilities in the transition to writing. Writing can liberate from the constraints of time and place to which oral communication is subject.[68] It can also set both the oral poet and his listeners free from their immersion in the immediacy of the recital situation and permit distancing from what is said and a more critical stance.[69] Writing can also bring relief from the burden of memorisation and from the limitations which this necessity had imposed and the mental energy which it had absorbed.[70] Finally, writing opens up the possibility of accumulating knowledge over time, of an incremental proliferation not subject to the 'structural amnesia' of oral culture.[71]

The wealth of this line of inquiry suggests that medieval studies stand to gain much from it, even if exaggerated claims were at first made for it.[72] Havelock claimed, for example, that the Greek intellectual revolution was accomplished not just by writing, but by the use of a simple, efficient alphabet. Goody now questions this, pointing out that not simply the alphabet, but writing of any kind was introduced to Greece, so that cultural features associated with widespread literacy should perhaps be seen in terms of writing itself.[73] Secondly, Havelock argued that the Greeks, by adding vowel signs to the consonantal ones already present in the Phoenician script, really invented the alphabet.[74] What the Greeks adopted, however, was the shapes of letters, most of the names given to these letters, and their sequence – and also a system which did not use a symbol to convey a word (as with logograms) or a syllable (as in a syllabary), but to designate a phoneme (as in an alphabet).[75]

Thirdly, Goody at first gave the impression of technological determinism, talking of the 'consequences of literacy', where now he prefers 'implications'.[76] Against this earlier view Finnegan sees rather opportunities provided, not consequences determined, and reminds us that cultural development is too complex to be subsumed under the mode of communication as a master-key, that the introduction of a new mode can work out differently in different historical situations.[77] Gough also suggests that literacy is at the most an enabling factor, permitting certain developments which only take place, however, in the overall historical context.[78] To apply such considerations to the Middle Ages means asking how far the opportunities held out by writing were grasped and what forces worked against them.

(d) Medieval literacy and illiteracy

Grundmann's essay on this topic supplements Thompson's evidence for lay literacy, but also surveys changes between antiquity and the Middle Ages in this area.[79] There are, however, grounds for thinking that his definition of literacy fails to do justice to the position in vernacular literature. Grundmann's definition comprises three points: medieval literacy was the prerogative, first, of clerics who, secondly, were able to read and write, and, thirdly, exercised these skills in the medium of Latin.[80] This definition serves him well, for his survey moves from classical usage to medieval evidence largely in Latin, but by taking account only of Latin literacy it excludes the position in the vernacular, where a layman could be ignorant of Latin, yet read a text in his own language.[81]

Of the claim that medieval literacy involved reading and writing we may ask whether someone who could read, but not write, must be termed illiterate,[82] but also whether Grundmann is anachronistically applying standards of literacy to the Middle Ages taken over from the modern period.[83] In the Middle Ages these two abilities belonged to different categories: reading was an intellectual attainment (no matter how elementary), whilst writing was more a manual skill and formed no part of the discipline of letters.[84] The medieval separation of two aspects which for us belong together means that we cannot assume that someone who could not write therefore could not read.[85] To call those priests illiterate who in the fifteenth century could not write[86] is to apply a modern yardstick of literacy.

However largely true Grundmann's second point (the equation of literacy with the clergy, of illiteracy with the laity) may be, it should not blind us to exceptions. Some clerics fall short of ideal literacy (amongst the monks Cassiodorus refers to them as *agrammati*), some know the psalms by heart through hearing the liturgy so often, but without knowing Latin, and at a later date Caesarius von Heisterbach still knows many exceptions to the postulate of clerical literacy.[87] More important for us is the converse, the growing range of evidence that some laymen could in fact read: although heavily weighted in favour of the French-speaking area[88] it is still relevant to assessing medieval literacy at large. How disturbing of the distinction which it was in the interests of the Church to maintain (and which Grundmann still retains) these literate laymen were is suggested by Matthew Paris's words of a lay member of the royal household: *miles litteratus sive clericus militaris*.[89] This remark is an attempt to save the appearances of the clerics' claim to an educational monopoly, but that is no reason why, with Grundmann, we should follow them in this reactionary attempt.[90]

Similarly, the equation of literacy with Latinity is calculated to prolong the medieval cleric's view of literacy as confined to his Latin cultural world.[91] The idea that the path to literacy in the Middle Ages involved learning Latin may be generally correct, but is subject to qualifications, since there are cases, no longer so few from the thirteenth century, where literacy was acquired without recourse to Latin.[92] By the fifteenth century, when there were many town schools in Germany which taught reading, but bypassed Latin, there are cases where the ability to read is expressly divorced from a knowledge of Latin (hardly surprising in the age when printing was invented).[93] More important are examples of a similar divorce already in the fourteenth century, as when a Grand Master of the Teutonic Order took account of the possibility that lay brothers in the Order might be *gelêret* (*litteratus*), but ignorant of Latin, so that they might say their prayers in German.[94] In the light of such cases Steer suggests that the earlier distinction between *litteratus* and *illitteratus*, as in Grundmann's definition, no longer holds water and that new terms take heed of a new situation: in place of the simple distinction between literate clerics and illiterate laymen, the latter now have to be divided between those who have some and those with no qualifications in literacy.[95]

This development can be followed back into the thirteenth century where Grundmann, in contradiction to his definition, sees the rise of religious literature in German as meant for a new class of recipient, mainly women (lay or religious) occupying an intermediate position. Like clerics they wish to read religious writings for themselves, but like laymen they have no Latin, so that reading-matter meant for them has to be in the vernacular.[96] The reading-matter of laymen, however, was not always religious, as when the author of *Von dem übeln wîbe* confesses that, although unable to understand Latin, he has read a detail in German.[97]

In one instance Grundmann's evidence goes back to the late twelfth century, where he suggests a parallel between religious and secular literature. The example concerns the conversion of Valdes to a life of apostolic preaching: under the impact of a recital of the legend of St Alexius he asks two clerics to translate the gospels and other works so that he may read them frequently for use in his preaching.[98] Valdes could therefore read, but not in Latin, so that by Grundmann's categories he was *illitteratus*. That is certainly how Walter Map saw it, terming the followers of Valdes *homines ydiotas, illiteratos*.[99] The arrogance which Grundmann here imputes to Walter Map rightly belongs to the clergy at large, scorning the pretensions of laymen by calling them illiterate because their reading did not embrace Latin.

Grundmann mentions secular alongside religious literature when attempting to accommodate Valdes and his followers within his definition. He says that, like the contemporary example of court literature, Valdensian literature was for illiterates who could read, but did not understand Latin.[100] This description of a complex position is unsatisfactory in using two key-terms in a sense taken from two different historical periods: 'Illiterat' in the medieval sense (unable to read Latin), but 'Leser' in the modern sense (able to read a vernacular). The terms of a definition which cannot be applied to a case like this (or, more pointedly for us, to court literature) force Grundmann to tie himself in definitional knots as much as did Lord when driven to say of some orally composed works that they were 'written composition without writing'. Steer's doubts about the adequacy of Grundmann's definition to the fourteenth century[101] can be extended to the thirteenth and even to aspects of the twelfth. Historical changes undermine what has been presented as a static view of medieval literacy.[102]

This view is also undermined by what Grundmann says of the contrast between a literacy of high culture (Latin antiquity and the twelfth-century renaissance) and a minimal literacy, for the tension between these can mean that someone who is literate in the minimal sense (he can read) will not be described as such by someone who regards literacy more ambitiously.[103] The most telling remark comes from John of Salisbury, for whom someone who does not measure up to his ideal of education is illiterate, even if he can read.[104] If even Grundmann's view of medieval literacy embraces two levels, we need to question whether the simple pair *litteratus* and *illitteratus* suffices for the many intermediate forms in lay society.[105] Some of the distinctions proposed by recent scholarship may be socially or linguistically determined,[106] but to tie a definition of literacy to one social group or to one language makes it difficult to follow through historical changes cutting across such boundaries.

(e) Hearing and reading

The study of the reading reception of medieval vernacular literature has been partly attempted for Germany by Scholz,[107] but other literatures lack anything comparable.

Gratitude for what Scholz has accomplished in a pioneer study does not mean that he satisfies us on all scores.

To his positive achievements belongs his critical review of MHG terminology. Although it was long ago realised that *sagen* meant 'to say', but also 'to recount' (it could therefore be used of an oral, but also of a written statement), Scholz has made it impossible to argue that verbs like *sagen* and *hoeren* necessarily reflect oral delivery and reception.[108] He has also demonstrated the frequency with which court authors appear to have readers in mind.[109] By systematically reviewing a wide range of different pointers he has put up for discussion the view that this literature was meant for readers. Here lies the novelty, but also the controversial aspect of his work, for vernacular literature for laymen had previously been seen in terms of recital to listeners, alongside whom the reader was exceptional. When Scholz establishes a reading dimension we need to ask who is doing the reading: is it, in addition to the occasional private reader, someone who recites from a text to listeners?

Among more particular issues chronology is strangely neglected. The dating of a reading reception of German literature is simply not discussed – when he asks at one point when the transition from hearing to reading was made in court literature he asserts, but does not demonstrate, that this must have been in the decades around 1200.[110] Nor is his method likely to have produced a reasoned answer, for Scholz proceeds by discussing a range of examples from different languages and periods, but not in chronological sequence. This method is well chosen to suggest a reading mode for court literature at large, but not to address the question when this mode is first found in Germany. Moreover, Scholz largely confines himself to the twelfth and thirteenth centuries.[111] By blocking off any prehistory he creates the ahistorical impression that vernacular reading began only in his chosen period, but if he were to reply that he is concerned with reading by laymen, then the monastic examples quoted by him have no place here.

Another omission concerns the question whether one genre might be more predisposed to one mode of reception than another.[112] Again, the method adopted could hardly have answered this question, for even within court literature a genre like the lyric is nowhere treated, and if Scholz were to seek refuge in a concern with narrative literature we face the huge omission of the heroic epic (absent, it might be thought, because it does not lend itself to the thesis of a reading reception). Scholz has also been criticised for not taking account of the difference between clerical and secular texts, as when Kartschoke points out that the clearest examples adduced for a visual reception largely come from clerical works.[113] By his educational background a cleric would have regarded his work as a book to be read, even if it was recited to laymen incapable of reading, but this can be extended to those clerics who composed the majority of court narratives.[114] For court clerics to regard their works as books for reading was justified in view of the literacy of many noblewomen,[115] but since these works were also received by largely illiterate knights the process of reception involved actual listeners as well as potential readers. The interplay between these two is almost entirely missing from Scholz's pages.

He is aware that the question how court literature was transmitted cannot be answered by a simple either–or, and criticises others for falling into this trap,[116] but does not escape this fate himself. The most telling example is his choice of title, for *hoeren unde lesen* was a double formula to indicate two ways in which a work could be received. It is paradoxical that he does not systematically discuss this formula,[117] but the reason is clear from the thrust of his argument: to show that court literature was meant to be read as opposed to the traditional view of a listening reception which he largely plays down.[118] He uses the double formula as evidence for reading, but ignores its implication that the same works could also be addressed to listeners. The recurrence of the double formula in medieval literature means that the transition from exclusive hearing to exclusive reading had not yet been made, that over a long period a manuscript was the basis of a public recital, but could also be read individually. To concentrate on reading alone and dismiss the further implication of the double formula means viewing the transition in oversimplified terms, creating the impression that it took place more quickly than is likely.[119]

His failure to pay attention to the possibility that a medieval work could be addressed to a twofold audience means that Scholz faces a recurrent difficulty with those works in which evidence for a reception by ear is found alongside evidence for reading.[120] He has devised two methods for coping with this, each calculated to resolve what he regards as a contradiction by undercutting the significance of one of its poles. One method is to invoke the difference between literal and figurative, and true to the tenor of his argument Scholz implies that, whereas the evidence for reading was meant literally, that for listening was only figurative.[121] He proceeds here from one of the strong points of the book (the critical analysis of terms too readily taken to suggest oral recital), but takes it too far: to establish the possibility that *hoeren* and *sagen* could be used figuratively is not the same thing as demonstrating that they must always be so used. The other method used to overcome an apparent contradiction is to appeal to an author's use of a 'Hörerfiktion', suggesting the pretence of a recital situation, but not its reality, conjured up for an audience of readers.[122] Scholz nowhere enlightens us on the function of such a fiction or why we must accept its presence. Indeed, with regard to the latter his argument proceeds in the same way as with figurative speech: to suggest the possibility of a fiction is apparently regarded as sufficient. Scholz's argument on both these points is unconvincingly conducted and unnecessary once we accept the implications of the double formula and the possibility of a twofold reception of literature in a society largely but not completely illiterate.[123]

(f) The introduction of printing

Like Guillaume Fichet we can also look at our problem with hindsight, from the invention of printing, particularly the arguments of Eisenstein and Giesecke, both of whom are concerned with the role of printing in introducing features of the post-medieval world.[124] To show this Eisenstein discusses how print culture differed from the manuscript culture which it displaced, whilst Giesecke radically draws printing and modern electronic media closer together, thereby drawing printing further away from manuscript culture. Both stress discontinuity between the Middle Ages and the post-Gutenberg world; both suggest that the discovery of printing was a revolutionary break.[125]

In sketching the salient features of print culture Eisenstein contrasts it with the manuscript culture of the Middle Ages so that, coming to our period from behind, we are shown it in a helpfully novel light. She also shows up the disadvantages of writing as a means of transmission in the Middle Ages, but implicit in this is the fact that the advantages of printing reduplicate many of those enjoyed by writing over orality.[126] Printing provided an escape from the threats to scribal culture (textual corruption, dependence on a restricted number of copies and continuous recopying),[127] but this parallels the answer given by writing to the deficiencies of orality (unreliable memory, the threat that one break in the chain could destroy the whole transmission). Printing may have brought release from the near exhaustion of scribal capacities available,[128] but the introduction of writing had meant liberation from the overloading of memory in oral culture. Whereas the fixity of a printed text made possible a series of improved editions (thus enabling energy to be devoted to new tasks rather than to preservation of the past),[129] writing also had a measure of fixity over against the spoken word, assuring not just survival, but its ability to be 'resurrected into limitless living contexts by a limitless number of living readers'.[130] Lastly, incremental knowledge and the changes it brings are common, to different degrees, both to writing and to print.[131]

These parallels between the earlier shift (from orality to writing) and the later one (from writing to print) can be placed in a wider context. In *Phaedrus* Plato reports Socrates' argument that writing destroys memory, causing the attrition of mental resources,[132] an objection which has recently been voiced by opponents of using pocket calculators on the grounds that they, too, weaken the mind by depriving it of the work that keeps it in training.[133] Similar misgivings greeted the introduction of printing.[134] Such parallels are not meant to suggest that an improvement in technology[135] must mean an improvement in knowledge, but that to the advantages enjoyed by writing over orality there correspond disadvantages suffered by writing in contrast to printing. By looking at both sides of the coin we see our problem in a longer historical perspective.

A substantive criticism can here be made of Eisenstein: her neglect of the prehistory of printing. She is aware of this prehistory, but abandons an evolutionary approach and nowhere discusses what lay literacy in the later Middle Ages may have contributed to the need for and success of printing.[136] How far she is from granting it significance is brought out by her contrast between the reading public (she has in mind the readers of printed books) and the listening public (above all before Gutenberg).[137] By implying a contrast between reading a printed book and hearing a manuscript recited she suggests too clean a break and ignores the hard core of Scholz's argument, that manuscripts could be read in the Middle Ages, not just Latin ones by clerics, but also vernacular ones by laymen. It is vital to look back before 1450, to the growth of lay literacy and lay readers. To the question why printing was invented around 1450 Clanchy has replied that it was because Western Europe had by then achieved a vigorous literate culture strong enough to sustain the mass production of printed books.[138]

Giesecke, too, overplays the importance of the break at 1450, not merely because his stress on technology places printing in an emphatically postmedieval context.[139] Another reason is because he takes *litteratus* in Grundmann's sense (restricted to a limited educational tradition) and ignores changes in the term around 1200 concerning laymen and the vernacular.[140] Following from this he argues that only the invention of printing led to the present hierarchy of reading over hearing.[141] This may have been a long-term effect, but for all that the double formula *hoeren oder lesen*, used in the Middle Ages of written texts, continued in use in the early modern period, applied to printed books.[142] When Giesecke quotes Ortolf Fuchsperger as contemporary evidence for the preference of the print medium for the visual rather than acoustic dimension he ignores Fuchsperger's ultimate dependence on Isidore of Seville, who used the same argument within a manuscript culture.[143] The argument concerns not the difference between printing and what went before, but between reading and orality at large, which significantly reduces the role of printing as a turning-point.

The same objection can be made when Giesecke attributes to the new medium features also attested in the manuscript tradition of the Middle Ages. He quotes from the *Kölnische Chronik* to the effect that as a result of the invention of printing people can no longer excuse themselves by ignorance of the scriptures, whether they are laymen who can only read German or depend on someone reading out to them.[144] Giesecke uncritically accepts as true a claim made by printing on its own behalf (this advantage is said to result from the invention of the new medium), but in fact a close parallel was provided already in the sixth century by Caesarius of Arles.[145] Not merely does Caesarius use writing to undermine the same excuse of negligent Christians, he also sees their access to the scriptures as twofold (personal reading and public recital). Between them these examples illustrate the continuity of the double formula from classical antiquity to the early modern period, but also continuity between manuscript and print culture.

Caesarius was concerned with a text written in Latin, whereas the *Kölnische Chronik* mentions printed books in Latin and in German. For such a reason Giesecke can suggest that the use of the vernacular was connected with typographical technology,[146] but to that we must reply that it was also connected with manuscript technology, for the argument of this book will be that the relationship of written German to written Latin was a recurrent problem in the Middle Ages. Giesecke concedes forerunners for printed vernacular Bibles in the demand of religious movements of the thirteenth and fourteenth centuries for religious texts in the vernacular, but dismisses them as trifling, confined to the *arcana* of sects.[147] This was hardly the attitude of the Church around 1200, facing waves of heresy, fearing to lose control over religious movements like the béguines, and using the new mendicant orders to deal with these symptoms of the religious crisis of the late Middle Ages.[148] When Giesecke sums up the dangers of printing as providing laymen with a direct (vernacular) access to God, dispensing with priests, this is how Walter Map had earlier seen the threat from Valdensians having their own written Bible in the vernacular.[149] An approach to Gutenberg's invention which takes full account of the medieval written codex still has to be written, but is called for to counteract claims made for the absolute novelty of printing.

(g) Avoiding anachronisms

To Graham's work on oral aspects of religious books we owe warnings of the dangers of anachronism. He stresses that, historically, our modern conception of reading is both 'limited and limiting', bedevilling our view of the past by imposing on it a conception which is recent and specific to Western culture.[150] For him our modern view of the book is not even the same as that of the sixteenth century, let alone the Middle Ages, classical antiquity or the literary cultures of Asia.[151] The recognition of such discontinuity between our modern book culture (a much later development than Gutenberg) and medieval manuscript culture is the precondition for understanding how medieval reading differed from modern reading.

Graham argues that the historian must rid himself of the notion that the written text has always been what the book is for us today (a written or printed text to which access is by private, silent reading) and he sees this notion as the culmination of the print revolution in the industrial society of nineteenth-century Western Europe.[152] By contrast with this recent development other cultures, including medieval Europe and even Europe for some time after the spread of printing, know the book more in its oral dimension (it is recited to others or the individual reads it aloud to himself) than as something merely written or printed.[153] This oral dimension was sustained by widespread illiteracy in the Middle Ages and beyond, only slowly pushed back by the emergence of lay literacy from the twelfth century on, so that the majority had access to books only by hearing someone else read aloud. Even in the case of the literate minority the practice of reading aloud to oneself, if only by murmuring, still ensured a link between the written and the spoken word.[154] That such coexistence of reading with hearing was not passing is suggested finally by the way in which it continues well beyond the Middle Ages, surviving the invention of printing by some time. Scribner has argued that the Reformation took place in a society still dependent on oral communication, in which 'printing was, in fact, an addition to, not a replacement for, oral communication',[155] whilst for Nelson the Renaissance author still wrote for the ear of his intended audience, whom he expected to hear him or hear his work read.[156] He regards the seventeenth century as the turning-point in this fading away of the spoken voice in literature,[157] but Schlieben-Lange reminds us that for French society the eighteenth century still knew of two coexistent cultures, one based on writing and reading and largely centred in Paris, the other oral and rural.[158]

The theme of Graham's book was the history of various religions, so that his approach to the problem was to stress the oral aspects of scripture. Our theme is not confined to religion, so that our concern must be with the oral aspects of reading and writing, of written transmission in the Middle Ages.[159]

A first approach has been provided by Köhn's analysis of medieval correspondence,[160] a practice which we today should regard as normally confined to the literate dimension (A writes a letter to B, who then reads it), but for which in the Middle Ages he is able to establish a number of oral aspects, divided between six features. Köhn stresses, first, that most letters until the thirteenth century were composed in Latin (as the language of education Latin was the language of writing, so that laymen who wished to correspond depended on the good offices of Latinate literates).[161] Secondly, a letter was the result of the sender dictating its content aloud to a scribe, word by word or with a few keywords.[162] Thirdly, as this last point implies, the sender was not identical with the writer, so that some oral communication between the two was unavoidable.[163] Fourthly, the messenger conveyed to the addressee not merely the letter, but also an oral message which could at times be more important than what had been entrusted to writing, thereby still betraying the conservative view that the spoken word was more trustworthy than the written.[164] Fifthly, the letter, once delivered, was not usually read by the recipient, but by someone else versed in Latin.[165] Lastly, the content of the letter was translated from Latin by this *confidant*, who read out his translation aloud to the recipient and those in his company.[166] Written communication by means of a letter therefore involved two translation processes, but also the use of the spoken word at three points (dictation, delivery, recital).

Warned that written communication in the Middle Ages need not be confined to the dimension of the written word, we may now ask whether anything comparable can be suggested for medieval literature. Following Köhn, we may divide the process of the written transmission of literature into a number of stages. The first, the act of composition, embraced three steps in Latin antiquity (note-taking, organising, dictating to a scribe),[167] so that the last step, *dictare*, could stand for the whole, as in the Middle Ages where, as Clanchy points out, 'reading and dictating' were usually linked together, not 'reading and writing'.[168] The next stage, the actual writing down of the literary text, could be performed by the author himself[169] or, more commonly, by a professional scribe, but in either case the act of writing with the hand was accompanied by the mouth speaking the words. As far as the author is concerned, Paulinus of Nola sees his physical activity in terms of *lingua et manus*, for Bernardus Morlanensis the conjunction is *et stylo et ori meo*, whilst Thomas a Kempis implied the same when concluding a letter (*lingua ergo manusque scribentis ... silescant*).[170] The activity of the scribe, when explicitly mentioned, is no different. Clanchy quotes a description of the physical labour demanded of the scribe, making of his duties in the monastic scriptorium a substitute for physical work (three fingers to hold the pen, two eyes to see the words, one tongue to speak them, the whole body to labour),[171] whilst it has been suggested of the scribe who entered musical notation into a manuscript that he may even have sung, however softly, to himself a section from the draft he was copying and then written from memory what he had just heard rather that what he had seen.[172]

The third stage is the reading of a literary text. Where, more commonly, this takes the form of one person reading to an assembled group orality is obviously involved, but this need not be absent when an individual reads to himself. Augustine and Ambrose may have read silently to themselves, but they occasioned enough surprise to deserve comment,[173] and there is ample evidence to show that the converse practice of reading aloud was continued through the Middle Ages.[174] If the Benedictine Rule recommends monks who wish to read by themselves to do so silently, so as not to disturb others, and if medieval monastic architecture takes account of this, it suggests that for a long time the usual practice was to pronounce the text as one read to oneself.[175] Finally, even that stage of the reception of a text which might seem to us most internalised and silent, meditation on a religious text, need not always have been completely voiceless, as Graham suggests ('Reflection on a text, like reading a text, was an audible and vocal, not a silent and purely mental activity').[176] On all four stages the transmission of written literature can involve the spoken alongside the written word. To concentrate on the latter, as with modern literature, is to miss an essential feature of the 'Alterität des Mittelalters'.

This confirms what Fromm has said of the symbiotic nature of the Middle Ages.[177] In society at large orality persisted alongside literacy (illiterates as well as literates, recital as well as writing, hearing as well as reading), so that instead of saying that literacy replaced orality in this period, we must see it as encroaching upon it. In medieval literature we must be similarly alert to two dimensions: illiterates need not be confined to their oral culture, for they could find access to written works by hearing a recital, whilst literates could attend recital, but in addition read the text (even here reading aloud ensured that orality was not completely excluded). This symbiosis suggests that Scholz would have been truer to the reality of medieval literature (and to the implications of his own title) if he had considered both modes of reception in their interaction.

(h) Guidelines

Our survey of recent work in the field of orality and writing has suggested a number of positive achievements, but also tasks which still need to be done. It can provide us with guidelines for the present book.

The first is the need to place our literary question firmly in the wider context of the symbiosis between spoken and written word.[178] We can no longer afford, with the Parry–Lord school, to devote ourselves to orality alone or, with Scholz, to reading alone, but must see both in their interplay, recognising that there may have been various fields, certainly not just the aristocratic court alone,[179] where the two had every opportunity to come together. If we combine this wider approach with a historical one, asking when changes came about within this symbiosis, this will lead us much further back than the twelfth century with which Scholz began, back to the beginning in OHG. It should also cause us to be suspicious of the view that, if there was a sequence oral–written, this could mean that oral communication was replaced by written, rather than by a long period of coexistence.[180]

A second guideline is to concentrate, as Scholz does, on the reception of German medieval literature. Like him I understand by 'primary reception' the manner in which medieval authors anticipated the reception of their works by the audience they were addressing.[181] To concentrate on this aspect is part of a general reaction against the almost exclusive emphasis given since the Romantics to the importance of artistic creation by the individual writer, neglecting his relation to patron, audience and the society of his day.[182] Seeing the author of the remote past in terms of the isolation of the modern author since the Romantics is an anachronism against which Bumke has worked with his study of the patron (who could be regarded as the leading member of the audience addressed), but also Scholz with his discussion of one aspect of the audience's relationship to the work meant for them. One may go further: the audience not merely plays a part in all literature,[183] it is even more important, because of its physical presence, in the case of orally delivered literature, whether this be destined for those who were only listeners or for those who were readers as well as listeners. With this recent switch of attention medieval studies are only now beginning to take to heart Schröder's suggestion, made in 1930, that we must try to identify the patron and circle of listeners and readers for which a work was meant,[184] with the proviso that, instead of identifying this circle, we are concerned with its composition (listeners, readers, or both).

This brings us to the third guideline, for we must go beyond the exclusive emphasis placed by the Parry–Lord school and by Scholz on opposite poles by taking into account both reception by the listener and reception by the reader, as well as the relationship between these two modes, best represented by the intermediate mode, present in those works destined for both types of recipient. To take account of these three possibilities the six central chapters of this book, making up Part II, fall into three groups, concerned with reception by hearing, reception by reading, and the intermediate mode. I regard the latter as particularly important (it introduces the possibility of reading alongside the traditional role of listeners and is well suited to illustrating the interplay between them), but this makes it incumbent on me to state not just how reading differed in the Middle Ages from modern practice (as we have in part just seen), but how the verb *lesen* was understood in medieval Germany. Scholz divides its semantic scope into three categories: 'lesen,' 'vorlesen', 'sagen, erzählen'.[185] Instead of beginning with a weighty semantic analysis under three headings it is more practicable to discuss these separately: *lesen* in the sense of the oral delivery of a written text ('vorlesen') is discussed in Chapter 3, and in the sense of an individual reading to himself in Chapter 5. By contrast, the more general sense 'to say, recount' is treated in an appendix, since inserting it elsewhere would have disrupted the course of the argument.

To these guidelines must be added two more special observations. The first concerns the nature of the material which is the object of this inquiry: do we confine our texts to literary ones or do we also include pragmatic texts ('Gebrauchstexte')? Schröder has stated this dilemma in the context of OHG literature: *either* the historian writes a history of orally transmitted poetry which has not come down to us, but which he can reconstruct with only some degree of reliability *or* he writes a history of the earliest writing in German, only occasionally of literary as opposed to linguistic or historical value and excluding the living (oral) poetry of the period.[186] Schröder asks whether any written text is to be regarded as literate and therefore a part of literature. The answer given by recent work has been to accept for the Middle Ages the need to include all types of written testimony in a definition of literature. Kuhn argues that it is yet another anachronism to impose a modern view of poetry, based on Romantic conceptions of individual creativity, on an earlier period,[187] and this has been accepted in practice in the second edition of the *Verfasserlexikon* with its broad criteria for what is to be included.[188] From his historical discipline Sprandel has recommended medieval literary scholars to define the concept literature in conformity to its Latin origin as meaning the written word, reminding us that a conception of literature as poetry divorced from any function or utilitarian purpose runs up against the fact that medieval literature is largely functional or utilitarian.[189] This has been adopted by Heinzle for the history of medieval German literature under his editorship. If its aim is to trace the development of a vernacular written culture, then no type of written text can be ignored[190] (one has only to imagine the volume by Haubrichs on OHG literature, restricted to the handful of 'poetic' texts in this period and ignoring all else, to see how impoverishing the result of a modern conception of literature would have been). For the historian of modern literature a view such as Heinzle's may seem absurd, but for the medievalist it is unavoidable. For reasons such as these our survey of the spoken and written word will have to take its material from any source, 'poetic' or not.

A last point has to do with the historical span of this inquiry. I have already suggested that Scholz creates an impression of absolute novelty for the twelfth century by beginning then and that we shall have to go back to the beginnings of written German around 800. Ideally, we should begin there and proceed through until about 1500, but the state of research and editions in the later Middle Ages, coupled with the fact that there is a limit to the number of centuries which can be tackled by one person and brought within the covers of one book, makes this a doctrine of perfection.[191] This inquiry is therefore taken only as far as 1300, a cut-off point which is not interpreted rigorously because of scepticism about the dating of some works and the need to accommodate authors whose works fall before and after this point.[192] The year 1300, moreover, is not meant as an attempt at periodising German literature,[193] but has been chosen since it includes the numerous important changes which the thirteenth century brought and represents enough of a turning-point in itself. At about this time changes affecting the court romance can be registered: its productivity as a genre ceases almost entirely shortly afterwards,[194] and by this date those who regarded themselves as successors to the classical generation have concluded their work,[195] whilst Bumke sees a significant change in the composition of the audience for the romance around 1300.[196] With regard to the court lyric Schweikle places its gradual conclusion around the same date with Hadloub and Frauenlob,[197] a point in time from which separate manuscripts for this genre are also to be dated,[198] whilst Schneider added the heroic epic to these two genres, saying that the eclipse of all three constitutes a caesura in literary history.[199] Corresponding to this negative assessment (the genres that come to an end) Janota has added a positive one in his survey of the fourteenth century (new developments which begin around 1300).[200] On both scores this date, whilst not necessarily opening a new period in literary history, is one at which a provisional survey may justifiably finish. However, before we start this survey from 800 to 1300 we must look at its prehistory, at the oral nature of Germanic and early German society before Charles the Great and at the ways in which it was slowly permeated by writing.[201]

2
The historical background

One of the ways in which the fall of the Roman Empire may be seen is to say that a literate culture was swamped by an oral one.[1] The Romans shared their literacy with the Eastern Mediterranean area which had seen the birth of writing (they had acquired their script from a Western Greek script, whilst the Greeks had taken over and developed the Phoenicians' script),[2] but in their expansion northwards, first in Italy, and then beyond the Alps, the Romans penetrated into an area dominated by an oral culture. One of the criteria by which Rome distinguished itself from barbarians was by its literacy. For Cato the superiority of the Romans to the barbarian tribes rested on the latters' ignorance of their own past which in the case of the Ligurians he attributed to their illiteracy,[3] whilst it has also been argued that the primacy of written law with the Romans formed another dividing line between civilised man and the barbarian dependent on oral tradition alone.[4] The expansion of the Roman Empire may have brought the written word to areas which had hitherto known only the spoken word,[5] but this merely pushed back a stage the same horizontal distinction between Roman written culture and barbarian oral cultures. With the transition to the Middle Ages this horizontal contrast gave way to a vertical one: now the literate clergy formed educationally an upper class with a monopoly of Latin culture, whilst the layman's cultural values remained confined to oral tradition in the vernacular.[6] As long as Latin in the hands of the clergy could perform the functions for which writing was required (religion, but also administration and knowledge) there was little impetus towards writing in the vernacular.

Along such lines Haug has sketched the position in the early Middle Ages.[7] He sees the antithesis between the literate and oral cultures as an emphatic one, lasting over centuries and made up of five basic contrasts: (1) Latin versus vernacular; (2) Written versus oral; (3) Religious versus secular; (4) Clerical versus lay; (5) Learned versus unlearned.[8] Our concern will be primarily with the first two contrasts: with plotting the way in which written literature in German emerged alongside oral tradition in German as well as written literature in Latin, as the precondition for determining whether this written literature in German was, like oral tradition, meant to be listened to and how far, like written literature in Latin, it was available to the occasional reader.

The long duration of this symbiosis of two traditions has been stressed by Fromm, who gives as one of its reasons the many intermediate forms between the oral culture of laymen and the literate culture of clerics.[9] The links between the two cultures have to be stressed much more than Grundmann was prepared to; we have to look for signs of movement and change within the five contrasting pairs listed by Haug, for without such changes, spread over however long a period, a German literature meant for laymen could never have found its way on to parchment, attracting the occasional reader alongside listeners. These connections between the spoken and the written word could take many forms: what was transmitted orally in the vernacular could find its way into writing either in the vernacular (e.g. the *Hildebrandslied*) or in Latin (e.g. *Waltharius*), whilst conversely what had originally been written in Latin could also be written in the vernacular for reader or listener.[10] The importance of seeing the links between these two dimensions has been stressed categorically by Kuhn, who claimed that every written German text of the Middle Ages, by the mere fact that it was written down, was the product of an attempt to mediate between the two cultures.[11] This must be borne in mind if we now turn to look at the two poles in our antithesis, native orality and a written tradition imported from the Mediterranean world, before considering ways in which the antithesis was undermined and changes were introduced.

(a) Native orality

If we may generalise on Cato's comment on the Ligurians or Otfrid's criticism of the Franks,[12] there can be no doubt how we must classify the Germanic tribes at large, for their orality and hence lack of any reliable (written) historical tradition stamp them as barbarians. This is how Tacitus, despite his use of them to castigate the Roman society of his day, saw them. He reported that they sang of their origins in songs which were for them the only form of historical tradition and that the deeds of Arminius were celebrated by them in one such song.[13] The survival of such lays in oral form, especially in the shape of heroic lays, from the period of the Germanic migrations to the time when, from about 1200, some provided material for heroic epics in written form, suggests the pertinacity of this oral tradition,[14] lasting from the oral society of Germania through the oral culture of laymen in the mixed (oral and written) society of the Middle Ages.

What Havelock has said of the function of oral poetry as a tribal encyclopaedia in archaic Greek society is not without its parallels in Germanic literature, especially if we take account of Klingenberg's division of Germanic 'Kleindichtung' into three genres according to the function they perform in preserving the knowledge necessary for a tribe to cope with the problems of life and to maintain its sense of identity.[15] His first genre, magic charms, can be seen as a primitive attempt to exercise a 'scientific' or even medical control over nature, whilst its oral, spoken dimension is revealed by the etymological evidence of some of its technical terms,[16] but also by suggestions that the pronouncement of the charm was accompanied by a ritual action, so that word and deed worked together in a context which was both audible and visible.[17] Klingenberg's second genre is gnomic or wisdom poetry, distinguished from magic charms in being entirely restricted to this world, encapsulating the practical experience necessary for life in the form of proverbial wisdom, practical saws, legal sayings, riddles, short mnemonic poems[18] (an example has survived in written form in the *Abecedarium Nordmannicum*, originally a device for memorising the sequence of the runic *futhark*, which found its way on to parchment because of the interest of a literate monk in various types of writing).[19] In a literate society, dependent on writing for storing its essential wisdom, poems belonging to this genre have largely lost their function and been pushed to the perimeter of literary interest, but in their original oral context their practical function was unassailed and their importance correspondingly greater.

The third genre, called by Klingenberg 'Merk-, Wissensdichtung', preserved essential tribal knowledge of another kind, theological or mythological.[20] The poems belonging to it recounted views of the beginning and end of the world, of tribal origins (as referred to by Tacitus), they could be memorial poems giving the genealogy of rulers or lists of names in a sequence which it was essential to store from one generation to another, they therefore preserved a tribe's historical knowledge in an easily recalled form.[21] Bloomfield and Dunn have said of such genealogies, found in archaic societies other than Germania, that their function was to support the legitimacy of the rulers and they display that structural amnesia which Goody postulated as a feature of oral tradition under pressure to discard what was no longer relevant to the present.[22]

In addition to this 'Kleindichtung' Germanic literature knew of two 'higher genres', cultivated at the ruler's court and with a clear political-military function. Encomiastic lays or praise-poems of rulers, legitimising their position, may not have come down to us in southern Germania to attest their earlier existence, but nonetheless praise-poems were composed later in medieval literature, whether in the form of the *Ludwigslied* (once held to be a Christian adaptation of the Germanic genre) or in some of Walther's political poetry.[23] For us the important feature of such praise-poetry is its essentially public nature: not merely in the sense that it glorified a public person, but that it did so publicly, in the warrior-leader's hall or the ruler's court, so that it was a genre for oral recital and collective reception.

With the second 'higher genre', the heroic lay, we are in a slightly better position, since at least the *Hildebrandslied* survives to attest it for southern Germania. In so far as events from tribal history could find expression in heroic legend and in heroic lays,[24] these lays helped to preserve tribal tradition and self-awareness, which explains why, in Latin form, they could be incorporated in written tribal histories, providing evidence for an early period before a written tradition.[25] The social-political function of these lays was similar to that of the praise-poems, for Haubrichs has taught us to take seriously references to them in Latin sources, mentioning their depiction of *veterum regum actus et bella* or of *avos et proavos*.[26] Literary praise of tribal rulers and forefathers demanded a public dimension,[27] and it is in this collective setting that we have to place the oral recital of lays mentioned by Tacitus and confirmed by so many references to their transmission by song through the Middle Ages.

Transmission by song, without recourse to written record, placed a burden on the memory and created the need for mnemonic aids. This need has been adduced to explain the use of the recurrent and the conventional in order to counteract the evanescent (proverbs, fixed sayings, standard epithets, and numerical sets),[28] but also, in origin at least, of formal devices which we might otherwise regard as poetic embellishments, such as rhyme, alliteration, metre, formulas.[29] That devices like these could have been used to assist memorising and storing information was already clear to Coleridge ('before the invention of printing, and in a still greater degree, before the introduction of writing, metre, especially *alliterative* metre, possessed an independent value as assisting the recollecting, and consequently the preservation of *any* series of truths or incidents').[30] Fry, concerned to do justice to the role of memorising in Germanic verse alongside the possibility of composition-in-performance suggested by the oral-formulaic school, has reminded us that formulas may have been employed because they were easier to remember.[31] If Gschwantler, in the title of one of his sections in a survey of the genres of Germanic literature ('Stäbe als Gedächtnisstützen'), sees alliteration as a mnemonic device,[32] we may agree, but go further and see this as a function of the other devices listed above. In looking at the oral poetry of archaic Greece Havelock has gone even further, suggesting that the onus of sheer repetition, necessary to the memory as a prop, was in part transferred to the metrical pattern retained tenaciously in the memory.[33] This metrical pattern could in turn be preserved, without attention to meaning, by a rhythm set up by the fingers of the singer playing upon a stringed instrument (in Greece as in Germania it had to be a stringed and not a wind instrument if the performance was solo).[34] How relevant this consideration is to Germanic oral poetry is suggested by the evidence that the poet accompanied his song by the harp,[35] and if Havelock goes yet another step (proposing that the mnemonic function of the rhythm produced by voice and musical instrument could be reinforced by the bodily rhythm of dance),[36] this reminds us of suggestions that dancing, ritual or otherwise, may underlie the origins of metre or such a technical term as OHG *leich*.[37]

Germanic poetry was essentially oral because the society for which it was produced was an oral culture, for whose members writing did not normally even cross their horizon (the use of runes was confined to specialist rune-masters and had no everyday pragmatic function). At this stage an attitude to writing, a rejection of literacy or resistance to it, did not exist as a problem, but came to the fore only after contact with the literate practices of the Roman Empire or, more decisively, within the symbiotic society of the Middle Ages where illiterate layman confronted literate cleric. In considering the layman's divorce from literacy and his resistance to it we are concerned with a massive survival of oral values and practices from Germanic society through to medieval society. It will not be our task to list the many cases where a layman, aristocrat or not, is described as illiterate (for that we can still turn to Thompson and Grundmann),[38] but rather to consider those cases which betray the layman's attitude to writing and why he would often have nothing to do with it.

In the early Middle Ages the layman's divorce from literacy was not simply the result of his exclusion from cultural values confined to the clergy; it derived more essentially from his conviction, inherited from Germanic antiquity, that the aristocratic ideal was a military one in which writing played no part. This does not mean that there was no educational programme for training the young aristocrat in his duties, and it is a prejudice of modern literacy to assume that an oral society knew nothing of culture, but the programme and the culture dispensed with the need for letters and saw them as a threat to the lay aristocrat's values. Haubrichs has stressed that the catalogue of qualifications which the young warrior must acquire was largely identical in Scandinavia, England and the continent in the early Middle Ages, because inherited from Germanic antiquity, giving pride of place to physical accomplishments (riding, hunting, running, swimming, above all skill in arms), but not to the neglect of the knowledge which an oral society can transmit (an awareness of genealogy and tribal history from praise-songs and heroic lays, of ethical norms from wisdom literature, of the law from the oral practice of law).[39] Towards Roman education the aristocrat's attitude could range from hostility to indifference, but in most cases it was certainly not regarded as appropriate to his own status. The layman's values were inculcated by an education which was essentially for peasants and warriors, and if it has been compared with that characteristic of Homeric society this is because both societies were military and oral.[40]

The gulf between these oral values and literacy could reach the point of hostility whenever the lengthy education in the latter was felt to jeopardise the amount of time required for training in the former (especially in its physical skills). As late as around 1200 the abbot in Hartmann's *Gregorius* is convinced that he has made a telling point to this effect (*swer ze schuole belîbe / unz er dâ vertrîbe / ungeriten zwelf jâr, / der müeze iemer vür wâr / gebâren nâch den phaffen*),[41] but this was a danger which the layman could see for himself.[42] An example of this attitude is provided by Procopius, who tells us that the daughter of Theoderic wished for a Roman education for her son, but ran foul of the Goths' disapproval, who insisted that their future ruler should be brought up in the traditional manner (i.e. in the values of an oral society) and not be trained to fear the schoolmaster's cane. They added that the boy's grandfather had founded a great kingdom without any knowledge of letters, so that in the end the Roman teachers were dispensed with in the child's case, too.[43]

Other examples may not be so explicit about the reason (learning to fear a schoolmaster is no good training for a warrior-ruler), but they still suggest opposition to literate values or contempt for them.[44] Hugo of Fleury dedicated his *Historia ecclesiastica* to the countess Adela because she was educated and knew Latin, rather than to illiterate princes who actually scorned the art of letters.[45] That such an attitude was more firmly entrenched in Germany is suggested by Wipo when he recommended Heinrich III as Emperor to require the wealthy to educate their offspring in letters, for he added that the Germans alone regarded it as a waste of time and even a disgrace to teach someone who was not to become a cleric.[46] The reputation of the German nobility in this respect was such that the same point could still be made by Petrus von Andlau in the fifteenth century.[47] This reputation of the Germans should not lead us to assume that their attitude was not to be found elsewhere, even if less frequently, as is attested by Walter Map's attempt to persuade the aristocrats of his day that as men of free birth (*liberi*) they had a special obligation to ensure that their sons were educated in the liberal arts.[48]

This statement by Walter Map is interesting in another respect, for he strengthened his appeal by warning negligent aristocrats that men of unfree birth by contrast were having their children educated, recognising in this a potential source of wealth and power.[49] The threat that education might enable unfree men to rise higher than the feudal hierarchy was willing to permit has another aspect, as Walter Map also recognised, for in his condemnation of the presumption of Valdensian laymen, illiterate yet daring to preach as if they were clerics, he pointed to the danger this presented to the hierarchy of the Church, undermining its claim to a monopoly of learning.[50] In other words, educated laymen (not merely heretics) may rival and outflank clerics, so that with this we reach the point that literacy and laymen may have been kept separate because this was the wish not merely of laymen, but also of clerics.

Goody has stressed that there may be factors restricting the full development of literacy, once this has been introduced into a society, amongst which he suggests that literates may have an interest in maintaining a monopoly of influence and power,[51] as Walter Map has shown for the twelfth century. Clerical reluctance to forgo a literate monopoly has also been suggested for the Carolingian renaissance, in that the Church, as the main beneficiary of this movement, was not anxious to favour the written development of the vernaculars, but was concerned to affirm the linguistic superiority which it enjoyed over laymen in three respects: as masters of one of the three *sacred* languages, of a *written* language, and, because of its restriction to a limited number of people devoted to a particular purpose, of an *esoteric* language.[52] It would have been surprising if such a carefully buttressed superiority had not occasioned a contempt for those excluded from the magic circle, as is suggested already in the Carolingian period by the contrast between *illitterati*, *idiotae* and *rustici* on the one hand and *docti et cauti* on the other, or by the claim by Amalarius of Metz that a layman, concerned with acquiring property, cattle and a wife, had no mind for learned study.[53] If the attempt by Charles the Great to bridge the gulf between the two cultures had no long-term success, this was due to the reluctance of laymen, but also to the resistance of clerics concerned to maintain their *sacerdotalis libertas* (the synod of Paris therefore abolished in 829 the institution of external schools for laymen in monasteries which Charles had encouraged).[54]

The attitude shown by Walter Map towards the Valdensians demonstrates the persistence of this division between laymen and clerics in the later Middle Ages in yet another respect. If the mendicant orders were called into being to deal with the same dangers of heresy, Berthold von Regensburg had every reason to maintain the clerics' literate primacy (*Wan ir leien niht lesen kunnet als wir pfaffen*),[55] from which he derived the Church's privilege to read, interpret and pass on religious writings in Latin and the layman's duty to accept his inferior status of recipient. As part of the same defence against allowing uneducated laymen to interpret theological writings for themselves, with all the dangers of heresy, the Church of the late Middle Ages made repeated attempts to prohibit laymen from reading the Bible in the vernacular, and Schreiner has followed this through into the Reformation period.[56] In this last transformation the orality which was characteristic of Germanic society, after becoming in the Middle Ages the orality of the layman by contrast to the cleric, persisted through to the early modern period.[57] Even after the spread of lay literacy in the later Middle Ages the Church attempted to confine the layman to his role as passive recipient of the Bible. His oral status was a long-lasting characteristic of the layman.

(b) Written tradition

We come now to the other pole in our dichotomy, to literacy and the function of the written word. Corresponding to the two different sources from which writing entered the medieval world, we shall be concerned with the function of the written word and reading in two spheres: Roman antiquity and Christianity.

If Germanic society could be described as an oral culture, Roman antiquity may be termed a written one, even though we may not know how far down the social scale we have to go before reaching those to whom writing meant nothing.[58] What can be said, however, is that it cannot be without a bearing on the nature of Roman life if the expansion of the Empire was accompanied by an expansion of inscriptions on tombs, triumphal arches, city gates, and everyday objects.[59] In cities attention was drawn to inscriptions, documents were posted publicly, trade demanded a measure of writing on the part of the merchant or the scribe he employed, whilst legal transactions required the drawing up of documents.[60] At Rome the secret ballot made it necessary for voters to be able to write the candidates' names, and slaves were taught to read if their duties called for it.[61] In view of this ubiquity of writing it is not surprising that Roman education was one in literacy, even though its methods have been described as 'slow, thorough, and relentlessly pedantic', involving from an early age the practice of writing and reading out the letters of the alphabet in all sorts of combinations before proceeding to syllables and complete words.[62]

Literacy was widespread enough to call forth two institutions for the benefit of readers: booksellers and libraries. The earliest mention of a booktrade is in the time of Cicero, before which books circulated as a result of private enterprise, just as it remained possible for an individual to make for himself a copy of any text to which he could gain access (whole libraries could be built up in this way by slaves for well-to-do Romans).[63] In this way, especially at Rome, a large number of books were available to anyone interested, which explains why, even if account is taken of a possible topos, readers could be encouraged by authors to follow up special interests in other works.[64] The size of the trade brought its disadvantages, however, as when Martial excused himself with the reader by explaining that errors were the work of copyists hurrying over their work.[65] Where private ownership was restricted or impossible, public libraries provided another possibility. The first such library dates from the time of Virgil, and Augustus himself founded two, each providing for Greek and Latin books.[66] Public libraries did not, however, displace private ones, considered a necessary part of any distinguished Roman household. Cicero wrote that, as a guest, he was browsing in his host's library,[67] but if Seneca denounced those who accumulated books for mere show, without reading them,[68] this implies the practice of private reading, even though it may have been honoured more in the breach than in the observance in these cases.

Some of these references have already suggested the existence of a reading class, however restricted. Apart from drama and rhetoric, addressed to a wider public, poetry was directed to a select group of readers who shared the poet's concerns and were able to judge his work.[69] Of Martial it has been said, for example, that his epigrams appear to be meant for a closed society of members well known to each other.[70] Exactly who constituted the readership for literature is largely unknown, but it must have included scholars and writers themselves, whilst in his letters Cicero recommended people to his friends who must be presumed to have had cultivated interests.[71] Legal works were popular in the upper class of Roman society and those in public life would regard historical reading-matter a requirement, as well as some works on political thought, such as Xenophon, whether in the original or in Latin translation.[72] Other readers have been suggested amongst freedmen trying to rise in the world, scribes and bureaucrats.[73] Of particular interest, because it parallels what we find in medieval literature, is one clearly defined group of readers, namely women. If Catullus, Propertius and Ovid refer to cultured women in their poetry, it is tempting to think that they had them in mind when composing it, whilst Juvenal's criticism of such women must have had some basis in reality if his satire was to be effective.[74] Those Roman women of the upper classes whose literary education can be documented may also be counted among potential readers.

The individual reader also had a role to play as a result of the adoption of *scriptura continua* in the second century and the abandonment of punctuation, for the fresh copy of a work now forced him to divide the words himself and supply his own punctuation, quite apart from the overriding need to correct slips of the copyist's pen.[75] More telling is the documentation provided by the poet himself, suggesting that he anticipated an individual reader whom he could occasionally address. In his *Tristia* Ovid addressed his readership in the singular (*lector amice*) or in the plural (*lectores*) and could appeal to those who sympathised with him in banishment by picturing them reading his work in tears.[76] In Persius the reader is to consign the poet's lessons to his ear,[77] whilst Martial can boast that he is read by young men and old, and even by ladies, and he recommends the reader to skip as it suits him, making his book as short as he likes.[78]

It is with this individual reader that the author attempts to insinuate himself in a variety of ways. Catullus adopts a pose of humility before the superior taste of his readers;[79] the reader can be flattered by the qualities imputed to him (he is therefore *amator et lector studiosissimus litterarum*, alternatively he is *delicate lector* or *lector* [*scrupulosus*]),[80] whilst the author must be careful not to impose on the reader too much.[81] Although, as we shall see, *lector* could also designate a professional reciter, he was in Roman society normally a slave in a wealthy household (*anagnostes*), so that the author can have had no cause to flatter him or seek his favours. Instead, in such passages he was concerned with the approval of those on whom he *was* dependent, on cultivated society at large and particularly on individual readers within it.

Two final indications of the individual reader have to do with phrases with a double application, only one of which concerns us at the moment. The first indication is provided by a double formula, in classical as well as medieval Latin, suggesting that a work was to be received either by listening to a public recital or by private reading. The background to this is provided by Pliny's statement that he preferred hearing a work recited by another to reading it for himself,[82] which explains why Fronto referred to the stylistic effect on those who hear or read (*audientium aut legentium*),[83] why Martial anticipated both recipients (*lector et auditor*) for his epigrams,[84] or why Lactantius mentioned the pagans' scorn for the unpolished style of the scriptures in terms of their refusal to hear or read (*Contemnuntur ab iis, qui nihil audire vel legere nisi expolitum ac disertum volunt*).[85] Whatever the other pole in these phrases may involve, they presuppose the existence of individual readers. The same is even more clear with the second indication, concerning the manner in which an individual read in antiquity, silently to himself (as is attested for St Ambrose) or aloud (murmuring or muttering).[86] We shall turn later to the comparable problem in medieval German, but for the moment may cut the Gordian knot by observing that, whichever manner of reading may be involved, we are dealing with an individual reader.

Literacy and reading were brought to Northern Europe, however, not merely with the expansion of the Roman Empire, but also by the spread of Christianity. Roman society was an essentially written culture, but Christianity must be seen similarly, for a Christian society cannot be wholly illiterate.[87] Christianity is a religion of the book, not merely in the eyes of Moslems, but also in its own eyes: in religious art Christ and the prophets and apostles are often depicted holding a roll or a codex,[88] books were needed for any serious preoccupation with Christian truths, and the Church instituted many different types of school, in every one of which mastery of books was an essential requirement.[89] Moreover, from the beginning the world into which Christianity was born was remarkably literate, not merely because the Middle East was part of the Roman Empire, but also because this was historically the area in which writing had been invented and practised in various forms, a tendency reinforced by the role of the book in the Jewish religion as well as by the Hellenisation of this area.[90] The Christian idea that books were an essential part of religion would have been nothing strange to the Jews, but was alien to the pagan world of Greece or Rome,[91] so that the expansion of the new religion brought a new impetus to the practice of reading, going far beyond the pragmatic use in Roman society hitherto.

The importance of the written transmission of a sacred text in defining the religion which it perpetuated was common to both Christianity and Judaism, and even if the written text was frequently recited or taught orally, so that the written word also survived as the spoken word, it was the written tradition which was regarded as the norm, for it was a revealed text stemming from God.[92] The reverence felt for a sacred text could transfer itself to its physical copy in book form, and the wish to set the Bible apart from other books may explain why the early Christians replaced the roll by the codex, which then became typical of Christian tradition.[93] Beneath this difference between roll and codex, however, there lies the more fundamental similarity between Hebrews and Christians: both make use of the book to transmit religious lore, the Christian idea of the book derives from Judaism, the prototypical religion of the book.[94] The nucleus of this idea was the belief that Moses proclaimed the words of God at Sinai, but also wrote them down, just as he recorded the laws in writing.[95] The use of the Hebrew word for 'writing' to denote holy writing in particular lies behind the Christian use of *scriptura* in a sense new to Latin. The early Christians followed this Jewish precedent for a very natural reason. As a Jew Christ appealed to the authority of the Jewish holy writings, which for more than a century constituted in the form of the Old Testament the only sacred book available to

Christians. Although Christians then went their own way in placing the New alongside the Old Testament, the underlying idea of claiming divine authority for a written book grew out of the Jewish context of earliest Christianity.[96]

This is important for the use of this sacred book as a text to be read by the individual, since this had already been the practice with the Jews (Christ could hope to be credible in telling them to search the scriptures for confirmation, and there is the example of Candace's Jewish treasurer who read Isaiah while riding in his chariot).[97] If Jewish scribes occupied themselves with the scriptures outside the context of worship, there is little surprise in seeing the same practice attested for Christians, as has been richly documented for the earliest Christian centuries.[98] It is presumably because this practice was widespread among Christians that there should be evidence (including the case of Augustine himself) of pagans being converted to the new religion as a result of reading its scripture.[99] Apart from this special type of case, when Origen recommended those who heard his homily to take the scripture in their hand and learn from it in accordance with what they heard in church he was recommending the same practice of private reading outside the context of worship for Christians as obtained with the Jews.[100] When Tertullian pointed out that when a Christian married a pagan there was no reading of the scriptures he presupposed that a Christian married couple was expected to read the Bible jointly.[101]

A particular type of private reading by Christians (once the new religion had spread into the Gentile world) has been suggested by Saenger.[102] He points out that amongst the Jews oral rabbinical learning coexisted with the stress on a book religion and that Christians of Jewish origin would be acquainted with the oral mnemonic techniques of their culture, whilst Gentile Christians, unversed in these skills, would need to go direct to the written text, especially that of the gospels. To facilitate this the New Testament canon was divided into chapters and paragraphs, a practice unknown to the textual tradition of the Torah, but enabling Christians to peruse the Bible and find any passage required. He suggests that this need to facilitate consultation may have also favoured the transition to the codex, in place of the roll, for the numbered leaves of the former gave reference points, whilst the margins provided the opportunity for notes to help the reader find his place in the book.[103]

Evidence for the individual Christian reader, as for his pagan counterpart, is also provided by the double formula suggesting reading as well as hearing, used in early Christian as well as classical literature. The situation in which this formula found a Christian application is that suggested by Origen, recommending Christians to read for themselves what they had already heard in church. From this biblical context the formula could be applied to other types of religious reading, meant to be heard when recited or to be read privately, so that Augustine could use phrases like *legendo et audiendo* or *leguntur et audiuntur*.[104] Much later, at a time in the Middle Ages when literacy had suffered an enormous, but not fatal setback, there were enough pockets of literacy surviving to give some meaning still to the formula: Bede therefore referred to an audience in terms of *auditor sive lector*, whilst Hrabanus Maurus saw the reception of a letter as involving *legere aut audire*.[105] What I have said of the formula here, as with classical literature, is only part of the picture, but enough to confirm the practice of private reading amongst Christians.

Private reading by Christians, if not by all, was feasible as long as the Roman society into which Christianity expanded remained literate, but the collapse of imperial education and the barbarian invasions meant that Christian literacy, too, was forced on to the retreat, finding its main refuge ultimately in the monasteries. It is characteristic of this restriction of literacy to relatively few centres that examples of the Christian use of the double formula should frequently come from monastic authors. Private reading played an important part in monastic life: two or three hours were set aside each morning for this purpose, in the afternoon on a personal basis, and also on Sundays.[106] In addition, during the Easter period every monk received a book from the library which he was to read *per ordinem ex integro*.[107] St Benedict, in laying this down, appears to have assumed that anyone becoming a monk would be literate, but if even Italy in the sixth century could not guarantee this the position could, in theory at least, be remedied within the monastic school. In principle, therefore, the Benedictine monastery remained a refuge for literacy and for individual reading.

(c) Orality within the written tradition

So far we have been concerned with two poles in an antithesis, Germanic or lay orality as opposed to Roman or clerical literacy, as if they were absolutes in watertight compartments. That is historically unrealistic since, if true, it could not explain the slow emergence of lay literacy in the vernacular during the Middle Ages, but I have started with this antithesis in order to bring out the full range of the cultural spectrum with which we are dealing. We must now look at ways in which this antithesis could be relativised already at an early point in history. The first consideration is that the literate culture we have just been looking at, Roman or Christian, was not completely literate (there is no such thing as an exclusively literate culture),[108] but existed within an oral dimension in a number of respects.

In classical times reading aloud to an audience was common practice. Among the Greeks publication was by means of public recitation (by the author or professional readers) and this continued even after books and the art of reading had established themselves.[109] Rome, too, retained this characteristic of an oral culture, so that a history of Latin literature reminds us 'that nearly all the books discussed in this history were written to be listened to',[110] a statement which need not exclude the possibility that readers were also anticipated. This context of public recital is suggested whenever *legere* or *lector* is used of public reading, as at a banquet[111] or when the listeners are mentioned.[112] The same is suggested when either word is used in close conjunction with a word of hearing[113] or of reciting.[114]

As with the Greeks, public reading could be given in Rome by the author reciting to a small group of chosen friends, with the intention that they should freely criticise what they heard. The more firmly established an author's reputation was, the more he preferred a small coterie of like-minded connoisseurs.[115] Suetonius tells us that the *Georgics* were read aloud to Augustus, but also some books of the *Aeneid* to the Emperor and Octavia.[116] Horace makes it clear that he preferred reciting to a select group of friends, valuing their criticism more highly than the flattery of many.[117]

Pliny speaks of his own and his friends' readings, commenting on the advantages which, as an author, he derived from honest criticism and admitting that if anyone of his audience should peruse the text he has heard him read he would notice such improvements.[118] The significance of this passage is that, without using the double formula, Pliny implies the possibility of a double reception: someone who had been his listener may well become his reader, the one did not exclude the other. This and other passages show that in Rome, as in Greece, the growth of literacy, books and libraries did not drive out reading aloud as a form of entertainment and publication. That this was far from being the case is confirmed by the widespread practice of *recitatio*, the public or semi-public reading aloud by an author, going far beyond the narrow circle of poet and friends, constituting a form of advertisement and a regular feature of literary life in the first century AD.[119] This practice aroused the indignation of satirists, but their attacks cannot have been without a target, one which demonstrates that a literary life as literate as that of Roman society had by no means dispensed with this oral dimension.

Why this should have been so has been suggested by Balogh. He is not concerned with the practice of reading a text aloud to others (whether a small group or a large gathering), but with the individual reading aloud to himself (rather than silently), yet the two situations share the common ground of reading aloud. He reminds us that reading aloud fitted well into the rhetorical ideal of classical antiquity, in which the well-turned spoken word was the basis of public life, education, literature and knowledge.[120] He sees in this rhetorical framework (the recognition that a book was destined to be read aloud to its audience) one of the reasons why the classical author chose to dictate his work to a scribe (or to write it down aloud himself), for this gave him an immediate check on its acoustic effectiveness.[121] Balogh regards the act of reading aloud as the logical endpoint of the various acoustic stages in the composition and transmission of a classical work between author and recipient, but it loses nothing of its logic if we see this reading aloud not confined, as with Balogh, to the individual reading to himself, but also in the context of recital to others. If public recital, as practised in antiquity, was passed on to the Middle Ages, it was drastically separated from the rhetorical ideal which sustained it in antiquity and to which the early Church was vehemently opposed, and was made necessary by other considerations, not least the drastic decline in literacy.

Written books found readers in Roman society, but also many listeners. This situation is captured by the double formula in Latin literature (*lector vel auditor*). If we used this earlier to establish the existence of the private reader, we must now turn the coin round and insist also on the public listener. Both together make up the literary scene. This twofold reception means that *lector*, like the verb *legere*, can be used in two senses, to denote the individual reader (as in the double formula) or the professional reciter who read out to his *auditores*. The lector in this latter sense (also known at Rome by the Greek word *anagnostes*) could be a slave attached to an aristocratic household, or a professional (especially at public *recitationes*), or, with the coming of Christianity, the holder of a particular office in the ecclesiastic hierarchy.[122] Whether in classical antiquity or in its medieval survivals, it suggests an oral dimension to written literature.

It is possible to identify some of the works which were recited (apart from those already mentioned). We should not know, for example, that the history of the Roman Empire written by Ammianus Marcellinus had been declaimed by him if he had not been congratulated on this in a letter by Libanius.[123] If the *Thebais* of Statius also belongs here,[124] this is significant for our medieval concerns, since the presence of neumes in medieval manuscripts of this work (as of the *Aeneid*) suggests that it was not merely recited, as in antiquity, but actually sung.[125] We also possess a tenth-century setting of an ode by Horace to a melody taken from a hymn, whilst metra from the *Consolatio* of Boethius were set down with musical notation by the ninth century.[126]

Leaving aside musical recital, we know of Latin works which were recited publicly in the Middle Ages. In the sixth century Arator recited his Christian epic on the acts of the apostles for four days in San Pietro in Vincoli, providing, as a Christian Virgil, what has been termed a last example of the classical *recitatio*.[127] It has been suggested that Smaragdus conceived his *Diadema monachorum* as material to be read out to monks in the *collatio*,[128] and the works recited to Charles the Great at table included St Augustine's *De civitate Dei*.[129] Hrabanus Maurus sent a copy of his *De universo* to Ludwig the German, expressing the expectation that the Emperor would have it read out in his presence (*coram vobis relegi illud faciatis*),[130] whilst Theodulf expected his poems to be read out as part of the literary entertainment at court in the evening by a *lector* to whom the recital had been allotted.[131] From the epilogue to Hrotswitha's *Theophilus* it seems likely that this verse legend, like her others, was meant to be recited in the refectory of the convent at Gandersheim,[132] and of the *Ecbasis cuiusdam captivi* it has been suggested that it was intended for recital in a monastic community over the Easter period.[133] In the twelfth century, despite what has been called its revolution of the book and the increase in literacy, the position is no different. Giraldus Cambrensis brought his *Topographia Hiberniae* before his public by reciting from it for three days at Oxford; Gervase of Tilbury, who dedicated his *Otia imperialia* to Otto IV, expected the copy he sent him to be presented to his ears; Ordericus Vitalis, wishing to summarise the *vita* of a saint, commented that, whereas a *cantilena* might be transmitted by minstrels, it was preferable to have an authentic account written by scholars read aloud to the monks; the Archipoeta reckoned with the recital of a poem by someone else.[134]

These are some of the examples which I have excerpted in the course of reading, to which many more could be added. One comes across isolated references to them in medieval Latin scholarship, but no systematic treatment of the phenomenon, presumably because of the anachronistic assumption that, since Latin literature was *ipso facto* literate, it existed exclusively in the modern literate dimension of private reading. Such exclusiveness was true neither of classical nor of medieval Latin literature: if the Middle Ages continue the practice of Roman antiquity in this respect, we cannot argue that the medieval examples illustrate medieval orality swamping classical literacy. Instead, both periods combine orality with literacy, even if to a different extent and for different reasons.[135] If even literate clerics retain the practice of oral recital of Latin literature, this practice must have been even more firmly entrenched amongst laymen, literate or not.

The oral dimension of literate culture was passed on to the Middle Ages not merely from classical literature, but also because it was present in Christianity from the beginning. Although the written authority of Hebrew law derived from Moses writing down the commandments of God, behind this there lay the words spoken by God to Moses on Sinai or, further back, God's spoken word at the beginning of time (Gen. 1, 3) or in Christian terms from the beginning of the fourth gospel: 'In the beginning was the Word.'[136] What we may call the theology of the spoken word, alongside that of the book, was reinforced by the two ways, oral and written, in which the Christian message was first transmitted. From the beginning the words spoken by Christ were preached by early Christians to the unconverted and this personal preaching took precedence for some time over the written authority of the Old Testament or of the Christian canon, as it gradually came to be established.[137] The words spoken by Christ were passed on as a spoken message long before they were written down as a book; they existed in oral transmission until, in the second half of the second century, the first Christian writings were put down,[138] occasioned by particular needs and circumstances (in the case of St Paul, for example, letters had been called for to bridge a geographical gap).[139] This early interplay between the spoken and the written word is not to be seen as an insight of modern biblical criticism, since medieval writers were aware of the contrast at least. Heinrich von Kröllwitz, for example, discusses Christ and the evangelists in just these terms (*vurwâr sô mach er ouch wol sîn / ein vil war evangeliste, / wan swaz iene schriben von criste, / daz hât gesprochen sîn munt*)[140] and the author of the *Passional* sees St Luke's written account as based on what Mary had told him by word of mouth.[141]

A theology of the spoken word and the importance of the oral transmission of Christ's words from the beginning are buttressed by oral features of Christian worship, such as collective prayers, hymns, sermons and readings from the scriptures. Graham has stressed this oral dimension of Christianity as a book religion, arguing that it is necessary to distinguish between oral and written uses of the scriptures or even, in shorthand, to talk of 'oral and written scriptures'.[142] Just as the semantic expansion of the word literature under the pressure of literacy (from meaning only written literature to literature at large) forces us to use the contradiction in terms 'oral literature', so is Graham driven to use his terms, even though 'oral scripture' is an oxymoron and 'written scripture' a redundancy.[143]

If Christianity took over much of its literate dimension from Jewish practice, the same is true of its oral dimension, for the reading of the Torah, the prophets, the psalms and other books of the Old Testament had played a part in Jewish worship.[144] For Christians before the rise of widespread literacy the common means of access to the scriptures was acoustic, in the framework of the liturgy, even in the case of those early Christians from whom private reading could be expected, quite apart from medieval laymen after the collapse of classical literacy. More important than private reading of the Bible, often resisted by the Church in the vernacular for laymen, was its oral presence in collective worship, such as the reading of lessons, the preaching of sermons based on a scriptural text, the singing of psalms and of hymns impregnated with biblical imagery, the recital of prayers largely derived from biblical passages.[145] If the authority acquired by the Church in standing between the individual Christian and the scriptures was what largely exercised the reformers of the sixteenth century, for us the aspect to be stressed is the emphasis placed on oral communication rather than reading.

Lessons, or the reading of scriptural passages to the congregation, were early established within the Christian liturgy. In so far as the passages were taken from the Old Testament, their reading can be compared with Jewish practice, even though the purpose was quite different. As far as the New Testament is concerned the reading of selected passages had an apostolic precedent, since not merely were St Paul's epistles, like other letters in antiquity and in the Middle Ages, meant to be read aloud, they were also read aloud in the church of the Christian communities to which he sent them, as he himself made clear (e.g. Col. 4, 16).[146] Indeed, the reading from books of the New Testament quickly assumed such importance that the use of a particular book within the liturgy, providing the text of a lesson, formed a criterion for accepting it into the canon of the New Testament.[147] Since the lesson formed the basis of the sermon, liturgical orality was important in a second respect. Any cleric of the early Church who knew the importance of rhetoric realised that preaching was an effective way to win converts, especially when a rhetorically effective performance in church could be applauded by Christian *cognoscenti* just as much as if they had been attending a classical rhetorician's recital.[148] Even when *cognoscenti* of this type became rarer and when illiteracy increased the sermon retained its importance, but in a new manner, because, as Gregory the Great stressed, it was the way to teach the illiterate what God required.[149]

Even in the monasteries, those centres of literacy which stood out all the more as other aspects of Roman literacy were swept away, orality continued to play an important role, quite apart from its presence in the liturgy, the focus of monastic life. Two recurrent points in the monastic cycle grant it a part to play. The first was the practice of having a *lector*, gifted with a good voice and knowledge of Latin, read out to the assembled monks at mealtime in the refectory from a book obtained from the librarian.[150] To this task he was appointed for a week at a time and the purpose of this practice was to ensure that the monks, eating in silence and listening to an edifying text, should reinforce themselves with spiritual pabulum as well as with material food.[151] The second occasion for reading aloud from a text was the evening *collatio*, at which a monk, appointed as reader, took as his theme a text from the scriptures or the Benedictine Rule or some patristic work, showed it first to his superior so that he might read it and prepare a commentary, then read out a few lines and allowed the superior to explain it.[152] The *collatio* developed out of the *confabulatio*, an early Christian practice which involved an intimate group of the likeminded who were explicitly distinguished from the public addressed by the Roman rhetorician, but who, like the Roman public, were brought together for an oral communication.[153] A third aspect of the monastery was the school or, more precisely, the oral dimension of teaching and learning. Given the expense of parchment, teaching was conducted orally in that the teacher would read out his text aloud and then comment on it. The orality of this process is captured linguistically by the fact that the word *lectio* has produced 'lesson' both in the liturgical and in the scholastic sense, that MHG *lesen* can mean 'to read out loud', but also 'to teach' (as well as 'to learn'),[154] and that in Medieval Latin *legere* had the same range of meanings.[155] In its vital educational function, as well as in the refectory and the *collatio*, the monastery was still closely involved with orality.[156]

(d) Writing in an oral society

We began the last section by observing that there is no such thing as an exclusively literate culture, so that the oral dimension of Roman and Christian literacy was latent within these two traditions from the beginning. By contrast, there is such a phenomenon as a completely oral society (even though the Westernisation of the world may soon call this into question) and in such a case (apart from the actual origin of writing as a historical problem)[157] writing has to be introduced from outside. This we observe in Germany, where writing was introduced from the Mediterranean world which saw its birth. That this faced considerable difficulties is clear: three separate attempts were necessary, of which only the third was ultimately successful, and even the achievement of that success took centuries, so that the acquisition of literacy for laymen in the vernacular is largely coterminous with the medieval period.

The first use of writing on German soil is the runes, an alphabetic system of writing derived from a North Italic script. When the runes were first adopted remains doubtful (opinions vary between the first and second century BC and the first century AD),[158] but roughly contemporary with our first information on Germania from classical sources, so that it might be argued that their presence destroys the case that Germania was an oral society, unacquainted with writing. Strictly speaking, that is true, but there are considerations suggesting that runic practice is not to be compared with writing as used by the Romans or in the Middle Ages. Fundamentally, this is because the possibilities of communication opened up by an alphabetic script were not seized upon in Germania, where the runic script was largely converted to other purposes.

In the first place, runic knowledge (the ability to write and read the signs) was restricted, confined to a small circle of rune-masters[159] and a sparse number of runic monuments, even though there was no theoretical reason why the Germanic language could not have been expressed in this script as regularly as was Latin in its alphabet – provided that the impetus towards literacy was there. Secondly, the inscriptions are short and terse, containing no text of any length (only three inscriptions on stone from Scandinavia in the period in which the script of twenty-four runes was used go beyond 100 letters); nor are there any other indications of longer inscriptions which suggest that perishable material is to blame.[160] We cannot count here references in the sagas to inscribing poems in runes on pieces of wood, for they come from a later period influenced by the use of the Latin script,[161] and the same is true of the fragments of the OE *Dream of the Rood* carved in runes on the Ruthwell Cross (the monument is under strong Christian and classical influence, and the runes may even serve a decorative, rather than communicative purpose).[162] This brings us to a third point, for instead of transmitting a communication the runes appear to have been used to conceal it, to wrap it up in mystery and magic.[163] Not by chance is the word rune connected with mystery or secret ('the *mystery* of the kingdom of God' was translated into Gothic by *rūna*, in OE the word can suggest secret meditation, whilst modern German *raunen* implies whispering secretively).[164] It might be thought that this semantic equation suggests the awe-struck reaction of an illiterate barbarian to an incomprehensible practice, but against this we have the testimony of initiated rune-masters, using runes for magical purposes and describing the process as an act of concealment (ON *fela*).[165] Above all in this context we have to seek the reason why writing was adopted not as a technology (which it was in the south), but as a mystery. Lastly, this distinction can be put in another way: in place of the pragmatic ends which writing served south of the Alps the runes were removed from the everyday world and used for monumental and epigraphic purposes.[166] There is nothing to suggest that they performed a function in Germania at all similar to that exercised by writing in Rome.[167]

Quite apart from the attitude adopted by the Church towards a writing practice associated with pagan magic, the growth of a need for pragmatic literacy meant that the Latin alphabet and its accompanying techniques were bound to win the day over the runes. Nonetheless, some linguistic continuity was preserved between the two writing systems in that three OE terms (in OHG only two) at home in runes came to be applied later to the use of the Latin alphabet. The fact that OE (followed by OHG and ON) distinguished between *rūnstæf* for the runic letter and *bōcstæf* for the Latin suggests that the Common Germanic equivalent of *stæf* had been used for the old script and the compounds became necessary only when the two scripts coexisted for a time.[168] If the word corresponding to OE *rǣdan* was a technical term of runic practice ('to interpret the meaning of an oracle with runes'), only in this language was the word transferred to reading the new script.[169] Finally, OE *wrītan* (and its equivalents in other dialects) was a runic term also used for the Latin script, regularly in England, but only on a few early occasions in Germany.[170] Continuity with the runic past is therefore most firmly attested in England, but only fragmentarily in Germany, and even the one word in which it is still evident ('Buchstabe') is a loan-word from OE which owes its existence to the juxtaposition of runic writing with the system which was to oust it.

To sum up: the runes had the advantage that it was the vernacular language which they recorded, but the disadvantages that knowledge of them was a closely guarded secret, they were used for short inscriptions and served a non-pragmatic purpose, concealing rather than communicating a message. With both the other attempts to introduce writing into Germany this position was exactly reversed.

The second attempt to introduce writing avoided these disadvantages in a drastic way, by simply taking over the Latin writing system itself, together with all its practical advantages, but with it the Latin language as well. The historical background to this cultural loan, well before the Christian mission brought ecclesiastical literacy to Germany, has been discussed by Rosenfeld, who explains why the adoption of the Latin script also involved the adoption of the Latin language.[171] He assembles evidence for the earliest contacts between Germanic leaders and Romans across the imperial frontier by means of messages (some personal, some written) and also the closer contacts resulting from Germanic mercenary service in the Roman army. In either case some knowledge of Latin was called for on the part of the barbarians involved: in the Roman Empire, as later in the British, it was the task of these others to learn the 'world-language' of the dominant power, and not vice versa. To some extent writing was also called for, but as a practical necessity quite different from runic usage: obviously in the case of written messages across the frontier, but also with mercenary service if we bear in mind that for officers in the Roman army (as some of the Germanic leaders were) an ability to read and write was indispensable, since the army depended on a flow of written intelligence and orders.[172] This writing was done cheaply and practically on wax-tablets (*tabellae*) with a wooden cover (for longer messages several could be tied together)[173] which were inscribed with a stylus and used in the army and by Roman merchants.

Tablets of this kind lie behind the OHG word *buoch* and its cognates, designated by the material (beechwood) out of which the cover was made and meaning originally 'document',[174] whereas its plural form (as attested in OHG and MHG) derives from the practice of using several tablets for a longer communication.[175] In accepting this origin of *buoch* we may agree with Rosenfeld that the Germanic word with this meaning did not originate with the Goths, but in western Germania where contact was first made with the Romans and their writing habits,[176] but also with Kuhn and Ebel that it had had no previous connection with runic practice.[177] On both scores we are dealing with a term belonging to a second wave of writing practice in Germany.

Two other words probably belong to this wave, but, unlike *buoch*, they bear the outward stamp of the Latin origin of this writing and fill the gaps created by the refusal in Germany, total or nearly so, to make use of the runic terms *rǣdan* and *wrītan* which OE had applied to the new script. The OHG verb *skrîban* is a loan-word from Latin *scribere*, presumably of some antiquity because, on the model of native verbs like *trîban* or *rîban*, it has been assimilated to the first class of strong verbs, driving out the runic term for writing almost entirely.[178] By contrast, the OHG verb *lesan* is a native word and the only one to be used for reading in German. Its original meaning was 'to pick, to gather', but the earlier view that it was associated with the runic oracle practice described by Tacitus is now questioned, mainly because the shift of meaning to 'to read' is precisely paralleled by Latin *legere*, so that we are probably dealing with a loan-translation.[179] Just as it is difficult to conceive that all the Latin names for the days of the week were not taken across into Germanic lock, stock and barrel as part of one process, so it is likely that *skrîban* and *lesan* were formed at the same time, even in conjunction with the creation of *buoch*. All three point to an early contact with Roman writing practice quite distinct from the connection between the runes and a North Italic script.

We come thirdly to another contact with Latin writing practice which on linguistic grounds must be placed later. Our best entry into this problem is to go back one stage, for we saw that the Germanic word corresponding to OHG *buoch* was probably coined to render the Roman writing-tablet, *tabella*. The later development of the vernacular word, first to 'document' and then to 'book' (assisted by outward appearances, in that the wooden covers of a lengthy communication on tablets resembled the covers of a book, wooden and bound in leather), created a lexical gap for the writing-tablet, in regular use in the Middle Ages as in classical antiquity. This gap could not be filled by the loanword *zabal*, taken over direct from *tabula* or *tabella*, since it had specialised its meaning to 'gaming board'.[180] Instead, the Latin word was borrowed into German a second time, producing now *tavala* with the technical meaning 'writing-tablet' (alongside occasional 'gaming board').[181] We can be sure that *zabal* was considerably earlier than *tavala*: it retained classical Latin *-b-* in place of Vulgar Latin *-v-*, and underwent the effects of the second sound-shift (*t-* > *z-*), whereas *tavala* was too late for this. Furthermore, the need for *tavala* could only have arisen once the introduction of books, as distinct from writing-tablets, had called forth the shift of meaning of *buoch*.

There is a group of other words, all to do with the practice of writing, which entered German as loanwords at a date later than *zabal* or *buoch*. A late loan is suggested by the absence of any effects of the second sound-shift in the case of OHG *tincta* 'ink' (< Latin *tincta*), *karta* 'papyrus' (< *charta* 'sheet of papyrus'), *pergamin* 'parchment' (< *pergamenum*). A slightly earlier dating is suggested by the evidence of Vulgar Latin in the case of two further words. In classical Latin a short written communication was termed a *libellus brevis*, shortened to *libellus* or to *brevis*. The former survives in OHG *livol* (which presupposes the development of classical to Vulgar Latin *livellus*), whilst the latter produces OHG *briaf* 'document' (where the diphthong presupposes an earlier long *e*, as in Vulgar Latin in this position, by contrast with classical Latin short *e*). In other words, apart from *livol* and *briaf*, all these words (including *tavala*) would have been exposed to the sound-shift if they had been borrowed early enough. If we accept the course of the sixth century as an approximate dating of the shift, these words were borrowed after this date, probably as part of one wholesale cultural innovation, involving the regular practice of writing, both in a provisional form (writing-tablet) and in a more permanent book form (papyrus, parchment, ink, book).

If we tie these words together and see them as a unified loan, the only institution in this period which was concerned with writing is Benedictine monasticism: established in the sixth century in Gaul (with pockets in Trier and on the Mosel), in the seventh century in Upper Germany (the Irish mission), and in the eighth century in Middle Germany (the Anglo-Saxon mission).[182] This suggests that our writing terminology, and with it the practice of writing, was introduced in the seventh or eighth century, probably (given the slowness with which writing established itself) in the eighth.[183]

We can go one last step further, since evidence for the institutional concern of monasticism with writing is provided by one more loanword. Classical Latin had used the word *schola* (with a short stem-vowel) with the meaning 'group of pupils, disciples, followers', and this word is attested in OS *scola* 'warrior-band' and OE *scolu* 'group of people', neither in a scholastic sense. However, the diphthong in OHG *scuola* ('monastic school', first attested in the OHG *Benediktinerregel*)[184] suggests a later loan, presupposing a Vulgar Latin long vowel (cf. *briaf*). The position with this word is therefore the same as with the writing terms we have been considering. The school was the context within the institution of monasticism which ensured the teaching and transmission of the practice of writing. It is the context which tied together our writing terms and created the need for them in German, as part of one cultural innovation.[185]

To sum up this third stage: in the early monastic context in Germany writing and reading were now institutionalised and more widespread, we witness the first beginnings of a written culture, concerned with the communication, pragmatic or not, of short or long texts. Nothing we have so far seen, however, suggests that these texts were in German; everything points to a monastic culture in Latin.

The dominance of Latin in the written tradition, even where the vernacular might seem to be called for, is also present in the codification of barbarian laws in this period. Germanic law was oral and committed to memory by experts, but after the migrations the usefulness of written law became apparent when judgment had to be given to those living under different laws.[186] The first to codify their law were the Visigoths, followed by the Burgundians, whilst the Salic Law of the Franks was written down at the beginning of the sixth century.[187] Common to these codifications (with the exception of the Anglo-Saxons and later the Scandinavians) is the fact that they were all in Latin. In view of these exceptions it is not enough to say that the continental codifiers used Latin because it was the appropriate language for written law,[188] but Wormald also suggests that legislation could be a matter of image-building and that one image was imperial Rome.[189] Einhard's description of Charles the Great committing the laws of his peoples to writing opens with the words *post susceptum imperiale nomen*, and Charles, like Einhard, may have known what Suetonius had written about Augustus, and was persuaded that written legislation went with his new imperial dignity, as at Rome.[190] Imitation of the Roman model, even down to the use of language, could only raise the status of the barbarian rulers. Wormald also points to a second model, however: Christianity (clerics were involved in the legislation as scribes, but also as royal advisers).[191] Christianity was not merely a religion of the book, but of the Bible as a law-book, with Christ as judge, frequently depicted holding a book. In this way barbarian written law could emulate Moses and strengthen the position of the king as a Christian ruler.[192] The two lines of transmission of literacy (Rome and Christianity) converge in this codification of Germanic laws – if the two lines saw literacy in terms of Latin, it is not surprising that continental Germanic laws were set down in Latin and that Germanic rulers sought to acquire its authority as the language of writing, of Empire and of religion for themselves as Christian rulers.

The different moves towards writing within German society considered in this section stand in a mirror-image relationship to one another. On the one hand we have runic writing in the vernacular, but with a number of disadvantages (restricted scope, non-communicative function, non-pragmatic use). On the other hand we have the use of writing-tablets, the cultivation of writing at monastic centres, and the codification of law, all of which avoid the disadvantages of runic practice, but miss its advantage, the use of the vernacular in writing. This is a gap which we have still to see bridged in the course of the early Middle Ages, but before that we must turn to two obstacles in the path of a written tradition.

(e) Obstacles to the written tradition

Our argument has suggested that written transmission was tied up with two factors: with monasteries as centres of literacy and with Latin as the language of writing. Neither of these factors could be taken for granted.

The cultural function which monasteries later exercised was not a foregone conclusion at the start of Western monasticism, a fact which we are prone to forget in the light of the cultural ascendancy of the Carolingian monasteries. The aloofness of monasteries is part of a deep-seated anti-intellectual strain within early Christianity, resulting from the Church's opposition to the surviving forces of pagan culture, amounting to a rejection of classical values embodied in grammar, rhetoric and the study of classical authors.[193] Forced to confront these earlier values with a rival set, the Church located its alternative values in monasticism, where education was subordinated to religious meditation and prayer, and excluded reference to the pagan tradition. Early monasticism has therefore been termed a counter-culture of outsiders rejecting the ideals which had informed the literate culture of Rome.[194] Unlike Cassiodorus (who found a place for liberal education within his monastery Vivarium), most monastic leaders of the time were anti-intellectual ascetics, concentrating on the liturgical and meditational cycle and avoiding classical studies.[195] This attitude is summed up by Jerome's nightmare vision of being accused by Christ of being a 'Ciceronian' (we should say an 'intellectual') rather than a Christian, and by Cassian's recommendation that a monk who wished to penetrate the meaning of the scriptures would succeed more by self-purification and mortification than by theological study of the commentators.[196]

If, despite this order of priorities, intellectual attainments were called for in the monastery, we must stress their restricted scope in this early period. St Benedict, in calling his monastery a *scola dominici servitii*, may have used *scola* in a military sense, equating it with *militia*, but it is also probable that, like others, he implied here a contrast with the school of classical learning which he had fled in his youth, exchanging it for the school of Christ.[197] Although the monk abandoned study of the classics, this does not mean that he abandoned learning altogether: he had to know the psalms and should therefore be able to read and the Rule of St Benedict set aside time for reading in private each day. Even this preoccupation with books should not be interpreted as an intellectual activity, for reading was regarded as an ascetic exercise; the goal of monastic education (apart from the grammatical minimum to understand the scriptures) was religious edification and a withdrawal from worldly values, so that St Benedict could be described as *scienter nescius et sapienter indoctus*.[198] In this early period of monasticism education (necessary to the extent that *pueri oblati* were admitted at an early age and had to be educated)[199] was not organised along the lines of what we should recognise as a school, but rested on the private encounter (*confabulatio mutua*) between monastic seniors and juniors and on the psalter as the central educational text, incorporating at once a religious document, history, grammar, and poetry.[200]

It is characteristic of this relationship between monasticism and the literate values of antiquity that, like St Augustine, St Benedict had begun by taking up studies, but then abandoned them, just as Caesarius of Arles renounced the instruction of a grammarian who was to give him the polish of secular learning.[201] A similar picture has been sketched for the major monasteries of the Merovingian period: their monks included many who, in withdrawing from the world, had inwardly distanced themselves from the rhetorical education they had been given.[202] If literary culture was to be found in these monasteries, it was not the result of education given there, but an inheritance from the world before *conversio*. As far as literacy and written transmission are concerned, the role of the monasteries in this period must be assessed negatively. Religious conviction brought about a break with the past; if anything of this past survived within the monastery it had been brought there from the world outside, not cultivated within. Monastic education was therefore at the best a secondary accretion.[203] St Benedict's monastery may have possessed a school, but it does not modify his monastic ideal.[204] What we regard as historically important about the later achievement of Benedictine monasticism (its cultivation, even rescue, of classical learning, literature and language) is a later achievement of the ninth century, not foreseen by the founding father, and strictly subordinate to bringing about a religious awakening and inculcating a monastic discipline.

If it took centuries to bring about an achievement by no means self-evident within early monasticism, what is it that, mainly in the eighth and ninth centuries, brought about such a change, making it possible for an institution which had rejected the cultural values of antiquity to be instrumental in saving them in written form in their scriptoria?[205] Two preliminary observations can be made before we come to the vital part played by the Carolingian renaissance.

We may start with a point made by von See (that the Benedictine order, founded at Montecassino in the first half of the sixth century, acquired its role as protagonist of written culture north of the Alps in the ninth century)[206] and ask what this geographical transposition involved. The expansion of monasticism from Italy to Northern Europe meant that it was now at home not merely in the urban context which had been the focus of the classical pagan culture from which St Benedict distanced himself, but also in an area with far fewer cities, with nothing like an urban culture to compare with Rome, and moreover, as monks were used for missionary purposes, even in regions with no cities at all, bordering on pagan kingdoms.[207] The dangers of an urban pagan civilisation against which the Church had reacted vigorously where it was exposed to them in Italy were not so acute north of the Alps, especially in large areas of Germany. Admittedly, here too Christianity faced the dangers of paganism, but Germanic paganism was an oral phenomenon, unlike Roman pagan literature, so that to busy oneself with that literature (if only as a means to an end) did not harbour dangers as it had in Italy. In now acquiring more of an educational monopoly the Church could afford to take up less of a defensive stance, to relax somewhat, and derive what value it could from Latin written culture.

In another sense, too, the switch of political activity northwards assisted the development we are tracing. In drawing attention to predecessors of the Carolingian renaissance Guerreau-Jalabert has stressed the importance of Ireland and Britain, especially their geographical position.[208] In these two countries (never, or only for a short time, part of the Roman Empire) the conversion to Christianity brought with it exposure to an ecclesiastical institution based on Latin, a language foreign to these countries as it was not to Gaul, so that the Church had to take in hand the necessary education for its clerics, achieving a purer Latin in the process,[209] because what was taught scholastically was not jeopardised by Vulgar Latin, as in Gaul. In that the Irish and the Anglo-Saxons were also active on the continent, founding monasteries in the seventh and eighth centuries, they took their pedagogic and intellectual values with them,[210] creating the conditions for a 'pre-reform' and, in the case of Alcuin, playing a part in the reform of Charles the Great.[211]

As a result of this Emperor's policy the systematisation of monastic education came about,[212] based on the school, scriptorium, and library in a form of organisation which goes far beyond what had been provided for by St Benedict.[213] Only now was there found, alongside the spiritual and edificational training of monastic life, a regularised promotion of literate studies, including the *artes* of classical education. Only now did the monastery acquire an educational function.

The second obstacle concerns Latin as the language of literacy, handed down from Roman antiquity and within the Church. We have seen that, apart from the short-lived exception of the runes, any attempt at writing in Germany involved the use of Latin. Whilst the authority of Latin could only strengthen such attempts, the converse possibility must not be disregarded: any threat to Latin involved a threat to writing, since there was no vernacular fall-back position in which writing could be rescued.

This position of Latin, unique as long as writing depended on it as a medium in Western Europe, has been well stressed by von See. He observes that in the pre-Carolingian period not merely were the Germanic vernaculars slowly approaching the possibility of being written down (a process which we are following for German), but also Latin was on the brink of retreating from the realm of writing or at least losing control over its full extent.[214] By that he refers to the growing dissolution of Latin into incipient Romance vernaculars, to the increasing 'oralisation' of Latin, detectable in what Fontaine has described as a linguistic crisis affecting both spoken and written Latin, traceable to an educational crisis (the disappearance of Roman schooling, a marked increase in illiteracy, a drying-up of literary activity).[215]

It is a pointer to the importance of the Carolingian renaissance that, as with the educational function of monasticism, so too with written Latin Charles the Great represents a turning-point, for he ensured that Latin was brought back to its correct written norm (why this should have concerned him as a ruler will occupy us shortly). Steps were taken to regularise the syntactical and orthographic chaos that characterised Merovingian Latin; the successful attempt was made to restore Latin to the position which it then occupied for some centuries: of being the only language in which a variety of intellectual themes (history, philosophy, science, theology) could be discussed or in which a legal or commercial transaction would be drawn up.[216] Latin as a written language recovered the full range of possibilities which it had possessed in Roman antiquity (from high culture to day-to-day pragmatism), but if Latin was restored to the realm of writing, this seems to have been at the cost of vernacular writing, since the more Latin was able to fulfil the tasks of writing, the less need there might have been to depute some of these to the vernacular.

By a development not foreseen by the organisers of the Carolingian reform this proved not to be so, certainly not in the case of the French vernacular.[217] Part of the reform of Latin had concerned pronunciation, an attempt to free it from the clutches of vernacular Romance and restore it to what was regarded as the norm of classical Latin (significantly the work of Alcuin, from a country where he had had to learn Latin as a 'foreign language', under no threat from a spoken Romance tongue).[218] An unexpected result of this was that Latin as now pronounced by clerics was no longer comprehensible to Romance laymen, an outcome which was a disadvantage in preaching, which is why a number of councils dealt with this difficulty and why the council of Tours laid down that the preacher was to *transferre* his sermon *in rusticam Romanam linguam*.[219] After this birth-certificate of French, this acknowledgment of a distinction between Latin and Romance vernacular, there followed isolated attempts to put the vernacular into writing (the *Strassburg Oaths, Sainte Eulalie*),[220] so that the Carolingian reform of Latin distinguished Latin from vernacular, but also indirectly led to the first attempts to put that vernacular into writing. What was true of the French vernacular can have been relevant to German (the council of Tours referred also to the *linguam Theotiscam*, also used in the *Strassburg Oaths* alongside French), so that we approach the possibility of encountering German in writing. Before this, however, we must look at the implications of the Carolingian renaissance for writing, for it is not by chance that this has proved to be a turning-point for the institutionalisation of monastic literate culture and for the reform of Latin as a written language.

(f) The Carolingian renaissance of literacy

Against the view that the period around 800 witnessed a renaissance of the culture of classical antiquity Treitler has urged that the goal of Charles's educational programme was literacy rather than literature, and that we are dealing with a renaissance of literacy and of the Latin language (revealing by that conjunction continuity with what we have seen in earlier periods).[221] However many classical texts were transmitted by the Carolingian scribes, they were collected and copied as part of a literacy programme, not for their own sake as literature. Together with scribal activity in other fields they made up what Treitler calls a 'script culture',[222] just as McKitterick argues that the written word was central to Carolingian society[223] (for the first time we return to the situation which had been true of Roman society). Charles's programme demanded a staggering amount of parchment, not just to gratify an interest in learning, but for very practical reasons.

There were also practical reasons why this production of writing was in Latin. In the first place, it was the language of the Bible, of the fathers, of the liturgy and of the Church, so that the Emperor's legislation dealing with ecclesiastical affairs, the education of the clergy, the improvement of Latin texts for their use, all provided religious support for the Empire and buttressed Charles's divinely sanctioned authority. Secondly, Latin was the language of the imperial tradition which Charles resumed in 800, so that the codification of written law in Latin on the model of the Roman emperors strengthened his political authority in yet another way. Two other factors are less ideological and more practical. Charles ruled over a multilingual society (his subjects spoke a variety of Germanic and Slav dialects, together with a number of Romance vernaculars more and more mutually incomprehensible), so that Latin served as the language of international communication.[224] Lastly, as the only known and tried language of pragmatic writing and reading, Latin assisted the administration of a widespread Empire, making for unity over time and space. Writing and the language of writing were linked as essential instruments in governing the Carolingian Empire, just as they had been for its Roman predecessor.

One detail assisted this process. By partly going against the earlier practice of itinerant kingship (the ruler held court at various places in his kingdom, travelling constantly to do so) in the creation of a permanent residential palace at Aachen, Charles created conditions which made possible a settled administrative apparatus relying on regular written communication.[225] This may be another way in which he imitated Roman models, but it is possible that he was stimulated in this by the tangible advantages accruing to bishops in the administration of their diocese from their cathedral city or by the way in which the production of writing was made easier for monasteries by their *stabilitas loci*.[226]

This explosion of writing made it necessary to recruit a class of *litterati* for the secular and ecclesiastical administration of a vast realm. Charles knew that to rule effectively he had to communicate with various parts of his Empire in writing and to maintain written records, but on his accession to the throne the state of illiteracy was such that he had to seek help in the only quarter where literacy, however imperfect, was to be found: in the Church, especially in the monasteries. The Church has been described as the common denominator in a realm of such size;[227] it was the body which, with whatever qualifications, had kept in touch with classical and Christian literate education, and was therefore the obvious means of providing the trained administrators required. If a programme of education was called for, Charles had little choice but to make use of whatever schools already existed: in the monasteries and to some extent in episcopal centres.[228]

The importance attached to script culture is clear from the imperial legislation concerned with it. The *Admonitio generalis* laid down the foundation of schools for teaching children to read, the philological correction of religious works to ensure that clerics prayed in a correct linguistic form, the accurate copying of liturgical manuscripts, as well as the study of the seven liberal arts as the foundation of good language and style. This concern for correctness (*rectitudo*) is visible in further details. If texts had to be recopied in a reliable form, this presupposed grammatical and orthographic accuracy, but also a form of writing, the Caroline minuscule, which avoided ligatures and achieved greater clarity and comprehensibility; in other words the needs of the reader were consulted as well as those of the scribe. From this range of features I select a few to consider for their relevance to the problem of literacy.

We may start, as the Carolingians must have done, with the foundation of literacy, the act of writing. Before their reforms the eighth century had known a variety of scripts within Europe, lacking uniformity and easy legibility, which were largely replaced by the Caroline minuscule, developed at Corbie in the 770s, diffused with the assistance of Alcuin at Tours, and achieving legibility by restricting ligatures and separating words by spaces and phrases by capitals.[229] With this new script went a system of punctuation, the aim of which was to facilitate understanding by the reader by indicating how clauses and sentences were articulated. The reader whose needs were consulted is not to be seen only in terms of modern reading, for this punctuation was meant to tell him when to raise or lower his voice, so that the listeners would not be confused.[230] That we are dealing with someone who read out to others, with the Church *lector*, was made clear by Alcuin who wrote on the importance of punctuation, saying that the object of correct punctuation was that the lector should read nothing false, nor suddenly fall silent when reading before the pious brothers in church.[231] Even in instructions for correct writing the dimension of orality was not lost to view.

Grammar, too, had a role to play in the literacy programme, not merely in the sense that the Carolingians realised that clarity of thought demanded an accurate use of language.[232] Much more revealing is what Einhard reported of Charles's policy after becoming Emperor, for he included in a list of various spheres in which oral tradition was to be put into written form the statement that the Emperor *inchoavit et grammaticam patrii sermonis*.[233] This remark was understood to mean that Charles encouraged the equivalent of a vernacular Donatus, but Matzel has pointed out how anachronistic this is (later parallels in the Middle Ages presuppose an already developed vernacular literature in written form, whereas with Charles we stand at the threshold of vernacular writing) and how it must have surpassed the capacities of this early period.[234] In proposing his alternative reading Matzel bases himself on what Grundmann said of this passage: that *grammatica* was used in the sense of the theory of a written language subject to due rules.[235] Hitherto a grammar had only been possible in Latin, because only Latin was written and possessed *grammata* or *litterae*, as opposed to the sounds of exclusively oral languages, for which by reason of their orality no grammar was conceivable. If Alcuin defined grammar in terms of letters and writing, with a possible influence on speech as well (*grammatica est literalis scientia, et est custos recte loquendi et scribendi*),[236] then the Emperor's concern was with making the vernacular subject to the same rules of written language as Latin, with making the vernacular capable of being written. The idea of a *grammatica patrii sermonis* could not have been conceived without the Latin model, just as the translation of Latin texts into OHG encouraged an awareness of the rules and norms which underlay the written use of the vernacular by recognising the similar rules elaborated for Latin.[237] Matzel goes one important step further, suggesting that a coherent regularisation of grammar and orthography was nowhere achieved in OHG more successfully than in the *Isidor* translations, which he sees as closely connected with the Emperor's policy.[238] In this sense grammar, the regularisation of a spoken language to make it fit for writing, may be said to underlie Charles's linguistic and educational policy.

Punctuation and grammar together account for another Carolingian innovation, the beginning of musical notation in the Middle Ages. Treitler has shown that writing down music arose in intimate association with the writing down of language and the teaching about language which played a prominent part in Carolingian culture.[239] He emphasises that although because of this association there are features shared by neumes, punctuation and grammar, we should not assume neumes to have been used earlier for musical notation,[240] in other words that with these neumes we witness the entry of writing into the domain of an oral tradition.[241] He dates this from early in the ninth century, locates its origin in the northern part of the West Frankish domain, in other words in the region which was a centre for the spread of Carolingian language-writing.[242] It may not derive from any specific legislation by Charles, but it is a Carolingian phenomenon, closely associated with the contemporary spread of literacy.[243] In so far as it was meant to exercise a control over oral tradition[244] and to provide guidance in the singing of texts[245] the writing down of music had just as much an oral dimension as had the use of the punctuation signs out of which it evolved.

An intelligible orthography, a clear punctuation and a regularised grammar all demand accuracy, but this will achieve little without accuracy of the texts to which they are all subordinate. It is therefore true to say that Alcuin's influence in editing ecclesiastical texts was as marked as in the fields of grammar and the Caroline minuscule. Here too he faced the problem of a range of variants inherited from the past, making it a necessity to prepare reliable texts for uniform use.[246] He therefore turned to editing a uniform liturgy, but also devoted his energies to the Bible itself, establishing a complete text, largely free of corruptions and widely accepted as authoritative.

Among the fields in which, according to Einhard, Charles busied himself with instituting a written tradition is law, important for the administration of a far-flung domain with different codes in different regions. A concern for the written codification of Germanic law in Latin went back well before his time, but Charles continued this process in several ways. He saw that the tribal law of the Saxons, Thuringians and others in his Empire was committed to writing and brought about a thorough revision of the *Lex Salica*.[247] As with previous codifications, the language of these written laws was Latin, even though the language of legal transactions remained the vernacular. Such a linguistic divorce rendered urgent the problem of translating and communicating this written law, as when Charles summoned to Aachen in 802 secular rulers together with those skilled in law, and ordered the laws of different parts of his realm to be read out in translated form to all those assembled (the fragmentary OHG translation of the *Lex Salica* has been associated with this).[248] Two points are of interest here. In the first place, as with punctuation to prevent the *lector* in church stumbling into error as he read out to others, we are dealing with an oral dimension of what has been written down. Secondly, as with medieval correspondence, we witness a to-and-fro between vernacular and Latin: in correspondence it was from dictation in the vernacular to writing down in Latin to reading out in translation,[249] and similarly in law (legal transaction or oral law in the vernacular, followed by a codification in Latin, reactivated by translating back into the vernacular). The transition from spoken to written in both cases involved a change in language. If this suggests that the vernacular was at home in the oral field and Latin in writing, the importance of the OHG fragment of the *Lex Salica* is that, unlike the position in correspondence, the translation back into the vernacular has found its way on to parchment.

The *Lex Salica* translation is an isolated exception and the language of literacy in the Carolingian period, as earlier, was regularly Latin. Haubrichs has made this point by emphasising that OHG texts occupied a minute area by comparison with the mass of written productions in Latin and that only at Reichenau did any of the monastic library catalogues list German writings amongst their holdings.[250] We have reached the same conclusion along a different path: whilst writing has been associated with Latin throughout this chapter, we have had occasion to mention writing in German only rarely. We know of no text which can be directly associated with the sermons in German mentioned at the council of Tours, whilst the *Isidor* translations occur in a bilingual manuscript (the implications of this we shall shortly discuss), the German text of the *Strassburg Oaths* is a vernacular 'quotation' in Neidhart's Latin text, and even the *Lex Salica* enjoyed no linguistic autonomy, but stood in the interplay between vernacular and Latin. All this suggests the slowness with which the vernacular found its way on to parchment, but also the fact that it managed this only in the shadow of Latin.

(g) The transition of Old High German to a written tradition

Before looking at the ways in which German had to break loose from the dominance of Latin in finding its way on to parchment we must recall that this process was slowed down by the persistence of oral tradition.

In the preface to her history of a later period Vollmann-Profe reminds us of the continuity of this oral tradition long after the Carolingian period, adding that it did not vacate the field to writing in German without putting up a struggle, and recommending us to keep it in mind when considering written works in the vernacular.[251] In his volume in the same series Haubrichs has devised a more effective method for calling this 'lost' dimension to mind by devoting two parts to the oral tradition of the lay nobility and to the written literature of clerics respectively and by giving pride of place in the former to themes of heroic literature which are known to have circulated orally in Germany during the period.[252] By going into such detail Haubrichs does more than improve upon Vollmann-Profe's reminder of oral tradition:[253] he presents it as coexisting alongside written literature and devotes a third part to the literary interplay between these two fields. By doing this his presentation also progresses beyond what Baesecke planned for his literary history. Although the earlier scholar's survey had the merit of presenting Germanic literature as oral and OHG literature as written, the division of these into two separate volumes had the result of suggesting that an oral tradition was replaced by a written one, that one was simply followed by the other. By contrast, Haubrichs is truer to the facts of literary history in implying that writing did not oust orality, but encroached upon it, so that oral tradition continued alongside writing. It is the ability of this orality to survive which qualified the rate of progress of German literature in written form.

Even greater difficulties, however, were caused by German having to make headway against the overriding claims of Latin as a written language. Problems arose, for example, on quite an elementary level by the decision, unavoidable since writing reached northern Europe in the form of Latin, to use the Latin alphabet, adapting it to the different phonetic requirements of the German language. Some isolated OHG texts show signs of the Anglo-Saxon script, and from this same source attempts were also made to meet some of the needs of a Germanic language which Latin could not (e.g. 'w' or 'th').[254] The failure of the Latin alphabet to meet these needs concerned fricatives in Germanic and affricates in German, some spirants and diphthongs, but also the need to distinguish between long and short vowels, as well as dialectal variations arising within OHG.

All this suggests that the application of an alphabet devised with the needs of Latin in mind to a language with a different phonetic structure led to problems and an awareness of deficiencies. Objectively, these deficiencies were those of the Latin alphabet, unable to adjust itself to new needs, but in view of the unquestioned superiority of Latin as a written language this is not how things presented themselves to German writers struggling with the problem, which they saw in terms of the primitive nature of their own language, resisting the discipline of Latin. The best-known statement of this attitude is in Otfrid's Latin dedication of his work to Liutbert. He accused the Frankish tongue of *barbaries*[255] because it had not been subjected to the discipline of grammar, quoting some of the hair-raising orthographic devices he had been driven to in writing Frankish in the Latin alphabet, saying that his use of 'k' and 'z' went against Latin usage (*extra usum latinitatis*), but fearing to quote other examples in his Latin epistle for fear that the reader would scorn the uncouthness of such a rustic language – rustic because the Franks did not use it in writing and had therefore not polished it by any rules.[256] In using criteria derived from Latin Otfrid is reproaching Frankish for not being Latin or for not being a written language like Latin. In the eyes of the Romans barbarians had been distinguished by their lack of literacy (so that Otfrid followed them in accusing Frankish of *barbaries*) and *grammatica* was conceivable only in a written language (which is why Frankish must be judged uncouth). The thrust of Otfrid's argument may go beyond this (he was presenting a book in which Frankish had been written down),[257] but the excuses he felt it necessary to make are revealing: he had to deal with the objection that the vernacular fell short of Latin, in its use of writing and even when it used the letters of the Latin alphabet.

Even where OHG did find its way into writing, this did nothing to call seriously into question the dominance of Latin (although once an advantage was seen in using the vernacular in writing, this must ultimately call into question one of the components in the superiority of Latin).[258] In the OHG period, however, such a threat was far from being realised. Latin as the language of the Church, of education and of learning, of political and legal administration and of poetry, enjoyed the immense advantage of being an international means of communication.[259] By comparison, the use of a vernacular was restricted in scope to the tribe which spoke it, but also in its inability to deal with the intellectual complexities of which Latin was capable.[260] The clerics, whose literacy at this time provided the only possibility of writing in the vernacular, were the first to see the advantages of an international language like Latin and the last to see any advantages in a written vernacular with no international scope which occupied only a small sector of intellectual life in the country that spoke it.

As Germanists we run the risk of inflating the importance of the OHG texts which provide the material of our discipline by neglecting the modest role they played in the cultural life of their time. Derolez has reminded us that the weighty volumes of the OHG glosses do not prove what we might like them to prove: they are not testimony to an interest in the German language (that is how we regard them), but evidence of ignorance of Latin and a means of coping with it.[261] For the cleric who compiled glossaries, mainly for use in monastic schools, German was a means to the end of teaching Latin, not an end in itself, as in modern scholarship. Only if we disabuse ourselves of this scholarly anachronism can we see the vernacular in its subordination to Latin. That this is true not merely of the everyday purposes of education,[262] but also of vernacular works of literature to which importance was attributed at the time has been suggested by a contrast drawn by von See. Whereas Otfrid's work and the OS *Heliand* have each been preserved in 4 manuscripts or fragments only, a Latin work such as *Waltharius* is attested in twelve manuscripts, Einhard's *Vita Karoli Magni* in 80, and the *Historia Langobardorum* of Paulus Diaconus in about 200.[263] Kuhn has suggested the true proportions with the image of isolated and experimental texts in the vernacular floating in a sea of Latin literature,[264] whilst Masser has illustrated the point with regard to literary activity at the court of Charles the Great: whereas authors in his circle composed hundreds of Latin *carmina*, not one of them composed a line in the vernacular.[265] If this court is regarded as not wholly characteristic, similar evidence is forthcoming elsewhere. The monastic library of St. Gallen contained an important array of Latin literary texts, classical and Christian, but included no German text (even though Otfrid sent a copy of his work there) apart from shorter pragmatic ones of a catechetical nature and works intended for the monastic school.[266] For the most part writing in OHG had only a secondary function, supplementing the vastly greater bulk of Latin writing which it served. This has justified Sonderegger in classifying the transmission of OHG texts in four groups, each dependent on Latin: translations of a Latin original, biblical poetry dependent on a Latin model, incorporation of vernacular words in a Latin text, and the inclusion of OHG texts in a Latin manuscript.[267]

This last phenomenon demonstrates that these vernacular texts existed alongside Latin, not in place of it, a juxtaposition which Masser has characterised as 'bilingual texts'.[268] He argues that in a text which consists of two versions, a Latin original accompanied by a translation into German, the status of the latter is more restricted than if it occurred autonomously, since the translation derives its function from the original and constantly refers back to it.[269] This is obvious in interlinear translations[270] such as the *Benediktinerregel* or the *Murbacher Hymnen*, where the non-German word-order is not meant to provide a consecutive text in the vernacular, but to help understand the Latin words in their sequence.[271] Where the two versions appear in two columns side by side attempts can be made to coordinate them by dividing them into sections and arranging that to each Latin section there corresponds its vernacular counterpart. Where however, as with *Tatian*, the division into lines is so carefully made that the lines of the German text correspond to those of the Latin, we can be sure that the latter is the reference-point to which German is subordinate, because the Latin text, but not the German, is divided into sections by the use of capitals.[272] Masser's observations on bilingual texts apply even to the *Isidor* translations (because of their high linguistic quality normally regarded as distinct from run-of-the-mill interlinear translations)[273] and even to the supreme achievement of Notker, since we know that he produced his work not to establish scholarship in the German language,[274] but to assist his monastic pupils to understand a Latin text.[275] It is the quality of these translations which tempts us to see in them more than was intended, more than vernacular versions geared to the needs of the Latin primary text.

The marginal function of German written texts can sometimes be established quite literally. That is the case where in place of interlinear glosses we have marginal ones,[276] but elsewhere the marginal preservation of a German text must be understood metaphorically. This is so whenever a text occurs as a page-filler when a Latin codex happens to leave space available, as with *Muspilli* or the *St. Galler Spottverse*, or on the endpapers of a codex, as with the *Hildebrandslied* or the *Merseburger Zaubersprüche*.[277]

Relegation of German writing to a subordinate position brings out the unique position of the *Heliand* and Otfrid's *Evangelienbuch*, for they are the only texts preserved in codices meant specifically for them, although there is probably a particular explanation for their privileged position.[278]

Where German works were written down which are not translations they are poetic texts such as the *Hildebrandslied* or *Muspilli* or alternatively biblical epics in verse where dependence on a Latin model is more remote than with bilingual texts. These belong to what Sonderegger has termed 'autochthonous texts',[279] some of which may represent survivals in writing from an oral past and all of which, as poetic works rather than translations, have understandably attracted the lion's share of scholarly attention. Even so, it is important to stress the relative rarity of these works (this despite the size of the biblical epics). If we forget this, we can be tempted by their intrinsic interest to concentrate on them and see them as largely making up Carolingian literature in the vernacular. As highlights they remain few and isolated, whereas the bulk of German literature stands in the shadow of Latin. Whether autochthonous or geared to the needs of Latin, however, the German language now slowly found its way on to parchment under the Carolingians, involving attempts to wrestle with the problems of writing and realise its potentialities for a hitherto oral language.

(h) The course of Old High German as a written tradition

To place this section at the end of the chapter is not meant to suggest a teleological determinism about German being used in writing, as if it were a foregone conclusion, but rather to re-emphasise the difficulties in the way of this. If up to now we have been considering the ways in which writing found its way *to Germany*, we must now sharpen our focus to writing *in German*, asking about the conditions under which this came about. Although we have to sharpen our focus, we can proceed by the same steps as in previous sections, in the sequence: runic inscriptions, wax-tablets, the codification of law, and monastic writing. Most of our attention will be devoted to monastic writing and to the place which the German language slowly found within it.

Runic inscriptions need not detain us for long. Although they are important as the first examples of writing in the vernacular, they are few and short and moreover the surviving examples in German date from a period (fifth to eighth centuries)[280] in which Christianisation and the use of the Latin script for a wider range of uses than was available for the runes meant that their days were numbered. It is a sign of the pressures to which runic writing was now exposed that a good proportion of German examples reveal Christian influence or that inscriptions should also be attested in the Latin alphabet, one from Cologne about 850 praising a library and the new educational possibilities it presented.[281]

We may pass over the evidence of wax-tablets quickly for two reasons. First, because although a number of writing tablets have survived from the Roman period complete with inscription (documents, letters, school exercises)[282] none is known to have played a part in communication between a German and Roman. The second reason is even more telling, since in this Roman context the language of writing was naturally Latin and remained so for some time even with medieval writing tablets (when they were used for German escapes us because of the flimsy nature of this material evidence).

Nor need the legal evidence detain us, for it mainly concerns scattered vernacular words in the middle of a Latin codification, representing personal and place names as well as technical terms of Germanic law for which there was no Latin equivalent.[283] This evidence is of linguistic interest, but it does provide pockets of German which have survived the transposition from oral law in the vernacular to written codification in Latin. Even where the result is a linguistically mixed document, as with the *Würzburger Markbeschreibungen*, the path to a completely German text was no quick one, since the second version, in which this was achieved, was written as late as the end of the tenth century.[284]

Only with monastic literacy does the evidence become frequent and informative, because the monasteries were involved in the two spheres into which Haubrichs has divided early vernacular Carolingian texts: their scriptoria with the production of pragmatic texts in German for catechetical use (baptismal formulas, creeds, prayers, confessions) and their schools with the teaching of Latin as the basis for writing, with the task of introducing pupils to the riches of the Latin intellectual world.[285] Haug has stressed that school practice could not ignore the vernacular completely, since it was the inevitable starting-point of those who were to be educated in Latinity.[286] Even in the case of more advanced pupils (such as Notker presupposed in his classroom at St. Gallen whenever he used a Latin term to explain a point)[287] the advantage of the vernacular was that a difficult argument could be more quickly grasped in German than in Latin (as Notker suggested in his letter to Bishop Hugo).[288] It is in this context that we have learned to regard the earliest vernacular texts in Germany (glosses, word-lists, interlinear translations): they were elementary aids to understanding a Latin text, keyed to the Latin which had to be taught and not concerned primarily with putting German into writing. This is also the reason why Haubrichs has discussed these texts in a section devoted to the monastic school, thereby implying an overriding pragmatic function for the majority of Carolingian works, for texts with a purpose in school as well as for those with a pastoral role.[289]

In looking at the ways in which the linguistic needs of the monastic schoolroom encouraged the writing of German I largely follow suggestions made by Feldbusch, even though these have been criticised by Knoop.[290] He objects to her sketch of the spread of writing in German, saying that she sees it as a mechanical development from smaller to larger (from glosses to glossaries and then to translations) and that she ignores the conflicting evidence that German literature begins with a glossary (*Abrogans*) and that by about 800 we already have a fully fledged translation of high quality (*Isidor*). This objection would be valid if Feldbusch had meant her pattern to be understood chronologically, rather than typologically. There is no suggestion that this is what she meant, and no need to accept her argument as anything other than a (non-chronological) outline of advantages and disadvantages in various ways of using OHG to provide a written aid to understanding Latin.

If, with Feldbusch,[291] we begin with isolated glosses (sometimes inserted between the lines of the Latin text, sometimes in the margin, occasionally in the same line as the Latin word to be explained)[292] as the simplest, but not in all cases earliest attempts to use German as an aid, it is to stress the gain for the scribe: having once written the German equivalent above an unknown Latin word, he will be confronted with this on any subsequent reading, and thus be absolved from having to rely on memory or consulting someone else. The use of writing in individual glosses thus makes the task of understanding the Latin speedier and more reliable; it enables the reader to concentrate his mental energies on the text itself. Moreover, since writing is a means of bridging time and space, it makes it possible for a text, glossed by a scribe for his own benefit, to be used and understood by others.

The next step is to use glossaries, i.e. glosses separated from the text they accompanied and listed so that the Latin word and the German term which explains it are grouped either thematically or alphabetically.[293] German–Latin glossaries are found already in the second half of the eighth century and as linguistic aids are based on classical and early medieval Latin–Latin glossaries whose aim was to explain difficult or rare terms or to provide synonyms for Latin speakers.[294] More important than this origin is a consideration, latent in the school practice of monasteries, which confers an advantage on glossaries not provided by separate glosses inserted in a Latin text. The benefits of glossing a manuscript were confined to reading that manuscript alone; the linguistic information it stored could only be released for other texts by two laborious methods: by transferring glosses from the first manuscript to a second where this used the same Latin word, or, after encountering such a word when reading the second manuscript, to look up its vernacular meaning in the first, wherever it might be found. Efficiency demanded that this process be speeded up by extracting the word-pairs (Latin and German) from the first manuscript and listing them in a separate text which was available to the reader of the second. Merely to extract these word-pairs from the original text and list them in a glossary was not enough, since the word-pairs occurred in the sequence of that text, which was not identical with that of another Latin work. Glossaries were therefore arranged thematically or alphabetically: the latter method in particular facilitated the understanding of new texts, using a feature of the writing system to increase the benefits of writing itself.

Glosses and glossaries have one thing in common: by glossing difficult words in permanent written form they make it possible for the text to be speedily understood by any number of people, even those whose knowledge of Latin is not up to the standards of the original scribe. There still remains a difficulty, however, for if we are talking of possible users whose Latin standards may vary (as is bound to be the case in monastic schooling) glosses and glossaries make the unrealistic assumption that every potential user will find difficulties with the same words and that no other words will cause problems. The solution to this was provided by interlinear translations of every word of the Latin text in the sequence of that text, as in the *Benediktinerregel* and the *Murbacher Hymnen*.[295] Translations of this type presuppose a reader whose imperfect command of Latin demands help at unforeseeable stages; the German text is there to assist him in reading the Latin – how far it is from representing a text to be read for itself is suggested by its slavish adherence to Latin word-order, so that the syntax is quite un-German.[296]

The last type of translation discussed by Feldbusch corresponds to what Sonderegger calls 'freie Übersetzungen'.[297] It occurs when all the words in the Latin text are rendered into German, as in interlinear translations, but with German word-order and syntax in place of Latin. That the last type is not the last in time is suggested by the fact that, although Notker and Williram belong to it, the same is true of the *Isidor* translations as early as 800. Quite apart from linguistic quality, the importance of this type is that it no longer clings slavishly to the Latin original, but produces a German text which could be read for itself. This is a decisive point, it means that, potentially, written German has reached a point of autonomy, where it no longer has to be read only with an eye to the Latin original and to assist in understanding a text in a foreign language.[298]

Typologically, but already passing beyond the context of schooling and translation, the next step is characterised by poetic texts, to some extent dependent on a Latin source or model, but with a poetic independence which goes beyond even the linguistic status of a Notker. Examples include Otfrid and the *Georgslied*, works more properly considered in Part II, where we deal with the reception of German works from 800 to 1300.[299] Even here cold water can be poured on any idea of teleology by the reminder that, however much scholarship has dwelt on works in this class, they were works without a future,[300] since they were followed by a period of 150 years in which writing in German practically ceased altogether.[301] The difficulties facing the use of German in writing on which I have dwelt in this chapter existed before the Carolingian renaissance (and needed its impetus to overcome them), during that period itself (in so far as literacy was still geared primarily to Latin) and also after it (the silence of 150 years means that in the second half of the eleventh century the task has to be undertaken again).

In this chapter we have been concerned with a historical development along two lines: with the course of orality from Germanic antiquity to the lay culture of the Middle Ages (but in addition as a dimension of literacy in Roman and Christian tradition) and also with the course of writing from Roman and Christian sources (together with its slow introduction to Germany and adaptation to the German language). We shall return to historical considerations in Chapters 9 and 10, but meanwhile, in Part II, we abandon the historical approach for a systematic survey.

PART II

Three modes of reception

Introduction

This part of the book consists of six chapters, arranged in three pairs. The first pair discusses reception by hearing, the second by reading, the last the possibility that hearing and reading were anticipated for the same work. In each pair of chapters the first evaluates the criteria for determining the mode of reception, whilst the second surveys the works which can be allocated to a particular mode in the period 800–1300.

The exception is Chapter 7. Since this chapter deals with works meant to be both heard and read, there is no point in repeating the criteria for these two modes. Instead, Chapter 7 is given over to a definition of the intermediate mode, to establishing the special criteria available, but above all to discussing selected examples.

In the following chapters, as Scholz also found unavoidable, we rely on the internal evidence of texts in assessing how it was expected that they would be received. This is unavoidable since historical sources (as distinct from literary ones) show little interest in medieval literature in the vernacular, let alone the way in which it was delivered or received. On the few occasions when they refer to this at all it is generally with regard to public recital and acoustic reception (because these were social occasions which a chronicler might deem worthy of report),[1] hardly ever with an eye to an individual reading a text for himself.[2] Although historical scholarship may prefer to deal with non-literary sources, we have no choice but to give priority to the evidence of literary texts. Without them our questions could not be answered at all.[3]

The occasions when an author may be expected to reveal how he anticipates his work being received are those passages where he stands back from narrating and turns towards the audience. They are above all the prologue, where he presents his work and seeks to gain their attention, and the epilogue, where he takes leave, recommending his work and hoping for their thanks.[4] Much of our evidence comes from these two exposed points, and it would have been helpful in amassing evidence if we could have assumed that it would be found only at these points. This is not the case, for evidence is often forthcoming from fortuitous references in the body of the narrative. The author of the *Gandersheimer Reimchronik* requests a prayer of intercession from his audience not in the epilogue, but midway through his work, formulating his request so as to suggest that his work was read out to an audience sitting around the reciter.[5] A similar example, this time of individual reading, is provided by *Die Erlösung*, where an acrostic, with instructions how the reader is to solve it, occurs in the body of the text, far removed from prologue or epilogue.[6] Passages like these must be judged fortuitous in the sense that, deprived of the information which they provide, but not where it might be expected, we should find it difficult to say how these works were received.[7]

Apart from examples like these, an element of chance attaches to a mention of how the author anticipated the reception of his work, even in the prologue or epilogue. An example is provided by Veldeke's *Eneide*, where the possibility of an individual reading the work is mentioned only in connection with the countess of Cleves borrowing the manuscript, in turn referred to only because of the accident that the manuscript was stolen on that occasion.[8] But for the chance theft we may wonder whether, even in his epilogue, Veldeke would have felt it necessary to refer to the reading of the countess. We must assume something similar at large: what evidence we have is likely to be fortuitous, so that we have no means of assessing the reception of many works whose authors make no allusion to it.

To illustrate how, even given the possibility of a prologue or epilogue, no mention of reception is made we may look at the range of cases where this is so. Although the classical device of a prologue was known to Carolingian literature in the vernacular (Otfrid provides us with information in his dedicatory letters and opening chapter I, 1), there are several works which deprive us of this by beginning, in accordance with OE biblical literature, with a phrase like *Dat gafregin ih* or, adapted to Christian literacy, *Lesên wir*.[9] These cases withhold from us the information which Otfrid gives us. The same is the case with works where we might have expected help from a prologue or epilogue, but whose fragmentary state denies us this.[10] Hartmann's *Erec* has reached us deprived of its prologue, whilst the uncompleted state of Gottfried's *Tristan* means that we are dependent only on his prologue and other chance remarks in the body of his work. Where a prologue or epilogue survives, this may be short, but still long enough to contain a pointer (in his twelve-line epilogue to *Lanzelet* Ulrich von Zatzikhoven finds room to mention his expectation that it will be heard or read)[11] or too short to be useful (Hartmann's abrupt termination of *Iwein*). Even where an epilogue is somewhat longer, as with Wolfram's *Parzival*, this may be uninformative. We should be hard put to it to judge whether Wolfram expected readers at all if we did not have, as it were, a 'misplaced' epilogue at the close of Book VI, where a break in composition is commonly assumed.[12] If we accept Bumke's suggestion that this may be connected with a change of patron,[13] then the vital information in this passage may be as much the result of chance circumstances as the pointer at the close of Veldeke's *Eneide*. If this information reaches us fortuitously, it is likely that many works were intended for hearing or reading without our being able to tell. This is an unavoidable gap in our evidence which we shall have to bear in mind.

A number of assumptions may be made about the reception of medieval literature as long as we recognise that they are general observations which cannot always be applied to a particular case. Thus, the oral dimension predominates in medieval literature, Latin or vernacular: for memorised or orally composed literature, for the recital of written works and for reading aloud to oneself. It could follow that references to an acoustic reception may be missing because it was regarded as so self-evident as not to warrant mention. It could also follow that the burden of proof lies with those who suggest a reading reception (this is the novelty within vernacular literature) and that unless evidence to the contrary is provided a pointer like *hoeren* may be meant literally. In addition, a literal meaning of *hoeren* is overwhelmingly likely in a genre like heroic literature, for whose oral transmission over the centuries we possess historical testimony,[14] or with clerical literature addressed to illiterate laymen, who could therefore only have access by hearing it recited.[15]

The best way to pass beyond such general surmise is to determine various criteria for a particular mode of reception (as in Chapters 3, 5 and 7) and then to evaluate what works contain more than one such criterion (as in Chapters 4, 6 and 8). In this we follow the method chosen independently by Bergmann and by Linke for determining whether texts of dramas were meant for performance or for reading.[16] Only rarely is a pointer so persuasive that it can be taken by itself as sufficient evidence. For the rest, we need multiple evidence, several pointers to establish the mode of reception, so that where these are lacking a measure of doubt must remain.

Nowhere is this more obviously the case than with *hoeren*, which we cannot accept in its literal sense without more ado as indicating an acoustic reception after Scholz's demonstration that it could be used metaphorically of a reader 'hearing' or 'learning' from a book. To overcome doubts we need to establish whether other pointers suggest an oral recital and therefore an acoustic reception. In Chapters 3 and 4 we shall frequently have to argue in this way, reinforcing the literal function of *hoeren* by other indicators.

We shall encounter cases where an author composed more than one work, including evidence about the mode of reception in one, but not the other, so that the question arises whether we may extend what we learn of one work to the other. Where the theme of both works is similar, as with the *Frauendienst* and the *Frauenbuch* of Ulrich von Lichtenstein, we may safely do this. We may even do this where the works are as different as romance and legend, if we recall Schnell's remarks about the extent of court taste and heed his warning against a simplistic equation of 'court' with 'secular' and 'clergy' with 'religious'.[17] There is thus little objection to applying what Hartmann says about the reception of his legends to his romances (where he is silent on this point), especially in view of the suggestion that his legends and romances were probably meant for the same type of aristocratic court audience.[18] A similar type of audience has also been worked out for Rudolf von Ems: in his case, too, what he says of one work may be applicable to another where he is more reticent.[19] Sometimes, however, different types of audience for different works make it doubtful whether we can proceed in this way. An example is Veldeke's *Servatius* and *Eneide*: not because of the distinction between legend and romance or the geographical distance between the Maas/Rhine area and Thuringia, but rather because, whereas his romance was intended for the court, the legend occupies an uncertain position between the court and the cathedral of Maastricht.[20] In view of this possible distinction it would be unwise to assume the same kind of reception for both works.

In those chapters where a survey of reception (by hearing, by reading and with both) is attempted, the material is arranged by genres (including subgenres) and within each genre chronologically. This raises the question of genres, which is present as a means of organising the material and of suggesting how far the relationship between hearing and reading may in part be peculiar to genres. It is as well that in the timespan covered the question of genres is not uppermost, for there are difficulties in the way of any neat differentiation. It has been argued that for more than the first century of the MHG period criteria for dividing works into distinct genres do not exist, that it is often possible to allocate a work to more than one genre, according to the criteria used, and that not even the broadest differentiation between secular and religious is always feasible.[21] To group material not merely from the first hundred years of MHG literature, but from 500 years in which some genres die out and others arise, but all undergo considerable changes, presents even greater difficulties. The following division therefore represents no more than an attempt to group the material so as to show which types of literature prove resistant to literacy and which more quickly seize the opportunities which it offered.

With this in mind I have arranged the works we have to consider in ten groups. (a) Functional literature ('Gebrauchsliteratur', an established but unhappy term if we accept that most medieval literature served a non-literary function).[22] Under this heading are included science (or what passed as such, so that magical charms and blessings also belong here), school literature, and didactic literature. (b) Literature of religious worship and instruction. Under this are included hymns, catechetical literature, sermons, what is called 'Reimpredigt',[23] and devotional literature. (c) Legal literature, including charters. (d) Historiography. (e) Biblical literature. (f) Legends, including legendaries. (g) Drama. (h) Heroic literature. (i) Court narrative literature. This is further subdivided into the 'court epic' (the so-called 'Spielmannsepen' and works whose theme derives from, or builds on the chanson de geste), the romance, and the 'Märe'. (j) Lyric, divided into love poetry and gnomic poetry ('Spruchdichtung'). The chapters that follow must demonstrate how far this grid, made up of genres and dating, in combination with other factors plots the changing relationship between hearing and reading over five hundred years of German literary history.

3

Criteria for reception by hearing

Recent work on the differences between the spoken and the written word has sharpened our understanding of the different types of communication and transmission which these two modes involve. Goody sums up these differences by saying that writing changes the channel of communicated language from auditory to visual: we hear speech and see writing; we speak with the mouth and listen with the ears, whereas we write with the hand and read with the eyes.[1] Since in this chapter we shall be concerned with evidence for hearing the spoken word we may start with the features of oral communication and transmission.

Oral communication presupposes a speaker and at least one listener at the same time and at the same place; together they constitute a group (as distinct from the individual writer or reader) which, because of its physical presence on the same occasion, can rely on deictic pointers to what is clear to both parties in order to reinforce the communication.[2] Since both parties share the same visual and acoustic space they are open to non-verbal communication: visual in the form of miming or gestures, acoustic in the shape of intonation or accentuation (aspects which cannot be conveyed in writing except by verbal additions or by postmedieval typographic devices such as italics or exclamation marks).[3] In that oral communication depends on the presence of both parties potential dialogue is always there, ranging from explanations given by the speaker in response to a look of incomprehension on his listener's face to interruptions from the latter.[4] This give-and-take element of oral communication, also dependent on unforeseeable details of time and place, imposes restrictions on the extent to which what is spoken can be planned ahead in detail and, in lengthy communications, grants an important role to memorising and mnemonic devices, but also to the need to extemporise.[5]

With the further transmission of an oral statement we register other features of the oral mode. It is tied to the acoustic space in which the original statement is made in a negative sense in that it is confined to the medium of sound, a fleeting phenomenon which dies even as it comes into being.[6] This transience of speech can be overcome in oral transmission only by memory and its ability to store an earlier communication over a shorter or longer period of time.[7] The limitations which this imposes are obvious, so that to support the individual's unreliable memory recourse is had to professional remembrancers, whose task is to store knowledge of the field for which they are responsible (shamans, oral poets).[8] Even this solution is not perfect, since knowledge will be transmitted orally only so long as there happens to be no break in the chain, and what is transmitted cannot exceed a certain amount of material or degree of complexity.[9]

These features of oral communication and transmission are centred on the acoustic dimension, and it is this which Goody likewise stressed in opposing the auditory to the visual. We can illustrate this clearcut antithesis from the Middle Ages, for Thomasin von Zerclaere applies it to the difference between cleric and layman, saying that the literate cleric absorbs information visually (by reading) which is available to the illiterate layman only acoustically: *gêt ez dem phaffn zen ougen in / sô gêt doch der selbe sin / den leien durch diu ôren*.[10] In this fundamental distinction between hearing an oral communication and seeing a written one qualifications are called for on both sides. As regards the spoken communication its non-verbal accompaniment may include the visual details of miming and gestures and the understanding of the spoken word may in part depend on visual aspects of the setting in which it is voiced, to which pointers can be made by the speaker and understood by the listener. To that extent the reception of the spoken word is not exclusively auditory.

That this was realised theoretically can be shown from Geoffroi de Vinsauf, who says of the reciter that he speaks with three languages: the first is the mouth, the second his features, and the third his gestures.[11] What Geoffroi divides into three we may regard as twofold, for his first feature is acoustic, the other two visual. The point behind this theoretical distinction was made clear in classical antiquity by Pliny. He stated a preference for hearing a work recited to reading it for himself, but gives as reasons for this preference not just the reciter's intonation, but also his expression, appearance and gestures.[12] I have also suggested elsewhere that pointers to medieval irony which elude us now because they were lost with the conclusion of each recital may have included greater vocal emphasis or change of tone (to which rhetorical handbooks refer), but also gestures.[13]

Two medieval genres by their nature often refer to both these dimensions. The medieval drama was meant to be seen as well as heard, as is made clear in a stage-instruction in the *Benediktbeurer Passionsspiel*, saying that Judas is to give a signal to the Jews and also to sing the following passage (between vv. 182 and 183). What is made visible as well as audible to the Jews is also meant to be visible as well as audible to the audience.[14] This is more obvious at the start of the *Wiener Passionsspiel*, where an opening request for silence is addressed to those who are about to hear and see the following drama (2f.).[15] The other genre is legal literature, on the grounds that medieval legal practice prescribed the utterance of a formula to be heard by witnesses to a transaction, but also the transfer of a symbolic object (knife or piece of turf) or a legal gesture which they could also see.[16] How the one was to accompany the other is best brought out by the gloss to the *Sächsisches Weichbildrecht: Doch sollit ir gar eigentlichen wissen, das alle gelobde sollen geschen mit vingern unde mit zunge, daz ist: wenne eyn eynem gelabit mit dem munde, daz sal er bewisen mit der hant, unde sol em syne hant daruff gebin; daz ist eyne bestetigunge der truwe*.[17] This double requirement underlies the occurrence of the double formula *hoeren unde sehen* in legal literature, as we shall see.

Despite these qualifications, implying visual aspects even of oral communication, the acoustic dimension was more important. The speaker's expression or gestures merely accompanied, reinforced or qualified what he had to say, so that Thomasin was justified in his emphasis on hearing, as opposed to the seeing of a reader. Moreover, we have no choice but to ignore the visual dimension in practice since this was irretrievably lost with the conclusion of a performance, whereas the oral communication, even though transposed to the foreign setting of a text which we now read, has at least come down to us. The lost visual dimension and the indirectly attested acoustic dimension[18] both suggest the presence of a group assembled at one time and place. In view of that physical fact of oral communication we may start with the collective context in which medieval literature was delivered and the acoustic reception which this presupposes.

(a) Collective function and reception

Against the position adopted by Scholz we have been reminded that court literature was intended for readers only to a limited extent in the high Middle Ages and that even these few readers more usually received this literature in the same way as their illiterate colleagues, by hearing it read out on a sociable occasion.[19] The reason for social reception Bumke sees in the social function of medieval literature, to create and sustain a sense of community,[20] in the political sense of a society grouped around a ruler and identifying with his display of power or in the social sense of a knightly class seeking cultural independence and self-awareness in emancipating itself from clerical tutelage. In either case, a literature meant to serve a sense of community will more readily achieve this by collective occasions on which the group reaffirms its cohesion by hearing this proclaimed to them in public than by private reading by isolated individuals.[21] This is not to deny the existence of private readers, however rare, or their significance for the author, but rather to suggest that the function of this literature, in the eyes of those who commissioned it and of most of those who received it, lay more in the public domain, including a public and hence acoustic reception.[22]

The occasions when a medieval ruler held court provided an opportunity for joint deliberation, legislation, political decisions, but also for a festive display of the ruler's wealth and power. Court literature belongs to this festive display in the sense that it frequently depicts such festivals, but more essentially in that this literature is part of the festival itself,[23] comes into its own when so many are gathered together to provide resonance for the renown of the ruler who commissioned it.[24] Even without the dimension of literature, merely to hold a court festival redounds to the credit of a ruler, even in the negative case of King Constantine in *König Rother*, who accedes to his daughter's suggestion that he hold a festival with the words (1559): *Ich wille haven geste, / daz man immer sage mere, / waz hie schales were / zo disen hochgecitin.* Where a literary dimension is also present in the festival the element of renown is heightened in the sense that generosity to minstrels brings literary praise by them as its reward, as Veldeke makes clear on the occasion of Eneas' wedding festival: *den spelmannen si gaven / grotlike ende so / dat si alle danne schieden vro / ende lof den koninge sungen / igelic ane siner tungen.*[25] The oral transmission of the ruler's praise by these minstrels continues the oral nature of the wedding festival itself, to which they must have contributed if they were rewarded.[26] The acoustic nature of the festivities at large, underlined here,[27] is of a piece with the minstrels' oral activity: a festival is of its nature a collective gathering which looks askance at anyone standing aloof and affords no opportunity to the private reader. At stake here is not primarily the personal enjoyment of literature by the individual (although this may well be possible), but public praise of the ruler on a public occasion,[28] an affirmation of group-identity on the part of those present at court. It is this public function of medieval literature which dictated its public reception, in other words its oral dimension. Jammers has made a point in connection with singing which is equally applicable to any form of oral delivery in the Middle Ages.[29] He says that the recital is directed not at the individual as such, but at a society whose communal sense it reinforces, making it impossible for the individual to stand aloof. He adds that the encouragement of a sense of community in this way is true of recital in the feudal lord's hall, but also in the refectory of a monastery or in church when epistles and gospels are declaimed.

The connection between a public display of political power and the public recital of literature has been shown for the *Rolandslied* as an example of 'Repräsentationskunst' encouraged by Henry the Lion. Mertens has suggested the relevance of the theme of Charles the Great around 1170: he had been canonised in 1165, Barbarossa proclaimed his imperial authority with reference to this predecessor, and Henry the Lion saw himself as *nepos Caroli*.[30] Given the political and genealogical implications of a theme like this, Mertens is reluctant to see the encouragement of a German version as a purely aesthetic concern, but sees in it the propagation of political interests by means of a suitable literary theme, not unlike the policy of Henry's father-in-law, Henry II of England, in encouraging a literature to the greater glory of his dynasty.[31] Ashcroft has taken this further, particularly with regard to Henry the Lion's expeditions against the pagan Slavs, listing a range of parallels between the Saxon duke and details to be found in the *Rolandslied* attributed to his Carolingian predecessor, including even, perhaps, the promotion of royal ambitions on the part of Henry the Lion.[32] These concrete political implications suggest that a public display of political power, as represented in this work (but also in the construction of Burg Dankwarderode at Braunschweig or the coronation illumination in the Helmarshausen gospel-book),[33] demanded public praise in literary form, which suggests a public recital. It is not by chance that, although there are no references to a reading reception of the *Rolandslied*, there are several pointers to an oral reception. In that respect there is no difference between how the author foresaw the reception of his work and the description given in the *Annales Stederburgenses* of how Henry was fond of having works read out to him: *Ipse antiqua scripta cronicorum colligi praecepit et conscribi et coram recitari*.[34]

The use of *coram* in this example captures the assembled audience for an oral recital not merely for the *Rolandslied*, but for other examples where a collective reception is attested. Already in Germanic literature the heroic lay and praise-poem were recited in the lord's hall (Priscus reports that what are taken to be two Gothic singers performed at Attila's court while he was at table, and a similar setting is presupposed by Apollinaris Sidonius of the practice at a Burgundian court).[35] A collective setting is also suggested repeatedly for the Middle Ages: the topical 'Sagelied' was delivered by singing,[36] but Otto von Freising was more explicit in placing this delivery at gatherings and at courts.[37] Bishop Gunther of Bamberg was criticised for paying too much attention to the recital of heroic poetry, specified as *fabulae curiales* and sung at his episcopal court,[38] but the example of this ecclesiastic is by no means unique, as is borne out by Wolfger von Erla's predilection for the performance of minstrels and singers[39] or by repeated fulminations by the Church against these practices at clerical centres, where references to recital at table (*comessationes, ad mensam, in mensa*) underline the persistence of this setting.[40] By contrast, recital in the monastic refectory may have been more acceptable, but it still combined oral delivery with an assembled audience.

If the collective function of medieval literature largely accounts for its collective reception, hence its oral delivery to listeners, we face the question: since this literature meant for listeners has come down to us in written form, how can the written text be used to supply criteria for oral delivery? We turn to the criteria available, grouped first under a non-lexical, then under a lexical heading.

NON-LEXICAL EVIDENCE

(b) Singing

Evidence for heroic poetry or the 'Sagelied' frequently refers to sung delivery, but this kind of delivery, implying an acoustic reception, is also attested for a wide range of other genres. I shall group examples under religious and secular, but also attempt to show how far the audience played a part themselves (whether they were merely sung to, or joined in to some extent, or did all the singing themselves).

The clearest early example of a religious song sung to the audience is the *Galluslied*, a Latin translation of a lost vernacular original, of which it is said in the prologue that it was intended to be sung to the people in praise of St Gallus (. . . *fecit carmen barbarum populo in laude s. Galli canendum*).[41] Osterwalder has established that *populus* refers to laymen as opposed to clerics, which explains why the song had to be (originally) in the vernacular (*carmen barbarum*).[42] He resolves the ambiguous verbal construction (was the song sung *to* the laymen or *by* them?) in favour of the former, on the grounds that the participation of laymen in the liturgy (even in what is here likely to be a paraliturgical hymn) was very restricted.[43] What we have here is likely to be a song sung by the clergy to the laymen, possibly on the occasion of a procession on the day of St Gallus.[44]

However restricted in number and scope, there were occasions when the lay congregation could play an active part in the liturgy (refrains, *Kyrie, Gloria*, etc.), so that we may expect some cases where laymen joined in the singing.[45]

Although refrains occur in the *Georgslied* they are too complex and variegated to be attributed to the laymen, so that this work (text and refrains), like the *Galluslied*, was probably sung by the clergy to the laity on a similar occasion.[46] Such a reservation cannot apply to the simpler example of the *Melker Marienlied*, where each stanza is concluded with the unchanging refrain *Sancta Maria*. This work is commonly accepted as a hymn[47] and was probably used in the liturgy *in quocumque festo Sanctae Mariae Virginis*, with the congregation singing the refrains as responsions.[48] For a more telling example of a sung refrain we have to turn to a secular example, the *Tanzlied von Kölbigk*, with its short concluding verse (*Quid stamus? Cur non imus?*) coming after the lines sung by the dance leader.[49] This line shows all the signs of a refrain: it differs thematically from what precedes, it shows a change of tense from imperfect to present and of grammatical person from third singular to first plural, it refers explicitly to the dance, and is termed a *regressus* or responsion.[50] We may be reasonably certain that, after the leader had sung his stanza (the German text can in part be hypothetically reconstructed on the basis of the Latin in which the event is reported),[51] the chorus sang this refrain in unison.

With the *Kyrie eleison* we range similarly from liturgical to secular usage. Berthold von Regensburg makes it clear that these words are to be sung by the lay congregation (*Daz solten die leien singen, daz waere iuwer reht daz ir daz kyrie eleyson singen soltet*).[52] To Haubrichs we owe the collection of evidence suggesting that the *Kyrie eleison* was sung by laymen in the litanies of numerous procession days of the Church,[53] a practice which he connects with an OHG hymn, the *Petruslied*, in which these words occur as a refrain and for which use in a procession has been postulated.[54] In agreement with Haubrichs' suggestion we also find references to *Kyrie eleison* in the *Galluslied* (in close association with the *populus* who take part) and in *Heinrichs Litanei*.[55] These words can also be sung outside the ecclesiastic context, especially in connection with battle. In the *Ludwigslied* they are sung collectively in response to the leader's solo performance (*sang lioth frano, / Ioh alle saman sungun 'Kyrie leison'*),[56] as in the liturgy, but elsewhere by themselves, very much as a battle cry on the eve of battle (Ottokar's *Österreichische Reimchronik* 62112f.).[57]

Other examples at home in the liturgy can sometimes divorce themselves from this context, but still imply collective singing. *Te Deum*, for example, is intoned in the *Rolandslied* to express thanks for the death of the pagan Binabel (8988ff.).[58] Likewise, the *Gloria* is retained as the response of the Christian warriors to Turpin's address (5278) and of the congregation in the coronation service for Charles the Great in the *Kaiserchronik* (14755f.).

Mertens has argued on behalf of the 'Ruf' or *acclamatio* as a distinct genre in medieval religious literature and locates it either within the liturgy or, as with the *Kyrie eleison*, in the context of battle or starting a journey.[59] In the former case he sees it sung by the congregation in response to an invitation from a cleric, generally at the close of a sermon, whilst in the latter it serves as a request for assistance. Whether liturgical or not, whether in response to a sung invitation or not, the *acclamatio* retains its character of collective song.[60] Collective singing of a hymn-like nature is also described by Otfrid on one occasion[61] and implied in the case of his own work (I 6, 15: *Nu síngemes álle*). We shall discuss the conditions under which the *Ezzolied* may have been sung, but for the moment may content ourselves with what Gerhoch von Reichersberg says of the Germans' predilection for vernacular hymns: ... *in ore Christo militantium laicorum laus Dei crebrescit ... tota terra jubilat in Christi laudibus etiam per cantilenas linguae vulgaris, maxime in Teutonicis, quorum lingua magis apta est concinnis canticis.*[62]

In those cases where singing is attested independently of a liturgical context laymen play a more prominent part, singing collectively themselves and not restricted to listening or responding to a clerical singer. The contexts where this is attested include battle, either just before its engagement (*Kaiserchronik* 5304 and *Rolandslied* 842)[63] or after its conclusion to give thanks for victory (Gottfried's *Tristan* 7102f.). Another context is a wedding, where bridesong can belong to a wedding procession (*Athis und Prophilias* C° 96: *Sus giengin die iungin / Hupphinde und springinde, / Von den brutin singinde*) or where the German word, used to explain epithalamion, presupposes German practice (Konrad von Heimesfurt, *Unser vrouwen hinvart* 1048f.).

The court is also a setting for collective singing, as is implied in *Virginal* (970, 3: *sî vür die vrouwen giengen / und sungen hovelîchen sanc*), but also for singing in unison after someone has sung solo (Heinrich von Neustadt, *Apollonius von Tyrland* 5341: *Si hub an und sanck / Ain liedel nach ir hertzen gier. / Si sungen alle gar nach ir*). Even in the court lyric, which one might expect to be dominated by the individual poet-singer, his song was so much part of sociable entertainment that it could be regarded as the prelude to joint singing. This is implied in one of Neidhart's *Winterlieder* (30, 7, 1: *Swenne ich an ein trûren wende mînen muot, / sô kumt einer unde sprichet: 'guote, singet etewaz! / lât uns mit iu singen'*). Collective singing at court is also implied in one of Ulrich von Lichtenstein's poems (52, 1, 1f.) and in the 'Leich' of Ulrich von Winterstetten (III 97: *Nu singen, nu singen; dannoch harte erspringen / Den reien, den reien, pfaffen unde leien*).

These suggestions of the singing of works by or to an assembled company, religious or secular, for the most part do not refer to singing the work in question, but to contemporary practice, which is presupposed and taken to be well known. There is little reason to assume that they all independently conjure up an entirely fictitious situation. Nonetheless, the occurrence of these references over a wide spread of genres does not exclude the possibility of *spoken* recital,[64] as we shall see when we discuss the evidence of such verbs as *sprechen, sagen, lesen*.

(c) Musical evidence

There are no grounds for assuming that the singing just considered must have had a musical accompaniment, but equally no cause for surprise where this is the case, as is attested for Germanic literature and different medieval genres.[65]

Recent work on the recital of Germanic alliterative verse has called into question Heusler's rejection of sung recital on the grounds that he regarded the singing in modern terms, not as the recitation-tone or *cantillatio* now invoked.[66] For all that, Heusler was aware of the musical accompaniment to Germanic poetry, the parallel between OE *hearpslege* and OHG *leodslakkeo* (the harp was plucked as the song was delivered) did not escape him.[67] Nor did the conjunction of the barbarian's *harpa* with songs (*leudos*) in the description by Venantius Fortunatus, or the reference by Jordanes to the Goths singing to the harp songs dealing with the exploits of their ancestors.⁶⁸ The harp is present in the recital of heroic lays in Alcuin's letter to Lindisfarne and in the account of the blind Frisian singer Bernlef in the *Vita Liudgeri*.⁶⁹ Continuity of sung performance beyond the time of Bernlef and Alcuin allows us to understand later references to singing heroic poetry literally, rather than metaphorically (as in Virgil's *Arma virumque cano*). This is true of the opening of the *Annolied* (1, 1: *Wir horten ie dikke singen von alten dingen*), where *hoeren* and *singen* combine to reinforce the oral dimension, *dikke* suggests the continuity of its tradition, and the following lines imply the heroic subject-matter.⁷⁰ The same dismissal of heroic song by a clerical author conscious of its rival attractions is present in *Vom Himmlischen Jerusalem* (26, 3: *swa man aine guote rede tuot, (daz ist) dem tumben ummare. / der haizet ime singen von werltlichen dingen / unt von der degenhaite*).⁷¹ That *singen* still has to be taken literally in medieval heroic epics is finally confirmed by recent work on their melodies, undoing Heusler's thesis that they were meant for spoken recital.⁷² (Whether sung or spoken, the fact of oral recital, and therefore acoustic reception, remains unchallenged.)

Sung recital must be assumed not only for heroic literature with its roots in the past, but also for genres that first appear in the Middle Ages. Relatively few German love-lyrics survive with their actual melody (by comparison with France or with the gnomic lyric in Germany),⁷³ but enough to suggest that they were meant to be sung and that the melodies were dependent on oral transmission far more than the texts themselves.⁷⁴ This possibility is borne out by what we learn of the delivery of love-poems in practice. Heinrich von Melk had every reason for accuracy in depicting the target of his satire, which makes it significant that he refers to the love-lyric being sung (*Von des todes gehugde* 19, 16: ... *da mit er diu trutliet chunde / behagenlichen singen*). The theme of love is associated with singing in a court festival in *Morant und Galie* (5550: *al da mochte man schouwen / danzen inde springen, / van minnen horen singen*), in a similar context in Der Stricker's *Daniel von dem Blühenden Tal* (8163ff.) or, in the context of named lyric poets and with a reference to the melody employed, in Hugo von Trimberg's *Renner* (1182f.).

With the gnomic lyric many more melodies have survived so that, whatever one may think of Schweikle's stress on the reading reception of the love-lyric at the cost of oral reception, he makes a useful point in saying that gnomic poetry, with its essentially public or even political subject-matter, was of its nature geared to public delivery.⁷⁵

A third genre for which sung recital (in part) must be postulated is the medieval drama. This is borne out by stage instructions for the singing of passages, solo or in chorus (*cantet* or *cantent*),⁷⁶ by the presence of musical notation in some cases,⁷⁷ but particularly by evidence for the contrafacture of melodies from secular works, adapting them to another purpose. Examples of contrafacture are the *Trier-Alsfelder Marienklage* (thought to derive its melody from the *Nibelungenlied*), or some stanzas in the *Zehnjungfrauenspiel* which may go back to the MHG *Walther* epic.⁷⁸ Such evidence has generally been used to cast light on the melody used for the heroic epics in question, but from our point of view its significance is to confirm that these dramas were meant to be sung.

Where the melody is not preserved a textual reference to its existence may be almost as telling. Of the vernacular *Galluslied* we are told in the prologue to the Latin version that its melody was sweet (*tam dulcis melodia*) and that his wish to preserve it was the reason for Ekkehart IV translating it into Latin.[79] The *Praefatio* to the *Heliand* mentions *cantilena* and *modulatio*, confirmed by the presence of neumes in one fragment of this work,[80] just as there are love-lyrics which refer to their melody (*wîse*) and whose musical notation happens to be preserved.[81] Cases like these suggest that we should not dismiss all references to *wort* und *wîse* as simply conventional. That is certainly not the case with the *Ezzolied*, where we are told of a division of labour between writing the text and composing the melody (1,4: *Ezzo begunde scriben Wille vant die wise*). If Sayce questions Walther's remark (26, 3f.), wondering whether it is merely formulaic,[82] her reservation is weakened by the fact that the melody for this particular tone happens to survive.[83] A conjunction of words and melody is also implied when Gottfried refers to Tristan playing the harp and singing (3631), when in Heinrich von dem Türlin's *Crone* a performance is given by fiddlers together with singers (29287ff.) or when Volker both fiddles and sings (*Nibelungenlied* 1705, 3).[84]

(d) Dance song

Some of the references made to singing and music have alluded to accompanying a dance,[85] thereby underlining their sociable nature, but it would be as well to look at this type of evidence by itself. I shall follow the threefold division proposed by Stevens: the popular dance, the courtly, and the clerical.[86]

The popular dance, accompanied by song, can be attested for Germanic antiquity by the semantic spread of the words cognate with Gothic *láiks*, originally denoting any kind of active movement, then specialised to dance, to combat, and, because the dance was accompanied by song, to musical playing.[87] In OHG *leih* is most commonly used in the sense of melody, but not to the exclusion of the meanings 'song' and 'dance'.[88] Of relevance here is the point made by Sayce that MHG *leich*, although it designates a specific lyric genre by the thirteenth century, is associated with dancing in some examples of the genre.[89] Before that point is reached we have an example of the popular dance song in the *Tanzlied von Kölbigk*, meant to be sung solo and in chorus, but also to be danced to. From the three versions reporting the occasion it emerges that we are dealing with a round-dance in which the dancers hold hands, stamp with their feet and leap.[90] It betrays its popular nature by these details, but also by being accompanied only by song, whereas a courtly dance was graced with instrumental music.[91] As to the song itself, Ehrismann has stressed its formulaic nature as a sign of its simple, popular type.[92]

The courtly dance song is seen by Stevens as 'acting out ... the forms of social life – ceremony, entertainment, game';[93] it performs a central sociable function in court literature which underlies the acoustic dimension in which it existed. How this contributed to the sense of cohesion of an élite has been stressed by Huot's comment on dance refrains sung on social occasions by members of the aristocracy, for she sees in this the gathering becoming 'a theatrical event in which there is no distinction between performers and audience. Rather, the society collectively acts out the code of values and manners on which it is based, through a code of diction and performance.'[94] That this remark can also be applied to German practice is confirmed by a passage in Jans Enikel's *Fürstenbuch*, referring to the Babenberg court in Vienna, at which duke Leopold VI was clearly in the habit of himself singing and leading the dance (2027ff.).[95]

Against this background of court entertainment we can interpret some of the references to song accompanying a dance in court literature. Most informative is Ulrich von Lichtenstein, nearly half of whose poems in *Frauendienst* are characterised as dance songs: twenty-six by the title *tanzwîse* in the manuscript, one by *reye*, and one by its opening (536, 9: *Disiu liet diu heizent vrowen tanz . . . blîdeclîchen man si tanzen sol*).[96] If Ulrich meant these poems as accompaniment to a court dance, we may assume the same with other poets. Neidhart MS c contains two relevant titles of poems (*raye*, as with Ulrich, and *stamph* = *estampie*),[97] just as Neidhart occasionally makes the kind of internal reference which we found once with Ulrich (e.g. *Sommerlieder* 22, 5, 1ff.; *Winterlieder* 17, 4, 10). References of this kind are found with other lyric poets, especially with Tannhäuser,[98] but not least with Walther, as when he combines his own new-found encouragement as a poet with a general invitation to dance (19, 37: *wol ûf, swer tanzen welle nâch der gîgen!*) or if the dance song 74, 20 gained piquancy by the poet's search for his lost beloved (75, 5: *Waz obe si gêt an disem tanze?*) being associated with an actual dance at the court at which it was recited.[99]

Stevens has drawn our attention to the ecclesiastical realm of dance,[100] but also to the fact that where, as in an example quoted from Honorius Augustodunensis, a clerical work claims 'to instruct us in the nature of the celestial motions by allegorizing dances on earth, in fact [it does] precisely the reverse'.[101] With this support we may see how descriptions of the celestial dance throw light on courtly dance-song. Mechthild von Magdeburg sees the mystic dance, like so much of her mystic experience, in courtly terms (28, 32: *ich mag nit tanzen, herre, du enleitest mich. / Wilt du das ich sere springe, / Sô muost du selber voran singen*). Bruder Philipp mentions the dance conducted by the souls of the blessed with the angels while Michael sings (*Marienleben* 9856ff.), but in the *Büchlein von der Himmelfahrt Mariae* the dance is by the angels and Mary, with Michael as the singer.[102] Whether in the court of heaven or in a court on earth, the dance-song is performed collectively and acoustically, binding together all those who take part.

(e) Processional song

The best-known early example of a song sung on a journey, if not a processional song, comes from the episode in *Beowulf* in which a song is extemporised, celebrating the hero's defeat of Grendel, by one of his followers on horseback amidst his armed companions.[103] Whether this can be regarded as an example of Germanic verse composed on the spur of the moment does not concern us here as much as the fact that it exemplifies oral delivery to a surrounding group of listeners.[104] In such a situation no other form of delivery and reception is conceivable – it is this which makes the song on a journey or the processional song relevant to our concern.[105]

A point touched upon more than once is summed up by Haubrichs when he suggests that in OHG the *Petruslied*, the *Galluslied* (original version), the *Georgslied*, and perhaps the lost *Ulrichslied* may be classified as hymns sung on festival and penitential processions.[106] He quotes contemporary reports of such occasions, where references to both clergy and laymen taking part account for the use of the vernacular, especially in the refrain which he sees as characteristic of hymns of this type.[107] The *adventus* of a ruler, ecclesiastic or secular, could also take the form of his being received by processional song.[108]

A song to be sung on a journey, more particularly a pilgrimage song, is possibly suggested by the *Ezzolied*. Freytag, in disagreeing with Vollmann-Profe's interpretation, attaches importance to the reference in the *Vita Altmanni* to a *scholasticus Ezzo* who took part in a pilgrimage to Jerusalem in 1064/5 and composed a vernacular song on Christ's miracles for that occasion, so that it was presumably sung to or by the pilgrims.[109] Here again the fact that they are made up of clerics and laymen would account for the use of the vernacular, a practice which Gerhoch von Reichersberg attests for Germany in particular.[110] Freytag goes further in seeing close links between the paschal theme of the *Ezzolied* and the corresponding timing of the pilgrimage, so that he finds it impossible to agree with the suggestion that the poem was composed to celebrate the reform of the Bamberg clergy in 1063 as a 'Festkantate' for that occasion.[111] Freytag's paschal connection between the poem and the pilgrimage is so precise that it cannot be fortuitous, but the line 1, 5 (*duo ilten si sich alle munechen*) conforms more to the Bamberg interpretation than to the pilgrimage one. If we accept the latter we must regard the *Ezzolied* as sung on a journey, but if the former as a paraliturgical hymn, perhaps sung as the reformed clergy processed to St. Gangolf. In either case we are dealing with sung delivery to an assembled audience.

Other types of religious processional songs include the litany with sung appeals for intercession to the saints, as described briefly in the *Passional* (III 199, 95: *an der processione / da man solde schone / mit der letanien / die heiligen anschrien*), but also, even though actual examples come later,[112] the particular form of the flagellants' procession accompanied by song, attested first in Ottokar's *Österreichische Reimchronik* (9440ff.).

Examples of singing in procession or on a journey are not lacking from the secular context of the court. Two of Ulrich von Lichtenstein's poems are entitled *ein ûzreise* (403, 25; 456, 25)[113] and in each case he makes it clear that (after presumably being learned by heart) they were sung by knights as they journeyed from one tournament to another (*Frauendienst* 405, 15ff.; 458, 8ff.). As a secular counterpart to ecclesiastical practice, there is evidence for courtly processionals accompanied by song and music (*Virginal* 675, 1: *Si zogten über den wîten plân. / die stolzen megde wol getân / begunden lûter singen. / dar under seitenspil dô klanc, / dâ mite gemischet wart der sanc: / man hôrt die harpfen klingen*; Heinrich von Neustadt, *Apollonius von Tyrland* 13171ff.). In these courtly, as in the clerical examples, song and procession form a unity, the acoustic dimension reinforces the visual.

(f) Court entertainment

Thus medieval literature was widely meant for public recital before an assembled audience and in courtly entertainment in particular this could include dance, music, and song. Frau Ava's description of the court entertainment (*wirtscaft*) arranged in his castle (*burch*) by Herod[114] casts more light on medieval practice than on conditions at the time of Christ: Salome's skill is that of a *spilwip* (*Johannes* 20, 7) and she combines dancing with music and song in her performance at the banquet (*Johannes* 26, 8: *si begunde wol singen, snellichlichen springen / mit herphin unde mit gigen, mit orgenen unde mit lyren*). The *Rolandslied* may have replaced suspect dancing by military training in its description of the various activities at Karl's court, but still finds a place for recitals with musical accompaniment (648: *Si sâhen guote knechte / schiezen unt springin, / si hôrten sagen und singin / vil manigir slachte seitspil*), whilst *Herzog Ernst* combines all three activities (3369ff.) and places emphasis not just on singing, but on the sheer noise of courtly entertainment (*ruofen unde schrîen; michel was der lût; grôzen schal; grôzer kradem*). What is here presented as a token of sociability at court is shown in its negative light at the Thuringian court by Walther (20, 4: *Der in den ôren siech von ungesühte sî, / daz ist mîn rât, der lâz den hof ze Dürengen frî*).

Noise and other acoustic distractions may have made it difficult for the poet-reciter to find a hearing, but at least this oral dimension of entertainment provided him with an opportunity, as is suggested when descriptions of festivities include the recital of songs. Albrecht von Halberstadt sees this variegated entertainment provided by minstrels (XII 14: *dar quam spillûte vil ... / nâch ir art sie spilden / vur den vursten milden: / dirre vacht, jener spranc. / man hôrte meisterlich gesanc*), just as does Hartmann von Aue in the description of a wedding festival (*Erec* 2151ff.; 2158). In *Laurin* the festival begins in general terms (1017ff.), but then the focus narrows down to literary entertainment (1045ff.).

We shall see that Scholz, seeking to play down the public, acoustic situation in favour of private reading, employs the concept 'Hörerfiktion', suggesting that what is described in the work had no real basis in the world for which the work was intended. This argument confronts us with the question whether passages like those just quoted are purely fictitious or corresponded in any way to medieval practice. Two examples argue against a fictional reading. The first is the description of the festival at the close of Veldeke's *Eneide*[115] where, for the first time in German literature, we have a detailed description of court entertainments, with stress on the acoustic dimension (13156f.), on the conjunction of music with song (13159ff.), and on the presence of minstrels (13107ff.).[116] However idealised the description, the author is concerned not with its fictitiousness, but with its correspondence to the reality of his day. When he mentions the attendance of minstrels Veldeke adds that they would have done just the same today, flocking there for the pickings (13110ff.), whilst an overriding link between past and present, between literary description and contemporary practice, is made when a comparison is drawn between Eneas' festival and that held at Mainz in 1184, at which Veldeke had been present and which made such an impression on contemporaries.[117] Whatever the element of idealisation, we cannot dismiss the minstrels and reciters as pure fiction: it is difficult to imagine that Veldeke was present at Mainz in any function other than as a poet, and in his chronicle account of the same occasion Gislebert of Mons also mentions the presence of *joculatores* and *joculatrices*.[118] These, and many other professional entertainers, also occur in a second example. If it is unlikely that the Church, in repeatedly criticising the practice of clerical dignitaries listening to minstrels at table, wasted its time on something purely fictitious, we also have testimony concerning one dignitary, Wolfger von Erla. We know something of his patronage of court literature, but the documentary evidence for Walther von der Vogelweide in his train at one point refers to a mixed crop of entertainers, including *cantatrices, ioculatores, ioculatrices*, a *discantor*, a *mimus*, to name only these.[119] The rewards given them are listed, so that the artistic service they rendered was a concrete one, certainly not fictitious.[120] If contemporary practice included such entertainers, we must hesitate to dismiss literary references as divorced from reality, certainly as long as no evidence for a fictional function is adduced.

(g) Collective audience

In his discussion of a narrator's request for the attention of his audience Scholz advances the view that what appears to be a direct contact between reciter and audience may be no more than a fictional pretence. Scholz quotes Drube, who long ago commented on passages in Hartmann's works where questions and answers at times amount to dialogues between reciter and listeners.[121] Drube said of these passages that Hartmann tells his story here in the fictitious guise of being surrounded by interested listeners who interrupt the course of his recital. We may agree with Drube's observation, while not accepting the use Scholz makes of it, for the fact that a narrator attributes fictitious questions to an assembled audience does not mean that the assembled audience is itself fictitious. All Drube doubted was the reality of the questions posed, but Scholz takes this as doubting the reality of assembled listeners. Indeed, one could argue that there is added point when an author attributes fictitious questions to listeners actually present at a recital.

The physical presence of listeners engaged in a joint discourse with the preacher is most obvious in clerical literature, where the priest invites the congregation to repeat a formula after him. This is the case, for example, with the OHG creeds which are to be recited after the priest (*St. Galler Glaube II* 343, 15: *unt spreche nâh mir; Münchener Glaube* 346, 15: *Nu sprechet nach mir*). A similar situation, presupposing an assembled congregation, occurs in several MHG sermons whenever the joint recital of the creed is included, as in the *Speculum Ecclesiae* (2, 19: *Vnde sprechet nach mir uil luterlichen*) or the *Wiener Predigten* (111, 33). Our task is to see, however, whether pointers to an assembled audience in literature with no liturgical function can likewise be taken literally.

A first pointer is provided whenever the recital of literature is placed in a specific context, to accompany or follow a meal at table, for we have come across examples where such a recital at an episcopal court, in agreement with the practice at secular courts,[122] was real enough to attract censure whenever the wrong type of literature was recited. In view of this testimony we need to be given a reason why we should not take it at face value when recital at table is mentioned in *Virginal* (217, 12: *vor den tischen manegen dôn mit rîcheme sang man an gevie*) or when the same is implied later in the same work, for the description of a recital (278, 4ff.) is here followed by the removal of the tables (279, 2: *dô man die tavelen ûf gehuop / und häte genomen wazzer*). On some occasions, however, the recital takes place after the conclusion of the meal, but still before an assembled audience, as in *Laurin A* (1125 ff.). Whether the recital actually accompanies the meal or not, we can agree with Salmen's multidimensional view of the medieval banquet, providing food for the palate, but also a feast for the eyes (jugglers and athletes) as well as for the ears (music and recital).[123]

On other occasions the physical presence of an audience at a recital is mentioned with so little ado that we may accept it as normal practice. In Konrad von Würzburg's *Engelhard* the courtly abilities of the two friends, including recital and singing (747ff.), are placed in a social setting before those who see and hear them (758: *swaz man nû kurzewîle sol / vor rittern und vor frouwen / hoeren unde schouwen, / daz lac an in mit voller kraft*). This makes it more telling when Konrad implies the same setting for the reception of his own work, for when referring to the negative recipient who has no patience with a work of this nature he says that this recipient does not *remain*, presumably with those who do listen to the work's recital (182: *wan der ungetriuwe zage / ungerne dâ belîbet / dâ man vil gerne trîbet / von triuwen guoter maere vil*). The place where he does not remain may not be specified, but the fact that it is a place suggests an assembled audience. That a similar situation can be assumed for clerical literature addressed to laymen is shown by Heinrich von Kröllwitz, who wished to make available in the vernacular what clerics had composed in Latin.[124] Despite Scholz's stress on readers,[125] there are also references to hearing the work,[126] so that recommendations to the man who is bored to depart and make room for others presuppose a place where the recital took place (*Vaterunser* 2834ff.; 2838ff.; 2850f.).

Other examples which mention the presence of listeners can be quite specific. Eberhard, the clerical author of the *Gandersheimer Reimchronik*, requests a prayer of intercession on his behalf from *we et lese edder sitte darbi* (881). The two possibilities suggested cannot be, as the editor proposes,[127] the reader or the listener (as the double formula normally implies), but rather the listener who sits close by the reciter ('Vorleser'),[128] so that both terms refer to the same recital situation. Informed by this, we are better able to interpret what Der Stricker says of the advantages for the listener (*Daniel von dem Blühenden Tal* 8125: *swie lange erz iemer hoeret*) in learning certain details (8132: *swie lange er sitzet dâ bî / und ez merket ebene*). If the audience hears the story, but at the same time sits in the vicinity (of the reciter), then *hoeren* is unlikely to have a merely metaphorical function. The same is implied by a narratorial comment in *Seifried Helbling* (VII 8): *ich hân ein maere für ze legen, / daz iz wol verstendic sî, / den die mir nâhen sitzen bî*. Although the two terms in the *Gandersheimer Reimchronik* are not used here, the implication is still that the author as reciter confronts his assembled audience.

On some occasions the listeners can be specified as ladies. In his *Apokalypse* Heinrich von Hesler can so far assume their attendance that he recommends the reciter to omit a detail when he comes to it so as not to give offence to their delicate ears (3711: *Des bit ich den lesere, / Swen her kumt in diz mere, / Daz her mit schonen witzen – / Ob dar vrouwen bi sitzen – / Antweder her entrumen / Oder obervar den lumen, / So daz her in icht durfe sagen; / Die man mugen iz baz vortragen, / Wen is mer get uf iren lip / Von schulden wen uf die broden wip*). Here *lesere*, like *lesen* in the *Gandersheimer Reimchronik*, refers to the reciter, while those who sit nearby are again his listeners. In the *Wartburgkrieg* (*Rätselspiel* 33, 1ff.) the prospect of a story being told makes it necessary to send for the ladies, so that they too may form part of an assembled company.

These last examples have in common the presence of reciter and listeners together at a particular time and place, a situation characteristic of oral communication, which makes it possible for deictic references by the speaker to shared time or space to be comprehensible to the listeners. Scholz omits any discussion of such evidence,[129] which can be treated here as reinforcement of a tangible recital situation.

Pointers to shared time (*hiute, nu,* etc.) are particularly significant. An author cannot dictate that his work will be read by an individual on a certain day, but the author as reciter can be aware when his work is likely to be recited, especially if it has a liturgical or paraliturgical function. Embedded in the liturgical year sermons frequently make use of such pointers linking preacher with congregation in shared time, as with the *St. Pauler Predigten* (3, 12: *an disem tage, dâ von wir heute lesen an der heiligen schrift*) or the *Rothsche Sammlung* (V 1: *Vns sait daz hilig ewaingelium, daz man hivt liset ze dem hiligen Ambt*). In both cases *lesen* is used in the sense of reading out the lesson to the congregation. Paraliturgical examples (connected with a particular point in the liturgical year, but not forming part of the liturgy itself) are provided by the *Millstätter Exodus* with its close associations with Easter (3309: ... *daz ich mohte chunden / mit tûtiskeme munde / die vrovde sîner liute / an disem tage hiute*)[130] or the *Trierer Osterspiel*, performed before spectators on a fixed day (194ff.).

Pointers to place which are as clear to listeners as to speaker (e.g. *hie, her*) are ambiguous by themselves, since they can also be used in the context of writing (to refer to a point in the text).[131] It is nonetheless possible to distinguish the two usages. This is the case with texts with a liturgical function, especially sermons: whenever the adverb of place is combined with another spatial indicator, such as 'gather together' (e.g. *Rothsche Sammlung* XX 1: *Alle, die sich hivt her in dem namen des almaehtigen gotes gesament habent*) or 'come' (*Speculum Ecclesiae* 88, 5: *Swer hivte her chomin ist ... durch got sine sunde ze clagine*) or 'sit' (Berthold von Regensburg 20, 34: *Ir morder, ir mordent iezuo nieman, ir sitzet iezuo mit guoten zühten hie ... Ir rouber, ir sît hie vor mir iezuo âne roub ... Ir schelter, ir fluocher, ir sitzet iezuo hie vor mir unde swîget vil stille*).[132] A paraliturgical example is given by Könemann von Jerxheim, addressing the 'Kalandsbruderschaft' of Eilenstedt, made up of clerics and laymen for whom he composed his *Kaland* (1: *Horet leyen, horet papen, / horet ritter, horet knapen, / De got here gesant / Hat an dissen Kalant / zo Eylsted*; 12: *Den leyen doch binamen / De man hir vindet / Desser selscap gesindet*). We may interpret the *Gandersheimer Reimchronik* similarly (1948: *is hir jemant, deme dit bok nicht behage, / et si under vrouwen, leien edder papen*), especially since we have seen evidence for reciter and listeners, but also examples establishing initial contact between reciter and audience, as with Rudolf von Ems (*Willehalm von Orlens* 17: *Wis ich nu ob ieman her / Dar uf waer komen das er / Hie saeze mit spotlichen sitten, / Den wolte ich vil gerne bitten / Das er geruochte gan hin dan*) or Eilhart von Oberge (*Tristrant* 1f.). Not to accept examples of this type as indications of public recital means suggesting that Eilhart anticipated only readers (possibly at the court of Henry the Lion, of whose predilection for recitals we are informed) and that clerics like Könemann von Jerxheim and Priester Eberhard, for whatever reason, preoccupied themselves with a 'Hörerfiktion'.

The public recital of a work of any length brought with it the problem how much could be delivered at one time without straining the reciter's voice or the audience's patience.[133] One solution is suggested in the Dresden manuscript of *Wolfdietrich A*, for the version has been drastically shortened from 700 to 333 stanzas with a specific purpose in mind: *das man auf einem sitzen dick müg hörn anfanck vnt ent* (334, 4).[134] How the strain on the reciter's voice was to be relieved at the end of a performance by means of a liquid reward is made clear at the close of *Virginal* (1097, 1: *Nu hânt ir daz ende vernomen: / heizent ein mit wîne komen, / daz er uns allen schenke*). Such demands for a drink for the reciter could possibly be dismissed as conventional flourishes without any basis in reality – but for one consideration.

The example from *Virginal* comes at the end of the work, where it makes good sense, but the demand also makes sense in the middle of the narrative, as long as we recognise that this generally coincides with a dramatic point of suspense in the action, when the audience's tension and wish to know what happened next were at their highest. The reciter, blackmailing his audience into giving him a drink if they wish him to continue, reminds us of the position in old silent films where the cliffhanger situation with which one instalment finished created enough tension to bring the audience to the next session. The threat not to continue with the story makes no sense in the context of a reading reception, for the reader has the complete text in his hands and can proceed at his own pace, reading as much as he chooses at one sitting and under no threat from author or reciter. It does make sense, however, in the context of oral recital, where the audience is dependent on the reciter, who can use this in order to extract a reward. Both the oral recital and the silent film presuppose an assembled audience: in the first case the cap is passed round before they are told what follows, in the second they have to be persuaded that it is worth their while to attend again.

Common to the medieval and modern poles of this comparison is the fact that pressure is effectively exercised on the audience not at any point in the narrative, but at a critical turning-point where suspense has been created. This is what our medieval examples often show. In the *Münchener Oswald* the reciter involves his listeners in the process of narration by pretending to ask them for advice on how to continue (381: *nu rat all an dem ringe, / wie wir den raben ab dem turen pringe[n]!*), but in MS I this has been reinforced by pressure to reward the reciter (p. 33, col. 2: *nu ratet alle an dem ringe / wie ich den raben ab der zinnen pringen / er mocht herab nicht chomen wol / man pring den dem leser ein chopff weins vol*). The author of *Orendel* likewise inserts a number of feigned requests to the listeners to help him over an awkward point (379f., 1157f., 2396f., 2512f.), but the concrete need behind them is revealed on one especially tricky occasion (2826: *wa ist nu der Grawe Roc der biderbe? / er lit vor dem kunige dar nidere / und muz verliesen sin leben, / man enwelle dem leser zu drinken geben*). Similar remarks occur at comparable points in *Herzog Ernst G* (61, 8ff.)[135] and in *Laurin* (1215ff.). In all these cases we have to make a distinction between the narrator who pretends to need advice (his need is clearly pretended, he knows more than anyone) and the listeners whom he addresses (only they, not readers, are exposed to this pressure). Like the other pointers, the demand for a drink performs its function best in the context of oral recital, so that we need positive evidence why it should be imagined as addressed fictitiously to a reader on whom it has no bearing.

(h) Request for attention

Here too we are dealing with a remark normally addressed to the audience and requesting them to listen or keep silent.[136] A remark of this nature can most easily be imagined in the setting of oral recital, but Scholz again argues that it could be meant fictitiously in a work for readers.[137] Scholz begins his argument on this kind of remark by asking how far its position in a work throws light on whether it was meant with regard to a real recital situation.[138] He lists examples where the request for attention opens a work, and concedes that this is the position where its literal function is conceivable. He shows doubts, however, when the remark occurs in other positions, doubts which we need not share. If the request comes *after* the prologue and at the beginning of the narrative, this may reflect a realistic awareness that many members of a medieval audience paid less attention to the theoretical tenor of a prologue and needed to be jollied into attention when the narrative was about to begin.[139] We should also hesitate to dismiss comparable remarks in the middle of a narrative as devoid of any practical function, as long as we remain ignorant about how much of a work was recited at one session, how far a request for attention may coincide with something resembling a 'cliffhanger situation', or even whether an audience could be expected to grow more restive and inattentive as the recital advanced. Reasons such as these, possibly accounting for the remark in the middle of a work, do not apply when it is used at the conclusion, where it does seem to have lost any real function, but even here Scholz quotes only one example.[140] The need to postulate a reception other than by oral recital, i.e. a reader, is therefore far less than Scholz suggests. What we may regard as 'fictitious' in these remarks is the fact that authors have written them in advance into their texts, not the need for their audience to keep quiet or their presence as listeners.

A fictitious use of these remarks can sometimes be accepted, but not to the exclusion of a literal use, namely in those works for which twofold reception, by readers as well as by listeners, can be assumed. When Ulrich von Zatzikhoven at a point far into his *Lanzelet* enjoins silence on his listeners (7584: *welt ir hoeren wie ez kam, / sô sult ir dar zuo gedagen*), we might feel tempted to question the necessity of this at such a point and to recall that *hoeren* can also be used of the reader learning from a written text. That may be so, but the author reveals that it is only part of the picture when, at the end of the work, he suggests a twofold reception by his audience (9440: *des sult ir alle biten in, / die diz liet hoeren oder lesen*). If both listeners and readers are anticipated, then the request to listen and to keep silent must have had literal force for the listeners, but metaphorical or fictitious force for the readers. One function does not exclude the other (especially if we bear in mind that a medieval reader could also attend a collective recital). To suggest a non-literal usage in these cases is not enough to prove that they were not also meant literally.

A final example of a request for silence applied to an actual audience is provided by medieval drama. In the *Wiener Passionsspiel* this request is directed to a public actually present and therefore able to see and hear the play (1: *Silete, silentium habete! / Hoeret ir hêrren unt ir vrowen, / di daz spil wellent schowen: / ir sult alle stille wesen, / sô muget ir von goete hoeren singen unt lesen!*). Since this remark comes at the opening of the drama, presumably Scholz would take it at its face value, implying an actual performance before spectators (on which we are richly informed for medieval drama).[141] The same must hold of the *St. Galler Passionsspiel*, even though the player who takes the part of Augustine acts as the equivalent of a narrator in making his request at several points in the drama (e.g. 374: *Swigent mit zuhten an dirre stunt, / so wollen wir vch machen kunt...*).[142] If there is no reason for assuming that this drama was not performed before an actual audience, then the insertion of such requests in the body of this text must cast doubt on Scholz's reluctance to accept them when similarly placed in narrative texts. The need for silence may not have been foreseeable either in the performance of the drama or in the recital of other texts, but this does not disprove collective listening in either case.

(i) *Tu autem, domine, miserere nobis*

We come now to a formula, discussed by Ohly, which was used with a number of vernacular works ranging from the ninth to the twelfth century.[143] He has shown that the formula was originally used to indicate the conclusion of a recital in the monastic refectory or for works with no evidence that their recital took place in that setting. Common to both situations is the fact of a recital to listeners.

The formula can be retained in its complete Latin form at the close of a vernacular work, as with the *Rolandslied* (9094).[144] The Latin wording together with the position at the close of the work are enough to evoke the function of the formula in a refectory recital, even though recital in this case took place at court. What the formula now suggests, apart from its appositeness to the religious dimension of the work, is its recital before listeners, a fact borne out by other indication in the text and by what the *Annales Stederburgenses* report on Henry the Lion's preference for recitals.

Elsewhere the formula can be used in a half-Latin, half-German form, as in *Memento Mori* (19, 1: *Trohtin, chunic here, nobis miserere!*),[145] again at the close of a work and, in that the work is addressed to laymen illiterate at that time,[146] in the context of oral recital. A completely vernacular version is found at the close of the *Petruslied* (*Pittemes den gotes trut alla samant upar lut, / daz er uns firtanen giuuerdo ginaden*), where the presence of neumes and refrains, together with the probability that the poem was sung in procession, all point to acoustic reception,[147] although the text does not lend itself to a refectory reading.[148] Underlying all the cases treated by Ohly, whether in the refectory or not, is the fact of oral recital.

The same is paradoxically true of a case where this formula is *not* employed, for Kartschoke has made the attractive suggestion that the *Wessobrunner Schöpfungsgedicht* (16, 1ff.) was entered fragmentarily (no more than the opening lines) in its manuscript for the purpose of calling it to mind, since the poem was regularly recited orally.[149] He proposes for the following *Wessobrunner Gebet* (16, 10ff.) the same function as the *Tu autem* formula: to indicate the close of the recital and to pray for the spiritual strengthening of those who have heard it. Thelen has taken this suggestion further: on the basis of parallels between the prayer and the theme of the poem he regards the former as composed with an eye to the poem (whereas the *Tu autem* formula was applied to various poems).[150] Thelen agrees with Kartschoke in seeing the prayer as concluding an oral recital of the poem.

(j) Memorisation

A final non-lexical criterion for oral reception may be dealt with briefly. We have considered memorisation as a possibility distinct from composition-in-recital, but its relevance to the present argument is that something remembered will not normally be read, but recited aloud, so that its reception is acoustic. When Otfrid says that the Franks were able to sing prayers and liturgical formulas by heart (I 1, 109: *iz úzana gisíngen*), there is no need of the verb *gisingen* for us to realise that something committed to memory, rather than to writing, will find its way vocally to recipients.[151] The same is true when the gloss to the *Sächsische Weichbildrecht* sees past law in terms of the medieval distinction between oral and written (211, 6: . . . *daz waz nicht ein beschreben recht, wenn sy kunden is allez uzwendig*), for law which is memorised, not written, can only be made public by oral proclamation. Whenever, as is normally the case with liturgical formulas, something has been memorised (e.g. *Exhortatio* 49, 2: . . . *calaupa, dera ir in herzin cahuctliho hapen sculut*) it is with its future function as spoken word in mind. A qualification is called for in the case of Latin *memoriae mandare*, which can be used of committing something to writing.[152]

LEXICAL EVIDENCE

Scholz is aware of the value of lexical evidence in shedding light on the mode of reception of medieval literature but devotes most attention to indicators for reading. We must now restore the balance by considering what the usage of various words tells us about hearing the works to which they refer.

(k) *Hoeren*

It can be dangerous to take this word at face value as implying an acoustic reception (the author of the *Mariengrüße* uses it in addressing his reader, 791: *Leser, wilt dû hoeren nû*).[153] When discussing this verb Scholz is mainly concerned to show that it could be used metaphorically and he thereby largely ignores a literal usage.

He comes closest to admitting a literal function in the case of the nomen agentis *hoeraere*, mainly because, one suspects, this form (applied to the recipients of a literary work) occurs seldom in MHG, so that he is not conceding much ground. He accepts the evidence of the nomen agentis because its infrequency suggests that it was less likely to be used conventionally, whereas the greater frequency of the verb *hoeren* exposed it to the danger of being employed long after the changed conditions of literary reception justified its literal meaning. Applied to the audience, Scholz has found three examples of *hoeraere*, only one of which (*Anegenge* 298) he accepts in the sense of an acoustic reception,[154] but his grounds for rejecting the others are hardly convincing. When Ebernand von Erfurt begs for the prayers of his listeners (*Heinrich und Kunigunde* 52: *ir reinen hôrêre guot, / ir sult mir ouch ze gote wegen, / daz er mir teile sînen segen*), Scholz drastically reinterprets *hôrêre* and claims that it refers to readers. He does this because Latin *auditor* can sometimes be used of a reader, but derives this information not from any specific work, but from dictionaries, without telling us why what was possible sometimes in Latin must be the case in this German text.[155] Moreover, if we can accept a monastic context for Ebernand, this suggests a parallel with the *Ulrichsleben* of Albertus von Augsburg, for which Scholz, uniquely, is prepared to accept a twofold reception on the grounds that this was common monastic practice.[156] Why therefore should he deny to Ebernand's work what is conceded with Albertus? If Ebernand likewise reckoned with a twofold reception there is no reason to see in his *hôrêre* anything other than listeners. Scholz is also suspicious of two references to listeners when the author of *Lohengrin* abbreviates what he has to say for fear of trying their patience (4267: ... *Der ich nande vil ob sîn die hoerer niht verdrüzze*; 4970: ... *und daz sîn lîht verdrüzze die hoerer harte*). The reason for Scholz's suspicion is the evidence for a reading reception of this work, which he sees in conflict with an acoustic reception. He resolves his conflict in favour of reading by arguing that here too the listeners are really readers. That hearing is likely to be meant literally, however, is suggested by the possibility of a melody for *Lohengrin*.[157]

Scholz's task would have been rendered more difficult if he had taken other examples of the nomen agentis into account. The Zwiefalten version of the MHG *Benediktinerregel* describes the monastic *collatio* in terms of someone reading out aloud for the edification of his *horare* (34, 4) who, from all we know of this practice,[158] certainly cannot be transformed into readers (the reading, aloud, is performed by someone else). Three other examples are decisive in another way. Brun von Schönebeck addresses his audience, seeing them composed of two types (*Hohes Lied* 12542: *ir horer und ir lesere*); the gloss to the *Sächsisches Weichbildrecht* sees its reception in similar terms (181, 8: ... *dorumme daz der leser und der zuhörer nicht beswert werden*); the same is true (with a present participle) when Hiltgart von Hürnheim addresses her audience (*Secretum Secretorum* 4, 34: ... *Euch losennden und hörenndenn mueß wol gelingen. Ich pit euch leser und leserinne / Das ir geleubig seit meinem krancken sinne*). Common to these three examples is their explicit reference to what was implicit in *Heinrich und Kunigunde* and *Lohengrin*, a twofold reception, by listeners and readers. This reception suggests that the listeners have to be understood literally.

Even taking account of these examples we are left with a total crop of listeners, on the evidence of the nomen agentis, which is remarkably small. To increase this we

CRITERIA FOR RECEPTION BY HEARING

turn to the evidence of the verb *hoeren* itself where, however conventionally it may be used, it can still occur with a literal function. In other words, Scholz's stress on a fictitious or metaphorical usage by no means puts an end to a literal use.

With Bruder Philipp's *Marienleben* the cards seem stacked in favour of Scholz's case. *Hoeren*, applied to the audience, is not attested by itself, but reference is made once to potential readers (10116), so that we might be tempted to see the work meant for them, as with a modern book. That this is only part of the picture is brought out by an isolated reference to a twofold reception (10083ff.). The *Ulrichsleben* of Albertus von Augsburg uses *hoeren* once only of the audience (1155), but against this suggests a reader explicitly (1206) and also by its employment of an acrostic (1ff.) and instructions on solving it (1574ff.). That we should be wrong to dismiss *hoeren* as conventional and outweighed by the reading evidence is suggested by a reference to the audience hearing the book read out to them (1546). In the *Rede vom heiligen Glauben* Der Arme Hartmann uses *hoeren* (and *vernemen*) infrequently, not enough to give us a lead. There is one reference to reading (95, 9), but in the same context as a reference to a twofold reception (95, 7f.), from which we may conclude that *hoeren*, however uninformative by itself, refers to actual listeners. In the *Livländische Reimchronik hoeren* is used of the audience's reception of the work six times in all, not often enough to be suspected of being conventional, but not in itself wholly convincing. More revealing is the precise way in which the author several times uses a construction like 5688 (*als ich ûch hie vor las*) with a specific reference to an earlier point in his narrative (5583ff.). We shall see that *lesen* is used with a dative object to denote reading out (aloud) to someone else, so that its recurrence in this work at points where reference is made to what had been recited earlier establishes a recital situation and therewith a literal meaning for *hoeren*.[159] Just after Rennewart's death has been recounted, half-way through his *Rennewart*, Ulrich von Türheim asks his audience to continue listening to the whole work (25702: *Über hoeret gar diu maere*, translated in the editor's glossary as 'vorlesen lassen'). As a final example of how this verb may point to an oral context we may take Albrecht von Scharfenberg's *Jüngerer Titurel*, where *hoeren* is used regularly – not excessively, but still in what could be taken to be stereotyped phrases. A decision in favour of a literal meaning, however, is suggested by phrases, describing the work's reception, like *lesen oder hoeren* (1663, 1: *Swer hie nu vreude si lesende oder hoere an disem buoche* or 6327, 4: *alle, di iz hoeren, lesen oder schriben*). This oral dimension is underlined when on one occasion Albrecht expands the first of these two constructions by adding a reference to singing the work to a melody (6077, 4: *diez lesen oder hoeren und der iz sag oder in dem done singe*) and by other references to singing to a melody (3205, 2ff.; 3812, 2ff.).[160]

These examples are enough to permit three conclusions about interpreting the verb to throw light on an actual recital of a work. First, no passage can be judged by itself, it must be collated with other evidence in the same work. Secondly, the evidence for *hoeren* must be collated with non-lexical evidence: for example, with the presence of an acrostic or with references to singing and a melody. Thirdly, the evidence for *hoeren* must be collated with other lexical evidence in the same work: repeatedly relevant are phrases which will occupy us later, such as *hoeren lesen* or *hoeren oder lesen* or *als ich ûch hie vor las*. These types of evidence are characteristic of the intermediate mode of reception, so that by ignoring this Scholz has made it difficult to judge the literal importance of *hoeren* and the continuing importance of acoustic reception.

(l) *Sprechen, sagen, singen*

Just as Scholz weakened the case for understanding *hoeren* literally by illustrating its application to the reader in the *Mariengrüße*, so does he undercut the verb *sagen* by an example from the same work (821: *Leser, ich wil dir sagen mê*).[161] This complementary example suggests that we should look at these three verbs in the same way as *hoeren*, discussing the evidence for the nomen agentis, then for the verb itself.

As with *hoeraere*, the nomen agentis *sprecher* is used with a technical function much less commonly than the verb *sprechen* with reference to the poet addressing his audience, so that there is less likelihood of *sprecher* being used conventionally. That it could be used of those who recited tales to their audience as part of court entertainment (with its acoustic as well as visual dimension) is made clear in *Laurin* 1045: *dar nâch sach man für gân / zwêne wol singende man, / zwêne guote sprechaere. / hovelîchiu maere / si sungen vor den fürsten vil, / daz was ir kurzwîle und ir spil.* Apart from this isolated example the *sprecher* is considered by Fischer as the term for a professional reciter who first comes to the fore in the thirteenth century and was particularly connected with the recital of 'Mären'.[162] Fischer points out that information on this reciter can be gleaned from the accounts of princely families and cities who record their expenses in rewarding entertainers just as meticulously as Wolfger von Erla, a suggestion which has been followed up by Mundschau with his focus on the fourteenth century, when the evidence becomes available.[163] The fact that the nomen agentis is applied to public reciters not just in *Laurin*, but in such account-books makes it clear that here there is no danger that it was used metaphorically, but that it designated a public performer associated with the 'Märe'.

By contrast, the verb *sprechen* was not restricted to this genre. As was the case in *Laurin* with the nomen agentis, Hartmann uses the verb without restriction to a genre when he refers to the rewards given to minstrels at Erec's wedding festival: *nû schiet mit rîcher hende / vil vroelîchen dan / manec wol sprechender spilman*.[164] Likewise in the setting of a court festival and minstrels the author of *Morant und Galie* refers to the activity of some who recite love-stories (5152: *sulche ouch da waren / die van minnen inde lieve / sprachen ane brieve*). The phrase *ane brieve* suggests that they learned their stories by heart and therefore delivered them orally, as is implied by the Provençal parallel in Jaufre Rudel: *Senes breu de parguamina / Tramet lo vers*.[165] A different context, showing that the verb cannot be tied down to one genre, is involved when Rudolf von Ems uses *sprechen* of his activity as reciter in his *Weltchronik* 2079 ... *als ich ê han gesprochen hie / dú arche von der ich é las*. If, as I argue in the next section, *lesen* in combination with *é* refers to the reciter having read out a detail at an earlier point (he refers back to 829ff.), this suggests that *sprechen* too indicates oral recital.

What we have seen of *sprechen* can also be shown with *sagen*. The nomen agentis *sager* is less common than the verb, even if we confine the latter to the context of reciter addressing audience. In its weak form the nomen agentis occurs in the context of professional entertainers at a court festival in *Dietrichs Flucht* (679: *gîger singer unde sagen*), but in its full form we find it in clear association with 'Mären', used by the author as reciter in *Drei listige Frauen II* (1: *Welt irz mit zühten hoeren / und den sager niht betoeren*) and in *Der Pfaffe mit der Schnur* (1ff.).

By comparison with these isolated examples the verb is used much more frequently of a recital situation which, if only because of the nomen agentis, we cannot simply dismiss as conventional. Hartmann uses *sagen* of Kalogreant's recital to the Round Table in *Iwein* (249: 'man verliuset michel sagen, / man enwellez merken unde dagen. / maneger biutet diu ôren dar: / ern nemes ouch mit dem herzen war, / sône wirt im niht wan der dôz') and sees the relationship between reciter and audience in terms of 'saying' and 'hearing' (256). The same is true of a recital situation depicted in *Die Klage* in which first the messengers give their public account of what happened (3771: *alrêrst hiez man dô für gân / die boten zantwurte stân, / daz si sageten diu maere, / wie ez ergangen waere*), then the minstrel gives his account (3776: *Swämmel stuont vor der schar; / er begunde in diu maere sagen*). The incorporation of a 'poem within a poem' is clearly a fictional device, but Curschmann has argued that the author of *Die Klage* depicts here an oral poet delivering his work without benefit of writing before an assembled audience, because this was the normal way in which heroic themes were transmitted.[166] Such a passage, while telling us little about the reception of *Die Klage*, does throw light on the transmission of heroic poetry and on the function of a verb like *sagen* in that process.

Like Hartmann's Kalogreant, Gottfried's narrator can use the verb *sagen* in addressing his audience (*Tristan* 239: *Und swer nu ger, daz man im sage / ir leben ... / der biete herze und ôren her*). If this part of the prologue is built on an analogy with the eucharist,[167] so that the reading of the story of Tristan and Isold is implicitly compared with the reading of the text of the Bible in the course of the liturgy, this implies a public reading of Gottfried's text to an assembled audience, no matter whether we also argue for a private reading on the part of some recipients. Public reading is also suggested in the case of *sagen*, as for *sprechen*, in the *Weltchronik* of Rudolf von Ems, when the author alludes to earlier points in his narrative (13803: *... als ich ê las / und offte han von im geseit*). Here too, if *lesen* together with *ê* indicates a reference to what has been read out to the audience at preceding points, this implies an oral context for *sagen*.[168] A similar implication is made by Hartmann in *Erec* when he refers to an earlier mention of Guivreiz (6821: *ich hân iu ê von im gesaget*), for this has to be compared with references such as 7179 (*als ir ê hôrtet sagen*, cf. 7148) and 7304 (*... sô disiu schilthalben was / von der ich iu nû dâ las*, cf. 7292ff.). Whether or not a potential reader may be involved, these reminders of past details are addressed to a listening audience.

The third verb, *singen*, might seem to be the clearest case of an acoustic delivery, but only if we ignore a metaphorical usage like Virgil's at the opening of the *Aeneid*, so that it is advisable to subject this verb to the same consideration as *sprechen* and *sagen*. Here too the nomen agentis, applied to the professional singer, occurs much less commonly than the verb, used of the poet. The genres in which it is used include gnomic poetry, as when Fegfeuer distinguishes wandering minstrels from their clerical rivals (1 3, 7f.),[169] but also love-poetry (Der Stricker, *Daniel von dem Blühenden Tal* 8163: *zweinzic singaere, / die durch vertrîben swaere / von minne lieder sungen*), the heroic epic (*Walberan* 1234: *man hôrte ouch manic guot gesanc / von guoten singaeren*), but also the 'Spielmannsepos' (as with a blackmailing demand for wine from the reciter in *Herzog Ernst G* 61, 8ff.).[170]

Although the corresponding verb is used more frequently in this technical sense, it occurs in the same genres as the nomen agentis, presumably therefore in the same literal sense which with lyric and heroic poetry is confirmed by their melodies. In view of this it would be rash to take *singen* as meant only metaphorically in gnomic poetry (as with Bruder Wernher 11, 1: *Ich hân sô vil gesungen ê, daz maneger nû geswüere wol, / ich hete gar gesungen ûz*), in love poetry (e.g. Ulrich von Lichtenstein, *Frauendienst* 592, 23: *ich wil si gerne loben mê. / swer welle daz ez hier an stê, / swenne ichz gesing, der schrîbe ez dran*), in the heroic epic (*Laurin* 1046: *zwêne wol singende man*, used of entertainers at court), and in the 'Spielmannsepos' (*Herzog Ernst G* 89, 13: *swer sîn mêr künne der singe ez baz*). In all such cases the parallel with the nomen agentis, less likely to be used in a conventional manner, and the evidence that the genres were equipped with a melody (less convincing only in the case of the 'Spielmannsepen') suggest a literal meaning of the verb *singen* and therefore an acoustic reception.[171]

(m) *Lesen*

With this word we come to a key-term for the reception of vernacular literature. The verb has a range of other meanings which are discussed in the Appendix (whose argument I presuppose in what follows), but in the present context *lesen* will concern us as the reading of a text not by an individual to himself, but aloud to others assembled to listen. It is a peculiarity of the medieval position that a verb which nowadays is used almost entirely of private reading could be employed of an audience, possibly entirely illiterate, but perhaps also including literates, listening to one person who alone was active in reading. That we are justified in distinguishing for this verb reading by an individual for himself from reading aloud to others is confirmed by what John of Salisbury says on the Latin equivalent *legere*, for to make the same distinction he proposes the two verbs *legere* and *prelegere*.[172] If the need to avoid ambiguity existed in medieval Latin, this suggests that *legere*, like *lesen*, could also be used of reading aloud to listeners, and if John does not always observe his doctrine of clarity, this shows how firmly entrenched was this linguistic practice.[173]

Before we consider the evidence for *lesen* used of public recital, we must look at the evidence for the nomen agentis, as in the case of the verbs *hoeren*, *sprechen*, *sagen* and *singen*. *Leser* is used of one who recites from a text to a listening audience in MHG versions of the *Benediktinerregel*, where it designates the monastic lector who reads to the other monks while they eat in the refectory. Where the Latin version of the Rule refers to the monk who has this task as *lector* and *legens*,[174] the Hohenfurth version in the vernacular refers to him as *leisere* (71, 4: *vnd michil stilnisse si cetische. daz da nieman gehorit werde. wene der eine leisere*), whilst the

Asbach version follows the other Latin model and uses the present participle (150, 4: *Vnd oberistiv swige sol zem tische sin, daz nimans cispizen oder stimme niwan aleine des lesendes da gehoret werde*).[175] This usage is not simply the result of imitating Latin usage, as can be shown by cases where a secular reciter demands liquid refreshment at a point in his performance as the price of continuing. This is so with MS I of the *Münchener Oswald* (*. . . man pring den dem leser ein chopff weins vol*),[176] with *Orendel* (2829), with *Laurin* at a well-chosen point (1218), and after v. 1488 in MS W of *Flos unde Blankeflos* (*dut bok is nu vtghelesen / me scal dem lezer drincken gheuen*).[177] To demand a concrete reward in such a context presupposes an acoustic situation for this secular *leser* just as much as with the monastic lector in the refectory. This is also the case with the recommendation of Heinrich von Hesler to the reciter of his *Apokalypse* to skip a passage if ladies happen to be present (3711: *Des bit ich den lesere* . . .). Even though the nomen agentis is used by itself in all these cases, the context indicates that reading aloud to others is implied, rather than for oneself: the need for silence in the refectory, the ability to blackmail an audience dependent on the reciter, or the presence of ladies whose ears must not be offended. Discussion of the verb *lesen*, however, begins best with those cases where its function is indicated by its conjunction with another pointer.

The first pointer, the employment of *lesen* with an indirect object in the dative to convey reading (or reciting) aloud to others, has been mentioned in passing by Scholz.[178] More telling is his quotation of the definition of *lectio* by Hugh of St Victor,[179] where only two of the three aspects given concern us at present: private reading is defined as *lego librum*, but reading out to others (as with the teacher in the classroom to his pupils) as *lego librum illi*. The addition of a dative object, suggesting that reading is to someone else or on his behalf, has parallels in German. In Veldeke's *Servatius* Charles the Great has the saint's life read out to him (4240: *di vite dede he sich lesen*), where the acoustic dimension is underlined by the conjunction of *lesen* with *horen* (4242). In Ulrich von Lichtenstein's *Frauendienst* the poet asks for a letter from his lady to be read out to him (195, 21: *den brief ich mir an der stat / vil snelleclîchen lesen bat*), so that he may *hear* it (195, 23).

Armed with evidence of this kind, we may understand the position when the construction is used of the reception of the author's own work. In *Ortnit* those who seek entertainment are recommended to have the book recited to them (2, 1: *Swer in freuden welle und in kurzwîle wesen, / der lâze im von dem buoche singen und lesen*), where the conjunction of *lesen* with *singen* underlines the acoustic dimension.[180] Ebernand von Erfurt refers to the heroine of his *Heinrich und Kunigunde* with the phrase (3789) *die vrouwe, darvon ich û las, / michel guote an ir was*, but since the audience addressed here in the dative are elsewhere described as listeners (52), we may be sure that they are read to aloud. When Rudolf von Ems describes the reception he anticipates for his *Weltchronik* at the royal court, he sees Konrad ordering the work to be read out to him (21700: *swenner im lesin hieze*), an oral reception which is confirmed by the use of *hoeren* (21707).[181] There are also cases where even without a reference to singing or hearing we may be confident of oral reception. In requesting the prayers of his audience at the conclusion of *Meier Helmbrecht* Wernher der Gartenaere sees them as having it recited to them (1929: *Swer iu ditze maere lese*), whilst Dietrich von Glezze makes the same assumption at the opening of *Der Borte* when he has his personified book say (7): *man sol mich hubschen luten lesen.*

A second pointer to public recital is provided when *lesen* is employed in conjunction with *vor*, implying the presence of others,[182] not in the improbable sense that, despite this company, someone withdraws antisocially into himself to read privately, but in the sense that he contributes to the sociability of the occasion by reciting aloud before them and to them. This vernacular construction is therefore the equivalent of what John of Salisbury registered for medieval Latin (*prelectio*). A well-known example is provided in Hartmann's *Iwein*, where a young noblewoman reads aloud to her parents in the garden of their castle: she sits in front of them (6455: *und vor in beiden saz ein maget*) and entertains them (6458) by reading (6461: *ez dûhte si guot swaz si las*), which can only be aloud.[183] A comparable situation is suggested in the *Wigalois* of Wirnt von Grafenberg (2713: *ein schoeniu maget vor ir las / an einem buoche ein maere, / wie Troje zevuort waere*). Here *lesen* stands much closer to the pointer *vor*, so that we approach a stage where the construction begins to resemble modern German 'vorlesen'. This is also the case with *Wolfdietrich D* with regard to reading out a letter (10, 27, 1: *Sie seiten im diu maere, den brief man vor im las*), whereas a similar context in the *Alexander* of Rudolf von Ems is noticeably more public (4266: *er nam und las sie [brieve] sâ zehant / offenlîche vor der schar / daz siez alle hôrten gar*). Our construction can also occur in a form identical with modern German, especially in the context of preaching a sermon or reading a lesson. *Das Passional* has an example concerning a bishop explicitly termed a *predigere* (III 232, 6): *do daz volc zur kirchen was / und in der bischof vorlas / unseres herren lere* (233, 81), whilst the *Wiener Predigten* use the verb of the liturgical lesson (78, 9).

These last examples serve as a bridge to the construction used of the reception of the author's own work. The author of *Diu vrône botschaft* expects any priest who has a copy of his work to read it out to his flock (384: *Und swelich briester geschriben hât / dise botschaft und si ungelesen lât / offenlîchen vor den liuten*). What is interesting is that the narrative action of this work (a miraculous letter is read out for the moral improvement of listeners within the narrative)[184] reflects the reception of the work itself (likewise to be read out to listeners). Of quite a different nature, but still implying oral recital, is what is said at the close of the *Schwabenspiegel Langform M*: *dicz puch ist gewizzen vnd weisen leuten gut vor ze lesen.*[185]

While we are dealing with the construction *lesen + vor* we may look briefly at the conjunction of other verbs with *vor* to suggest a public recital. Of the verbs considered in the previous section *sprechen* occurs infrequently in conjunction with *vor*. An example is provided by Bruder Hermann in his *Leben der Gräfin Iolande von Vianden*, when he refuses to speak or write the wording of an angry curse (3826: *dy wort, der ich nyt sprechen mach / noch ôich enwil nyt schrîven / vor allen reinen wîven*), where I take the construction *sprechen + schrîven + vor* to imply recital from a written text to assembled listeners, perhaps religious women.

Sagen occurs rather more frequently in conjunction with *vor*. We have seen it applied to an oral recital in *Die Klage* (3776: *Swämmel stuont vor der schar: / er begunde in diu maere sagen*), but it is also used in *Herzog Ernst* of preaching (5919:

der bischof trat ûf den lector / und sagt der kristenheite vor / die süeze gotes lêre). Applied to the delivery of the author's own work we find it in Wolfram's *Willehalm* where the narrator has to observe certain decencies in the presence of ladies (153, 4: *die namn het ich bekennet, / ob ich die wolte vor iu sagen: / nu muoz ich si durch zuht verdagen*) or in Johann von Würzburg's *Wilhelm von Österreich* (19502ff.).

Most frequent, in lyric poetry, is the construction *singen + vor*, where the presence of melodies suggests a literal use of the verb. In *Minnesangs Frühling* Kaiser Heinrich reckons with the possibility that his poem will be sung in the presence of his lady and convey his greetings to her (IX, III 1, 5: *Swer nu disiu liet singe vor ir*). Boppe sums up the art of the lyric poet as singing to others (11, 10: *... unt kan er hoflich singen vor den liuten*),[186] just as does Rumelant von Sachsen (VI 12, 4: *Er hat den jungen vor gesungen unt dar zuo den alten*). In some cases the construction can be used with reference to someone acting as precentor or choirleader: although *vor* can have a temporal meaning in such cases (his singing precedes that of the others), this need not exclude the spatial function which is our concern. Neidhart uses the phrase of someone who leads the dance in song (*Winterlieder* 17, 4, 10: '*er het uns an der wîle ein liet ze tanze vor gesungen*'), as does von Stamhein (11, 6: *dar nâch huop sich des meien ein vil michel tanz. / den sanc in Bêle vor*), whilst Jans Enikel refers to Leopold VI performing the same role at the court of Vienna (*Fürstenbuch* 2027).[187]

The three verbs of recital considered in the last section can therefore all be combined with *vor* to suggest a public setting, but other verbs can be used to the same effect. When Brun von Schönebeck, combining *komen* with *vor*, says that his work may come before princes, public recital is what he has in mind (*Hohes Lied* 1124: *sint ditz buch uf einen tag / vor di vursten wol komen mag, / so daz si iz lesen horen*). In the *Rheinisches Marienlob*, presumably composed by a cleric for nuns or religious women,[188] the conjunction of *dúden* with *vür* (meaning 'vor' rather than 'für')[189] implies that the author is to interpret his work in the presence of his audience, as part of a recital situation (4373: *Ler mich, vrow, die gemmen dúden / schön vür allen godes brüden!*).[190] When the author of the *Trierer Silvester* opens his poem by appealing for silence and referring to hearing his work he suggests that the combination of *bringen* with *vor* (4: *eine uil suze rede uuore bringen*) refers to recital of the work ('vortragen').

This example ties up with Kartschoke's suggestion concerning *vor tragen*[191] and *fur bringen* in the epilogue to the *Rolandslied* (9022, 9032).[192] He considers the semantic function of these verbs in MHG, distinguishing between a concrete spatial meaning ('to bring forward, to serve up, to produce') and a metaphorical ('to express, to convey, to recite'). Whereas dictionaries give few examples of the latter meaning before the later Middle Ages, Kartschoke suggests that when what is brought forward in the spatial sense is a book the possibility of reciting from it to an assembled public is not far removed. In the light of this he sees a parallel between the two phrases in the *Rolandslied* (9022: *daz buoch hîz er vor tragen*; 9032: *daz man [iz] fur brâchte*), where the common ground is not the spatial meaning, but the metaphorical one, suggesting recital,[193] an interpretation reinforced by other pointers in this work to oral recital. That this was possible is borne out by the occurrence of *uor tragen* in the metaphorical sense in a contemporary example not quoted by Kartschoke, in the *Speculum Ecclesiae* (139, 2: *Wir ewarten sculen iv sagen allez, daz gan gote gezivhet, wir sculen den laigen offenen, wie si sculen leben, unde sculen wir in daz bilde gvoter werche uor tragen*).

After this excursion into the use of *vor* with verbs other than *lesen* we return to this verb, this time in conjunction with a third pointer to oral recital, the adverb *offen* or *offenlîche*.[194] Implied by the addition of this adverb is not just reading *in* public, as opposed to reading in private, but also reading *to* an assembled public. We have considered one example from the *Alexander* of Rudolf von Ems (4266ff.) where the public dimension suggested by *lesen* + *offenlîche* is reinforced by *vor der schar*, just as a little later a comparable phrase (4588: *dô hiez er die brieve sâ / lesen offenlîche*) is confirmed by 4595 (*vor allem dem gesinde*).[195] Since what is read out to all and sundry is the content of a letter, we may recall what Köhn has shown of medieval correspondence: that a letter was commonly read out loud to the addressee, but also to others gathered around him.[196] The same construction is used in the epistolary context when Thomasin criticises Walther for his unjustified attack on the pope: he says that he heard the papal missive read out (*wan ich bin dâ gewesen / dâ ich hôrt offenlîchen lesen / sînen brief* ...)[197] and makes the public setting clear (11189: *des bâbstes bote den brief las / dâ manic biderbe man was*). Outside the context of letter-writing the combination of *lesen* with *offen* occurs in the *Väterbuch* with reference to the daily reading of saints' lives, epistles and gospels in church (3972ff.).[198] From this it is a short step to the same construction being used with regard to the reception of an author's own work, for the author of *Diu vrône botschaft* hopes that it will be read out publicly by the priest (384: *Und swelich briester... si ungelesen lât / offenlîchen vor den liuten*). In all these cases the public setting shows that *lesen* is used of an oral recital.

A fourth pointer to this situation can be present when *lesen* is used together with a verb with causative force, meaning 'to cause' (*tuon, lân*) or 'to request, to order' (*biten, heizen*). How this construction can imply an acoustic dimension can be shown by a Latin parallel from the dedication of his *De universo* by Hrabanus Maurus in which he addressed Ludwig the German: *ipsum opus vobis ... transmisi: ut si Serenitati Vestrae placuerit, coram vobis relegi illud faciatis*.[199] Here *relegi faciatis* corresponds to a vernacular *lesen heizen*, but the addition of *coram vobis* points to an assembled audience and therefore oral recital.[200] This is how the following examples have to be interpreted. Whereas the modern implication of such a construction would be 'to ensure that a work is read by as many people as possible', the social dimension of medieval literature and widespread illiteracy imply something different: 'to ensure that a work is recited to as many listeners as possible'.

The linkage of *lesen* with *tuon* can be illustrated from Gottfried Hagen's *Chronik der Stadt Köln* (4110: *sinen breif den doit uch lesen*), where medieval practice in correspondence and the use of *lesen* with a dative object suggest that the letter was meant to be read out loud. The same construction occurs in a similar context in the prose *Lancelot* (I 492, 6), where the physical presence of listeners (*vor allen*) is reinforced by a scribe reading out the letter as loudly as possible (492, 15: *Der konig nam den brieff und gab yn eim schriber das ern lese so er allerlutest mocht*). When *lesen* is linked with *lân*, this can be in the same context of having a letter read out publicly, as in *Alexius F* (1390: *der bâbest nam / den brief von im andaehteclîch / und liez in lesen offenlich*), where *offenlich* points in the same direction.²⁰¹ It can also occur in a more intimate context, involving two people and presumably a work of court literature, as in *Mai und Beaflor* (230, 29: *'welt ir lenger hinne wesen, / ich lâze iu mîne tohter lesen / swelch maere ir welt in franzois'*), where the indirect object *iu* confirms the oral nature of the reading.

That *biten* in the same construction can imply an oral dimension is shown by Ulrich von Lichtenstein having a letter read out to him (*Frauendienst* 195, 21: *den brief ich mir an der stat / vil snelleclîchen lesen bat. / den brief ich hôrt*) or by *Das Passional* (III 338, 96: *do bat si alda vor ir lesen / die passion, die Lucas schreib*), where *vor ir* conjures up the spatial setting of the recital. *Heizen* can be used to the same effect, as when Ulrich von Lichtenstein has a letter read out (*Frauendienst* 231, 21: *Ich dâht 'ich sol den brief wol mir / hie heizen lesen'*), where *mir* implies that someone else is to read to him. A clear case is provided by the *Jüngerer Titurel* of Albrecht von Scharfenberg, where a scribe is instructed to read out the inscription on the leash (1871, 1: *Einen schriber wol geleret man lesen hiez di strangen*) and an explanation added that, since so many were present, there was no choice but to read it out. The same dependence on a literate scribe, who as reciter stands in front of his audience, is attested in *Esther* (1373: *sîne schrîbere er dô rief / und hiez vor im die bûch lesen*) or in the *Schwabenspiegel Langform M (Königebuch* 17c).²⁰²

In these cases where *lesen* is combined with a causative the oral aspect of reciting aloud is made quite clear. The implication of the causative is not simply to request or command, but to stress the necessity of a public reading, either because the recipients may be illiterate or because a collective reception is called for. The examples may have to do with situations within the narrative framework, but the constructions can also indicate how the author anticipates the reception of his own work. As an example with the verb *lân* I quote the *Hamburgisches Stadtrecht (1270)*, where provision is made that, if anyone objects to a decision, he has the right to have the lawbook read out at the meeting of the city-council to establish his claim (VI 30: *... vnde he schal to deme negesten dinge, also de rad uppe deme hus is, dat bock lesen laten, vnde bewisen eyn recht ordel*). An example with *heizen* is provided by Otfrid in his dedications to Ludwig the German, where the poet expresses the hope that the latter will order his work to be read (Lud. 87: *Themo dîhton ih thiz búah; oba er hábet iro rúah, / ódo er thaz giwéizit, thaz er sa lésan heizit*).²⁰³ Although Otfrid reckoned with individual readers, it is doubtful whether he has them in mind at this point. A work serving the public interests of a ruler can do this best in the public setting of oral recital at court; the parallel with a similar dedication by Hrabanus Maurus to the same ruler (where *relegi faciatis* corresponds to *lesan heizit*) reinforces the public setting; the poet's wish for his work to be known amongst as many Franks as possible was better served by public recital than by any number of private readers.

A fifth indicator of an oral recital goes beyond the use of *lesen* with a dative object with which we began. The present pointer is made up of *lesen* combined with a dative, but also with a temporal adverb (*ê, hie vor, nu* for the most part) indicating a point in the recent or distant past, so that the whole construction amounts to a reciter's reminder to his listeners, recalling a previous point in his narrative relevant to the present. If we register this construction as typical of a recital in which the reciter reminds his listeners of what he told them earlier, ideally three separate points need to be clarified. First, the conjunction of *lesen* with *iu* (dative plural of the second person, the listeners addressed) shows that recital aloud to these listeners is taking place. Secondly, the conjunction of the verb in the past tense with a temporal adverb draws the listeners' attention to an earlier passage in the work. Finally, the verb *lesen* must have the meaning 'to read a text' (so that its conjunction with *iu* means 'to read out from a text'), rather than, in the more general sense, 'to narrate, to tell' (which need not imply a recital). As I discuss the distinction between these last two possibilities later, I presuppose my conclusions in what follows.

This construction can be illustrated from a passage, referring to Semei who had earlier cursed David, in the *Weltchronik* of Rudolf von Ems (30320: *Ouh kam, als ich gelesin han, / Semey der ê beschalt / Daviden den degin balt, / do er, als ih iuh hie vor las, / Absalone entwichin was*).[204] I take the phrase *als ich gelesin han* as referring to the biblical source (II Reg. 16, 5 and 13), but read the second phrase *als ih iuh hie vor las* with reference to what the poet had earlier said in his own work (29600ff.). That we are justified in reading these examples of *lesen* in two different ways is suggested by the syntax. The first example conjoins the pronoun *ich* with the verb to indicate the poet's task of consulting his written source in solitude, whereas the second, dealing with his relationship as reciter to his audience, brings them into the picture by means of the dative plural *iuh* (they are being recited to). Whereas the first example uses the past tense alone, the second underlines this by *hie vor*, drawing attention to the earlier passage of which the listeners are to be reminded. With this second example we witness the poet, in his role as reciter, reading out to his audience from what is conceived as a written text.[205] How precise the nature of such a back-reference can be is shown repeatedly in the *Livländische Reimchronik*. Our construction is used at one point (3116): *den hatte des meisters her geslagen / binnen des, dô irgangen was / zû Rîge, als man ûch ê las* (*man* is revealed in the next line as identical with *ich*). Whereas Rudolf von Ems simply referred back to an earlier episode, the *Reimchronik* also provides a verbal echo, for the words *zû Rîge* hark back to 3014ff. and 3008 (*kein Rîge*).[206]

These references to what was recited earlier can be so precise that sometimes the dative *iu* can be dropped, so that the construction now consists of *lesen* with a temporal adverb. This can be illustrated from two works which use the full construction. In his *Weltchronik* Rudolf refers to a point which he has frequently narrated by the temporal adverb *ofte* without a dative (26363: *... und das sîn eit / so dicke mit unwarheit / ubirgie und zerbrah / mit wanche dú wort dú er sprach, / als ich ofte han gelesen*).[207] In a work which uses the full construction (*lesen* + dative object + temporal adverb) to imply an earlier recital of a point the same is likely to be the case with the shorter construction. This is also true of the *Livländische Reimchronik*, whose author makes frequent use of the shorter construction, with verbal echoes just as explicit as with the longer one, as with 6242, referring back to 6213ff. and with the word *gewunnen* (6231) providing the explicit link. In the light of such examples it is possible to interpret shorter constructions in the same way, even in works which do not also employ the longer counterpart, as with Gottfried's *Tristan* (17421: *Der jäger, von dem ich nu las*), a back-reference to 17331ff. which Schröder has interpreted, together with other examples, as a 'Vorleserformel'.[208]

This construction can sometimes be used even more contractedly: *lesen* alone, without dative object or temporal adverb. Where the works in question also use the full construction we can be confident that we are dealing with an abbreviated usage, as is implied by the *Livländische Reimchronik* (9831: *dô ich von las*), referring back to 9809f. and with echoes in *kummentûr* and *enpôt*. The method is so much the same (*lesen*, a back-reference, a verbal echo) that *lesen* by itself is used just as much of a recital as when it is conjoined with other pointers.[209]

This last point is important, for it leads to the possibility that *lesen* by itself might be used to indicate recital. We have seen this already with the nomen agentis *leser*, but this is a special case: whereas a verb can be qualified by additions (dative object or temporal adverb), this is not always so easy with a nomen agentis. We have to ask, in other words, whether the verb by itself can be used in the sense of recital. OHG *lesan* can occasionally render Latin *recitare*,[210] but Gottfried still uses the verb in this sense (*Tristan* 19192: *er seite ir schoeniu maere, / er sanc, er schreib ir unde las*) in a compressed passage rendered by Schröder as 'er erzählte schöne Geschichten, sang ihr Lieder vor, schrieb selber etwas und las es ihr vor'.[211] A similar recital situation is implied when Konrad von Würzburg describes the hero's courtly attainments in providing sociable entertainment (*Engelhard* 1846: '*lesen unde schrîben, / harpfen unde singen, / tanzen unde springen, / kan er ûzer mâzen wol. / dâ mite er alle stunde sol / kurzewîle machen dir*'). If the activities *harpfen* and *singen* belong together, like *tanzen* and *springen*, we can assume the same of *lesen* and *schrîben*: like Tristan, Engelhard writes and recites. The indirect object (denoting the recipient of this entertainment) is expressed by Gottfried as *ir* in regard to *sagen* and *schrîben*, but has to be understood for *singen* and *lesen*, whilst Konrad's *dir* stands even further removed from *lesen* and has to be mentally transferred there from *kurzewîle machen*. Although the dative pointer may not be entirely missing, it is no longer an integral part of the construction.

To conclude this section on the oral dimension of *lesen* we must consider this verb denoting an oral recital (together with *sprechen*, *sagen* and *singen*) in combination with *hoeren*. The acoustic implications of *hoeren lesen* have been conceded by Scholz, but where it is used in a work which also contains evidence for reading he is inclined to dismiss it as a 'Hörerfiktion'.[212] Moreover, he considers this phrase mainly with regard to the author's relationship to his source, whereas our concern, the reception of a work by its audience, demands that we restrict ourselves to cases where the audience are the grammatical subject of *hoeren lesen*. In addition, to exclude the medieval situation of someone reading aloud and hearing himself as he reads, we have to focus on cases where two different people are involved (someone reads out and someone else listens), as is exemplified, in a passage where *lesen* and *hoeren* are used together, by the preference of Charles the Great for hearing a work recited to him, as expressed by Veldeke (*Servatius* 4242: *her horde gerne dat man se las*).

Behind the vernacular *hoeren lesen* there lies a Latin usage which shows that even clerical literacy did not exclude reciting Latin works orally. Peter of Blois contrasts the oral recital of themes of the *matière de Bretagne* with that of religious literature, describing the former as *fabulae recitatio* and the latter in the terms *de Domino aliquid pium legi audire*, so that both meet on common oral ground.[213] The key-term *legi audire* also occurs in such variants as *legentem audire* and *legentes audire*,[214] but it is the former which is most commonly imitated in the vernacular. Where *hoeren lesen* is used in conjunction with a term meaning book, this suggests not simply that, in one meaning of *lesen*, the reciter 'tells' or 'narrates' to the listeners, but that he reads out to them from a written text. This is the case with Veldeke's request for the prayers of his audience (*Servatius* 6210: *Goede lude alle te samen / Die dit boeck hoeren leesen*) or with the *Hohes Lied* of Brun von Schönebeck (1124: *sint ditz buch uf einen tag / vor di vursten komen mag, / so daz si iz lesen horen*) or with Johann von Würzburg's *Wilhelm von Österreich* (10848: *ez si vrawe oder man, / swaz gern hort von tugenden lesen, / dem muoz ich deste hoelder wesen*).[215]

Although *hoeren sprechen* occurs less frequently, the possibility of the phrase being used literally is suggested by Rudolf von Ems (*Weltchronik* 4282: *als ir mich hortent sprechen ê*), given the similar function of this back-reference to what we have seen of *lesen* in this same work and also the oral recital situation for it described in some detail.[216] *Hoeren sagen* is used more frequently, but a difficulty is presented by Scholz's view that both *hoeren* and *sagen* can be used figuratively.[217] Although he concedes that *hoeren sagen*, like *hoeren lesen*, points to an acoustic reception,[218] he illustrates this for each phrase with two examples only without placing them in the context of oral recital. Some examples may demonstrate an oral context. The author of *Morant und Galie* uses this phrase in referring to a point elsewhere in his narrative (608: *als ir mich hat horen sagen*), but he also uses *horen lesen* in the same way (3874). If we accept an oral dimension in the latter phrase, we must also accept it for *horen sagen*, at least in this work. The same is suggested in the epilogue to the *Rolandslied* (9086: *Swer iz iemer hôre gesagen*), a part of the work with other references to an oral recital (*vor tragen; fur bringen; Tu autem domine miserere nobis*). When Hartmann refers to a past detail (*Gregorius* 3296: *von dem ir ê hôrtet sagen*, an allusion to 3094ff.) we may take this literally as a pointer to acoustic recital, not merely because the function of this phrase is similar to the construction *lesen* + dative object + temporal adverb (e.g. *Erec* 7305), but particularly because a later reference to the audience receiving *Gregorius* in two ways (3995: ... *die ez hoeren oder lesen*) places an oral recital beyond all doubt. When Rudolf von Ems, amongst the literary genres demanded of him, mentions the Arthurian romance (*Alexander* 20670: *von Artûses hövescheit / wil ouch einer hoeren sagn*), it would be difficult to deny this any basis in contemporary literary life in the light of the description of a typical recital situation for the romance given by Peter of Blois: the work is to be recited (*recitari*), received by ear (*auditus*) and the recipients are listeners (*audientes*).[219]

The possibility that *hoeren singen* should be understood literally is suggested whenever it is used of a work or genre for which there is other evidence for a musical delivery. The fact that this was the case with heroic literature throughout the Middle Ages makes it significant that the *Annolied* begins with a reference to the type of literature with which it is in competition (1, 1: *Wir horten ie dikke singen von alten dingen*). That various types of delivery, including singing, all belong to oral recital is suggested by the *Jüngerer Titurel* (2958, 1: *Swer ritterlich geverte sol ritterlichen triben / in schimpf und ouch in herte, der sol daz nimmer gerne lan beliben, / ern hoere da von lesen, sagen, singen*). To accept the oral implications of *hoeren lesen* and *hoeren sagen* means that we cannot dismiss it for *hoeren singen*, especially when singing belongs to the entertainment provided while a meal was in progress (*Dietrichs Flucht* 5321: *vor den tischen hôrt man singen*). A similar assessment of the value of literature is given in the *Frauendienst* of Ulrich von Lichtenstein (112, 8: '*si giht ez sî guot ritters site, / die gerne hoeren bî ir tagen / singen lesen unde sagen / waz hie vor die biderben man / durch werde vrouwen habent getân*').[220]

The combination of *lesen* (and other verbs) with *hoeren* reinforces the oral dimension of reading, but there is another combination of *lesen* with *hoeren* with which we must conclude this chapter on acoustic reception: their conjunction in the double formula so far considered only in its Latin form.

(n) *Lesen oder hoeren*

We considered the occurrence of the formula *audire vel legere* in classical Latin and Christian literature, where the first pole denoted an acoustic reception foreseen by the author. We must now look at the vernacular equivalent, leaving until later such questions as when and under what conditions it was introduced.

As in other cases we are not concerned with the application of the formula to the poet. When Thomasin von Zerclaere says of himself (141): *Ich hân gehôrt unde gelesen*, he refers to his acquisition of source-material in two different ways without mentioning his audience.[221] Nor are we concerned with the employment of the formula to indicate any type of learning process for anybody, as when Thomasin recommends knowledge of certain works in the education of the young (762: *si suln lesen unde hôren / vil wundergerne guotiu maere*).[222] However significant such examples may be for the wide scope of the formula, we must confine ourselves to cases where it indicates the two ways in which an author's work may be received, suggesting two different types of recipient for one work (or the same people receiving it in different ways on separate occasions).

The earliest example of what comes close to being our formula is given by Der Arme Hartmann (*Die Rede vom heiligen Glauben* 95, 7: *iz ist alliz gescriben / ze gehorenne unde ze gesihte in dutiscer scrifte. / swer daz buch wille lesen*).[223] The conjunction of *gesiht* with *lesen* indicates that the noun is meant in the sense of 'reading', but alongside this an oral dimension, as an alternative means of reception, is envisaged. If an element of ambiguity attaches to this example (could not the dimensions, acoustic and visual, belong together as complementary aspects of the same process, implying someone reading aloud to himself?), this doubt is removed whenever *und* is replaced by *oder* to imply alternative modes of reception (e.g. Ulrich von Zatzikhoven, *Lanzelet* 9441: *die diz liet hoeren oder lesen* or Rudolf von Ems, *Barlaam und Josaphat* 16075: *swer ez hoere oder lese*).[224] This formula can sometimes be expanded to the fuller form *lesen oder hoeren lesen*. Scholz refers in passing to the second pole in this form,[225] but accepts it as implying listeners only in those works which use *hoeren lesen* without any reference to reception by private reading, under the mistaken impression that one mode of reception must exclude the other. The importance of the double formula is that it denotes two types of reception for the same work, perhaps by different people, perhaps by listeners who can occasionally be readers. These two dimensions are implied when in Wetzel von Bernau's *Margaretenleben* the saint prays on behalf of the audience for her legend who have preoccupied themselves with her example (1054: *'wer von mir gerne höret lesen / oder selber liset . . . '*) or when a similar request for intercession is made of Mary in *Unser Vrouwen Klage* (62: *. . . allen, die diz büechelîn / lesen oder hoeren lesen*). Whether or not the verb *lesen* used by itself in this expanded form refers to the reciter (and not to a private reader),[226] the phrase *hoeren lesen* clearly implies an oral recital.

In this chapter we have been occupied with the collective function of medieval literature (for religious literature in a liturgical or paraliturgical sense or in the context of the monastic refectory or *collatio*, for secular literature at the court to sustain group-consciousness or provide social entertainment). This collective function was underlined by a collective reception by an audience gathered together as listeners and as spectators. Our concern has been with them primarily as listeners, since the visual aspect of their activity did not concern their potential role as individual readers, but reinforced what they were listening to.

4

Survey of reception by hearing

The evidence for this mode of reception must now be discussed under the ten genre headings listed on p. 60, within each of which works are listed chronologically. Some cases are much weaker than others, but conversely many works, probably received by hearing, cannot be included for lack of evidence. Wherever possible works are discussed separately, but where the material is repetitive they are treated generically. The internal evidence for hearing works recited is largely focused on a verb like *hoeren*, which can however be used conventionally or metaphorically, so that we shall have to establish whether it is used literally of a given work: either when other criteria for hearing are present or when those for the intermediate mode are found (the audience is seen as reading or hearing the work, or as hearing it recited). This supplementary evidence helps to establish when *hoeren* is to be understood literally.

(a) Functional literature

Magic charms and blessings had to be voiced to be effective. They were intended for one kind of recital or another: chanting or a low whisper.[1]

For the latter cf. *Ad equum errehet* (373, 10: *tu rune imo in daz ora*) or, as a Christian parallel, the *Züricher Arzneibuch* (384).[2] This written transmission of oral practice (normally resting on spoken contact between master and pupil) is quite exceptional.[3]

Works meant for use in the monastic school are governed by the oral dimension of teaching, where the teacher may use a text as the basis of what he says to his listeners. If writing was also present (the teacher's text, notes made by pupils on writing tablets), the bridge between these two possibilities was the oral lecture. Anomalously, the monastic school which preserved written transmission of knowledge cannot be conceived without this oral dimension.[4]

With reference to the requirement of the *Statuta Murbacensia* that the Rule be recited and explained to the monks for them to learn by heart and recite in turn interlinear translations like the OHG *Benediktinerregel*, *Altalemannische Psalmenübersetzung*, *Murbacher Hymnen* show how orality can bypass the written dimension, while still depending on it.[5] For the *Carmen ad Deum* use in the monastic school, and therewith the possibility of the oral dimension of medieval teaching, is also likely.[6] In the thirteenth century German translations of *Cato* differ from the Latin source[7] in implying an oral dimension (having the text read out aloud instead of reading it oneself): the Z version 256 (*lesen* + dative and with a causative verb), the Silesian version p. 206, II Praef. 21 (*hore leßin*) and the *Rumpfüberlieferung* 1ff. (*hôrten sagen*, a request for silence, *lesen* + dative). In these cases individual reading in Latin gives way to recital in German.

Didactic literature is less formal in its educational function.[8] The *Lucidarius* makes an uncertain allusion to a hearing reception in the rhymed prologue (4ff.: *vernemen, horen*), but this is strengthened by Henry the Lion's known preference for recital at court and a later reference, in the context of instruction for laymen, to hearing this book read out (36, 23ff.).[9]

In the *Welscher Gast* Thomasin von Zerclaere refers more frequently to hearing his work, but also addresses knightly aristocrats seen predominantly as illiterate and therefore dependent on recital, and anticipates listeners as well as readers (7).[10] In her *Secretum Secretorum* Hiltgart von Hürnheim implies recital as one possibility in referring both to those who hear and to those who read her work (4, 24).[11] In *Seifried Helbling hoeren* is reinforced by other pointers (the physical presence of seated listeners;[12] XI 107, p. 236: the *Tu autem* formula; IV 281, p. 138: *hoere lesen*). In his *Renner* Hugo von Trimberg refers to listeners whom he requests to keep silent, anticipates listeners as well as readers (19), as he also does in his Latin works.[13] He likewise makes several references to the acoustic reception of contemporary literature with a wide range of themes.[14]

(b) Literature of religious worship and instruction

Of the hymn, the first example in this section, it can be said that there was no place for the medieval layman in liturgical singing at Mass, hence no call for vernacular versions of Latin texts.[15] However, the congregation could join in vernacular songs not regarded as part of the liturgy, e.g. before and after the sermon or especially on paraliturgical occasions (the eve of saints' feasts or major feastdays in the form of processions, within the parish or for pilgrims further afield).[16]

Ekkehard IV says of Ratpert's *Galluslied* that it was meant to be sung to listeners (by a trained choir?).[17] The use of *canere* is confirmed by Ekkehard's wish to preserve a *tam dulcis melodia*.[18] Although no neumes are preserved for the *Georgslied* a sung performance is commonly accepted, possibly on a procession on this saint's day in which laymen as well as clerics took part, although the variability of the refrains suggests that it was sung by a precentor.[19] By contrast, the unchanging simple refrains of the *Petruslied* imply that laymen may have sung them.[20] Singing is implied by neumes in the MS, collective recital by the phrase 103, 7, and a paraliturgical occasion by the *eleison* of the refrain.[21] For a possible pilgrimage song we have to wait for the *Ezzolied*, whose sung nature is suggested by its designation as a *cantilena* and the reference to a melody (Vorau 1, 4).[22] Whether we associate its composition with Bamberg or with Gunther's pilgrimage, a public occasion confirms delivery to assembled listeners.[23]

The (para)liturgical context of four hymns to Mary suggests public delivery of another kind. The *Vorauer Marienlob* issues in hymn-like praise of Mary, so that a paraliturgical function (before or after divine service) has been proposed.[24] The *Melker Marienlied* is more clearcut: each stanza concludes with an identical refrain and it is commonly regarded as a hymn, for which a liturgical function has been proposed.[25] Choral singing may also be true of the *Mariensequenz aus Seckau*: the MS calls it a sequence, it partly renders a Latin sequence, and it has been connected with the feast of the Annunciation.[26] The *Mariensequenz aus Muri* is also specified as a sequence in the Muri MS; in form and melody it corresponds to the same Latin sequence as the text from Seckau, and its sung nature is borne out by its inclusion in the Engelberg codex (largely devoted to liturgical use) and its liturgical association.[27]

A second group is made up of catechetical literature. The oral dimension of such instruction of laymen is made clear in Carolingian legislation enjoining priests to instruct their flock: they do this orally (*vivo sermone annuntiare*), whilst the laymen remember by heart what they have heard (*memoriter tenere*) and recite it in turn (*recitare, reddere*).[28] Orality is as unavoidable here as the vernacular: together they represent the only way for *illitterati* to gain knowledge of salvation.

The written form of the *Sächsisches Taufgelöbnis* was meant for oral use: the priest instructed his flock in such a basic text,[29] whilst the baptizand had to repeat the formula (20, 1ff. *respondet*) just recited to him. Other catechetical texts perform a similar oral function.[30]

Prayers too may belong to this context. The *Arnsteiner Mariengebet* has references to the feast of the Purification for which it may have been meant as a paraliturgical *oratio*, recited by a nun to her sisters and with no suggestion that it served the private devotions of an individual.[31] If the *Gebet einer Frau*, like most MHG prayers on parchment, was written for nuns unversed in Latin and if this 'illiteracy' went as far as an inability to read at all, this prayer was likewise meant to be read out to assembled nuns.[32] Vocalisation of prayers is also implied when they are seen in the context of the spoken or sung word (e.g. *Gebete und Benediktionen von Muri* 270ff.).[33] To assume silence for medieval prayer, even when solitary, is to impose a postmedieval view on our material.

A particular form of prayer is represented by *Heinrichs Litanei*, designated a litany in the MS title and in the text (24, 1). The oral nature of any litany consists in a series of supplications voiced by the priest, to which the people respond with *Kyrie eleison*, recurring throughout this poem (e.g. 1, 36). This public setting agrees with the use of litanies on feastdays and in processions. The poem's variations on the formula *Tu autem*[34] likewise suggest that a concluding allusion to *sprechen* and *zunge* (24, 4f.) is to be understood literally.

Another type of functional text meant for recital and tied to collective worship is the sermon, whose public dimension is captured by Alanus ab Insulis, for whom it is both *manifesta* and *publica*.[35] Its relevance to our concern lies in its role as a link between the Latin, literate world of the clergy and the vernacular, illiterate world of laymen:[36] the homily proceeds from a biblical passage read out in the Latin of the Vulgate, then rendered into German before it is commented on.[37]

The *Exhortatio ad plebem christianam* may have been meant as a model sermon to help parish priests,[38] but behind them the ultimate addressees were the laymen exhorted to learn the Credo and Pater Noster and to pass on this knowledge to their godchildren, presumably by word of mouth. The Carolingian sermon here conveys orally (in two stages) essential catechetical information. The *Homilie Bedas*, treating the feast of All Saints, was possibly recited on that feastday to the canonesses of the community at Essen, largely unschooled in Latin.[39] The *Predigtsammlung A, B, C* has also been linked with a religious community of women, but we lack any pointer to delivery aloud or to individual reading.[40]

Of fundamental importance is the division of sermons written in German into two types, one of which is a 'Musterbuch' (model sermons to guide the priest in sermons which he gives orally),[41] so that behind the written text is to be seen the outline of a sermon actually given. Priester Konrad says explicitly that his collection was meant for such clergy, whose economic and educational status made his help necessary (*Predigten* 3, 14ff.). The *Speculum Ecclesiae* gives instructions on how to use a sermon on different occasions (90, 21) and the *Oberaltaicher Predigten* contain similar pointers (e.g. 171, 6).[42] These pointers, addressed to the priest, are in Latin, as distinct from the sermon in German, meant for the lay congregation. In this the priest acts as mediator between written text and listening congregation, so that the frequent references to the preacher speaking and his congregation listening have to be taken at face value, even though written into the text in anticipation.[43]

A branch of literature which stems from the sermon, the so-called 'Reimpredigt', also offers many examples where acoustic reception is likely.

The *Memento Mori*, addressed to laymen, contains the *Tu autem* formula in German (19, 1) characteristic of public recital.[44] The *Summa Theologiae* is assumed to be meant for noblemen, for whom an acoustic reception was most likely around 1120.[45] When the author of *Vom Himmlischen Jerusalem* suggests rivalry between his religious work and secular competitors (26, 3ff.) the oral dimension of this secular heroic poetry (*haizet* + *singen*) implies the same for its clerical rival.[46] *Die Wahrheit*, also meant for laymen,[47] indicates that public recital was foreseen (10, 1ff.: *horet singen oder sagen*). In his *Loblied auf den heiligen Geist* Priester Arnold also addresses laymen (38, 1f.) and therefore translates Latin quotations into German, so that verbs like *vure bringen, gesagen oder gesingen* (2, 1ff.) are probably indicative of actual recital.[48] The close connection of *Von der Babylonischen Gefangenschaft* with the liturgy (Septuagesima Sunday) makes likely a collective function as a call to penitence in the period before Lent.[49] Der Arme Hartmann addresses laymen in his *Rede vom heiligen Glauben* (2, 4f.) for whom he has to translate any Latin quotation (6, 2f.): that *horen*, used of their reception (e.g. 192, 1), was meant literally is borne out by a reference to both listeners and readers (95, 7f.).

Public delivery of the *Deutung der Meßgebräuche* is rendered likely by its transmission with German sermons meant to be delivered and with liturgical texts.[50] The rivalry of *Die Hochzeit* with secular poetry differs from that of *Vom Himmlischen Jerusalem* in its attempt at a contrafacture, taking its audience's taste into account[51] by meeting them on the field of oral recital (cf. 1, 1). The so-called Heinrich von Melk also addresses laymen, to whom his work is to be recited, so that a request to listen was probably meant literally.[52] *Das Anegenge* is likewise meant for laymen, whose possible role as listeners (475f., 1230) is confirmed by their being termed *hoeraere* (298).[53] A weak suggestion for the auditory reception of Alber's *Tnugdalus*[54] is strengthened by his remark that he wrote for the illiterate (63f.). *Diu vrône boteschaft* works with a parallel between the narrative action (an angel reads out a miraculous letter) and the work itself, meant to be read out by the priest to his flock.[55] In the *Visio Philiberti* Heinrich von Neustadt uses *horen* of his audience (5), but also says more specifically that they are to hear the work recited (587ff.).[56] A solitary reference to listening to *Der Seele Rat* of Heinrich von Burgeis (220ff.)[57] is similarly underlined by a closing reference to hearing or reading this book (6540).[58]

A final group in this section concerns devotional literature for reading out in the refectory or to groups of pious laymen or *religiosae*.[59] That such literature was not confined to individual reading in privacy is suggested by the monastic practice of *collatio* or by the hope of Heinrich von Neustadt (*Visio Philiberti* 587ff.) that *andaht* might be encouraged by hearing his text read aloud.

The *Altsächsischer Psalmenkommentar* may have been read out to the inmates of the convent of Gernrode as devotional matter in the refectory or the chapter-house.[60] In *Die vier Sciven* Werner vom Niederrhein conventionally requests silence at the start (2,1), but in having to translate Latin quotations he presumably faces laymen for whom listening would be normal.[61] If the *Benediktbeurer Gebet zum Meßopfer* was meant for meditation before Mass[62] the deictic stress in 1,3 suggests a particular place where it was read before the liturgical ceremony. The physical presence of listeners is implied in another way in *Das Rheinische Marienlob*: the priestly author presents and interprets (*dúden*) his work *vür allen godes brüden*, in the presence of nuns.[63] The possibly conventional use of *hoeren* by Lamprecht von Regensburg in *Tochter Syon* is given literal force by a reference back to what has earlier been recited (1142).[64] Heinrich von Kröllwitz suggests a listening reception of his *Vaterunser* in a number of ways: frequent use of *hôren*, appeals for silence, suggestions that the uninterested should leave the place of recital, a deictic pointer like *hie*, and a reminder of what the audience has already heard him say.[65] With David von Augsburg we have an isolated use of *sprechen* for the author and *hoeren* for his recipients,[66] but the latter are more persuasively expected to read or hear his work (375, 23). In the *Geistlicher Herzen Bavngart* an isolated use of *hoeren* (198, 92) similarly acquires new force in the light of *hoeren lesen* (ii 40).[67] The frequent recommendation in *Die Lilie* to listen is given literal force by a pointer to a twofold reception (9, 29),[68] while recital of the *Alemannische Tochter Syon* is made probable by means of *lesen* + dative (592f.).[69] With *Der Sêle Cranz* the same conclusion is suggested by a pointer to hearing a recital (307).

(c) Legal literature

In Germanic law the legal act was oral: a binding pronouncement or oath was made, accompanied by prescribed gestures,[70] so that the act was both heard and seen, two dimensions which were recalled by witnesses testifying to what they had heard and seen. The oral dimension survived amongst laymen into the Middle Ages, but now alongside written canon law of the Church (in Latin) and the possibility, acquired from Rome, of attesting legal transactions in written Latin,[71] with written German occurring only from the middle of the thirteenth century.[72] Oral law is reflected in German literature at many points. The *Sächsisches Weichbildrecht* exemplifies the two dimensions of an oral transaction; the *Schwabenspiegel Langform M* was to be read out to its recipients; it was accepted that written law should be read out to the ruler.[73] The Middle Ages were therefore characterised by two legal traditions (oral and vernacular as distinct from written and Latin), so that whenever law was written down in German we stand at a meeting-point of these two traditions.[74]

Initially, orality could be so much taken for granted that it need not be mentioned, so that we lack internal evidence. As protocol texts the *Hammelburger* and *Würzburger Markbeschreibungen* capture a legal transaction which has already taken place.[75] Where the former text is in Latin (normal at this time), the second Würzburg text, serving the same purpose of recording land made over to the monastery of Fulda,[76] is in German, probably because of the need to read the text aloud to all those affected by the handing over of land.[77] This use of the vernacular anticipates the oral reactivation of the text in the future; we move from oral transaction to written copy to oral recital, whenever called for. An oral delivery is also likely for the fragment of a translation of the *Lex Salica* if it was meant, like other tribal laws, for reading out at an assembly.[78] With the *Priestereid* the vernacular was used in a ceremony otherwise conducted in Latin to make it clear to the parish that a legal obligation was being incurred to which they were witnesses.[79]

The vernacular was also used for bystanders as witnesses in the *Straßburger Eide*, for laymen would scarcely have understood the oaths in Latin.[80] They were politically important enough not to have been formulated impromptu by the two rulers, but were drawn up beforehand in writing in their chanceries, then read out to the rulers for them to learn by heart or repeat on oath. In either case the written text served an oral function.[81] Public recital is also likely with the *Trierer Capitulare*, a law which made it possible for a freeman to make over property to the Church instead of kinsmen — since this brought an advantage to the clergy it was in their interest to have the text recited to laymen in their tongue.[82] The *Erfurter Judeneid* is a type of oath sworn in public (in the synagogue on the Torah) and parallels the practice of a judge pronouncing a formula to be repeated by the swearer of the oath.[83] Even though the *Schwäbische Trauformel* may stipulate that a document (*widembuoch*) be made out, this follows an oral transaction with the handing over of symbolic objects characteristic of oral law.[84] With the *Mainzer Reichslandfriede* of 1235 we reach a turning-point: it is the first imperial legislation written in German as well as Latin, but it was the German text which was read out to the assembled princes and to which they agreed.[85]

When written law in German sets in comprehensively in the thirteenth century orality could no longer be taken for granted and must therefore be mentioned expressly.

In view of the division of the order into literates and illiterates[86] the *Statuten des Deutschen Ordens* specify that the Rule and statutes are to be read out to the brethren (74, 9), who learn by hearing in this way (71, 13ff.; 74, 25ff.).[87] The *Hamburgisches Stadtrecht (1270)* indicates that it was to be read aloud to the council whenever a judgment was questioned, whilst the *Sächsisches Weichbildrecht*, although it uses *horen* with what could be stereotyped frequency, refers to two modes of reception (181, 8).[88] The *Schwabenspiegel Langform M* also sees its audience hearing (p. 179), but recommends more convincingly that it be profitably read out loud.[89]

A special group within legal literature is formed by charters, appearing in German with any frequency only from 1250. This late appearance derives from the oral nature of German law as described by the *Mainzer Reichslandfriede* as late as 1235:[90] accordingly, of the more than 3,500 German charters of the thirteenth century none is dated earlier than 1235. German charters also agree with the orality of German law at large in stressing the reliability of witnesses who both saw and heard: what is stated in general terms in the *Sächsisches Weichbildrecht* recurs frequently in the charters.[91]

(d) Historiography

With two exceptions works in this section all come from the thirteenth century, a belatedness which suggests that the laymen could for long meet their need for historical orientation elsewhere within the oral realm. For centuries this need could be satisfied by the heroic lay (providing knowledge of the past) and the 'Sagelied' (dealing with more recent history).[92] Historical knowledge in the religious sense ('Heilsgeschichte') was provided by clerical literature, in genres such as biblical literature and legends conveyed to the layman by oral recital.[93] The question this raises is why historical works made the transition not simply from oral to written, but also from Latin to vernacular (and were then conveyed to their audience by oral means).

References to *hören* in the *Gandersheimer Reimchronik* may be taken literally in view of the pointer to a recital situation, complete with reciter and listeners seated nearby, and the use of deictic *hir* which this makes possible.[94] That the *Livländische Reimchronik* was a history of the Teutonic Knights in this region, an order with a high degree of illiteracy among its knightly brethren, has to be taken into account in assessing the import of *hören* constructions, of a solitary request for silence and of what the audience has heard recited earlier.[95] These pointers suggest that the chronicle was read out to members of the order.

The list of world chronicles opens with two examples from before the thirteenth century. The inclusion of a historical survey in a clerical work like the *Annolied*[96] may explain why the author opposes his view of history as 'Heilsgeschichte' to the claim of heroic literature to transmit history (1, 1ff.), but if his wish is to drive out secular poetry which is sung he presumably took up the challenge by at least orally reciting his own work.[97] The other example before 1200, the *Kaiserchronik*, contains few pointers for all its length, but an indication is given by the way in which the author, as in the *Annolied*, distances himself from secular rivals, for he too confronts them not merely on the field of history,[98] but also as a reciter. They recite orally and a wise man refrains from listening to them (41), but the clerical author meets them on the same ground, intends his own work for recital, and is prepared for *die tumben* to refuse to listen (11).[99] The *Sächsische Weltchronik* occasionally uses *horen* of its audience, but its literal force may be surmised from a reference to what they have heard recited (285, 22).[100] In his *Weltchronik* Rudolf von Ems is more informative: his *hören* constructions are likewise confirmed by what the audience has already heard, but they are also presented as listeners in the sketch of the reception anticipated for his work at the court of Konrad IV, where a number of different criteria all point emphatically to public recital.[101] Jans Enikel frequently uses *hören* in his *Weltchronik*, but its literal function is suggested by two references to recital before an audience by means of the verb *vor sagen* (2818, 27394) in the sense of 'to say in someone's presence'.[102] With the *Christherre-Chronik* the position is less certain, but still probable: *hoeren* occurs occasionally,[103] but in the sense that concerns us if we take into account a remark about the audience having heard earlier (sinful) works of the author recited (1171). This could be a topos, but it betrays how the author conceived the reception of literature and therefore presumably of this work.[104]

(e) Biblical literature

Biblical literature (i.e. biblical themes in poetic form) has to be distinguished from translations of the Bible.[105] Apart from special purposes (monastic teaching, exegetical commentary, the biblical text of a sermon) the latter are largely absent in our period: the need for a vernacular Bible was first voiced in heretical circles, the Old Testament was translated into German only in the fourteenth century, and the question of the layman's direct access to the Bible was still a bone of contention in the Reformation.[106] Where the word of God, as in the Vulgate, was not at issue (with poetic versions of a biblical theme) these difficulties were not encountered: such biblical literature could be addressed to the layman, but orally because of his illiteracy. The earliest Germanic biblical literature, as already with Caedmon, therefore betrays its links with the realm of orality,[107] but our question is whether this early oral dimension is to be found later, at least in the form of oral delivery to listeners.

To the parallels between the *Wessobrunner Schöpfungsgedicht* and native poetry belongs the opening formula (16, 1: *dat gafregin ik*), but this tells us only that the poet stood in an oral tradition (towards his 'source'),[108] not that the audience stood in the same tradition towards him, as listeners. Oral recital has been proposed, however, on two grounds: the suggestion that the prayer following the poem has the same function as *Tu autem* (to close a recital), but also the proposal that the MS title *De poeta*, like the liturgical formula at the start of a lesson, points to a reading to listeners.[109] Of the oral recital of the OS *Heliand* there can be little doubt if we accept that it was meant for the illiterate as well as the literate, that it was composed in the vernacular specifically for listeners, and that its designation as a *cantilena* with its *modulatio* is borne out by the neumes in MS M.[110] We shall see that among the pointers to an oral delivery of Otfrid's *Evangelienbuch* music likewise plays a part. The occurrence of an oral opening formula in *Muspilli* (68, 37) resembles what we saw in the *Wessobrunner Schöpfungsgedicht*: it tells us more about the poet than about his audience whose status may be that of aristocrats with legal obligations.[111] With *Christus und die Samariterin* the utilisation of spoken language and dialogue form suggest ballad poetry and vocal differentiation in recital, whilst the paraphrase of *Psalm 138* (beginning with a formula 105, 1, this time concerning the audience) may have been meant for edificational recital at a Carolingian court.[112]

For the *Wiener Genesis* oral recital is likely: it addresses its audience in the manner of a sermon (1), the use of *fore tuon* in the following line, like *fure bringen*, implies an oral situation, whilst the suggestion that the work was divided into sections to be read out as lessons implies a paraliturgical function in view of the role of the biblical *Genesis* in Lent.[113] Oral recital for the *Lob Salomons* is suggested by a vernacular equivalent of *Tu autem* and by narrative elements reminiscent of lay oral poetry.[114] An assembled audience is suggested by the use of *vorgelesen* in the *Friedberger Christ* (29, 2f.), where the prefix points to their presence.[115] Frau Ava's works may be seen similarly: an oral dimension is suggested by her reference to the 'outer ears' and the inner ones of her audience (*Leben Jesu* 210, 4ff.) and by the paraliturgical use of her work in largely following selected pericopes of the Christmas and Easter cycles.[116] That the author of the *Millstätter Exodus* addresses listeners (2907f.) is borne out by his use of *vurebringen* (927f.) and of a deictic pointer to recital at Easter (3309ff.) and by the suggestion that the liturgical formula 3315f. indicates reading out as 'Reimlektionen' in association with the liturgy.[117] For the *Jüngere Judith* we rely on no more than the spatial implication of 15, 3, suggesting an assembled audience,[118] just as *horen* references in Lamprecht's *Tobias* can be taken literally if combined with a deictic pointer to shared space.[119]

References to *horen* in the *Millstätter Genesis* are reinforced by the sermon formula at the opening (1, 1) and by the prefix in *vorbriefen* in the following line suggesting listeners in front of the reciter.[120] Although the *St. Trudperter Hohes Lied* lacks clear internal evidence it can be regarded both as a monastic sermon and as a text for the *collatio*, whilst Ohly argues for oral recital as part of the nuns' *lectio divina*.[121] The *Linzer Antichrist* implies that many refuse to listen to the recital of clerical works (1, 3ff.) and this oral dimension is confirmed by the work being addressed to laymen, for whom Latin quotations need to be translated.[122] For the *Wien-Münchener Evangelienübersetzung*, meant for recital at points in the liturgical year, the presence of neumes indicates that it was not merely read out or spoken, but sung in the *tonus lectionis*.[123]

Hoeren references in the *Urstende* of Konrad von Heimesfurt are to be taken literally in view of an allusion to a twofold reception (12)[124] and we shall see that the same is true of Brun von Schönebeck. In his *Apokalypse* Heinrich von Hesler underpins his allusions to a listening audience by a request for silence (13494), a mention of the reciter (3711: *lesere*) and the physical presence of his audience.[125] Accordingly, he addresses his audience as laymen and as illiterate.[126] As elsewhere, *hoeren* references in *Gottes Zukunft* by Heinrich von Neustadt and an isolated request to listen in *Der Saelden Hort* (2386) are given added weight by pointers to a twofold reception.[127] Finally, *Die Erlösung* contains a number of stereotyped references to *hôren*, meant literally if its use of *lesen* is equated with recital aloud.[128]

(f) Legends

Etymologically *legenda* suggests that a saint's *vita* or *passio* was read out aloud on the saint's day,[129] so that our question is how far this oral potential was realised in vernacular examples. That German legends are attested only from the middle of the twelfth century has been associated with the rise of court literature at this time: the

THREE MODES OF RECEPTION

presentation of a secular ideal called forth a clerical reaction in a genre rejecting the world.[130] If the encounter between these two genres took place in the vernacular, can they also be said to share an oral dimension?

The opening lines of the *Trierer Silvester* include a request for silence (1), a reference to *horen* (7) and *uuore tragen* in the sense of 'to recite', but more telling is the contrast between secular and clerical literature suggesting a shared oral realm (13 and 31) and reminiscent of the rivalry detectable in the *Annolied* and the *Kaiserchronik*.[131] Persuasive pointers are given by Heinrich von Veldeke in *Servatius*, where examples of *horen*[132] are strengthened by the foreshadowing of the work's reception in Charles the Great listening to the *vita* (4240ff.: *lesen* + causative verb and dative, *horde*). That this is applicable to Veldeke's vernacular text is made likely by the mention of *her Hessel*, in charge of the treasury and pilgrim lodgings at Maastricht and interested in having the legend recited to pilgrims,[133] as well as by the author addressing his work to laymen (178ff.; 6210f.).[134] Priester Wernher makes regular use of *horen* in his *Maria*, confirmed as probably literal by *fure bringen* for the act of recital (C 5394) and especially by the evidence for a collective occasion for recital (the work is connected with Augsburg, where the monastery of St. Ulrich and Afra introduced a new festival devoted to Mary at about this time, so that the need to reach as many as possible implies public delivery).[135] The *Kindheit Jesu* of Konrad von Fussesbrunnen refers to what its audience has previously heard recited (2349) and also suggests a twofold reception (96f.).

Soon after 1200 we return to Augsburg with the *Leben des heiligen Ulrich* of Albertus von Augsburg: a solitary example of *horen* (1155) seems unpromising, but there is also a reference to the audience hearing a recital (1544ff.) and the likelihood that the work was connected with the transfer of the saint's bones to St. Afra, its reconsecration in 1187 and the revival of the saint's cult: a public occasion again suggests public recital.[136] Ebernand von Erfurt employs *hôren* frequently in *Heinrich und Kunigunde*, but also, more significantly, *hôrêre* of his audience, who can be appealed to for silence and to whom a point has previously been read out.[137] The *Unser vrouwen hinfart* of Konrad von Heimesfurt has an isolated example of *hoeren* which can be taken literally because applied to *illitterati* (50ff.).[138] With the *Barlaam und Josaphat* of Rudolf von Ems an isolated reference to *vernemen* is underlined by the mention of a twofold reception.[139] The same argument can be used of the *Margaretenleben* of Wetzel von Bernau and of the *Sanct Franzisken Leben* of Lamprecht von Regensburg.[140]

As so often, an uninformative use of *hoeren* in the *Silvester* of Konrad von Würzburg is more revealing in the light of *hoeren sagen* and *hoeren lesen*, and the same is true of his *Alexius*.[141] More is forthcoming from the *Passional*: the usual run of *hoeren* examples is reinforced by what the audience has already heard, by their being physically present, above all by the arrangement of the saints' lives in the sequence of the church year, suggesting a (para)liturgical recital to an assembly.[142] In the *Väterbuch* the use of *horen* is supported by a request for silence, by the opening sketch of a recital situation, but above all by hearing the text read out.[143] In his *Martina* Hugo von Langenstein combines a frequent use of *hoeren* with a reference to the physical presence of listeners and the employment of *lesen* + dative.[144] The *hoeren* formula in the *Marienleben* of Walther von Rheinau is rescued by references to a twofold reception; the same is achieved in the *Leben der heiligen Elisabeth* by hints at what has been previously recited; in *Sante Margareten Marter* a passing allusion to its recital is underpinned by the saint's prayer for those who hear her story recited or read it themselves.[145]

(g) Drama

Examples of this genre exist in Latin from the eleventh century, but in German only from the first half of the thirteenth for Latin drama with vernacular insertions and from the second half for exclusively German examples.[146] If the drama has been compared with the sermon as an effective way for the Church to influence laymen the rise of vernacular drama may be seen in connection with changes in the sermon at the same time.[147] Just as the sermon could be listened to collectively or read by an individual, so could the drama be received in either of these ways. There are, however, no vernacular examples of dramas meant for reading before 1300, so that the texts in question were composed with an oral performance and acoustic reception in mind.[148]

The oral dimension of the *Klosterneuburger Osterspiel* is conveyed by directions for passages to be sung (solo or in chorus), the presence of neumes and the way in which the vernacular passage 220, sung to the *populus universus*, is in effect addressed to the audience.[149] The evidence for the oral dimension of the *Benediktbeurer Passionsspiel* is precisely the same.[150] In the *Osterspiel von Muri* the three Marys sing the antiphon of the *visitatio*, and again the *populus* addressed by Pilate (I 41) and to whom the merchant praises his wares (III 51ff.) can be equated with the audience of the play.[151] The *Wiener Passionsspiel* refers to sung delivery, gives the melody in part, and opens with a plea for silence which captures the oral situation in addressing the audience as listeners and as spectators.[152] The *St. Galler Passionsspiel* gives instructions for *cantare* and *dicere*, gives no notation (although singing has been assumed) but has Augustine act as a 'narrator' come to dramatic life in demanding silence from the audience.[153] The *Amorbacher Spiel* has instructions for solo and choral singing, but also musical notation.[154] Finally, the *Trierer Osterspiel* refers to singing, gives the melody in part, regularly translates Latin verses into German, and has Mary Magdalene address the audience in the vernacular as assembled on a particular day.[155]

(h) Heroic literature

Before the *Nibelungenlied* was written down around 1200 only one German heroic work, the *Hildebrandslied*, found its way on to parchment (first half of the ninth century). This gulf in time between heroic poetry and writing is symptomatic of the oral nature of heroic tradition.[156] We have seen reflections of the oral nature of secular poetry (likely to be heroic poetry) whenever the authors of clerical works react against their rivals by meeting them on the same ground of oral delivery.[157] An idea of the oral poetry lost to us may be gained from 'Sagelieder' to which we have references in Latin chronicles or in contrafactures betraying the theme of the original (e.g. *Modus qui et Carelmanninc*).[158] The sung recital of this original is suggested by the imitation of its melody, just as a 'Sagelied' dealing with Adelbert is described by Ekkehard IV as sung.[159] This agrees with reports on heroic poems: they were not merely heard (*audire* can be used),[160] but were songs set to music and sung by a singer.[161] This aspect of orality is still relevant to written examples of heroic literature from the thirteenth century for many of which a melody is attested,[162] which raises the as yet unanswered question whether the musical delivery attested for some texts was true of them all.

The opening formula of the *Hildebrandslied* (1, 1) places the poet, but not his audience, within oral tradition,[163] but in pointing back to a collective memory of 'Vorzeitkunde', to an unbroken chain of oral tradition in which this lay is the latest link, this opening is unlikely to herald a sudden switch to a reading reception. Whatever the motive behind writing down this lay,[164] all we know of Carolingian literature suggests oral recital. The position is clearer with the *Ludwigslied*:[165] its political function suggests a public dimension, its royal image-boosting points to public recital at a celebration of the Frankish victory at Saucourt.[166] Whether the concluding *acclamatio* of Ludwig be associated with liturgical *laudes regiae* (in the form of ceremonial procession) or with an *adventus* of the ruler,[167] anything but public celebration is unthinkable. The *laudes* are not merely narrated, but actualised in celebratory song.

What had to be surmised for the *Hildebrandslied* is made clear in the *Nibelungenlied*: it uses the same phrase *hoeren sagen*, but applied to the audience, not the poet, often enough to suggest stereotyped usage.[168] That this is not the whole story has been shown by Curschmann's analysis of the opening stanza: reciter and also audience belong to an impersonal tradition and the movement is towards what the latter are to hear recited.[169] To oral recital belongs acoustic reception, so that other references to a listening audience may be granted full value, especially since the work, like stanzaic epics at large, was meant for sung recital.[170] Where this work does represent a novelty is in its being the first heroic epic in written form, but even this does not count against its oral dimension, for the oral transmission of the heroic epic continues alongside the written,[171] and written transmission is still associated with oral recital.[172]

Ortnit: an isolated *hoeren* formula, but also an opening suggestion of reading aloud (2, 1f.: *lesen* + dative and causative verb).[173] *Wolfdietrich A*: evidence of oral recital in the Dresden MS, sung to the melody of the *Jüngeres Hildebrandslied*.[174] *Eckenlied*: *hoeren*, 'Bernerton' melody, included in a travelling minstrel's repertoire.[175] *Laurin* and *Walberan* belong together: the reciter of the former, termed a *leser*, demands a drink at a turning-point.[176] *Biterolf und Dietleib*: *hoeren*, physical presence of the audience, allusions to what they have already heard recited.[177] *Wolfdietrich C*: *hoeren*, opening request for silence in which the recital of the work to listeners is announced.[178] *Laurin A*: *hoeren*, but some MSS also include a request for a drink by the reciter (*leßer*) at a well chosen point in the narrative.[179] *Laurin D*: *hoeren*, an opening deictic reference to shared space, a request for silence, a suggestion that the recital was to be heard.[180] *Virginal*: *hoeren*, the reciter requests a liquid reward at the conclusion, composition in the 'Bernerton'.[181]

SURVEY OF RECEPTION BY HEARING

(i) Court narrative literature

Under this heading we deal with three types: what may be called court epics (with one exception, 'Spielmannsepen' or German adaptations of chansons de geste), court romances (classical, Arthurian, Grail or Tristan themes or romances of love and adventure) and 'Mären'.

If we accept the 'Spielmannsepen' as clerical attempts to influence courts by a literary propaganda making use of the legend,[182] we may expect the orality of clerical genres to be continued here, too. For all their written form these works do not cut loose from orality since, to reach the court, they had to be recited to laymen. Orality concerns these works in a further respect: the prehistory of the themes treated was largely oral, so that the task of converting oral material into written form was quite different from dealing with written sources,[183] as largely in religious literature or in the court romance. This group of works illustrates a novel encounter between oral and written.

König Rother may use *horen* conventionally, but its recital is attested as popular by its inclusion in the repertoire from which Der Marner was expected to sing.[184] The written dimension of the work (oral material has found its way into book form and the poet uses this to establish its historical veracity) does not exclude oral recital.[185] References to *hoeren* in the *Münchener Oswald* are reinforced by a request for silence, by the sketch of a recital situation, and by the recommendation in MS I to bring the reciter (*leser*) wine if he is to continue.[186] The case for the *Wiener Oswald* rests on an opening request for silence where, however, *hore zu* is rather more emphatic than *hore* alone.[187] With *Orendel horen* is reinforced by a sketch in which the assembled audience shares the reciter's difficulties and is to provide liquid refreshment for him.[188] In addition to these internal pointers the work's connection with the deposition of the seamless robe of Christ in Trier cathedral suggests an attempt to publicise this, hence, as with Veldeke's *Servatius*, the use of the vernacular for public recital.[189] *Herzog Ernst B* accompanies a few cases of *hoeren* by only a deictic pointer to an assembled audience; the *D* text supplements its cases of *horen* with a mention of what has earlier been recited; the *G* text supports them by a reference to the singer of the poem and his need for wine.[190]

The earliest German example from the *matière de France* is Pfaffe Konrad's *Rolandslied*. Its importance as a book epic dependent on another written text, but in another vernacular, does not alter the fact that this book was meant for oral recital: it concludes with *Tu autem*, it uses *vor tragen* and *fure bringen* in the sense of public recital, and *hoeren sagen* of the audience's reception.[191] Wolfram's *Willehalm* makes frequent use of *hoeren*, but also provides a sketch of a recital situation and a reference to what has already been recited.[192] Wolfram's reluctance to speak bluntly on one occasion before his audience may be related to the suggestion that certain topics are not fit for the ears of ladies.[193] Der Stricker's *Karl der Große* combines *hoeren* with a back-reference with such close verbal agreement that conventional usage is hardly likely.[194] *Morant und Galie* supplements *horen* by a request for silence and *lesen* in the sense of what the poet is to read aloud, so that the audience explicitly hears what is read out to them.[195] In *Karl und Galie horen* is reinforced by a request for silence, a frequent use of *lesen* + dative, and again a reference to what the audience earlier heard recited.[196] Ulrich von Türheim uses the *hoeren* formula in *Rennewart*, but this has to be seen in the light of a concluding pointer to a twofold reception.[197]

German examples of the romance seem to lack an oral feature present in their French counterparts. However much Chrétien may have stressed his literacy (his clerical training and dependence on the written material of Geoffrey of Monmouth), he nonetheless derived his actual narrative from oral tales of Celtic origin,[198] whereas his German followers were dependent on his written version alone. Their task was to transfer a written text from one vernacular to another,[199] whereas his had been more complex: to fuse a written tradition with an oral one. Yet this discrepancy concerns only the authors' sources and their act of composition, whilst in the reception of their works the oral dimension was present for the German as much as for the French works. The German authors' stress on literacy (their source is written, their work is a book, open to reading)[200] does not exclude orality, especially with noblemen, for the most part illiterate, of whom Baldwin II of Guines as *quasi literatus* may be regarded as representative.[201]

This is already clear from what Peter of Blois reports on reciting romances as opposed to religious readings in the Anglo-Norman realm.[202] For the former (Arthur, Gawein and Tristan are mentioned) a typical recital is sketched: the genre consists of *carmina poetarum* and *joculatorum cantilenae*, they are to be recited (*recitari*) and received by ear (*auditus*), their recipients are listeners (*audientes*). In Germany, where lay literacy was less advanced, this was all the more true. The author of *Der Saelden Hort* intended it for recital in competition with court literature (Wigalois and Tristan are mentioned as rivals),[203] likewise meant for recital (5411ff.). In his *Alexander* Rudolf von Ems refers to various genres requested of him by his audience,[204] including the heroic epic in the form of the Dietrich cycle for which an acoustic reception is implied (20667f.), but also the Arthurian romance, equally for oral recital (20670f.). Hugo von Trimberg likewise details in his *Renner* the repertoire of a minstrel, including works which his audience might expect him to recite (16183). This repertoire embraces a number of romance themes: Tristan, Parzival, the Round Table, Alexander and Wigalois. The written form of the romance did not therefore mean that it was not also destined for oral recital.[205]

The first example from romances with a classical theme is Veldeke's *Eneide*.[206] The frequent use of *hoeren* is not enough, because not supported by other types of evidence.[207] Instead, the probability of hearing arises where reading is suggested (13436ff.: the unfinished MS was lent to the countess of Cleves to read). Veldeke's patron may possibly have brought the MS to Cleves to boast of it on a public occasion, not by simply showing it to largely unlettered noblemen, but by having it recited (public recital would fit in with the public occasion of wedding festivities).[208] As so often, Herbort von Fritzlar uses *horen* of the audience for his *Liet von Troye*, but also more specifically in a way reminiscent of the court of Baldwin of Guines (18449ff.): laymen are given access to a written tradition which has passed from Greek to Latin and then to French by having it rendered into German and then recited.²⁰⁹ In *Alexander* Rudolf von Ems grants more force to *hoeren* by suggesting that the ill-wisher depart and leave the recital free to those ready to listen, by using *hoeren sagen* of what the audience has already heard recounted and the variant *hoeren lesen* in the sketch of the ill-wisher.²¹⁰ Ulrich von Etzenbach likewise uses *hoeren* in his *Alexandreis*, but alongside allusions to an assembled audience and to what they hear recited.²¹¹

The first two examples of the Arthurian romance, Hartmann's *Erec* and *Iwein*, we shall consider later. In the next case, *Lanzelet*, Ulrich von Zatzikhoven couples *hoeren* with other pointers: a request for the ill-wisher to keep away from the recital, a plea for silence from those who remain, but above all the anticipation of a twofold reception.²¹² From *Der Saelden Hort* and Hugo von Trimberg we know already that the *Wigalois* of Wirnt von Grafenberg was transmitted orally, and the poet himself combines a request for silence with *hoeren*, but also refers more convincingly to a twofold reception.²¹³ In *Daniel von dem Blühenden Tal* Der Stricker supports *hoeren* with a request for silence, a pointer to the physical presence of listeners, sketched as sitting by the reciter, as in the *Gandersheimer Reimchronik*.²¹⁴ A remark like 3303 (*Nû muget ir gerne hoeren sagen*) may be taken literally in the light of this sketch, but also because a twofold reception is suggested.²¹⁵ In *Die Crone* Heinrich von dem Türlin implies a listening reception by *hoeren* confirmed by two vignettes of a recital situation and by the spatial function of *vor sagen* (recital in front of listeners).²¹⁶ For all its length, the evidence for the acoustic reception of the prose *Lancelot* is singularly weak, for the *hören* formula is supported only by occasional references to passages recited earlier.²¹⁷

The earliest German Grail romance, Wolfram's *Parzival*, will be considered later for its reception by listeners as well as readers. Its thematic development, *Titurel*, may be included here: its few *horen* examples are given persuasive support by the view that its stanzaic form implies a sung recital.²¹⁸ The same consideration is true of the *Jüngerer Titurel* of Albrecht von Scharfenberg. Support for *hoeren* is provided by the adaptation of Wolfram's *Parzival* prologue, where Albrecht refers more specifically to the acoustic dimension.²¹⁹ General remarks on the oral recital of knightly themes (917, 4; 2958, 1f.) need not be inapplicable to this particular work, as is suggested by a concluding wish (6327, 4) or by explicit references to two modes of reception.²²⁰ Orality of a particular kind is implied by the presence of a melody in MS A.²²¹ In another thematic development of Wolfram's *Parzival*, *Lohengrin*, the possibly stereotyped *hoeren* is reinforced by the nomen agentis *hoerer* and by the composition of the work in the melody of the 'Schwarzer Ton'.²²²

In the earliest Tristan romance Eilhart von Oberg supplements *hören* by an allusion to the audience's presence, an appeal to them to assist in telling the story of a type characteristic of orality with the 'Spielmannsepen', deictic references to shared space, and appeals for silence.²²³ His version may have acquired book form (9447), but this did not exclude oral recital. Gottfried's version will be discussed in the context of twofold reception. The supplementary evidence in the *Tristan* of Ulrich von Türheim is difficult to interpret, for 3170f. might imply a contrast between individual reading and public recital, but 3577ff. suggests recital, certainly with Ulrich's forerunners and probably with him as well.²²⁴ In his version Heinrich von

Freiberg uses *hoeren* only occasionally, but supports it with *lesen* to refer to what he had earlier read out.[225]

There remain the romances of love and adventure for a brief listing. Konrad Fleck, *Flore und Blanscheflur*: *hoeren*, a pointer to a twofold reception.[226] Rudolf von Ems, *Der guote Gerhard*: *hoeren* together with a deictic pointer, public recital in sketches of court entertainment, the potential recipient as a listener.[227] Rudolf von Ems, *Willehalm von Orlens*: *hören*, presence of an audience from which any ill-wisher is to withdraw, request for silence, audience to hear recited or read out.[228] Konrad von Würzburg, *Partonopier und Meliur*: invitation to listen, request for silence, suggestion of the oral dimension of poetry, reference to what has already been read out.[229] Konrad von Würzburg, *Engelhard*: *hoeren*, public recital in shared space, reference to hearing the book recited.[230] *Reinfried von Braunschweig*: the audience hears, the reciter says with tongue or mouth, in the presence of his audience.[231] *Flos vnde Blankeflos*: *lesen* in the sense of 'to recite aloud'.[232] *Apollonius von Tyrland*: *horen*, references to what has earlier been recited.[233] Johann von Würzburg, *Wilhelm von Österreich*: *hoeren*, requests for silence, references to hearing a recital, a verb of communication with *vor* (before an assembled audience), *hoern lesen* applied to the recipients of this work.[234]

The 'Märe', with which we conclude court narrative literature,[235] is a form so short that memorising and therewith the oral spread of such material have been considered possible.[236] This would account for the variety of different versions in which some examples have reached us, with a textual instability unknown to longer narrative types which found their way earlier into the fixed form of writing.[237] Oral transmission was so central to the 'Märe' that, at a time when writing was impinging more on the oral realm, doubts were expressed about the truthfulness of mere hearsay, so that authors of 'Mären' reacted by using a mode of proof known to medieval law and historiography, invoking what witnesses had heard and said.[238] Doubts about orality were thus set at rest by a procedure which was itself embedded in orality.

In this genre the use of *hoeren* by itself is as unreliable as elsewhere, although the information in account-books about *sprecher* as professional reciters of 'Mären' implies that the verb can be understood literally.[239] A recital situation is also implied by another phrase in such sources (e.g. *en spreker, die vor mijns heren tafel sprac*), implying an audience at table.[240] Hence also the occasional request by the reciter for a drink or a quasi-dramatic recital dependent on a skilled change of voice in dialogue (the MS evidence of *Meier Helmbrecht* has been plausibly interpreted in the light of different requirements for oral recital and individual reading).[241] Like other genres meant for oral recital the 'Märe' can encourage ill-wishers to depart or request silence.[242] This public dimension also explains the use of *lesen* with the dative or in referring back to what has been previously recited.[243] Other examples suggest that although the 'Märe' may have found its way into written form it was still meant to be recited to listeners.[244] Whether the 'Märe' existed in oral or in written form, its reception, as far as our evidence shows, was by listening to a recital.

(j) Lyric poetry

German love-poetry starts essentially with *Minnesangs Frühling*,[245] for which orality can be postulated on several grounds. Whereas the longer narrative poem was created as a written work which found its way into orality by being recited, text and music belonged together with the lyric, which was conceived as a song to be sung, so that it found its way on to parchment only later and more by chance.[246] Whereas the MS transmission of narrative literature often goes back to the lifetime of its authors, love-poetry composed from the middle of the twelfth century was preserved in writing only in MSS put together from towards the end of the thirteenth century.[247] The initial oral transmission which this suggests is reflected in the textual instability of this genre by contrast with narrative literature[248] and by references to the recital of love-poetry in narrative literature as belonging to court entertainment.[249] Gottfried's lovers entertain themselves in this way, and in a more social context Der Stricker recruits singers at a festival for this purpose, just as Rudolf von Ems includes the recital of love songs within a court festivity.[250]

In such examples there is no reason not to take *singen* at face value, so that references in lyric poetry itself to *singen* and *sanc* (and also to *hoeren* of the recipients) mean literally what they say.[251] Internal evidence also suggests that recital could be by the poet or by someone else, that duet or even collective singing took place, amounting to a public function, and hence acoustic reception, of a genre which has been seen in terms of court ceremony and display.[252] Moreover, musical accompaniment is brought out by references to the melody (*wîse*, *dôn*) and the occasional presence of musical notation, but also by internal references to musical instruments or the evidence of illustrations in the Manesse MS.[253] The social dimension of the love-lyric is also indicated whenever it accompanied a dance – the public occasion and collective entertainment presuppose a listening reception by the court.[254]

This is just as true of gnomic poetry – and would be even more so if we accepted Schweikle's suggestion that the public (even political) themes of this poetry go better with a public recital than with what he sees as the more esoteric nature of love-poetry.[255] All we can safely maintain is that the public, oral dimension is attested for both types of lyric poetry.[256] Further, whereas German love-poetry was largely the domain of aristocratic amateurs, gnomic poetry was mainly practised by travelling minstrels who lived by performing from their repertoire at court. Their dependence on an oral repertoire has been used to explain the association of gnomic poets with lesser courts where patrons could more easily afford poets not dependent on the appurtenances of writing.[257]

The oral dimension of gnomic poetry is not called into question by the use of parchment rolls for recording it and their depiction in the Manesse MS.[258] The association of roll with wax-tablet suggests that both types of written record served a more practical and provisional purpose than the luxurious codex, that the roll was meant for everyday use by a reciter when performing (just as the roll of the *Osterspiel von Muri* was meant for a souffleur at a performance).[259] Oral transmission would also account for the textual instability of gnomic poetry as for love-poetry, the variability of form both in wording and in the order of stanzas.[260] Variants can arise unconsciously in oral tradition from gaps in the reciter's memory, but gnomic poetry is also subject to conscious variations, for the poet, wandering from court to court, would confront different audiences and different political interests, making it advisable to suppress or replace an occasional stanza.[261] These two types of variability underline the orality of this genre: unconscious changes because the reciter depends on a sometimes faulty memory, conscious ones because in recital he confronts an actual audience to whom he must adapt or perish.

In this chapter we have considered examples of an acoustic reception over a span of more than five hundred years. The total number of separate texts is 270,[262] the evidence for some of which is far weaker than for others, but against that we may set cases where we have treated the genre as a whole, rather than its individual texts.[263] From this it is clear that the acoustic reception was much more widespread than this total might suggest. It remains a constant factor in all genres in this period.

Some genres continue to be received by hearing without also being read by individuals. On the other hand, although a reading reception of the court romance is markedly well attested this is not at the cost of an acoustic reception. Any survey of the primary reception of medieval literature, including the possibility of reading, cannot afford to disregard reception by hearing.

5

Criteria for reception by reading

If oral communication rests on the presence of a speaker and at least one listener, together forming a group, written communication normally separates them and sees them as individuals (even if the author does not write himself, but dictates to a scribe, he is still separated from the reader who, even if he reads in or to a group, is separated from the writer). Written communication, freed from the restriction to shared time and place to which the spoken word is tied, can extend to past and future, but also to other places, yet suffers the drawback that deictic pointers intelligible in face-to-face communication are now excluded and have to be replaced by explicit linguistic references.[1] This applies also to non-verbal aspects of oral communication: visual ones, like miming or gestures, cannot be conveyed in writing, whilst acoustic ones, such as intonation or accentuation, have been captured partially in writing, and even then only by means of modern typographic devices.[2] This greater explicitness forced on the writer if he is to achieve what the speaker does in front of his listeners is unavoidable in another respect, for the potential element of give-and-take dialogue in direct oral encounter is missing from writing.[3] A written text remains silent beyond what is written and cannot be asked questions by its reader (this was the gist of Plato's criticism of writing),[4] so that the careful writer has to anticipate such questions and write his answers into his text in advance.[5] On the other hand, his medium makes it easier to do this. If the unforeseeable give-and-take of oral encounter imposes restrictions on the extent to which the spoken word can be planned ahead, the writer is freed from the immediacy of a direct confrontation, can plan at his own pace, even revising as he thinks fit and inserting details which may occur to him only with the more considered pace of written composition.[6]

Written transmission differs from oral transmission along similar lines. No longer tied to the fleeting medium of sound, writing can be reactivated at any point in time or space independently of the writer.[7] Where the spoken word could only overcome its inherent transience by memory and mnemonic devices, to whose reliability and ability to cope with a large amount of material there were definite limits set, the written word can outlive its originator and those for whom it was first intended, surviving as long as the material text remains intact.[8] Whilst an oral society depended on training professional remembrancers, a community based on writing has to rely on professional scribes and literate reciters, which necessitates an organised education in literacy. Finally, whereas the spoken word, transmitted by memory, could cope with only a certain degree of complexity, writing is subject to no such limitations: it may be introduced as a means of dealing with the growing complexity of a society's needs, but in turn brings about even more differentiation.[9]

These features are informed by the visual dimension, which underlies both the writer's encoding of language in script and the reader's decoding. It is this dimension which led Thomasin von Zerclaere to contrast the *clericus* reading with his eyes (*Der welsche Gast* 9445: *gêt ez dem phaffn zen ougen in*) with the illiterate layman dependent on his ears. It also lies behind Goody's statement of the change wrought by writing, 'involving the transfer from sound to sight, from ear to eye'.[10] We saw when dealing with oral communication that Thomasin and Goody viewed the contrast with writing too absolutely and that qualifications were called for as regards the equation of orality with hearing. The same is true of their equation of writing with seeing, for this ignores the oral dimension of literacy before the modern era: the practice, in classical antiquity and in the Middle Ages, of someone reading to himself, but aloud (even if only muttering or whispering), and also the fact that a written work for which there were readers may also have been meant for public recital. Even with these qualifications, however, it is still justifiable to link reading with seeing, because the oral utterance of the reader or the reciter depends upon the message which he registers with his eyes.

This appears to confront us with a difficulty if we take into account the isolated position of writer or reader as opposed to the group situation of speaker and listener (to listen to a recital is a collective experience, whereas to read, even if not in solitude, isolates the reader who buries himself in the text and cuts himself off from others).[11] Our difficulty lies in this: if we accept the argument about the collective function of medieval literature and hence the social, even sociable occasion of its delivery, it is difficult to imagine where an opportunity could be found for the unsocial, isolating act of reading for oneself. We shall return later to this question, but for the moment may content ourselves with a general point.

In his survey of late medieval literature Cramer says that the reception of literature, particularly in narrative and didactic genres, gradually withdrew from the social, ceremonial context, became more the object of private reading and continued the transition from public recital to a literature read by individuals.[12] The period Cramer has in mind covers the fourteenth and fifteenth centuries, but the transition to which he points may have begun before 1300, even though its speed and extent increased only later. This was likely if we recall that public recital could be expressed by *lesen* combined with *offenlîche*, especially in the light of Hölscher's observation that to describe anything as taking place in public presupposes that it can also take place apart from the public gaze, in secret.[13] The contrast between public and secrecy has been discussed by Wenzel with regard to the work which promises most for this approach, Gottfried's *Tristan*, and he emphasises the possibility of reading it 'from without' (the point of view of Marke's court, the public domain) and 'from within' (from the point of view of the lovers, with their need for secrecy).[14] Where Hölscher makes the point that in the late Middle Ages the advisers of a ruler were known as 'Heimliche', corresponding to Latin *secretarii*,[15] Wenzel reminds us that Gottfried, referring to Marke's court, talks of *des küneges heinlîchaere*, translated by

CRITERIA FOR RECEPTION BY READING

Hatto as 'the King's secretary'.[16] The conjunction of a sphere of secrecy, set apart from the wider world, with literacy is suggested by Hölscher for Ulrich von Lichtenstein, whose *schrîber* is associated with *heimlîche* (in the sense of a private room),[17] and agrees with his suggestion that reading which is explicitly described as done in public implies the possibility that it could also be done more confidentially. It also agrees with what we shall later see: individual reading (and writing) can be seen in the context of a room (*kamer, heimlîche*) separate from the court at large, by no means reserved only for the use of administrators, but available also for other literate members of the court.[18]

That an area to which the individual could withdraw to read or write was to be found elsewhere can be illustrated from what we have seen of monastic practice. Not merely did it provide for recital in the refectory and in the *collatio*, it also specified hours in which the monk was to read in his cell and regulated the course of his reading programme.[19] However much the need to establish a corporate sense of identity may have given priority to recital to the assembled monks, this did not exclude individual reading. The argument in support of an audience to which works were read out aloud does not therefore conflict with potential readers to be found amongst these listeners. Less frequent than listeners they may have been, but there are traces of them before the fourteenth and fifteenth centuries.

The criteria for a reading reception are divided into three groups: ambiguous criteria (points where I am more sceptical than Scholz), less ambiguous ones (where we are more in agreement), followed by lexical pointers.

AMBIGUOUS CRITERIA

Scepticism is called for concerning a number of points for two reasons. In the first place, Scholz is too ready to assume that establishing a work as a written text is tantamount to demonstrating that it was read by an individual,[20] whereas it could equally well be read out to listeners. Secondly, some criteria used by Scholz to suggest an individual reader are also applicable to works meant to be received by listening, so that they cannot be taken automatically in the sense in which Scholz reads them. Taken together, these reservations suggest that by largely ignoring reception by listeners he has not always been able to judge reception by readers correctly, because the two modes cannot be divorced from one another, but must be seen in their interplay. In what follows I indicate examples where the criteria used by Scholz to establish a reading reception can also be found outside the context of exclusive reading. What for him was a sufficient indication of a reader turns out in many cases to be ambiguous, in need of further confirmation.

(a) *Wir lesen; man liset*

These phrases are discussed briefly by Scholz, who places them in the context of MHG *lesen* with the modern meaning (reading by an individual to himself).[21] He interprets Der Arme Hartmann, *Rede vom heiligen Glauben* (79, 1: *Wir lesen in den scriften der vier evangelisten*) or Frau Ava, *Johannes* (14, 1: *Man liset von Johanne*) as indicating a unity of author and public, constituting together an ideal community of readers or Christendom at large.[22] It is, in fact, highly unlikely that 'Christendom' can be equated with 'community of readers' because the clerical nature of the works quoted suggests that the Christian community involved is more likely to be a congregation to whom the biblical texts were read out as part of the liturgy.[23] The reading involved is more probably that of a priest to his flock than that of members of his congregation as individual readers.

The liturgical function of these phrases, suggesting the collective knowledge of Christendom conveyed in written form, but with no indication that it was read by anyone other than the priest, is particularly clear when they occur in a sermon, referring to the lesson for that day, as with the *St. Pauler Predigten* (4, 12: *Wir lesen heut an dem heiligen êwangêliô*). Here the priest who had read the gospel text links himself with the congregation, so that they may be said to have read the text indirectly, through his mediation. The use of *wir lesen* in such a context can be seen as evidence of one reader only (the priest), there is no suggestion that the segment of Christendom addressed is a 'community of readers' except in the metaphorical sense that, literate or illiterate, they are given access to written Christian tradition by the priest reading out to them.[24] How drastically this indirect reading of the congregation can exclude their reading for themselves is suggested by the *Speculum Ecclesiae* collection of sermons, where one of these phrases (55, 11: *Wir lêsin*) has to be seen in conjunction with the priest's allusion, at another point, to the illiteracy of his flock (35, 22: *Wan ir der bvoche niht kvnnet*). Revealing is the use of *man liset* with a dative object for the recipients (e.g. *Anegenge* 1859: *nû liset man uns an einer letzen*). Not merely are we placed in the liturgical context of the lesson, but the use of the dative points to what is read out to a listening congregation.[25] Although the evidence of sermons, as part of the liturgy, can most easily undermine Scholz's interpretation of these phrases, the same can also be suggested by paraliturgical works (not part of the actual liturgy, but tied to a definite point in the liturgical year). As an example we may take the *Millstätter Exodus* (35: *Ein buoch heizet Exodus, / dar inne lesen wir sus*), a passage which derives its force from the association of this work with Easter and from the role of the book of Exodus in the liturgy of Easter.[26]

Even beyond the liturgical and paraliturgical context these phrases indicate knowledge of what was transmitted in the Middle Ages in written form, while leaving it open who had access to it as readers. They are also used in a secularised context, applied to what has been handed down from classical antiquity and also, once court literature establishes itself as a written tradition, to what an aristocratic public may be expected to know of that literature. Lamprecht, the clerical author of the Vorau version of the *Alexanderlied*, refers to knowledge about the Trojan War (1329: *man list von gûten chnehten ... in Troiâre liede*), just as Thomasin alludes to Julius Caesar (*als wir lesen*),[27] without these remarks meaning anything other than what has been transmitted in writing and should be common knowledge as the result of reading or hearing. The same is true even of a work for which the author anticipated readers. When Gottfried says of his *Tristan* towards the end of his prologue: *wir lesen ir leben, wir lesen ir tôt: / und ist uns daz süez' alse brôt* (235f.), the allusion to the eucharist makes it clear that the liturgical use of *wir lesen* has been secularised and that we have no justification to read this less generally (court society is made acquainted with this written version, but it is left open whether this took place directly or indirectly) than we did the liturgical examples. If we argue in terms of readers for Gottfried's romance, it cannot safely be on the basis of these two lines.[28]

Far from implying that individual members of the audience read a work, these phrases generally suggest an acoustic reception by the majority (the work was read out to them). They belong more to *lesen* to imply recital aloud to others. If we are to claim them for individual reading, it can only be in conjunction with other pointers.

(b) *Schríben* + dative

Scholz devotes a short section to this, arguing that a phrase like Konrad Fleck's *ich muoz iu leider schríben* implies not just that the author is writing for his audience, but that he conceives them as potential readers.[29] About this assumption we may have doubts. Theoretically, there is no reason why an author should not write a work for listeners who hear it recited as much as for those who read it themselves, and if the conjunction of another verb of literacy, *lesen*, with the dative was used to denote recital, as Scholz himself concedes,[30] we need to be told what the force of *schríben* may be which transfers this construction to the realm of individual reading instead. Finally, Scholz admits that, whereas an author's use of *schríben* of his own activity may decide whether his work was composed orally or not, it tells us nothing about how he imagined its reception.[31]

These considerations make us cautious, yet the problem is best considered with regard to concrete examples. We may start with a case which Scholz could have used to support his contention, for Mechthild von Magdeburg, for whose *Fließendes Licht der Gottheit* there is evidence that it was meant to be read,[32] but none that it was intended for recital, addresses her potential reader with this phrase (32, 94: *Lieber gottes frúnt, disen minneweg han ich dir geschriben*; 106, 3). Against this must be set other examples, however, which cast doubt on a necessary equation of this phrase with a reading reception. When the author of the *Millstätter Reimphysiologus* says: *diu heiligen wort ... / diu uns sint gescriben unde gechundet* (85, 1f.), he is making the same kind of remark as later (96, 1): *In dem salter lesen wir*. In neither case does he mean that the biblical text will be read by those with whom he groups himself, but that this written text is available to us, directly or indirectly.

More telling are cases where our phrase is used in connection with works for which a twofold reception is indicated, i.e. they were meant for the individual reader and for assembled listeners. Hugo von Trimberg says of his *Renner* (12760): *Diz büechelín ich iu schríbe*, but makes it clear elsewhere that he expects it to be received by individual readers as well as listeners (19: *Swelhe ez lesen oder hoeren lesen*). Whereas the readers anticipated by Hugo confirm Scholz's point, the author's reckoning with listeners as well agrees with our suggestion that a work could be written as much for listeners as for readers. The position is no different with Priester Wernher, who says of his *Maria* (A 170): *waz Matheus schreib dort / den ebrayschen levten, / daz wil ich iv bedevten, / sagen vnd schreiben / mannen vnd weiben*. Here we may agree that *schríben* + dative anticipates a reading reception of a work for which elsewhere the possibility of readers is entertained (A 137ff.). Alongside this, however, we have to set the evidence for a listening reception of this work,[33] so that the conclusion is that *schríben* + dative is at the most a neutral construction, employed with regard to listeners and to readers, and not a sufficient pointer to a reading reception. Other works which use this phrase and for which a twofold reception can be postulated[34] (including the *Flore und Blanscheflur* of Konrad Fleck with which Scholz began) point in the same direction: if this phrase can be used as a criterion for a reading reception, it is only in combination with other pointers.

(c) *Hie stân*

Whether in this form or expanded to *hie geschriben stân* Scholz regards this as indicating a written text: he observes that the adverb of place *hie* implies that the written work must be in front of the audience and visible,[35] but might have added that *stân* also suggests that the passage referred to occupies a spatial dimension, is found in a manuscript or book. From this Scholz goes one step further and suggests that the passage is for the benefit of readers. I do not deny this possibility, which can be confirmed by a text which Scholz does not mention, for in his *Hohes Lied* Williram von Ebersberg refers to an earlier passage (49, 1: *daz selbe vers stêt ôuh da vora ad tale signum X*). Although the adverb *hie* has been replaced by *da* (*vora*), the construction is comparable, and the fact that the earlier passage is made easier to find by being marked with an X reinforces the visual dimension in which a reader is presupposed. Since Williram's work contains other pointers to a reading reception[36] and none to listeners, we may agree so far with Scholz.

Beyond that it is difficult to agree with him. If an author refers to the spatial dimension in which a passage is to be found it is possible that he is writing into the text the situation of a reciter addressing listeners and pointing to his text, saying that what he is reciting is to be found there in black and white and therefore acceptable as the truth to an illiterate audience. Scholz mentions this possibility,[37] but dismisses it in the case of Ulrich von Lichtenstein's *Frauendienst*[38] by reference to this author's anticipation of readers. We shall return to this example, but must now do what Scholz neglects to do, namely consider the implications when this phrase is used of a work meant for listeners. The *Wiener Oswald* calls up the situation of an audience listening to a recital from a written text (1: *Deme nach fremden meren / stat alle sin begere, / der hore zu gar eben / von sinte Oswalden leben, / daz alhi geschriben stat*). Scholz elsewhere concedes that *zuohoeren* has more force than the simple *hoeren* as evidence for an acoustic reception:[39] if we accept that in this case (there is also no evidence for a reading reception of the *Wiener Oswald*), then the position here is that of a literate reciter brandishing his copy before his listeners, selling his wares by convincing a largely illiterate audience of the superiority of his written text. *Hie stân* may indicate a written text, but not necessarily individual readers.

A reference to a written text, but equally one for which a reader is not expected, is found in Priester Arnold's *Loblied auf den heiligen Geist* where, with reference to Latin *consilium*, it is said: *so iz an den puochen gescriben stat, / in unser zungen chut iz rat* (9, 3). Not merely does this Latin word have to be translated, so do others elsewhere in this work,[40] so that if *geschriben stat* refers to a Latin source there can be no hope that it is to be read by Arnold's audience. By underlining his knowledge of a learned written source the author can hope to establish his own work as true. The same applies even to an audience, such as monks, of whom reading might normally be expected. When Notker uses the construction *dâ stân* of what is to be found in the Bible, there is no reason to assume that he expected the biblical passage in question to be read by those addressed (even though he may reckon with this on other occasions). In his *Psalter*, for example, he says: *Daz líset man an danihele. Dâr stât* (712, 2) and then gives the Latin text as part of his own commentary. Whether or not Notker's work itself was read or heard, there is no indication that he expected the Book of Daniel to be consulted by a reader, for if *man liset* is ambiguous in this respect, the same must be said of *dâr stât* with which it is associated.[41]

The suggestion that this phrase implies a reading reception is weakened whenever it occurs in a work for which a twofold reception can be established. Unfortunately for his case Scholz correlates an example from Ulrich von Lichtenstein (*Frauendienst* 592, 20: *daz vint man hie / allez an dem buoche stân*) with a reading reception by quoting a subsequent passage which presupposes a reader (592, 24). This is only part of the picture, for a few lines earlier Ulrich also refers to the possibility of his work being heard in recital (592, 6: *dô man ditz buoch hôrt niwez lesen*). If *hie stân* reveals itself as neutral, applicable to either mode of reception, it oversimplifies the issue to register it simply as a criterion for reading. This objection is not confined to Ulrich's work, for there are other examples in which the phrase occurs and for which a twofold reception is likely, such as the *Weltchronik* of Rudolf von Ems and the *Sanct Franzisken Leben* of Lamprecht von Regensburg.[42] In such cases *hie stân*, whilst reconcilable with a reading reception, does not suffice to establish this mode as distinct from another.

(d) *Suochen; vinden*

Under this heading Scholz includes references to looking for, or finding, a particular piece of information, which he interprets as involving a reader invited to confirm what the author has said or to find more than he can give.[43] Certainly this is possible. An example is provided by the *Kaiserchronik*, not for the reception of this work, but with reference to a work mentioned in an episode (2361: '*dû vindest ouh gescriben stân . . . / in der selben lineâ vindest dû gescriben dâ*'), where the precise reference (*in der selben lineâ*) suggests a reader checking up a passage. The same conclusion can be drawn from *Reinfried von Braunschweig* with regard to the reading of a letter in the narrative (24519: *den brief der im dâ was gesant, / den brach er ûf, dar an er vant / geschriben . . .*). When this action is later summed up in the words *Dô er den brief alsus gelas* (24685), the equation of *gelas* with *vant* tells us that the latter verb, as in the *Kaiserchronik*, involves reading.

This need not necessarily be true on every occasion, since theoretically an author who employs a recommendation to look or find need not address potential readers; he could equally well intend the words for listeners, not as a recommendation, but as an indication of the truth of his account (it derives from a written source in which the truth could theoretically be confirmed). If the words do not refer to another work, they could be addressed to the listener to whom the reciter points out his own text where the words are to be found (a possibility admitted by Scholz).[44] In looking at these possibilities I exclude two types of evidence as not relevant. The first is when the verb of seeking or finding, involving reading, is used of the poet consulting his source, as in Veldeke's *Eneide* (13520: *alse he't geschreven vant*, paralleled by 13523: *alse'r ane den buken las*).[45] However revealing such usage may be about the author's literate process of composition, it tells us nothing about how his work was to be received. The other class to be excluded consists of cases where a verb of seeking or finding is used in the first person plural as a pluralis societatis, as in the *Linzer Antichrist* (32, 1: *Die altin scribaere / sagint uns ze maere: / (wir vindinz an den buochin, / welle wirz suochin*)).[46] A case like this corresponds to *wir lesen*, and does not imply that the audience in the *wir* are expected to consult the books, but merely that such reliable written information transmitted down the ages lies behind the author's account.

Apart from that we find, for example, that Gottfried uses one of these verbs in a context where reading aloud to an assembled company is involved (*Tristan* 13232: 'heizet küneges reht lesen: / und vindet ir ez niht dâ ...'). The law may be written, but in having it read out Marke can only 'find' a point by receiving it acoustically, so that *vinden* cannot be a sufficient indication of reading. A distinction between *vinden* and reading is also made by Heinrich von Melk in V*on dem gemeinen lebene* (13, 30: *swaz wir von dem tode wellen sagen, / daz vindet ir gescriben hie bi*), for he does no more than announce his following work, its presence in written form, which is not the same thing as expecting it to be read (his works contain no reference to a reading reception).

As with other criteria, Scholz's argument that *suochen* and *vinden* can be accepted as indications of reading is weakened by their occurrence in works meant for a twofold reception, thereby anticipating listeners on some occasions. His reference to two examples from Otfrid is a case in point, for the *Evangelienbuch* is one of the first works which can be shown to be addressed to listeners as well as readers,[47] so that the 'finding' associated with a far from homogeneous audience may involve reading (as in the *Kaiserchronik* and *Reinfried von Braunschweig*), but equally listening (as in the episode from Gottfried's *Tristan*). The same openness to either interpretation is present when Notker refers in his text to an illustration given at an earlier point (*De interpretatione* 522, 13: *Sih târuore an die descriptionem, târ uindest tu ...*), for references of this kind may imply a reader, but also listeners to whom the illustration may be shown by the reciter (in this case the teacher), and that Notker designed his work both for readers and for listeners.[48] Ebernand von Erfurt may address his audience using the same verb (*Heinrich und Kunigunde* 1104: *diz sult ir an der schrifte / hier nâch wol ervinden baz*), but since he later mentions a reader and implies listeners as well,[49] it is difficult to claim for the verb more than that it can be equated, but not identified with reading. Ulrich von Lichtenstein uses the phrase *hie stân*, but combines it with *vinden* (*Frauendienst* 592, 20f.) in such a way as to suggest both readers and listeners. By ignoring this recurrent intermediate mode of reception Scholz has been led to regard this usage exclusively in terms of reading.

(e) *Obene; dort vorne*

After indicating the use of *quod supra dixi* and *persequar inferius* in Latin literature[50] Scholz discusses their counterparts in medieval German, pointing to their frequency already with Otfrid (e.g. V 12, 4: *thísu selba rédina, thia wir hiar scríbun obana*).[51] Strictly speaking, all these examples establish is that the works in question were written ones, because of the spatial point to which reference is made (Otfrid thus wrote something above). They give no information on how the works were received. Admittedly, a pronouncedly bookish phrase like 'saying something above' makes better sense in the context of literacy than of orality, but as long as the phrase concerns what the *author* said above (not what the *audience* heard above) we are in the context of literate composition: what the author wrote above may be something which his audience heard earlier. Only when *obene* is applied to the audience (what they heard above) can we talk of a careless use of language (bookish in a non-bookish context), but we are not concerned with whether language is used consistently or not, but with what the choice of wording may indicate about the reception of a work. If Otfrid can be inconsistent enough to put this phrase twice into the mouth of Christ when talking with the disciples,[52] it is also possible for him to use it of the reciter delivering a work to listeners – indeed with more justification, since Otfrid's words, unlike those spoken by Christ, were at least written.[53]

What this implies for the reception of a work can be illustrated by two examples. Towards the end of his *Liet von Troye* Herbort von Fritzlar refers to a point made earlier (18276: *Da obene gesaget ist / Mit welcher not mit welcher list / Vlixes von circen schiet*). The author of a work which he terms a *buoch*[54] is justified in talking of what he said above, but this says nothing about his audience: they are nowhere implied as readers, but are seen as listening to a recital (13670: *Die diz horent lesen*). The use of *lesen*, combined with *buoch*, constitutes the written dimension which justifies the use of *obene sagen*, but *horen* indicates that the audience as listeners have only indirect access to literacy. Such a use of *obene* tells us nothing about their possible role as readers. The situation is similar with the *Sächsische Weltchronik*. Here too reference is made to an earlier point (267, 33: *Aver de erste Liberius, de ovene bescreven is ...*), but again with the suggestion, at least in the *Sächsische Fortsetzung*, that the audience could listen to a recital of the work (285, 22: *als ir davor habet gehort lesen*). In both cases the literacy of the author is not necessarily shared by his audience – if they are conceived as potential readers, it will have to be established on other evidence. Only slightly less clearcut is the position in *Morant und Galie*. The author of a *buoch*[55] is again justified in talking of what he said above (2144, 5482f.), but his audience is nowhere seen as potential readers, and indeed the evidence points to their receiving his work as listeners.[56]

Made sceptical by such examples we may now look at one example where the construction occurs in a work meant for a twofold reception. The *Sanct Franzisken Leben* of Lamprecht von Regensburg represents something new, since the author uses the construction of his audience (1380: *als ir dâ oben hânt vernomen*). Scholz is right to defend the author against the charge of inconsistency by pointing out that Lamprecht anticipated readers, for whom *oben* was as justified as with a literate author.[57] His wording ('daß seine Dichtungen (auch) an Leser gerichtet sind') is accurate, but revealing, for he refers to Lamprecht's pointer to a twofold reception of his work (90: *die diz buoch hoeren oder lesen*). Scholz marginalises the twofold reception by placing it in brackets and concentrates on readers, but if we also take the listeners into account, it will be to recall that *obene* can be used by an author who has listeners in mind. Lamprecht's literate composition, together with this anticipation of some readers, may dictate the use of *oben* with his listeners, but this still means that the construction cannot be taken by itself as an unambiguous indication of readers.

The other possibility is for an author to use a phrase such as *dort vorne* or *hie vor*, whose spatial implication is taken by Scholz as a pointer to a passage found further forward in a written text, as in Wolfram's *Parzival* (788, 14: ...*der troestenlîche trôst, / den Trevrizent dort vorne sprach*).[58] Here two points need to be made. The first is, once again, that this construction confirms only the presence of a written work, whilst saying nothing about its reception. Secondly, a difficulty is presented by the semantic difference between *hie obene* and *dort vorne*.[59] Whereas the former has an exclusively spatial meaning (it refers to a passage written above), *dort vorne* can be interpreted either spatially (it points to a passage on an earlier page) or temporally (what was said before need not be present in written form, a possibility to be reckoned with even more with *da vor*). Whereas *hie obene* can strictly be used only by the author of a written work, *dort vorne* or *da vor* can occur in connection with writing and in the context of oral recital. These latter phrases, because of this ambiguity, can only be claimed for literacy when a further pointer is added, either to the writer (e.g. Otfrid V 24, 4: *thiu wir hiar scríbun fórna*) or to the reader (e.g. Otfrid II 3, 29: *Maht lésan ouh hiar fórna*). Once again, a criterion which Scholz takes as sufficient evidence for readers in itself must be seen at the most as not contradicting that.

This last reservation, illustrated from Otfrid, confirms a point made before, since his *Evangelienbuch* was composed with listeners as well as readers in mind, a situation in which the examples quoted must have had a different force for those who could only listen as opposed to those who could also read. When Gottfried refers to a detail mentioned earlier (*Tristan* 8741: *und als daz maere hie vor giht*) it is not *hie vor* which tells us that he anticipates readers, but the following line in which he recommends that this earlier passage should be looked up (8742: *der dâ vor an daz maere siht*).[60] In this last line *dâ vor* has a spatial sense (further back in the book), whilst *hie vor* in the preceding line is more likely to be temporal, because it lacks the visual support of *sehen*. This need for an additional pointer to establish a reading context for *hie vor*, together with the fact that Gottfried reckoned with a twofold reception like Otfrid,[61] is in line with what we have seen elsewhere. It also agrees with Wolfram's back-reference to what Trevrizent had said *dort vorne* (786, 4; 788, 15). Whereas Bartsch and Marti read this as a temporal, not a local construction,[62] I should argue that it is strictly neutral. In either case, we cannot be sure that it is meant locally (although this is likely) and even if we had such certainty, this would establish no more than a written text, not the manner of its reception. For that we need confirmation from other points.

Where we are dealing with works meant for two modes of reception a reference to an earlier passage intended for the reader (reminding him of what he has already read and even inviting him to turn the pages back) must have passed over the heads of those who could only listen, bringing home to them aspects of the work from whose appreciation they were excluded. These cases suggest an audience which in educational and literary terms was far from homogeneous: some were left behind while others enjoyed a more advantageous position.[63]

(f) Recommendations to collate, copy or skip the text

Under this heading I group recommendations made by the author which share the common factor of suggesting how his audience should react to his work. What is involved can be shown by the recommendation to collate two passages to appreciate their bearing on each other, for we have just seen an example of Gottfried doing this (*Tristan* 8741: *und als daz maere hie vor giht, / der dâ vor an daz maere siht*). What concerned us in the last section was the author's phrasing (*hie vor, dâ vor*), but what interests us now is the fact that he recommends his audience to collate two passages at all. To 'look up' a past passage in oral recital is only possible by the laborious and improbable process of a repeat performance, whereas the reader has only to turn back a few pages. Collating is therefore much more easily performed by a reader, as is suggested by Gottfried's stress on the visual dimension (*sehen*), and I have no wish to deny that such recommendations generally presuppose a reader. This can be illustrated by Williram's use of *da vora stên* to indicate where an earlier passage is to be found (*Hohes Lied* 49, 1), for the sign X as a pointer indicates the visual dimension of reading as much as Gottfried's *sehen*. The same dimension is apparent in the prose *Lancelot* where a back-reference is reinforced, for ease of consultation, by specifying in what gathering the passage is to be found, on what page, alongside what date, and the medieval scribe's equivalent of bold type used (II 689, 20: ... *und sagten im alles das, wie es im ergangen was und beschriben stet an dem allerersten blat diß qwinternen by dem datum mit grober schrifft geschriben*).[64] Such a plethora of literate details presupposes a reader to follow these instructions.[65]

However, not only the reader is implied by such references. The author of the *Sächsische Weltchronik* anticipates a point he will later make by saying: *also men hir vorbat gescreven vint* (81, 22).[66] The construction *gescreven vinden* is the equivalent of *lesen*, but since the subject of the verb is *men* we are reminded of what we saw with *man liset*: that it is dangerous to take it as an indication that the person in question actually read. The involvement of listeners in this kind of recommendation is clear when the work is intended for them as well as readers. That is true of Gottfried's back-reference and, given the twofold reception of Otfrid's work, listeners cannot be divorced from his recommendation to the reader (II 3, 29: *Maht lésan ouh hiar fórna* ...).[67] The same is true of *Das Leben der heiligen Elisabeth* (9926ff.)[68] or *Die Apokalypse* of Heinrich von Hesler (8875ff.).[69] These examples suggest what we saw at the close of the last section: the listeners to whom they were also addressed, by overhearing instructions given to readers, were made aware of a dimension of reception which was closed to them.

The second recommendation (to copy a text or to have it copied)[70] could be addressed as much to a listener as to a reader, so that again it establishes a work in written form, but leaves it open whether public recital or individual reading is at issue. How the literate process of having a copy made can be associated with oral recital is exemplified by *Diu vrône botschaft ze der christenheit*, a work whose narrative action (a miraculous letter is read out for the moral improvement of listeners) reflects the reception of the work itself (881: *die ditze buochel hôren lesen*). When the narrative therefore praises the copying and propagation of the letter (482: *Der si schrîbet und vurbaz sendet, / des chumber sî verendet, / über den sî ouch getân mîn segen*) we can equate this copying with the oral recital for which it was intended. Walther von Rheinau associates the copying of his *Marienleben* with readers, but also with listeners (16152: *Alle, die diz buoch lesen / Ald hoeren ald des flîzes wesen, / Daz ez geschriben werde...*) and thereby shows that the wish to have a written copy can proceed as much from one to whom it is read out as from one who reads it himself.[71] The same is true when the suggestion to copy a text occurs in works which imply a twofold reception, as with the *Histoire de la Bible* of Herman de Valenciennes, quoted by Scholz,[72] or with Priester Wernher's *Maria*.[73]

The third recommendation (to skip a passage) may strike modern literates, exposed to the risks of speed-reading, as associated with the reader, but since MHG *leser* can also mean 'Vorleser', it is possible that listeners may be involved. This can be illustrated from the *Apokalypse* of Heinrich von Hesler who recommends the reciter to omit a passage if he finds ladies present (3711: *Des bit ich den lesere, / Swen her kumt in diz mere, / Daz her mit schonen witzen – / Ob dar vrouwen bi sitzen – / Antweder her entrumen / Oder obervar den lumen, / So daz her in icht durfe sagen*). The decision which falls to modern readers is here entrusted to the medieval performer facing a listening audience. When Rudolf von Ems makes a similar point in his *Weltchronik* (2390: *swem niht behagt der paragraf / und von dem Rine dirre klaf, / der sol das ze lone han: / er sol ez ungelesin lan / und leber allir sorgen bar*) we may take that as an instruction to the individual reader[74] as long as we bear in mind that, in view of the twofold reception of this work (21731), listeners cannot be dismissed, so that the reader involved, as with Heinrich von Hesler, could also be the reciter who addresses them.

(g) Recommendations to consult the source or further texts

Heinrich von Veldeke is representative in suggesting that whoever doubts the truth of what he says may easily confirm it by checking his source (*Eneide* 376: *weme so des wundert... he kome tut den buken / di men da heitet Eneide. / na suliker warheide / alse't dar an geschreven is, / so mach'er's werden gewis*). The question with testimony of this kind is whether it was intended to affirm the truth (Veldeke's work derives from a written source, shares its kudos and can be checked) or whether the author expected the doubter to read his source (imputing to him an ability to read either the Old French *Enéas* or Virgil's Latin). If Gottfried can recommend a reader to look up an earlier passage in his own work (*Tristan* 8741f.), can he also expect him to consult his source (which again may embrace Latin works alongside

French)? If we take this as a serious possibility, we face the difficulty of deciding how many books were available for consultation in the Middle Ages outside a few chiefly clerical centres. This suggests that rather than take these recommendations at face value we should consider that their function is to confirm the truth of the author's work (as necessary for him to establish with listeners as with readers) and to impress his (largely illiterate) listeners by demonstrating that this vernacular work belongs to a literate tradition.[75]

It would be wrong to deny in principle that this recommendation could be addressed to readers expected to do what the author suggests, but examples of this come largely from monastic literature. Otfrid repeatedly enjoins members of his audience to read in the Bible a detail which he has given them in his work (e.g. II 9, 71: *Lis sélbo, theih thir rédion, in sínen evangélion, / thar lísist thu*; III 13, 43f.), whilst Notker does the same in a more pedagogic, but still monastic context (e.g. *De consolatione* 46, 26: *Lis orosium, er saget tir iz*; *De interpretatione* 511, 24: *lis mîne metaphisica, dâr lêro ih tih iz*; *Psalter* 685, 8: *Sih dir selbo lector uuio Augustinus* ...).[76] These passages can combine *lesan* with the pronoun *selbo* or with the reflexive dative (sometimes both together), usages which we shall see are pointers to individual reading, so that we may conclude that members of the monastic community are recommended to take their studies further in this way.

What could be expected in some centres of literacy was not practicable in all, let alone in the world outside. An example of the scepticism necessary in reading these recommendations comes from Priester Eberhard's *Gandersheimer Reimchronik*. He suggests that anyone who wishes to learn more may consult a text at Bamberg (1898: *is hir ok jemant, de von en mer wetten wil, / de vare to Bavenberch, da vindet he des gescreven vil*). We may doubt how seriously the suggestion to travel from Gandersheim to Bamberg was meant, but there is a further reason for questioning whether a reader is being invoked. At an earlier point reference is made to another source (588: *also an sünte Jacopes boke gescreven steit. / we de wil, de mach et wol vinden alda*), which is followed by the Latin quotation and German translation. If Eberhard finds it necessary to translate the Latin quotation for his audience, it is difficult to conceive them as readers of the Latin text to which he refers them. A reference like this differs from Otfrid and Notker: the Saxon author does not envisage his audience as potential readers, but as people to impress by the display of literate learning which lies behind his work. That Bamberg's renown as a centre of clerical learning[77] exposed it to use for such purposes is brought out by *Herzog Ernst*, where in versions B and D the sceptical reader is likewise sent on his way to the cathedral library at Bamberg to consult a Latin text which will confirm the vernacular work,[78] whose reliability is further underlined by the the 'Waise', the jewel in the imperial crown brought back by Ernst from his travels. If Kartschoke says of such a reference that there is no point in looking for these lost 'sources',[79] it is equally pointless to imagine medieval readers consulting them.

In other cases, too, what lies behind these remarks is not the recommendation to read another work, but an affirmation of truth and adherence to a literate tradition conceivably more effective when addressed to illiterate laymen than to those able to read. Werner vom Niederrhein may not send his audience on a wild goose chase to

Bamberg but, like Priester Eberhard, he suggests a task for which he knows them to be unequipped. If anyone registers doubts about his work he is to consult a particular page of the psalter (*Die vier Sciven* 5, 1ff.). When this is followed by the relevant psalm text in Latin and then in German (other Latin quotations are regularly translated in this work)[80] Werner reveals that he is dealing with an audience with no Latin, whom it made no sense to refer to a Latin source. The force of this is to show that the author's point can be confirmed, not that the reader is called upon to do it for himself. Similarly, the remark by Der Wilde Mann (*Vespasian* 10, 3: *des vundin si urkunde gnuch, / bisehin si di aldin buch, / so solden si si wol birihten, / dat ich di warheit dihten*) is more an argument for the truth of the author's version.[81]

(h) Text and illustration

Scholz devotes several pages to the question of vernacular works preserved in illustrated manuscripts.[82] The question is relevant because it can be looked at in two ways. On the one hand, text and illustration could reinforce one another; the text could explain the illustration, whilst the illustration clarified the text, so that the visual illustration would reinforce reading as a visual reception. On the other hand, the illustration could be a replacement for the text, in the sense meant by Gregory the Great when he said that pictures are for the illiterate what books are for the literate[83] or by Thomasin (*Der welsche Gast* 1097: *von dem gemâlten bilde sint / der gebûre und daz kint / gevreuwet oft: / swer niht enkan / verstên swaz ein biderb man / an der schrift verstên sol, / dem sî mit den bilden wol*).[84] In the one case, the illustrated manuscript would suggest that its text was to be read, but in the other the lay recipient would have access to the picture, but need to have the text read out to him.[85]

Although there must have been many cases where the meaning of a medieval picture was intelligible to a layman, we cannot generalise this. Camille, who has looked at the visual implications of medieval literacy and illiteracy from an art-historian's point of view, emphasises the position (to which Bäuml first drew attention)[86] of someone standing between the fully literate and the fully illiterate, someone who relied on the literacy of another for access to written transmission.[87] He applies this to art-historical material by reminding us that the *tituli* or inscriptions of most twelfth-century images are crucial in understanding their meaning,[88] so that these images could not function as a book for the illiterate in the way suggested by Gregory and Thomasin, since they referred to written signs from which the illiterate were excluded. (A similar point has been made by Wenzel with regard to an illustrated *Bible moralisée* of the early thirteenth century.[89]) To gain access to the writing without which they could not understand these pictures laymen were dependent on explanations given by clerical literates, and in the case of one illustrated manuscript Camille suggests that 'the owner might want to look at the drawings while the underlying text was read aloud to her by a clerk'.[90]

That this situation was known in Germany is suggested by the episode in the prose *Lancelot* in which King Arthur finds himself in the room in which Lancelot had been held captive and on the walls of which he had depicted the lives of Arthur and

Guinevere (III 462, 12ff.). However, Lancelot had also equipped these pictures with an inscription which provided a commentary, and it was only thanks to this inscription that Arthur understood the pictures and recognised that Guinevere and Lancelot had committed adultery (III 465, 7: *Da begunde der konig zu sehen umb sich und sah das gedichte das Lanczlot hett gemacht die wyl daz er da gefangen was gewest. Und der konig kuond als viel der schrifft das er das wol laß und verstund. Und da er die buchstaben gesach die da bezeichent die gescheffniß von den bilden, da begunde er sie zu lesen als vil das er schinbarlich erkant das die kammer gemalt was von Lanczlot ... 466, 2: 'Off myn trúwe, ist diß bedútniß ware von dißer schrifft, so hatt mich Lanczlot geschant mit der konigin'*). It is not the pictures alone which convey their message to the king, but pictures accompanied by their written commentary, which Arthur can understand only because he is literate (*kuond als viel der schrifft*). If Arthur had been illiterate he would have failed to understand the pictures or been dependent on a literate's assistance. From this and from Camille's argument we may draw the conclusion that the presence of an illustration need not mean that the text it accompanied was meant for individual reading, but that text and illustration could be explained by a literate reading the text aloud.

An example that hearing as well as seeing may be involved in the conjunction of text with picture (or diagram) occurs with Notker. In three works he clarifies his argument by inserting a diagram into his text, but also a verbal pointer to the diagram, so that he reckoned with readers who will be guided by the text to the diagram, which in turn allows them to understand the text more easily.[91] This is only part of the story, for Notker anticipated not merely readers, but listeners as well, best imagined in the oral context of the monastic school, in which the teacher possessed a copy of the text for instruction, while the pupils depended on his reading it out to them, and commenting on it, in the classroom.[92] Wherever the text contained a diagram he had to hold out his copy so that they could see the diagram as he commented on it from his text. Notker's pupils at St. Gallen resemble the English noblewoman mentioned by Camille: they see the image without reading the text, which is instead read out to them. If individual readers could be expected in Notker's monastic school, this was less so (without being impossible) at the court for which Thomasin composed his treatise. When he discusses pride and avarice as conducive to hell he reminds his audience that he has previously mentioned their relative position on the rungs of the ladder leading to hell (11970: *ir habt ez an der helle stiege / gemâlt, als ich gesprochen hân, / ob ir sín war habt getân*).[93] As *gemâlt* suggests, this earlier passage was accompanied by an illustration,[94] so that, in so far as Thomasin anticipated a reader, this image was seen by him as he read the text, whereas the listeners are best imagined being shown it by the reciter at the relevant point.[95] Again, the presence of a picture need not always presuppose a reader.

Two examples from the Millstatt manuscript are also discussed by Scholz.[96] The first concerns the *Millstätter Reimphysiologus*, which says of the lion (73,2): *daz selbe tier hat ubilen list, ez ist getan, als hie gemalet ist*, and accordingly has a picture over 73,1.[97] The second example comes from the *Millstätter Genesis*, where the tree of life in the Garden of Eden is mentioned in the text and illustrated by a picture (9, 23: *Von dem holze des lebenes des guoten und des ubeles, / uon dem holze der gewizzene uindet hie geschriebene*). Scholz points out that the idea of including illustrations must go back to the poets, because they are referred to in their text,[98] but for interpreting this conjunction of text with illustration he relies mainly on what Voss said about the *Millstätter Genesis*. About this doubts are called for.

Voss argues, surely correctly, that the pictures in the *Genesis* text are not self-explanatory, but need to be clarified by relation to the text.[99] That could mean one of two things: *either* an individual reader who studies the text and the pictures together, *or* a reciter who reads out the text and shows the pictures to the audience. Referring to two other points in her book Voss opts for the former explanation, claiming that the text was intended for an individual reader, not for a recital audience.[100]

The first point to which Voss refers is not convincing, for she says that the *Millstätter Genesis* already existed in written form, whereas the *Wiener Genesis* pointed to an oral recital.[101] This betrays a confusion between composition and reception: from the fact that a work exists in written form we cannot conclude that it was meant for individual reading. Moreover, the evidence on which this antithesis is based is equally shaky. If the opening phrase of the Millstatt version (1,1: *eine rede ... uorbrieuen*) suggests a text in written form, whilst the formulation of the Vienna version (2: *aine rede fore tvon*) is neutral, this still tells us nothing about the delivery of the written Millstatt version (was it read or recited to others?). Indeed, in that both verbs have the prefix *vor-* they could both suggest oral delivery to an assembled audience, as with *vortragen* and *vorbringen*.[102]

At the other point in her book Voss quotes two passages from the *Millstätter Genesis*,[103] one the pointer to the tree of life quoted above and the other an indication of a new section (28, 1: *Hie heuet sich daz andir buoch*). Both suggest a written text, but again this tells us nothing about its reception. The pointer to the tree of life could be said to the audience as the picture was shown by the reciter, while the reference to a new section could be an announcement by the reciter to his listeners. If Scholz's reliance on Voss is therefore misplaced, we conclude that the conjunction of text with illustration may suggest readers, but equally illiterate listeners.

(i) The book or story in the first person

Scholz begins a section 'Das Buch als Sprecher' with an interpretation of the opening of the *Wigalois* of Wirnt von Grafenberg which illustrates the relevance of this section to our problem.[104] Wirnt's first line (*Wer hât mich guoter ûf getân?*) leaves it unspecified who is meant by the first person singular, but the next lines make this clear. They indicate that we are dealing with a personification of the book for which individual readers (and not just a reciter) are envisaged. In a case like this we can accept that the employment of this device indicates that the work was meant for readers. There are however cases where the device indicates no more than that the work existed in book form and could equally well be read out to a listening audience. The device itself is no sufficient pointer, only the context in which it is used, its conjunction with other indicators.[105]

In only two examples[106] other than *Wigalois* is the device used in a work conceivably meant for a reading reception. *Der heimliche Bote* begins, like *Wigalois*, with a first-person statement (1: (*bin*) *ein heinlich bote*) coming from the work which names itself, rather than from the book. That we are dealing with a written work for which a reader could be imagined is suggested a little later (7: *nv sih wie gescⁱbe stat*). The other example, *Der Minne Frigedanc*, begins with a first-person statement coming from the work, but makes it clear that it is in written form (1: *Ich bin ein minne büchelîn*).[107] Again, reference is made later to the possibility of an individual reader (88: *Da von halt' ain iedlich man / Der er hernach vint geschriben stan*).

With that we exhaust the works which could be reconciled with Scholz's thesis and turn to those which can better be linked with listeners. The clearest example is *Der Borte* of Dietrich von Glezze. This work opens with a first-person statement giving the title (1: *Ich bin der Borte genant, / hubschen luten sol ich sin bekant*) and its written nature is implied when, with a switch of the first person from work to author, the latter refers to his writing (20: . . . *dar umbe ich von im schriben wil*). As regards the reception of this work, there is no reference to any reader, but instead an indication that the author foresaw his written text being recited to listeners (7: *man sol mich hubschen luten lesen*), where *lesen* + dative has the function discussed in Chapter 3. This example has not escaped Scholz's attention: he interprets it along the same lines, adding that this counter-example indicates that not every case where the work or book is personified in the first person can be claimed for individual reading, but that this can only be assumed when other criteria point in that direction.[108]

This is relevant to the remaining cases, for they concern works addressed to readers, but above all to listeners before whom the reciter would have to perform what Scholz terms a 'Rollenspiel', pretending to play the part of the work or book.[109] An example is the *Rheinisches Marienlob*, registered one-sidedly as meant for readers.[110] Once again, the work opens with a personification, this time addressed to Mary (5: *Ich bin geschriven zuo dinem love*), where the verb (together with other pointers)[111] indicates its written form. Scholz also adduces criteria suggesting a reading reception for this written work, which I do not contest, since they are reconcilable with what we know of the context for which the work was produced: by a priest for nuns (or possibly béguines).[112] This background opens up another possibility, however, for nuns, like monks, not merely read devotional literature for themselves, they also heard it recited, which would explain the author's phrasing on two occasions (he interprets his subject-matter in the presence of these nuns, *vür allen godes brüden*).[113] If we accept this, it suggests that this device could be employed with two modes of reception in mind: as a criterion it could refer to listeners as well as to readers.

The same conclusion can be drawn about the two remaining works listed by Scholz in support of his case. The point in the *Willehalm von Orlens* of Rudolf von Ems where the reciter suddenly slips into the role of the personified book (2143: '*Wer hat mich guoter her gelesen?*') is reconcilable with the criteria for individual readers to be found in this work, but also has to be seen in connection with the evidence for listeners.[114] By concentrating on the former Scholz has suggested one-sidedly a reading reception,[115] whereas the position is more complex. He may correctly say that Rudolf's *Wer* refers to the individual reader, but this does not mean that the device indicates only a reading reception. Exactly the same is true of Wirnt's *Wigalois*, for which listeners as well as readers were anticipated.[116] With that our argument for this section has turned full circle.

With that we have also concluded our survey of ambiguous criteria for reception by reading. If reservations recur only in a minor key with Scholz, this is because he is too ready to assume that a written work presupposes readers, but also because he pays too little attention to criteria for works intended for two types of recipient. Taken together, these points amount to a neglect of the intermediate mode of reception. However, if a work presupposes readers as well as listeners this suggests that it might be possible to find less ambiguous pointers to the individual reader.

LESS AMBIGUOUS CRITERIA

(j) Recommendations to correct the text

Theoretically, the request to make a correction could proceed from someone, such as the patron, who had heard the work recited and was critical of a point, even though, in the case of a written work, the correction would have to be made by a literate individual, reading and then improving the text. In practice our examples show us authors concentrating on the literate aspect: the request proceeds from a reader, the literate status of the corrector is underlined, and reading or writing is mentioned, even in the case of works which may also have been meant for hearing. For these reasons I include this evidence under less ambiguous criteria for reading.

To this I know of only one exception, with which we begin. When Priester Eberhard suggests that whoever finds fault with his *Gandersheimer Reimchronik* has the right to improve upon it (1948: *is hir jemant, deme dit bok nicht behage, / et si under vrouwen, leien edder papen, / unde wil he von düsser rede eine betere maken* ...), we have to remember that there is no suggestion of readers and that there is a pointer to a recital for this work.[117] This is, however, the only case where a reference to correcting a text occurs in a work meant for listening rather than reading, for already in the *Braunschweigische Reimchronik*, where correcting the text appears to be placed in an oral context (96: *is ouch hi eman dher is ghehort / me habe, wan ik, odher baz, / dher sol ... richten min getihte*), we are dealing with a work for which readers were also expected.[118]

Elsewhere a literate reception is made unmistakably clear. This can be suggested when the act of correcting the text is associated with someone who is a reader. Otfrid sees his work as a written text which can be improved by having its faults cut out from it (v 25, 37 and 42), but the corrector is seen as a reader (v 25, 41: *joh hiar iz lísit thuruh gót*). Heinrich von Hesler announces his readiness to correct any faults in his *Apokalypse*[119] to those whom he specifies as readers (1319: ... *die diz buch / Lesen*). The same readiness is expressed in *Die Rede von den fünfzehn Graden* (158, 30ff.). Bruder Philipp requests those into whose hands his *Marienleben* might come to erase any untruth they may find in it (10094ff.)[120]

Where the potential corrector is not seen as a reader, he can be described as learned, therefore literate and qualified to improve a written text after studying it. Williram presents his *Hohes Lied* for improvement to those who are more learned (*Prologus* 41: *Opusculum hoc... doctioribus emendandum offero*) and whom he sees as readers (*Prologus* 24: *studioso lectori*; 37: *quivis legens*). Walther von Rheinau places his *Marienleben* in the hands of those who are learned enough to judge whether it conforms to the truth (12316: *Nu sî von mir diz büechelîn / Gesant dien, die gelêret sîn, / Und bitte si flîzeclich, / Ob die wârheit iender ich / Dar an übergangen habe, / Daz ir kunst daz widerstabe / Ald snîden ald verbrennen, / Swâ si den valsch erkennen*)[121] and sees their task as involving a preliminary reading of his book.[122] We are probably justified in understanding Johannes von Frankenstein's reference to the *klûge man* in the same way (*Der Kreuziger* 11467ff.). It is also part of the corrector's literate task when its scribal nature is stressed, even in a negative context, as when Konrad von Heimesfurt mentions the scribe's materials (*Urstende* 13: *... daz ich ez sô besniten habe / daz mir iemen iht dar abe / mit pumz oder mit mezzer / schabe und mir bezzer / in dem margine dâ bî / des in dem blate vergezzen sî*).[123]

On occasions the task of correction is left to someone else who can write poetry, but is specified as skilled or literate in one way or another. Hugo von Trimberg concludes his *Renner* by leaving it to such a person to improve his rhymes (24518f.), but sees him as literate: what he is to put right largely stems from the errors of scribes (24520: *schrîber unverstandenheit*) and therefore demands scribal knowledge from the corrector, who can be called *ein wîser man* (24607) in the context of reading (24602). If Otte, the author of *Eraclius*, who calls himself *ein gelerter man* (Prologue 140), grants leave to *die guoten tihtaere* to correct his work (Prologue 124ff.), we may feel confident that they were learned and able to perform this task in a literate way.

For the rest, an invitation to correct the author's written work occurs in three texts meant for a twofold reception, but in a context dealing with reading or writing. Albertus von Augsburg allows anyone qualified to improve his *Ulrichsleben* (1578ff.), but does this in the same context as his instructions how the reader is to solve the acrostic (1574ff.).[124] Heinrich von Kröllwitz grants similar leave to his audience (3975: *si ihtes dâ gebrochen, / des muget ir iuch irgezzen / und anders dar sezzen*), but the ability to 'put' something in place of what he has written (together with 40: *swer dise rede lesende sî*) suggests their literacy.[125] A similar remark by Könemann von Jerxheim (*Der Wurzgarten Mariens* 6528ff.) comes shortly before he addresses *Du leser* (6557).

With one exception (the *Gandersheimer Reimchronik*) this criterion is repeatedly tied to literacy, presupposing a written text subject to correction, but also a literate recipient in charge of the corrections and more clearly visible than with any of the criteria considered earlier.

(k) Acrostics and anagrams

We may agree with Scholz[126] that the acrostic is essentially a visual device, appealing to the eye and not the ear.[127] As Bertau, discussing Gottfried's acrostics in *Tristan*, engagingly says: 'Wie die Liebe, nach der zeitgenössischen Theorie, geht dieser Klang nämlich durch das Auge in Herz und Ohr; denn er wendet sich nicht an ein hörendes, sondern an ein lesendes Ohr.'[128] He points out that with Gottfried we can hear the stanzas with their rhymes, but not the initial letters which constitute the acrostic.[129] If this is true of the acrostic, Scholz concludes, the same must be true of works which make use of it: they too are meant for the eye of a reader.[130] If we stress this visual dimension of the acrostic we must be aware how this device differs from the visual conjunction of text with illustration, which we placed among the ambiguous criteria. An illustration could be shown to listeners who, even if illiterate, could grasp something of its meaning as it was explained to them, but the same is not true of acrostics, the solution and appreciation of which involve letters, their combination in a novel way, and reading, from all of which an illiterate was excluded by definition.

Understandably, the three works whose authors give instructions about the acrostics they employ all refer to the literate dimension. Albertus von Augsburg conceals his name in an opening acrostic (*Ulrichsleben* 1ff.) and refers his audience to it at the close of his work (1574: *Swer wizzen welle sinen namen / der sol setzen ze samen / an dem ersten blate die buoch staben / die die roten varwe haben*).[131] Only the literate can read these letters and put them together to produce a new meaning. By not having his acrostic altogether at one point, but by spacing it over a succession of chapters, each of which begins with the relevant letter, Ebernand von Erfurt illustrates Bertau's point that an acrostic cannot be made apparent by a reciter addressing an audience, but can only be grasped by a reader able to refer to the beginning of each chapter.[132] Ebernand also confirms that it is the reader he has in mind (*Heinrich und Kunigunde* 4453: *ist der leser kluoc, / hât er an kunste die gefuoc, / er lese die houbtbuochstabe / von êrst wan an daz ende herab, / darmit die verse erhaben sint*). An acrostic is also employed in *Die Erlösung* (1771ff.) and instructions are given on how to read it (1837: *Wer die houbitbûchstabe / von oben an biz niden abe / ordenlîchen lesen kan, / dâ schouwet unde sihet man / in kriechen, in latînen / gar ordenlîche erschînen / dise namen grundelôs*). What is stressed here is not merely the visual dimension (*schouwen, sehen, erschînen*) which this device shares with the conjunction of text with illustration, but more particularly aspects of the reading process (*houbitbûchstabe, lesen*).[133]

These three works can be explicit in their instructions to readers because their authors all anticipate a twofold reception,[134] including therefore readers who may cope with the acrostics, whereas the instructions must have passed over the heads of listeners who were not also readers. This twofold reception is true of the other cases where acrostics occur in German works up to about 1300:[135] although Scholz discusses most of them, he does not dwell on this point and the presence of readers which it implies. If these works differ from the three just considered in giving no instructions, this suggests readers who could be expected to pick up the acrostics without any mention in the text, possibly because they were made apparent in the manuscript, as is the case with Otfrid's telestichs (they are written in capitals and moved over into the right-hand margin, where they stand out and can be read vertically more easily.)[136] One further work, *Die sieben Tagzeiten* of Hartwig von dem Hage, includes an acrostic giving the author's name (1ff.), but no instructions.

If we assume the same mode of reception for this work as for his *Margaretenlegende*, the suggestion of individual readers for the legend would imply them also for the acrostic.[137] Finally, the *Willehalm* of Ulrich von dem Türlin stands quite alone with its acrostic, but only because there is no clear evidence for its mode of reception, whether for listeners or for readers.[138] The evidence of all the other works should incline us to think that here, too, acrostics and readers belong closely together.

Scholz's view about the second formal device (he claims that only readers can ascertain the presence of an anagram)[139] can be confirmed by what two authors of a *Tristan* romance say about how an anagram, behind which the hero hoped to conceal his name, was resolved. With Heinrich von Freiberg Tristan hides behind the name Peilnetosî when he returns disguised to Marke's court, and mutters the word *Tosî* to himself. Isold 'decodes' these names by reading them backwards: 5332 (*Isôt die küneginne kluoc / den namen widersinnes las . . . / Isôtenliep sie drinne vant*) and 5366 (*sie greif aber an daz ort / des wortes unde las hin wider; / dô vant sie verborgen sider, / als ir wîsheit gebôt / ir selbes namen Isôt*). What lies behind Isold being called *kluoc* and gifted with *wîsheit* is made clear when an enemy likewise decodes Tristan's assumed name (5539: *Pfelerîn geléret was; / den namen er widersinnes las, / dô wart der name im rechte bekant, / Isôtenliep er drinne vant*), for *geléret* is used in the sense 'educated' and therefore 'literate'. No reading of an actual text is involved here, *lesen* means mental reading, based on a literate's awareness of individual letters and the possibility of rearranging them to produce a new sense. Gottfried's Tristan conceals himself even more primitively under the name Tantris, but Isold 'breaks this code' because chance has led her to compare the minstrel Tantris with the Tristan of whom she has heard (10115: *nu geviel si an die buochstabe, / dâ man si beide schephet abe, / und vant in disem al zehant / die selben, die si in jenem vant. / nu begunde s'an in beiden / die sillaben scheiden;* 10124: *vür sich sô las si Tristan, / her wider sô las si Tantris*). Again the process of solving the anagram is seen as literate: Isold reads the names, sees them in terms of letters and syllables.[140]

If these two authors imply that the ability to resolve an anagram is a literate skill (operating with the letters and syllables which make up words), this may be confirmed in reverse by the position in oral cultures. Lord says of an illiterate singer asked for impossible precision: 'When asked what a word is, he will reply that he does not know, or he will give a sound group which may vary in length from what we call a word to an entire line of poetry, or even an entire song. The word for "word" means an "utterance".'[141] Lest we suspect that what applies to oral-formulaic poetry may not be true of oral poetry at large, similar testimony is forthcoming from elsewhere. Havelock reminds us that in Greek neither *epos* nor *logos* originally meant the separated word,[142] and that syllabic or alphabetic writing depends on 'atomising' linguistic sound into abstract components,[143] which were therefore grasped as such in oral culture only at the stage when a script was being evolved. This process of abstraction has also been stressed by Coulmas.[144] When the actors in the *Tristan* romances break down names into syllables and letters they are doing what is possible for them as literates and inaccessible to members of an oral society.

For Gottfried's work von Kraus has proposed an anagrammatic game of hide-and-seek in the prologue.[145] If we accept this, our reasons may include the fact that this part of his work is marked out by acrostics, but also the consideration that, in later demonstrating how Isold deciphers the name Tantris, the author presupposes an audience possibly acquainted with this literate device. The same must hold good of the *Braunschweigische Reimchronik* if there was any chance of the necessary groups of letters being read out of vv. 53ff. to produce the name of the patron (*in Brunswich hertzoghe Albrecht dher erste*),[146] a task which the author could expect from the readers for whom his work was intended[147] just as much as Gottfried could from the literate members of his audience. Otto von Freising, the author of the *Laubacher Barlaam*, includes an anagram allusion to himself at the close of his work (16678ff.) which, as long as we can accept vv. 13f. (... *daz ez ein iegelîcher man / wol vernimet der iht lesen kan*) as referring to his own work, would also tie this device to a reading reception.[148]

(l) Physical contact with the book

Under this heading I include two types of reference which, as regards German material, Scholz has discussed desultorily: the situation of an individual reading to himself presupposed whenever he is said to take a book in his hands or sit with it in his lap.[149] It is conceivable that a book could have been picked up by an illiterate, who could admire any pictures, gaze wonderingly and uncomprehendingly at the closed world of the text, or even receive it as a patron before ordering it to be recited aloud. Yet these situations are not what primarily interested the medieval author, for he was more concerned with the reception of his written work, involving either the reciter or the individual reader, i.e. *lesen* in either of its two main senses. We shall see that the examples where someone takes a book in his hands all suggest that the reader was primarily envisaged (he was more important to the author than the reciter).[150] The position is no different where a person is depicted with a book in his lap: this suggests a longer preoccupation with the book than an illiterate looking at it without understanding. With both types all our examples suggest an individual reader, first in terms of a reading situation described in the narrative and then with regard to the reception of the author's own work.

When Otfrid depicts Mary reading the psalter at the Annunciation (I 5, 10: *mit sálteru in hénti, then sáng si*) the traditional privacy of this scene means that she is reading to herself, not to others.[151] Veldeke describes how Eneas found the Sibyl alone (*Eneide* 2714: *ein buc hadde si an der hant, / dar ane sach si unde las*), where the conjunction of *lesen* with *sehen* stresses the visual more than any acoustic dimension.[152] Hartmann's Gregorius is given the tablet on which he reads the secrets of his birth (*Gregorius* 1744: ... *unde gap im in die hant / sîne tavel, daz er las / wie allem sînem dinge was*): he may read this in the company of the abbot, but the way in which their conversation is resumed (1756ff.) suggests that he read to himself, not to the abbot who already knew the content of the tablet. Wolfram's Sigune resembles Otfrid's Mary in holding a psalter in her hands for devotional reading in solitude (*Parzival* 438, 1: *Si truoc ein salter in der hant*), whilst the reading attributed to Wirnt von Grafenberg by Konrad von Würzburg is secular, but just as solitary (*Der Welt Lohn* 52: *Sus saz der hôchgelobte / in einer kemenâten ... und haete ein buoch in sîner hant, / dar an er âventiure vant / von der minne geschriben*). These examples from within the narrative suggest the possibility of individual reading whenever an author uses this phrase of the reception of his own work, especially since there is further evidence that a reader was foreseen. Addressing his book, Thomasin sees it coming into someone's hands to be read frequently (*Der welsche Gast* 14705: *... unz du dem kumest ze hant / dem du wirst lîht baz erkant / und der dich dicke überlist*).[153] The author of *Unser Vrouwen Klage*, who anticipated readers and listeners,[154] had the former in mind when he hoped for frequent use (128: *ir sult ez dicke nemen zehant, / sô mügent ir goes minne / erkennen wol dar inne*). When the clerical author of *Der Saelden Hort* sees his work in opposition to the claims of court literature, he imagines these secular works in written form in the hands of the women addressed (4407: *fúr Wigoleis, Tristanden / in megten, witwen handen / den usser welten dinen / ez tuo lutzellig schinen!*).[155] Finally, Bruder Philipp equates those into whose hands his *Marienleben* may come (10095: *... den ditz buoch ze handen kumt*) with those who read it (10116: *alle die an disem buoche / lesent*).

The second type of situation (a person sits with a book in his lap) was already present in Konrad's sketch of Wirnt reading to himself: he had the book in his hands, but we also have to link his seated position (52: *Sus saz*) with v. 58 (*dar obe haete er dô vertriben / den tag*) for a complete picture of the reader bent over his text. A similar scene is depicted in *Reinfried von Braunschweig* (21300ff.)[156] and in the *Göttweiger Trojanerkrieg* (319: *... Da er ob ainem büch sass / Und von astromyen lass*).[157] In view of these examples within the narrative and the link with the first type of situation provided by Wirnt we may take the use of the same phrase with regard to the author's own work as a pointer to a reading reception. Thomasin reinforces this mode of reception by imagining his work in the lap of someone who peruses it unhurriedly (14692: *wan dich sol ein biderbe man / müezeclîchen an gesehen: / sitze ûf sîn schôz*).[158] Both types of reference in this section suggest not merely a text in book form, but also an individual reading it to himself.

LEXICAL EVIDENCE

From now on we shall largely be concerned with *lesen* and how far it could be used to indicate someone reading to himself (whether silently or aloud is for the moment beside the point, since what concerns us is the possibility of individual reading, not its manner). In Chapter 3 we considered this verb in a different sense (to read aloud or recite to others) indicated when a verbal pointer was added, such as *lesen* governing a dative object, *lesen* + *vor*, or in conjunction with an adverb like *offenlîche*, to name only these. Theoretically it might be possible to argue that where we encounter *lesen* without additional pointers to public recital the verb means 'to read to oneself'. Unfortunately, this easy way out is blocked to us by the fact that *lesen* could be used by itself to convey reciting aloud to others.[159] In other words, the verb *lesen* is essentially ambiguous: it could mean 'to recite to others', but it can also be used of the individual reading to himself. We need not be surprised by the lack of semantic clarity in this vernacular word, for the same is also true of Latin *legere*: John of Salisbury was conscious enough of its ambiguity to propose a distinction between *legere* and *prelegere*,[160] whilst Hugh of St Victor distinguished three meanings for the noun *lectio*.[161]

A comparable ambiguity exists with *lesen* in medieval German, one which it is not always possible to resolve. A difficulty confronts us even in those apparently clearcut cases where the conjunction of *lesen* with the noun *munt* seems to imply reading aloud to others. At times the context gives us the clarity we need, as in Wolfram's *Parzival* when Queen Guinevere reads a letter (650, 23: *er gap der küneginne den brief, / des manec ouge über lief, / dô ir süezer munt gelas / al daz dran geschriben was*), for if those standing around weep over its content, this implies that she read the letter aloud for them to hear. The position is not always so unambiguous, especially if we take into account the medieval practice of an individual reading to himself, but aloud and therefore using his *munt*.[162] This renders ambiguous the meaning of certain hyperbolic phrases used by Wolfram of Condwiramurs (224, 12: ... *daz munt von wîbe nie gelas / noch sus gesagte maere, / diu schoenr und bezzer waere*) or of Ither (315, 14: '*wan munt von rîter nie gelas, / der pflaeg sô ganzer werdekeit*'). With phrases like these it is uncertain whether the surpassing of a literary model concerns texts which the addressee may have read himself (but aloud) or heard in recital. The position is no clearer in a work of a different nature, in the *Pariser Tagezeiten* (2482: *Waz alle wisheit ist gewesen, / Daz alle meister hant gelesen, / Waz wiser muont noch ie gelas, / Die schrifte alle erfuollit waz*), for we are left in doubt whether *muont* ... *gelas* is in parallel with *hant gelesen* (individual reading) or in contrast to it (reading to others). The question is rendered even more open by the fact that the author of the *Pariser Tagezeiten*, like Wolfram in *Parzival*, saw his own work as being either read or heard.[163]

The ambiguity of *lesen*, even when the addition of *munt* might promise help, forces us to look for other indicators. In the following sections I discuss, first, examples from within the narrative and then cases where the phrase is applied to the reception of the author's own work.

(m) *Lesen* + reflexive dative

In Chapter 3 we saw that one criterion for hearing was the construction *lesen* + dative object.[164] At this point we must specify this more precisely: where the indirect object (in the dative) is grammatically a different person from the subject of *lesen* we have the situation of someone reading to someone else, a recital from a written text. However, where the indirect object is the same person as the subject (i.e. where we have a reflexive construction) the situation is of someone reading to himself, withdrawn from the collective context of public recital to a solitary communion with the text. It is irrelevant whether this reading takes place silently, in a whisper, or aloud — what counts is the fact of an individual reading to himself.

A good example is supplied by the Benedictine Rule, especially where provision is made for a regular programme of reading by each monk by himself. When this reading is mentioned after the meal at the sixth hour it is described as reading to oneself and by oneself (*aut forte qui voluerit legere sibi*).¹⁶⁵ How this was meant to be by oneself is made clear by what follows (*sic legat ut alium non inquietet*) – by reading to oneself silently or softly one reads by oneself, withdrawing from the others in their cells and therefore not disturbing them. This construction *legere sibi* has its counterpart in various MHG versions of the Rule, as in the Hohenfurth version (75, 8: ... *oder der da lese wolle. der lese ime also. daz er einin anderin icht vnrvwic mache*).¹⁶⁶ The position can be made clearer when, in addition to the reflexive, *selbe* is also used, for we shall see that this is another pointer to reading by oneself. An example of this fuller construction is given by the Asbach text (154, 8: *oder der leiht lesen welle. der les im selben also. daz er einen andern niht vnrvowe*).¹⁶⁷

It might be thought that these examples from the German *Benediktinerregel* have been dictated by the Latin original, but this is unlikely to be the whole story since we also find this construction, applied to the reception of their own works, with such (admittedly monastic) authors as Otfrid and Notker. Otfrid uses the reflexive to address someone who is to read to himself, not a reciter who is to read to others (II 3, 68: *so thu thir hiar nu lesan scalt*; Hartmuat 125: *Lís thir in then lívolon thaz sélba, theih thir rédinon*).¹⁶⁸ Like the *Benediktinerregel*, but independently of it, he can reinforce this with *selbo* (III 19, 16: *selbo lísist thu thir tház*; IV 28, 18: *zi zéllenn ist iz láng, in wár; lis thir sélbo iz rehto thár*).¹⁶⁹ Employing the verb *sehan* instead of *lesan*, but combining it with the vocative use of *lector*, Notker, too, reinforces the reflexive with *selbo* (*Psalter* 685, 8: *Sih dir selbo lector uuio Augustinus ...*). A *lector* who is to read for himself must be seen as an individual reader rather than as a reciter performing before others.¹⁷⁰

(n) *Lesen + selber*

The use of this pointer, which could be combined with a reflexive construction to suggest individual reading, can be illustrated from the *Margaretenleben* of Wetzel von Bernau, in which the saint intercedes with God on behalf of those who preoccupy themselves with her legend (1054: '*wer von mir gerne höret lesen / oder selber liset den lausse in din riche*'). Those who have learned about her example are divided into those who listen to it recited and those who read it for themselves (in a context like this the author is not concerned with the solitary reciter, but with as wide a range of his audience as possible). If *selber* provides emphasis here, it highlights the reader by contrast with the listener.¹⁷¹

A parallel construction is *schríben + selber*, as with Pfaffe Lamprecht's *Alexanderlied* (Vorau version 1129: *Diz sazte man dô allez an einen brief, / daz was dem chunige Alexander lieb. / er screib in selbe mit siner hant*) or *Herzog Ernst B* (318: *mit sîn selbes hant er schreip / einen brief*). What lies behind this construction and that with *lesen* is that in a largely illiterate society in which reading and writing were performed by professionals it was necessary to point out the infrequent occasions when a non-professional did either. In a clerical context where, as in a monastery, individual reading coexisted with recital the stress conveyed by *selber* can point to the former.

The vernacular construction *lesen* + *selber* has a Latin counterpart. William of Malmesbury, talking of the leisure hours of Robert of Gloucester, says: *aut ipsi legere, aut legentes possitis audire.*[172] This parallels the vernacular phrasing in Wetzel's *Margaretenleben*: the act of individual reading is emphasised, and as in the legend William is not concerned with the reciter (he did not picture the earl demeaning himself by taking over this task at his court),[173] but with an aristocrat as occasional reader, even though there might be flattery in that. Another way in Latin to indicate individual reading is to combine a verb for reading with *per se*. The threefold definition of *lectio* given by Hugh of St Victor defines private reading (*lego librum*) as the act of *per se inspicientis*,[174] whilst for John of Salisbury the same activity is characteristic of *per se scrutantis scripturas*.[175] *Per se* suggests greater privacy, while *ipse* or *selber* highlights the reader as opposed to the listener.

German examples can be explicit about what lies behind this highlighting. When Marsilie in the *Rolandslied* reads a letter from Karl (2113: *selbe er den brief las*), the context makes it clear that he must have read it first to himself, since he only then communicates its content to his followers (2116ff.). The use of *selbe* does more than indicate that he read to himself, however, it also hints at why he was able to dispense with a scribe reading to him, for in the next line we are told: *wande er wole geléret was* (2114), where *geléret* means 'educated' and therefore 'literate', as in Der Stricker's corresponding passage (*Karl der Große* 2627: *selbe er den brief las, / wan er diu buoch geléret was*). The position is slightly different in the *Tristan* of Heinrich von Freiberg, where the hero receives a message sent by Arthur, first in an oral communication by the messenger, then in the letter which he hands to him. About the latter we are told (1408: *der wol geléret Tristant / an den brieven selber las, / daz alle die rede wâr was, / die der knappe het gesaget*). Here Tristan is able to read to himself without assistance because he is literate, but *selber* also stresses that he reads for himself to confirm what the messenger has just announced by word of mouth. The use of a letter to confirm what a messenger says orally is also illustrated in the *Alexandreis* of Ulrich von Etzenbach, when Candacis receives a messenger with a letter (20271: *dô er vür die frouwen kam / und sie die brieve genam, / dô gienc die saelden rîche / an ir heimelîche, / die schrift selbe sie besach* ...). In place of *lesen* Ulrich uses another visual verb for the queen's reading, but by placing this in the seclusion of a room apart, rather than in full view of the messenger, he implies that Candacis read to herself.[176] The same need for confidentiality which only private reading can guarantee is expressed in Konrad von Würzburg's *Partonopier und Meliur*, where a messenger is dispatched with strict instructions on delivering a letter (4772ff.). The use of *gehoeren* with *lesen* here may be metaphorical ('to learn by reading') or suggest reading aloud to oneself, but of the privacy of the reading there can be no doubt.

Applied to the reception of the author's own work, this construction occurs infrequently. Apart from the *Margaretenleben* of Wetzel von Bernau, it is only Otfrid and Notker who employ it at all significantly. Otfrid makes use of it to reinforce the reflexive construction with *lesan* (III 13, 43: *thaz zellu ih híar nu bi thíu, / thaz thu thir sélbo leses thár thaz séltsana wuntar*), where the emphasis provided by *selbo*, as in the examples concerning a message, implies a differentiation between hearing and reading: what the author (anticipating a recital to listeners) has just told them may be read for themselves by some.[177] The same differentiation is made in IV 28, 17 (*Sagen mág man thes ginúag, wio alt giscríb er thes giwúag; / zi zéllenn ist iz láng in wár; lis thir sélbo iz rehto thár*), for what the author himself says is only a fraction of the whole, which may be read up individually. The example from Notker likewise reinforces a reflexive dative construction (*Psalter* 685, 8: *Sih dir selbo lector uuio Augustinus* . . .). Again, *lesan* is replaced by another verb of seeing and *selbo* emphasises that the reader should do his own further reading, outside the oral context of the classroom.

(o) *Lesen, sehen, schouwen*

The last example from Notker suggests that in the predominantly visual dimension of reading *lesen* could be associated with, or even replaced by, a verb of seeing (*sehen, schouwen*). Where the visual dimension is emphasised in this way we may suspect reading rather than the acoustic dimension of public recital, a contrast which can be exemplified from Wolfram's *Parzival* and *Die Heidin*. In the former case Guinevere's reading of a letter brings tears to the eyes of bystanders (650, 24: *des manec ouge über lief*) because they hear what she reads aloud, with her mouth (650, 25: *ir süezer munt gelas*). In the latter case, where no bystanders are mentioned, the eyes that weep are those of the reader (2. *und 3. Redaktion* 1005: *Mit weinden ougen si daz las, / Dar an alsô geschriben was*). To reinforce the idea of reading by mentioning eyes (or seeing) has different implications from associating it with the mouth (or speech).

Of the Sibyl in Veldeke's *Eneide* who has a book in her hands for reading it is said (2715): *dar ane sach si ende las*, and the same is said of Eneas reading a love-letter (10933: *Du he'ne gesach ende gelas / dat dar ane geschreven was*). When Jans Enikel describes how he studied his source-material in Vienna (*Fürstenbuch* 1091: *dô las ichz unde hânz gesehen*), *sehen* in such a double formula does not mean simply 'see, look at' (no amount of mere looking at a manuscript would have acquainted a reader with its content), but instead reinforces the visual dimension of private reading. The same is true of the *Urstende* of Konrad von Heimesfurt, where the religious testimony of Leoncius and Karicius is tested by having them write down their respective accounts 'in examination conditions', in isolation from one another, with the result that when compared they are found to be miraculously identical, a state of affairs which would make a modern examiner suspicious. Comparing these two versions (1686: *dô man die schouwet unde las*) must have involved a critical correlation, so that *schouwen* strengthens *lesen* and means more than 'to look'. The association of *lesen* with the eyes for highly private, secret reading is present when Hartmann's Gregorius reads the tablet with the shameful facts about his birth (2282: . . . *an der er tegelîchen las / sîn süntlîche sache / den ougen ze ungemache*), for he consults the tablet in a hiding-place (2277ff.). Ulrich von Etzenbach gives an example of privacy in reading when he describes how Aristander, up early while others are still asleep (*Alexandreis* 23449f.), reads in his room by the window (23451ff.), is distracted by a woman in the garden and has to turn his eyes away and back to his book (23463: *der meister die frouwe gerne sach, / doch er die ougen von ir brach / und sazt sich ze dem buoche wider*). Of course, the eyes are also involved whenever someone reads aloud to others, but for the recipients the reciter's mouth is more important than his eyes, which is why Wolfram mentions her mouth as Guinevere reads aloud. Where the eyes are mentioned instead and where the context points in the same direction we may assume individual reading.

To illustrate that this phrasing can suggest that an author envisaged a reception of this kind for his work we may turn again to Heinrich von Veldeke, who uses *sehen ende lesen* of the Sibyl and Eneas within his narrative, but also employs a variant when he describes how the countess of Cleves read his unfinished manuscript (*Eneide* 13445: *he le et einer vrouwen / dore lesen ende dore scouwen / ere men't volschreve*). Schwietering rejects the idea that *scouwen* might here suggest looking at the pictures of an illustrated manuscript and sees it instead as reinforcing *lesen*.[178] The occasion for Veldeke to lend his copy was provided by wedding festivities at Cleves, a context in which public recital was likely, as is also the possibility that Veldeke's patron may have brought the manuscript and the poet with him to Cleves as a form of self-advertisement on so public an occasion.[179] If we accept this, then it is conceivable that the countess first heard the work recited which she wished to read for herself at greater leisure and that we face here a situation which we shall encounter with Wolfram's *Parzival*: the act of reading for oneself arises out of public recital.[180] When Veldeke stresses the visual dimension (*lesen*, but also *scouwen*) he draws attention to the countess doing for herself what for others was performed by the reciter. This emphasis is comparable with the conjunction of *lesan* with *selbo* with Otfrid and Notker, who likewise imply a reader acting for himself after listening to a reading of the work. Whereas in their case the recommendation to the reader proceeds from the author, in the situation at Cleves the initiative apparently lay with the countess.

Other examples of individual reading are given by Priester Wernher (*Maria* A 138: ... *daz ez alle mugen lesen / die gotes chint wesen / vnd auch mugen schowen / phaffen, layen, vrowen*), where the clause with *lesen* parallells that with *schowen*, and by the author of *Die Erlösung*, who sums up the action of the reader in resolving his acrostic by using the verb *lesen*,[181] but also *dâ schouwet unde sihet man* (1839f.). Particular importance attaches to a passage in the *Rede vom heiligen Glauben* of Der Arme Hartmann, who refers to the reception of his work in more detail (95, 7: *iz ist alliz gescriben / ze gehorenne unde ze gesihte in dutiscer scrifte. / swer daz buch wille lesen* ...).[182] Here the visual dimension of reading is underlined by linking *lesen* with a verbal noun (*gesiht*) as well as by their contrast with the acoustic dimension (*gehoren*).

So far we have been concerned with cases where *lesen* is reinforced by the addition of a visual term to suggest reading to and for oneself, but there are examples where *sehen* and *schouwen* can be employed without *lesen* in that sense. For example, whether or not he expects any potential reader to follow up what he says, Veldeke claims that a detail in his account may also be found in the Latin *Vita* which is his source for *Servatius*, but uses sometimes the verb 'to see' in this context (e.g. 3130: *alse men in siner viten sit*), and sometimes the verb 'to read' (e.g. 460: *di di vite hebben gelesen*).[183] A similar equation of *sehen* with *lesen* is present when Thomasin makes use of Gregory the Great's distinction between cleric and layman (1103: *der pfaffe sehe die schrift an / sô sol der ungelêrte man / diu bilde sehen*), for the point of this contrast is that, whereas the illiterate layman can only look at pictures, the cleric actually reads, which is the force of *ansehen* here. The same is true in Gottfried's *Tristan* when Isold reads what has been carved on the chips of wood (14677: *Isôt diu vie si und sach sie an, / si las Isôt, si las Tristan*), for *ansehen* is an integral part of reading, as is the case with *schouwen* in *Wolfdietrich A* (201, 2: '*habt ir den brief geschouwet, saget uns waz stêt dar an*'), where the verb means more than just 'look at' if the content of the letter is now known. When Ulrich von Etzenbach sums up Alexander's reaction on reading[184] a letter from Darius (5547: *Dô Alexander gesach / die schrift, der im der brief verjach, / der drô er lützel erkam*), *gesehen* implies that he has taken in its meaning (he recognises that the letter constitutes a threat).

We may now turn to cases where the author's work is involved. When Gottfried recommends that a point can be confirmed from an earlier passage (8741: *und als daz maere hie vor giht, / der dâ vor an daz maere siht*), he is making a precise back-reference (7208ff.) the point of which would be lost if it did not involve actual reading of the earlier passage and collation with the present one. Thomasin, when he conceives his work as resting in the potential reader's lap,[185] uses the verb *schouwen* of this reader's activity (14667ff.) and a little later equates this with reading (14677ff.).

Finally, another visual substitute for *lesen* is the phrase *geschriben sehen*, used not in the sense of seeing or registering something in written form, but of actually reading it. A general example is provided by Veldeke's *Servatius*, where the author makes a reference to his source[186] on one occasion with *also alse ich't geschreven sach* (1560) and on another with *alse ich et las* (4808).[187] A similar parallel is provided by what Wolfram says about Kyot consulting his written source, for this can be expressed either by *geschriben sehen* (*Parzival* 416, 26: *der dise âventiur von Parzivâl / heidensch geschriben sach*) or by *lesen* (431, 2: *ich sage iu als Kyôt las*).[188] Applied to the author's own work the same construction is used in *Parzival* of the ladies whom Wolfram imagines as potential readers (337, 1: ... *swelch sinnec wîp, / ob si hât getriwen lîp, / diu diz maere geschriben siht*),[189] but also, for example, by Rudolf von Ems of someone qualified to assess his *Alexander* by reading the Latin sources on which it is dependent (8059: *daz beide der und der iht jehe, / der die latîne geschriben sehe, / ez sî ein künstelôser man / der des getihtes êrst began*). This comparative task involves close reading, no mere looking at a written text.

(p) *Lesen oder hoeren*

The passage by Der Arme Hartmann which we looked at (*Die Rede vom heiligen Glauben* 95, 7ff.) has far wider implications than the context within which we considered it, since it is chronologically in German literature the first example of something resembling the double formula *lesen oder hoeren*. If this is sometimes varied by *sehen oder hoeren* this need not surprise us after what we have just seen, whilst the variation between *oder* or *unde* is a point to which we shall come back later.[190] We have already looked at this double formula with regard to *hoeren* (suggesting the possibility of hearing a recital),[191] but we must now, as earlier with *legere aut audire*,[192] turn this formula round to consider *lesen*. Theoretically, two possibilities exist.

The first is to take *lesen* in the sense 'to read out, recite'. In this case the formula refers to two simultaneous and complementary poles of the recital situation: the reciter reads out and/or the audience listens. This has been suggested by Kartschoke: 'Ich sehe keinen Grund, weshalb wir die sehr häufige Doppelform "hoeren unde/oder lesen" nicht auf Vorleser und Zuhörer bzw. natürlich auch die – aber wie weit verbreitete? – mehrfache Rezeptionsmöglichkeit sollten beziehen können'.[193] By mentioning the second possibility as an afterthought and by questioning how widespread it may have been Kartschoke conveys the impression that he finds the first more convincing, as is confirmed when he quotes the *Gandersheimer Reimchronik* (881: *we et lese edde sitte darbi*) as a reference to reciter and listeners ('Vorleser und Hörer').[194] That may be so,[195] but the fact remains that this particular conjunction of reciter with listeners is *not* expressed by the formula which concerns us. We might argue in the opposite direction (although examples are so rare that it is difficult to reach a decision) that wherever the transmitter of a work (i.e. the reciter), rather than the recipient, has to be expressed by this formula an additional pointer is called for. This is suggested by the manner in which the two types of recipient and the reciter are summed up in the *Jüngerer Titurel* (6077, 4: *diez lesen oder hoeren, und der iz sag oder in dem done singe*) or by the fact that when in the *Stadtbuch von Augsburg* the formula happens to be used of a public reading this has to be indicated by the addition of *offenlich* (293 (41): *das dise erkantnüs alle iare uff weyhennachten in dem grossen rate offenlich verlesen und verhoert werden sol*).[196] If such additions are called for to make clear the position suggested by Kartschoke we need to hesitate before accepting his reading of the double formula as an overall explanation.

The other interpretation of the double formula is to take *lesen* in the sense 'to read for oneself'. In this case the formula refers to two alternative modes of reception, at different times and in different circumstances: an audience listens to a recital, but some have the opportunity of reading the text for themselves. Scholz nowhere faces this or discusses the formula systematically, and we have seen that Kartschoke plays down its importance in favour of the first interpretation. To anticipate the next stage in the argument: I regard the double formula as referring to two alternative modes of reception. If we accept this, then in the cases where the double formula is employed *lesen* is used in the sense 'to read for oneself'.[197] With the rise of this formula two modes of reception were envisaged, whereas previously oral tradition had involved only reception by ear.

(q) The individual reader

Up to now we have been concerned with *lesen* to indicate the activity of someone reading for himself, but have not looked at the individual reader himself. Nor have we considered reasons why *lesen* should be seen in terms of individual reading, rather than in the sense of reading to others.

In a religious context the individual reader must be assumed whenever private devotions and the reading which accompanied them are mentioned, as in *Die Klage* (3682: *Uote diu vrouwe hêre / ze Lôrse in ir hûse was, / dâ si venjete unde las / an ir salter alle ir tagezît*). Although Uote may have said her devotions aloud or murmured them, it makes no sense, in view of their private nature, to imagine them addressed to anyone but God. Solitary reading is also suggested in the case of literature which, although conceivably secular, has a religious dimension, as when Brandan is subjected to divine punishment for refusing to believe the geographical miracles which are an aspect of God's omnipotence. Brandan's reading is for himself: he consults out-of-the-way books (*Sanct Brandan* 21f., 26) and reads them for his own purposes (44: *er enwolde noch enmohte / des iht geloubic wesen / wie er ez hette gelesen*). In a secular context Thomasin recommends the man who cannot understand what is intellectually profound to content himself with reading court romances (1107: *daz selbe sol tuon ein man / der tiefe sinne niht verstên kan, / der sol die âventiure lesen*). They may be regarded as second best, but at least they are presented as reading-matter.[198] How secluded such individual reading can be, even in a secular context, is suggested by Konrad von Würzburg's sketch of Wirnt von Grafenberg reading a work of court literature (*Der Welt Lohn* 52ff.). He holds the book in his hand and bends over it to read it, but spends the day doing this in a private room (53: *in einer kemenâten*).

Acquaintance with such reading-matter as the result of individual reading is suggested whenever the author appeals to the literary knowledge and interests of an audience whom he regards as readers. Gottfried feels confident enough to make such an appeal concerning a detail (2016: *diz maere, der daz ie gelas, / der erkennet sich wol, daz der nam / dem lebene was gehellesam*),[199] whilst Rudolf von Ems can assume with his audience a similar reading knowledge of Gottfried's work (*Alexander* 3159: *sîn Tristan! swer den ie gelas ...*). Rudolf can also recommend his audience to read a version of *Cligés* (*Willehalm von Orlens* 4390: *Das hat min frünt her Uolrich / Von Turham mit wishait / An Clies wîslich gesait. / Das sol man lesen!*), whilst Ottokar's *Österreichische Reimchronik* contains a similar recommendation to read *Tristan* (19919: *swer des kunde welle hân, / der sol Tristramen lesen*). No matter how uncertain it may be whether the author expected these suggestions to be followed up, merely to make them implies the practice of reading romances, however restricted.

These readers can be addressed in a number of ways, but whereas our task up to now has been to isolate evidence for the reader by distinguishing him from the listener, from now on our problem will be to suggest reasons why the individual reader is addressed rather than the reciter reading aloud to others. We saw that *leser* could indicate this reciter, but there are also cases where the individual reader must be meant. In early monastic literature the term for reader may occur in Latin even with a vernacular work. In his letter to Liutbert, even though he also uses *legentes* in the sense of those who recite his work orally,[200] Otfrid employs the same word to denote the individual reader, for with Patzlaff it makes little sense to say that the meaning of the text should be made clear to the reciter (*Liut.* 86: *ut legentibus (quod lectio signat) apertior fiat*) if the reciter is not at the same time seen as a recipient.[201] If the sense 'reader' were not meant here we should expect something like *audienti-*

bus instead. The author of the *Praefatio* to the *Heliand* similarly mentions *lector*, saying that the chapters of the work have been equipped with headings so that an episode may be found more easily (*Ut vero studiosi lectoris intentio facilius quaeque ut gesta sunt possit invenire, singulis sententiis ... annotata sunt*). On this Kartschoke comments that *studiosus* implies a careful reader who wishes to learn more, not simply a *lector* in the sense of 'reciter',[202] but even if the latter were involved we should still have to apply to him what Patzlaff has said of Otfrid's *legentes*: that he is regarded here in terms of his function as a reader. When Notker recommends the reader of his psalter to consult Augustine he addresses him as *lector* (685, 8: *Sih dir selbo lector uuio Augustinus*),[203] a term glossed by the vernacular *léso*, whilst Williram refers in the prologue to his reader as *studioso lectori* (and as *quivis legens*).[204] That an individual reader is likely here is confirmed by the reference to an earlier point marked by the sign X.

Elsewhere the reader is designated in the vernacular as *leser*. Ebernand von Erfurt gives instructions about his acrostics to one whom he qualifies (*Heinrich und Kunigunde* 4453: *ist der leser kluoc*). We have seen that this is the task of a reader and in this case it is impossible to imagine a reciter reading out acrostics spread over sixty-one chapters in the work. Albertus von Augsburg, in telling his reader that he will learn something more elsewhere (1206: *fuore baz wirt daz deme lesêre kunt*), may have taken this from his source,[205] but we cannot on that score dismiss the reader, who is also implied in the *Ulrichsleben* by acrostics. The same argument can be used of the *Rheinisches Marienlob*, whose author refrains from giving further details in order not to tax his reader unduly (4699: *wan ich möcht den leser besweren*), for here too the presence of acrostics points to individual reading.

In other cases, with a variant of the double formula, the author can see his audience as made up of listeners but also of readers. They are addressed by Brun von Schönebeck as *ir horer und ir lesere* (*Hohes Lied* 12542), by Hiltgart von Hürnheim as *euch leser und leserinne* alongside *Euch losennden und hörenndenn* (*Secretum Secretorum* 4, 34), and in the *Sächsisches Weichbildrecht*, with a motivation resembling the *Rheinisches Marienlob*, as the reader and the listener (*Glosse* 181, 8: ... *dorumme daz der leser und der zuhörer nicht beswert werden*). For all three of these works there are other criteria suggesting a reading reception in agreement with the readers whom these formulas suggest,[206] who cannot be dismissed in favour of a reciter as easily as Kartschoke suggested. This does not mean that the reciter is absent from these works (if they are also heard by listeners, this must be thanks to him), but that he is not designated by the word *leser*.

The term *leser* for the individual reader[207] can be replaced by two circumlocutions. The first, which takes the form *swer ditz buoch lese*, may be illustrated by a variant from the conclusion of Ulrich von Türheim's *Tristan* (3658: *swelhe vrouwen an disem buoche lesen*). Given their degree of literacy in the Middle Ages we can imagine noblewomen as readers[208] (especially of a love-story), but hardly as reciters. Moreover, this request for thanks for the author, taking the form of wishing him success or religious salvation (both could be implied by *heil*), could more effectively be directed at an aristocratic audience, capable of helping him at least towards material success, than at a socially low-placed reciter.[209] The second circumlocution, (alle) die ditz buoch lesent, can be illustrated from *Judith*, which, mainly because of the indication of a clerical audience, even Kartschoke is prepared to regard as meant for readers.[210] The passage on which he bases this is the one which concerns us (2725: *Du und alle die da mitte / Die in geistlichem sitte / Lesen vlizeclich diz buch*). Not merely are there other pointers to a reading reception,[211] it also makes greater sense for the author to address all those who may read his work carefully for themselves than all those who may recite it.[212]

Examples such as these suggest that despite the predominance of oral recital in the Middle Ages (where *leser* has the force of 'reciter'), there are cases, perhaps initially confined to the monastic context but later found beyond it, where an individual reader is involved. On occasions, given the ambiguity of a term like *leser*, we can be assisted whenever the context is more intelligible in terms of a reader. In this respect Scholz uses an argument which we can make fully our own, for when discussing the prologue to *Wigalois* he maintains that what the author hoped for (a readiness to ignore blemishes and to refrain from *valsche rede*) are reactions more commonly ascribed to the audience than to a reciter.[213] The author's aim is to achieve direct contact between himself and his audience, to minimise intervention by the scribe (prone to mistakes)[214] or by the reciter (unreliable whenever someone other than the author performs this role). In view of this: why should the author keep on appealing, in the examples which follow, to the interests, advantages, and importance of the reciter rather than the reader? It is *a priori* much more likely that these features concern the author in his relationship to audience and patron.[215]

The author frequently recommends his work to the attention of others, both when his theme is secular, as with Ulrich von Lichtenstein (*Frauenbuch* 660, 28: *die frowen süln ez gerne lesen*), and when it is religious, as with *Das Leben der heiligen Elisabeth* (20: *Wer nu daz beste priset / Geistliche zu genesene, / Der flize sich zu lesene / An tugentliche mere*). That both these works were also recited is beside the point, for they are recommended to potential readers, to groups who may be expected to read (noblewomen; members of a monastic community)[216] and whose support the authors have to gain. By comparison, the reciter sits well below the salt at court and occupies no position of permanent importance in the monastery, so that authors have little interest in selling their wares to him.[217]

The author can also request the exercise of critical judgment on his work by those who read it[218] (e.g. Heinrich von Hesler, *Die Apokalypse* 1319: *Des bit ich uch, die diz buch / Lesen ... / Ob ir icht vindet dar an / Wandelberiger sache, / Daz ich daz bezzer mache*; or Walther von Rheinau, *Marienleben* 16140ff.). A public appeal for well-informed criticism is a flattery of those in a superior position, whilst critical judgment is better exercised by a private, close reading than in the act of reciting. In cases like these *lesen* is more likely to refer to readers than to reciters.[219]

At times the author can consult the convenience of his readers, as can be illustrated by two examples considered under another heading: *Das Rheinische Marienlob* (4699: *wan ich möcht den leser besweren*) and the *Sächsisches Weichbildrecht* (*Glosse* 181, 8: *... dorumme daz der leser und der zuhörer nicht besweret werden*).[220] In the second example listeners may be invoked as well, but it is the audience, and not the reciter, whose convenience is the author's concern.[221] From the Latin examples quoted by Scholz (Ovid's *Candide lector* or *lector amice*; the authorial wish *ut legentibus fastidium non generem*)[222] it is clear that the author is flattering his audience and insinuating himself with them.

The audience can be guided through the ramifications of a work by an author reminding them that a point has already been made or will recur later. In itself, such guidance is as desirable for readers as for listeners, but the former are addressed, for example, in Ottokar's *Österreichische Reimchronik* (84946: *waz er an im tet, / daz habt ir vor gelesen wol, / dâvon ez nû belîben sol*)[223] or in *Judith* (2535: *Nu hast gelesen wol da vor / Wi* ...),[224] works for which there are other indicators for a reading reception.[225] It would be ludicrous to maintain that in these works, each of which contains a number of such passages, the author constantly interrupted a narrative in order to address a remark to the reciter – instead, he speaks to his audience all the time, but shows that he reckons with readers among them. We have here a reader's counterpart to a phrase which we saw in Chapter 3 was also addressed to an audience conceived as listeners (*als ich iu ê las*).[226] The occurrence of both types of phrase suggests that alongside works meant for listeners there were some whose authors presupposed readers.[227]

In promoting himself the author can promise the acquisition of knowledge from his work. This is so in religious terms in *Judith* (2334: *Wiltu nu wisheit gute / Dir bekennen lerne, / So saltu lesen gerne / Dicke an dissem buche / Und in witzen such / Sine geistliche kunst*) or in secular in *Lucidarius* (15: *Suuer diz buoch gerne lesen wil, / Der gewinnet wistuomes vil, / Der uz den buochen nith lithe wirt ervarn*). It is difficult to imagine why an author should sell his wares to a reciter, instead of his audience, or how this knowledge was better acquired in reciting than by reading. The gain held out to readers can also be seen as moral improvement, as in the *Barlaam und Josaphat* of Rudolf von Ems (157: *... und bite, swer diz maere lese, / daz er sich bezzernde wese ... / und durch got gedenke mîn*). Since the same hope for moral improvement is expressed at the close of the work on behalf of those who hear or read it (16077: *swer ez hoere oder lese, / daz er sich bezzernde wese*) we may take the reader of v. 157 to be a member of the audience to whom Rudolf recommends his work,[228] not a reciter whom he can safely ignore.

This example from Rudolf von Ems has suggested that the author could also request a prayer on his behalf from his readers (*durch got gedenke mîn*), a request found elsewhere in association with the reader, for example in *Das Rheinische Marienlob* (1528: *Ir sult al gebeden wesen / die dit gedichte sulen lesen, / dat ir min vrowe bit vür mich armen, / dat si sich üver mich wil erbarmen*) or in Bruder Philipp's *Marienleben* (10116: *alle die an disem buoche / lesent, der genâde ich suoche, / daz si wellent haben staete / mich durch got an ir gebete*). Such a request was more effectively directed to an audience (especially of higher rank) who could offer up many prayers, by comparison with a solitary low-placed reciter. In these examples, to regard the latter as involved is to grant him an importance which was not his and for which we have no other evidence.[229]

We have been considering evidence for the individual reader where Kartschoke was more inclined to detect the reciter, but we have also qualified the arguments for the reader put forward by Scholz, whom Kartschoke also criticised. This is less of a self-contradiction than might appear, for the reception of vernacular literature was neither by listeners alone nor by readers alone. Both could be anticipated for one and the same work, so that the readers in this chapter could also be the listeners in Chapter 3. This state of affairs is reflected in what we have to consider in the last section.

(r) Oral aspects of reading

This feature of medieval reading we considered earlier where we dealt only with Latin testimony.[230] I wish now to illustrate that in the vernacular literature of Germany, too, writing addressed to an individual reader was not confined to the written word, but also had an oral dimension. We may best divide written communication into several steps which in conditions of modern literacy are almost entirely confined to the visual realm, but which in the Middle Ages were characterised by an interplay between the spoken and written word.

The first step concerns an author's relationship to his source-material, which nowadays is mainly by reading.[231] A medieval literate author could of course also read his sources, but alongside this for various reasons his access to sources may have been by oral means.[232] The first reason may be that he had an oral informant or claimed to have one, as is true of 'Mären', whose authors use the eyewitness account, common in historiography, for their own purposes.[233] This is the case in *Der Ritter unterm Zuber* (8: *hiebî nemet einre maere war, / Wie einiu âventiur' beschach / eime ritter, den ich sach, / Der mir'z mit sînem munde / seite ze einre stunde*) and with Herrand von Wildonie (11 10ff.). More interesting is the position in *Mai und Beaflor*, where we are told that the oral informant's account goes back to a written text (3, 10ff.). Here the movement is from written original to the informant's oral account, then to the poem as we have it (without any indication that it was meant for listeners or readers). Another explanation of orality behind a written text is the fact that its author may depend on assistance from others with access to written texts closed to him. (An early example of this is Bede's account of Caedmon: clerics wrote down what he recited, but his composition rested on what they read out to him for turning into verse.[234]) This situation is implied by Hugo von Langenstein (*Martina* 292, 9: *Daz seiten mire zetiute / Guote geistlich liute / Die es geschriben lasen*)[235] and by Lamprecht von Regensburg's expression of what he owes to bruoder Gêrhart (*Diu Tohter von Syon* 55: *man darf mich niht dârumbe loben, / er ist der rede ein urhap. / von sînem munde er mir gap / die materie und den sin*). Of the lay poet Der Wilde Mann it has been suggested that he may have drawn his (often faulty) theological knowledge from sermons and his position has been compared with religious laymen and heretics acquiring their knowledge from those who were literate.[236] A third reason for depending on oral transmission may be not the poet's inability to read, but his ignorance of a particular language, so that he must rely on someone else to translate a source-text. Konrad von Würzburg knew Latin, but not French, so that he was dependent on the oral offices of a translator for *Partonopier und Meliur* (208: *daz buoch er schône diutet / von wälhisch mir in tiutschiu wort. / er hât der zweier sprâche hort / gelernet als ein wîser man. / franzeis ich niht vernemen kan, / daz tiutschet mir sîn künstic munt*), and a similar explanation has been advanced for Wirnt von Grafenberg (*Wigalois* 11689: *niwan eines von sînem munde / enpfie ich die âventiure*),[237] so that we should hesitate to take this as evidence for the poet's illiteracy.

For transposition into written form the author could dictate to a scribe or perhaps write it down himself. The first possibility, with its obvious orality, is attested for lyric poetry in some illustrations in the Manesse manuscript (Bligger von Steinach, Reinmar von Zweter and Konrad von Würzburg are depicted dictating to scribes who write on a roll or writing-tablet),[238] but also in occasional verbal references. At the close of *Die gute Frau* the author says that he has completed his work, but must now have it written (3053: *nu wil ichz heizen schrîben / ze êren guoten wîben*),[239] whilst Johann von Würzburg occasionally addresses his scribe directly in *Wilhelm von Österreich* (884, 3596).[240]

After dictation the next step is writing itself, whether by the scribe to whom the author dictates or by the latter in person.[241] In either case, we have to reckon with the medieval practice of writing aloud, saying to oneself what one writes, attested for Latin[242] and also for German. Alber sums up his task in composing *Tnugdalus* in written form (10: *wir suln sî gerne schrîben, / daz unser hant und unser zunge / sî ein warnunge / der armen und der rîchen*), where the co-operation of hand and tongue resembles what Paulinus of Nola said much earlier of writing (*lingua et manus*).[243] Johann von Würzburg reveals this oral dimension of writing in an episode within his narrative, when the need to write a confidential letter demands absolute solitude for fear that the oral act of writing be overheard (*Wilhelm von Österreich* 6674: *den hiez er balde bringen / tinten und birmit; / uf sin bett er da mit / saz und hiez in uz gan: / sin sin was also getan, / er wolt ein brievelin schriben*) and also when writing a letter (6988) is accompanied by the writer dictating aloud to herself (6983: *getihtet von ir munde*). What for us is a silent activity had an oral dimension in the Middle Ages.

The transmission of a written text to its recipient could take place in two ways: it could be read out loud to him by someone else or he could read it himself. The first possibility resembles its mirror-image (the author dictating to a scribe) in its obvious element of orality, especially in connection with a phrase like *hoeren lesen*. Even the individual reading to himself, no less than someone writing, commonly did this aloud. The devotional work *Geistlicher Herzen Bavngart* sees the nun's acquisition of religious knowledge in two ways, hearing (a recital) and reading (25, 17: ... *swaz du gehoret oder gelesen hast*), but is more specific about reading (25, 31: ... *die du hörst von sinen worten sagen, vnd di dv liesst mit dinem munde*). The same is implied by Bruder Philipp of private devotional reading (*Marienleben* 766: *swaz sî las mit dem munde, / daz verspartes in des herzen grunde*) and again Johann von Würzburg gives us an informative sketch of someone wishing to read a letter, yet keep its content to herself, and having to send others out of the room (*Wilhelm von Österreich* 9976: '*ich wil doch vor mim ende / daz brievelin lesen daz er mir / gap*' ... / *und hiez do von ir gan / die dri juncvrawen wol getan. / Si wolt ir hainlich nie gesagen / kaim liut*). Having to do this presupposes reading aloud, even to oneself.

Written transmission, from the author's work with his sources through to reception by an individual reader, can therefore be accompanied by a variable element of orality. To dismiss this in practice, as does Scholz, is to see medieval reading too much in terms of modern reading, yet to play down the possibility of individual reading, as does Kartschoke in what he says about the double formula, is to risk missing the historical beginnings of vernacular literacy. The readers we have been concerned with cannot be separated from the listeners considered earlier. This is why some examples of reading in the following chapter also appeared earlier as examples of listening, since organising our material in this way is the best hope of avoiding the oversimplification of an either–or explanation.

6

Survey of reception by reading

That evidence for reading in this chapter occurs less frequently than earlier for hearing shows that recital and listening were predominant modes in the Middle Ages, persisting alongside individual reading, which gained importance only towards 1200 and increasingly after that. Had this survey covered the fourteenth century as well it would have yielded very different results.

With the acoustic reception in Chapter 4 we began each section with some words on the role of orality in that genre. In this chapter we shall preface each section with remarks on the way in which the genre found its way on to parchment before considering works with pointers to an individual reader. Strictly speaking, writing underlies not merely a text read by an individual, but also one read out to listeners, but it is more fitting to include this literate aspect in a chapter devoted to the literate act of reading. Whereas in Chapter 4 the argument often turned on the verb *hoeren*, now the problem lies with *lesen*. The act of reading is suggested when this verb implies reception of a work by someone for himself, rather than transmission to others by recital. The reasons suggesting the former instead of the latter were discussed at the close of the last chapter.

(a) Functional literature

If magic charms and blessings had to be pronounced to be effective they have reached us because they were also written. How this could happen with pagan charms at a time when writing was a clerical monopoly can be seen in the light of their medical function: several OHG examples are preserved in a medical context, just as medical texts can also contain a charm.[1] Medicine inherited from antiquity was studied in monasteries and in so far as classical medicine was imbued with magic monks were indirectly engaged in magic.[2] Even where such magic was officially condemned it could still be associated with clerics, as at an early synod at Agde.[3] This has been confirmed from the codicological evidence of vernacular charms and blessings, falling largely into two groups, either contained in a collection of medical texts or preserved as additions to MSS with sermons, prayers and liturgical texts, pointing to the practical needs of a priest.[4] Given this zone of contact between magic, medicine and the clergy we may understand how charms could find their way on to parchment as part of written medical lore.[5]

The linguistic evidence which earlier showed that German charms were pronounced orally also demonstrates that they could be written down, specifically as amulets or talismans. The use of writing for such a magical purpose is attested for runes as well as by the opposition of the Church to amulets or *phylacteria*, translated by *zaubargescrip* or *prieueli*, implying a written amulet scrap.[6] Although no German charm has been identified as an amulet there is evidence for the use of writing in Christianised magical blessings in a medical context in the *Münchener Wundsegen*, a Latin blessing for toothache, another cure for toothache in the Bartholomäus tradition, Erhart Hesel's *Arzneibuch* and a MLG medical book.[7] In these examples literacy is involved in a restricted sense: only certain formulas were to be recited orally, while the rest of the text was meant for reading by the priestly practitioner or exorcist. A reader of a much more pragmatic kind is foreseen by Meister Albrant in his self-recommendation to the recipient.[8] Scientific knowledge is conveyed in the *Mainauer Naturlehre*, frequently by a diagram referred to in the text: although this correlation in itself is ambiguous, we may assume an individual reader, for some mnemonic verses are interpreted with regard to their letters and syllables, presupposing an analytic view of language possible for a reader, but not for an illiterate listener.[9]

A second group consists of works for the monastic school, where the use of writing is as understandable as the recourse to the vernacular in the acquisition of Latin (hence the use of glosses, glossaries, interlinear translations).[10] Such vernacular texts served a practical educational goal, whilst more ambitiously Notker's novelty was to transfer the mixture of two languages in the classroom to parchment. If we treat him later, but other OHG texts for the monastery school at this point, this is because only Notker makes clear the possibility of both hearing and reading his works.

OHG examples are the *Benediktinerregel*, the *Altalemannische Psalmenübersetzung*, and the *Murbacher Hymnen*: all were probably used in the monastic school, where individual reading was also involved, as with Notker.[11] It is also likely that the *Carmen ad Deum* was meant for the same context, specifically for teaching metrics.[12] The *Abecedarium Nordmannicum* may not have been used in schooling, but was certainly at home in monastic scholarship and illustrates an interesting interplay between writing and orality.[13] As a *litteratus* Walahfrid Strabo included it among various alphabets and an extract from Isidore of Seville on *litterae*, but it contains the runes of the later Scandinavian futhark accompanied by a short gnomic poem to assist memorising their sequence. The movement is therefore from writing (runes) to oral memory (gnomic poem, alliteration as an aid to memory), then back to writing (Walahfrid). Gnomic verse also found its way from orality to writing in short vernacular verse examples used by Notker to exemplify points in teaching logic and rhetoric.[14] Finally, unlike other versions of the medieval *Cato*, for which listeners were expected, the version Z^1 reckoned with a reading reception.[15]

Didactic literature, amounting to a more informal type of instruction, often takes the form of a cleric teaching laymen by passing on the riches of written Latin tradition in the vernacular, addressing them either as members of his flock or as belonging to a court at which he was active.[16] In neither case need the use of writing surprise us, nor the incipient possibility that a text might be available to the potential reader.

Wernher von Elmendorf makes no such explicit allusion, but the accessibility of his work to reading is borne out by a reader's marginal notes in the Berlin fragments, including quotations from sources used.[17] Although Wernher refers to his work being heard it also found a painstaking reader. These two possibilities recur with the *Lucidarius*: listening to a recital was anticipated, but also the possibility of an individual reader.[18] The evidence for a reading reception of Thomasin's *Welscher Gast* is more detailed. Neither a recommendation to consult other texts nor a correlation between text and illustration, even if it goes back to Thomasin, is of itself convincing.[19] More telling is a reference to the recipient having the work in his lap, especially in combination with the visual dimension employed in the sense of reading.[20] Giving the work to someone to look at (14670: *schouwen*) is thus varied by giving it to read (14673ff.: *gelesen*), just as the knights, ladies and clerics envisaged as looking at the work (14695f.: *schouwen*) are those who read the book (14635ff.). Readers are also implied at the opening and the close of the work.[21] Thomasin, a clerical *litteratus*, envisaged readers for his work, whether clerical or not.[22]

Two other didactic works may not have been meant by a cleric for a court, but reckon with readers. In her *Secretum Secretorum* Hiltgart von Hürnheim refers the potential reader to various headings in her book and mentions, in addition to listeners, readers of both sexes.[23] In *Der Renner* of Hugo von Trimberg the evidence is more variegated. Recommendations to consult a source are often more precise than would be called for if he were arguing that his text is reliable because it follows a written source.[24] When Hugo agrees that his errors should be corrected the *wise man* who is to do this must count reading among his qualifications, since these lines follow a reference to the reader of an earlier work, presumably also anticipated for *Der Renner*.[25] This will be borne out by Hugo's use of the double formula to suggest readers as well as listeners.

(b) Literature of religious worship and instruction

Two genres in this section treated under reception by hearing (hymns and catechetical literature) offer no evidence that they were also meant for individual reading, presumably because they were so much at home within the liturgy. The most we can say is that the participation of laymen in the hymns and the use of catechetical literature in instructing laymen account for the use of the vernacular without implying individual reading.[26]

The position is different with sermons and the 'Reimpredigt'. A collection of sermons could be written down either to assist a priest in his pastoral task by supplying models or to provide a text for personal meditation.[27] The latter possibility concerns us now. It was not confined to Germany and its importance lies in the fact that written sermons appeal to addressees other than spoken ones: they are meant for reading, whether reading aloud to others in the monastic refectory or devotional reading in the monk's cell or the literate layman's home.[28] This last case, historically later, concerns an intermediate public of religious laypeople able to read, but not in Latin (which is why the sermons are written in the vernacular),[29] who as béguines or *religiosae* belong neither to the lay world nor to the clerical, who have renounced the world without abandoning it entirely.[30] Written sermons addressed to such groups have found their way from the pulpit to the book, from hearing to reading.[31] The same transition could also be made within monasticism by nuns whose Latin was often shaky and whose sex likewise placed them on the borders of the clerical world.[32] That vernacular sermons were written for their reading needs is accepted for the eight sermons of Berthold von Regensburg belonging to the *Z group, addressed to nuns.[33]

In view of this marginal position of nuns (unlike béguines they have fully withdrawn from the world, but unlike monks they are not always literate in the sense of Latinate) they have been proposed as readers of isolated earlier vernacular sermons. The *Predigtsammlung A, B, C* was possibly connected with a nuns' convent, its transfer to parchment providing them with reading material, either individual or collective.[34] It has been suggested that the OS *Homilie Bedas*, connected with a community of canonesses at Essen, was meant for reading out on All Saints' Day, but in such a context a vernacular text could also have been meant for individual reading.[35] Devotional reading of sermons in German was also important among the *religiosae* of the thirteenth century, as reflected in a decision by the Dominicans in 1242 forbidding the translation of such literature into German, which points to a practice before this date.[36] We are not told whether the reading needs of these *religiosae* involved individual reading or reading to a small circle, but since these women practised reading aloud at table and private reading like monks we may assume that written sermons in the vernacular addressed to them also found individual readers.[37]

Despite the historical importance of this genesis of a new class of readers in the religious movements of the thirteenth century, we have been warned against exaggerating the speed at which it was established. This class of readers became large only in the fourteenth century; before this these groups were so small and scattered that vernacular works meant for them survived in written transmission only if they reached the wider readership of the fourteenth century.[38] As so often with the literacy of the thirteenth century, historical beginnings detectable here reach full efflorescence only later.

The 'Reimpredigt' thus offers only two examples where an individual reader is likely. In foreseeing a twofold reception of his *Rede vom heiligen Glauben* Der Arme Hartmann is explicit about the act of reading (*lesen* is reinforced by *gesiht*).[39] About a century later *Die heilige Regel für ein vollkommenes Leben*, written by a monastic author probably for Cistercians, anticipates a reading reception as private spiritual communion conducted inwardly with God.[40] The inwardness of this reading withdraws it from the collective situation of public recital.

Devotional literature could be read aloud to small groups without excluding private readers, even though these are largely attested only in the thirteenth century when the mendicant orders assumed responsibility for the religious needs of laymen, especially for those whose incipient vernacular literacy demanded a new type of literature to meet a novel situation.[41]

Only two works before this century can be tentatively placed here, the *Rheinfränkische Psalterübersetzung* and the *Altsächsischer Psalmenkommentar*, for both of which use in a nuns' convent has been suggested as well as the possibility of reading out to the community, say in the refectory, but in such a community reading of a vernacular text by an individual nun is also conceivable.[42] Clearer cases, however, arise only from the religious turmoil of the thirteenth century.

When the author of the *Rheinisches Marienlob* claims that a detail can be established in 'the books' (3157f.) there is no proof that he actually expected a reader to consult these texts. More persuasive are the presence of acrostics, accessible only to a reader, and two explicit references to potential readers.[43] By contrast, since the recommendation by Lamprecht von Regensburg in his *Tochter Syon* to consult the Bible (2816ff.) in no way establishes the truth of Lamprecht's own text, it has the appearance of a genuine suggestion for further reading.[44] Heinrich von Kröllwitz concedes that anyone finding fault with his *Vaterunser* is at liberty to correct it (3973ff.), but by using the verb *sezzen* of this act of correction he implies someone able to write and therefore also to read his text beforehand. That readers were anticipated is stated emphatically at the close of the work and at a point where Heinrich names himself so that the reader may pray on his behalf.[45] In suggesting that Mechthild von Magdeburg reckoned with readers for her *Fließendes Licht der Gottheit* we are not dependent on recommendations in the foreword and at the opening of the text whose genuineness has been questioned.[46] What has not been doubted is her wish that her work may not be read by Pharisees and that it continue to be read after her death.[47]

The *Geistlicher Herzen Bavngart* anticipates a listening, but also reading audience and refers explicitly to the reader of this book.[48] *Die Lilie* informs the reader of what he may find on one folio and of a more general theme of the work,[49] whilst *Die Rede von den fünfzehn Graden* ends with the author's readiness to correct errors pointed out by readers.[50] A similar invitation by Könemann von Jerxheim in his *Wurzgarten Mariens* may not allude to readers, but this deficiency is made good elsewhere.[51] In *Unser Vrouwen Klage* the recipients recommended to take *ditz kleine büechelîn* (125) into their hands frequently for devotions are seen as individual readers.[52] Although the author of the *Mariengrüße* may 'say' something it is a reader whom he addresses.[53] A reading reception of the *Sieben Tagzeiten* of Hartwig von dem Hage and of *Von dem englischen Gruoß ein leich* is suggested by the use of acrostics.[54]

(c) Legal literature

When written in German, law represented a meeting between two traditions because the oral legal transaction normally took place in the vernacular, whilst its written record was in Latin, the language of writing. This was already the case with early Germanic tribal laws and remained usual practice for centuries,[55] so that with written law in German our question must not be why writing was adopted, but why a written tradition in Latin gave way to one in German.[56]

For the earlier period special reasons and occasions account for laws having to be read out and, for that reason, needing first to be written down in German: for long law found its way in German on to parchment only exceptionally.[57] By contrast, written law in German from the thirteenth century forms a continuous tradition. For the *Sachsenspiegel* the universalism of law in the process of territorialisation has been suggested (writing helped to bridge space and guaranteed the uniformity of law everywhere)[58] and this model found an echo not merely in North Germany, but also under Franciscan influence in the south (*Schwabenspiegel, Deutschenspiegel*).[59] The immediacy of this echo reflects the needs which law written in German now met and is confirmed by the agreement in dating between the *Sachsenspiegel* (1220–35) and two other written legal texts in German, the *Mühlhäuser Reichsrechtsbuch* (1220–35) and the *Mainzer Reichslandfrieden* (1235).[60]

The continuity of written tradition inaugurated by these texts is illustrated in another way in the *Schwabenspiegel*, with its repeated references to historical precedents for written law, stemming from the Old Testament and classical antiquity.[61] This is reminiscent of early Germanic legislation, recorded in Latin, seeking ideological support for barbarian kingship from the precedents of Moses as a lawgiver and from Rome, but the *Schwabenspiegel* goes a step further in also including Charles the Great and Ludwig the Pious among its exemplars.[62] By joining this line the *Schwabenspiegel* illustrates what written law accomplished from 1235 on: the vernacular has joined a written tradition of some antiquity hitherto confined to Latin (and Hebrew).

From this point the opportunity, however rarely attested, of an individual reading a German legal text now existed. In the *Sächsisches Weichbildrecht*, alongside ambiguous pointers, a twofold reception is alluded to: the reader as well as the listener was anticipated.[63] Nor are most indications in the *Schwabenspiegel Langform M* clear beyond doubt, apart from cross-references between (or within) the 'Lehnrecht' and the 'Landrecht', for these suggest a reader making practical use in consulting various parts of the text for his own purposes.[64] In view of this, the reference to a twofold reception of the *cronica*, judged too long for inclusion, may also be applied to this work.[65] In addition to uncertain indications the *Deutschenspiegel* is fully informative only when castigating the wrong type of reader.[66] The *Stadtbuch von Augsburg* contains cross-references which suggest a written work, not necessarily a reader, but more force attaches to those indicating a precisely defined point in the text:[67] here too a reader consulting the text for a specific practical purpose is suggested.[68]

The problem with charters is the same as with legal literature at large: why did charters in Latin begin to give some ground to German in the thirteenth century? As in so many aspects of German finding its way into writing this process takes place in the shadow of Latin and on the margins of a written tradition still predominantly Latin.[69] The charter records in writing the orality of a legal transaction, so that, as long as the transaction was in Latin (say, between clerics), there was little danger of a discrepancy between transaction and Latin record. When laymen were involved and the transaction was in their vernacular, linguistic and legal difficulties arose in transposing the vernacular transaction into a Latin record (and back again whenever reactivated in place of witnesses). Reactivating a charter meant recital in public, so that once more, if laymen were involved, there were advantages in composing the charter in German in the first place.[70] The rise of the German charter is therefore tied up with a growth in charters issued by laymen with no Latin (or no literacy, if the text is read back to them).[71] Because of the difficulties of Latin greater trust was placed in German documents:[72] the decision to write a charter in Latin or German rested not simply on the status of those involved (cleric or layman), but on the state of their education (Latinate or not).[73] This impetus towards charters in German could come from the lay aristocracy, especially the lower nobility (they lacked chanceries of their own with a tradition of writing in Latin and were not hindered by convention in making the transition to German),[74] but also from the town[75] as a social centre of novel importance, especially regarding the encouragement of a pragmatic literacy and constituting a major source of German charters in their first century.

Of the legal genre of the oath it has been asked what happens when an oral transaction is transposed into writing, what changes does this bring about.[76] The two dimensions of the original legal transaction (witnesses heard what was said and saw what was done) were captured in the two dimensions of the charter's reactivation as evidence (it was heard when read aloud and the document could be inspected). Hence the Latin charter formula *visuris et audituris*, together with its German counterpart (*Swer dise schrift siht. alde horet*).[77] With the visual dimension of reading out a charter as evidence there is no reason to equate 'seeing' in these formulas with individual reading, but the transition to reading lay close to hand, since written charters could be heard as they were read out, but also read by anyone literate. Alongside the formulas just quoted we therefore find *lecturis et audituris* or *lesende oder hoerende*.[78] The introduction of written charters, especially in German, made possible a change in the visual dimension from seeing at large to reading in particular.

(d) Historiography

Our examples all come from the thirteenth century after a long practice of Latin historiography, so that we face the same question as with charters: why did German written texts arise alongside Latin in this period?[79] One reason was the difficulty experienced by medieval vernaculars in gaining acceptance as reliable vehicles of truth in face of Latin, involving points of criticism such as oral or written and *fabula* or *historia*.[80] Heroic poetry, a source of historical awareness for laymen, was attacked by clerics as untrustworthy because of its oral form, so that once this criticism was accepted by laymen the way was open to providing vernacular history for them in written form.[81] What was true of written law in German is also relevant here if we take account of the close connections between legal literature and some historical works. Just as the *Schwabenspiegel* presented contemporary law against a historical background, so was historiography conversely linked with a number of lawbooks, e.g. the *Buch der Könige* with the *Deutschenspiegel* or possibly the *Sächsische Weltchronik* with the *Sachsenspiegel*.[82] The transition of law to writing may therefore have assisted the similar move with historiography.[83]

A written form for historical works opens up the possibility of individual readers, even though, as with the *Kaiserchronik*, this may not always be realised in practice. Some pointers in the *Sächsische Weltchronik* may not be fully persuasive, but more clearcut is a reference to those who may read or write the author's work or a general allusion to reading which has a particular bearing on this chronicle.[84] Fewer doubts attach to the *Weltchronik* of Rudolf von Ems: it contains acrostics meant for the reader's eye, but also a recommendation to skip a *paragraf*, if desired. However we interpret *paragraf*, it was only visually recognisable as such, and when its omission is left to the discretion of a reader who may not like it (*behagt*) this differs from the recommendation to the reciter in the *Apokalypse* of Heinrich von Hesler, who has to regard not his own dislikes, but those of his listeners.[85] In addition, Rudolf's expectation of a reader, we shall see, is underlined by his use of a double formula for the reception of his work. In the *Weltchronik* of Jans Enikel doubts as to whether the recommendation to consult the *korônik* for further information really implies a reader can be laid to rest by references to what the audience have read elsewhere in this book.[86] The author of the *Christherre-Chronik* appeals, with an eye to his patron, to those who read his work.[87] In the *Braunschweigische Reimchronik* the uncertainty of references to consulting a chronicle for confirmation gives way to the more persuasive evidence of an anagram and a pointer to what recipients 'see' (meaning 'read') elsewhere in the book.[88] Finally, Ottokar's *Österreichische Reimchronik* refers to what has been said above, but the reader perhaps implicit here only comes clearly to the fore when what he reads at various points in the chronicle is expressly mentioned or when the author hopes for a favourable reception from his reader.[89] However belated their appearance in the vernacular, these written historical works quickly found readers alongside listeners.

(e) Biblical literature

Nothing like an uninterrupted tradition of biblical literature in German can be traced up to 1300. Instead, three discontinuous centres of gravity are found (Carolingian, early MHG, the Teutonic Order), which imply particular reasons why this literature acquired written form at different times, rather than a sustained development towards writing through the centuries. Again, this literature has to be seen against the tradition of Latin biblical literature (Otfrid already saw himself in this light),[90] so that here too we have to ask what forces made for a biblical literature in the vernacular alongside Latin.

The leading Carolingian examples (the *Heliand* and Otfrid) have been associated with the cultural programme of Ludwig the German, in which the distinction between tribes east and west of the Rhine led to a stress on the vernacular in place of a universal Latin suggesting no such distinction.[91] The shorter biblical works in early MHG are connected with writing in a sense not true of these two Carolingian works (preserved in MSS devoted to them alone), for the shorter works survived only by being protected in the large-scale collective MSS of the twelfth century.[92] Other examples, likewise meant for oral delivery, may have perished through not being incorporated in these larger MSS.[93] The literature of the Teutonic Order concentrated on biblical literature, history and legends, genres which could be termed *historia*,[94] the first two of which, in the form of Old Testament themes, were important in providing biblical precedents for the Order in the wars of Israel.[95] This granted a new importance to biblical literature of this type, but the illiteracy of most knightly members of the Order meant that, although this literature may not have found many readers, the need for recital in the refectory still encouraged the growth of written biblical literature.[96]

Elsewhere the transposition of biblical themes to vernacular writing found individual readers.[97] The twofold reception of Otfrid's *Evangelienbuch* we shall look at later, but readers were also anticipated for the OS *Heliand*. The *Praefatio* says that this work is divided into *capitula* with headings for the benefit of the *studiosus lector* wishing to find his way.[98] In the *Hohes Lied* of Williram von Ebersberg a reference to an earlier passage implies a text in written form, but is followed by a remark suggesting the visual dimension of a reader guided to this passage.[99] This is confirmed by prologue allusions to the *studiosus lector* and to *quivis legens*, to the learned recipients of the work (*doctiores*), conceived as much as readers as Williram regarded himself in perusing his work with satisfaction.[100] With Frau Ava the one pointer to a reader is a reliable one when she asks for prayers on her behalf from her audience.[101] In the *Windberger Psalter*, an interlinear translation used like its OHG predecessors in the context of school teaching, there is a clear indication of reading: in the margins by Psalm 94, 3 instructions are given how the reader is not to understand a phrase.[102] There is no Latin counterpart: it is an independent vernacular addition suggesting that a Latin work with interlinear glosses presupposed use by a reader.

In his *Urstende* Konrad von Heimesfurt guards against alterations to his text by leaving the margins too narrow: in foreseeing an uninformed corrector (erasing what he has read) he reckons with a reader as much as in his acrostics.[103] The author of *Judith*, in hoping that his work will be copied correctly, leaves it open whether a reader or listener is envisaged, but the former is apparent in references to what the recipient has read already in this book and in the expectation of frequent reading.[104] The *Hohes Lied* of Brun von Schönebeck we shall consider later as an example of a twofold reception, but the three biblical works of Heinrich von Hesler can be discussed together now. A cross-reference in his *Apokalypse* to what came earlier is so precise as to suggest the convenience of a reader,[105] but more convincing is the author's readiness to correct faults pointed out to him, especially by readers.[106] In his *Erlösung* Heinrich invites corrections from other poets who are to *setzen* their improvements in his book (if they can write, they may also be seen as readers), just as readers in more general terms are anticipated.[107] They are also expected for the *Evangelium Nicodemi*.[108]

Heinrich von Neustadt apologises to readers for shortcomings in his *Gottes Zukunft*.[109] The author of *Der Saelden Hort* hopes that his work will be found in the hands of young women and widows (as readers) in preference to court literature.[110] For *Die Erlösung* readers are implied by the presence of acrostics and their pointedly literate explanation.[111] In *Der Kreuziger* Johannes von Frankenstein qualifies one who is to correct his work as *ein klûger man* (11467ff.): that this includes an ability to read is suggested by a Greek word which the recipient saw written at an earlier point and by the author's request for the prayers of those who read him.[112] Finally, in *Das Leben Jesu* the Dominican nuns for whom it was meant are seen as potential readers, an indication to be confirmed by the twofold reception foreseen for this work.[113]

(f) Legends

The competition between legends and court literature involved a measure of common ground: in stating a rival message to laymen the authors of legends addressed them in their oral dimension. It could be that this also led to a reading reception of legends, for there is evidence for this especially in the court romance. Several court authors wrote both legends and romances, and a number of courts commissioned legends,[114] so that if we are right to assume the same kind of audience for both genres the expectation of readers for the romance makes it likely for the legend. Indeed, the boot may be on the other foot and we may be better informed about the reading reception of an author's legend than about his romance, as we shall see in the case of Hartmann von Aue.

First to suggest readers is Priester Wernher in *Maria*. Some pointers may be dubious, but the author also refers to those who read his work, using two visual verbs to stress this dimension.[115] Of interest here is the reference to laymen, which must include laywomen in view of the talisman value of having the book in the house to guarantee safe childbirth.[116] Although this betrays a magical conception of the book and writing (from which Brun von Schönebeck breaks loose in favour of a pragmatic attitude), it is unlikely that this book was kept in a house solely for that purpose, so that Wernher seems to have reckoned with laywomen as possible readers. Albertus von Augsburg also anticipated readers for his *Leben des heiligen Ulrich*. When he invites the correction of any errors the qualifications of the corrector probably include literacy, since the passage comes immediately after the 'literate' instructions on interpreting an acrostic.[117] At one point the reader is told what he will learn later in the book: although Albertus follows the *Vita* here, this cannot be the sole explanation, as his vernacular acrostic makes clear.[118] Ebernand von Erfurt implies the same in *Heinrich und Kunigunde* by the repeated use of acrostics, together with instructions for solving them for *der leser*.[119] Rudolf von Ems makes an early remark in *Barlaam und Josaphat* about his reader in agreement with the reading reception of his other works and taken up at the conclusion as part of a double formula and by the presence of an acrostic at the close of the work.[120] Konrad von Würzburg expects a reader (as well as listeners) for his *Alexius*.[121]

For all its length *Das Passional* does not abound in evidence, but the ambiguity of a *schríben* + dative construction is resolved by what we shall see of a twofold reception for this work.[122] Hugo von Langenstein makes a passing reference to readers in *Martina*,[123] whilst Hartwig von dem Hage suggests reading indirectly in his *Margaretenlegende* by depicting the saint praying for those who write or read of her martyrdom and by claiming that childbirth will be easier wherever this book is read in the saint's honour.[124] The author of the *Märterbuch* promises that it will bring spiritual betterment to the reader.[125] In the *Leben der heiligen Elisabeth* a reference to calculating a date previously given is of itself indecisive, but the recipients are said to 'see' something happen in the book, presumably in the sense of reading, which is in any case meant in an opening recommendation.[126] Bruder Philipp gives leave to erase offending passages from his *Marienleben*, significantly in the vicinity of a request for the prayers of those who read him.[127] Finally, those who encourage copies of the *Marienleben* of Walther von Rheinau are associated with those who read or hear it, which suggests a twofold reception.[128] Among the invitations to correct the text are some which link this explicitly with literacy, whilst those to whom Walther sends a copy are asked to read the whole work.[129] Whether belonging to a monastic setting or associated with a secular court the legends considered in this section were destined for individual readers.

(g) Drama

Here too we face a preliminary question encountered elsewhere: given the time-lag between Latin dramas from the eleventh century on and German ones from the thirteenth (at first with isolated vernacular insertions only), what reasons lie behind the penetration of German into these texts at this point in time? An informative approach has been to consider those examples where German first appears in particular contexts and to ask about the nature of these contexts.[130]

The nucleus for this linguistic encroachment has been seen as the religious experience of Christ's passion, confirmed by the use of German in Mary's lament in the *Benediktbeurer Passionsspiel*, conveyed directly to the layman in his mother tongue, but also in the episodes of Longinus, as a model for conversion addressed to laymen, and Mary Magdalene, typifying worldly sinfulness and repentance.[131] In the *Osterspiel von Muri* German is not confined to isolated passages,[132] but importance still attaches to the scene of Mary Magdalene's encounter with the risen Christ, with features reminiscent of the new piety of the thirteenth century.[133] The use of German is not to be equated with the sinfulness of this world,[134] but is the language of laymen to whom the religious appeal is directed: in the *Benediktbeurer Passionsspiel* Mary Magdalene abandons her dramatic role at one point to address the audience directly, using the vernacular for the same reason as in a sermon.[135]

In the *Benediktbeurer Passionsspiel* Mary Magdalene typifies not simply worldliness,[136] but is depicted specifically as a courtly figure, while the text of the *Osterspiel von Muri* is similarly impregnated with courtly vocabulary.[137] When Mary Magdalene uses this vocabulary as a seducer her sinfulness is equated with the contemporary ideal of court literature, which is also shown up negatively when the merchant's wares in the *Osterspiel von Muri* are exposed as aphrodisiacs.[138] This suggests at least an audience including members of a court and implies a late parallel with the vernacular legend: both genres made the transition to the vernacular under the impetus of court culture and the need to counter its rival claims.

This is not called into question by the likelihood of a monastery setting for some dramas in the thirteenth century (*Klosterneuburger Osterspiel, Amorbacher Spiel*).[139] As in other genres, the location of a work in a monastery need not exclude the vernacular or the presence of laymen: the Klosterneuburg example is thought to have been performed on the occasion when duke Leopold VI visited the monastery at Easter in 1204, while in the case of Amorbach the alternation of Latin and German (the latter paraphrasing the former) implies the presence of some unable to follow the Latin alone (lay guests or lay brothers).[140] That such plays could be performed before an audience of secular aristocrats (not necessarily in a monastery) is clear from the report of Caesarius von Heisterbach on a performance at the castle of Eisenach in 1227 for landgrave Ludwig IV of Thuringia.[141]

Several factors thus combine to account for the gradual emergence of the vernacular in clerical dramas of the thirteenth century.[142] Yet the existence of written German dramas does not mean that, in addition to performance, they immediately found a reading reception.[143] We owe to Linke and Bergmann useful discussions of the differences between the text of a drama meant for performance and one for the individual reader.[144] Stressing that one criterion alone is not enough, but only the combination of several, they list a number of features characteristic of texts of these two types. The application of their criteria to dramas of the thirteenth century leads to the conclusion that, apart from the special case of the *Osterspiel von Muri*, none can safely be classified as meant for reading. Admittedly, the *Benediktbeurer Passionsspiel* has been claimed for this class,[145] presumably on the grounds that it is transmitted in a mixed MS and in incomplete form, so that it was hardly meant for performance. However, to argue that a text was not meant for performance is not the same as showing that it was meant to be read, and the text does contain a pointer to performance in the presence of neumes.[146] Given this uncertainty we should hesitate to regard this solitary text as meant for reading and recognise that, conceivably because of their sheer dramatic impact, these written dramas may have been slower than other genres in finding individual readers.

(h) Heroic literature

Heroic literature and medieval drama proceed from very different starting-points: oral vernacular as opposed to written Latin. Once we reach the period when both genres are written in the vernacular (for heroic literature this is also the thirteenth century) they now resemble each other in that a reading reception for heroic literature is as uncertain as for the drama. We have to distinguish, in other words, composition and transmission of heroic works (which may make use of writing) from reception (there is no internal evidence for reading).

Die Klage, in addition to containing a typical recital situation for this genre,[147] has also been used to shed light on the move to writing in the *Nibelungenlied*.[148] It recounts how a bishop of Passau heard the news of the downfall of the Nibelungen from an oral singer Swämmel (3350ff.), was struck by it (3480f.) and ordered it to be written down (3464ff., 4295ff.) by his scribe (4314f.), although other versions still circulate (4316ff.). There are also indications that this transition from oral to written was accompanied by an interplay between vernacular and Latin. Swämmel's initial account, like that in the typical recital situation (3776ff.), must have been in the vernacular, but the written version ordered by Pilgrim was in Latin, the language of writing, whilst the versions which still circulate were in German (4316f.). The parallel between this linguistic interplay and what we have seen elsewhere is so close that it is difficult to dismiss this account as completely fictitious.[149]

In dealing with the question why this move to writing began we are helped by the comparative aspect of this process, pursued by Wolf with admirable tenacity.[150] He looks at the problem in its European context and acknowledges that, whilst writing may sometimes remove heroic poetry from its natural oral habitat and show it up in a problematic, fractured light, there are also cases where it can be written down without its substance being questioned.[151] In these latter cases writing is meant simply to preserve for posterity (Einhard says of the written collection ordered by Charles the Great: *scripsit memoriaeque mandavit*),[152] not to subject these heroic poems to criticism by divorcing them from the oral realm in which they had hitherto found their function and justification.

Apart from isolated examples around 800,[153] the real question about heroic literature and writing arises four centuries later with the *Nibelungenlied* and the impetus it gave to transposing other heroic themes to writing. For this process Wolf suggests influence from the chanson de geste and the romance: since both these genres had begun their transition to writing before 1200, their influence on the *Nibelungenlied* may well have included an impetus towards written form,[154] a development given urgency by clerical criticism of an unreliable oral tradition.

Turning now to the heroic epics which, following the lead of the *Nibelungenlied*, were transferred to writing during the thirteenth century we base ourselves on the distinction between their composition and their reception. Concerning their source and their own work the authors of these epics repeatedly stress the written dimension.[155] The claim that a written source has been followed is made in a number of ways: the audience can hear what is said by an author expressly dependent on a book; the author has heard a book say or has heard from a book; the book recites a detail or informs us; it has been read in a book; the tale has been handed down in writing; a detail can be confirmed from a written source or from those with access to it.[156] Recurrent formulas like these suggest that the authors of heroic literature no longer justify their works from within oral tradition. In place of the oral formula of the *Hildebrandslied*, *ik gihorta ðat seggen*, we have *an einem buoch hôrte ich sagen*.

Almost as frequent are suggestions that the heroic epic is itself to be regarded as a *buoch*. References can therefore be made to 'this book', to 'the book here', to 'this German book'.[157] Without a demonstrative the book in question can be shown to be the present one when its recital is begun or conversely its conclusion is announced.[158] A written text, likewise in the context of oral recital, is implied for *Wolfdietrich A* when in the Dresden MS it is calculated precisely that a version of 700 stanzas has been shortened to 333.[159]

Occasionally the written version can be made more respectable by association with known centres of writing. According to *Die Klage* the *Nibelungenlied* found its way on to parchment at a bishop's court,[160] but elsewhere monasteries are chosen. In *Kudrun* the written privileges of a monastery act as testimony to the battle fought at that site, in *Wolfdietrich C* a written version is associated with the monastery of Eichstätt, whilst in version D the concluding *moniage* and miracles of the hero give a legendary turn to the epic.[161] This *moniage* suggests where these references may have come from, for the chanson de geste also underlines its literate status by claiming clerical associations (St Denis plays a part similar to Bamberg) and invites respectability by the theme of *moniage*.[162]

The literacy of composition in heroic literature, however, has no counterpart in reception, which remains firmly in the oral sphere.[163] This is suggested not merely by the evidence for acoustic reception, but also by the striking lack of internal evidence for reading as a complement to writing.[164] For this we have no direct evidence other than *Wolfdietrich C*, where the claim for a monastic original is buttressed by statements that it was read by a bishop (2, 1ff.; 3, 1ff.) and an abbess (5, 2ff.). If we regard the references to Eichstätt as source-fictions as much as in the chanson de geste, these isolated readers cannot be used to suggest a reading reception of heroic literature at large. By contrast with the romance there are no internal pointers to readers, which must be significant. Why this should be so is difficult to explain, although something must be ascribed to the force of inertia latent in an oral tradition which had lasted over centuries and had proved effective enough in meeting the layman's needs.[165] Because of this the move towards literacy could not be made completely in one go, it was effected first in composition, while reception came later.[166]

(i) Court narrative literature

No evidence for readers is found in the 'Spielmannsepen', where we also have to distinguish between the literacy of composition and of reception.[167] These works, too, repeatedly stress the written dimension. A written source is referred to as a book, as writing, as something to be transferred to writing, as something in Latin, the language of literacy.[168] The written status of the German works themselves is suggested similarly: they are 'this book' or simply 'the book', something written or a text to be recited by a *leser*.[169] These parallels with heroic literature go further, for this written status is associated with clerical centres of literacy: the cathedral library at Bamberg or Trier cathedral.[170] Like heroic epics these 'Spielmannsepen' were meant for an acoustic reception, but give no hint of an individual reader.

Of works with a theme from the *matière de France* only three suggest a reading reception. Although Wolfram's *Willehalm* contains no internal pointers, it may be included here because of his expectation of readers for *Parzival*.[171] In *Rennewart* Ulrich von Türheim refers to earlier works of his which were read and makes it clear that he anticipates a reader for this work, too.[172] Readers can also be argued for the *Willehalm* of Ulrich von dem Türlin on the basis of its acrostics.[173]

With the court romance we must first ask what factors assisted its immediate passage to parchment, whereas several genres had to wait centuries for that move. The emergence of the romance as a novel genre coincided with an explosion of writing which impelled it in this direction,[174] but other factors account for the central position of the romance in this process. A first impetus came from court literature being written in its early stages by clerical authors.[175] Neither they nor their use of the vernacular was new, but novelty attached to their addressing a court audience rather than a religious community and treating a secular theme.[176] A second incentive was the special appeal of this literature to women:[177] the superior role granted them in the love-lyric, if not in feudal patriarchalism,[178] the theme of the love romance, and the place for love alongside chivalry in the Arthurian romance. Given the noblewomen's ability to read,[179] a literature addressing their interests was impelled towards literacy as much for this reason as because of its composition by a cleric. Thirdly, clerical authors at court were brought into contact, even collision, with oral minstrels (already in the case of Chrétien),[180] so that literate poets would naturally stress their literacy in putting forward their claims in the best light. This amounts to re-drawing the line dividing lay from clerical in favour of a distinction between illiterate and literate: court authors set themselves apart from mere minstrels by belonging to a literate tradition.[181] Finally, an important precedent was given by French models: like Latin literary models hitherto largely followed they were in written form, but in a vernacular, which provided an incentive to use writing in German adaptations.[182] This now gave German works the chance to insinuate themselves into a literate tradition from which they had previously been excluded. This tradition was originally at home in clerical literature (e.g. Priester Wernher's *Maria*),[183] but is progressively taken over by secular literature in the vernacular. In tracing the written transmission of his theme in the *Liet von Troye* Herbort von Fritzlar includes two vernaculars (French and German) alongside Greek and Latin.[184] In Veldeke's *Eneide* the predominance of the vernacular is more marked (French and German alongside Latin) and is exclusive in the prose *Lancelot* (French, Flemish, German).[185] With the *Tristan* of Ulrich von Türheim, continuing Gottfried's work with assistance from Eilhart, the written tradition is entirely German: written literature in German has by now established its own independence.[186]

What writing could mean for the romance can be shown elsewhere in the Tristan tradition. The initial oral transmission of this story is clear,[187] but although Béroul and Thomas, like Eilhart and Gottfried, present book versions,[188] not every one of them is aware of the compositional opportunities offered by writing. Inconsistencies have long been registered with Béroul and Eilhart, but Wolf suggests that this is because they stand closer to the episodic narrative style of the oral performer, concentrating on the matter in hand and unable to take other episodes sufficiently into account.[189] If Thomas and Gottfried seek to remove contradictions it is because they have realised the possibilities of patterning and structure open to the poet who uses writing.[190] As poets they act in the same way as Gottfried hopes his critical reader will act when he recommends him to compare one passage with another.[191]

That this individual reader was possible can be shown even where no specific authors are named. Thomasin recommends young people at court to seek ethical exemplars in their reading of romances.[192] The author of *Der Saelden Hort* hopes that his work will fall into the hands of women readers in place of stories of Wigalois and Tristan, implying readers for the latter, too.[193] Konrad von Würzburg sees a literate fellow-poet, Wirnt von Grafenberg, as reading an *âventiure* in the privacy of a room.[194]

In romances with a classical theme Veldeke's *Eneide* contains a pointer by chance: the theft of his MS arose from the wish of the countess of Cleves to read it for herself.[195] Readers for the *Alexander* of Rudolf von Ems are suggested by acrostics and the remark that it will be read and readers will see what is written in it.[196]

Arthurian romances yield a richer crop.[197] The prologue to the *Wigalois* of Wirnt von Grafenberg has been analysed as an example of the personification of the book addressing the individual reader.[198] In *Die Crone* Heinrich von dem Türlin employs an acrostic and refers to the reader of his book.[199] The written status of the prose *Lancelot* is made clear by a reference to what has been said above, but more force attaches to one reference because of its precision (at what point in the gathering the passage may be found), and also because the passage is made recognisable by bold letters.[200] As with Williram von Ebersberg (*ad tale signum* X) a reader checking back is implied. In the prose *Lancelot* this is confirmed by an explicit reference to readers, presumably taken over from the Flemish version, but left intact.[201] A last Arthurian author is Der Pleier, who in *Tandareis und Flordibel* requests readers to pray for him.[202] Although his other romances (*Meleranz* and *Garel von dem Blühenden Tal*) have no internal pointers they were probably written for the same kind of audience, including readers, too.

Apart from Wolfram's *Parzival* the only example of a Grail romance belonging here is *Lohengrin* on the basis of an acrostic and an explicit reference to reading, revealingly in close conjunction with *reine vrouwen*.[203]

After Gottfried's work, the first Tristan romance meant explicitly for readers, there are two other examples. Ulrich von Türheim had readers, particularly women, in mind for his work, whilst in his version Heinrich von Freiberg, besides also expecting listeners, appealed to readers in particular at a point where close attention is called for.[204]

The romance of love and adventure is well represented in the thirteenth century. *Der guote Gerhart* of Rudolf von Ems is attested as a written work only elsewhere and readers may be assumed for it because of explicit references to them in every other work of his.[205] They are certainly present in his *Willehalm von Orlens*, a highly literary work (divided into books, each with a prologue) whose artistry could be appreciated only by a literate reader.[206] Rudolf personifies his book, as Wirnt von Grafenberg did, and has it address the individual reader, implied also by the acrostics which open each book and by the reception which Rudolf foresees for his work in which the visual dimension is stressed by the equation of *lesen* with *sehen*.[207]

Of the three romances of Berthold von Holle only *Darifant* refers to his readers (as critics), but the likelihood of the same kind of audience suggests that his *Demantin* and *Crane* found a similar reception.[208] The opening verse of the *Engelhard* of Konrad von Würzburg, paralleled by another self-advertisement in his *Silvester*, can be interpreted as individual reading only if we see it as imitating Konrad's *meister*, Gottfried von Strassburg, who uses a similar phrase in his prologue for which individual reading is most likely.[209] The evidence for *Reinfried von Braunschweig* is an isolated allusion to what the audience have earlier read in this work.[210] Heinrich von Neustadt, like many other authors, requests a prayer from the audience for his *Apollonius von Tyrland*, but sees them in terms of reading.[211] Johann von Würzburg hopes that his *Wilhelm von Österreich* will give instruction to those *die ez lesen gern*.[212]

'Mären', possibly composed by clerical and clerically trained authors for court consumption, initially at least, are likely to have been a written literature.[213] Various steps in their written transmission from author's copy to collective manuscript have been proposed,[214] including the possibility of a dedication copy attested for Holland.[215] Evidence of this type is lacking for Germany, but many 'Mären' contain indications of their written nature. An author can refer to his work as a 'book', as something which he writes or transfers to parchment and which can be read out to a listening audience in fixed form.[216] However short (and capable of being memorised) these texts may be, there is no reason to question their having been written down as well.

Difficulties arise if we wish to proceed from writing to individual reading since, as *Frauentreue* 353 illustrates, the written form could just as well serve as the basis of a public recital. When Fischer argues that the written form perhaps originally served this function of recital, but also made private reading possible, thereby opening up the path from a sociable gathering to the individual reader,[217] we may agree in principle, but add that this tells us nothing about when this path was first trodden. This difficulty is enhanced by the internal evidence of 'Mären' for, like heroic literature and the 'Spielmannsepen', they contain evidence for writing, but none for readers.

Two apparent exceptions confirm this. In *Karl der Große – Liebeszauber* the audience may be recommended to read a written source,[218] but we have had ample opportunity to observe that this kind of remark may only underline the reliability of this text; it need not suggest that someone actually read this source, let alone the author's own work. The other example concerns the *Meier Helmbrecht* of Wernher der Gartenaere. Kolb's interpretation of the MS evidence suggests that a work originally meant for oral recital of a quasi-dramatic kind (the partners in a dialogue are distinguished by change of tone or gestures on the part of the reciter) was adapted to the needs of a reader by the later insertion of *inquit* formulas in some MSS.[219] This illustrates the path from recital to reading suggested by Fischer and shows that this work later found readers, not necessarily that its author expected them.[220] They may well have existed after 1300 for this example or for the genre at large, but we have no evidence for them before this date.

(j) Lyric poetry

Several reasons account for love poetry finding its way on to parchment in the thirteenth century, even though the transition from performance to writing was slower than with narrative literature.[221] One reason for the development may have been precisely this time-lag in writing between the two genres: by 1200 various branches of court literature had begun this move ('Spielmannsepen', romances, heroic literature, and soon after 'Mären'), which could not be without an effect on the love lyric. This interplay was assisted by the activity of authors like Veldeke and Hartmann in both genres, so that their literate status in one field gave an impetus in the other. Another impetus has been suggested from the Romance source of the love lyric: it is scarcely fortuitous that the first French *chansonniers* are dated around 1250, the date ascribed to the (hypothetical) written predecessors of the leading German collective manuscripts (*AC, *BC, *EC).[222] A third suggestion has to do with what we have seen with the romance, the emergence of an awareness of a vernacular literary tradition in written form. Kuhn has stressed that for all the differences between narrative literature, love lyric and gnomic poetry these genres meet on common ground: from 1230 they acknowledge a classical tradition of *meister* in German literature whose achievements now constitute a norm.[223]

How these songs were written down is shown from the collective manuscripts which preserve them: the MSS A, B, and C are all connected with towns, in which writing established itself in the thirteenth century, and probably associated with episcopal courts, another focus of writing.[224] The period in which these collections were written was ca. 1270 – ca. 1300, but earlier datings are possible for their hypothetical predecessors, dated about 1250, and the *Carmina Burana* collection with German and Latin examples, around 1230.[225] In one form or another German songs found their way into writing from about this date, a process reflected in some illustrations in MS C, where a poem is taken down on a writing tablet or sent to the poet's lady in written form on a roll.[226]

Does the written form of these lyrics mean that they were intended for reading? How careful we must be is shown by Der Taler, who sends a written poem to his lady by a messenger, but makes it clear that it is to be sung to her, or by Ulrich von Lichtenstein instructing a messenger to sing or read out a poem, so that sending a written text need not always mean that the recipient read it for herself.[227] Sometimes, however, Ulrich shows that he anticipated the lady doing this or even, going beyond one recipient, that his 'Leich' was well received by listeners and by readers, again female.[228] The explicit example of Ulrich is an isolated one, dated as late as about 1255, so that for the rest we are dependent on surmise.[229] Our conclusion must be that, although readers were anticipated for the German lyric, there is no certain evidence before about the middle of the thirteenth century.

These qualifications need to be greater with gnomic poetry. It was codified later than the love lyric and the special conditions explaining isolated early examples in writing are reminiscent of OHG fragments: anonymous transmission in predominantly Latin texts, written in monastic centres, incidentally rather than as a purposeful collection as later with the collective manuscripts of love poems or the Jena MS for gnomic examples.[230] Even though three gnomic stanzas come from a collective manuscript from Zürich (ca. 1200), this MS contains an assortment of nearly 400 texts, predominantly Latin, in prose and verse and of secular as well as religious content,[231] so that there can be no talk of a systematic early codification of German gnomic poetry.

The folio in the MS containing *Ubermuot diu alte* gives musical notation,[232] suggesting recital, and gnomic poetry at large is marked by a total absence of pointers to a reading reception such as we found in the love lyric with Ulrich von Lichtenstein. Instead, German gnomic poets stress their literate, learned status,[233] granting laymen an indirect access to knowledge. They read their written source, refer to this source, stress that their own work is a written one and are confident that few laymen will understand them.[234] The transmission of gnomic poetry to its audience from a written basis has been confirmed by the discovery of fragments of Reinmar von Zweter in a roll (as depicted for this poet in MS C), presumably meant for use by the reciter in performance, as well as by other rolls from the thirteenth century containing gnomic poetry.[235] In these cases the written text was meant for a listening audience so that, as far as our internal evidence goes, we have to distinguish literacy of composition from orality of reception in this genre as in some others.

The total number of texts up to 1300 for which a reading reception can be made possible has amounted to 110. This total has to be increased, as was the case with the acoustic reception, whenever we had to treat the genre as a whole (e.g. charters or love lyric) or where works still to be discussed show by the double formula that reading was one of the modes of reception foreseen. Such factors have to be taken into account for reading as for hearing, so that the total in this chapter for reading, as opposed to the total for hearing (270), suggests that despite the move towards literacy in the thirteenth century reading was still far from catching up with listening.

As followed through here, the transition to writing took three different forms. The first, affecting heroic literature and to some extent the 'Spielmannsepen', illustrated a change from an oral tradition in German to written transmission in German, so that the problem was one of communication, a change from orality to writing. In the second form of transition the change was from literature previously written in Latin to literature written in German, so that the problem was a linguistic one, the emergence of the vernacular alongside a hitherto dominant Latin. The genres concerned were legal and biblical literature, historiography, legends and drama. Thirdly, a historically important form of evidence occurs with new genres (no direct predecessor in the oral vernacular or in written Latin) which find their way with little delay into written German. Here the examples are in court literature: with the narrative genre the adoption of writing was immediate, with the lyric it was somewhat slower.

Another set of conclusions concerns the reading reception of works now available in writing. Genres in which the expectation of individual readers is expressed with little or no delay include biblical literature (already in OHG), legends and romances from the twelfth century and historiography from the thirteenth. Secondly, in the case of the love lyric readers are attested with some delay (middle of the thirteenth century, nearly a century after this genre made the first tentative steps towards a written form). Thirdly, and not always to be explained easily, come those genres which, despite their transposition to writing, show no signs of being addressed to potential readers, at least before 1300. These include hymns and catechetical literature (presumably because of their (para)liturgical context), drama (more at home within performance), heroic literature (still traditionally oral, at least in reception) and the 'Spielmannsepen' (closely akin to heroic literature), but also 'Mären' (whose brevity lent them more to memorising and oral delivery) and gnomic poetry (whose public themes went with public delivery). Whatever the reasons may be, these genres all demonstrate that the transition to writing did not lead automatically to a reception by readers, that the reading with which we have been concerned, despite its historical importance, still had obstacles to overcome at the close of our period, centuries after the obstacles it had faced before and during the Carolingian encouragement of literacy.

7

Criteria for the intermediate mode of reception

We have so far been concerned with the reception of German literature under two headings, by listeners and by readers. The reason for discussing these in separate chapters was clarity of presentation, but this should not lead to the conclusion that listening and reading were so opposed to one another that one could not coexist with the other. An obvious example is the Benedictine monastery, where monks heard works recited in the refectory, but were also expected to follow a fixed programme of reading for themselves. The same conjunction of listening with reading is why certain works have been mentioned in the preceding chapters under the heading of hearing and under that for reading. So far, such examples have been mentioned without any discussion of what is involved. Now we must make this good, discussing the implications when a work was intended for both modes of reception and how we may determine when this was the case.

It is necessary to stress this conjunction of hearing with reading against attempts to depict them as mutually exclusive. The firmest statement of the opposing view has been made by Lord, who says of the two techniques, oral and written, that they are 'contradictory and mutually exclusive ... The written technique ... is not compatible with the oral technique.'[1] Finnegan has expressed doubts about the evidence for Lord's conclusion and has questioned whether his binary model on the basis of Yugoslav material can be transferred to other traditions as a universal explanation.[2] Proceeding from the opposite pole and concentrating on literacy rather than orality, Scholz is aware that the reception of medieval literature cannot be presented in terms of an either–or antithesis.[3] In practice, however, he remains under the influence of a binary model whenever, on encountering a work with pointers to hearing as well as reading, he resolves what he regards as a contradiction by arguing one of the pointers, generally that to hearing, out of existence. Although he has chosen for his title a double formula on which we shall concentrate as primary evidence for the intermediate mode of reception, Scholz nowhere discusses it in this light. Proceeding from opposite poles, therefore, Lord has denied that orality and literacy can be usefully regarded in their interplay and Scholz, although conceding that this is wrong, has failed to convert this insight into practice.

To argue in terms of orality and literacy may be a useful first step in organising a mass of material,[4] as in the last four chapters, but only if we recognise that seeing them as exclusive opposites is historically false as far as the Middle Ages are concerned.[5] Finnegan argues that most known cultures do not conform to the binary model, that a mixture of oral with written is more typical than a reliance on one alone, and that this 'kind of mixture is and has been a common and ordinary feature of cultures throughout the centuries rather than the "abnormal" case implied by the ideal types model'.[6] When she says that by now it would be difficult to find actual examples of a purely oral society, untouched by the written word,[7] this is true of the twentieth century with its westernisation of the world in technology, but is also applicable to the past. Not even prehistoric Germania is accessible to us as a purely oral society (although it was dominated by preliterate values), since our earliest testimony comes from classical sources reporting on the Germanic tribes when runic writing and writing in Latin were not unknown to them.[8] If even Germania must be regarded as combining orality with a minimum of writing, the same is more true of the Middle Ages, where the spread of restricted literacy amongst the clergy was accompanied by orality with laymen. Connections between these groups (priests preaching to laymen, lay brothers in monasteries) led to a coexistence of oral with written. It is within this coexistence that we have to place the intermediate mode of reception.[9]

(a) Diagonal channels of communication

The possibility of an intermediate mode, together with its linguistic importance in the early Middle Ages, has been suggested by Romance philologists. Lüdtke criticises the assumption that there are only two channels of linguistic communication: the medium of sound (a transfer of information from speaker to listener) or the medium of writing (a transfer from writer to reader).[10] He points out that, in addition to these direct transfers of information, there also exist two indirect possibilities: the first is 'Vorlesen' or reading aloud from a text (the information proceeds from the writer *via* the reciter to the listener), whilst he terms the second 'Protokoll' or making a written record of an oral proceeding (the path of information is from the speaker *via* the record-taker to the reader). In between the two poles of what may be called pure orality and pure literacy room has been found for two further means of communication, one proceeding from writing to hearing and the other from speaking to reading.

Lüdtke's suggestion was refined by Wunderli, who used the term 'diagonal channels' to describe the two additional means of communication.[11] Wunderli accepts both possibilities, but argues that taking a written record in the vernacular (as opposed to Latin) was a relatively late phenomenon in the Romance vernaculars, dependent on their slow development as written languages.[12] By contrast, recital from a written text to listeners occurred much earlier, because of widespread illiteracy and also because the preparation of a text before its recital allowed the writer time to cope with the problems of writing in the vernacular, time not available to someone recording the spoken word.[13] The situation is similar in Germany, where reading from a text to listeners is much more common from the beginning than the other process. Despite this distinction, each of these diagonal channels bridges the gap between pure orality and pure literacy and represents what Schlieben-Lange terms 'semi-orality'[14] and what I, seeking neutrality, call the intermediate mode (of communication, hence also of reception), partly also because I understand by this rather more than she does by semi-orality.

CRITERIA FOR THE INTERMEDIATE MODE OF RECEPTION

The intermediate mode of reception can be partly identified with semi-orality: both provide a hinge between readers and oral tradition[15] and both include the reading out of a written text to a listening audience. For our purposes, however, the intermediate mode acts as a bridge between reception by reading and reception by hearing; it combines the two modes of reception which we have so far considered largely in artificial isolation. The intermediate mode is potentially present whenever an audience listens to a reciter deliver a work from a manuscript in front of him. This type of delivery shares with the exclusively acoustic situation the presence of assembled listeners, reception by the ear, and dependence on a reciter, but it also shares with the exclusively literate situation the fact of a manuscript and the possibility of reading: for the reciter, but also for any literate member of the audience who might gain access to the text. This description of the intermediate mode should make it clear where it differs from the semi-orality of Romance philologists. To establish this mode it is not enough to show that a written text was meant to be read out aloud to listeners since, whatever the difference between a written text and a work memorised or extemporised, in either case the reception is by the ear alone. This is why examples of *lesen* + dative, meaning 'to read to someone else', were included under reception by hearing.[16] To allocate a work to the intermediate mode we need not merely the possibility that a written work meant for recital could fall into the hands of a potential reader, but also an indication that the author reckoned with the reader. Only then can we talk of the intermediate mode.

To describe the intermediate mode in this way underlines its difference from oral and from written communication, each of which is symmetrical. In oral communication an audience hears collectively a reciter who composes or recalls in front of them, a situation whose immediacy sets limits to the quantity and complexity of what the listeners can take in and the reciter extemporise or memorise. Each party is bound to the limitations of the recital situation. With written communication the solitary reader, freed from dependence on a reciter, can proceed at his own pace, just as the author, freed from the presence of an audience, can write and revise at his own pace. Neither party is tied to the limitations of a face-to-face encounter.

In the intermediate mode of reception the symmetry of these types is replaced by asymmetry, as in two types of situation whenever communication takes place, not from speaker to listener or from writer to reader, but from writer *via* reciter to listener. The first situation is present whenever an audience hears collectively a reciter reading out a work, behind whom stands an author who had previously composed at his own pace. The result of this asymmetrical situation is that potentially a gap opens up between listeners and author. To this the author may react by speaking over the heads of his audience, who lose touch with him and fall behind, or by urging some of his audience to greater efforts of understanding. These two reactions need not be mutually exclusive; they point to varying attitudes of different members of the same audience, as is suggested by Gottfried's distinction between the *edele herzen* and *ir aller werlt* or Wolfram's between the *wîse man* and *tumbe liute*. In either case we are dealing with a potential differentiation of the audience.

This can be taken further in the second situation characteristic of the intermediate mode. Once more, the reciter reads out a work previously composed by an author writing at his own pace. The difference lies instead with the audience, who may still collectively hear the work recited but may now also be represented by the solitary reader, who, unlike the listeners and like the author, can proceed at his own pace. Although the difference between the two parts of the audience is not absolute (there is no reason to assume that readers held themselves aloof from any public recital), it is more accentuated than in the first type. The author must have been conscious of the need to appeal to both parts: to listeners (comprising his total audience), but also to readers (of whose greater powers of appreciation, because they proceeded, like him, at their own pace, he must have been aware).[17] In that the author addresses these two parts of his audience on different levels of communication (as listeners and as readers) his task is of greater complexity, but the discrepancy he faces provides him with greater possibilities of irony, distance from court values, and questioning of convention.[18]

(b) Criteria for recognition

We now have to establish criteria for recognising the presence of the intermediate mode, basing our argument on internal evidence, which falls into three classes discussed in a descending order of convincingness.

First must come those explicit cases where the author says how he expects his work to be received, seeing this in terms of reading and hearing as complementary possibilities, suggested by a double formula, as with Ulrich von Zatzikhoven in *Lanzelet* 9440: *des sult ir alle biten in, / die diz liet hoeren oder lesen*. For the moment it may suffice to say that this formula, long at home in Latin as a pointer to two modes of receiving literature and finding its way into German only at a particular point in time, is the clearest indicator that an author reckoned with his work being received in two ways.

The second class consists of works where, independently of one another and without any explicit link, evidence for a reading reception is found alongside evidence for hearing. If Scholz has shown himself to be worried by this kind of situation,[19] we need not share his worry, for it arises from his neglect of the double formula (i.e. our first class of evidence) and from his tendency to ignore the recital situation in favour of the reading reception.

The third class, made up of two subclasses, is present whenever the reciter reads from a written text to his listeners or, conversely, whenever the audience hears the text recited to them. These complementary situations belong to the last class since, although hearing is involved, the only reading is by the reciter. It is conceivable that the occasional listener, if literate, may have gained access to the manuscript, but this remains no more than a theoretical possibility unless evidence from one of the first two classes is also forthcoming. This is in fact often the case, so that works do not always belong to this third class as if it were a limbo of unrealised potentialities. In many cases the potential reader was an actual reader, present in the listening audience, but capable of dissociating himself in the act of reading.

However clearcut these three classes appear to be, restrictions are imposed on attempts to allocate any work to one or other of them, mainly because of ambiguities in our evidence. I shall illustrate these difficulties in each of our three classes.

With the first class we have to protect ourselves on two flanks in order to meet two suggestions from opposite directions. Where we cannot protect ourselves we are in no position to allocate the work to this class. In one of the brief passages where he does consider the double formula Scholz relates it to reading aloud to oneself.[20] He seeks support from classical scholarship, in particular from Balogh.[21] We shall return to Scholz's argument later and do what he does not do, namely consider the examples of the German double formula before about 1300, where we shall see that the great majority of cases imply two alternative modes of reception (reading or listening) rather than the unity of reading and hearing (the individual reads aloud to himself).[22] Even for the remaining handful of cases the possibility of a twofold reception will be seen still to exist.[23]

The other suggestion was made by Kartschoke who is inclined to interpret the double formula in terms of reciter and listener, thereby taking *lesen* in the sense of reading out to others, rather than to oneself.[24] There are grounds for doubting this (as long as no specific pointer is present) in cases where *lesen* by itself refers more probably to the individual reader,[25] but now we have to extend the argument to cases where the verb forms part of the double formula. An example is provided by Walther von Rheinau, who reckons with readers (*Marienleben* 16114: *Diz getihtes büechelîn . . . / Daz siz ruochen überlesen*; 16140: *swer ez lese*) to whom, rather than to a lector, he grants the privilege of correcting or even destroying his work if they find errors in it (16126ff.). When elsewhere the double formula is used of its reception[26] we may be sure that *lesen* refers to those same readers anticipated by the author as critical judges of its quality and truthfulness.[27]

This may be equipped with flesh and blood if we turn to a passage in the *Weltchronik* where Rudolf von Ems describes its reception at the royal court[28] and uses the double formula of his audience (21731: . . . *des bittich die / dú mere lesin und horent hie*). In this description the reciter lurks behind the phrase *horte lesin* (21695), but is not expressed linguistically. For the rest, the passage is concerned with three figures, each of whom is expressed linguistically: the poet (in the first person singular pronoun throughout), his patron (21663, 21720) and the audience (21711f., 21728f.). This coherent relationship, as well as the fact that the reciter is too negligible to merit mention, makes it unlikely that *lesin* in the double formula refers to anything but the audience, especially since noblewomen, about whose reading ability we do know something, are mentioned among them (21712, 21729).

What I have suggested in this case (the author was much more concerned with appealing to his aristocratic patron and audience, all of whom could listen and some read, than to a solitary professional reciter) is also likely to be true of most cases where the double formula is employed. In classical Latin the author likewise addressed patron and select audience, seeing them as listeners and potential readers, but did not deem it necessary to take the slave-reciter into account. In monastic examples in medieval Latin it is conceivable that the reciter in the refectory might be included in the formula, but much more likely that the author had in mind all who, in addition to hearing his work recited, would preoccupy themselves with it in the devotional reading required by the Rule. Likewise, vernacular examples from court literature addressed the court in all its groupings, including the literate minority, especially the reading noblewoman: among these groupings the reciter was not so important as to be the regular addressee of these double formulas.[29]

As regards the double formula I occupy middle ground between Scholz and Kartschoke, maintaining that it implies works intended for public recital and for individual reading. With that we turn to our second class of evidence: works in which pointers to reading are juxtaposed with indications of hearing, without any express conjunction.

We shall see that Otfrid, without using the double formula, reckoned with two types of audience or two groups within the same audience (he implies that some know Latin, but others do not) and that he anticipated a variety of reception situations.[30] Amongst these we may include the monastic refectory (a background to recital), the cell (in which private reading could take place), but also the school (in which the teacher read to his pupils from a text to which they could at times have access). An example like this, where evidence for reading is present alongside evidence for listening and where it is possible to reconstruct the situations which called forth a twofold reception, must cause us to doubt whether a contradiction, of the type assumed by Scholz, is involved.

Our disagreement with Scholz must proceed one step further, with regard to his readiness to assume a figurative usage for *hoeren*, suggesting that it is not meant literally and therefore acoustically. Kartschoke sees this as arbitrary[31] and puts his finger on the lack of balance in Scholz's procedure, who takes references to a reading reception as literally true, but ignores references to listening or empties them of real content by suggesting a figurative function.[32]

What this amounts to can be shown in the *Marienleben* of Walther von Rheinau. This author reckoned with readers who would peruse his text critically and to whom he conceded the right to delete any offending passage. Alongside such pointers there are also invitations to the incredulous to listen patiently (4168: *Swen diz dunke ungloublich, / Der hoere ez doch gedulteclich*) and to those who may wish to learn more (6560: *Swer wiste und gerne erkande ... / Der hoere zuo*). This is the kind of situation in which Scholz perceives a contradiction, resolved by suggesting that, since a reader can be invited to listen metaphorically to a book, we are dealing with a reading reception only. That such onesidedness will not do can be shown by the recurrence of our double formula in this work, in every case with the *oder* construction implying alternative modes of reception. Early on Walther addresses his audience of men and women with the phrase *Die diz buoch hoeren ald lesen* (67), whilst towards the close the same distinction is made as part of a threefold formula (16152: *Alle, die diz buoch lesen / Ald hoeren ald des flîzes wesen, / Daz ez geschriben werde*; 16237f.). If in such passages we grant a real import to reading the book or having a written copy made, seeing in this a reflection of the reception by readers foreseen by the author, we must also grant an equally real import to listening to this same text. The presence of the double (or threefold) formula confirms that we must take the isolated references to listening as seriously as Scholz takes the evidence for reading. If this conclusion can be reached in the case of a work which happens to contain a double formula, there is no justification for suspecting a contradiction between pointers to reading and evidence for hearing in works which do not employ this formula.

We come now to the third class of evidence and the qualifications which have to be made before we can accept it as a safe pointer to the intermediate mode of reception. The overriding qualification is that evidence from this class does not suffice in itself to establish this mode; it suggests the possibility, not its actual realisation. For final certainty evidence from this class needs to be supplemented from the other two classes. Apart from this special qualifications are required for each of the two subclasses.

The first subclass is the situation in which the reciter reads from a written text to his listeners, as with the *Weltchronik* of Rudolf von Ems (15727: *als ich ez iuh hie vor las*).[33] Quite apart from other points which need to be clarified about this construction,[34] we have to be assured that *lesen* means 'to read out from a written text', rather than 'to narrate, to tell', for only the former, combined with evidence from the first or second class for individual reading, can establish the intermediate mode. This has been made clear by Schröder's discussion of Gottfried,[35] who used the wording *als ich ê las* (*Tristan* 7155, translated by Schröder as 'wie ich gerade (vorhin) vorgelesen habe') as long as he saw himself as a reciter as well as a poet or as long as he entertained the possibility of a recital at all. For the private reader, however, for whom Gottfried also hoped, such a phrase changed its function: it now referred to the narrator 'telling', rather than the reciter 'reading out'. Schröder stresses that the ambivalence of this verb, brought about by the twofold reception foreseen by Gottfried, does not mean that *lesen* was now the equivalent of *sprechen*, for it still implied communication from a written text. This written text is the basis of both modes of reception: it is what the reciter has in front of him as he faces his listeners and what the literate member of the audience reads to himself.

In the second subclass the emphasis lies on the listeners hearing a text recited to them. In his *Renner* Hugo von Trimberg tells his audience to listen to his written account (7727: *Nu hoert ein wâr geschriben mêr*),[36] where the written text agrees with his terming his work elsewhere a *büechelîn* (15, 611). In *Unser Vrouwen Klage* divine favours are requested for those who hear this work recited (76: *den die dîn clage hoerent lesen*), where *lesen* as recital from a written text is suggested by the author's equation of poetic composition with writing.[37] The author of the *Passional* refers to those who hear his book read out (III 5, 92: *swer daz buch horet lesen*), and the same is imagined of a member of his audience by the author of the *Väterbuch* (41448: *Ob er ditz puch hort lesen*).

In these cases it would be theoretically possible to argue, with Scholz, that *hoeren* refers equally well to the reception of a work by a reader and that *lesen* denoted not reciting a work, but the metaphorical possibility of a work 'telling' a reader something. We can meet this objection in the same way as with the other classes of evidence. It is possible to show that *hoeren* is meant literally in such cases if we take into account the evidence of the double formula. All the works just listed contain examples of the double formula (it is anticipated that they will be read or heard in recital).[38] The double formula, where hearing a recital is meant as literally as the act of reading, reinforces this second subclass and suggests that here too hearing reflects a possible reception and cannot be dismissed as merely figurative.

With that we conclude our survey of the three classes of evidence suggesting a twofold reception. Of the double formula it can be said that, despite the need to define its status on two fronts, it presents the least doubtful evidence for twofold reception. In this German follows the precedent of Latin and imitates the Latin formula only at a point when conditions in German came to resemble those hitherto obtaining in Latin sufficiently to make the imitation feasible. The second class of evidence (the juxtaposition of pointers to reading and pointers to hearing) is less convincing only because less explicit, but the mere existence of the double formula testifies to the reality of a twofold reception and shows how unjustified it is to regard pointers to hearing as contradicted by pointers to reading. Instead, the two sets of evidence are complementary. Moreover, when works with evidence of this second class also make use of the double formula,[39] we can be sure that the implicit evidence is reconcilable with the explicit, that both can be used to establish a twofold reception.

By contrast with these classes the third is less convincing, for neither subclass actually establishes a twofold reception, as distinct from the possibility that a literate listener might gain access to the text. That this possibility could at times be realised in practice is suggested in two much discussed passages: in Veldeke's *Eneide* 13445f.[40] and in Wolfram's *Parzival* 337, 1ff.[41] More important, however, is the overriding qualification which we have to demand from this third class: its evidence is only relevant when the recital it suggests can be supplemented by evidence for reading from either of the other classes.

This is important in another respect, concerning how we classify works as meant for listeners, readers, or both. We have to be clear exactly how, in grouping our material, we distinguish works meant for reception by ear alone (dealt with above in Chapters 3 and 4) from works also meant for listeners, but as part of the twofold reception with which we are now dealing. The need for making this distinction arises from the fact that in our third class of evidence in this chapter we have come across *lesen* in the sense 'to read aloud' and *hoeren lesen* in the sense of listening to someone read aloud, terms also discussed in Chapter 3 in the context of reception by hearing. By what criteria may we judge whether a work whose reception is described by one of these terms is to be allocated to the intermediate mode rather than to simple reception by hearing?

Where the work contains no reference to its existence as a written text we have no certainty that *lesen*, used of the reciter's delivery, must denote reading from a text (as opposed to simply telling) and equally no certainty that the work was available for individual reading. In such a case the work may have been received by listeners, but we lack knowledge of readers. An example is the *Friedberger Christ* whose author refers to his audience with the words: ... *daz ich nemac noch newil / necheineme dumben vorgele(sen) noch gesagen* (29, 2f.). Since this work contains no reference to its being a written text (or to the existence of a potential reader) we have no justification for understanding *vorgelesen* as reading out loud from a text or for classifying this work in the intermediate mode. The position is similar in *Dietrich und*

CRITERIA FOR THE INTERMEDIATE MODE OF RECEPTION

Wenezlan: there is no reference to a written text or reader, so that, when the audience is addressed (283: *ouch hoert die âventiure lesen*) we lack grounds for seeing in this anything more than the reciter telling his story. This work likewise belongs to reception by hearing, not to the intermediate mode.

Secondly, where the work contains a reference to a written text and to recital from it, but no suggestion that an individual reader was anticipated, it must be classified under the hearing reception alone. The *Millstätter Genesis* contains internal references to its book form,[42] so that the author's reference to an earlier point (82, 12: *als wir da vor lasen*) may suggest a reciter reading from the book, whilst the absence of any hint of a reader confines the work to reception by hearing. The *Liet von Troye* of Herbort von Fritzlar is instructive as a reminder of the limitations of our evidence. There are references to the work's written form[43] and also to its being read out to listeners (13670: ... *Die diz horent lesen*), but for want of indications of individual readers we cannot assume a twofold reception. This may mean that we thereby exclude from our list a work which belonged to the intermediate mode since, although Herbort does not refer to them, individual women readers can be presupposed for the Thuringian court for which he wrote just as much as Wolfram implies them for Book VI of *Parzival*, written at the same court at about the same time.[44] This assumption remains a surmise, so that only reception by listeners can be safely accepted for Herbort's work.

We may now consider some selected examples in more detail. Since vernacular works follow the example of Latin (classical, early Christian or medieval), it will pay to look briefly at Latin precedents first.

(c) Latin examples

We must content ourselves with a few illustrations only, passing beyond what we saw in Chapter 2 (the world of Latin literacy from antiquity through to the Middle Ages knew of two dimensions, orality and reading) to consider how individual works were meant for public recital and individual reading and how individual recipients could be listeners and readers.

When looking at evidence for the individual reader in classical Latin we saw him implied, even if pushed into second place, by Pliny's preference for hearing a work recited by another to reading it for himself.[45] Whatever the reasons for his preference (the rarity value of a good oral performance, reinforced by a skilled exploitation of the visual dimension), it presupposes two possibilities open to him for the same work. That these alternatives were not available to Pliny alone is clear from what he elsewhere says about his audience. Talking about the advantages of a public *recitatio* for an author, who can become a keener critic of his own work on registering the reactions of the audience before him, he makes the interesting point that if anyone amongst his listeners should be curious enough to read the work which he heard Pliny recite he would come across revisions made as a result of the public occasion.[46] Whether many listeners became readers in this way is beside the point, for what counts is that Pliny could reckon, with his audience as in his own case, with the possibility of receiving a work in two ways.

Individual reading was also to be found in early Christianity as well as reading aloud to others, especially in the liturgy, so that it is hardly surprising if, here too, the two practices came together to constitute a double reception. An early example comes from Origen, who enjoined those who heard him preach to take up the Bible and learn from it what they had been taught in church.[47] As with Pliny, it makes little difference if this happened only rarely, the decisive fact is that this double possibility existed and could be referred to as credible. A similar implication is present in a sermon by Caesarius of Arles, who argues against the excuses of the illiterate in his flock that they are unable to read the scriptures by suggesting that they can arrange to have them read out to them, that they should follow the example of others and pay for this reading.[48] In recommending this practice to those whom he designates as illiterate (*Non novi litteras; aliquis nesciens litteras non potest legere; illi qui litteras nesciunt*) Caesarius is suggesting a solution called for by their uneducated status which was not necessary for the educated. This implies an assumption on his part that the literate would read the scriptures to themselves, supplementing the readings which they had heard in the liturgy.

Examples from medieval Latin are not hard to find. Bertholdus Augiensis, describing the intellectual attainments of Herimannus Contractus, included the practice of reading either to himself or to others (*sive sibi vel aliis lectitabat*), so that the works in question were open to a twofold reception.[49] Jonas of Orléans recommended Matfrid of Orléans either to read his *De institutione laicorum* frequently for himself or to have it read out to him (*ut hoc crebro legas, aut tibi legi facias*).[50] Vollmann interprets the concentration of neumes in some groups of the *Carmina Burana*, but not in others, as suggesting that some were meant for public recital, others for reading.[51] William of Tyre described two aristocratic brothers, Baldwin III of Jerusalem and Amalric, saying that both were literate (the former *commode litteratus*, the latter only *modice*) and devoted what spare time they could find to reading.[52] Nonetheless, William described them both as keen listeners to literature (Baldwin: *historiarum precipue auditor*; Amalric: *Historiarum, prae caeteris lectionibus, erat avidus auditor*), so that for him, as for these two aristocrats, the reception of literature by reading existed side by side with public recital. The necessary condition for this was of course the presence of written texts and literate recipients, but these examples demonstrate that even so there were still occasions enough for the recital of literature to an assembled audience.

The persistence of this twofold reception even in the literate world of Latin is reflected in the traditional use of the double formula *audire aut legere*. How closely the two are in fact connected can be shown from some of the examples just listed. One of the excuses which Caesarius of Arles had to meet came from a country-dweller who argued that he had no opportunity to read scripture or to hear it recited (*Ego homo rusticus sum ... lectionem divinam nec legere possum nec audire*),[53] whilst Jonas of Orléans, after recommending to Matfrid two possibilities of receiving his work, summed them up by the double formula (*in eo legentes, sive audientes*).[54]

The double formula occurs frequently in Latin to denote the prolonged coexistence of these two possibilities. For classical Latin we have met Fronto wishing to surprise his listeners or readers (*audientium aut legentium*) and Martial's concern with the approval of his *lector et auditor*,[55] whilst in early Christianity Lactantius hoped for a patient reception in similar terms (*aut legat patienter aut audiat*), just as Augustine saw his own reception of a psalm in one of two ways (*lego, vel audio*).[56] From medieval sources we may quote Ludwig the Pious rejecting the pagan classics and refusing to read or hear or teach them (*nec legere, nec audire nec docere voluit*),[57] the preoccupation of Kunigunde, the wife of Henry II, with literature (*legere aut legentem audire*),[58] or John of Salisbury's anticipation of a double reception for his *Policraticus* (*lector vel auditor*).[59] Particularly revealing is a remark made with regard to Count Ayulf, but intended as a general observation: *Haec et horum similia legere vel audire princeps mente nobilis non fastidit*.[60] In this Philip of Harvengt resembled William of Tyre: both testify to the incipient literacy of aristocrats in the French-speaking world, but also to the survival of recital at their courts. The use of the double formula in Latin sources is a reflection of this situation.

If even the literate culture of Latin anticipated public delivery as well as individual reading, how much more likely is it that the medieval vernacular, making its first major inroads into literacy from the second half of the twelfth century, should have retained links with the oral realm from which it was emerging, at least in the form of public delivery alongside individual reading. To the vernacular we now turn, looking at six authors where a twofold reception can be shown to be likely. In selecting these examples I have cast my net as widely as possible, ranging from the ninth century until around 1300 and taking my texts from the three areas (monastery, court, town) where literacy primarily established itself and thereby made a twofold reception at all possible.[61]

(d) Otfrid von Weissenburg[62]

The written text indispensable for both aspects of the intermediate mode (the reciter reads from it, the reader has access to it) is made clear by Otfrid in a variety of internal references. He uses *scríban* (and its Latin counterpart in his dedication to Liutbert) to designate poetic composition or the general purposes which lie behind his work,[63] but also when making cross-references, reminding his audience that a detail has already been given them (e.g. II 2, 6: *iz ungidán ni bileip, soso ih hiar fórna giscreip*).[64]

An author who writes produces a book, a product of literacy which Otfrid expresses in his dedication to Liutbert by Latin terms (*volumen, liber, lectio, scriptio*), denoting the whole of the written work[65] or, in the case of *liber*, one of the five books into which, following Latin literary tradition, the author has divided the text.[66] The vernacular equivalents *buah, giscrib, livol*, and *lekza* (loaned from *lectio*) likewise designate either the complete work or one particular book.[67]

Scríban could, however, be meant metaphorically in the sense of composing a work,[68] whilst Otfrid's *buah*, given the fact that he frequently equates his own work with the Bible, may mean simply that he regarded the Bible as a written text.[69] This objection can be met by evidence that Otfrid regarded his book as a concrete, physical object, so that neither *scríban* nor *buah* can be used only metaphorically.

One indication comes in the dedications to Liutbert and Salomo where Otfrid says that he is sending a copy to each of these dignitaries, asking them to judge the work (Liut. 1, 122; Sal. 5f.). This implies that the work existed in written form from the beginning in more than one copy.[70] Another indication is Otfrid's claim to monastic humility and dependence on the superior judgment of others, for in the concluding section he requests his audience to take the good parts of his book to heart, but to cut out whatever may be unacceptable.[71] That we are dealing with a literal meaning of the verb *snîdan* and therefore with the physical alteration of a manuscript is borne out by the evidence assembled by Scholz for a later period, where similar references to correction imply the existence of a physical text.[72]

The presence of a text as a visual object is suggested whenever Otfrid refers to something previously said in an essentially bookish way: 'as I said above'. He does this at one point in his Latin dedication, but several times in his vernacular text,[73] even forgetting himself by twice using this phrase not of himself, but illogically of Christ speaking to the disciples within the narrative.[74]

These examples presuppose Otfrid's work as a text present in a spatial dimension, a visual object whose separate parts may be referred to as passages to be looked up by those who used it.[75] The same is true of acrostics and telestichs (both standing out by capitals, the latter highlighted by being aligned in the right-hand margin, so that the consecutive text is more easily legible).[76] Whereas Latin and later German literature can sometimes draw attention to this device, saying how it can be resolved, Otfrid is silent on this (even though he is the first vernacular author to employ the device), presumably because the telestichs stand out so obviously.

With that we reach the point nearest to an actual reader so far. Otfrid may have written, but this need not imply that his writing was read by individuals, for their relationship to the book could have been indirect, listening to a recital. Phrases of the type 'as I said above' establish no more than that the author made cross-references, as easily to listeners as to readers. When the book as visual object is seen in terms of corrections we draw closer to readers, for we have seen that later such corrections are explicitly linked with readers.[77] Finally, acrostics and telestichs are not merely a visual, but a literate device, for no amount of mere looking at them will reveal their meaning to someone who cannot read. Amongst Otfrid's back-references (normally in the form of what he said or wrote earlier) we are therefore not surprised to come across one to what a recipient may read earlier (II 3, 29: *Maht lésan ouh hiar fórna*).

This reader can be glimpsed elsewhere in the *Evangelienbuch*. He can be implied by *lesan* + reflexive dative (e.g. II 3, 68: *so thu thir hiar nu lesan scalt*),[78] by *lesan* + *selbo* (e.g. Lud. 44: *sélbo maht iz lésan thar*),[79] or by a combination of both (e.g. III 19, 16: *selbo lísist thu thir tház*).[80] In the Latin dedication such readers are referred to as *legentes*.[81] Who these readers may have been we cannot tell, but from his dedications, mentioning the sending of a copy, we may assume that Otfrid hoped for readers at the imperial court,[82] at the courts of Archbishop Liutbert and Bishop Salomo, and at the monastery of St. Gallen, quite apart from Weissenburg. For the rest, these readers remain anonymous, with the exception of one named by a later hand in the Heidelberg MS (*Kicila diu scona min filo las*).[83] It is perhaps not by chance that, as with Notker, the reader whose name we learn should be a woman.

CRITERIA FOR THE INTERMEDIATE MODE OF RECEPTION

The activity in which Otfrid encouraged these readers is shown by his urging them to turn to the Vulgate for confirmation or fuller details, implying therefore that they are Latinate.[84] Quite distinct from these passages, incorporated into the vernacular verses, are marginalia whose wording is from the passage in the Vulgate which is the basis of the *Evangelienbuch* at that point.[85] These marginalia are pointers for the reader, showing him what verses of the Latin source underlie the vernacular text, but many have the words *et reliqua* added, suggesting that the reader is not to content himself with the keywords in the margin, but is directed to the rest of the Vulgate which Otfrid has rendered.[86] The reader may be compared with the *studiosus lector* of the *Heliand Praefatio*:[87] he read Otfrid's text, but was encouraged to further reading in the Vulgate to which Otfrid regarded his own work as subordinate. Patzlaff has therefore concluded from his analysis of the Latin dedication: 'so ergibt sich aus dem Text des Liutbertbriefes die wichtige Feststellung, daß Otfrid hinsichtlich seiner Evangeliendichtung, wenn nicht ausschließlich, so doch auch an ein privates Lesen gedacht hat'.[88]

Patzlaff's formulation reveals that he acknowledges another mode of reception for Otfrid's work, recital to assembled listeners. Ohly has argued that an entry at the close of the Freising MS contains two variant vernacular forms of the prayer *Tu autem, Domine, miserere nobis*,[89] slightly expanded to accommodate them within the Otfridian line, so that in Freising at least Otfrid's text was recited in the refectory.[90] As the Freising MS was probably completed at the beginning of the tenth century, this tells us nothing about Otfrid's intention, but light is thrown on this by two dedications. In that to Liutbert, although *legentes* can refer to individual readers, it is also used in the context of oral delivery of the reciter.[91] Otfrid hopes that Ludwig will give instructions for his book to be read (Lud. 88: *thaz er sa lésan heizit*). The conjunction of *lesen* with a causative generally refers to public recital rather than private reading,[92] but Otfrid's wording may be compared with that used by Hrabanus Maurus in sending a copy of his *De universo* to the same ruler (*ipsum opus vobis ... transmisi: ut si Serenitati Vestrae placuerit, coram vobis relegi illud faciatis*). Here the words *relegi faciatis* correspond to *lesan heizit*, but the addition of *coram vobis* shows that Hrabanus had oral recital in mind, so that Otfrid, too, may have been thinking of the spread of his work by public delivery rather than by any number of individual readers. A public recital is also suggested by *lesan* where Otfrid provides an exegetical commentary on Christ's crown of thorns, details of which had been previously narrated (IV 25, 6: *thie wír hiar lasun fórna*).[93] The conjunction of *lesan* with *hiar ... forna* as a back-reference is a clear sign that these words have nothing to do with what Otfrid read in his source, but recall what he had previously told his audience. *Lesan* here means not the preparatory reading of his source by the author, but the reading out of his own version to listeners.[94]

How Otfrid conceived recital of his work is suggested by the rivalry he indicates between his vernacular Christian poem and another kind of poetry.[95] The vernacular poetry of laymen which Otfrid is attempting to drive out was not merely oral, but specifically sung poetry,[96] whereas his Christian poem was literate in a double sense (it rested on the written gospels and was itself a written work),[97] so that we have a contrast between *illitterati* (laymen clinging to traditional oral poetry) and *litterati* (clerics with a monopoly of Latin and writing).[98] Yet this contrast was not an absolute one between exclusively oral and exclusively written, for Otfrid used *cantus* of laymen's poetry, but also of his own (*hujus cantus lectionis*). If he hoped to drive out secular poetry he had to meet it on its own vocal ground, since to confine his own work to the written context would have meant avoiding the challenge from oral poetry.[99] This oral poetry was sung poetry, so that Otfrid could not afford to make his appeal less persuasive than his rivals; for him to have reckoned with speech by contrast with their use of song (and music) would have undermined the force of his attack.[100] This sung dimension of Otfrid's work, as he himself conceived it, has been confirmed by musicological interpretations of the key-phrase *hujus cantus lectionis*,[101] the presence of isolated neumes in the Heidelberg MS,[102] the sporadic use of Romanus letters as musical notation in the Vienna MS,[103] and the similar function of accents found systematically throughout Otfrid's text and interpreted musicologically with reference to the *accentus Moguntinus* in use in the archbishopric to which Otfrid's monastery belonged.[104] Singing is also suggested by refrain stanzas in the *Evangelienbuch*, implying sung performance by more than just a reciter, no matter whether it involves antiphons (two choirs alternate) or responsions (the lector alternates with his listeners).[105] That choral singing must be considered is made clear at two points where *singan* is used with *wir*, used as a collective plural (implying joint singing) rather than an authorial plural (suggesting poetic composition).[106] Choral singing of this kind, scattered over several passages in the work, takes it out of the context of the refectory and shows that recital was not confined to that occasion.

Within the variety of ways in which Otfrid's work could be received there is a basic distinction between the individual reader and assembled listeners, but the latter must be differentiated according to the various recital forms suggested by different notations, and also in the light of the distinction between a solo reciter and choral singing. This variety has created difficulties, leading McKenzie, for example, to talk of contradictory statements by Otfrid.[107] McKenzie has shown that Otfrid regarded his audience as knowing Latin (if he wished to guide them from his text to the Vulgate),[108] but against this has to be set the apparent suggestion that this audience was ignorant of Latin.[109] The search for the recipients of Otfrid's work and for the modes in which they received it seems to have brought us to a quandary, confronting us with an audience which was both acquainted with Latin and ignorant of it, or which consisted both of readers and of listeners. To resolve this we have to consider whether the contradiction may be only apparent and yield to a difference between various types of audience or various groups within the same audience. Corresponding to the different ways in which Otfrid's work was received (reading, various types of recital, choral singing) we also have to take account of various reception situations.

Two situations imply the possibility of reading. Ernst has mentioned the monastic cell as background to the private reading implied when Otfrid referred his reader to the Vulgate,[110] and has also suggested that the work could have been used in the Weissenburg *schola*[111] for, as with Notker, this could mean that the text was read out by the teacher, but also read separately by some of the pupils. Otfrid's almost scholarly cross-references make this credible.

Other situations imply oral delivery. This is the case with recital in the refectory, and Ohly observes that such recitals were commonly meant for the *insipientes*,[112] which would account for the use of vernacular texts, especially given the presence of lay brothers, secular guests and others unable to follow a recital in Latin.[113] The same is true of the suggestion that the reception of the work may not have been confined to the monastery, implied by the dedication to Ludwig the German and by the author's hope that it would be recited among the Franks.[114] Royal interest in the work has been suggested as one of the reasons why it was composed in the vernacular in the first place.[115]

Different reception situations imply different modes of reception. The monk's cell and the monastic school suggest the possibility of individual reading, of the Vulgate as well as of Otfrid's text, whilst public recital is implied by the refectory and the ruler's court. Statements about the ability and inability of his audience to understand Latin do not amount to a contradiction, but are evidence for the various modes of reception and the variegated audience which he anticipated. Reducing this variety to a basic formulation: Otfrid was aware that his work would be recited, in one way or another, to a listening audience, but also hoped for and encouraged a reading reception, even though this may have involved fewer people. Once we recognise the twofold nature of this reception, we can accept that reading and listening need not be in contradiction, but can complement one another (the reader can on occasions be present as a member of a listening audience).

(e) Notker the German[116]

With Notker we have to take account of the conditions in which he worked in a monastery school and which cannot be equated with those applicable to Otfrid (except in so far as the *Evangelienbuch* may also have been used in the school). If most of Notker's surviving works fall within the trivium, the elementary level of instruction, this is the level on which the need for translation and explanation existed.[117] Even so, his method implies that he was not dealing with beginners, for the mixed language (German with Latin key-terms) used even in translation and commentary suggests that his pupils understood these technical Latin terms. By using the vernacular Notker meets the needs of his pupils, as implied by the words written above the first line of the Latin commemorative poem in the *Liber benedictionum* of Ekkehart IV.[118] His activity as a translator and commentator was devoted to this pedagogic goal, so that we may regard his works as intended for the same classroom situation. His teaching methods involved a preoccupation with a written text meant for the individual reader and an oral delivery, as in a modern lecture-room.[119]

In his additions to the texts which he translated and explained Notker made it clear that the trivium embraced book disciplines. He translated *septem liberalium artium*[120] by *tero siben bûohlisto* (*De consolatione* 73, 22); where Boethius referred to *libellos*, Notker was more specific (*De consolatione* 12, 4: *bûoh. târ liberales artes ana uuâren*); with reference to rhetoric Notker said: *tes sint ciceronis pûoh fol. diu er de arte rhetorica gescriben habet* (*De consolatione* 80, 24). These disciplines were therefore book disciplines for him, presupposing reading and writing. The same is true of the two works listed by Notker in his letter to Bishop Hugo of Sitten[121] which do not belong to the liberal arts, his translations of the psalms and the book of Job. These presuppose learned written commentaries and it is said in a gloss to the *Liber benedictionum* that the Empress Gisela had copies of these works made for her personal use.[122] All of Notker's work belonged to the world of books.

Accordingly, Notker referred to his works as written[123] and, more commonly, to be read. He could imply the act of reading either as an organised curriculum of study (*De interpretatione* 499, 15ff.) or in a sense close to 'textual reading' (e.g. *Canticum Ezechie Regis* 1060, 3).[124] On occasions reading could be personalised in an allusion to the individual reader, even though the Latin *lector* was used in the middle of a German sentence (e.g. *Psalter* 685, 8: *Sih dir selbo lector uuio Augustinus chede* ...).[125]

A written text meant to be read constitutes a book, which is how Notker could sometimes refer to his own works (e.g. *De consolatione* 162, 27: *Pediu chît ter titulus tisses pûoches*).[126] The phrase 'this book' constitutes a problem, however, if we take into account *De interpretatione* 499, 8 (*tero uersuîgêt er an disemo bûoche*), where *er* refers to Aristotle as the author of the book which Notker was translating. It would be possible to interpret 'this book' in all cases belonging to this group as denoting the classical work rather than the medieval, but that captures only part of the situation in Notker's classroom, for he did not have in front of him a manuscript containing only the classical text. Instead, the text before him was more complex, consisting of the classical text, but also a vernacular translation and commentary. Whilst 'this book' might still refer to the classical work, it also included Notker's vernacular text, presented as a book just as much as its classical predecessor.

There are other ways in which Notker's reader can be implied. If in the early Middle Ages knowledge of Latin involved an ability to read,[127] it is significant that Notker was often ready to give an explanation in Latin, assuming that he would be understood. The implications of this are revealed by the converse technique where clerical authors, addressing illiterate laymen, explained Latin terms by a vernacular translation.[128] This technique, made necessary by the audience's lack of Latinity or literacy, was not unknown to Notker,[129] but not for the same reason since it is outweighed by the frequency with which a Latin term provided an explanation (e.g. *Psalter* 977, 15: *an selbemo dinge. nals in gedingi. Daz chit in re. nals in spe*).[130] Such cases suggest an audience capable of understanding Latin and therefore able to read.

Notker was able to give readers instructions for further reading, telling them where to find further information or confirmation (e.g. *De consolatione* 46, 26: *Lis orosium. er saget tir iz*).[131] It could be objected that this recommendation might be made by the Lady Philosophy to Boethius, not by Notker to his readers. Against this it can be argued that the equation between the instruction received by Boethius and that given in the St. Gallen school is no mere assumption, but is a parallel drawn explicitly by Notker (*De consolatione* 179, 8ff.). Similarly, although in one example (*De interpretatione* 511, 24ff.) the subject is Aristotle, those whom he teaches are not just his personal pupils, but also those introduced to his arguments at St. Gallen. Aristotle's bibliographical reference is therefore Notker's, which confirms the suggestion that 'this book' covers both Aristotle's original and its medieval adaptation.[132]

That a visual reception of his works was anticipated by Notker is clear whenever, to clarify his argument, he inserted a diagram, but also a pointer to the diagram into the text. He reckoned therefore with readers who would understand his argument more easily by consulting the diagram and who would be guided to the diagram by what they read in the text.[133] It could be that these cases are ambiguous, that *De consolatione* 235, 2 (*sô du hîer sehen maht*) could be addressed equally well to a listener in the classroom to whom the teacher displayed the diagram. Against that another example can be set, *De interpretatione* 522, 13: *Sih târuore an dia descriptionem*, which tells the reader to look at a diagram, but also informs him that it will be found not at the same point in the text, but further back.[134] This passage conjures up a reader who looks at a diagram, but who has to turn back to do this – it shows that Notker did not simply expect a classroom situation, but also the individual reader.

The literate nature of these works can also be confirmed by Notker's use of technical terms to indicate their various parts or rhetorical subdivisions (e.g. *Psalter* 872, 3: *Andere codices chedent; Martianus Capella* 132, 9: *An demo êreren libello ist taz kesaget; Psalter* 384, 5: *Diser uers triffet ad passionem*).[135] In employing such concepts as book (a part of the whole work), chapter, prologue, verse etc. Notker as a learned author followed established practice in Latin literature, and his terms owe much to Latin models. To divide a work in this way, as Otfrid had done, is an indication that the work was under learned, Latin influence and belonged to the realm of writing, a realm which included individual readers (his audience was literate; he referred the potential reader from text to diagram; he equipped him with cross-references to other passages).

There is however a sense in which the equation of a teacher's works with readers is not self-evident, for the situation in the classroom also has to be considered, the possibility that Notker may have used his text as the basis of lectures, addressing his pupils as listeners in front of him. In view of the expense of books pupils did not possess their own copy: only the teacher commonly had this, whilst they made do with copying on to writing-tablets points read out to them.[136] However much individual reading may have been possible outside the classroom, within it we have a typically oral situation: a text was made available by the teacher reading it out.

These comments have been drawn from what is known of medieval teaching methods at large, so that our difficulty is to tell whether they can be applied to St. Gallen in Notker's day. For de Boor there is apparently little difficulty, since he regards Notker's works as lecture notes for his own use,[137] meant to be read out loud by the teacher.[138] This gives us no reasons why we must regard Notker's written works in this oral light, so that to bridge the gap between written text and oral reception we still need firm evidence. This is not provided by the rare occasions on which Notker referred to his pupils 'hearing' what he had to tell them – because of the paucity of these occasions[139] and because a verb of hearing cannot be taken as reliable evidence for an oral situation.

Paradoxically for one renowned as a translator into the vernacular our search for Notker's listeners is assisted by an indication which he frequently gave in Latin. It consists of a word or phrase added to his source, but not rendered in his German translation: it therefore comes between his source (Latin text) and his audience (vernacular version),[140] so that we may associate it with Notker himself. It reflects his position as a mediator. These additions normally come at the end of a Latin sentence or clause isolated for subsequent translation and commentary before the Latin text is continued, and they generally extend over several such sentences or clauses, but sometimes less. An example from *Martianus Capella* (109, 11) reads:

> Ni nostra astrigeri nota benignitas. conferre arbitrium cogeret intimum. Suspensio. Ube mih nescunti mîn gûotwilligi. mînen tougenen uuillen mit iu ahtôn. Et quicquid tacito uelle fuit satis. id ferre in medium collibitum foret. Et hic. Unde ube mih nelusti fure iuuih pringen. des mir suîgentemo samo-uuola spûoti. Possem certa .i. mea decreta meis promere ductibus .i. sententiis. Depositio. Anderes-uuîo mahti ih einrâte gefrummen mîne beneimedâ.

Here each sentence is given first in Latin and then in German, but in between something is added (*Suspensio* ... *Et hic* ... *Depositio*), missing in the Latin and in the translation.[141] As a rhetorical term *depositio* denotes the conclusion of a period,[142] while *Et hic* stands for *Et hic suspensio*, meaning that the *suspensio* runs on. The problem lies with understanding *suspensio*. As variants we find *Suspende vocem*[143] and *Suspensio vocis*,[144] telling us that the function of *suspensio* is connected with *vox*. This suggests that the speech or discourse was to be suspended or interrupted, whilst the imperative *suspende* in a context concerning Notker (as opposed to source or recipients) implies that these additions were reminders to the lecturer, telling him at what points to pause.[145]

Why he should want to pause is suggested by two variants. At one point[146] Notker hints at a reason (*Categorien* 440, 23: *hic suspende uocem. quia pendet sensus*): the lecturer must pause here because the meaning of his argument is unclear. The second variant is more revealing, for after adding *Hic suspensio vocis* and twice using *Et hic* Notker employs two variant forms (*De interpretatione* 535, 27: *Hic remisior uox. quia interposita ratio est*;[147] 536, 3: *Et hic remissa*) before concluding this group.[148] If *remissus* (as opposed to *astrictus*) means 'in free speech', this suggests that the teacher extemporised, inserting an *ad hoc* argument (*ratio*) at a point where difficulties were likely to arise in view of the uncertainty of the meaning. What is true of these two passages where Notker is more informative may apply to the more succinct ones: at difficult points this pedagogue paused in his prepared delivery and met difficulties in his pupils' comprehension by extemporising a further explanation. This suggests that de Boor was correct in stressing that Notker's texts cannot be separated from oral delivery and that 'sie waren Vortragsgrundlage, an die weitere Erläuterungen anknüpfen konnten und sicher angeknüpft haben'.[149] The importance of these passages lies in the indication that, however much Notker may have addressed the individual reader, the conditions of teaching made it impossible to abandon the oral context of the classroom.[150]

(f) Hartmann von Aue[151]

We shall be concerned with this author's Arthurian romances and court legends (however persuasively Mertens has sketched the position of the *Klage-Büchlein* between lay and clerical,[152] this work contains no suggestions of how the author anticipated its reception). In considering these four works I make no distinction of kind between them, but approach them as if they were meant, if not for the same audience, at least for the same kind of lay aristocratic audience of whom the author could make the same assumptions about public recital and ability to read. This assumption is justified with the two Arthurian romances in view of Gawein's advice to Iwein about the danger of not taking the example of Erec to heart[153] – the reference is so concise that Hartmann must have assumed that his audience for *Iwein* knew his first romance. The same assumption can be made for the legends if we accept the argument of Mertens that *Gregorius* was meant for lay aristocrats who knew the author's secular works, including *Erec*, the *Klage-Büchlein*, and some lyrics.[154]

Hartmann's *Armer Heinrich* seems to promise little about oral reception, since it contains only one possible pointer in an author's address to his audience (356: *von der ich iu ê hân gesaget*) where it is uncertain whether *sagen* is meant literally or metaphorically. On that uncertain note we may leave this aspect for the converse dimension of literacy, raised by the author in the prologue in two respects, concerning himself and those whom he addresses. The narrator, who refers to himself as Hartmann von Aue, describes himself as literate (1: *Ein ritter sô gelêret was / daz er an den buochen las*), which Wapnewski brands as naïve in the conjunction of *sô gelêret* with no more than an ability to read.[155] Such an impression is created only if we do not take v. 3 into account: *swaz er dar an geschrieben vant*, for this goes beyond a mere ability to read and tells us that Hartmann read (and understood) all that he came across in his source studies,[156] which in his literary career means texts in French and Latin. The poet's educational standing is therefore presented on a higher level than elementary literacy, so that he is justified in drawing attention to it.

This opens the way to the second aspect of literacy: whether the author reckoned with a reading reception. This question is answered from two lines in which he requests the prayers of a future audience, saying of them: *und swer nâch sînem lîbe / si hoere sagen oder lese* (22f.). Here we may agree with Scholz that *lesen* is used in the modern sense ('to read to oneself'), so that v. 23 refers to different ways of receiving the work, by listening and by reading.[157] If the author requests prayers on his behalf from all who learn of his work, he is not likely to address his request first to 'all who listen to its recital' and then, fussily and anticlimactically, to 'the one person who recites it'. The situation demands a conjunction of 'all who listen' with 'all who read', making up the totality of Hartmann's audience. This is also suggested by later examples in court literature, where this double formula denotes two types of reception. Talking of the reception of Wolfram's work, Gottfried says: *als man si hoeret unde siht* (*Tristan* 4685), where *sehen* instead of *lesen* makes it clear that reading rather than recital is involved.[158]

The double formula does more than enlighten us about the reader, for if we take *lesen* seriously in its literal sense, we must do the same with *hoeren sagen* and cannot demote it to a mere metaphor. If it points to an audience listening to a recital, this in turn throws light on the isolated pointer to an oral reception (356), suggesting that we understand it literally. Or rather, to do justice to the complexity of twofold reception, this line is to be understood literally when listeners are addressed, but metaphorically when readers are involved.

Concerning this twofold reception we have to go further than Scholz. He used Hartmann's passage as an illustration that court literature was meant to be read, but ignored Hartmann's anticipation of two modes of reception. With this author we are far from having made the transition from exclusive hearing to exclusive reading. Hartmann's assumption of a reader implies that he regarded his work as much as a written text as the written sources he consulted, whilst his conjunction of reader with listener places this work within the intermediate mode of reception. The novelty is not that he anticipated readers for his work, but that he reckoned with two kinds of reception and indicated this by the double formula.

The same can be shown for *Gregorius*. Here, too, the pointers to an oral delivery and reception are ambiguous. When the author refers to 'hearing' this story (53: ... *daz si vil starc ze hoerenne ist*), to 'telling' the story to his audience (1843: *als ich iu ê gesaget hân*) and to their having 'heard recounted' a detail (3296: ... *on dem ir ê hôrtet sagen*), none of these phrases is precise enough: each could be used literally, but equally well in a figurative sense of written communication. As with *Der Arme Heinrich* assistance is provided from elsewhere, but only if we regard the oral dimension in conjunction with literacy.

Even if *Gregorius* lacks the self-satisfied tone of the prologue to *Der Arme Heinrich*, the author still presents himself as someone who has consulted a book source and must possess more than elementary literacy. He does this twice, using the phrase *als ich ez las*, when stating that he has derived a point from his source:[159] since the point has not been mentioned before, the phrase cannot mean 'as I recited (at an earlier point)', but is used to show that the author read the detail in his source. This indication of the author's literate status is complemented, as in *Der Arme Heinrich*, by a passage in which a reading reception of the work is anticipated. As with the other legend, this concerns a request for prayers on behalf of the author by his audience, defined by the two ways in which they may receive the work (3994: ... *von in allen / die ez hoeren oder lesen*). The parallel between the two legends is a close one: the context of the audience requested to pray for the author is the same, the contrast between the two modes of reception is suggested by *oder* (more persuasive than *und*), and the distinction in each work is between *hoeren* and *lesen*. The use of *hoeren* in this double formula is enough to suggest that this verb in the ambiguous pointers to oral delivery (and by extension *sagen*) can be interpreted literally. These pointers are not so much ambiguous as twofold in application – in this they reflect the twofold reception of the work.

Again the double formula has revealed itself as vital in detecting the intermediate mode. Scholz does not discuss this passage from *Gregorius*, but from it we may draw the same conclusion as with *Der Arme Heinrich*. For both legends Hartmann reckoned with possible readers, but also with public recital.[160] Both belong to the intermediate mode.

In *Erec* we encounter many more references to the author consulting a written source, perhaps because in this first example of a new genre he wished to stress the new literate ideal to which he subscribed. Two are of the type found in *Gregorius*

CRITERIA FOR THE INTERMEDIATE MODE OF RECEPTION

(*als ich ez las*)[161] and a third is more explicit, for the author claims to have followed his source, specified as a book he has read (7491: *als ich an sînem buoche las*). In this *an sînem buoche* corresponds to *ez* in the other references, but makes explicit what they implied. In a fourth reference Hartmann attributes responsibility for the truth to his written source (8698: *ob uns daz buoch niht liuget*). The literacy involved in all these references concerns the German author reading his source, but also the author of this written source, Chrétien,[162] described as a *meister* (7299, 7893), a *magister* educated in the schools. The relationship between these authors is presented in literate terms; together they incorporate the new literate ideal of court literature.

This literacy has so far not touched Hartmann's audience and their reception of *Erec*. Light is thrown on them by a remark in the description of the horse given to Enite. Having shown how one flank was white, the narrator starts his depiction of the other: *alzan genzlîchen wîz / sô disiu schilthalben was / von der ich iu nû dâ las* (7303ff.). This phrase differs from *als ich ez las* in that Hartmann no longer refers to his source, but is addressing his audience (*iu*),[163] drawing their attention to what he has recently told them (*nû dâ*): the point takes up what has been said in vv. 7292ff. *Lesen* in this passage refers to the relationship of the author/reciter to his audience and denotes the act of reading out to an assembled audience, so that we may agree with Cramer's translation: 'So weiß die linke Seite war, von der ich euch eben vorgelesen habe.'[164] As a literate poet Hartmann saw his work as a written text as much as Chrétien's and as such it was potentially available for the literate members of his audience to read (that he reckoned with this possibility at court we shall see from a vignette in his *Iwein*). Hartmann might not say that he expected readers, as in his legends, but if we assume the same kind of audience for all his works he must have anticipated that *Erec* would find some readers, besides many listeners,[165] at court. This first romance, like the legends, was meant for two modes of reception.

In *Iwein* Hartmann places less emphasis on literacy in two respects. The first concerns his literacy as an author: although this is mentioned (21: *Ein rîter, der gelêret was / unde ez an den buochen las*), it is pushed into a subordinate clause, by contrast with the main clause in *Der Arme Heinrich*. In another sense, too, the *Iwein* statement fails to go as far. Although the author's ability to compose poetry (25, 30) may result from his literacy (he is therefore a literate poet), his *maere* is not said to result from reading any book. The books which he reads in v. 22 illustrate his literacy but are not necessarily the sources consulted, as in *Der Arme Heinrich*.

Hartmann is also less emphatic in *Iwein* concerning the literacy of his audience, for he has included no reference to their reading his work. Despite this there is an indirect suggestion in the vignette of the young aristocratic lady reading to her parents in the garden (6455: *und vor in beiden saz ein maget, / diu vil wol, ist mir gesaget, / wälhisch lesen kunde: / diu kurzte in die stunde*; 6461: *ez dûhte si guot swaz sî las*; 6470: *ir lesen was eht dâ vil wert*). That the daughter could read French is a token of her literacy, illustrated in a vernacular rather than in Latin.[166] The other two examples of *lesen* point in another direction, for thanks to her literacy the daughter can read aloud to her parents. They derive satisfaction not from her ability to read, but from the content of what she read (*swaz sî las*), her reading is a performance meant for this restricted audience (*vor in beiden saz ein maget*). Since the young noblewoman is neither a poet nor a court entertainer, she illustrates how a work of court literature, when not recited in public, could be read by an individual, if not in complete privacy, then at least in family privacy. In this vignette *lesen* catches two aspects: the personal literacy of the noblewoman and her recital aloud to her parents. It is difficult to imagine Hartmann sketching such a vignette if it had no connection with how he expected his own work to be received, so that we may conclude that with *Iwein*, too, he reckoned with a recital,[167] but also with the possibility that the literacy of some might enable them to do without a reciter, either acting as one for others or reading the work for themselves.

The intermediate mode of reception, as reconstructed for Hartmann's works, is closely tied up with genre:[168] although this mode is referred to explicitly in his legends, he is more reticent in the romances, so that we can include these only on the likely assumption that they were meant for the same kind of audience, readers alongside listeners. If the double formula occurs only in the legends, on both occasions in a prayer on behalf of the author, this is probably because such intercessions occur for the most part in works with a religious theme.[169] Hartmann may be readier to use the double formula in his legends, because at this time a twofold reception was at home in the context of clerical literature: he could feel safeguarded by these precedents in his legends, but still hesitated to say the same of his romances.

(g) Wolfram von Eschenbach, *Parzival*[170]

Wolfram's relationship to the orality and literacy of his day, raised by his claim to have no knowledge of letters (*Parzival* 115, 27), was for long discussed in personal or biographical terms as tantamount to asking whether Wolfram himself was literate or not.[171] Recently a second aspect has come to the fore, arising from a switch of attention from whether he composed his work orally or in writing to the wider question of the cultural world, lay or clerical, to which he belonged and its function within the symbiosis of lay and clerical, oral and literate.[172] A third aspect has not yet been treated systematically: it consists in taking the question of literacy one stage further from the author, asking it now of his audience. Were some members of Wolfram's audience able to read and did he take account of this, as did Hartmann, in anticipating readers alongside listeners?

If we begin our answer by assembling evidence for reception of *Parzival* by a listening audience, we find that much of it has already been collected by those who argued the case for the author's personal illiteracy, on the grounds that an author who composed orally must also have delivered orally, so that his audience received his work by ear. Whatever our reservations about this approach, they concern its application to the author himself (Can he be confidently equated with the narrator? Can oral composition have produced a work of such complexity?) and are not necessarily valid when the question is asked of his audience. If we take the intermediate mode seriously, the rejection of Wolfram's illiteracy need not mean that his *Parzival* was intended only for readers.

Horacek sought support for her view that Wolfram composed orally in the many source-references in which he remarks on what he has 'heard' or 'heard said', on what he has been 'told', but nowhere on what he has read (as with Hartmann).[173] She supplements this by arguing that Wolfram was so far from envisaging a reading audience that he constantly addressed his audience as listeners, requesting them to 'hear', to 'listen', to 'pay attention' etc.,[174] but nowhere (apart from one exception which Horacek nowhere mentions) referring to a potential reader. The two questions addressed here (the presumed illiteracy of the author and his audience's reception of his work as listeners) are not strictly complementary, as can be seen if we introduce the question of the possibly fictional function of such remarks which has been raised by Scholz. Nellmann uses the concept fiction in this context, saying that the solitary hint of a potential reader does not really destroy the fiction of a recital situation.[175] His use of 'fiction' here is unfortunate, since elsewhere he makes the point that the picture of the audience which emerges from internal references in *Parzival* cannot be equated with the real audience which faced Wolfram as reciter, but that there is a measure of common ground between real and fictitious audience.[176] In the fact of common ground at all we must recognise that Wolfram reckoned with an assembled audience (addressed by himself or another reciter)[177] on which he could build what fictional aspects he found useful for the rhetorical control of his audience.

There is also a characteristic contrast between Wolfram and other poets who addressed potential readers and put themselves forward as literate. Whereas Hartmann and Gottfried give cross-references to other passages by a verb suggesting recital from a written text (e.g. *Tristan* 7155: *als ich ê las*) alongside various verbs which need not imply a manuscript, Wolfram uses only the latter (e.g. 414, 1: *Welt ir hoern, ich tuon iu kunt / wâ von ê sprach mîn munt*, refers back to 402, 1ff.; 426, 21: *wan als ir selbe hât gehôrt*, refers back to 425, 15ff.). Finally, whereas a literate author like Rudolf von Ems can strengthen his position as a vernacular author by placing his work in an uninterrupted written tradition from Greek to Latin and thence to German,[178] Wolfram stresses the way in which his story was handed down, but makes no mention of the literate dimension to which Rudolf attached such importance.[179]

Of all such passages with Wolfram the question could be asked whether they might not be fictional in intent, implying in a literate work an imaginary recital situation not to be taken literally. If in the 'Selbstverteidigung' (*Parzival* 114, 5ff.) the narrator proclaims allegiance to the cultural ideal of laymen and denies all contact with book literature, it is incredible (because it would have destroyed the effectiveness of this passage) that he could have said this of a work which, whatever the manner of its composition, did not enjoy a reception by listeners and did not share at least this aspect of the oral tradition of laymen. If such literate authors as Hartmann and Gottfried made it clear that they anticipated readers and also listeners, is it not likely that Wolfram, rejecting all association with reading and writing, reckoned at least with a listening reception? Can his poetic intentions be conceived as more literate than those of Hartmann and Gottfried, so literate that he could dispense with public recital altogether? Can he be imagined as so free of the conditions of literary patronage and its need for a public dimension of literature that he could choose for himself to do without recital? We do not have to go as far as Curschmann's assumption that Wolfram as reciter appeared before his audience equipped with certain 'stage-props'[180] to see the force of his suggestion that a passage like the 'Selbstverteidigung' was conceived with an eye to recital.[181]

The real problem lies elsewhere: with the question whether Wolfram also had potential readers in mind, which we shall see means women readers in particular. Noblewomen have long been recognised as an exception to the medieval equation *laicus = illitteratus*, and we know much about their role in encouraging literature, religious and secular, and influence as readers to whom court authors paid special regard.[182] This is above all true of *Parzival*: Wolfram hints at having composed it at the request of a woman,[183] and as narrator he addresses women on various occasions,[184] not least in the 'Selbstverteidigung' and the epilogue to Book VI which will shortly engage us. One of the ways in which the author brings home his critical reservations about knighthood is by depicting its negative effects suffered by women as its primary victims.[185] When at the close of Book VI women in particular are addressed, emphasis falls on the suffering of female characters like Belakane, Jeschute, Herzeloyde, Ginover and Cunneware. If a theme of such importance to the author as knighthood has light cast upon it from the point of view of women this suggests how much importance he attached to this group within his audience.

In view of this it is hardly by chance that a hint of a reading reception should come in the epilogue to Book VI, addressed to women and assessing events from their point of view. Seeking to justify himself in the eyes of women, the narrator entrusts himself to their reception of his work: *Nu weiz ich, swelch sinnec wîp, / ob si hât getriuwen lîp, / diu diz maere geschriben siht, / daz si mir mit wârheit giht, / ich kunde wîben sprechen baz / denne als ich sanc gein einer maz* (337, 1ff.). The key-words (*diu diz maere geschriben siht*) are normally interpreted as 'who reads this story',[186] but Nellmann objects that, strictly speaking, the ladies see the story in written form (*geschriben siht*), yet do not read it.[187] He leaves unexplained how they are to have their doubts about the author's attitude to their sex put at rest by seeing that his story exists in written form, rather than by reading it in all the details concerning the women whose fates are recalled in the names that follow. In addition, there is ample evidence that *geschriben sehen*, and even *sehen* by itself, are employed in the sense 'to read'.[188]

These parallels to Wolfram's phrase suffice to confirm the meaning 'to read' for this passage and to suggest that, whatever distance he may keep from bookishness in the 'Selbstverteidigung', his work existed in written form and he reckoned with its circulating independently and hence being read by women in his audience.[189] The written form of *Parzival* can also be shown in a detail to which Scholz has drawn attention.[190] When drawing the threads of his narrative together towards the end of the work and reminding his audience of the links between past and present the narrator twice reminds them of an earlier detail by the words *dort vorne*, a spatial pointer indicative of a written text.[191]

Two distinct modes of reception, listening and reading, have thus emerged for this work, but, as with Otfrid and Notker, these are suggested by separate classes of evidence, not conjoined as two complementary possibilities, as with the formula *hoeren oder lesen* used by Hartmann. Can we, on the basis of two separate classes of evidence, claim that *Parzival* also belongs to the intermediate mode? If we saw no

CRITERIA FOR THE INTERMEDIATE MODE OF RECEPTION

necessary contradiction between them with Otfrid and Notker, the same must hold of Wolfram. Curschmann has implied the same in different terms. He says of the same passage 337, 1ff. that it is an invitation to women in the audience to check, by private reading, whether the author's claim to praise women in an exemplary way was justified.[192] In that case the private reading which they are encouraged to do arises out of public recital, the audience for which included these same women as listeners. They both hear the work recited and read it themselves, they are invited to compare their impressions from the one act with the conclusions they draw from the other. In short, they incorporate the intermediate mode of reception for Wolfram's work. That this possibility is no mere surmise is confirmed by Gottfried's remark on the reception of his rival's work (4685: *als man si hoeret unde siht*), where *sehen*, as elsewhere, stands for *lesen*.[193]

We still lack the explicit evidence, given by Hartmann, showing that Wolfram, too, expected a twofold reception, but find it in the 'Selbstverteidigung', that other digression addressing the women with whom he associated his readers. The passage comes just before the narrator's claim to knightly status (115, 11) and shows him submitting to women's judgment of his position: *swelhiu mîn reht wil schouwen, / beidiu sehen und hoeren, / dien sol ich niht betoeren* (115, 8ff.). They can judge this as a result of hearing and reading the author's work: *sehen und hoeren* is the phrase which Gottfried used of Wolfram's *Parzival*, and is a variant of Hartmann's *hoeren oder lesen*. Wolfram's use of *sehen* may be regarded as the semantic, if less explicit, equivalent of that used by Hartmann. These two authors differ in another detail, however: where Hartmann links *hoeren* and *lesen* by *oder*, Wolfram joins *sehen* with *hoeren* by *und*. On this we may recall the comment by Scholz on the similar variation between *aut* and *et* in the Latin double formula: whereas *aut* must always imply two alternative modes of reception, *et* is ambiguous, sometimes implying reading aloud to oneself, sometimes the same two modes as with *aut*, seen as complementary possibilities.[194] Just as *sehen* was less clearcut than *lesen*, so is *und* less explicit than *oder*.

Wolfram's position emerges as deliberately open to two interpretations. Outwardly, he uses *sehen und hoeren* in its preliterate sense: because his work was recited, he could stress this amount of contact with a completely oral literature (composed and delivered without the aid of writing) and imply that what his audience saw was the visual dimension of oral recital.[195] By doing this he could suggest that his poetic activity (with no mention of writing or reading) was not in conflict with his knightly status. Behind this, however, it is possible to detect signs that the transition to writing has already been made: his work existed in written form (despite his denial) and some readers were envisaged. The author safeguarded his position, in which he may be said to have his cake and eat it, by using an all-embracing terminology. He made use of a double formula which was itself wide-ranging (it could be used of hearing and seeing an oral recital, but also of reading a written work alongside hearing it read out); he avoided the explicit *lesen* and used *sehen* instead (which could mean 'to read', but 'to see' as well); he used the less clearcut and more permissive *und* instead of the more precisely discriminating *oder* (the conjunction chosen by him could, but need not always, imply two modes of reception). Wolfram's attachment to the lay culture of his time means that, even though he anticipated a twofold reception of his work, he drew back from expressing this as openly as one who boasted of his literacy.

(h) Gottfried von Strassburg

Of this author's educational standing, going far beyond simple literacy, there has never been any doubt.[196] Internal evidence suggests a high degree of book learning, so that in addition to consulting his book source, Thomas, it is more than likely that Gottfried drew on further written material in composing his own book. There are no grounds for disbelieving him when he refers to detailed preparatory study of books, both French and Latin.[197] His reference to Latin sources, together with his wish to present himself as a historian dutifully consulting his sources, suggests that they could well have been medieval Latin texts, perhaps chronicles, but this need not exclude classical Latin reading, particularly Ovid and the classical rhetoricians.[198]

A literate author like Gottfried, but also like Thomas (to whom Gottfried attributed the same kind of concern with written sources),[199] dealt with the *Tristan* theme at a time when it had just made the transition to written form in French and German. This has been stressed by Wolf who, within this context of writing, sees a difference between Gottfried and Thomas on the one hand (for whom writing involved an overall detailed plan, possible only as 'Schreibtischarbeit') and Eilhart and Béroul on the other (whose conception and style were closer to oral poetry).[200] It is of a piece with Gottfried's advanced position as a literate author (he realises more of the potentialities of literacy than did Eilhart) that he placed so much stress on the written nature of the *Tristan* tradition to which he attached himself.

In passing over in silence various knightly exploits of Tristan for which he has no taste Gottfried refers to their transmission in written form (18463: *... alle sîne tât, / die man von ime geschriben hât*). When stating how his account of Tristan's combat with Morold differs from others Gottfried leaves us in no doubt that he has written versions in mind (6878: *swie ich doch daz nie gelas / an Tristandes maere, / ich mache ez doch wârbaere*). In reporting the alternative version of the swallow with the golden hair on which he pours his scorn he refers to it: *Si lesent an Tristande* (8605). This rival work is presented as a written text, as is confirmed by the criticism (8626: *waz rach er an den buochen, / der diz hiez schrîben unde lesen?*).

The literacy of the *Tristan* tradition acquires particular importance for an author anxious to stress this dimension whenever true of his own source, allowing him to argue that his version is true because he follows a reliable written source. Gottfried implies this in what he tells us about his consultation of written sources, suggesting that he used these as a check on Thomas, helping him to establish the veracity of the version which appealed to him (155ff.). His ultimate source is a written book (164: *unz ich an einem buoche / alle sîne jehe gelas, / wie dirre âventiure was*), so that the version which Gottfried presents can be summed up as the fruits of his reading (167: *waz aber mîn lesen dô waere / von disem senemaere: / daz lege ich mîner willekür / allen edelen herzen vür*). Behind this reading by Gottfried there lies the reading which Thomas had done for his version (152ff.) and what Thomas read can be adduced to establish the correctness of his version (326: *nu tuot uns aber Thomas gewis, / der ez an den âventiuren las* . . .). Literacy, and therewith truthfulness, is thus established over two literary generations. However, it can also extend over a much longer timespan, as when Gottfried presents a detail as deriving from his reading of Latin literature. If Isold surpasses Helen in beauty, this is meant to show that a medieval literary figure was superior to what Gottfried had read in classical literature (8267: . . . *des ich ie waenende was, / als ich ez an den buochen las, / diu von ir lobe geschriben sint*).[201] When Gottfried says *ich hân doch dicke daz gelesen* (19436) of a detail paralleled in Ovid's *Remedia amoris*,[202] we may take that as a pointer to his reading of the Latin poet, and he goes so far as to say that another point apparently deriving from Ovid must be true because he has read it (17900: *deist wâr, wan daz hân ich gelesen*).[203] What for us seems uncritical must have appeared in a different light at a time when vernacular literature was finding its way onto parchment and claiming something of the cultural prestige which had hitherto been enjoyed by written Latin alone.

In the literate tradition so far established for the *Tristan* story reading has emerged only in connection with the author, Gottfried or Thomas, not the audience. This question is still left open in what Wolf says about the higher degree of literacy in the versions of Gottfried and Thomas, for he describes their reception as implying 'immer noch vorwiegend Vorlesen', implying thereby the possibility of some individual reading.[204] That this question can be asked of the *Tristan* tradition, even on the basis of Gottfried's text alone, is clear in the prologue where the author discusses other versions, unsatisfactory in his eyes. Of these he says: *Ich weiz wol, ir ist vil gewesen, / die von Tristande hânt gelesen, / und ist ir doch niht vil gewesen, / die von im rehte haben gelesen* (131ff.). No matter whether we follow Hatto, who understands the first *lesen* here in the sense 'to tell' ('who have told the tale of Tristan'),[205] or Schröder, who takes it in the sense of individual reading ('die Berichte über Tristan gelesen haben'),[206] both are in agreement over the second *lesen*, which each interprets in the latter sense ('who have read his tale aright'; 'die sie richtig gelesen haben'). Both concede that individual reading, going beyond reading by authors preparatory to composing their work, had a place in the *Tristan* tradition, as sketched by Gottfried.[207] The German author goes further, for he implies readers not merely in this tradition at large, but in regard to his own contribution, which he recommends to his audience, or at least the *edele herzen* among them:[208] *ez ist in sêre guot gelesen* (172), which Hatto and Schröder agree in seeing as personal reading ('They will find it very good reading'; 'Es ist für sie sehr nützlich zu lesen').[209] With that we reach the possibility of readers anticipated by Gottfried, which we must now expand to include reception by listeners as well.

As with Hartmann, the evidence for listeners to Gottfried's work is ambiguous as long as we remain uncertain whether terms are employed literally or figuratively, i.e. as long as we regard this evidence by itself, without regard for a twofold reception. When the narrator decides not to dwell too long on the lament for Blanscheflur's death and refuses 'to say' something which may offend 'the ears' of his audience (1855: *wan ez den ôren missehaget, / swâ man von klage ze vil gesaget*), it would be possible to take this literally (implying a recital), but equally possible, with Scholz, as a 'Hörerfiktion' built into a work addressed to readers. The same ambiguity attaches to the reminder of a detail which has been 'heard' earlier (4276: *als ir wol habet gehoeret wie*)[210] or when the narrator pretends to invite someone in his audience to take over storytelling in his stead (5660: *lât hoeren, wie sol ez ergân?*). Rather more persuasive is an example where *sagen* occurs in conjunction with *ôren* to suggest a possible oral situation. This comes in the appeal to the audience at the close of the prologue (239: *Und swer nu ger, daz man im sage / ir leben, ir tôt, ir fröude, ir klage, / der biete herze und ôren her*). If reading the story of Tristan and Isold is here equated with reading the Bible, but if this passage is based on an analogy with the eucharist,[211] it is likely that, as in the liturgy, the reading anticipated is aloud, to listeners. While regarding this interpretation as a probable one I must also concede its weakness, for it is an interpretation based on another interpretation, and stands or falls with it. It is a weakness which this passage shares with other suggestions of an acoustic reception: none is wholly convincing by itself, but stands in need of confirmation.

This is not the case with evidence for readers, which is more clearcut (which need not imply that Gottfried had only readers in mind, but rather that he addressed them with more fellow-feeling, conscious that it was with them that a literate author should concern himself). It is to the élite represented by the *edele herzen* that the author commends his work as reading-matter (*ez ist in sêre guot gelesen*), but if individual reading is a possibility alongside the public recital available to society at large, this suggests a link between two select groups, the *edele herzen* and the individual readers whom Gottfried has in mind. To the qualifications for being one of the *edele herzen* we might have to add the ability to read and to pay the close attention to Gottfried's written text for which he hoped.[212]

Such is the case in a passage where we are reminded that a point has been made earlier, but with the addition that this can be ascertained by the reader turning back (8741: *und als daz maere hie vor giht, / der dâ vor an daz maere siht*).[213] We, too, have discussed this passage before, but instead of referring the reader back to an earlier page I shall content myself with the observation that this attention to detail and the ability to collate one passage with another are to be expected more from a reader than from a listener. That readers who could scrutinise the text were anticipated by Gottfried is suggested by his use of acrostics.[214] Even if we assumed that listeners might be shown the acrostics in the prologue by the reciter displaying his manuscript to them, these capitals would mean nothing to them unless they were readers, and this assumption could not be made of the names of the lovers, for the acrostics which constitute them are spread over wide stretches of the narrative which could only be embraced by one who had the manuscript in his hands as a reader.[215]

Concerning the intermediate mode of reception we could argue that the evidence for listeners in conjunction with that for readers amounted to the second class of evidence for this mode, but only if the evidence were beyond all doubt. Yet this was not the case with listeners, so that we must approach this question from the other two classes. The first (the double formula) was certainly known to Gottfried, for we have seen him apply it to the reception of Wolfram's work, but more telling is its application to his own. After recommending the *edele herzen* to read his work to their profit (172) the narrator argues that a work whose theme is perfect loyalty cannot fail to commend this and other virtues to the audience, whom he now sees in terms of listeners as well as readers (177: *wan swâ man hoeret oder list, / daz von sô reinen triuwen ist* ...). From this we may conclude that reading formed only a part (however important) of the total reception of *Tristan* and that, as with the women in Wolfram's audience, the readers were probably also listeners, but enjoyed an advantage over those who were only listeners.

This suggestion of listeners alongside readers is enough to remove doubts as to whether indications of hearing could be meant literally, but we can go further by turning to the third class of evidence for the intermediate mode. One form which this took was to suggest that the audience heard the story read out, which we find towards the end of the prologue when the work's theme of loyalty is stressed (230: *wan swâ man noch gehoeret lesen / ir triuwe, ir triuwen reinekeit* ...). If the *edele herzen* in this passage[216] listen to a recital, whereas in v. 172 they are recommended to read it for themselves, we can claim that in v. 177 the double formula links these two possibilities together. The other form which this third class took was the indication that the reciter read out his written text to his listeners.[217] Frequent use is made of this when the audience are reminded that a detail has already been given them earlier. This pointer backwards can be expressed by different temporal adverbs: *ê* (7155: *als ich ê las*), *iezuo* (16493: *alse ich iezuo las*)[218] or *nu* (17421: *Der jäger, von dem ich nu las*). Common to these cases is the fact that the earlier passage can be determined[219] and that, given a literate and carefully constructed work, *lesen* must imply that the text was read out to the listeners. This recital situation does not exclude the individual reader – if it did, we could not include Gottfried's work in the intermediate mode. Conversely, however much importance Gottfried attaches to readers, however much he may expect understanding from the *edele herzen*, their reading reception is only part of the whole to which public recital also belongs.

For this reason a remark by Bertau in his discussion of Gottfried's 'cryptogram' use of acrostics calls for qualification. He says: 'Das ehedem zum Anhören durch eine Gesellschaft bereitete, rezitierte Werk sähe sich im "Tristan" abgelöst von einem wesentlich intimen Werk, das der allgemeinen Gesellschaft (*ir aller werlde* 50) und ihrer Rezitationskultur sozusagen den Rücken kehrt.'[220] As an indication of the direction in which Gottfried was moving and of those to whom he was primarily appealing this is correct, yet it would be mistaken to think that Gottfried turned his back on society in any sense other than where his sympathies lay, to conclude that, however close the bonds between himself and his readers, he had the freedom to ignore the social setting of medieval literature. Public recital may have been a second-best for him and for others who knew that their artistry could only be appreciated by readers, but it was a dimension of literature which they could not escape. To ignore it means exaggerating the speed with which the transition from exclusive listening to exclusive reading was made, a transition prolonged by the persistence of the twofold reception of literature.

(i) Brun von Schönebeck, *Das Hohe Lied*

With this author we come to the latest text in our survey. Brun was a layman belonging to the fraternity of the 'Konstabler' and a member of the Magdeburg patriciate (he refers to his lay status in the *Hohes Lied* 1824ff.). This status is underlined by remarks which indicate a certain distance from the clergy, as when Brun claims to have derived certain details from clerical informants (e.g. 4598: *als mir jahen wise pfaffen*) or when he observes that the meaning of a Latin term is known to clerics (9715: *daz wort palma ... / daz hat vil gute bedutunge. / daz wizzen di wisen pfaffen wol*). Yet Brun, too, knows the meaning of this term, which could have been taught him, together with much else, by the monk Heinrich von Höxter to whom he expresses thanks for assistance in composing his work (12458ff.). This monk cannot have been the sole source of Brun's knowledge, for he refers to what he read or learned at school (e.g. 9756: *sus las ich nehest in der schule*),[221] in his *Ave Maria* he says that he attended a clerical school,[222] and the *Magdeburger Schöppenchronik* describes him as educated (*de heit Brun van Schonenbeke, dat was ein gelart man*) and as the author of many vernacular written works (*... makede sedder vele descher boke*).[223] When Brun disclaims literate knowledge for himself (1824ff.) we may take this as a humility formula in the light of this other evidence, especially since it occurs in a context where he is comparing himself as a layman with clerics, about whose superior literacy there can be so little doubt that they can be termed not simply *di wisen* by contrast with Brun, who is *tump* (7283ff.), but even *di obirwisen* (7330ff.). We are dealing with a lay author who was literate and possessed some degree of book learning, which need cause little surprise towards the end of the thirteenth century in view of the increasing reliance of towns on writing for a commercial and administrative purposes.[224] In literary culture these towns were largely influenced by the literature of the courts (the *Schöppenchronik* reports that Brun also instituted a Grail festival at Magdeburg to which merchants from other towns were invited),[225] so that we may ask whether Brun, like the authors of court literature, reckoned with a twofold reception of his work.

Pointers to a listening reception are too uncertain to be acceptable, as long as we regard them by themselves. We face the usual difficulty of deciding between a literal and a figurative meaning whenever it is said that Brun's audience 'hears' his work (e.g. 773: *ditz sint gar vremde wort, / di ir hie habit gehort*; 944f.; 10816ff.). The same difficulty exists with the other pole of an oral relationship when the author addresses his audience, even where orality might seem to be implied by reference to the reciter's *munt* or *zunge* (e.g. 3837: *daz saget uch min zunge*; 8288: *ditz mere sage vort min munt*). Slightly more convincing evidence, but still not enough in itself, is provided where the author refers back to a point he has just made (3521: *... ab si ein stein si als ich las?*, a reference back to 3515). Against the suggestion that *lesen* here may mean no more than 'to tell, to narrate' we may adduce the frequent references to Brun's work as a book (e.g. 778; 1016ff.), which make it likely that *lesen* used of the reciter has the more precise meaning 'to recite from a written text', which would imply a listening audience. Even if we accept this, we are left with a meagre crop of mainly uncertain pointers to an acoustic reception which, as with Gottfried's *Tristan*, need to be supplemented from other sources.

Turning now to evidence for a reading reception we find that some pointers are equally uncertain when taken by themselves, but that some are more convincing. On one occasion the author says that he has written something not merely for himself, but for 'you', i.e. for his audience (2130: *daz schribe ich mir und vobis*), but we cannot accept the idea of writing for someone as evidence that the person actually read the text, as distinct from possibly hearing it read out.[226] Rather more convincing is a passage where Brun refers back to an earlier point, telling his audience where they may find it in rather more detail than Gottfried on a similar occasion (6150: *daz schreib ich an deme stucke / werliche des andren buches, / du vindest iz ab du iz suches*, a reference back to 464ff.). Here the audience is not being sent on a wild goose chase from Gandersheim to Bamberg in search of a Latin source which they cannot read,[227] they are instead given precise instructions where they can find a detail in Brun's own book. If Gottfried's recommendation implied a potential reader whom he had in mind, the same must be granted in this case. Whether the same conclusion must be drawn from references to other works (e.g. 3126: *davon vint man an den buchen / geschreben vil, welle wir iz suchen*;[228] 6708f.) is rather less certain, for references of this type may simply underline the truth of Brun's work.[229] Finally, the most convincing suggestion of an individual reading occurs with instructions for spelling out the letters of a name (3379: *di buchstaben schribe ich uch so ... / wer daz kan zusamene binden / der mac sinen namen vinden*). Here the author singles out from his audience those who can combine the letters to produce a name, who must therefore be regarded as readers of his work.

The position so far resembles that with Gottfried's *Tristan*: the evidence for a reading reception is more persuasive than for listeners. To be sure that they, too, were anticipated and that the *Hohes Lied* likewise was intended for a twofold reception we have to look at the classes of evidence for the intermediate mode. We cannot adduce the second class (conjunction of evidence for listening with pointers to reading) because the evidence for listening is ambiguous. Instead, we must concentrate on the other two classes.

As far as the first class (the double formula) is concerned, Brun refers to the reception of his work not in terms of the variant *sehen und hoeren* which we have come across with Wolfram and Gottfried, but by a further variant, using *schouwen* instead of *sehen* (*schouwen* can be used equally well in the context of reading).[230] Brun refers to these complementary modes of reception when announcing to his audience what they will learn (5351: *als ir sullet horen und schouwen*; 6102: *daz sult ir horen und schouwen*). Where Veldeke referred to the private reading of the countess of Cleves by stressing the visual dimension alone (*lesen* and *schouwen*),[231] Brun stresses the two possibilities open to his audience (*horen* and *schouwen*). That Brun, like Veldeke, meant *schouwen* in the sense of reading can be shown from a third example of the double formula in which he uses the nomen agentis in place of the verb, and *lesen* in place of *schouwen*: *ir horer und ir lesere* (12542). If in these cases *schouwen* and *lesere* confirm what we saw earlier of a reading reception, we must be prepared to take *horen* and *horer* as an indication that the ambiguous evidence for listening can be interpreted literally.

A similar clarification of ambiguous evidence is given in the third class of evidence. One type of construction in this class (to hear a work read out) suggests that hearing is not employed metaphorically. Brun foresees the day when his work might be recited before princes (1124: *sint ditz buch uf einen tag / vor di vursten wol komen mag, / so daz si iz lesen horen*). *Horen* and *lesen* are similarly combined when the author refers back to an earlier point in his work (2299: *als wir hie vor horten do ichz las*, cf. 2199ff.): in *wir* the author includes himself since he heard himself recite, but also the audience to whom he read out. Listeners to an oral recital are also addressed when the author requests their prayers on his behalf (12508: *wer ditz buch hore lesen, / sus suln si mine maner wesen / zu got und sprechen vorholne / ein pater noster*). If these listeners are seen a little later as part of a wider audience (12542: *ir horer und ir lesere*), this indicates that the recital of a work need not preclude readers. The twofold reception to which this amounts was foreseen by Brun in composing his work.

The other construction in the third class (the reciter reads out to his audience) likewise implies listeners and confirms interpreting pointers to them literally. Again, this occurs especially in authorial references to what has gone before, e.g. 5744: *als ich uch e vore las* (refers to 2709ff.). We have seen enough of *lesen* + dative to recognise that a recital (and therefore listeners) is involved here. We may recognise recital from a written text: because *lesen* to describe the delivery of what is elsewhere termed a book[232] points in that direction, but also because of the parallel between the reference just quoted (5744) and one coming shortly afterwards, 6359: *also ich uch schreib da bevorne* (refers to 6193ff.). This parallel suggests that *lesen* does not simply mean 'to tell': what was read was in fact something written. A final example also suggests an acoustic situation (11317: *also ich uch e las und sang*), for the orality of *lesen* + dative is underlined by the suggestion of singing.

Although the evidence for a listening reception at first seemed ambiguous, it has proved possible to settle the issue by taking into account the evidence for the intermediate mode, with its testimony for listeners alongside readers. What is important about this mode is not merely its evidence for two modes of reception, but also the suggestion that listening persisted alongside occasional reading and that it is anachronistic to concentrate on the novelty, which cannot be understood except in conjunction with what it slowly replaced.

Before we leave Brun's *Hohes Lied*, we may make use of this opportunity to look at the attitude to writing which he exemplified. This has been discussed by Hagenlocher,[233] whose starting-point is a passage, surprising to anyone who comes to it from a clerical attitude to writing, in which writing is accused of potential falsity and is even compared with a harlot: *iz ist um di schrift also geschaffen, / als um ein elich wip / daz do treit doch velen lip / und sich vremden mannen leget bi* (953ff.). Hagenlocher is concerned to establish a possible source for this, but also to propose parallels from the thirteenth century and to place them, together with the attitude they betray, in the context of the rise of vernacular writing.

Brun's attitude is clearly different from what Hagenlocher regards as the clerics' attitude to writing, for whom this activity, especially within the tradition of exegesis, was invested with the authority and sacrality of the Bible as the word of God.[234] Theology and exegesis were so dominant in written culture until the twelfth and thirteenth century that they imparted their authority to writing,[235] so that writing itself, whatever existed in written form, remained largely unchallenged (a reflection of this attitude, adapted to very different ends, may be detectable in Gottfried's claim, 17900: *deist wâr, wan daz hân ich gelesen*). If Brun, together with other examples adduced by Hagenlocher, betrays a different attitude (more critical or realistic), this is because the thirteenth century saw writing practised by social groups other than the clergy who had an interest in its practical advantages and disadvantages for specific purposes.[236] What is decisive in this change of attitude is the spread of writing beyond the clergy. Where clerics saw writing in an exegetical context as the basis of a spiritual truth within it, the layman's pragmatic use of writing for everyday purposes made him conscious that it could be used for any purpose and was adaptable to lies as much as to truth. This change of viewpoint (writing was no longer judged by those who subjected it to exegesis, but by those who made practical use of it and were aware of its shortcomings)[237] is characteristic of a period in which writing was about to pass beyond the restricted ranks of clerical literacy to become more of an everyday phenomenon.[238] The thirteenth century, once a more pragmatic and critical attitude had arisen, but not yet ousted the clerical view, represented a period of transition: 'Auf der einen Seite steht die Scriptura als von Gott gesetzte Wahrheit, der sich Menschen mit ihren schwachen Mitteln im besten Fall exegetisch nähern können, auf der anderen Schrift als bloßes Medium, für sich völlig wertfrei, das für jeden Zweck verwendbar ist.'[239]

It may not be by chance that a drastic statement of a new, pragmatic view of writing comes from a writer at home in the patriciate of Magdeburg and in close contact with other towns in Saxony. It was in the German towns of the thirteenth century that writing began to establish itself on a broader front for the practical purposes of long-distance trade, town administration, charters and lay schools.[240] For Rörig it is symptomatic that, whereas the literate culture of antiquity perished when the use of the everyday cursive script for charters died out about 700, the thirteenth century saw its re-emergence, above all in the towns.[241] Brun von Schönebeck did not have the cursive in mind, but his attitude towards writing was every bit as utilitarian.

These examples of the intermediate mode were chosen to cover as long a period as possible, from the ninth to the thirteenth century. By confining clerical examples to Otfrid and Notker I did not wish to suggest that this mode of reception was not found in clerical literature after Notker, for the conditions under which these two authors worked still obtained in later centuries. Nor did I wish to imply, by restricting examples of lay literature to the hundred years between Hartmann von Aue and Brun von Schönebeck, that the twofold reception of this literature lasted no more than a century. The period around 1300 may be our cut-off point, but it would not be difficult to find later examples of the twofold reception.[242] Even though the examples from lay literature occur later than those from the clerical sphere, the intermediate mode lasted throughout the Middle Ages.

This raises a question about German literature which Goody has asked in more general terms.[243] When reading is available, why should written texts continue to be transmitted orally to listeners over so long a period of time? One answer has come up from time to time: the double formula implies that not all members of the audience were able to read. For them there was no alternative to an oral recital, the need for which persisted long after the first readers were envisaged. For the rest we may assume answers such as those suggested by Goody. One situation where the oral delivery of a written text is appropriate is the pedagogic one considered in the case of Notker and present in any work with a didactic slant: it can be an advantage for the teacher to receive questions from his audience, to see where they encounter difficulties and need more explanation.[244] The immediacy of this give-and-take means that a written text, when delivered by its author, could answer questions, an ability which Plato denied to writing.[245] A technological consideration concerns the Middle Ages as a manuscript culture, in which manuscripts were rare and expensive, so that, in view of restricted literacy, the most effective access to them for many was listening rather than reading. Finally, we should not underestimate the importance to the clergy of maintaining their monopoly, which they were able to do so long as a written text was transmitted to laymen only through their literate services, which explains much clerical resistance to the spread of religious knowledge in the vernacular, bypassing the priest in many cases.[246] None of these features remained free from change, but together they explain the slowness of the transition from orality to reading and the persistence of a twofold reception.

8

Survey of the intermediate mode of reception

We have so far discussed the intermediate mode of reception not for itself, but for the light which the double formula, the clearest evidence for this mode, throws on the two modes hearing and reading. Only in Chapter 7 was it suggested that the double formula was to be equated neither with individual reading nor with public recital alone, but with both modes of reception as complementary or alternative possibilities.[1] The rest of that chapter was devoted to illustrating this in six vernacular authors from the ninth to the thirteenth century, so that we now have to take this further by asking: in what works does the internal evidence suggest that the author anticipated a twofold reception?

First comes a survey of the works which can be allotted to this mode, arranged according to genres. Secondly, because the twofold reception was not governed exclusively by the genre to which a work belonged, there follows a section on five different contexts of reception for medieval literature, illustrating how the type of audience and its social setting also explain the conjunction of two different modes of reception for the same work. We conclude with a section on the double formula *hoeren oder lesen*, the most obvious pointer to what we are concerned with.

GENRES

Our material is grouped under the same ten headings as in the surveys of reception by listeners and by readers. Under each heading the works for which a twofold reception can be argued are listed chronologically. For each work the evidence is given as cursorily as possible and in the light of the three classes of evidence, in a descending order of persuasiveness, discussed in the last chapter. In other words, priority is given to the double formula, wherever this occurs, as the least doubtful pointer. Next comes the evidence of those works for which pointers to a listening reception are independently present alongside indications of reading, in other words those works which have already been discussed both in Chapter 4 and in Chapter 6. Where the evidence in one or other chapter was weak this makes the case for a twofold reception correspondingly weak, but that is no reason for calling into question this class of evidence at large, for regarding two modes of reception as constituting a logical contradiction. That these two modes could coexist is amply borne out by the double formula itself. The third class of evidence consists of indications that the reciter read to listeners from a written text or that the audience heard a text recited to them. Even though not convincing by itself, this evidence is given briefly because it demonstrates that the potential reader could at times become the actual reader anticipated in the first two classes.

(a) Functional literature

In this section only works used in the monastic school and didactic literature provide evidence for a twofold reception.

Of only one author from a monastic school can this be argued explicitly, for although the *Benediktinerregel*, the *Altalemannische Psalmenübersetzung* and the *Murbacher Hymnen* were used in that context, probably as the basis of oral instruction as well as the object of individual reading, there is no evidence for this. The case is different with Notker: he expected his works to be read, but there were also pointers to reading them out in the classroom. This amounts to the second class of evidence for a twofold reception, the relevance of which to teaching at St. Gallen there is as little reason to doubt as in modern university instruction, where a text can be read out in the lecture-room, but also (so it may be hoped) read privately by students.[2]

A few more examples come from didactic literature. The earliest, *Wernher von Elmendorf*, is weak: not because it simply contained a suggestion of hearing as well as a pointer to reading, but because the former was not free from doubt.[3] With the *Lucidarius* there was no doubt about either hearing or reading, whilst a reference to hearing it read out (36, 23) reinforces the evidence for hearing and confirms that private reading need not exclude recital. Thomasin von Zerclaere gave pointers to hearing and to reading, but links these two modes by means of a double formula.[4] Hiltgart von Hürnheim referred in the prologue of her *Secretum Secretorum* to listeners as well as to readers in two consecutive sentences not so concise as a double formula, which does occur much later as part of a triple formula.[5] Finally, Hugo von Trimberg, for whose *Renner* there was evidence of both an acoustic and a reading reception, compresses them into a double formula.[6] That a vernacular work could be read is confirmed by his allusion to the sinfulness of writing or reading Arthurian literature (21651). Hugo also shows that reading did not exclude possible listening by using the double formula (as part of a triple one) in one of his Latin works:[7] if this shows evidence of both, the vernacular *Renner* was hardly meant for the reader alone.

(b) Literature of religious worship and instruction

Collections of sermons could be intended as the basis of sermons to be given to an actual congregation, but also at times for private devotional reading.[8] These two possibilities need only be registered for the genre as a whole: the number of sermons is too large to permit individual treatment.

For the 'Reimpredigt' we have only two examples. In the *Rede vom heiligen Glauben* Der Arme Hartmann used a phrase close to a double formula, confirming both a hearing reception (*gehorenne*) and reading (*gesihte, lesen*).[9] The *Visio Philiberti* of Heinrich von Neustadt contained evidence for listening as well as reading.[10]

Devotional literature is rather more productive. None of the three earliest cases (the *Rheinisches Marienlob*, the *Tochter Syon* of Lamprecht von Regensburg,[11] the *Vaterunser* of Heinrich von Kröllwitz) employs the double formula, but all had clear pointers to listeners as well as readers. With David von Augsburg the presence of a double formula (375, 23) helped to establish a listening reception, but also the possibility of readers.[12] In the *Geistlicher Herzen Bavngart* listeners and readers were anticipated, but are connected with one another by the double formula.[13] *Die Lilie* combines these alternatives in the same way.[14] Könemann von Jerxheim has built into his *Wurzgarten Mariens* suggestions of readers as well as listeners, and confirms this by a double formula which is part of a triple one.[15] *Unser Vrouwen Klage* contained an indication of the individual reader, but no reliable hint of the listener, yet it belongs to this chapter because of its double formulas.[16] Four remaining works all agree in containing no separate pointers to either listening or reading, but suggest both modes by a double formula: the *Büchlein von der Himmelfahrt Mariae*, the *Buch von geistlicher Lehre*, *Der Seele Rat* of Heinrich von Burgeis, and the *Pariser Tagezeiten*.[17]

(c) Legal literature

For this genre in the widest sense there are only four cases of a twofold reception. The first is weak: although the *Deutschenspiegel* contained pointers to listening and to reading, the former were uncertain. The *Sächsisches Weichbildrecht* is somewhat more convincing, not because the two sets of pointers were any more persuasive, but because each is borne out by a double formula.[18] The evidence for listening and reading was rather more telling in the *Schwabenspiegel Langform M*, so that the use of a double formula in regard to a part of the source which was judged too long to incorporate could well be applicable to this work, too.[19] The *Schwabenspiegel* itself had only weak indications of listeners and readers so that for want of a double formula it is uncertain whether it belongs here at all.

The yield from German charters in the thirteenth century is so rich that a detailed survey is out of the question. Once legal transactions were put into writing their two dimensions (witnesses hear and see) were gradually changed into hearing a charter read out as evidence and inspecting the document, from which it was a short step to reading it. Alongside the ambiguous formula *sehen oder hoeren* (*sehen* could mean to inspect or to read) we find a more explicit use of a double formula (*lesen oder hoeren*) or even a triple one (*sehen, lesen oder hoeren*).[20] These formulas indicate that whenever a charter was reactivated as evidence it was to be read out loud, but was also available for private reading. From Wilhelm's *Corpus* it emerges that the double formula was used 340 times in the thirteenth century[21] and the triple one 301 times. For fully pragmatic reasons the twofold reception established itself in this branch of written German firmly, if later than in other genres.

(d) Historiography

Six works show clear signs of a twofold reception. The *Sächsische Weltchronik* gave indications that it was meant for listeners, but also that readers may have been taken into account: these two possibilities are correlated in an early remark combining *horen* with *lesen*.[22] The position is clearer with the *Weltchronik* of Rudolf von Ems, where the evidence for listening and for reading was subject to no doubt and is confirmed by a double formula in an authorial address to the audience.[23] In this work it would be difficult to play down the implications of *horin*, for Rudolf makes it repeatedly clear that oral recital was counted on as well as individual reading.[24] Such a detailed correlation of recital with reading underlies the use of the double formula.

Other works dispense with the double formula, but contained the two types of evidence suggesting a twofold reception. This was the case with Jans Enikel's *Weltchronik* and with the *Braunschweigische Reimchronik*. In the *Christherre-Chronik* the author's reference to an audience hearing his earlier works recited (1171) presumably throws light, for all the topos nature of the passage, on how he foresaw the reception of his present work, so that recital, coupled with the suggestion of a reader (291), amounts to a twofold reception. Evidence for both modes was also found in Ottokar's *Österreichische Reimchronik*: the acoustic dimension is underlined by a reminder of what the audience had earlier heard recited (73512) and has to be coupled with indications of readers as well. These works may not use the explicit formula, but the remaining evidence is sufficiently beyond doubt.

(e) Biblical literature

The earliest examples are the *Heliand* and Otfrid's *Evangelienbuch*, both of which had separate suggestions of listeners as well as readers. Neither uses a double formula, but Otfrid has the first example of an author referring back to a passage previously recited.[25] The next evidence comes from Frau Ava who reckoned with an acoustic, but also a reading reception.

There follow eleven examples from the thirteenth century, for all of which (except two) there was separate evidence for both modes of reception and in some of which the double formula occurs. The *Urstende* of Konrad von Heimesfurt had pointers to listening and to reading, but also refers to its reception with a double formula.[26] The case for *Judith* is somewhat weaker because, although the evidence for reading was persuasive, that for listening was less so. More convincing is the *Hohes Lied* of Brun von Schönebeck. References to *horen* are confirmed by statements that the audience hears the book recited and by allusions to what has been earlier recited in the work,[27] but such acoustic evidence was accompanied by clear indications of a reading reception, and the two modes are combined in the occasional double formula.[28]

Both the *Apokalypse* and *Evangelium Nicodemi* of Heinrich von Hesler contained evidence for listening as well as reading, whereas his *Erlösung* fragment had indications of reading alone. However, the assumption of the same type of audience for all three works would imply a twofold reception for his *Erlösung*, too. The *Gottes Zukunft* of Heinrich von Neustadt, like the *Saelden Hort*, provided evidence for listening and reading, but also links them together in the double formula.[29] For two other works pointers to listeners as well as readers were forthcoming: *Die Erlösung* and the *Kreuziger* of Johannes von Frankenstein (although the latter work is more uncertain because of doubts about listeners). Finally, although a solitary reference to reading *Das Leben Jesu* was not matched by hearing, the two modes are again brought together in the double formula (1, 1; 1, 9).

(f) Legends

Twenty examples of this genre imply a twofold reception. The earliest, Priester Wernher's *Maria*, had signs of a listening reception alongside reading, with no contradiction between the two. This is followed by the *Gregorius* and *Der Arme Heinrich* of Hartmann von Aue: both contained evidence for a reception by listeners, but none for readers, yet make this good by a double formula embracing both. This may be applicable to *Die Kindheit Jesu* of Konrad von Fussesbrunnen: evidence for hearing was not matched by reading, but the latter is included in a double formula used of a work on the same theme.[30] The *Leben des heiligen Ulrich* of Albertus von Augsburg, like the *Heinrich und Kunigunde* of Ebernand von Erfurt, had separate indications of an acoustic and reading reception, even if not reinforced by a double formula.[31] In the *Barlaam und Josaphat* of Rudolf von Ems listeners and readers can be accepted when confirmed by a double formula (16077). The *Margaretenleben* of Wetzel von Bernau included a number of inconclusive *hören* references and no indication of reading, but the references are substantiated and the missing dimension is supplied by the terms of the saint's prayer to God.[32] Lamprecht von Regensburg suggested hearing in his *Sanct Franzisken Leben*, not reading, but again the double formula provides the missing indication.[33]

For the *Silvester* and *Alexius* of Konrad von Würzburg evidence for an acoustic reception was present,[34] but also the possibility of reading. The fragmentary *Ave Maria* of Brun von Schönebeck may also be included: it is suggested that a written text was read out to listeners,[35] some of whom may also have been readers (by analogy with the author's *Hohes Lied*). The *Passional* and the *Väterbuch* were alike in providing evidence that listeners were expected and no clear indication of reading, apart from the double formula which both employ.[36]

Hugo von Langenstein equipped his *Martina* with suggestions of a listening and a reading reception.[37] The *Märterbuch* had clear indications of both in the prologue, but explicitly binds them together in a formula.[38] The *Leben der heiligen Elisabeth* also contained pointers to both, but places its listeners in a recital situation by referring to what has been read out to them earlier.[39] By contrast, our last three examples are much more explicit because of the double formula. Bruder Philipp expected readers for his *Marienleben*, gave no sign that he also reckoned with listeners, but fills this gap by incorporating the double formula into a triple one.[40] In *Sante Margareten Marter* the position is the converse: there was a pointer to an acoustic reception (confirmed by *hoeren lesen*, 667), but no independent suggestion of reading but for the wording of St Margaret's prayer with its application of the double formula to this particular legend (575f.). In the *Marienleben* of Walther von Rheinau there were separate indications of listening and reading, reinforced by their conjunction in the double formula.[41]

(g) Drama

(h) Heroic literature

In neither of these genres was there any evidence, at least before 1300, that their acoustic reception was accompanied by the possibility of readers. For neither can a twofold reception be postulated.

(i) Court narrative literature

In this section the twofold reception is attested more clearly and more frequently (thirty-two examples in all) than in any other.

For four examples of the court epic the case can be argued with some probability. In Wolfram's *Willehalm* there was evidence for a listening reception and the likelihood of reading, even if the latter rested on an analogy with his *Parzival* and what it tells us of women readers at the Thuringian court. For *Karl der Große* of Der Stricker the evidence was internal: indications of an acoustic reception, but none for reading, yet the position is made good by an opening generalisation with a particular application and a double formula.[42] Ulrich von Türheim provided evidence in *Rennewart* for both listening and reading, and confirms this with a double formula in a wish for the prayers of his audience (36510f.). The *Willehalm* of Ulrich von dem Türlin is not so clearcut: although there were suggestions of listeners as well as readers, the case for the former was weak and is not strengthened by a double formula.

A twofold reception seems likely for three romances with a classical theme. In his *Eneide* Heinrich von Veldeke included suggestions for listeners, but also described reading in the case of the countess of Cleves.[43] Although Rudolf von Ems does not use the double formula in *Alexander* he made it clear by separate types of evidence that he reckoned both with listeners and with readers.[44] The case for the *Trojanischer Krieg* of Konrad von Würzburg is nothing like so strong (neither listeners nor readers were free from doubt).[45] For all its length this work is astonishingly poor in internal evidence.

We may begin the Arthurian romance with the *Erec* and *Iwein* of Hartmann von Aue, recalling that both works included evidence for listeners,[46] but none for readers. His legends likewise suggested hearing, but not reading, although both legends remedied the position with the double formula. If we accept that Hartmann addressed the same kind of audience in all four works this implies a twofold reception of his romances, too.[47] That this was possible in Hartmann's day is shown by Ulrich von Zatzikhoven in *Lanzelet*. Like Hartmann in his romances Ulrich gave pointers to listeners and none to readers, but like Hartmann in his legends he suggests reading by a double formula.[48] The same reception is true of the *Wigalois* of Wirnt von Grafenberg: separate pointers were present both to listeners and to readers, but are combined in a double formula describing the reception of his work.[49] Der Stricker in *Daniel von dem Blühenden Tal* resembles Ulrich von Zatzikhoven: he provided evidence for listening, none for reading, but makes this good with a double formula.⁵⁰ In *Die Crone* Heinrich von dem Türlin gave pointers to both modes of reception which are persuasive enough even without such confirmation. The intermediate mode was implied for the prose *Lancelot* by separate indications of hearing and reading, even though the former were weaker. The *Tandareis und Flordibel* of Der Pleier is also weak: although there were allusions to possible hearing and an indication of reading, the former were much less certain and there is no backing from any other class of evidence.⁵¹

Amongst Grail romances Wolfram's *Parzival* can now be seen to reveal a pattern detectable elsewhere: it contained pointers to a listening reception, one isolated suggestion of readers, but links the two together in a double formula used of its reception by women (115, 8f.). In however isolated a light Wolfram depicts himself (a knight who disdains contact with books),⁵² the internal evidence shows *Parzival* to be close to other works whose authors made no secret of their literacy or of the readers they anticipated. The *Jüngerer Titurel* of Albrecht von Scharfenberg shows no such qualms: the author supplied a range of pointers to an acoustic reception and little for reading, but stresses the written dimension of his work and links this explicitly with a double formula.⁵³ Lastly, even though *Lohengrin* dispenses with the double formula, its evidence for listening as well as reading was conclusive.

Of Gottfried's *Tristan* romance all we need recall is that it contained evidence for listeners as well as readers, but that these two modes are connected by a double formula which is also applied to another author, generally taken to be Wolfram.⁵⁴ This application to another author suggests that the twofold reception was becoming widespread at this time. Both Ulrich von Türheim and Heinrich von Freiberg in their versions gave evidence for each mode of reception without using a double formula.⁵⁵

The first of the romances of love and adventure, Konrad Fleck's *Flore und Blanscheflur*, contained some uncertain references to hearing and none to reading, but rectifies this by a double formula (7979). Although *Der guote Gerhart* contained no relevant evidence it may be included here by analogy with Rudolf's other works, for all of which there is evidence of a twofold reception.⁵⁶ By contrast, his *Willehalm von Orlens* contained evidence of both modes of reception and a double formula which, even if applied to another work, reveals how the author conceived the reception of contemporary literature.⁵⁷ The *Engelhard* of Konrad von Würzburg had pointers to hearing and reading, if with reservations about the latter. The three romances of Berthold von Holle are weak for the opposite reason: their evidence for hearing was unconvincing by itself (and not confirmed by a double formula), but the clear allusion to reading in *Darifant* is probably applicable to *Demantin* and *Crane* as well. In the last three examples of this subgenre (*Reinfried von Braunschweig*, the *Apollonius von Tyrland* of Heinrich von Neustadt, the *Wilhelm von Österreich* of Johann von Würzburg) the double formula is nowhere employed, but all contained separate pointers to hearing as well as reading.⁵⁸

There remain the *Frauendienst* and *Frauenbuch* of Ulrich von Lichtenstein: they belong together thematically and were meant for the same kind of audience. Although the double formula is not used, the case for a twofold reception is clear, resting on pointers to listening (including *hoeren lesen*) and to reading which there was no call to doubt. These works illustrate that, however useful we have found the double formula in this survey, we are not dependent on it alone in deciding whether a work was meant for a twofold reception.

We may conclude this survey of court narrative literature with a word on the 'Märe': whether it existed in oral or in written form, this narrative genre was delivered by recital to listeners and there was no internal indication of the individual reader. It cannot therefore be included under the twofold reception.

(j) Lyric poetry

With this genre we can be almost as brief as with the 'Märe', for there was little or no evidence of reading, hence no grounds for assuming a twofold reception.

That the love lyric was meant for public performance and acoustic reception there was little reason to doubt, but from the fact that some poems found their way into writing from about 1230 we could not deduce the necessity of reading. It was certainly possible, as with Ulrich von Lichtenstein, and in such cases we confront a twofold reception, even though, as in his 'Leich', no double formula may be used.[59] The example of Ulrich is isolated, however, no doubt because of the nature of his *Frauendienst*, a narrative including lyric poems, to which there was no other parallel in Germany at that time.[60] How relevant this is is borne out by 426, 4f.: these lines come not from the 'Leich', but from the narrative following it, where such information can be given without disrupting the hermetic nature of the poem. Since the German love lyric is nowhere else incorporated into a narrative we lack any indication that it may have been read as well as heard.

This negative conclusion has to be accentuated for gnomic poetry, which found its way later into writing and for which there was no internal evidence for readers and nothing external (as with Ulrich's 'Leich') to suggest this possibility. Before 1300 there is no reason to regard gnomic poetry as falling within a twofold reception.

In these ten sections 100 works have been proposed as possibly addressed to listeners as well as readers. It is conceivable that some might need to be subtracted (I have indicated whenever I think the argument is weak), but equally that the total might need to be increased (it takes no account of genres which we regarded as a whole, so that such a rich source of double formulas as charters is not included). This total for the intermediate mode is no different from the totals for hearing and reading, for they too included weaker cases and excluded figures for some genres. Subject to these reservations, there is no reason why we should not compare the total for this chapter with those for hearing (271) and for reading (110), at least to reach the conclusion that the intermediate mode compares numerically well enough with the reading mode. Although neither is strong enough to challenge hearing, each points to important changes taking place in the primary reception of German literature.[61]

CONTEXT OF RECEPTION

So far we have considered the intermediate mode of reception with regard to various literary genres which may assist or impede the practice of reading alongside listening. This is only one approach to our problem, for the mode of reception also depended on the recipients themselves and the social context in which reception took place. We shall return to the recipients later, but must now consider the contexts in which a work could be both listened to and read, asking why an author may have reckoned with two modes of reception for it.[62] The works which we have just surveyed are now divided into five categories, arranged in a descending order of frequency, representing five contexts of reception: the court of the secular aristocracy, the monastery, the town, the religious lay community, and the episcopal court.[63]

There is often uncertainty in categorising these works in this way, because there are interconnections between contexts, so that a clear line of demarcation is not always possible. Is Mechthild von Magdeburg to be placed in the context of a religious lay community in the light of her early life as a béguine in Magdeburg or under the heading of a monastery in view of her later entry into the Cistercian convent of Helfta?[64] Are we to connect Priester Wernher's *Maria* with the monastic sphere because of its associations with the house of St Ulrich and Afra in Augsburg or with the town because he also addressed secular women (possibly inhabitants of Augsburg)? Although this kind of difficulty arises, we need not be worried by it, for what counts is not the rigid choice between one possibility and another, but the recognition that all the works we are concerned with can be allocated to one of these five categories, for each of which reasons can be given why works produced in them were addressed both to listeners and to readers.

Listing these five contexts of reception establishes a number of centres where, in addition to *illitterati* dependent on listening to a recital, there were also *litterati* present. The suggestion that those able to read actually read the works produced for their centre is admittedly an assumption, but no more of an assumption than the author's own hope, implicit in his use of a double formula or expressed in his request for the prayers of readers, that his work would indeed be read. If the author could realistically work on this assumption, so may we.

(k) Court of the secular aristocracy

To this largest category forty-four works belong for which we have seen the likelihood (in varying degrees) that they were composed with an eye to twofold reception. In this section, as in the following ones, I shall list those works for which reception at this particular centre is likely, and then discuss the features of the secular court which explain the fact of listening, but also the possibility of reading.

Under didactic literature two examples are associated with the court: *Wernher von Elmendorf* was addressed to the secular aristocracy,[65] but with *Lucidarius* we can be more specific in seeing it commissioned by the court of Henry the Lion at Braunschweig.[66] Only one text in devotional literature possibly belongs to this kind of centre: Heinrich von Kröllwitz appears to have been active at the court of Count Gunzelin III of Schwerin, for whom he presumably composed his *Vaterunser*.[67]

The interest of courts in historiography ('höfische Geschichte') is shown by four examples. Rudolf von Ems composed his *Weltchronik* for King Konrad IV,[68] whilst the *Braunschweigische Reimchronik* is closely connected with the ducal house of Braunschweig-Lüneburg.[69] The precise affiliation of two other texts is not certain, but the *Christherre-Chronik* has been associated with landgrave Heinrich of Thuringia,[70] and Ottokar's *Österreichische Reimchronik* with Otto II of Lichtenstein or, more generally, with the Styrian nobility.[71]

Two examples of biblical literature have been judged as meant for a courtly aristocratic audience in general terms (*Die Erlösung* and *Der Saelden Hort*),[72] but rather more legends, so that these two genres indicate how misleading it would be to see the literary interests of a secular court merely in terms of secular literature. The legends that belong here include the *Gregorius* and *Armer Heinrich* of Hartmann von Aue, meant like his other works for a court of the secular nobility,[73] but also the *Kindheit Jesu* of Konrad von Fussesbrunnen, for which a court public has been suggested.[74] Rudolf von Ems composed his *Barlaam und Josaphat* for senior Hohenstaufen ministerials,[75] and Wetzel von Bernau his *Margaretenleben* for a court audience,[76] whilst the *Märterbuch* was commissioned by the countess of Rosenberg, presumably for her court.[77]

Only now do we come to secular works meant for a secular court, beginning with the court epic. In this group the position is reasonably clear: Wolfram's *Willehalm* was composed for the court of landgrave Hermann of Thuringia,[78] Der Stricker may have written *Karl der Große* for the counts of Rieneck and Loon,[79] whilst the *Rennewart* of Ulrich von Türheim was closely connected with the Hohenstaufen court circle,[80] and the *Willehalm* of Ulrich von dem Türlin with the court of King Ottokar II of Bohemia.[81] In such cases it would be difficult to divorce patronage from the circle where the audience was to be found, so that these epics are fully at home at court.

The same is true of the twenty-five romances to which falls the lion's share in this section. Because of the theft of his uncompleted MS the composition of Veldeke's *Eneide* is connected with two aristocratic courts: the circle around Margaret of Cleves (possibly also Agnes of Loon?) and the Thuringian court of landgrave Hermann I.[82] The two romances of Hartmann are thought to have been addressed to a court of the secular nobility, with opinions shifting between the house of Zähringen and Hohenstaufen or Welf circles.[83] The Hohenstaufen court of Heinrich VI was possibly addressed by Ulrich von Zatzikhoven in his *Lanzelet*,[84] whilst references in Wolfram's *Parzival* point to a number of courts of the secular nobility, including that of the landgrave of Thuringia.[85] The *Wigalois* of Wirnt von Grafenberg may have been written for duke Otto I of Andechs-Meran[86] and Der Stricker's *Daniel* for the counts of Rieneck and Loon.[87] Rudolf von Ems composed *Der guote Gerhart* for Rudolf von Steinach, a ministerial knight of the bishop of Konstanz,[88] whilst Heinrich von dem Türlin may have written *Die Crone* for the court of duke Bernhard of Carinthia.[89] Ulrich von Türheim in his *Tristan*, like Rudolf von Ems with his *Alexander*, addressed the Swabian court circle around Kings Heinrich VII and Konrad IV,[90] whilst in his *Willehalm von Orlens* Rudolf reveals connections with Johann von Ravensburg, Konrad von Winterstetten, and count Konrad von Öttingen, again a circle of Welf and Hohenstaufen noblemen.[91] The patron and audience of the prose *Lancelot* are unknown, but it is perhaps significant that the other historical works listed by Heinzle in this connection should all be literature intended for the court.[92] Since the lyrics of Ulrich von Lichtenstein were recited to court society and the contemporary figures inserted in his narrative are members of the court aristocracy it is reasonable to suppose that his *Frauendienst* and *Frauenbuch* were meant for a court of the secular nobility.[93] It has been suggested that Konrad von Würzburg wrote his *Engelhard* for the counts of either Cleves or Brabant,[94] whilst the three romances of Berthold von Holle were probably addressed to the Welf court of Braunschweig.[95] The circle for which Albrecht von Scharfenberg intended his *Jüngerer Titurel* is unclear in its details, but he mentions duke Ludwig II of Bavaria and three princes, so that the Wittelsbach court is conceivable.[96] Of the romances of Der Pleier we know only that they were presumably commissioned by a nobleman,[97] and for *Lohengrin* the case for Ludwig II of Bavaria as patron has been made.[98] Heinrich von Freiberg dedicated his *Tristan* to a Bohemian nobleman, Reimund von Lichtenburg, as his patron,[99] whilst Johann von Würzburg dedicated his *Wilhelm von Österreich* to the dukes Leopold I and Friedrich der Schöne of Austria and shows contacts with noblemen close to their court.[100]

Of the hundred works for which a twofold reception was shown to be likely forty-four stand in some sort of connection with a court of the secular aristocracy, high or low: sometimes the patron is actually named, sometimes his identity has been shown or surmised by scholarship, sometimes the evidence points to a circle of individuals at a particular court or close to it, but on other occasions we have to content ourselves with the suggestion that a court audience in general terms was addressed. None of these examples comes before the closing decades of the twelfth century and most belong to the following century as part of the rapid explosion of court literature. The question this raises is: was there anything about the composition of the court of the secular aristocracy in this period which could account for literature addressed to it being both heard and read?

Hearing presents little difficulty: given the widespread illiteracy of the lay nobility in Germany around 1200 vernacular literature addressed to them had to be recited. Although criticisms of royal illiteracy begin to be voiced about this time, we do not know how far it yielded practical results amongst the royalty, let alone at other levels of the aristocracy, and in any case this criticism seems to have been voiced more in the educationally advanced Anglo-Norman realm than in Germany.[101] Even if we disregard the uncertain factor of the ruler, this leaves him surrounded by laymen who are still illiterate: secular attendants and officials at court, as well as the lord's knightly retinue and any feudal subordinates attendant at court. Some members of this lay court circle may have acquired a measure of pragmatic literacy (a possibility increasingly to be reckoned with during the course of the thirteenth century), but nothing we know of these courts leads us to regard their officials and knightly members as more literate than lay society had been in the early Middle Ages.

There is another reason for the hearing dimension of literature at court, to do not with illiteracy, but with the social function of literature. Much medieval literature sustained a sense of social and political community (it praised and reinforced the power of a ruler or patron) and praise was conceived as a public occasion, advertising its object by the means best known to a society without widespread literacy, by public communication.[102] Public communication presupposed a public assembly of those who heard what was proclaimed.

This public and acoustic dimension of literature need not entirely exclude the possibility of individual readers. At this point, the argument for the dominant illiteracy of the secular court has created difficulties, making some reluctant to accept the possibility of a reading reception. For example, in discussing how the audience for Hartmann's *Gregorius* may have reacted to the depiction of a knightly hero enjoying a literate education Mertens observes that we cannot reckon on a feudal audience resembling Hartmann in being *sô gelêret ... / daz [ez] an den buochen las*.[103] This is correct, but does not go far enough. By equating an audience at court with a feudal audience, i.e. with those laymen whose knightly training left little room for an education in literacy, Mertens restricts the audience at court to knights and therewith to illiteracy. This restrictive equation must be called into question, for there are two other groups belonging to the audience for court literature which must be taken into account, since they provide potential readers. To achieve this differentiation of the audience it is helpful to take the term laymen literally. These laymen, the knights at court, may well have been illiterate, but this does not follow for clerics attached to a court or for aristocratic laywomen. In other words, in addition to an illiterate majority at court (lay officials, knights, feudal subordinates) we have to reckon with a literate minority (clerics and noblewomen).[104] Educationally court society was far from being homogeneous: it included *illitterati* who could only listen, but also *litterati* who could both listen and read. Against such a background the transition of vernacular literature to written form granted relevance to two modes of reception.

For all their personal illiteracy secular aristocrats did not live in total divorce from writing and secular courts stood in close connection with private or dynastic monasteries ('Hausklöster') which frequently provided written histories (in Latin) of the aristocratic family to which they were attached, but also chaplains and clerics for service at the court.[105] These court clerics not only served a religious function, they were useful also by virtue of their literate skills in the chancery as scribes, lawyers, and administrators. In the institution of their own chanceries by secular courts Bumke sees the decisive step in the entry of writing into the life of the court: no longer was the lay ruler dependent on the literate services of a monastery in the vicinity, he now disposed of scribes and secretaries at his own court.[106] This is a reflection of the growing complexity of administration, best met by writing, and is in turn reflected in the tendency towards a fixed residence, in place of itinerant rulership, where an incipient bureaucracy, however modest its apparatus, could exercise control.[107] There is a chronological parallel between the earliest courts to introduce chanceries (and the regular practice of writing) and those which first commission vernacular literature in written form.[108] This was not without effects on the composition of the court, even in the narrowest sense. The *Raitbücher* of the counts of Tirol include a chaplain and a teacher amongst the members of the court; from the Wittelsbach court we learn of a *chamerschriber*, a *chapplan* and an *oberist schriber*.[109] In her translation of the *Secretum Secretorum* Hiltgart von Hürnheim regards those endowed with knowledge of *puech kunst* as more than a mere adornment, for they illuminate the whole court.[110] However restricted in numbers the permanent inner court circle may have been, constituting the audience for works whose recital would necessarily extend over a period of time,[111] it included court clerics. They constituted potential readers of works recited to the court at large.

The same is true of the noblewomen, whose interest in literature (religious and secular) and whose literacy are well documented.[112] It had never been beneath their dignity, as it was with their menfolk, to busy themselves with reading, which is why authors who stress the written dimension of their work and anticipate readers should often address noblewomen in particular. Even Wolfram, who denies his literate status, admits that his *Parzival* may fall in written form into women's hands and the work is pervaded by a series of cryptic remarks about a woman for whom he may have composed it. Other references underline a special relationship between poet and lady, not merely in the love lyric, the genre whose idealisation of her sex may be expected to have aroused her interest, but in other genres, too.[113] Ulrich von Lichtenstein says that his *Frauendienst* belongs to noble women,[114] Heinrich von dem Türlin undertook his *Crone* on behalf of women,[115] and Ulrich von Türheim begins his *Rennewart* in God's name and for the sake of a good woman.[116] These references cannot be dismissed as mere topoi, for it is likely that the women in the court audience played an important part in literary judgment and could not be ignored by the poet.[117] Their presence in the court audience constitutes a second group of potential readers.

These women, like court clerics, have been referred to as potential readers. The point to which the argument has brought us is this: on the one hand we have works for a court audience, whose authors make it clear that they expect readers as well as listeners, and on the other hand we find within the audience at court (all of whom can be conceived as listeners at a festive recital) two groups able to read, whatever difference there may be between their forms of literacy.[118] It is a natural assumption that the readers who were expected were found in these two groups, and this assumption is no less realistic than the author's hope for readers. How this remaining gap may have been closed, how far these two groups actually supplied readers, we must discuss later.

(l) Monastery

We come now to the second largest category (thirty works) of twofold reception. The speedy growth of court literature accounts for its outstripping literature for the monastery, but against that monastic examples begin in the ninth century and persist through to 1300, so that there can be no talk of their having been ousted by the rise of literature for the courts. Court literature was not exclusively secular (it also included a number of religious works)[119] and it can even be argued that, in the novel form represented by the Franciscans and the Dominicans, monastic examples came to dominate the literary scene again as the thirteenth century advanced. We must now list those works for which a twofold reception at a monastery can be argued, before considering aspects of monastic life which explain the juxtaposition of listening and reading.

Within functional literature works meant for the monastic school are represented by Notker,[120] and didactic literature by the Cistercian nun Hiltgart von Hürnheim.[121] Literature of religious worship and instruction is present in two subgroups: a 'Reimpredigt', the *Heilige Rede vom Glauben*, which Der Arme Hartmann is thought to have addressed to aristocratic *conversi*,[122] but more fully in devotional literature. Under this heading the *Rheinisches Marienlob* was meant for use in a Rhenish nuns' convent,[123] Lamprecht von Regensburg composed his *Tochter Syon* for the Franciscans of Regensburg,[124] and *Unser Vrouwen Klage* was addressed to *religiosae*.[125] The *Büchlein von der Himmelfahrt Mariae* was possibly conceived for a monastery or convent,[126] and the *Buch von geistlicher Lehre* was meant for Cistercians.[127]

Legal literature may be included here: the Franciscans of Augsburg probably composed the *Deutschenspiegel*,[128] the *Schwabenspiegel*,[129] and the *Schwabenspiegel Langform M*.[130] This leaves on one side, for want of internal pointers, the question of the use to which these texts were put and by whom: was this outside the monastery (as suggested for the court of King Rudolf I of Austria in the case of the *Schwabenspiegel*)[131] or still within the monastery? The evidence for connecting this literature with monasteries is therefore more persuasive regarding its composition than it reception. Historiography is represented by the *Sächsische Weltchronik*, possibly composed in a similar way by the Franciscans of North Germany (Lüneburg?), again with the possibility of a (Welf) court in the background.[132] Even in view of this uncertainty about the context of reception for these works, the task of accounting for their twofold reception is not made more difficult: at the most, they would have to be transferred from this section to the previous one (the secular court) with its own reasons for hearing as well as reading.

A monastic context is most clearly present in biblical literature and in legends. The former is represented in the ninth century by the *Heliand* (opinions vary as to whether it was composed at Fulda or Werden, but not as to its monastic origin)[133] and by Otfrid's *Evangelienbuch* (composed at Weissenburg and meant for monastic consumption there and at St. Gallen, even though copies were also sent to dignitaries outside the realm of the monastery).[134] The works of Frau Ava are by someone attested as an *inclusa*, possibly connected with the monastery of Melk or nearby.[135] *Judith*, but also the three works of Heinrich von Hesler (*Apokalypse*, *Erlösung*, *Evangelium Nicodemi*), are all thought to have been composed on behalf of the Order of Teutonic Knights,[136] the *Kreuziger* of Johannes von Frankenstein for the Order of St John,[137] and the *Leben Jesu* for the Dominicans of Cologne.[138] These examples from the thirteenth century and from orders which cannot be called traditional ones, bear witness to how active monastic life as a centre of literature still was towards the end of our period.

The first legends for which a twofold reception can be argued, Priester Wernher's *Maria* and the *Leben des heiligen Ulrich* of Albertus von Augsburg, are connected with the Benedictine collegiate foundation of St Ulrich and Afra at Augsburg.[139] The legend of *Heinrich und Kunigunde* by Ebernand von Erfurt is tied to the Cistercian monastery of Georgenthal between Erfurt and Gotha,[140] whilst Lamprecht von Regensburg composed his *Sanct Franzisken Leben* (like his *Tochter Syon*) for the Regensburg Franciscans.[141] The *Leben der heiligen Elisabeth* was addressed to a monastic audience, which need not exclude an audience at a princely court as well.[142] Finally, with varying degrees of certainty, four legends or legendaries are associated with the Order of Teutonic Knights: the *Passional*, the *Väterbuch*, the *Martina* of Hugo von Langenstein, and the *Marienleben* of Bruder Philipp.[143] In a way quite different from biblical literature these legends illustrate the same persistence of monasteries as a focus of literary activity: they start in the vernacular only in the twelfth century, but continue to hold their own and outlive the heyday of their secular rivals.

The borderline between works produced for a monastery and those produced for a secular court is often very uncertain. We saw the possibility of a private monastery, attached to an aristocratic dynasty, meeting its literate needs, so that it is an open question whether a work produced there is to be associated with a secular court or a monastery.[144] Similarly, we have just seen that, although some legal literature was composed at Franciscan centres, this need not exclude use at a princely court. Such overlaps prompt the question whether the monastery may not resemble the court in also providing conditions under which literature was both heard and read.[145]

Private reading at monasteries is the easier part of this problem. Reading was already provided for by the Benedictine Rule, both certain hours set aside for this each day and also over a longer period in requiring each monk to take out a book from the monastery library for devotional reading on which he could be questioned.[146] This monastic *lectio*, described in its devotional implications by Leclercq and contrasted with the novel concept of reading introduced by the cathedral schools, is a hallmark of monastic literacy.[147] However many monks may have fallen short of what was required (in the quality of their reading, in their ability to write),[148] the monastery cannot be divorced from literacy, particularly in the form of *lectio*. Careful preparations were made for this in the monastery school: Notker explicitly addresses his reader, and in the *Murbacher Hymnen*, an interlinear translation representative of other texts used in the monastery in teaching Latin, the linkage of Latin text with vernacular glosses allows us, as it were, to trace the eye-movements of the reader who consulted them.[149]

This renders urgent an answer to a further question: how did the monasteries, as centres of reading and Latinity, also attract a vernacular literature not meant exclusively for private reading? The answer concerns two points: the oral dimension (in recital aloud) and the use of German.[150] The oral dimension of monastic life has already been touched on. It is present in the daily practice of reading a text aloud in the refectory at mealtime, so that spiritual nourishment may be provided as well as physical, and the evening *collatio*, in which a religious text is read out and commented on to the assembled monks.[151] To these must be added the monastery school, now in another guise, for teaching was conducted orally in the medieval classroom, as in the modern lecture-room. The written text was taught in the medium of the spoken word.

To account for the use of the vernacular we must bear in mind that the monastery as an institution was by no means entirely divorced from the world outside.[152] This is clear in the siting of Dominican and Franciscan centres in towns, as distinct from the remote countryside favoured by other orders, but can be shown for the latter, above all in the fact that a monastery which still maintained contacts with the world at large was in no position to dispense entirely with the vernacular. First, laymen (and with them the vernacular) are present within the monastery as laybrothers or *conversi*,[153] especially in the late eleventh and early twelfth centuries as a result of a flood of laymen, including noblemen, called to a religious life and accommodated in this intermediate status, no longer of the world but not fully monastic, in which they served as a point of contact between the monks and the surrounding world.[154] Laymen who became laybrothers[155] brought with them to the monastery a feature of their lay status, their illiteracy and ignorance of Latin (here they differed from *oblati*, placed in monasteries in youth and educated in the school), so that account now had to be taken of their educational status. The rise of this novel aspect of monastic life in this period[156] has been associated with the renewal of religious literature in German.[157] The monastic origins of much of this literature and its renewed use of German suggest the need to appeal to a group within the monastic community which, unlike the monks, could not be addressed in Latin. It means that an impetus was given to a vernacular literature for listeners in a setting which also contained readers.

A second link between the monasteries and the world outside is the position of many of them, especially the imperial abbeys, within the feudal hierarchy. For its upkeep and for the maintenance of its political position a monastery disposed of landed property, for which peasants and manual workers were necessary, but also knights and vassals to defend it and to allow the monastery to fulfil its feudal obligations.[158] These laymen belonged, not to the monastery, but to the monastic *familia* in the widest sense, which must therefore be assessed in social and political terms as well as spiritual ones. Ekkehard IV of St. Gallen describes how an abbot appointed knights to serve in a weekly cycle as steward and cupbearer at his table,[159] showing in these offices that as abbot he presided over a court, as much as when the abbot of Fulda in the twelfth century instituted the conventional court offices as a token of his political authority.[160] This authority, even when wielded by an abbot, brings military obligations in its train, as expressed in the instructions of Charles the Great to the abbots of royal monasteries, listing the equipment their men are to bring on military service.[161] This involvement of monasteries with feudalism, to the extent of being able to talk of a *curia abbatis* alongside *curia principis* and *curia ducis*[162] and with secular vassals forming part of the wider monastic community, suggests that monastic literature, composed in the vernacular with an eye to laybrothers, may also have been addressed to these vassals as well. We possess evidence of this in the *Gandersheimer Reimchronik* of Priester Eberhard. This chronicle was meant for listeners,[163] but was rendered into German for the sake of *ungelarde lüde* (83), described as *densthaft unde underdenich man* (82), ministerials of the foundation of Gandersheim. The need to address these laymen and involve them in the claims of the house to be freed from the jurisdiction of the bishop of Hildesheim in favour of the more advantageous because more distant authority of Rome has been suggested by Heinzle,[164] but this particular reason for using the vernacular need not mean that monasteries did not find other occasions for addressing laymen in the only language they could understand.

Thirdly, one such occasion may well have been the monastic practice, laid down in the Benedictine Rule, of providing hospitality for guests, including laymen. We have seen this in the suggestion that the *Klosterneuburger Osterspiel* was meant to be performed on the occasion of a visit to the monastery by duke Leopold VI[165] (although the effect this had on making room for the use of the vernacular was minimal). In his commentary on the Rule Hildemar of Civate complains that some monasteries hold a *lectio* only on a guest's first visit, but when he says that an explanation of what has been read out to them is given to these lay guests this could involve the use of the vernacular if they are ignorant of Latin.[166] On feastdays laymen may sit in the refectory as guests of the abbot, where they hear the reading normally given at mealtime.[167] This leads us to wonder whether any linguistic concession was made to the presence of laymen of high rank. What Haubrichs says of the contacts between monasteries and the lay world around them on feastdays of the Church year, involving processions and hymns in the vernacular because of the participation of laymen, suggests that this was possible.[168]

In our list of works whose twofold reception took place in a monastery some examples were related to the Order of Teutonic Knights, where a reason peculiar to this order made for the use of the vernacular. The order recruited its members as mature knights, of an age when the years of training for knighthood were already behind them. The knights joined the order at an age when, like the laymen who became laybrothers, they would not become pupils in the monastery school and therefore remained as illiterate as they had been in lay society. Grundmann has investigated this in its implications for the German literature of the Teutonic Order[169] and demonstrated that, although the order's monasteries had literate clerics necessary for administrative purposes, the presence of illiterate members demanded two things in the literary practice of the order: a concentration on works to be read out aloud and the use of German, rather than Latin.[170] (He also points out that if later more members of the order were literate, their ability to read was restricted to German, so that in their case Latin literacy was bypassed).[171] The literate members of the order (the clerics and those who acquired an ability to read in German) constituted the potential readers of the order's works, whilst those who remained illiterate in any language were confined to listening.[172]

The literature of the Teutonic Order illustrates what is true of monastic vernacular literature at large. It was composed by a *litteratus* knowledgeable in Latin for the benefit of *illitterati*, within the monastery or attached to it, who were dependent on a vernacular recital. It presupposes a monastic context in which some are literate and others not, some know Latin and others do not, so that the possibility of a twofold reception would meet these disparate needs as much as at secular courts.

(m) Town

The next largest group is made up of works intended for a twofold reception in the town, e.g. Strassburg in the case of Gottfried, Vienna for Heinrich von Neustadt, Goslar for Könemann von Jerxheim and Magdeburg for Brun von Schönebeck. They number nineteen and all come from the thirteenth century.

Didactic literature (as part of functional literature) is represented by *Der Renner* of Hugo von Trimberg, a secular teacher at Bamberg who also composed in Latin. Although a resident of an episcopal city, he did not teach at the cathedral school but wrote for the laymen of the town.[173] Literature of religious worship and instruction is represented by one example of a 'Reimpredigt' (the *Visio Philiberti* of Heinrich von Neustadt, an academically trained doctor at Vienna)[174] and two examples of devotional literature. The first is the *Wurzgarten Mariens* of Könemann von Jerxheim, dean, canon and head of a school at Goslar, who wrote his *Kaland* for the 'Kalandbruderschaft' of Eilenstedt (composed of clerics and laymen) and whose *Wurzgarten* was meant for the unlearned.[175] The second example is *Der Seele Rat* by Heinrich von Burgeis, a Franciscan with the cure of souls at Bozen who addresses laymen in his work.[176]

Legal literature is present in one example: the *Sächsisches Weichbildrecht* incorporates the town law of Magdeburg[177] and was presumably meant for town use (whether there is any association with a monastery, as we saw with the *Schwabenspiegel*, for example, is uncertain). Historiography also shows only one example: the *Weltchronik* of Jans Enikel, addressed to the patriciate of Vienna.[178]

Religious themes are treated in biblical literature and legends. The first example of biblical literature is the *Hohes Lied* of Brun von Schönebeck, a learned member of a leading Magdeburg family who wrote for laymen.[179] The second work is *Gottes Zukunft* by Heinrich von Neustadt who, we have seen, was active at Vienna. The legend is present in five examples, of which two are by Konrad von Würzburg, both in connection with Basel. He wrote his *Silvester* after being commissioned by Liutold von Roeteln, canon and later archdeacon and cathedral provost (and therefore a member of the cathedral chapter at Basel), but for a wider town audience.[180] His *Alexius* was commissioned by two members of town families, Johannes von Bermeswil and Heinrich Isenlin, who also belonged to the literary circle in the town which was the wider audience for *Silvester*.[181] Brun von Schönebeck composed his *Ave Maria* for the same Magdeburg setting as his *Hohes Lied*. A town background is not quite so clear for the two remaining legends. The author of *Sante Margareten Marter* addresses *man und frouwen* (661) without any aristocratic title, but location in a town is suggested only by the parallel between the help provided in childbirth by having a copy of the book in the house (585ff.) and the similar statement by Priester Wernher at Augsburg, who addressed towndwellers as well as the collegiate foundation there. Of the *Marienleben* of Walther von Rheinau we can say no more than that he was a professional scribe and may have worked for a town.[182]

Four romances may be associated with towns, two with more certainty than the others. Whether or not Gottfried von Strassburg was an actual cleric or had merely enjoyed a clerical education, the present consensus is that he addressed his *Tristan* to a mixed town audience in Strassburg,[183] whilst Heinrich von Neustadt composed *Apollonius von Tyrland*, like his other two works, at Vienna. The less certain cases are Konrad Fleck's *Flore und Blanscheflur* (was this work, like Gottfried's, meant for a town audience?)[184] and the enigmatic *Reinfried von Braunschweig* (can the description of its author as a 'bürgerlicher Literat'[185] be taken to imply a similar background for his audience?). Despite these doubts the evidence for this genre confirms what is known from other sources: the literary public in towns, centred on a patriciate with connections with the local nobility, were keen consumers of court literature.

This brings it home that literature meant for the town cannot be regarded in isolation (meant for the taste of burghers alone) and that it is difficult to distinguish works under this heading from those under others. An interplay between town and monastery, for example, is true of the Franciscans and Dominicans, who deliberately sought out towns as centres. Schnell has reminded us of what the similar interplay between town and aristocratic court meant for the rise of court literature in France and of what this may tell us of the literary taste of towns in Germany[186] (if Gottfried composed his work in response to the court literature of his day this suggests that his audience at Strassburg were likewise acquainted with it).[187] In the light of these connections between works meant for aristocratic courts, monasteries and towns we must ask whether conditions making for a twofold reception at court and in the monastery may not recur in the town. To answer this question let us follow the Upper Rhine upstream, starting with Gottfried's Strassburg, moving on to the Basel of Konrad von Würzburg, and then across to Hadloub's Zürich. What is there about these three representative towns which produced both listeners and readers for works produced there?[188]

For the Strassburg of Gottfried's day Bertau, in his search for the poet and the Dietrich mentioned in the opening acrostic, gives a survey of the leading inhabitants who could have constituted the audience for *Tristan* and for whom there is documentary evidence.[189] They fall into several groups: the senior clergy of the cathedral chapter (sons of baronial families),[190] members of the collegiate foundation of St Thomas (from patrician families), ministerial knights of the bishop of Strassburg, but also senior citizens of the town and members of the town council. This list is made up of clerics (senior or not), secular aristocrats and members of the patriciate, forming a group in which some could certainly read, but not all. This spectrum has been narrowed somewhat by Tomasek in his discussion of trading motifs in Gottfried's work, which he sees as a fusion of the author's own clerical education, the interests and mentality of merchant patricians, and the knightly culture which found its way into the town.[191] He postulates a mixed circle of recipients, dominated by clerical and trading interests,[192] whilst Krohn places his emphasis differently, suggesting that Gottfried's work was calculated to appeal to patricians, but also to a genuinely courtly (i.e. aristocratic) audience, offering something of interest to each.[193] The truth is likely to lie between these two suggestions, in a mixed audience at Strassburg composed of clerics, ministerials and patricians, as in Bertau's list. If their common interests brought them together on social occasions, including a recital of *Tristan*, all must be regarded as listeners, but amongst them were also to be found the potential readers for whom Gottfried hoped.[194]

An audience similarly homogeneous in its literary taste, but heterogeneous educationally is to be found at Basel at the time of Konrad von Würzburg. He names his patrons there, the documentary evidence for whom has been analysed by Schröder,[195] who sums up by saying that they embrace all the influential classes of Basel, including the senior clergy in the person of Liutold von Roeteln, town ministerials and burghers.[196] The patrons listed all took part in the public life of Basel, as is shown by the appearance of several together as witnesses in charters, so that, as in Gottfried's Strassburg, their common interests were the basis of their forming a group with similar literary tastes. If Bumke has criticised Schröder's wording, pointing out that Konrad's patrons were no representative cross-cut of Basel, but belonged only to a thin upper crust,[197] this has no bearing on what is important for us. However unrepresentative this circle was, however similar their literary interests may have been, they resemble the earlier grouping in Strassburg in their different educational backgrounds, for if the clergy could read, we have no evidence that this was true of all the patricians and ministerials involved. Their reception of literature may still have been as acoustic as with Baldwin of Guines, and in any case a literary circle which came together on various occasions met to hear Konrad's works recited to them. His works found listeners at Basel, but also the possibility of readers.

A similar composite picture emerges for Zürich, thanks to the persons named by Hadloub in three poems and to what we know of their social and educational background.[198] Again, this Zürich circle was homogeneous in its literary taste, but variegated in its background. It was made up of clerical members, male and female (Heinrich von Klingenberg as bishop of Konstanz, the abbot of Einsiedeln, the abbess of Zürich, the abbot of Petershausen), but also contained secular aristocrats (upper nobility as well as ministerials) and patricians of Zürich, above all the Manesse family, whose residence was so much the literary focus of this group that it has been possible to see it as a town *curia* or court.[199] Although Renk stresses that the unity of this circle prevents us from dividing it into three social groups, nonetheless their different walks in life have different educational implications: we know that some were literate, but are ignorant how far this extends to the laymen. Even if all were literate, this would not alter the fact that the poems recited to this group in Zürich were available to readers as well as listeners.

What emerges for the three towns we have considered at different periods of the thirteenth century may be taken as representative of others about which we are not so well informed. The audience for literature in towns was as far from being educationally homogeneous as it was at the nobleman's court and the monastery: in the audience at towns, too, whilst all could listen to a recital, we cannot assume that all could read.

(n) Religious lay community

Only four works for which a twofold reception is attested belong here. David von Augsburg composed his German works for laybrothers, nuns and lay communities.[200] Despite this wide spread, which makes allocation to any one group arbitrary, I place them here because the religious lay community is the novelty in our categories which would go by default if we simply registered this author as belonging to monastic literature. The *Geistlicher Herzen Bavngart* was composed for *religiosae*, whether Tertiaries or laywomen,[201] *Die Lilie* for *religiosae* and laywomen (possibly béguines),[202] and the *Pariser Tagezeiten* were meant for the private devotions of laymen.[203]

However short, this list shows that there is an indeterminate zone between this category and works meant for the monastery in that one and the same text may have been meant for both. Grundmann has discussed how the Church sought to regularise these lay communities by transforming them into convents subject to the Rule of an order,[204] but even before this the communities shared features with monastic life in that the members regulated their daily life according to monastic practices. To these belong recital at table and private devotional reading,[205] even if the lay status of members means that reading in either sense had to be in the vernacular. What was described by St Elisabeth as *a vita sororum in seculo*[206] underlines their intermediate position, relevant to our problem, as it was in the case of laybrothers. They lived in the world without being of it and followed monastic practices without being subject to a monastic Rule. Translated into the terms of our argument, this means that, like monasteries, these communities had a need for religious reading-matter, but that their reading had to be in German. The fact that David von Augsburg composed works in Latin alongside works in German has been interpreted as suggesting a heterogeneous public in his case, too: Latin works were presumably destined for theologically trained and literate members of his Franciscan order, whilst vernacular writings were for those who had no Latin, for laybrothers in his order, but also for nuns, members of the third order, religious lay communities living in the world under Franciscan supervision.[207] How much the Church regarded such supervision as necessary and with what suspicion it viewed the layman's preoccupation with religious writings in the vernacular emerges from a Franciscan report on the béguines of northern France in 1274. They are accused of *subtilitates* and *novitates*, which they imbibe in their conventicles and hidden corners,[208] but it is the fact that they have uncontrolled access to reading-matter in their own tongue which arouses the fear of heresy.

(o) Episcopal court

To this section, the last of our five, only three works with a twofold reception belong. Thomasin von Zerclaere composed his *Welscher Gast* as a canon at Aquileia for Wolfger's court, including clerics, laymen and ladies.[209] The *Urstende* of Konrad von Heimesfurt has been judged as meant for a court audience,[210] but how careful we must be in interpreting 'court' has been shown by Gärtner and Hoffmann, who argue that the author was a ministerial of the bishop of Eichstätt, at whose *curia* the work has to be placed.[211] The third example is the *Trojanischer Krieg* of Konrad von Würzburg, who was supported in this work by Dietrich am Orte, *cantor* at the cathedral of Basel, so that it is possible that the recipients of the work were the episcopal court.[212] Given the nature of the literary scene at Basel, however, this work, like Konrad's legends, could just as well have been placed in the category of the town. This qualification reminds us of the impossibility of hard and fast divisions and prompts the question how the episcopal court, like the town in which it is situated and like the court of the secular aristocracy with which it shares so much (including ties of blood kinship), found room for two modes of reception.

Even though only three works come under this heading, the importance of the episcopal court in the history of court literature is far greater than this suggests. By that I mean not merely the role played by this type of court in the rise of *curialitas* at large, but also its literary function.[213] We have known this for some time in the case of bishop Gunther of Bamberg with his predilection for recitals of heroic poetry from the Dietrich cycle,[214] where we have oral delivery alongside the Latinate culture of Meinhard at the same court,[215] but also, in Meinhard's criticism of Gunther's literary preferences, a clash between two cultural worlds. Although it is unlikely that Gottfried numbered the episcopal court of Strassburg among those whom he addressed in *Tristan*, the bishops and their entourage are not so easily excluded from the literary scene elsewhere: at Basel in the days of Konrad von Würzburg in the persons of Liutold von Roeteln and Dietrich am Orte, and at Zürich in the participation of the bishop of Konstanz. In addition there is circumstantial evidence associating the writing of three collective manuscripts of German love-poetry with different episcopal courts, where presumably this poetry was also cultivated in oral form.

The importance of these courts lies in their being a mirror-image of secular aristocratic courts: whereas the latter depended on clerics for written administration, the feudal political interests of princes of the Church, even more pronounced than those of abbots of royal monasteries,[216] meant that they were surrounded at court by knights as well as clerics and that their cultural interests were often just as secular as those of their kinsmen who had remained in the world.[217] The coexistence of laymen with clerics has been analysed for the court of the archbishop of Cologne on the basis of documentary evidence from the high and late Middle Ages.[218] The presence of literate clerics for administrative purposes (*capellanus, cancellarius, scriptor, notarius, secretarius*) need not surprise us, but equal importance attaches to laymen who cannot all be presumed to be Latinate or literate. These ministerials are also court officials (*summe officiales curie*), they look after the landed property and income of the archbishopric and they occupy the offices at the archbishop's court which we have already encountered in the *curia abbatis*.[219] Other offices for laymen include *burggravi* and the archbishop's vassals (*beneficiati homines sancti Petri*). My point in listing these offices is to suggest not a clean break between clerics and laymen, but on the contrary their joint presence at one centre, to underline that an episcopal court was bilingual and bicultural in its interests: Wolfger von Erla encouraged Latin literature (Buoncompagno, Eilbert von Bremen)[220] as well as German (Thomasin, Walther von der Vogelweide, probably the *Nibelungenlied*).[221] Literature in two languages suggests a culturally heterogeneous court at which Thomasin could reckon with a twofold reception of his work.

This is how we must sum up these five categories. It is as mistaken to assume that a clerical or religious community contained only *litterati* versed in Latin as it is to argue that a feudal court consisted only of illiterate laymen. If we extend this point about education to literature, then the presence of laymen, in one form or another, in monasteries, religious communities and episcopal courts encouraged the reception of literature by listening even at centres of literacy, just as conversely the presence of clerics (as well as literate noblewomen) at secular courts or alongside a town patriciate insinuated the presence of readers amongst otherwise illiterate groups of laymen. In these five contexts we face a cultural symbiosis between clerical and lay,

SURVEY OF THE INTERMEDIATE MODE OF RECEPTION

between literate and illiterate, which makes it historically unrealistic to argue in terms of exclusive reading or exclusive listening.

THE DOUBLE FORMULA

When discussing reception by hearing our argument frequently depended on how we interpreted the verb *hoeren*, just as in reception by reading the key-term was *lesen*. Unsurprisingly, in this chapter a major role was played by the phrase *hoeren oder lesen*. This double formula was not the only indication of a twofold reception, but the clearest one, a pointer which we could have wished for where the alternative suggestions were ambiguous. We conclude this chapter by looking at how this formula found its way into German.[222]

(p) *Hoeren oder lesen*

Three separate strands in the use of the formula can be distinguished. It occurs, first, with regard to the reception of a work of literature; secondly, in testifying the truth of a historical event (it was seen and heard by witnesses); thirdly, in legal testimony (as with the historical usage, its reliability depended upon what was seen and heard by witnesses). This sequence (literary, historical, legal) is in fact the chronological sequence of the different contexts in which this formula is adopted into German. In each strand, however, there are Latin parallels earlier than their German counterparts, sometimes centuries earlier, so that Latin usage provided a precedent for German. In other words, with the transition of German literature, historiography and law to written form in the twelfth and thirteenth centuries a formula previously at home in Latin finds its way into German.

In what constitutes this formula we must be guided, given its priority, by Latin usage. Latin achieved succinctness by neatly combining two verbs (*audio et lego*) or by repeating the verb for reading in a causative construction (*lego et legi facio*, 'read and cause to be read out'). In addition, it could combine the two corresponding nomina agentis (*auditor et lector*) or two verbal abstracts (*auditus et visus*). From this last example it is clear that *lego* can sometimes be replaced by *video* (both share the optical dimension which distinguishes a reading reception from hearing), just as MHG *sehen* was sometimes synonymous with *lesen*. All these Latin constructions have their counterparts in German,[223] and together they constitute insignificant variants within the formula.

One such variant concerns the manner in which the two modes of reception are linked in the double formula: with 'or' or with 'and'. In Latin Fronto talks of *audientium aut legentium*, but Martial refers to *lector et auditor*,[224] whilst John of Salisbury refers in one passage to *lector vel auditor*, but in another to *lector et auditor*.[225] These variations are reflected in German: Hartmann von Aue uses *oder* (*Gregorius* 3995: *hoeren oder lesen*), Rudolf von Ems employs *und* (*Weltchronik* 21732: *lesin und horent*), whilst both possibilities occur in *Der Saelden Hort* (3984: *hóren oder lesen*; 75: *hoerent und lesend*). The agreement between Latin and German in these variants raises the question of what may lie behind them.

In discussing this question Scholz quoted the classicist Balogh on this point: *'Legere* et (aut) *audire* heißt: "selbst lesen" oder vorgelesen (vorgetragen) bekommen.'[226] Scholz, perturbed by the way in which Balogh lumped together the two constructions, attempted to differentiate them. He suggested that *aut* must imply two alternative modes of reception (either reading or listening), but that the position was not so clearcut with *et*: this could imply either the unity of reading and hearing (the situation of an individual reading aloud to himself) or the same two modes of reception as with *aut*, but now linked together as complementary possibilities, rather than exclusive alternatives.

If we apply this differentiation to the forty-two examples of the double formula in German literature up to 1300 the following emerges. The construction with *oder*, implying listening to a recital or reading for oneself, occurs in twenty-nine works,[227] whilst *und*, suggesting the same situation or conceivably reading aloud to oneself, occurs in eighteen.[228] Even this imbalance in favour of the twofold reception has to be taken further, since there are six cases where both constructions are used in the same work. In these cases the German authors, like John of Salisbury in Latin, can have been conscious of no telling distinction between one and the other. Since *oder* implied two alternative modes of reception, *und* must also have been used here in this sense. There remain only twelve cases out of forty-two which could conceivably presuppose reading aloud to oneself, but even here it is possible that some may imply a twofold reception. It is this situation which is most frequently suggested by the double formula, whose entry into German we must now consider.

Chronologically we start with the reception of literature, which we have already seen illustrated for classical Latin, medieval Latin and Middle High German. There is no need to repeat the examples given for Latin, except to make the point that if even the literate culture of Latin, in antiquity as in the Middle Ages, anticipated public delivery as well as private reading, it was much more likely that the medieval vernacular, making its first inroads into literacy, should have kept links with the oral realm from which it was emerging at least in the form of public delivery alongside private reading. The earliest example in German, about 1150, is Der Arme Hartmann in his *Rede vom heiligen Glauben* (95, 7: . . . *iz ist alliz gescriben / ze gehorenne unde ze gesihte in dutiscer scrifte. / swer daz buch wille lesen* . . .).[229] Here *lesen* confirms that the verbal abstract *gesiht* means reading, but I should hesitate to call this a double formula in the strict sense found in Latin (and soon after in German, too), because it combines verb with noun, not verb with verb or noun with noun. Nonetheless, it shows an author anticipating two modes of reception in German by the middle of the twelfth century and indicating this by something close to the double formula.

The second possibility of using this formula attests the truth of a historical event. With the Latin evidence we start relatively late, with Isidore of Seville, since, although he may depend on classical precedents, it was he who formulated a definition of history handed on through the Middle Ages.[230] He based his definition on the etymology of *historia*, which he saw as going back to a Greek verb meaning 'to see', and argued that in antiquity no one wrote history who had not witnessed the events himself.[231] For Isidore, as for classical antiquity, history was reliable only if perpetuated in a written record: he uses *conscribere* in its literal sense here, but also sees history pertaining to grammar because 'anything which is worthy of memory is committed to letters'.[232] In a double sense Isidore's conception of history was visual, resting on the presence of an eyewitness and on written, rather than oral transmission, so that Konrad von Hirsau follows him in pithily defining the *historiographus* as *rei visae scriptor*.[233]

Where in this doubly visual conception of history is there room for a formula suggesting hearing alongside seeing? Such a reservation is apparently borne out by some medieval definitions of *historia* which, like Konrad von Hirsau, follow the lead given by Isidore. Thus, Hugh of St Victor says that among the ancients only those who had seen the events could write history[234] and Robert of Melun uses the same argument.[235] That this definition need not be confined to the one (visual) dimension, however, but can be based on witnessing by ear as well, is suggested by Otto von Freising. He widens the scope of his definition already at the start by claiming that classical historians based their written accounts not only on what they had themselves seen, but on what they had witnessed with their senses and is then more explicit in referring to what a witness may have seen and heard *(ea quae vidit et audivit)*.[236]

That Otto's derivation of a historical account from what had been seen and heard is no isolated agreement with the implications of the double formula can be shown by evidence in German. Towards the end of the twelfth and through the thirteenth century authors of historical works in the vernacular seek to establish historical veracity by making implicit use of Isidore's definition.[237] When the author of *Herzog Ernst*, for example, describes at the close of his work how the Emperor had Ernst report his adventures and gave orders for it to be taken down in writing, he is projecting into his narrative what anyone with a clerical education would have known of the definition of *historia*: it was an account given by an eyewitness involved and put into trustworthy written form. Again, there is no mention of witnessing in two dimensions and this is true of the majority of these works, in which only the visual dimension is involved, as in most of the Latin evidence.

There are, however, four works among them which agree with Otto von Freising by using the double formula to suggest two dimensions of historical attestation. The earliest example is *Die Klage*, whose author suggests that bishop Pilgrim of Passau had the events of the downfall of the Nibelungen preserved for posterity in written form on the basis of what was reported by Swämmel, a minstrel who had witnessed the catastrophe, but then specifies the nature of his testimony (4312: *wand erz hôrte unde sach / er unde manec ander man*). In the *Barlaam und Josaphat* of Rudolf von Ems, as in *Herzog Ernst*, a ruler involved in the events narrated orders at the close of the work an account of Josaphat's life to be preserved in writing, but, unlike *Herzog Ernst*, this work is explicit about the nature of his witnessing (16028: *als erz hôrte und als erz sach*). *Das Passional* suggests the historical veracity of Christian martyrdom by saying how deacons and subdeacons were sent out to the lands where Christians were persecuted in order to take down an account in book form, based on the reports of those who had witnessed the sufferings of the martyrs (III 100, 59: *die da horten unde san, / waz guten luten wart getan*). Of the examples of the double formula in the *Väterbuch* I quote only one, where historical reliability is insinuated by the report that an account was written by the deacon James who had personally witnessed the events he narrated (30529: *Diz mere screib durch Gotes lob / Der selbe diakon Jacob, / Der da horte, unde sach / Begen unde ende, wie ez geschach*).[238]

It is clear that the need to testify historical truth is present in the fourteen works in question, for they all have a historical theme. Some are concerned with classical history (the Trojan war, as depicted by Herbort von Fritzlar and Konrad von Würzburg, and as alluded to in *Moriz von Craun*), one with Germanic history (*Die Klage*), some with medieval history (*Herzog Ernst*, Der Stricker's *Karl der Große*, the prose *Lancelot*,[239] *Der guote Gerhart* of Rudolf von Ems, and the *Kreuzfahrt Landgraf Ludwigs des Frommen*). The theme of *Das Passional* is the history of salvation in the widest sense, and with *Barlaam und Josaphat* and the *Christi Hort* of Gundacker von Judenburg their legendary subject-matter implies no diminution of their historical claim if we recall that *historia* was used to designate a legend in the Middle Ages.[240]

However, the double formula, when used to establish historical truth, was employed in a manner different from the reception of literature. Whereas the historical formula suggests that the original events which form the basis of a written transmission were seen and heard by witnesses, the literary formula refers to the other end of this written transmission by showing how it was received, by readers and listeners. In these different cases the visual and acoustic aspects apply to different ends of the written transmission, but the gap apparently opened up can be largely closed by one last observation. Of the four German works with the double formula in this historical sense only *Die Klage* is uninformative about the manner in which its author anticipated its reception, whereas the other three expected their work to be both read and listened to (*Barlaam und Josaphat*, *Das Passional* and *Das Väterbuch*).[241] Three out of the four German works which use the double formula in its historical application establish a parallel between both ends of the transmission in writing, suggesting that both depend upon two dimensions: seeing and hearing with those who witnessed events, reading and hearing with those who gain access to the written report.

This opens the way to the third strand in the double formula, legal testimony, where a similar point can be made. Under this heading the earliest Latin examples come from the early Middle Ages when Germanic legal practice found its way into written Latin records, and then in Latin charters of the twelfth and thirteenth centuries. By contrast, German examples occur only in charters of the thirteenth century. Informing the use of the early medieval Latin formula was the need for legal testimony in the double form of seeing and hearing: seeing the symbolic objects and gestures accompanying the transaction and hearing the words of the oath or promise.[242] The act of witnessing is therefore repeatedly described in two dimensions, e.g. *Traditiones Patavienses* 41 (*qui audierunt et viderunt*),[243] *Lex Baiwariorum* 13, 2 (*qui audiant et videant*),[244] *Traditiones Frisingenses* 33 (*et ceteri audientes et videntes*),[245] *Annales Xantenses* a. 864 (*audientibus et videntibus*).[246] In such cases *videre* means literally 'to see' and has to be kept apart from reading, but this is not the case with Latin charters of the twelfth and thirteenth centuries, where a written document has been drawn up to bear witness to those who hear it read out or read it for themselves. Early examples come from: Kloster Reun, 1173 (*Universis ... huius paginae seriem lecturis et audituris*), Bredelar, ca. 1210 (*omnibus qui legerint sive qui audierint recitari huius pagine continentiam*), Zürich, 1219 (*omnibus hanc paginam audientibus vel inspicientibus*), Cologne, 1237 (*universis, quibus presens scriptum inspicere contigerit vel audire*).[247] The first two examples refer specifically to hearing and reading, which was not possible with the early medieval examples, because the original witness saw and heard the transaction performed, whilst only the reactivation of a written record in the present opens up the prospect of hearing or reading it.

German charters follow the Latin model in applying the double formula to the two possibilities of reception. The earliest example is dated 1251-4 (*Allen dien die disen brief werdent lesende oder hoerende ...*), others occur in 1263 and 1265 and then, with a rapid take-off, frequently throughout the rest of the century.[248] Slightly later in beginning (1263), but also growing rapidly in frequency, a triple formula expands on the double one, e.g.: *allen den die disen brief an sehent lesent oder horent.*[249] The frequency of these formulas (340 examples of the double, 301 of the triple) shows that, however late the evidence for the vernacular formula in charters may start, it soon establishes itself as more frequent than the other two strands.

The early medieval Latin examples (of the type *qui audierunt et viderunt*) agree with examples testifying historical truth in referring to what original witnesses (of the legal transaction as of the historical event) saw and heard themselves. By contrast, the examples from charters, Latin or German, agree with the literary examples in referring to a later reception of what has been committed to writing, by readers and listeners. Once more we find our evidence divided between two poles of the written transmission, between original witnesses and later recipients. Here too it is possible to bridge this gap.

We may do this by following through, typologically if not chronologically, the stages by which writing and reading inserted themselves into originally oral transactions and, in doing so, influenced the formula. In the still oral stage of early medieval law 'seeing and hearing' referred to witnesses hearing the donor utter the formal words of his grant and seeing him make the transfer by means of time-honoured object or gesture.[250] This position changes with the coming of written records: now hearing is applied to anyone hearing the charter read out at any time, to the recipient as opposed to the original witness, whilst seeing gradually moves towards the meaning 'reading'.[251] This semantic shift is still invisible when the formula *sehen oder hoeren* is applied to the recipient,[252] for this could suggest both a continuation of the oral situation and also, because of the ambiguity of *sehen*, the possibility of 'reading'. With a slight change in the formula to *sehen oder hoeren lesen*[253] literacy enters explicitly, but confined to delivery aloud from a written record, since *sehen* is still too ambiguous to mean reading of necessity. With the triple formula *lesen, hoeren oder sehen*[254] three aspects of the reception are stressed, two of which are traditional (seeing and hearing), but one is new in its explicitness, for *lesen*, now distinct from *sehen*, causes the latter to lose its ambiguity and drives it back on to its original ground ('to see a transaction performed'). Finally, with the double formula *lesen oder hoeren* (or its variant *lesen oder hoeren lesen*)[255] this traditional function of *sehen* is no longer important: what counts is the fact of literacy, both in delivery and in reception. For these semantic changes to be possible, for what 'witnesses saw and heard' to become what 'recipients read or heard read', the act of seeing (whatever its precise function) must have been present at both ends of the transmission process, which are not so separated from one another as appeared to be the case.

This last point is important in drawing the three strands together in which the double formula is employed. Clearly, there is enough to distinguish these strands and to suggest a different development for them. The literary formula is attested already in classical Latin, the historical formula arises from a definition established by Isidore, whilst the legal formula is entirely medieval in origin. Similarly, different lines of development are suggested by the dates for the entry of the formula into the vernacular: 1150 for the earliest literary evidence (if we accept the example from Der Arme Hartmann), about 1200 for history, and 1251 for charters. If we have been dealing with three separate developments which all use the same formula in different contexts, this suggests a unifying factor drawing them together.

It is easiest to grasp the parallel between the historical and legal strands. Schematically, the historical strand can be presented as follows. At the outset we have the historical event, seen and heard by a witness. Secondly, the experience of this witness only bears fruit for the future if conveyed in the reliable medium of writing and not exposed to the vagaries of oral transmission. Finally, this written record is received by a later generation, by means of reading or hearing recited. In this three-stage pattern writing provides not merely a reliable link between the first and third stages, it is also the means by which the double activity of the original witness (seeing and hearing) is echoed in the double activity of the later recipient (reading and hearing). This is also the pattern with charters. Here we have, first, a starting-point in the legal transaction which is both seen and heard by a witness; secondly, transmission to the future by writing; and, thirdly, reactivation of legal memory by a later reception in two ways, where the possibility of seeing and hearing gradually also accommodates reading and hearing. Here, too, the presence of writing is crucial in permitting the double activity of the witness to be resumed in the double activity of the recipient.

With the literary strand, however, the first to find entry into the vernacular, this parallel is not quite complete. Here, too, we have three stages where, if we work backwards in this case, the last two agree with what we have just seen: a third stage in which the literary work is received by reading or by hearing recited, preceded by a second stage at which the work is entrusted to writing. Instead, it is at the first stage that the parallel breaks down in this strand, for the work which is committed to writing does not proceed from an actual event, historical or legal. What these works of literature (especially of court literature in which the double formula first establishes itself at all frequently) go back to is not a real event, but another written text, their source, whose reliability lies in its written nature.[256] On all three stages works in this literary strand dwell on the fact of writing because they cannot be traced back to anything outside their own sphere of fiction, however many pseudohistorical trimmings may be added to conceal this. This deficiency need not always be a source of embarrassment, for the leaders in German court literature (precisely those who first make recurrent use of the double formula) are concerned to substitute the novel idea of fictional truth for historical truth. Not content with being unable to use the formula in its historical function, they suggest how different their conception of literary truth is from that held by those who follow Isidore's definition. With that we reach the theme of Chapter 9.

Conclusions for Part II

Despite the importance of the intermediate mode of reception there are two restrictions on the role it played. On the one hand, some genres were received by hearing and, although their written form may be stressed, they contain no evidence that readers were expected.[1] These genres were therefore excluded from the possibility of a twofold reception.

There is, however a number of individual works which have to be excluded for the opposite reason: they contain evidence of a reading reception, but not listening. Although their being read out loud is conceivable, there is no indication that this was anticipated. It is significant that these works suggest reading for a specific pragmatic purpose.

This is true, under the heading of functional literature, of four medical texts for all of which the need to consult them for a practical purpose may explain their suggestion of a reader, without any hint of recital.[2] To this group the *Mainauer Naturlehre* may also belong for the same reason, although it may be attached to a second group, under the heading of school literature, made up of *Cato Z^1* (evidence for reading, but not for listening) and, if we include monastic scholarship here, the *Abecedarium Nordmannicum* (whose runes could only be read, not heard in recital). A third group to be consulted by the reader for a practical purpose is made up of the *Deutschenspiegel* and the *Stadtbuch von Augsburg*: neither contains any suggestion of listeners, whilst the latter meets the purposes of the reader who consults it by giving cross-references to other points.[3] A final group with an allusion to reading alone serves purposes of a different kind, for it contains texts meant for private devotional reading within a religious community.[4] Although devotional literature could also be for recital the importance of individual reading within the monastic community is enough to explain this focus on reading.

Common to these four groups of texts (amounting to fifteen cases in all) is the fact that a special reason can be adduced for private reading: the everyday needs of a medical or legal practitioner, the pedagogic requirements of schooling, the discipline of monastic *lectio*. If we discount these examples, there remains only a handful of texts for which the preceding chapters have suggested readers, but not listeners. All but one of these cases are open to doubt.

In his *Erlösung* Heinrich von Hesler suggests reading, but although listening is not mentioned it is likely if we take into account the twofold reception attested for two other works by him.[5] Two works by Konrad von Würzburg, *Silvester* and *Engelhard*, belong here, but the evidence for reading is only circumstantial.[6] There remains the *Margaretenlegende* of Hartwig von dem Hage, the only text with an unequivocal pointer to reading and no suggestion of an acoustic reception.

The conclusion is clear. Apart from a small number of texts for which special reasons account for reading we are left with only one example where individual reading, unaccompanied by a hint of listening, was expressly anticipated. Elsewhere reading was a possibility which existed alongside reception by hearing. This implies that reading was considered as one of two possible alternatives. Up to 1300 reading as an independent mode of reception was extremely slow to establish itself.

This is in agreement with Street's argument against what he calls the autonomous model of literacy (as proposed by Goody and others).[7] Street is opposed to any 'great divide' between orality and literacy, to any theory which gives insufficient attention to the reality of 'mixed' and interacting modes.[8] He accepts Clanchy's argument that the shift from the oral to the literate mode was a gradual one in which writing, instead of immediately undermining orality, was for some time adapted to oral practice, and that this prolonged conjunction allowed the transition from oral to written to take place.[9] This view underlies the organisation of the last six chapters: the stress on an intermediate mode in addition to hearing or reading, the suggestion that the literate culture of Roman antiquity or Christianity also found a place for orality, just as the oral society of Germania was not completely impervious to writing, and the argument that the five types of centre at which medieval literature found a reception all granted a place to listening alongside reading.

Street also doubts whether literacy is a neutral technology which can achieve results independently of specific social contexts.[10] He is sceptical about claims for the greater objectivity of written language and in place of Goody's 'technology of the intellect' suggests socially constructed technologies devised for particular purposes within a given social framework, involving the promotion of certain vested interests and the overcoming of the prejudices of other groups.[11] It should be clear that this view parallels certain points in our argument: the use of literacy as a political instrument of the Carolingian or the territorial princely state, the clergy's clinging to literacy as their educational monopoly and the power this conveyed to them (traced by Schreiner right up to the Reformation),[12] as well as the prejudice against literacy shown amongst laymen, above all by aristocrats and knights.

Against Goody's account of the intellectual consequences of the transition from one means of communication to another (the development of logic, the distinction of myth from history, the emergence of scepticism, all supposedly made possible by writing) Street brings forward counterarguments.[13] As a token of my disagreement with Goody it may suffice to point out that, when listing theoretical differences between oral and written communication or transmission, I nowhere mentioned features such as the development of rationality, logic or scepticism. By contrast, what Goody says about the distinction of myth from history will shortly come up for discussion.

This mention of history is important in two respects. The first concerns Goody's suggestion that writing makes for historical objectivity, the ability to compare the past with the present instead of sloughing it off or incorporating it into the present, as in oral transmission. To this Street replies that even literate historians are the products of their time and society[14] – which can be confirmed in the following chapter, where we consider historical truth within the interplay of oral and written. The second respect in which history plays a part in Street's argument concerns the historical dimension of the rise of logic and objectivity, claimed by Goody for Greece as products of literacy. Street points out that literacy was already present in early Greece before these products developed, that the later generation of these features must be due to something other than the intrinsic qualities of literacy alone.[15] The problem of orality and literacy must therefore be seen in its historical dimension, a task attempted in the concluding chapter. With the two following chapters we therefore return to the historical approach temporarily abandoned at the close of Chapter 2.

PART III

Conclusions

9

Literacy, history and fiction

Of the three themes in the title of this chapter two have often been linked together. History and fiction could be contrasted with one another by a play on words between *res factae and res fictae*.[1] The two concepts could also be brought together in medieval theoretical discussion (as treated by Knapp)[2] where *historia* may be defined as *res gesta*, but is still differentiated from *res ficta*.[3] In recent scholarship the same conjunction has been made, not merely by Knapp or von Moos,[4] but also by Haug's argument that the emergence of fiction represents an attempt by court literature to emancipate itself from the dominance of the clerical view of historical, factual truth.[5] My purpose is to insert a new element into the discussion, the fact of literacy, and to inquire how far the relationship between history and fiction may have been influenced by the transition of German vernacular literature from the oral to the written realm.

HISTORY AND LITERACY OR ORALITY

We may start with theoretical definitions of *historia* in late antiquity handed on to the Middle Ages by Isidore of Seville.[6] For him, as for classical rhetoric, *historia* is one of the three subdivisions of *narratio*, connoting what actually happened, as opposed to *argumentum* (what did not happen, but could conceivably have occurred), but also to *fabula* (an untrue account which is not even conceivably possible).[7]

(a) The Latin conception of written history

Isidore is also important because of his etymological definition of history as resting on what the writer had seen himself.[8] Isidore's argument is well attested in the Middle Ages. Hugh of St Victor, for example, repeats the Greek etymology (*historeo quod est video*), but also the description of historiographical practice.[9] Other examples of Isidore's argument are to be found with Robert of Melun, Konrad von Hirsau, Vincent of Beauvais and Remigius of Auxerre.[10] All these cases concern Latin theory of the Middle Ages, whereas by contrast the earliest direct echo in the German language occurs as late as about 1300 in the *Buch von geistlicher Lehre*.[11] This example is not so isolated as it might seem, however, since we shall come across indirect echoes in German vernacular works whose clerical authors, introduced to Isidore's definition as part of their Latin education, make use of it to suggest the historical veracity of their own works.

CONCLUSIONS

Strictly speaking, Isidore's founding of history on what an eyewitness had beheld for himself should have confined it to contemporary history, but in practice he distances himself from this view by regarding history as an account of what took place in the past.[12] In this he is in agreement with the *Rhetorica ad Herennium*.[13] If a gap thus opens up between the original eyewitness and the historian's account, this has to be bridged in a reliable way if his account is to be as reliable as if composed by the eyewitness. Isidore sees this reliable bridge in writing. For him history belongs to the realm of grammar because anything worthy of memory is committed to letters;[14] historical accounts are *monumenta*, or written texts,[15] which transmit a record of what happened in the past, so that reliable written sources may replace eyewitnesses in a civilisation whose historical consciousness is matched by a high degree of literacy.[16] How important written tradition was felt to be alongside eyewitnesses in the Middle Ages is shown by the preference given to Darius over against Homer as a reliable source for the Trojan War. For Benoît de Sainte-Maure both were 'clerics' and used writing, but whereas the first was an eyewitness of what he wrote, Homer, because he was born later, lacked this advantage.[17] Nor is it said in his case that, although his own version was written, it also derived from a written source which bridged the gap between him and any eyewitness of the events at Troy. His written version lacked therefore both eyewitnesses and any written transmission from them to him. Its historicity was therefore doubtful. Writing, however, not merely linked eyewitness to historian by means of written sources, but was also an essential aspect of the historian's task, as described by Isidore (*conscribere*), an aspect which all his medieval followers listed above likewise maintain.

In a double sense Isidore's conception of history may therefore be described as a visual one: it rests on an eyewitness and on written rather than oral transmission. In both respects the visual dimension is felt to be more trustworthy than the oral. Of the witness Isidore says that what we perceive with the eyes is more reliable than what we merely hear.[18] As far as writing is concerned, the fact that Isidore sees it bridging the gap between eyewitness and historian, but also transmitting the latter's account to posterity is a pointer to how unreliable he regarded oral transmission. It is also in full agreement with the Romans' conviction of the superiority of their culture because, unlike illiterate barbarians, their historical knowledge was reliably transmitted by writing.

This doubly visual conception of history, continued from Isidore by clerical authors of the Middle Ages, is summed up by Konrad von Hirsau, who defines *historia* as *res visa* and the *historiographus* as the *rei visae scriptor*,[19] as one who writes an account of what was seen to take place, perhaps by the historian himself in the case of contemporary history, but if not by someone who transmitted a written record to him.

We saw that one reason why the Romans could look down on the barbarians lay in the superiority of a literate culture to an oral one. Cato's view of the Ligurians, however, criticises them for their illiteracy, but more specifically for their lack of a written tradition about their past,[20] so that a reliable historical dimension is missing from their culture. With a change in focus from barbarians without to the uneducated within Roman society Cicero can equate *homines litterati* with *historici* by arguing that those able to read written annals learn more about the past than those who depend on hearing *ex sermone hominum recenti*.[21] Examples such as these confirm that the view of history summed up by Isidore was no merely theoretical insight, but a reflection of Roman society as an essentially literate culture.

(b) Oral history

If the literacy of Roman society was reflected on the small scale in its conception of history as a written transmission descending from an eyewitness, it can also be shown that the oral society of Germania possessed knowledge of its past only in the form of orally transmitted history. Cato's disdain for the Ligurians' ignorance of their own history is just as applicable to the Germanic barbarians north of the Alps. What Tacitus reports of Germanic lays, meant for song and reception by listeners, reveals their function as perpetuating tribal history,[22] comparable to what Einhard later refers to as *veterum regum actus et bella*.[23] The historical function of these oral lays is made quite clear by Tacitus (*quod unum apud illos memoriae et annalium genus est*), but by comparing these lays with the written genre of the Roman annals he suggests that they attempt to meet the same needs as annals,[24] but by oral rather than by written means.

That Tacitus viewed the historical reliability of oral transmission in Germania with as little trust as Cato did that of the Ligurians is suggested by a qualification which he later adds (*in licentia vetustatis*), implying the wide scope offered to conjecture about the past in the absence of fixed written records.[25] This distance between what barbarian tribes and someone with a literate education could regard as historically trustworthy is similar to the attitude shown by Jordanes to the *prisca carmina* of the Goths about their migrations. He describes these oral lays as *pene storicu ritu*,[26] where *storicu ritu* captures their function as history, but *pene* suggests how they fell short of true history. What is available to the Germanic tribes as oral history failed to meet Roman standards for written history.

How far the deficiencies of oral history could disqualify it in the eyes of *litterati* can be shown in the case of Otfrid. Like Cato in regard to the Ligurians, Otfrid argues that the Franks have no record of the history of their ancestors because their language has not yet found its way into writing.[27] This demands an explanation in view of Einhard's report about Charles the Great having lays with a historical content collected and written down.[28] In place of Vollmann-Profe's suggestion of rhetorical exaggeration in this passage we may have to read Otfrid's words as a refusal to acknowledge that an oral transmission deserves the title of history.[29] If so, his attitude would be comparable with the statement of Saxo Grammaticus that the Danes had developed no historical tradition because of their ignorance of Latin, i.e. because of their illiteracy.[30]

On the other side of the cultural frontier, however, amongst the Germanic tribes precisely the age-old tradition of these lays, for Tacitus one of the grounds for doubting them, was a reason for taking them seriously as historical truth, passed down the generations from their forefathers,[31] whilst the other cause for doubt felt by Tacitus (that these lays had not been handed down, like the Roman annals, in a fixed written form) was irrelevant to the possibilities of a still oral culture. In such a culture these lays were, as Tacitus saw, the only form of historical memory available and therefore indispensable. In the mixed oral-literate society of the Middle Ages they were also indispensable even to critically minded historians as the only information on early history available for incorporation in their written histories,[32] whilst sufficient historical-political force still attached to them to make it worthwhile for aristocratic families to trace their descent from characters in these lays.[33] There were reasons enough, then, for this oral transmission to mould the historical consciousness of the layman and to be questioned as little by him as was customary law, handed down likewise by word of mouth.[34]

Clanchy has reminded us, however, that there are limits set to what can be transmitted from the past in this way. In an oral society the distinction between history and myth is less clear because all knowledge of the past is conveyed by the speech of contemporaries. Two conflicting reports of an event cannot easily be compared objectively with each other, since there is no record other than the equally fallible memories of different contemporaries.[35] Moreover, memory tends to transform the information which it stores, so that an oral culture discards or reinterprets historical facts which have become incomprehensible. The professional remembrancer's task is not, as it is for the historian, to study the past objectively, but to recollect it for his fellows when called upon to do so, adapting historical facts under the pressure of present needs. An oral society requires its history to be meaningful to the present, rather than an objective record of the past.[36]

In arguing thus Clanchy is in full agreement with others who have studied historical awareness in oral societies. With reference to preliterate Greece Havelock says that 'oral memory deals primarily with the present; it collects and recollects what is being done now or is appropriate to the present situation' and reminds us that, with the past continuously contaminated with the present, living memory preserves what is necessary for present life and discards what has become irrelevant.[37] With an eye to oral traditions in Africa Vansina maintains that tribal genealogies show what the relationships are between groups in the present and are used to prove the continuity of chieftainship and legitimise it today.[38] These oral traditions are no accurate record of past reality, but are subject to adjustment to the needs of the present.[39] Vollrath has applied these findings to the Middle Ages as an oral society, maintaining that 'die Vergangenheit ist also gar keine eigene Größe, der man sich von der Gegenwart her mit der Frage zuwendet, wie es eigentlich gewesen ist' and that the past was not so much history as the present projected back in time.[40] For her this contamination of past with present presupposes that the memory of the past was constantly adaptable, a condition brought about by orality with no fixed written transmission, whereas a view of the past as distinct from the present is possible only in a literate culture.[41]

Two illustrations of this attitude to the past in an oral society have been given by Goody on the basis of West African fieldwork.[42] One example concerns the Gonja people of Ghana who, like the Germanic tribes, set great store by an oral account of their origins, according to which the founder of the state had himself enthroned as chief, whilst his seven sons were set up as rulers over seven territories within the state. This is how British colonial administrators, recognising the political importance of this tradition, recorded it in writing at the beginning of this century, but sixty years later, when political changes had led to the disappearance of two territories, the native oral tradition knew of only five sons of the founder of the state. This tradition is therefore no faithful historical record of the past, but serves as an explanation of the present and it illustrates what Goody has termed the 'homeostatic tendency' of oral tradition to see the past in terms of the present.[43] Within this tradition there is no contradiction between what was once said and what is now said (in the other example discussed by Goody the Tiv people of Nigeria even maintain that their oral memory is correct, not the written record of the British),[44] because this tradition disposes of no enduring records from the past to set against present views.

A similar realignment of historical facts in oral transmission is known to heroic tradition in the Middle Ages, particularly in the development of epic cycles, as attested in the chansons de geste, but also for Germania.[45] Different heroic themes from different historical periods can be amalgamated in the development of heroic legend. Haubrichs has pointed out how Ermanaric and Witege enter the legend of Theoderic, how Witege is also linked with the Wieland tradition, how the *Hildebrandslied* makes use of the Theoderic story for its background, how Attila's court is a centre for exiles and hostages in the Theoderic and Walther legends.[46] The result of this amalgamation of different figures in a common 'heroic age' is that oral transmission brings together persons and events originally separated in time or space. Heroic figures can attract events to themselves which are felt more properly to belong to them, or particular events can draw figures about whom something similar is already recounted.[47] This means that persons can be linked as participants in the same events, even though they may have had no contact with one another in historical reality. To the medieval listener, for whom, if he was a layman, this heroic tradition represented historical knowledge, such discrepancies were as little apparent as contradictions as they are for the Gonja of Ghana, for in neither case do they have access to a fixed written tradition against which divergencies could be registered as such. Haubrichs sees this oral tradition, with its blurring between different historical events and figures, as characteristic of what Vollrath has said of the contamination of past with present in an oral culture ('Die Vergangenheit ist nicht abgeschlossen und damit der Veränderbarkeit entzogen, sondern steht in unmittelbarem Funktionszusammenhang mit der Gegenwart').[48]

Of particular interest to us, because they are figures later seized upon by clerical critics of the unreliable historicity of heroic literature, is the mention of Ermanaric, Theoderic and Attila in Haubrichs' list. Although these three historical figures were separate from one another in time (Ermanaric died about 375, Attila in 453, Theoderic in 526) their different historical periods have collapsed together into one shared heroic age, in which they can all participate in the same events in the Theoderic legend.[49] This amalgamation is quite unhistorical, but came about as part of an overriding wish to integrate originally separate heroic themes into a unified heroic age.

In this transformation of history into heroic legend the decisive point was the idea that Theoderic must have spent his exile with the Huns at Attila's court, an idea in which an event has been attributed to Theoderic which was originally true of his father Thiudimer,[50] even though this meant placing Attila and Theoderic in the same period, a conjunction which caused offence only for those who regard time as a linear chronological sequence. It has also been suggested that the third figure in this anachronistic grouping, Ermanaric, was introduced because of the structural similarity between his legend and the Theoderic legend, which allowed Ermanaric, as the tyrant *par excellence*, to take over the role of driving Theoderic into exile.[51] Whether this explanation is acceptable or not, a heroic tradition which goes back to originally historical events can no longer be judged historical when it makes contemporaries of two figures whose deaths are separated by 151 years.

(c) Written and oral history

In the last two sections we have repeated in regard to history what we saw in general terms of orality and literacy: the literate tradition of Roman society stressed the reliability of written historical sources and of a written transmission of history, whilst the oral features of Germania and of laymen in the Middle Ages passed on knowledge of the past by word of mouth. We must take this parallel one stage further, however. Just as it was false to regard orality and literacy as confined to watertight compartments and without interpenetration either in Latin antiquity or in the Middle Ages, so must we acknowledge mutual contacts between the two attitudes towards the past which we have so far considered separately.[52] In this section we shall be concerned with how far the historiography of *litterati* took account of oral tradition and its view of the past, whilst the following section will pay attention to the penetration of clerical views of history into vernacular literature meant for laymen.[53]

With the coming of Christianity and a written Latin tradition to Northern Europe we encounter a juxtaposition of two types of historical tradition in medieval society comparable to that exemplified by Cicero for Roman society in his distinction between the annals available to the *litterati* and the dependence of others on hearsay. Whereas for Cicero the difference was an educational one (literacy or not), the position in the Middle Ages embraced that contrast, but also one between clergy and laity for as long as the latter remained unable to read. That is why Otfrid, from the superior position of literacy in Latin, can look down on his mother-tongue for not yet having produced a written historical account of the Frankish past, thereby suggesting that the oral vernacular poetry of laymen had no claim to being regarded as history. Otfrid's rejection of an inferior, because oral, historical tradition continues in a Christian context the attitude shown by Cicero.

Even apart from such a consideration medieval historians reveal a preference for written as against oral tradition, perhaps on the assumption, as with Isidore, that the former goes back to an eyewitness.[54] Despite its uncertainty oral tradition could sometimes be indispensable, when no written information at all was forthcoming, in which case the oral testimony of eyewitnesses was given preference or the testimony of those whom the historian regarded as trustworthy (they can be described as *fideles, probati* or *veraces*).⁵⁵ Other types of oral information were regarded with mistrust, but precisely how these reservations could be expressly contrasted with the reliability of writing can be shown in the the *Getica* of Jordanes. He rejects a story about the early history of the Goths, justifying this by saying that he has nowhere come across it in written form and that he prefers to believe what he has read in sources than what he has heard in old wives' tales.⁵⁶ In this case the contrast between what can be accepted as *historia* and what is rejected as *fabulae* is seen in terms of reading and hearing.

The juxtaposition of an oral tradition of history for laymen and a written tradition for clerics persisted for the greater part of the Middle Ages, but as long as laymen could regard the clerical tradition as something quite separate, not meant for themselves, but for the clergy, little change would come about. This must still have been the case with Frutolf von Michelsberg around 1100 who as a reader of Jordanes' history of the Goths was accurately informed of the lapse of time separating Ermanaric from Attila and from Theoderic, so that they cannot all have belonged to the same period and participated in the same events, as is put about by the oral tradition of vernacular lays.⁵⁷ Frutolf proceeds with logical care here, suggesting various explanations, and although he reaches no clear decision himself, but places the facts before his reader, he puts his finger on a chronological contradiction which was only apparent to someone with access to Jordanes' written work. Although he makes a clear distinction between the literate status of Jordanes (he is termed a *hystoriographus*, but more explicitly a *grammaticus*)⁵⁸ and the oral tradition from which he differs (*vulgaris fabulatio, cantilenarum modulatio*),⁵⁹ the force of Frutolf's argument was restricted to the clerical, Latinate audience addressed and escaped the layman because of its written Latin form.

Basing himself on Frutolf, Otto von Freising also criticises two aspects of the Theoderic tradition which he qualifies as a *fabula* in vernacular form.⁶⁰ He rejects the popular view that Theoderic met his end plunging on horseback into Etna (making clear his preference for the clerical version of this in Gregory's *Dialogues*), but also the view that Theoderic, Ermanaric and Attila were all contemporaries.⁶¹ Even though Otto's rejection of heroic tradition may be more emphatic than Frutolf's, the contrast between oral and written is less explicit with him: the vernacular and Latin traditions referred to in the case of Theoderic's end must also be assumed to lie behind the different views about dating.

A similar attitude is shown in the fourteenth century by Jakob Twinger von Königshofen. In his chronicle he mentions the oral tradition about Theoderic (*Dieterich von Berne von dem die geburen singent und sagent*),⁶² where *geburen* may be taken, like Latin *rustici*, to refer to *illitterati*.⁶³ That need not imply any criticism in itself, and a little later the chronicler expresses his agreement with Gregory's version of Theoderic's end, emphasising the written nature of this version,⁶⁴ still without reference to a rival oral transmission. This is made good in what follows, where the miraculous exploits attributed to Theoderic in heroic poetry are dismissed as untrustworthy because they are attested in no written source.⁶⁵ As with Frutolf, an oral transmission is here judged by the standards of literacy, incorporated for the earlier historian in the *grammaticus* Jordanes, for the later in the *magister* (*meister*) who writes.

CONCLUSIONS

The novelty in Jakob Twinger lies in his formulating his criticism in the vernacular, thus making it accessible to laymen. He is not the first to do this, however, for the argument crossed the language barrier at the latest by 1150, in the *Kaiserchronik* which, even though it may not mention Jordanes expressly, makes use of the kind of argument against oral heroic tradition which his written history had made possible. When dealing with Theoderic the clerical author of the *Kaiserchronik* follows loosely the version of Gregory without polemicising against other traditions,[66] but then takes issue with oral poetry on the question of chronology, maintaining that Theoderic and Attila cannot have been contemporaries (*Swer nu welle bewaeren, / daz Dieterich Ezzelen saehe, / der haize daz buoch vur tragen*),[67] establishing their different dates (14179ff.), and dismissing the rival view as untrue.[68] The cleric knows himself to be on safe ground here, for by 1150 heroic poetry had not yet made the transition to parchment, was still exposed to the same inconsistencies as with the Gonja of Ghana, and could therefore be argued out of court by one who had the support of written evidence.[69] Now that this argument, conducted in German, was carried into the layman's camp, he was forced to react to a criticism which brought about radical changes in what was regarded as historical truth.

If written sources thus make possible a critical attitude towards historical transmission which is beyond the reach of orality, it is important to stress that we are dealing with a possibility not always realised. The amalgamation of past with present, even the subordination of the past to the present, can occur in written history as well as in oral. Fuhrmann says of Hincmar of Reims and Burchard von Worms that they allowed Augustine to speak 'as he ought to have spoken' and that a legal provision was valuable only in so far as it accorded with one's own times.[70] Arguing against Goody's view that historical objectivity follows from writing Street makes the general point that a society's representation of its past is tied up in the present ideological concerns of particular groups[71] (the medievalist thinks of the rise of the Arthurian legend in connection with Anglo-Norman political interests). For this reason, too, Vansina is doubtful about the sharpness of Goody's break between oral and literate, suggesting that the homeostasis of oral transmission is not always complete and that we are rather dealing with tendencies towards homeostasis.[72] As with Goody's argument at large, we should talk of the implications of literacy rather than its consequences.[73] Even with this qualification, however, there is enough evidence to suggest that, although they could meet on common ground, the oral and literate views of history in the Middle Ages were different enough to attract contemporaries' attention.

(d) Written history in the vernacular

The criticism of the layman's oral tradition by clerical *litterati* has to be seen in connection with another phenomenon in the twelfth century: history, previously written by clerics in the language of literacy, Latin, now came to be written by them in the vernacular as part of an attempt to win the secular aristocracy for a clerical view of history. Apart from an early beginning in the late eleventh century (*Annolied*) in the second half of the twelfth century works such as the *Alexanderlied*, the

Kaiserchronik, the *Rolandslied*, *König Rother* and *Herzog Ernst* plot the development of historical works of quite a different kind from those hitherto available to the illiterate laity.

These works all have a historical theme, generally the history of the Empire, as had been made topical by the accession of Barbarossa.[74] Despite its earlier dating the *Annolied* places the biography of a saint in the context of the modern Empire whose descent from the Romans it traces in detail.[75] The historicity of the *Alexanderlied* is assured by the mention of the hero in the Old Testament, by embedding the theme in the history of salvation, and by the relevance of the replacement of Persian by Greek rule to the prehistory of the Empire.[76] Historical events in the rule of Charles the Great were transmitted exclusively in Latin historiography until finding their way first into French epic poetry, then into the *Rolandslied*, written with the contemporary Empire very much in mind.[77] *König Rother* is linked with imperial history by the claim that Rother was the father of Pippin and therefore the grandfather of Charles the Great,[78] whilst *Herzog Ernst* treats of a rebel against imperial authority and seeks acceptance as a historical account by explaining the origins of the 'Waise' jewel in the imperial crown.[79]

If much of the historical material in these works had previously been confined to Latin historiography it is not surprising that their authors should be clerics. A member of the monastery of Siegburg is assumed as the author of the *Annolied*, with access to the *Vita Annonis* and Latin historiography, and writing in the interests of the monastery or the archbishop of Cologne.[80] The authors of the *Alexanderlied* and the *Rolandslied* designate themselves as *pfaffen*.[81] For the *Kaiserchronik*, whether commissioned by the ducal or the episcopal court at Regensburg, its size and the range of sources required presuppose the resources of ecclesiastical institutions and its author is to be regarded as a Regensburg cleric.[82] For *König Rother* a number of clerical aspects, not least the wish to give the work the stamp of history, suggest an educated clerical author,[83] whilst the dependence on Latin material for parts of the *Herzog Ernst* implies the same for this work, too.[84]

Clerical authorship implies literacy. This is true of the authors' relationship to their Latin sources, but in addition references can be made to a *buoch* as source in every case,[85] whether this written text be in Latin or, as in the case of the *Rolandslied*, in another vernacular rendered into German *via* a Latin version. Literacy can also be claimed of the author's own work. Written status is implied for the *Kaiserchronik* by the phrasing of a reference made to someone mentioned 'above',[86] the author of the *Rolandslied* sees it as his task 'to write the truth',[87] whilst the enigmatic reference to the author of *König Rother* as *rihter* has been interpreted as implying a 'schreibender Dichter', one who ensures a correct, because written, form for his material.[88] It is of a piece with this literate status of clerically composed works that two of these six works should polemicise against the shortcomings of oral tradition (*Annolied*, *Kaiserchronik*).[89] The need to do this arose from the fact that these clerical authors were treating secular not biblical history and therefore had to keep themselves apart from a heroic tradition which also regarded itself as transmitting knowledge of the past.[90] For the clerics their rivals handed down *lugene* or *ficta*, not *wârheit* or *facta*.

CONCLUSIONS

We must be careful not to see this development towards vernacular written history as proceeding solely from clerical motives, for the facts of patronage (secular courts probably stand behind these works,[91] to which the connections with imperial history would have made an ideological appeal similar to the classical past claimed for the Anglo-Norman dynasty by their historical writers)[92] suggest that the lay aristocracy may have had its own ambitious reasons for moving into a literary field, albeit in the vernacular, previously occupied by the clergy. It is significant that the large-scale vernacular chronicle first occurs from about the middle of the twelfth century both in Germany (*Kaiserchronik*) and in the Anglo-Norman realm (*Lestorie des Engles, Geste des Bretuns*),[93] roughly contemporary with the first beginnings of vernacular literature with secular themes and registering a similar move to written form and heightened historical awareness on the part of laymen.

If this historical awareness was served by clerics it is not out of the way that in two of the six works a specifically historical argument, as known to medieval theory in Latin, should be used to establish their veracity. At the close of *Herzog Ernst* it is claimed that the Emperor had his former opponent Ernst report his adventures and gave orders for them to be taken down in writing (6002ff.). From this we are invited to believe that the Latin codex at Bamberg, on which the German author bases his version and which is the guarantee of its truth,[94] goes back directly to this dictated report. In other words, what we have here is a projection into the narrative of what a cleric would have known about Isidore's definition of *historia*: an account by eyewitnesses involved (Ernst, and the Emperor too), put into trustworthy written form.

With *König Rother* a different attempt at historical verification is made. At three points in the narrative it is claimed that the hero was the father of Pippin, hence the grandfather of Charles the Great,[95] but two of these passages are linked with an explicit claim for the work's truthfulness (3491f.; 4794ff.). This grafting of Rother onto the Carolingian ancestral tree is a means of granting historical credibility to the work, suggesting that it deals with *facta*, not *ficta*. Even though no distinction is made here between written and oral, the other works which cannot be compared with *König Rother* for truthfulness are reminiscent of the oral tradition attacked in the *Annolied* and the *Kaiserchronik*. If *König Rother* claims historical reliability for itself by reference to Charles the Great we are reminded of the argument of Hugh of Fleury at the beginning of the twelfth century that events which cannot be coordinated with particular rulers or dates cannot claim to be regarded as history, but only as stupid fables.[96] By using this kind of argument the author of *König Rother* hoped to establish his work's historical veracity as much as did the author of *Herzog Ernst* in making use of Isidore of Seville.

If we take these last two observations together (clerical criticism of the historical unreliability of oral tradition and the growing need for vernacular history to acquire the written form hitherto reserved for Latin historiography) they suggest increasing doubts about the historicity of oral poetry, a threat to its function of transmitting knowledge of the past which was best met by accepting the clerical challenge and moving into the field of writing. At this point, where history and writing are now felt to belong together, Isidore's definition acquires a significance which has not been sufficiently appreciated. We have seen that his view of *historia* lay behind *Herzog*

Ernst, but something similar is attested in heroic tradition, namely in the *Klage* when commenting on the events of the *Nibelungenlied*. We are told that Bishop Pilgrim of Passau ordered Swämmel to recite the events of the final catastrophe at Attila's court and that the bishop's scribe Konrad took this report down in Latin (4295ff.).[97] Of Swämmel it is said expressly that he had personally seen (and heard) the events which he reported (3469f.; 4309ff.) and Pilgrim even questions other possible eyewitnesses (3471ff.).[98] The written Latin version resulting from this is said to have reported how things had taken place and deserves to be regarded as the truth (4300). Once again, this passage incorporates the two aspects of Isidore's definition: the historical account derives from what an eyewitness has seen and its subsequent transmission is in written form.[99]

So close is the resemblance between the accounts given in *Herzog Ernst* and in the *Klage* that a causal relationship has been postulated.[100] This would be acceptable if it did not rest on an isolated argument which ignores many other cases in the twelfth and thirteenth centuries where historicity is likewise claimed on the basis of an eyewitness account taken down in written form. The range of these examples is so great that it suggests clerical (or clerically trained) authors making use of Isidore to buttress their trustworthiness.

Isidore's argument that *historia* demands both an eyewitness and written transmission can be illustrated by a number of examples spread over genres regarded as *historia* in the Middle Ages.[101] In *Seifried Helbling* the general point is made that the author will praise what he has seen, unlike the praise lavished on Gahmuret and Parzival by Wolfram *dẽr ir einen nie gesach*.[102] In the legend[103] the force of *Sanct Brandan* is to confront the doubting hero unexpectedly with what he had requested in his initial refusal to credit the miracles he had read, *er ensêhez mit den ougen sîn* (47),[104] whilst Konrad von Fussesbrunnen refuses literal-mindedly to report on what was eaten on one occasion *durch daz ich was dâ niht zehant*,[105] thereby heightening trust in what he does choose to recount. In the genre of history two battle poems with a historical basis claim eyewitness veracity: in the *Böhmenschlacht* it is the poet himself, in the *Schlacht bei Göllheim* a knight who took part is claimed as informant.[106] In his *Österreichische Reimchronik* Ottokar maintains that he is dependent on the reports of those who were present.[107] That this argument could also be used against fictional literature (with the implication that one's own work was not affected by it) is made clear by Herrand von Wildonie (*Âventiure swer die seit, / der sol die mit der wârheit / oder mit geziugen bringen dar: / ob ez ein hübscher habe für wâr / sô wil lîhte ein unhübscher jehen, / ez enhabe nieman gesehen*).[108] An example like this suggests a widespread reaction to romance fiction, not confined to *Seifried Helbling* in regard to *Parzival*.[109]

Isidore's conception of history, however, demanded written transmission as well as an eyewitness, so that we now have to consider those cases, in addition to *Herzog Ernst* and the *Klage*, where both points imply historical reliability. The most frequent are examples from legends. Admittedly, when three separate versions of a legend of St Margaret all make this point (e.g. *Sante Margareten Marter* 51: *alsô tet der guote Theotimus / ... der die marter ane sach: / der schreip ez als ez dô geschach*)[110] their force could be weakened by the objection that they all go back to a common source, but against this speaks the recurrence of this argument in many other legends. *Sanct Brandan* belongs here again, for it suggests its derivation from what the saint himself wrote of his experiences (814ff.), but also Alber's *Tnugdalus*, an expressly written version[111] which rests on an eyewitness account (27f.). The *Heinrich und Kunigunde* of Ebernand von Erfurt is likewise expressly a written text[112] deriving from eyewitnesses (82f.), whilst Rudolf von Ems sketches the transition of *Barlaam und Josaphat* from eyewitness experience to written transmission in a manner reminiscent of *Herzog Ernst* and the *Klage* (16021ff.). Similar examples are found in the *Passional*, the *Väterbuch*, *Alexius A*, and the *Leben der heiligen Elisabeth*.[113] In all these cases the legend is presented as a doubly authenticated *historia*.

Similar attestations are made in biblical literature.[114] Werner vom Niederrhein refers to the (written) gospel of St John as based on his visual testimony, and a similar authentication is made on behalf of St Luke and St Mark in the *Passional*.[115] When Gundacker von Judenburg bases his *Christi Hort* on Nicodemus,[116] this is again because the latter wrote an account of what he had personally seen and heard, just as the same point is made independently of Nicodemus by Heinrich von Hesler.[117] In his *Marienleben* Walther von Rheinau says the same of St Luke as was said in the *Passional*, whilst Heinrich von Neustadt attributes the written text of Alanus ab Insulis to what he had seen in his vision.[118]

Unsurprisingly, purely historical works avail themselves of the same argument. Whether, like Benoît de Sainte-Maure, they contrast him favourably with Homer or not, three German versions of (or references to) the Trojan War (*Moriz von Craun*, Herbort von Fritzlar, Konrad von Würzburg) all make the point that Dares both took part in the events and wrote them up.[119] A conjunction of eyewitnesses and written transmission of his *Alexander* is implied at one point by Rudolf von Ems, in Ottokar's *Österreichische Reimchronik*, and in the *Kreuzfahrt des Landgrafen Ludwigs des Frommen von Thüringen*.[120] If we may also include a German adaptation of the chanson de geste, similarly regarded as history, under this heading, Der Stricker's *Karl der Große* also claims a similar origin for itself, for the reliable witness is even replaced by an omniscient angel, dictating to St Giles what had happened.[121] In the heroic epic native to Germany, with its own claims to historicity, one example only is known to me, in *Virginal*, where it is suggested that the warriors themselves should write up their exploits for the ladies to read.[122]

By contrast with these three genres (legend, bible, history) only one example of this Isidorean technique occurs in a romance, in the prose *Lancelot*. We shall discuss this exception later.[123]

From *König Rother* we also saw that history could be established by linking events to a historically attested ruler or, from Hugh of Fleury, by giving an actual date. A ruler, often a pagan Roman, is frequently mentioned in legends: Nero in an early twelfth-century legendary, Claudius in Hugo von Langenstein's *Martina*, Patrinus in the *Märterbuch*.[124] On occasions the ruler in question can be a Christian (e.g. Theodosius in the *Passional*) or even a medieval one (e.g. Otto IV and Philip of Swabia in the *Leben der heiligen Elisabeth*), including the Pope (e.g. Innocent I in *Alexius A*).[125] Among historical works proper the *Kaiserchronik* is an obvious example, arranged according to named emperors, but also Ottokar's *Österreichische Reimchronik* (e.g. an event can be related to the papacy of Urban IV).[126] Hugh of Fleury would have had no difficulty in acknowledging these legends and chronicles as *historiae*.[127]

The same is true where the events related are given a historical dating. Examples are confined to legend and history. Cases of the former include the early twelfth-century legendary which also refers to the Emperor Nero, Alber's *Tnugdalus*, the *Heinrich und Kunigunde* of Ebernand von Erfurt, *Der heilige Georg* of Reinbot von Durne, and the *Passional*.[128] Examples under the latter heading include the *Kaiserchronik* (where time is organised not by absolute dates, but by the number of years in an emperor's reign), the *Livländische Reimchronik*, and Ottokar's Austrian chronicle.[129] Again, the prose *Lancelot* has to be registered as a solitary exception from the romance genre and will be discussed later.

The spread of genres in which these two techniques (summed up as Isidore and Hugh) are used covers various types of history (classical antiquity, the Germanic past, imperial history, even contemporary history), but also events recorded in the Bible and legends, likewise considered historical. (It is noticeable that, apart from the prose *Lancelot*, the romance does not put itself forward in this way as history.) With such historical themes it is not surprising that these works should include a suggestion of their historical reliability, and the position is no different with comparable references in French literature, for they too fall within the same spread of historical genres.[130]

To sum up: the general medieval symbiosis (an oral alongside a literate culture) is reflected on the smaller scale in two different views about knowledge of the past and what constitutes historical truth. By the second half of the twelfth century, however, with the rise of court literature in the vernacular dealing with secular themes and meant for laymen, but in written form, we see signs of an interpenetration of these two cultures: clerics criticise the historical truthfulness of oral tradition in the light of their written values and introduce these into vernacular works composed for lay listeners.[131]

FICTION AND LITERACY OR ORALITY

As a result laymen came to see the advantages of accepting literate values, the possibility of rivalling clerical culture on its own ground and of acquiring a measure of cultural independence for themselves. It is with this emancipatory movement that the future in court literature lay, producing results which could not be foretold from what we have so far seen.

(e) History and fiction in Arthurian material

We start with the manner in which Arthurian material was first made available in the Latin form chosen by Geoffrey of Monmouth. At first sight his work appears to belong to the clerical, literate tradition which claimed an exclusive right to historical reliability for itself. Writing in Latin and as a *magister* teaching at Oxford he certainly had enjoyed a clerical education,[132] and in giving his work the title *Historia regum Britanniae* he claims for it the rank of historical scholarship.[133] This suggestion of clerical historiography is apparently borne out by Geoffrey's dependence on other works of historical scholarship such as Gildas' *De excidio et conquestu Britanniae*, Bede's *Historia ecclesiastica*, and the anonymous *Historia Britonum*.[134] If Geoffrey also makes use of Virgil and the Bible,[135] this need not tell against the historical claim of his work, for the Middle Ages regarded the *Aeneid* as a historical account of Rome's Trojan origins[136] and the Bible was held to be historically true. Geoffrey's historical construction implies that, just as Rome traced its origins back to Aeneas, so did the rulers of Britain descend from Brutus, another refugee from Troy.[137] By suggesting that the Norman rulers fulfilled this British and Trojan prehistory Geoffrey supplied them with a historical nimbus which enabled them to compete with other royal ideologies, particularly the role played by the figure of Charles the Great in buttressing the claims of the Normans' rivals, the kings of France. In this sense Geoffrey's *Historia* was what he called it: a work of history as the Middle Ages understood that term.[138]

Accordingly, it is not surprising to see his work accepted as the historical truth. Soon after its appearance Alfred of Beverley wrote an epitome with the title *Historia de gestis regum Britanniae*, Geoffrey Gaimar translated it into Anglo-Norman and used the word *estoire* in his title, Ralph de Diceto took Geoffrey's account about Arthur as historically useful enough to justify English claims to Normandy, whilst Robert of Gloucester refashioned it as a rhymed chronicle.[139] The extent to which Geoffrey's work was regarded as historiography can often be shown by its MS transmission, as with an Exeter MS of the second half of the thirteenth century, containing the *De excidio Troiae* of Dares, Geoffrey's *Historia*, and the *Historia Anglorum* of Henry of Huntingdon, thus constituting a compendium of British history from its Trojan origins to the twelfth century.[140] Equally, when the figure of Arthur was used in support of English claims against Scotland, even the Scots did not reject the historicity of Arthur, but merely his place within the historical tradition of which the English made such use.[141]

The importance of Geoffrey's work, behind which oral tradition of Celtic origin is to be detected,[142] lies in the fact that Arthur has now found his way into a large-scale written work, has made the transition from oral to written,[143] a fact which, together with all the trappings of clerical historiography, enabled Geoffrey to pass it off as historically reliable. How important writing was in establishing historicity may be shown not from Geoffrey's work itself, but in a fifteenth-century reflection of it to which Johanek has drawn attention. The English chronicler John Hardyng, concerned to support English claims against Scotland, describes how the written tradition about Arthur began at the king's court itself: *And euery knight his auenture that stounde / Had tolde the kyng as his order was founde; / Whiche aduentures the kyng made all be written / In his register, euer to be knowen and weten.*[144] Johanek comments that transferring the knights' accounts into written form transposes them to the realm of historicity and he draws a parallel with the passage from the *Klage* where bishop Pilgrim issues similar instructions. We can go one step further, however, and relate this passage to all the other German works which establish their historicity in the same way, but also, ultimately, to Isidore's definition of *historia*.

Just as the German examples all occurred in various types of historical work, so does Hardyng's passage come from a rhymed chronicle, testimony to the acceptance of Geoffrey as a historian still in the late Middle Ages.

If that were all, there would be little reason to include Geoffrey under fiction and every reason for placing him under history. Yet doubts about the historical truth of Geoffrey's work were also expressed, since the historical sources used by him contained almost nothing about Arthur to justify the world-historical position granted him by Geoffrey.[145] William of Malmesbury, basing himself on the *Historia Britonum*, distinguishes between the historical figure of Arthur as a warleader and the untrustworthy Celtic tales circulating about him: *Hic est Artur, de quo Britonum nugae hodieque delirant; dignus plane quem non fallaces somniarent fabulae, sed veraces praedicarent historiae.*[146] Perhaps alerted by this contrast between *fallaces fabulae* (in what must still be oral tradition) and *veraces historiae*, other writers express reservations about Geoffrey's written *historia* which makes use of this Celtic tradition. For William of Newburgh Geoffrey's work is *figmenta ridicula*, Merlin's prophecies are *divinationes fallacissimae*, and the Avalon legend a *fabula*.[147] In passing judgment on Geoffrey's whole work (*contra fidem historicae veritatis deliravit*) William criticises him for his offences against chronology, presenting early British history in a manner which did not harmonise with all that was known from other sources.[148] In accusing Geoffrey of offending against historical truth and in contrasting him with the *historiographi veteres*[149] William not merely undermines his status as a historian, his attack also parallels the criticism of heroic lays dealing with Theoderic for their confused chronology.[150] Whereas Otto von Freising criticised an untrustworthy oral tradition, William of Newburgh criticises Geoffrey's written work, in part because it was based on oral tradition.

Giraldus Cambrensis goes further than William of Malmesbury in expressing his reservations about Arthur, for not merely does he stamp him (even in Geoffrey's written version) as transmitted in a fabulous story which lies (*sicut fabulosa Galfridi Arthuri mentitur historia*), he even goes so far as to question whether the figure of Arthur is historically true (*Et Arturi nostri famosi, ne dicam fabulosi ...*).[151] Aelred of Rievaulx refers to *fabulae mendaciae*, but also attests as early as 1141 the fictional nature of Arthurian material (*fabulis, quae uulgo de nescio quo finguntur Arthuro*).[152] His testimony antedates the passage from Peter of Blois in which Arthurian material is seen as *fabulae recitatio*, meant for delivery by mere *histriones*.[153] Passages such as these, written by the clerical opposition, point to the fascination exercised by Arthurian material on court society and are best interpreted in terms of the culture of laymen alongside that of clerics.[154] The Arthurian legend in England acted as a focal point for the two cultures to grow aware of the difference between them, just as the Theoderic legend performed a similar function in Germany.

We can approach the possibility of the fictional nature of the Arthurian romance if we look at a feature of the history of this genre common to France and Germany. The earliest attempts to appeal to the interests of the secular aristocracy concentrate on romances with a classical theme (e.g. Alexander, Troy, Aeneas) and only later pass on to Celtic or Arthurian themes.[155] A classical theme gave the poet a ready means of authorising his version as history. Benoît de Sainte-Maure boasts that his sources are historically more reliable than Homer and establishes this by means of Isidore's view of *historia*, so that his romance is as much concerned with the history of antiquity as the chanson de geste was felt to be with Carolingian history.[156] Likewise Wace, who begins his *Brut* by insinuating British history into classical history, affirms his role of telling the truth as a historian by recounting the succession of king after king[157] in a manner which Hugh of Fleury would have recognised as the mark of the historian.

Conversely, the choice of a classical theme restricted the court poet in adapting this traditional, pre-formed material to the expression of topical chivalric interests. With the transition to Celtic themes, previously circulating orally in no fixed form and not so well known on the continent that they had been made unadaptable to new needs, the court author acquired freedom of scope, but at the cost of losing historical legitimation.[158] In short, the transition from classical to Celtic romances was tantamount to an abandonment of historical truth as a justification. What results this could have amongst the clerical opposition has been shown in the case of Giraldus Cambrensis by Bezzola.[159] He points out that although Giraldus, as a member of the court of Henry II, shows himself abreast of works with a classical theme (Thebes, Troy, Aeneas) commissioned by that court, he keeps silent on the subject of the stories of the *matière de Bretagne*. Bezzola interprets this striking contrast as an indication that for Giraldus the Arthurian material must have lacked the historical basis which the classical themes enjoyed.[160]

How unhistorical, malleable and fictional these new themes were is seen in the inventiveness with which Chrétien de Troyes rings the changes on an earlier narrative plot, composing *Yvain* in part in reaction to *Erec*, or *Cligés* in response to *Tristan*.[161] If by a stretch of imagination one were to concede historicity to the earlier work in either case, the same could not be said of the later, constructed artificially by changing original presuppositions. Haug sees such poetic freedom to indulge in structural variations as constituting the history of the Arthurian romance and as tied up with the discovery of fiction. What Haug says of the unreal optimism of the prologue to Hartmann's *Iwein* is applicable to other romances, too: its optimism can only be at home in a fictional world in which merit and reward neatly correspond.[162] Not by chance have utopian elements been traced in Gottfried's *Tristan* or folktale structures in the romance at large:[163] in either case the gap between romance and historical reality is pronounced.

So far the clerical opposition to Arthurian material has been voiced only by Latin writers, but a turning-point is reached with Wace, who expresses his criticism in the vernacular, thereby carrying it into the camp of laymen. In this he occupies a position similar to that of the *Kaiserchronik*, whose author was likewise the first to voice clerical criticism of unreliable oral history in German.[164]

In his *Roman de Brut* Wace occupies an intriguing position between history and fiction. We have already mentioned his intention as a historian to recount the succession of rulers in Britain, and this concern for historical truth is also implicit in his scepticism about the *liber vetustissimus* which Geoffrey claimed as his source, and his decision to omit as unintelligible the prophecies of Merlin which William of

Newburgh dismissed as *fallacissimae*.[165] None of this directly affects Arthurian material itself, but it does suggest that Wace's view of his task as a historian was undercut by the nature of the work he translated.

In two respects Wace's scepticism extended to the Arthurian legend itself. He repeats the kind of criticism of Celtic tales about Arthur voiced by William of Malmesbury when he, too, dismisses them as fables (*... la Reonde Table / Dunt Breton dient mainte fable*),[166] but shortly afterwards goes into further detail. Wace says of the adventures of Arthur's knights in a long period of peace that they are neither completely a lie nor completely the truth, neither complete folly nor complete wisdom, and that the minstrels have recounted them and the storytellers recited them in order to embellish their tales so that they all now appear as a fable.[167] In the last lines the word *fable* and its variants occur so insistently (four times in seven lines) that, despite his role as a historian and although he concedes a partial element of truth to these tales, he creates the impression that his work is founded on a partly fictional tradition, so that he undermines the authority which an accurate conservation of the past conferred upon him.[168] Moreover, in so far as the adventures which fell in this period of peace are those which constitute the themes of the Arthurian romance with Chrétien the doubts raised by Wace accompany these themes, located in the middle ground between truth and lie, from the beginning.[169] In itself this does not stamp them as fictional, but it points in this direction.

In his *Roman de Rou* (a chronicle of the Normans which again underlines his role as a historian) Wace points to the unreliability of a Celtic motif found in the Arthurian romance. When mentioning the forest of Brecheliant (for which the young Parzival sets out in search of Arthur's court) Wace introduces his doubts (*... Donc Breton uont souent fablant*),[170] as he had in *Brut* when dismissing Celtic tales about Arthur. He then describes the marvel which is supposed to occur at the spring of Berenton in that forest, but undermines our trust by making the marvel depend on whether the truth is spoken about this spring.[171] As a critical historian Wace was not prepared to take this at face value, so that he describes how he personally went to the site, went through the required motions and was of course disappointed (*La alai io merueilles querre, / Vi la forest e ui la terre, / Merueilles quis, mais nes trouai, / Fol m'en reuinc, fol i alai, / Fol i alai, fol m'en reuinc, / Folie quis, por fol me tinc*).[172] If Wace was a fool to go to the spring in the first place, expecting to experience a marvel, but came away feeling a fool in his disillusionment, this implies the folly of believing in the reality of what is recounted in Arthurian romances. They are fables because, in Isidore's words, they are *contra naturam*.[173]

We saw in the last section that clerical doubts about the reliability of heroic literature in conveying knowledge of the past led to two results: the adoption of a clerical view of history in vernacular literature, but also the transposition of heroic literature to written form. Similar doubts about the historical reliability of Geoffrey's *Historia*, however, led to quite a different result, to the development of a concept of fictional, as opposed to historical truth. We shall see that Isidore's insistence that *historia* is a written record of past events going back to an eyewitness is frequently the focal point of the argument.

(f) Examples of fiction in the romance

At the end of a chapter devoted to three works which deal with a historical subject-matter Haug states that the development of an autonomous status for literature depended on its freeing itself from the restrictions of history ('heilsgeschichtlich-politische Konzeptionen').[174] In his following chapter he is engaged with the first romance of Chrétien de Troyes, whom he sees as decisive in this process. Not merely does he compose the first Arthurian romance, he also marks the point at which Arthurian vernacular narrative passes from oral to written transmission (from *jongleur* to educated cleric) and the emergence of a conscious awareness of fiction. With Chrétien fiction is not simply uncritical history-writing (as could be said by critics of Geoffrey of Monmouth), but rests on an awareness of the distinction between historical and fictional truth. The authors with whom we are now concerned make this distinction clear by showing that where fiction differs from history it does not fall short of it, but has its own positive function.

Medieval historical works were scrupulous in maintaining their agreement with their source, since this written source was the reliable link with the original eyewitness. Zink has stressed just how different Chrétien's attitude is already in his first romance (*Des or comancerai l'estoire / Qui toz jorz mes iert an memoire / Tant con durra crestiantez: / De ce s'est Crestiiens vantez*).[175] The novelty is that Chrétien does not turn towards the past the memory of which will be preserved in his work, but towards the future which will preserve the memory of his work, so that it is not the author's intention to perpetuate truthful knowledge of the past by faithfully following a source. The authority for this work is not a source linking it with the past, but the author who proudly puts himself forward in giving his name. Nor is this an isolated example, for in his *Perceval*, a work whose religious dimensions might have been expected to induce more humility, Chrétien also puts himself forward as the ultimate source or 'sower' of his work.[176] An author who can so stress himself as originator is hardly likely to be slavishly subject to a source with its own subordination to the past.

What results this can have for the difference between Chrétien, consciously aware of his own fiction, and Wace, factually critical of Arthurian fables, has been well brought out by Wolf in an interpretation of the Calogrenant episode in Chrétien's *Yvain*.[177] This work is unique in lacking the usual rhetorical prologue, but instead a delayed prologue is given within the narrative by Calogrenant introducing the account of his past adventure to the Round Table. Calogrenant stands in for Chrétien the narrator and his prologue contains topoi normally found in the prologue to the whole work. When Calogrenant promises to speak the truth (*Car ne vuel pas parler de songe, / Ne de fable ne de mançonge*), but adds to this a broadside (*Don maint autre vos ont servi*),[178] this addition serves no purpose within Arthur's court, but is the type of polemical thrust at rivals which an author normally inserts in his own prologue.[179] Calogrenant's promise not to indulge in a dream or a fable or a lie is therefore tantamount to Chrétien's own promise about his narrative.

The importance of this is revealed in Wolf's demonstration that we have in this passage a quotation by Chrétien from Wace to underline the full difference between the two. It is not merely that Calogrenant's (= Chrétien's) words *songe, fable, mançonge* recall words used by Wace and other clerical sceptics to denigrate the Arthurian legend (*somniare, fabula, mentiri*),[180] for these parallels are too general. Much more telling are those between Calogrenant's account of his adventure and Wace's account of his visit to the spring in the *Roman de Rou*. Like Wace, Calogrenant seeks an adventure in this forest and, like him, finds it at a magic spring. Where Wace sought marvels (*La alai io merveilles querre*), Calogrenant sought adventures (*Que je ... / Aloie querant avantures*);[181] just as Wace recounted what he saw personally (*Vi la forest e vi la terre*), so does Calogrenant make the same claim (*Ainz vos dirai ce, que je vi*).[182] More important is the parallel between the conclusions of the adventures, for where Wace repeatedly accused himself of folly in going to the spring and in coming back, Calogrenant blames himself in similar terms (*Einsi alai, einsi reving, / Au revenir por fol me ting*).[183] These parallels and Wolf's suggestion that Chrétien is quoting Wace throw light on how Chrétien regarded his narrative. Wace's account was meant to throw a critical light on the untruthfulness of the Arthurian legend, so that for Chrétien to refer to this account in his *Yvain* might seem to undermine the truthfulness of his own work. If Calogrenant, however, speaking on behalf of Chrétien, underlined the truthfulness of his account, this cannot be used to suggest that the clerically trained and intellectually alert Chrétien was more naïve and credulous than Wace.[184] Instead, it implies that on the elementary factual level Wace may well be right, but that Chrétien is here dealing with fictional truth on quite a different level.[185]

This does not mean that Chrétien could dispense with any legitimation, now that he had cut himself free from historical truth. Instead, he seeks this in the other element of Isidore's definition, in the written status of his works, deriving some (or details in them) from a *livre* or designating his own work as such, thereby insinuating for himself the authority of written tradition.[186] He does this in the prologue to *Erec*, at the beginning of the Arthurian romance. Not merely does he turn away from the past, he also establishes the superiority of his work to the version of those who earn a living by telling stories which they mutilate in the presence of kings and counts.[187] In attacking his rivals Chrétien is also attacking the oral mode of these minstrels,[188] inferior to what emerges as his written mode because they know nothing of his *conjointure* – a word which, whether it goes back to Horace or to Alanus ab Insulis, stems from the world of literacy and Latinity to which Chrétien belonged, but not his rivals.[189] This difference allowed Chrétien to scorn his oral rivals, just as any cleric was convinced of the superiority of his cultural world to that of laymen, even though Chrétien may have drawn the raw material of his new version from what these rivals had transmitted orally.[190] Convinced of the superiority of fictional truth to historical truth, Chrétien must have been aware that in the eyes of clerical sceptics his position was endangered by his abandonment of eyewitness testimony and needed to be reinforced by the written status of his works.

Once the concept of fictional truth had arisen alongside historical truth, the attitude adopted by Wace must have seemed impossibly literal and matter-of-fact to an author like Chrétien. This was even more true with his German followers, not merely because a historical tradition was more firmly established in German literature (and with it the view of historical truth),[191] but also because of Germany's backwardness at this time in literary matters by comparison with France.[192] This did not prevent German authors from seizing the opportunity which the discovery of fiction afforded them, but it does mean that, more emphatically than Chrétien, they found it necessary to point out the nature of fictional truth in the hope of training their audience to it.

Hartmann von Aue is far from shirking the problem of historical truth and goes out of his way to meet it head-on, showing that he has shifted the ground of debate from history to fiction. He does this in his *Iwein* when he refuses to give a description of the combat between the hero and Ascalon, which ended in the latter's death, on the grounds that Iwein, the survivor, was too well-bred to have boasted of what happened and no one else had been present as a possible eyewitness informant (*sî wâren dâ beide, / unde ouch nieman bî in mê / der mir der rede gestê*).[193] What starts by looking like a *brevitas* formula turns into a question of principle: whether a description of the combat is feasible, if nobody was there to report on it.[194] Hartmann confesses here that he is recounting an event on which no eyewitness report is possible, but what is said here of this episode is true of his whole work (if the criterion used here were generally valid, the work would not have come into existence)[195] and equally of Chrétien's version (what the German text reports on this episode is presumably applicable to the French). This passage therefore shows that the literate and clerically trained German author turns Isidore's definition on its head, for by his own argument his written version cannot go back to an eyewitness. In other words, it is possible for Hartmann to write responsibly and instructively on events about which he cannot possibly know that they actually took place and which cannot be designated as *historia*. In explaining his inability to describe this combat Hartmann may well have had various considerations in mind (to avoid a lengthy description, to present Iwein in flattering terms, to show himself as an almost pedantic and therefore trustworthy author),[196] but to these we must add the wish to bring home to his audience the fictional status of his work. How fictional it was can be shown by contrasting it with the refusal of Konrad von Fussesbrunnen in his *Kindheit Jesu* to describe the details of a meal on the grounds that he was not present.[197] What for lack of an eyewitness was not possible for Konrad in the historical genre of a legend was perfectly possible for Hartmann in the fictional genre of an Arthurian romance.

Elsewhere, too, Hartmann points provocatively to the fictional dimension of his work, as when, in answer to an imaginary question by a listener in *Erec*, he playfully refers this invented figure to the servants of Mabonagrin's mistress if he wishes to learn more about her dress.[198] By adding that he did not see the dress himself because he never went there the narrator stresses the gulf between his work and any external reality by which it can be checked, in order to imply the fictional nature of his narrative. Moreover, as Schultz has pointed out,[199] a passage like this where the narrator is unexpectedly ignorant of a detail threatens the integrity of his work: he tells us about the mantle which the mistress wore, but professes ignorance about her dress. For more than eight thousand lines he could describe what everybody wore, but now suddenly declares his ignorance: 'these sudden twists subvert the entire narration: if he cannot tell us now, how did he know before?'[200] By feeding these critical questions to his audience Hartmann is alerting them to the fictional nature of his work.

This last passage has been compared with an earlier one in *Erec* where the audience are recommended whom to consult if they wish to learn the names of the wonders of the sea just mentioned.[201] This time the narrator makes clear the futility of this wild goose chase. The inquirer is sent off to someone (unspecified) who might supply the information, but is then told that his task is in vain.[202] If we apply these disillusioning comments to the comparable situation with Mabonagrin's mistress it will be to register that such appeals to the 'world outside' are mistaken, because this world has no bearing on the fictional world of *Erec*. The same is true of another passage coming shortly before. The narrator undermines his description of a saddle (after having just described the horse at length) by suddenly pleading inability because he has not seen it.[203] This raises the kind of question put by Schultz (if the narrator is ignorant about the saddle, how did he come to be so knowledgeable about the horse?),[204] but there is more to it than that, as we see when we take the description of the saddle into account. This description opens with a general statement which for all its hyperbole is perfectly acceptable: no one ever possessed or saw a more beautiful horse (*daz doch nie dehein man / dehein schoenerz gewan / noch solde beschouwen*).[205] It closes with a comparable statement which is subtly different (*ez enkam doch phert nie sô guot / in deheines mannes gewalt*).[206] The narrator says here that no one ever possessed so beautiful a horse, but if we supplement this with the other verb employed in the opening statement ('no one ever *saw* so beautiful a horse') the implication is that this is because this horse does not exist in reality, but only in the fictional world constructed by Hartmann.[207] This conclusion is in agreement with Worstbrock's assessment that Hartmann's depiction of this horse belongs to the realm of fiction, that he means his audience to participate in this game with fiction, and that the horse and the saddle belong neither to a *historia* meriting factual belief nor to a tissue of lies, but are legitimate elements of a meaningful poetic (we might say: fictional) work.[208]

Hartmann's position within the development of fiction in the romance can be compared with Chrétien's (even though he found it didactically necessary to present this new departure more obviously to his German audience). Common to all the passages considered is the impossibility of seeing what is narrated or described: no one else was present at the combat between Iwein and Ascalon, Hartmann did not himself see the dress of Mabonagrin's mistress, or the saddle of Enite's horse, and he even suggests that no one ever could see it because of its unreality. If no one ever saw these details this means that, as with the single combat, there never was any eyewitness who could have reliably reported them. If one of the elements in Isidore's definition falls out, as with Chrétien, this means that with both a greater importance attaches to the written dimension of their work as legitimation.

Of Gottfried von Strassburg it has been said that he adopted the guise of a *historiographus*, rather than a *poeta*, but it has also been suggested that he may not have meant this guise to be taken seriously.[209] He creates the impression that he is a historian when he describes how he consulted a variety of sources in preparing his

Tristan,²¹⁰ but distances himself from what was regarded as the historian's method by not collating these sources, like a historical writer, but by finding his truth in one text alone, the version of Thomas.²¹¹ (How far Gottfried's method really is from being a historian's has also been shown by Brackert's contrast with what Rudolf von Ems says of his method in *Alexander*, a work with a historical theme for which Rudolf employed the procedure of a medieval historian.)²¹² In other words, Gottfried starts by apparently using a historian's method, but falls back on the poet's privilege of choosing a text closer to his own wishes. He also uses the key-term *istôrje* (for the first time in German literature) to refer to his source on four occasions, just as he can also employ *geste* in the same way, another term with historical implications (cf. *Rhetorica ad Herennium* 1, 8, 3: *Historia est gesta res*).²¹³ Three of the four occasions when Gottfried uses *istôrje* belong to a historical context within the terms of reference of Gottfried's work: he employs it when describing the foundation of Marke's rule as a result of internecine warfare in the history of England and Cornwall, the historical tribute rendered by Cornwall to Ireland, and the political situation of the duchy of Arundel. It is possible that by referring to his source(s) as *istôrje* on three historical occasions Gottfried wished to create the impression that these sources were *aller der lanthêrren leben* (153) which Thomas, and following his example Gottfried, has consulted.²¹⁴ He implies the procedure of a critical historian when, immediately before describing the political situation in Arundel, he refers briefly to Tristan's knightly exploits in the historical context of the German Empire, but refuses to treat them on the grounds that the relevant sources, although written, are not all trustworthy.²¹⁵ By such means Gottfried puts himself forward as a historian, and even the slight doubt occasioned by his opting for one source alone is clear only in retrospect (by contrast to his successor, Rudolf von Ems) or exclusively to those in his audience who were versed in medieval historiography.

In view of this historian's guise it is not surprising that another passage has been interpreted in a manner which, although Isidore has not been mentioned, apparently draws Gottfried close to his definition of *historia*, whereas it can instead be shown that he is in reality flying in the face of this definition. At the close of his description of the love-grotto the narrator says: *Diz weiz ich wol, wan ich was dâ*,²¹⁶ thereby apparently putting himself forward as an eyewitness to what he has just written, doing what Hartmann had claimed was impossible in the case of his own romances. However, this apparent personal testimony is undermined when the narrator says that he had known the love-grotto since his eleventh year, but adds: even though he has never been in Cornwall.²¹⁷ This passage has been interpreted as an *attestatio rei visae*, as a claim to have seen a particular detail (one of the components of Isidore's definition),²¹⁸ but Gottfried uses this topos in a special way, for what he claims to have registered is something in his own personal experience, not the love-grotto in Cornwall to which Tristan and Isold gained access. Since he never came to Cornwall, Gottfried's passage cannot be compared, say, with the testimony to the truth of a legend in the *Väterbuch* on the grounds that the martyr's sepulchre has actually been seen.²¹⁹ Whatever may be attested by Gottfried, it is not a detail which occurs in his story, and by suggesting, on the allegorical level, the timeless nature of the grotto he removes it effectively from the realm of history.²²⁰ Yet the use of allegory concerns not merely the grotto itself, but also the narrator who inserts himself into its description, thereby underlining the fact that his *attestatio* is meant figuratively, not literally or historically. He does not claim to have 'seen' the grotto (as Wace saw the forest of Brecheliant), but rather to have 'known' it (*erkant*), which Christ interprets as implying a knowledge of love ('ich kenne mich in der Liebe aus'), so that the allegorical interpretation of the grotto in terms of the nature of love distinguishes the grotto 'von der historischen Eigentlichkeit der sonstigen Fabel'.[221] How far the rest of Gottfried's narrative may be seen as historical is another matter, but this central episode transcends the merely historical and puts forward Gottfried's message in allegorical terms which are Gottfried's own, not deriving from his source and certainly not from history. Indeed, Gottfried's suggestion that despite his knowledge of love neither he nor anyone else is capable of meeting its absolute demands implies a strongly utopian aspect of this view of love,[222] a conviction that it is as little to be found in the real world as was the perfection of Enite's horse described by Hartmann.

Gottfried's fiction is also reflected in his readiness to employ symbolism as opposed to what is rationally probable in the contingent world, whenever the former suits his book. He is perfectly ready to adopt a pose of rejecting what is rationally improbable, especially when this concerns rival versions of the Tristan story, but, like Chrétien rising above the matter-of-factness of Wace, he is ready to abandon this pose when need be. An example of Gottfried's criticism of an improbable motivation is his rejection of the motif of the swallow with the golden hair[223] which has even found its way into written versions of the Tristan story,[224] so that there can be no talk of writing leading automatically to a more rational motivation. Gottfried's rejection of what is empirically improbable is a rhetorical pose not to be seen as a mark of literary realism: this is suggested by episodes where he is quite ready to retain improbable elements if he finds that they can be adapted to an overriding purpose.[225] Bertau talks persuasively of Gottfried's 'imaginäre Historizität', of an appearance of being historical-critical which is no more than an attitude, a rhetorical move to create the impression that *res fictae* are in fact *res gestae*.[226]

The force of this argument depends on the cases where Gottfried himself employs a rationally improbable motivation. One such example is Tristan's combat with Morolt where the author takes issue with the Tristan tradition, goes his own way against the source on which he elsewhere claims to depend, and says that he can establish the truth of his variant version.[227] He proceeds to do this, but on an allegorical, rather than literal level, thereby suggesting that the truth of his work is anchored not in any humdrum view of reality, but in a readiness to leave this behind at times for the higher purposes of fictional truth. Gottfried does more than just make his case, he also insinuates that he has taken his audience with him in his demonstration: whereas they once thought that his version was improbable, now they perceive its truth.[228] Like Hartmann, Gottfried is engaged in training his audience to a realisation that poetic truth need not be subsumed under factual, historical truth. The purpose which poetic truth is meant to serve is made clear in the love-grotto episode, not merely in the allegorisation of the grotto, but in a radical differentiation between factual and poetic truth. This example concerns the question how the lovers fed themselves during their woodland banishment, a question attributed to a fictionalised audience (*Genuoge nimet hier under / virwitze unde wunder / und habent mit frâge grôze nôt* ...)²²⁹ whose scepticism may reflect, as was also the case with Herrand von Wildonie, the uphill nature of the poet's task in educating them towards his view of fictional truth. When Gottfried explains that the lovers' food was the food of love, claims that it was enough for him, and challenges his audience to make a better suggestion,²³⁰ he is again bringing it home that this central scene is not to be judged by realistic standards, but in terms of a timeless allegory. Behind the critic of what is rationally improbable, adopting the attitude of a *historiographus*, there stands a *poeta* ready to switch his argument to another level whenever this suits the purposes of his fiction.

In yet another respect the fictional nature of Gottfried's work can be suggested. If the historian's agreement with his written source, providing a link with an original eyewitness, was the guarantee of his truthfulness, it is striking that in his description of the combat between Tristan and Morolt Gottfried differs from his source and makes no secret of it, which prompts the question: if Thomas spoke correctly on the basis of the historical sources he had consulted, how are we to assess Gottfried's deviation from him? An example is provided by the scene in which Tristan is clothed in readiness for his knighting ceremony (a scene which is once more transposed to the allegorical level).²³¹ Recently, when it was a case of clothing Tristan's companions for the same ceremony, Gottfried was ready to conform to his source in his description,²³² but with Tristan he adopts a different attitude, for now the criterion for his description is no longer conformity to his source, but rather the agreement of his audience and conformity to the overall meaning of his own story (*wie gevâhe ich nû mîn sprechen an ... / daz man ez gerne verneme / und an dem maere wol gezeme?*).²³³ With this shift of *maere* from the poet's source to his own version²³⁴ the poet's attitude has changed: his truthfulness depends no longer on a reliable source (and the historical sources behind that), but on his own careful dispositions and the complicity of his audience (*mac ich die volge von iu hân, / sô ist mîn wân alsô getân, / und weiz daz wol*).²³⁵ The truth of fiction now depends on the author making it probable and in conformity with his overall intentions, but also on his rhetorically establishing the complicity of his audience, so that both parties now work together (*so bevelhen wir in vieren / unsern friunt Tristanden*).²³⁶ A truth so far divorced from what the source transmitted as to be dependent on collusion between author and audience can make no claim to be historical, but must be seen as fictional. A case like this, where an initial agreement with the source is transposed to an allegorical level, is characteristic of a literature seeking autonomy by cutting loose from its ties to history.²³⁷

In his discussion of Tristan's accounts of his origins, adjusted to the varying circumstances in which he finds himself, Grosse has shown how the account he gives the pilgrims after he has been set ashore in Cornwall is in the literal sense untrue, because he does not recount what is factually true.²³⁸ In two other senses, however, it can be said to be true. First, because it is so plausibly concocted that the pilgrims are convinced by it, Tristan obtains their acceptance as much as the narrator does in describing Tristan's preparations for his investiture (*mac ich die volge von iu han* is said by the narrator, but could just as well describe Tristan's skill as storyteller).[239] Tristan's account is true, however, in yet another sense, for what he puts forward as a fabrication, namely that he was born in Cornwall, is in fact true in that he was conceived there and is related to Marke. In a similar way his invented claim to have been separated from a hunting party unwittingly anticipates the huntsmen who soon come on the scene. In a double sense, therefore, what is literally untrue turns out to be true: rhetorically convincing to his listeners and in conformity to the overall pattern of the work, the two criteria invoked by Gottfried for the knighting ceremony. In devising his story in this way Tristan has no awareness of its actual truth (he is ignorant of his Cornish origins and cannot know that a hunting party will soon come into view), he is as much an unwitting spokesman in the hands of the narrator as are Herzeloyde and Gurnemanz in Wolfram's *Parzival* when each gives the hero advice with a double application: to situations arising in the immediate future which they could be expected to foresee, but also to situations over a far longer timespan which they cannot possibly have foreseen, but which have their fitting place in Wolfram's fictional construction.[240] If Tristan as a story-teller can be paralleled with Gottfried as an author, then the way in which the former's fabrication reveals an unexpected truth suggests that Gottfried's fiction, although likewise no *historia*, also yields a truth on another level.

With Hartmann as with Gottfried fictional truth arose from their breaking free from the suggestion that their works went back to an eyewitness who transmitted an account to them, as in historiography, and the same is true of the *Parzival* of Wolfram von Eschenbach. Among the examples where the narrator says he lacks an eyewitness our first one seems innocuous enough. It occurs at the start of Book x after the preceding Book has been devoted entirely to Parzival so that Gawan's exploits have been lost to view. Of Gawan in this intervening period it is said: *Wiez Gâwâne komen sî, / der ie was missewende frî, / sît er von Tschanfanzûn geschiet, / op sîn reise ûf strît geriet, / des jehen diez dâ sâhen*.[241] By omitting any account of Gawan's travels and by implying that he himself had no first-hand report the narrator suggests that he recounts only what witnesses have reported to him, although this still leaves unanswered the kind of question raised by Schultz about Hartmann (if he is ignorant of some details how is he knowledgeable about others?).[242] Elsewhere Wolfram can claim that he has no witnesses for a particular detail, but depends on his source, as with the places on Gahmuret's travels or with a combat in which Gawan is engaged.[243] The throw-away tone of this last remark (reminiscent of Hartmann in *Erec* 9209f.) hardly reinforces the necessity to believe this detail, and in any case simply passing on responsibility to a source still leaves open the question whether witnesses were available for this source. On another occasion the narrator, passing over details of a wedding celebration, recommends members of the audience who wish to know more to ask those who received gifts on that occasion,[244] a narrator's trick which was probably borrowed from Hartmann's unhelpful suggestion to seek information from the servants of Mabonagrin's mistress. If Hartmann's purpose was to suggest the fictional nature of his narrative the same is likely to be true of Wolfram as well. That is how Seifried Helbling judged the matter, who contrasts a description of a combat personally witnessed with Wolfram's praise of Gahmuret and Parzival, neither of whom he ever saw.[245]

For Wolfram to fall back theoretically on the argument that, although he had not seen it himself, he nonetheless follows a reliable source not merely avoids the question whether witnesses had in fact been available one stage back, it also implies that he faithfully followed his source whenever he said he was doing so. Precisely this has been called into doubt by Lofmark's analysis of Wolfram's source-references, which demonstrates the unreliability of the narrator's pretence to be recounting what he has found in his source.[246] The claim to take a piece of information from the source is in most cases false, the narrator deceives his audience precisely when he says that he is faithfully following his source, and he inserts a source-reference whenever he seems to go his own way. The position is no different when Wolfram uses the word *âventiure* in the sense of 'source'.[247] Of the thirty-two cases only two have a counterpart in Chrétien's *Perceval* to which they could refer. Elsewhere, *âventiure* can refer to a source in episodes which are not included in Chrétien's (incomplete) text[248] or to a Kyot whose account cannot be checked or, even more remotely, to Kyot's own source. The majority of these references, especially those confirming points of no significance, is not intended to be taken seriously and the narrator shares with some of his audience a humorous disrespect for the rule of source authority.[249] If the narrator distances himself from his source he thereby also keeps his distance from any historical veracity which might be claimed for it. At this point the possibility of fiction comes into play, which rests on the author inviting his audience's collusion in a willing suspension of disbelief.

How far these examples could be seen by a contemporary audience as not to be taken seriously is uncertain. Lofmark suggests cautiously that only some of Wolfram's audience would have shared his disrespect for source authority, which agrees with Mohr's suggestion, relevant to any awareness that the source-references have no counterpart in the French text, that some of his audience had knowledge of Chrétien's work.[250] For the rest, only some of the examples may have been immediately apparent (the imitation of Hartmann or the matter-of-fact tone in which the audience is left to believe the Gawan combat or not), whilst others may have been taken at face value by a credulous or literal-minded audience not yet trained to the niceties of fiction. To make them aware of what is afoot, which is the basis of their complicity in accepting a fictional construct, two other methods are employed by Wolfram.

The first concerns the narrator, in particular the suggestion (already encountered in two of Chrétien's prologues and with Gottfried) that he disposes of the details of his narrative, for this radically subverts the view that the narrator conscientiously transmits a faithful version of a narrative already reliably set out in his source.[251] Examples of this are the narrator boasting of the courtesy with which he has arranged for Utepandragun to be unhorsed and fall on grass rather than rougher ground or, of far greater import, the suggestion that the narrator is in overall charge of events, guiding Parzival from one encounter to another, as with his combat with Feirefiz, and also to his climactic success at Munsalvaesche.[252] Wolfram may not pointedly look towards the future as did Chrétien in the prologue to *Erec*, but he puts himself forward just as much as the ultimate originator of his work as the Frenchman had done in his *Perceval* prologue. Each turns away from the past, from absolute dependence on a source for which historical veracity could be claimed. If the German narrator is in overall control he can also claim responsibility for details, even in the suggestion that he has lied in describing the plain of Dianazdrun as covered with more tent-poles than the Spessart has tree-trunks.[253] By raising the possibility of untruthfulness over an unimportant detail (he can use hyperbole elsewhere without undermining it) Wolfram suggests that the truth of his fiction is not to be judged on the factual level, that a 'lie' on this level need not exclude a truth on another.

This last remark was addressed pointedly to the audience (*iu*), which brings us to the second method used by Wolfram, his involvement of the audience in the task of storytelling by pretending to seek their advice over the next stage in the narrative, suggesting that some control over the narrative might lie with them, rather than with the source. Of this technique it has been said that while 'it seemed presumptuous of the narrator to claim to be able to affect the course of his true story, it seems preposterous that his audience should possess that same ability'.[254] From two directions the supposedly unassailable authority of the source is called into question.

Wolfram involves his audience in his fiction in three ways. The first is to pretend that he has their agreement to a particular detail, so that partial responsibility falls to them, as with the change in Gahmuret's coat of arms when he sets out on his adventures or when the course of Parzival's combat with Orilus depends on the audience's agreement.[255] These points are minor ones, but they help to establish a complicity between audience and author. This is taken further in a second way when it is suggested that the audience not merely agrees with the author's dispositions, but dictates them to him: in passing his responsibility on to them the author suggests that they are partners in his fictional enterprise. According to this argument a detail of the narrative has to meet not the claims of a pre-established source, but the decision of the audience,[256] a detail of the narrative has to be settled by them,[257] the choice is left to them,[258] their wishes have to be consulted,[259] the fact that Cundrie should hurry to bring her news to Parzival and the Round Table is shown to be under their control.[260] Such passages are fictional not merely in the sense that the narrator makes up audience demands on his work (what Scholz has termed a 'Hörerfiktion'), but also in the sense that, by pointedly involving them in the task of fiction, he teaches them what it is all about. As collaborators they share one final responsibility with him, for if he could be said to 'lie', then so must they. In a detail of the meal served at Munsalvaesche, where hyperbole is the order of the day, the narrator's oath to speak the truth is calmly passed on to his audience, so that the possibility of his lying can also be imputed to them.[261] With that the audience is fully implicated in and made aware of Wolfram's fiction.

For a last example we return to Chrétien's *Yvain*, not in order to add to the sketch of fiction with him, but because what can be shown in his case is also applicable to all the romance authors who anticipated a twofold reception, readers as well as listeners. The passage is once more Calogrenant's introduction to the account of his adventure which he gives to the Round Table as listeners. We saw that this stands in for the theoretical prologue missing from this work and that Calogrenant gives recommendations to Arthur's company normally conveyed by the author to his audience (a request to listen, an affirmation of the truth, the need for close attention, the right understanding of the tale).[262] If only a short way into the narrative Calogrenant belatedly brings what the author might have been expected to deliver at the start, this gives force to the suggestion that Chrétien has played a trick on his more superficial listeners, interested only in what happens in his story and ready to skip the first five minutes of recital with its prologue.[263] By confronting these latecomers with a deferred prologue he still confronts them with a lesson in how to receive his work, but his ability to play this trick at all presupposes that his work was meant for recital and that for his listeners the recital situation depicted between Calogrenant and the Round Table was a reality in which they, too, were involved.[264] The suggestion made by Scholz (that this passage appeals to Chrétien's readers and their sense of superiority to the Arthurian listeners in the narrative)[265] need not be seen in conflict with an actual recital situation if we assume a twofold reception for Chrétien's works as for those of his German successors. The recital situation which was a reality for those who listened to Chrétien's romance becomes an element in his fiction for those who read it. In other words, an element of fiction enters for the reader which is not always present for the listener; the change in the mode of reception can reinforce this element of fiction, in this as in other works.

We have been concerned with the gradual emergence of fiction and its possibilities in Arthurian material, first (more in a critical sense) in Norman England, then with Chrétien in French literature, and finally in Germany. This emergence can also be confirmed the other way round, by seeing it as a progressive loss of history in the Arthurian theme in moving from England to France and then to Germany. Even those in England who questioned the reliability of Geoffrey of Monmouth did not cast doubt on the historicity of Arthur.[266] The discussion about Arthur largely took place in chronicles, and his use to support political claims makes better sense if both parties share acceptance of him as a historical figure. For France on the other hand the Arthurian romance seems to oscillate between 'historical' truth and fiction, at least to judge by the nature of MS transmission, where Wace's *Brut* can be handed down in conjunction with chronicles, but also Chrétien's romances can be inserted into *Brut*, just as an early fourteenth-century MS combines 'historical' works such as *Eneas*, *Brut* and chansons de geste with Chrétien's *Yvain*.[267] In Germany the position is different again and has been sketched by Ott in terms of Heinrich von München in particular and the MS transmission of chronicles at large.[268] He points out that in the practice of conflating a chronicle text with other non-chronicle vernacular texts these other texts are of a 'historical' type (romances of classical antiquity, material from chansons de geste, biblical literature), but not examples of the Arthurian romance, which implies a distinction between what was acceptable as historical and what was regarded as fictional, a conviction that Arthurian material did not conform to the claims for historical truth expected from a chronicle. In this respect Germany differs markedly from England.

THE RETURN TO HISTORY

To withdraw from the realm of history into a fictional world meant establishing an autonomous realm of literature which is the counterpart to the attempt to establish autonomy for a knightly culture in process of emancipating itself from clerical ascendancy. If we admire this development because of its emancipatory force, we must also accept the unpalatable fact that it was relatively short-lived and was thwarted by a return to historical themes, as opposed to fictional ones, in the course of the thirteenth century.

(g) Thirteenth-century developments

If narrative literature in Germany around 1200 was dominated by the new genre of the romance the thirteenth century shows the re-emergence of literary forms, particularly the chronicle and the legend, earlier present in the twelfth century, but temporarily overshadowed by the romance.[269] In making themselves felt again they represent a threat to the autonomy of the new fictional genre: the chronicle by restating the claim of historical truth, the legend by stressing the fact of religious truth. Although the *Kaiserchronik* was composed around 1150, it remains isolated in the twelfth century as a chronicle in German, but in the thirteenth an avalanche of such works sets in: monastic chronicle (Eberhard for Gandersheim), city chronicle (Gottfried Hagen for Cologne), territorial chronicles (Jans Enikel for Austria, the *Braunschweigische Reimchronik* for the Welf dynasty) and world chronicles (Rudolf von Ems, Jans Enikel again, the *Sächsische Weltchronik* and the *Buch der Könige alter ê und niuwer ê*).[270] The frequency of such chronicles testifies to a need for historical orientation on the part of laymen which the romance could not satisfy. These chronicles also establish continuity with the pronounced historical tradition of German literature before the interlude of the romance,[271] and demonstrate how much the new concept of fiction had to contend with and why it eventually gave way to *historia*.

The literary history of the thirteenth century abandons the fictional interlude and reverts to an earlier tradition of the twelfth century in another sense, too. Around 1220 the interest in French court literature, especially the romance, underwent a decline in Germany, in that none of the many new French verse romances was now imitated in German, by contrast with the readiness with which the most important examples had been adapted before.[272] This change has been connected with a growth of didactic and religious literature (hardly well disposed towards the new concept of fiction), pointing to a function of literature in conveying knowledge of what is factually true, rather than an aesthetic presentation of secular values.[273] Seen in this light many texts of the thirteenth century stand closer to those of the first half of the twelfth century than to those of court literature around 1200, a factor which informs Schnell's study of the literary continuity of the twelfth century and the late Middle Ages, bypassing the interlude of the court romance.[274] In place of the French sources of the romance the literature of the thirteenth century turns once more to the mainly Latin sources which had lain behind vernacular literature in Germany before about 1150,[275] which means a retreat from fictional sources to largely historical ones, reflected, even in the romance itself, in its greater element of historicity in this period.[276] Corresponding to vernacular treatments of such historical themes as Alexander and the Trojan War which had preceded fictional Arthurian themes we find thirteenth-century authors reverting to these themes: Rudolf von Ems and Ulrich von Etzenbach deal with Alexander, whilst Konrad von Würzburg and the *Göttweiger Trojanerkrieg* resort to the Trojan theme. Where French sources remain unchallenged, as in Der Stricker's *Karl der Große* or the Willehalm cycle, it is in connection with the chanson de geste tradition for which a historical function had long been claimed.[277]

This tendency can be illustrated in the two most important court authors after 1220, Rudolf von Ems and Konrad von Würzburg.[278] Both experiment with a range of narrative genres and with both three types are represented: legend, history, and love-romance. In other words, apart from the last, they concentrate on the two literary forms which re-emerge in the thirteenth century, but significantly keep their distance from the Arthurian romance. What lies behind this shift of emphasis has been established in greatest detail for Rudolf von Ems: unlike Gottfried he presented himself as a historian, but wished to be taken seriously as such.[279] His lack of interest in the Arthurian romance is the consequence of his view of literature more in terms of *historia* than of *fabula*,[280] his *Weltchronik* draws on historical sources of the twelfth century,[281] and his overall conception of imperial history served the purpose of placing Konrad IV within world-history.[282] This historical emphasis explains why, amongst the German works whose historical reliability was proposed in terms of Isidore's definition, we find two by Rudolf: *Barlaam und Josaphat* and *Der guote Gerhart*. This is also the reason why the latter work, purportedly dealing with a none too distant event in German history, contains a phrase (*diu geschiht der selben zît*) which even corresponds to the stricter view of *historia* as contemporary history.[283] Finally, this is why in his *Alexander* (by contrast with other medieval versions) Rudolf appeals to Aristotle as the guarantor of historical truth, Alexander's teacher to whom the pupil reported his adventures in writing, so that here too, although not formulated expressly, the view of history agrees with Isidore.[284]

A further change in the thirteenth century is closely connected with historiography, both in France and in Germany, namely the transition in the vernacular from verse to prose. For France the discussion about the truth of prose as opposed to the untruth of verse was conducted in connection with vernacular versions of Latin historiography. The primary interest in vernacular prose proceeded from a wish for an accurate rendering of historical facts, and this discussion took place in the vernacular because here the verse tradition represented the obvious rival to prose.[285] For Germany Schnell has shown that if the vernacular chronicle makes the transition to prose around 1260 this is because it stands closest to Latin literature in which prose predominated for historiography,[286] whilst Heinzle has pointed out that the prologue to *Lucidarius* illustrates that this concern with prose as a vehicle for truth (if not specifically for historical truth) is attested even earlier in Germany.[287]

To associate this change from verse to prose with historiography might seem dangerous in view of the *Lancelot* as the most impressive example of prose literature, an Arthurian example for which Heinzle, however, has made the case for clerical, indeed Cistercian authorship.[288] We are no longer dealing here with an Arthurian romance on the model of Chrétien, but with Arthurian material appropriated by a cleric who, conscious that prose guarantees truth, whilst verse adorns a lie,[289] establishes the veracity of his narrative by writing prose and by presenting it as history. (How different these clerical ends can be is suggested by the downfall of Arthurian chivalry depicted and by leading figures ending their days in penance for their sins.)[290] In various ways the narrative is depicted as history, amongst which must be included frequent references to the French source (and on one occasion to the German version) as a *historie*, but also to the written nature of this source (*buch* or *schrifft*).[291] If this implies historicity on the basis of one element in Isidore's definition, it is significant that the author also builds references into his narrative showing King Arthur ordering his scribe to take down, as a permanent record, a written account of a knight's experiences on his quest.[292] Passages like these (e.g.: *Und der konig gebot vier schribern die darzu gesaczt warn, das sie all die abentur schriben die in sim hofe geschehen*)[293] represent an exact parallel to John Hardyng in England: just as his example occurs within a chronicle, so are the passages in the prose *Lancelot* meant to establish its historical truthfulness. On one occasion this technique is used of Bohort's adventures, but with the addition that this was just as he had seen things himself:[294] in this we now recognise the two aspects of the conventional definition, the historian as a *rei visae scriptor*. When in every case the knight-informant is able to give an accurate first-hand account we also recognise the difference between this technique and that of Hartmann in describing Iwein's combat with Ascalon. Whereas Hartmann was able to give a (fictional) account even though no eyewitness had reported the event, the author of the prose *Lancelot* can give his (historical) report only because an eyewitness stood at the beginning of the written tradition. This is the first occasion when this technique to establish historicity is used of Arthurian material in Germany, but only because that material no longer forms part of a fictional romance, but has been made to serve historical (and religious) ends by a cleric. These historical ends also explain the other exceptional position of the prose *Lancelot* within Arthurian material, the fact that, true to the criteria laid down by Hugh of Fleury, it also provides an absolute dating for its events.[295] By conforming both to Isidore and to Hugh the clerical author returns Arthurian material to the realm of history from which it had sought to free itself in the form of the romance.

(h) The Grail romance

Not by chance did this conversion of romance into history take place in a work dominated by the theme of the Grail, for in this subgenre the reversion from fiction to history is well attested (already the *Estoire dou Graal* of Robert de Boron is informed by the trinitarian historical speculations of Joachim of Fiore).[296] The openness of the Grail romance to this is not surprising, for if the dominant literary forms of the thirteenth century are history and legend, the Grail theme imposed a religious dimension on Arthurian material and already in Wolfram's version historical features are present.[297] However, we have to wait until later in the thirteenth century to observe the full appropriation of Grail material by history in the *Jüngerer Titurel* and *Lohengrin*.

The first of these is devoted not to an individual hero, but to suprapersonal events set in a historical dimension by tracing the history of the Grail dynasty back to Troy and Rome, two points of reference frequently employed for historical orientation in the Middle Ages.[298] Whether we are also justified in regarding the chronological gradation of events as constituting a historical dimension, instead of making it possible, is more open to doubt.[299] If Erec's adventures are presented in the *Jüngerer Titurel* as already in the past, whilst Iwein's still await the future,[300] this betrays a concern for time, but not necessarily for history: although these points of reference lie outside Albrecht's work, they still fall within the fictional realm constructed by Hartmann. Only a point outside the fictional realm in this widest sense, such as the reference to a ruler or date demanded by Hugh of Fleury, can supply this historical location. This is what we find elsewhere in the *Jüngerer Titurel*, for the author uses a method foreign to the Arthurian romance in pinpointing the reign of Arthur as falling a number of years before that of Charles the Great.[301] This restitution of Arthur to the realm of history is underlined by the inclusion of his campaign against Rome, a 'historical' detail deriving from Geoffrey of Monmouth,[302] so that with this motif Arthurian material has returned to the historical setting which Geoffrey had supplied for it. These elements of secular history are then reinforced by features of a clerically inspired 'Heilsgeschichte' to be found in the work.[303]

With *Lohengrin* this return to history is more obvious, for its sources include the fictional work of Wolfram, but also the *Sächsische Weltchronik*, followed over long stretches.[304] In addition, the political purpose which underlies the work means that the narrative action is placed in the reign of Heinrich I against the background of imperial history, so that at its close the action passes over to a chronicle-like survey of the Saxon dynasty.[305] Of this work it has been said that it represents the end of the Arthurian romance as a genre.[306]

With this abandonment of fiction in favour of religious and historical truth thirteenth-century literature reverts to the position in the twelfth century before the rise of the Arthurian romance.[307] The development we have been tracing started, first, with a written literature conceived as historically true, which was followed, secondly, by the discovery of fictional truth in the Arthurian romance, a discovery of relatively short life (until it was made again by Cervantes, significantly with recourse to the medieval romance)[308] which was, thirdly, superseded by a return to history. If we see this in terms of Isidore's definition we may say that the historical literature of our first and third periods was ready to use him to establish its veracity, whilst the Arthurian romance of the second period established its fiction by turning Isidore upside down and dispensing with authentication by an eyewitness.[309]

How far may this interaction between history and fiction be seen in terms of the relationship between orality and literacy? It is remarkable, although the implications have been contested,[310] that the rise of the Arthurian romance, in which the novel concept of fiction is first presented, is also marked by the feature of literacy. It is also of interest that the rise of fiction in classical Greek literature has been associated with the beginnings of literacy[311] and that, although the focus of discussion there was the truth of philosophy, this could also include the historical dimension important for the medieval development of fiction.[312]

The written word, in its contrast with the spoken word, was constantly present in the argument of this chapter. In the first part the question of historical reliability was tied up with the distinction between orality and literacy in so far as the latter alone guaranteed a reliable transmission from the eyewitness to the present. Where, in the second part, fictional literature dispensed with the need for an eyewitness, it was all the more necessary for it to stress the second element with Isidore, the written dimension. It would be wrong, however, to attach too much importance to writing and to see in it alone the factor making for fiction (rather than possibly justifying it). Greater importance attaches to the interplay between oral and written, since the chance of realising the possibilities of fiction arose in the Arthurian romance when Celtic themes previously circulating orally (and therefore not set in a fixed written form) were taken up by clerically trained authors and put into written form as an expression of current interests.[313] Freedom of fictional manoeuvre was also created on other occasions when orality and writing came together, as has been suggested by Vollmann-Profe in the context of 'Spielmannsepen'.[314] Here too she sees a hitherto oral tradition being discovered by literate authors who transpose it into writing, but enjoy a large measure of structural freedom in that task. Nonetheless, the difference between these works and the Arthurian romances is clear: the former are still presented as if they were historically true and develop no awareness of the possibilities of fiction. Out of this fruitful meeting of the spoken with the written word in the romance medieval fiction was born, not out of either one or the other. This was also true on the smaller scale, as in the case of Calogrenant's delayed prologue, where the reader's awareness of fiction depended on his knowledge that the work was also destined for listeners. In either case fiction arose at the meeting-point of oral with literate.

10

Recital and reading in their historical context

In the last chapter we were concerned with the part played by history within the relationship of the spoken to the written word and with the change in the conception of history which literacy could bring about. In this chapter we must turn the coin, looking at the position of orality and literacy within history, in their historical dimension in Germany from 800 to 1300.

(a) Historical factors in the rise of vernacular written literature[1]

In Chapter 2 we followed the emergence of written German to the Carolingian period, but must now continue this to about 1300. This confronts us with the problem of 'die große Lücke' in medieval German literary history, the fact that OHG texts start just before 800, but largely cease from about 900 so that, with the exception of Notker, we know of no written texts until about 1060, when they start again, with no further interruptions.[2] This gap of one and a half centuries has called forth explanations, none of which is satisfactory. Ehrismann conceals the problem by inserting into his survey of OHG texts Latin ones written in Germany in the tenth and eleventh centuries, suggesting thereby a literary continuity, but not in the vernacular.[3] A converse method is used by Stammler, who adduces oral tradition in the vernacular to bridge the gap between Otfrid and Ezzo, but the continuity proposed is one of literary production in German, not of *written* literary production.[4] A third solution was suggested by Meissburger, who denied the problem by dismissing vernacular Carolingian texts as 'European' and by regarding Ottonian literature as international, because composed in Latin, so that for him German literature begins only about 1060.[5] Yet to shunt off OHG literature into the sidings of a 'prehistory' would only make sense if that literature had been oral,[6] but since it remains obstinately written we cannot amputate it from the body of German literature and we still confront the problem of this gap.

Such attempts have run into difficulties because they have asked the wrong question, trying to explain the silence which began around 900. If we do not compare Germany with the anomalous situation of England (where a written vernacular tradition does start early), but regard it in its continental setting, the continuous vernacular written tradition from the second half of the eleventh century loses its strangeness, for apart from isolated forerunners a continuous tradition is attested for France only from the eleventh century and for Italy and Spain even later.[7] We have to ask not why the one and a half centuries before 1060 are silent, but why written texts began as early as about 800. We need to ask what historical reasons account for written OHG texts, but also why this tradition largely ceases by 900, and then what historical causes lie behind the emergence of a now continuous tradition from 1060, first in clerical literature in early MHG, then in new developments in the twelfth and the thirteenth centuries.

If the seamless unity proposed for OHG texts by Baesecke has now been abandoned,[8] a lesser unity can be seen in their connection with the legislation of Charles the Great.[9] Behind such legislation there stands a union of kingship with Christianity, a theocratic conception in which Charles intervened in ecclesiastic affairs, but also imposed duties of state upon the clergy,[10] so that there was little division between Church and state.[11] These interventions by Charles in the affairs of the Church may have assisted the spread of Christianity, but they also served his political ends (as with the war of conversion against the Saxons) and the unity of his Empire.[12] Legislation to ensure the Christianisation of his subjects strengthened the authority of their ruler,[13] which is one reason why many vernacular versions of catechetical texts, meant to be recited by the priest to the laymen, can be connected with imperial legislation.[14] In another pragmatic sense the Emperor depended on the Church and imposed duties upon the clergy, for the geographical spread of his Empire made written communication and legislation necessary which could only be carried out by the clergy, the *litterati* amongst his subjects,[15] whilst the need to communicate between the various languages of his territories set a premium on their command of Latin. The Emperor's concern to raise the level of education of the clergy[16] explains why most OHG texts are connected with a monastery as their place of origin.[17] As these were by and large the only centres of learning on which the Emperor could rely for his vernacular programme he had to divert monastic centres from their proper function and employ them for purposes which, had conditions permitted, would have been better met by the secular clergy.[18]

Although most Carolingian texts have such a pragmatic purpose, there remain two major texts of which this is not true, for the *Heliand* and Otfrid's *Evangelienbuch* are literary texts connected with a later ruler, Ludwig the German.[19] Although imperial impetus still lies behind them it is directed towards a different end, cultural rather than religious politics. This ruler took an active interest in the intellectual life of his day, but these works suggest that this was not confined to Latin. They were composed in the vernacular, for this was the language of the *regnum in orientali Francia*, beginning to establish itself as a separate entity after the dissolution of Carolingian unity.[20] Works in the vernacular, rather than Latin, served to underline the separateness and sense of unity of the tribes east of the Rhine, whilst their ambitious literary nature could be set in the scales against the cultural superiority of Charles the Bald in the west.[21]

In asking why this written tradition did not last we can proceed from the point so far established: to use the vernacular for writing was still so unusual that it only stood a chance when the centralising will of a ruler like Charles the Great or Ludwig the German stood behind it.[22] Where this was lacking the need to put German into writing was absent.[23] We see this with Ludwig the Pious,[24] whose encouragement of the monastic reformer Benedict of Aniane meant a withdrawal of monasteries from the non-monastic tasks given them by Charles the Great, an abandonment of the supply of written texts in the vernacular.[25] This same period saw a clash of interests between Emperor and Pope, and between the Emperor and his bishops, so that the unity on which Charles's theocracy had rested was threatened and with it the cultural programme he had pursued.[26]

Apart from such general reasons what is now stressed more than Baesecke's coherent unity is the isolation, geographically[27] and in time, in which OHG texts were produced, the opposite of any continuity necessary if the 'große Lücke' was to be avoided.[28] It is on discontinuity in time that we must concentrate, seeing both subjective and objective evidence for it. Subjectively, Otfrid shows in his dedication to Liutbert that he sees his undertaking as a novelty,[29] not just concerning his final rhyme, but in suggesting that he was encouraged by others on the grounds that, whereas classical poets sang of their great men and Christian Latin poets glorified Christ, this had not been done in German.[30] More than a hundred years later Notker sees the position no differently, for he tries to persuade his bishop to accept the same novelty of a work in the vernacular,[31] and his pupil Ekkehard IV praises him as the first to write in the vernacular and make it acceptable.[32] Nor is the position objectively different. Even a linguistic achievement like the OHG *Isidor* had no direct successors (other than its Bavarian copies) and sixty years later Otfrid knew nothing of its orthographic rulings.[33] Otfrid's lead in final rhyme was followed for only a short time by a handful of short works[34] so that, even though he sent a copy of his work to St. Gallen, it was lost to posterity: Notker knew nothing of his precedent and was unable to use it to justify his own undertaking.[35] The same repeats itself with Notker: after his death written literature in German ceases for fifty years and starts again after 1060. Only one copy of Notker's work appears to have passed beyond the walls of St. Gallen,[36] and even here Ekkehard IV wrote in Latin, not German.[37]

The history of this first stage of written literature in German is one of discontinuity, of new starts, of authors working in isolation and using the vernacular as an exception. Impetus from an imperial centre was generally necessary to produce this literature, but even when the vernacular was used without political encouragement, as with Notker, the results were just as shortlived. What must cause wonder is not the almost complete absence of vernacular texts for a century and a half, but their presence before 900 at all.

This places greater weight on the resumption of a written tradition in 1060, this time with greater force (because not stifled at birth) and without imperial encouragement. At a first glance this resumption appears as isolated and exposed to discontinuity as was OHG literature, for it is represented by scattered works appearing around the same time in different places: the *Ezzolied* at Bamberg, the *Annolied* at Siegburg, and the *Wiener Genesis* in Carinthia.[38] Behind these scattered reappearances of the written vernacular something new is to be detected: each inaugurates a continuous tradition in time not found in the Carolingian period which compensates for any geographical isolation. The *Ezzolied* is reworked in expanded form in the twelfth century, but also introduces a series of works with a dogmatic theme; a part of the *Annolied* is incorporated in the *Kaiserchronik* and the work is followed by others with a legendary or historical theme; the *Wiener Genesis* is reworked later and is succeeded by other biblical epics. In both senses (reworking or incorporation, and inaugurating a traditional genre) these works after 1060 attest a continuity in time previously lacking in vernacular literature.[39]

This makes it necessary to find good historical reasons for this new departure, which we can do by going back to the converse phenomenon, the abandonment of Charles's policy in the reign of Ludwig the Pious, one of the reasons for which lay with the monastic reform of Benedict of Aniane and the withdrawal of monasticism from affairs of state. This suggests the possibility that the renewal of a written tradition might be connected with the movement of monasticism back into contact with the world. Whereas monasticism around 800 had been recruited for state purposes by the Emperor, now it is brought back into affairs of this world by the reform-movement of Pope Gregory VII, so that the central encouragement of a written tradition which had earlier been provided by the state now proceeds from the Church.[40]

The concern of the reform-movement was to permeate the world more with Christian principles than earlier, when the Christianisation of society had proceeded little beyond the office of kingship.[41] This movement involved a reform of monasticism, but also of the episcopal church (freeing it from control by lay rulers) and of feudal knighthood.[42] Under these last two headings the Church was brought face to face with secular society and the need to proselytise laymen, which involved addressing them in their vernacular. The Church's penetration of the world is now much greater than around 800. Whereas Charles had used its literate resources for his administrative and educational programme and, in view of the poorly educated state of his secular clergy, had contented himself with little more than an elementary Christianisation of lay society, the eleventh century carried this a decisive step further in attempting to win the knight for a Christian view of his office.[43] If the papacy's attempt to free the Church from interventions by the lay ruler leads to a collision with the Empire, this occasions a mental stocktaking within lay society.[44] The institutional, religious and ethical problems brought to the fore by this movement called forth a wave of polemical literature composed in Latin,[45] but could not avoid addressing the layman in his mother tongue. Against this background of a reassessment of the layman's role in society clerical literature in the vernacular starts again in the eleventh century with a wealth of themes, genres and problems going far beyond what had been attempted in OHG.

The reform Church left its imprint on lay society not merely under the headings of the Investiture Contest and a reform of feudal knighthood, because this concern with the world also paradoxically characterises the reform of monasticism. At issue here was recruitment to the monastic life, previously by *oblati*, children offered by noble families at an early age and educated in the monastery before taking vows.[46] To the reformers this practice was suspect (monasticism was being exploited by laymen for their own purposes)[47] and preference was given to entry into monastic life by free choice as an adult, so that the layman now joined the monastic community as a lay monk or lay brother,[48] too late for an education in literacy which would equip him as a fully fledged choir monk. The monastery is open to the laity in two forms, constituting a body within the community which is illiterate, ignorant of Latin and the primary addressees of monastic literature composed in the vernacular.[49]

Moving from the monastery to the world outside we may note Grundmann's observations on the rise of a new idea of the *vita apostolica* from the eleventh century, an apostolic task in the world rather than in the monastery.[50] From the close of this century this term embraced monks and canons regular, as hitherto, but also monks and hermits who became itinerant preachers, so that those who had earlier withdrawn from the world now left the monastery to preach a new way of life.[51] In Germany Hirsau monks were active as preachers beyond the confines of the monastery, and as a result countless laymen, including noblemen, entered monasteries or constituted religious communities without becoming monks.[52] This period also sees the founding of new orders (Cistercians and Premonstratensians), even though they in turn withdraw from the world and leave the religious needs of laymen unsatisfied, so that these latter are an easy prey for heretical preachers.[53] These developments all finish in a withdrawal from the world (the laymen converted by Hirsau as much as the new orders), but at an earlier stage in each case monks had left the monasteries to preach to laymen. This attracted censure, as when Hirsau itinerant monks were equated with the *gyrovagi* condemned by the Rule of St Benedict[54] or when Bernard of Thiron had to defend himself against criticism.[55] On this front, too, the monk who enters the world as a preacher addresses laymen in the vernacular.

The heart of the Investiture Contest, as it affects literacy, has been summed up as involving a lay ruler, whose chancery is made up of literate clerics and who himself owes to the Church the aura of being the Lord's anointed, enjoys no literate education, but abrogates to himself the privilege of appointing clerical dignitaries who command the knowledge which he lacks.[56] Expressed in this way, literacy plays a central role, stimulating the ruler to see one answer to the reproach levelled against him in the acquisition of a literate education. Simony also played a part within the Investiture Contest and was important for society at large, raising the question whether the sacraments administered by simonistic priests had any validity.[57] It is unlikely that the polemical discussion of this problem was confined to the clergy alone, hence to Latin, and indeed the work *Memento mori* has been interpreted in this light.[58] Since there are also grounds for relating this work to the Hirsau reform-movement and the winning of noblemen for the monastic life,[59] it represents several tendencies making for a direct appeal to the laity on the part of those writing in German.

The fact that literature in German never breaks off again after 1060 makes it difficult to periodise this continuous tradition and to suggest that new causes explain why German literature (or certain genres) find their way into writing. Nonetheless, even though vernacular works continue to be written by clerical authors new factors are at work from about the middle of the twelfth century. These have to do with the reason why Bumke begins his survey of literary patronage about 1150, when clerical authors, in addition to addressing their audience as a religious community, also address them as members of court society. We come now to the historical reasons why court literature in German acquired written form.

The overriding reason must be sought in an explosion of writing in the twelfth century at large,[60] mainly in Latin, but with effects on the vernacular. Three transformations contribute to this. Fundamental is an educational one: the rise of urban schools of a novel type, challenging the supremacy of monastic schools and leading to universities as equally novel institutions.[61] Secondly, the book revolution of the twelfth century,[62] often understood as the *pecia* system of book copying (allowing a greater number of manuscripts to be produced for the growing needs of the new schools),[63] can also be seen as a new attitude towards the book as a working tool.[64] In place of monks copying a text as penance and ruminating on it as an act of devotion we have a 'desacralisation of learning' for practical purposes: professional *stationarii* cater for mass needs by new means of production, but also for new needs by introducing rubrics, tables of contents, cross-references, and an alphabetic arrangement of points in the argument for ease of reference.[65] Thirdly, underlying these changes was one in the incidence of writing: whereas scriptoria before the twelfth century were largely confined to monasteries and bishops' residences, now their centre of gravity switches to towns and chanceries of secular rulers, which amounts to an enormous increase in centres of writing.[66]

This explosion of writing, although largely confined to Latin, did not leave secular courts unaffected, which raises the question how far literacy, Latin or vernacular, may be found here too. We shall see that the spread of the ideal of *curialitas* or courtesy was closely tied up with the spread of lay literacy. For the moment we may content ourselves with Bumke's observation that in the French and Anglo-Norman realms court literature arose first at those centres where the patron himself was literate.[67] If the position is different in Germany, where the nobility clings longer to the tradition of lay illiteracy,[68] this may well be connected with the fact that courtesy comes later to Germany as an import from France and that even then German authors cannot presuppose as much understanding with their audience as could their French counterparts. Positively or negatively, literacy plays a part in the genesis and acceptance of this new secular ideal.

Another overriding reason lies in the growing sense of its cultural independence shown by European knighthood from the twelfth century.[69] A literature appealing to its interests could only arise when this section of lay society was sufficiently aware of its own importance to put forward its literature in rivalry with the religious works which had hitherto enjoyed a monopoly of writing,[70] when the court was sufficiently developed as a centre of social life to provide conditions of literary production and reception, and when the means were available for literature to be delivered orally, but also preserved in writing (and when the need for preservation was felt).[71] This suggests that writing was now practised at such courts and was no longer confined to the imperial court. Writing, as a feature of an increasingly complex administration, found its way from ecclesiastic and royal scriptoria to princely courts, an extension assisted by bishops who, in their function as territorial princes, were the first to use the document with seal previously used only by kings. In other words, these bishops first applied a feature of their clerical writing practice to their secular functions and were then followed by their colleagues, the secular princes.[72] If the equations *clericus* = *litteratus* and *laicus* = *illitteratus* were still at this time largely valid, the layman had no choice but to see the advantages and learn the practice of writing from the cleric. This placed particular importance on the court cleric,[73] long known at imperial and episcopal courts, but then at princely courts as these centres could no longer dispense with written administration. The result was that institutionally provision was already there for the writing of court literature once the need for it arose in the twelfth century.

That need, too, is a reflection of the growing cultural rivalry between layman and cleric. Secular courts keep up with ecclesiastic ones by transacting some of their business in writing, but also seek the kudos of written literature for themselves.[74] In this the cleric stands in an ambiguous relationship to the secular court which employs him. On the one hand he may attempt to impose religious values on the court and continue the literary approach of his colleagues since 1060 (even if they had not written specifically for the court). On the other hand the cleric is employed by the court to propagate its view of itself and put its values into lasting written form, values informed by rivalry with the Church in that these courts are attempting an act of cultural emancipation.[75]

The cleric who imposes religious values on the court is doing what could be advanced to justify his function outside the Church: utilising an opportunity for educational influence upon secular society.[76] This argument is no different from the preoccupation of the reform-movement with lay society from the eleventh century, but something new is also present. Works under this heading from the middle of the twelfth century deal with a secular theme appealing to lay noblemen: two works with a classical theme (Lamprecht's *Alexanderlied* and the *Liet von Troye* of Herbort von Fritzlar) find room for the topics of knighthood and love and suggest the ancestry of knighthood in antiquity, but *König Rother*, for example, may have appealed because of its possible political implications. This is but the sugaring of a clerical pill, because the purpose behind it is not always one which laymen would have been happy to swallow. Thus, the *Alexanderlied* is critical of the knightly exploits performed by the hero and qualifies love as little more than transient *vanitas*.[77] The course of the narrative in the first half of *König Rother* is repeated in the second so as to replace the earlier themes of bravery and cunning by resignation and dependence on God's grace.[78] In the *Liet von Troye* the criticism is even more radical, for knightly combat is depicted as an unrelieved bloodbath and love is seen in very negative terms.[79] These works treat themes which capture the attention of a court audience, but use them for a still clerical message.[80] The procedure is more skilled than if the authors had stuck to religious topics and thundered against a decline in morals,[81] but in their feeling it necessary to meet secular listeners on their home ground we may see a sign that the taste of the courts was becoming a power to be reckoned with.

This is also true of the historically more important works in court literature whose clerical authors embrace the ideals of the court. Here lay culture emancipates itself by ransacking the cultural arsenal of its clerical rivals, making use of details which, transposed to a new context, enrich this emergent culture. Where the Church had conceded that the knight who went to the Holy Land had a positive role to play,[82] court literature now puts forward the view that this can be true of knighthood at large, whether on a crusade or not. Where the Church, by drawing a parallel between Old Testament wars and crusading present,[83] had insinuated a biblical ancestry for medieval knighthood, court authors now claim an ancestry in classical antiquity, affording more scope to secular interests.[84] Claims are made for secular works in the vernacular which could previously be made only of religious ones. Whereas the latter had claimed authority by deriving from a written source (*buoch* designated the Bible or theological and historical literature), now the same word is used in court literature to denote a written source (which may be no more than a work of fiction).[85] Just as religious authors could refer to their source as *historia*, so now can Gottfried see his written but fictional source as an *istorje*.[86] Where a theological source, especially the Bible, incorporated the truth, but could also be termed *diu warheit*, Gottfried uses the same word of his fictional source.[87] Examples like these suggest that central to the values which court culture took over from the Church for its own purposes was the fact of written literature, with all the authority which the Middle Ages saw invested in it.[88]

So firmly established was this written tradition by now, serving a religious or a secular end in the vernacular, that the reasons applicable to court literature from 1150 continue to be relevant in the thirteenth century. In this century other forces come into play,[89] not always for the first time, but with noticeably greater effect, impelling literature in German more strongly in the direction of writing.

The first is the political and constitutional development known as territorialisation, which, although its beginnings go back earlier, acquired importance for writing and vernacular literature only later. By this term is meant a long-term process of rounding off scattered properties, held by counts, dukes or kings, so as to produce as far as possible one continuous territory in which the centralised authority of the territorial ruler could be exercised systematically.[90] To achieve this the ruler had to proceed against the special interests of local rulers, but also, if he was not a king himself, against the centralising tendencies of kingship. This produced, in place of the fragmented pattern of local feudal interests, a more unified form of state which could take the first steps towards the more tightly organised and bureaucratically administered state of modern times.[91] The territorial state thus brought the beginnings of a more complicated form of society with the need for more differentiated ways of running it. At this point the question of writing becomes crucial, providing the means of bridging a gap in time or in space, the latter dimension once a society passes beyond the easily surveyable limits of the tribe, and the former once a state claims historical continuity. From its historical beginnings writing had made possible the running of large-scale empires (Mesopotamia or Rome);[92] it was indispensable for the Carolingian Empire and acquired renewed importance with the process of territorialisation. Heinzle has argued that the *Sachsenspiegel* is representative of this new process in placing territorial above tribal law and guaranteeing a unified form of law by being composed in the vernacular and in written form.[93] Corresponding to this unification in space, made possible by writing, we find evidence for the temporal dimension which writing also opens up: the *Sachsenspiegel* and the *Schwabenspiegel* independently called forth written histories in the vernacular, meant to provide historical antecedents for these codifications and for the territorial states to which they applied.[94]

An important factor in the territorialisation process was the rise of towns as centres of trade and wealth, but also of writing. This latter feature was no absolute novelty in view of the episcopal court, a centre of clerical writing situated in the town,[95] or of the cathedral school, established in the early Middle Ages, but supported afresh since the twelfth century.[96] What is new is the rapid growth of different educational institutions in towns from the late twelfth century, most pronouncedly in northern France, where the growth of cities provided legal liberties as well as accommodation for teachers and growing numbers of students attracted by career prospects opened up by the bureaucratisation of Church, court and town. As centres of trade towns now grew in importance, which also involved writing,[97] an association which is again nothing new, since writing was developed in Sumeria for the purposes of trade and passed on from the Phoenicians to the Greeks in the same commercial context.[98] For medieval Germany it has been suggested that the invasion of the clerical realm of writing by laymen was made as much by towndwellers as by the feudal aristocracy,[99] especially since merchants operating over long distances came to see the advantages of writing already in the twelfth century.

The merchants' need for writing in the conduct of business is illustrated in *Der guote Gerhart* of Rudolf von Ems, when the merchant hero, setting out on a journey, includes in the crew a scribe to write down expenses.[100] Medieval trade relied more on writing as it moved from travelling merchants to those operating from a fixed base, for the latter became dependent on regular communication with distant colleagues, powers of attorney made out for third parties, credit notes, bookkeeping in general.[101] Oral messages and a good memory could provide a solution within modest limits, but with the growing volume of trade writing could not fail to show its advantages. The importance of this goes far beyond the individual merchants. Other callings were drawn into the realm of writing, for example the carrier whom the no longer itinerant merchant used to deliver his goods, for if the carrier could cut expenses by taking goods from several merchants on one journey a bill of lading became necessary to avoid confusing different deliveries.[102] In the merchant's home town the growth of writing around his needs, dictating the nature of town policy, is evident. The merchant needed to send his sons to schools run by the clergy so that they might acquire enough literacy to help in their father's business, which led to towns developing a policy for schooling, seeing it as a collective concern of the town and not of individual merchants.[103] In the further developed towns of Flanders and northern Germany we find the first evidence for their preoccupation with schooling, at first under clerical supervision, but then giving rise to quarrels with ecclesiastic authorities as the towns seek control for themselves, including the first steps towards schooling in the vernacular.[104] This development has been termed a secularisation of schooling, but it would be more accurate to say that education now begins to serve laymen's interests and to pass more into their hands.

Other developments include legal transactions carried out by towns in writing,[105] or the rise of such offices as the town-clerk and the schoolmaster, often held by the same person, in many cases a cleric who served the town by virtue of his literacy just as many of his colleagues served secular courts in a similar way.[106] With the growth of trade and the political importance of towns a whole realm has been won for writing, so that when vernacular literature is associated with the towns (Konrad von Würzburg at Strassburg and Basel, Jans Enikel at Vienna)[107] its written form can be taken as much for granted as at the feudal court.

The third force working towards written literature in the thirteenth century is represented by new religious movements.[108] They demonstrate continuity with what we saw earlier, before the rise of court literature, but also something new. These movements are now represented by newly founded orders which influenced education in the thirteenth century, the Dominicans because they needed theological training for their task of fighting heresy (their centre for this was the University of Paris) and the Franciscans who, after initial reservations about scholarship, were soon found at Paris, Oxford and Cambridge.[109] Both are mendicant orders, in direct contact with the lay world, above all in towns whose rapid growth had placed strains on the secular clergy and whose inhabitants were increasingly unchurched and exposed to heretical currents.[110] In seeking contact with laymen the mendicants, leaving the cloister and enjoying freedom of movement,[111] repeat what was earlier true of the eleventh-century reform-movement, but the Cistercians and Premonstratensians had subsequently withdrawn into monastic seclusion, so that the task of dealing with religious currents among laymen fell to these new orders.

Part of their task was the obligation, forced upon them against their will, to accept responsibility for religious communities of laymen, especially laywomen or béguines, a fact of importance for the genesis of a new religious literature in German.[112] If previously there had been little devotional literature in German meant for private reading, as opposed to public recital, by comparison with the mass available in Latin, this is because this literature could arise in the vernacular only once these lay communities provided a bridge between those who, like the clergy, could read and those who, like the laymen, could not read in Latin.[113] There are indications that the Dominicans provided these religious laywomen with reading-matter,[114] but these are confirmed by official prohibitions on translating religious texts from Latin into German for use by untrained women.[115] That it had to be forbidden shows that it was done – this is a new development in religious literature in the vernacular, something not brought about by earlier movements.

Over five centuries, therefore, writing repeatedly acted as a catalyst in the development of medieval literature. The Carolingian beginning, however important historically, was shortlived, but once German finds its way onto parchment again around 1060 it is for good, with new factors repeatedly coming into play for different reasons and impelling it irrevocably into the literate realm monopolised hitherto by Latin.

(b) Education and literacy

In this section we shall be concerned with the role of literate education in three periods (the Carolingian and Ottonian, then the twelfth century) as the precondition for texts composed in writing and destined for a reader.[116]

CONCLUSIONS

The educational focus of the Carolingians was the Benedictine monastery, above all the school, responsible for spreading an often merely elementary education amongst monks, clerics and some laymen.[117] Left to themselves these monasteries could have achieved only restricted, local influence, so that the Emperor's decisive step was to centralise their efforts by linking the educational programme of the monasteries with the imperial court and to use their literacy to carry out his legislation.[118]

Alongside the monasteries the episcopal school also played a part, but a restricted one: its task was largely confined to educating clerics to perform their pastoral and liturgical tasks (sometimes it also instructed laymen in reading the Bible).[119] This restricted function can be seen in the context of OHG literature. Whereas most vernacular texts were produced in monastic scriptoria, the role of episcopal schools is not so clearcut. If on occasions a bishop seems to have been involved in the preparation of a work, as with Heito, bishop of Basel, it is significant that he was also abbot of the monastery of Reichenau.[120]

Whereas Charles conscripted monastic *litterati* and scriptoria for providing religious texts in the vernacular, Ludwig the Pious, in embracing the reform ideas of Benedict of Aniane, occasioned a withdrawal by monks from literate tasks of state.[121] Accordingly, a capitulary of Ludwig restricted the educational function of the monastery to its own ranks and under him the state abandoned its involvement in education and left the initiative to the Church.[122]

Despite this inward turning of monastic education the impetus given by Charles still allowed it to play a new role in the tenth century.[123] The renewed synthesis between Church and state established by Otto the Great, an imperial encouragement of educated monks and clerics for political purposes, reveals a shift of emphasis within apparent continuity with the policy of Charles. Whereas Charles had relied largely on the resources of the monastery, Otto discovers a role for the bishops. To strengthen their position against the nobility Ottonian rulers develop an imperial–episcopal alliance, granting administrative and military responsibility to the bishops in exchange for being chosen by the crown, a system which ensured for Germany the best government in Europe.[124] As a result the Ottonian ruler, relying on his bishops for regional administration, also depended on them for the educational training required for administrators.[125]

Episcopal schools, in the shadow of monastic ones in the Carolingian period, flourish from the middle of the tenth century (twelve cathedral schools rise within sixty years) and acquire a specific function: to educate future statesmen and administrators, especially bishops in the imperial church system.[126] The Ottonians discover that cathedral schools could function as a more secular educational alternative to the monasteries. What was provided by these cathedral schools was not the training of clerics in their pastoral functions, but the preparation of talented young noblemen for service at court as administrators and eventually as bishops.[127] This change means, on the one hand, that education was geared more to secular ends: although the Carolingians used the monasteries as much for the secular ends of imperial administration as the Ottonians exploited episcopal schools, the latter incorporated secular clergy rather than monks. In Ottonian episcopal schools secular educational purposes are achieved within a markedly less otherworldly institutional framework than monasteries.

On the other hand, there now exists an institution for cultivating the qualities demanded of someone expected to serve at a court (secular or ecclesiastic) and then possibly, by holding the office of imperial bishop, to be ruler at a court himself. These qualities embrace religious ones, but also include such non-religious features as literacy, noble birth, military prowess, administrative efficiency. In addition, these are supplemented by a range of qualities expected of the Ottonian courtier bishop, summed up by the phrase *litterae et mores*,[128] the intellectual attainments and seemly manners of one who attends at court, a combination of literacy with courtesy. With this educational ideal the Ottonian episcopal school introduces qualities which later play a part in the education of the feudal aristocrat.

Just as Carolingian educational practice stood with the state's use of the resources of monasteries and fell when monastic reform withdrew them from its service, so did Ottonian practice stand and fall with the alliance between Emperor and bishops. When this was defeated by papal opposition to lay investiture of ecclesiastics, to the Emperor's appointment of bishops for non-ecclesiastic purposes, the basis of the success of the cathedral school was destroyed. Germany was the main target of the papal attack in the Investiture Contest, but France was largely spared this break-up, at least long enough for the cathedral schools of France to acquire a new purpose.[129] From these different developments in the two countries, above all from the destructive results of the Investiture Contest in Germany, setting it back for decades, there follows a cultural reversal: whereas the Empire had been in the lead, from now on the French-speaking world, France and the Anglo-Norman realm, maintains the intellectual ascendancy.

Whilst the Investiture Contest largely destroyed in Germany the educational function of the cathedral school, in France it survived by changing its nature. Here the freedom of a teacher to move from one centre to another and the growth of student numbers led to a rapid disengagement of higher education from cathedral schools.[130] This educational explosion, passing beyond what episcopal schools could cope with, was clear to contemporaries,[131] as was the advantage of education for a career at secular and episcopal courts and in cities, all of which constituted a market for those with a literate training. The changed function of the school is captured by Guibert de Nogent, for he witnesses the flourishing of studies neither in the monastery nor in the cathedral, but in cities (*villas...urbes...oppida*),[132] so that it is as justified to talk of city schools as of cathedral schools, even though they may often be neighbours, overlapping or identical. That this educational growth took place in cities (twenty-five are counted within not too large a radius from Paris, all of which attracted students from afar)[133] is understandable, for their resurgence allowed them to offer advantages unavailable elsewhere. To this must be added, negatively, the closure of monastery schools to outsiders,[134] but also, positively, the demand of Gregory VII that bishops set up schools in their cities of residence.[135] Since both features stem from the reform-movement, the changes which brought about a crisis for episcopal schools in Germany provided novel opportunities for their counterparts in France.

The adaptability which enabled cathedral schools in France to survive as city schools also helped to rescue a humanism eclipsed by scholasticism. The education given by the cathedral school (the combination of training for high office with courtly virtues) sought refuge elsewhere: in the courts of lords, secular or ecclesiastic. Jaeger describes this handing on of an educational function: 'The fading of the old learning at cathedral schools coincides with the rise of an education which we must now call "courtly", and no longer merely "for the court".'[136] The ideal of *litterae et mores* passes from the cathedral school to the court, but the court where it most readily found shelter was that of the bishop himself. The significance of literate culture at bishops' courts goes far beyond their patronage of literature,[137] for they also acted as a model for the courts of secular lords, from whose families they themselves came. If bishops transferred to their responsibilities as feudal lords the writing practice of their ecclesiastic administration and were imitated in this by their secular kinsmen,[138] the position will not have been different in written literature. We now have to consider, after the extension of education and literacy from monastery to cathedral school (or city school) and to episcopal court, its final transfer to the lay court.

The dealings of aristocratic courts with the Church (especially if at all exacerbated) compelled secular noblemen to find a place for one branch of knowledge within their incipient bureaucracy, for they needed someone versed in canon law if they were not to be outwitted by trained clerical opponents.[139] In employing court clerics for this and other literate purposes they could choose from the clerical unemployed. Similarly, at the beginning of court literature in France, England and Germany the authors of most works were court clerics,[140] producing a written literature for court consumption, so that the audience was slowly won for the intellectual standards of literacy. This pervasion of lay courts by clerical education was not confined to literature, for a high proportion of scholarly writing in the twelfth century came from the courts (especially of the Normans).[141] How the court could supplement the school has been shown with William of Conches, who taught at a French school, but then took up a post as tutor to the future Henry II of England.[142] He refashioned a work composed for teaching in the schools, writing it now as a *speculum principis* with an eye to his new position at court. He also wrote the *Moralium dogma philosophorum* which, rightly or wrongly, has been regarded as the basis of the ethical system found in vernacular court literature,[143] but which was probably dedicated to the young Henry II. The new developments in French schools (their move towards scholasticism) drive William away, but he finds a new home as teacher and writer at a court, one which encouraged the rise of court literature.[144]

The reasons why courts were willing to accept clerical standards of literacy are manifold. An obvious one was their wish to acquire learning as part of their emancipation from clerical tutelage by employing renegade clerics against the clerical monopoly of literacy,[145] much as a modern firm employs a former tax inspector as its own accountant. Another reason is the growth of literacy amongst laymen especially in the French-speaking world: it has been suggested that the nobleman's adoption of the ideal of courtesy from the educational programme of the courtier bishop was as closely tied to his literacy as were *mores* to *litterae* in the courtier bishop's training.[146] Although this educational ideal had been evolved in Ottonian

Germany, in the French-speaking west it acquired a new importance when adopted by the feudal nobility: not merely by the ruler (the ideal of the *rex litteratus* goes back to Augustus, Constantine and the Carolingians),[147] but also by the prince, the duke, the count and the knight. One reason why an ideal evolved in Germany reached fruition in France lies in this linkage between courtesy and literacy, for German noblemen were far behind their French counterparts in recognising the need for schooling and literacy.[148] This need came to be recognised in Germany, too, partly as a result of adapting French court literature,[149] but meanwhile the lead in propagating the ideal of the *miles litteratus* had long since passed to France and England.[150]

With this ideal an education in letters has found its way from the monastery to the lay court, and within lay society it extends in principle from the ruler down to the knight. If we look for evidence of literacy amongst secular aristocrats, particularly with knights, the references for Germany are markedly fewer than for France and England,[151] and only in the west do we come across explicit statements of principle, suggesting not merely that a particular knight was literate, but that the conjunction of letters and prowess, of *clergie et chevalerie*, was to be aimed at.[152]

The achievement of this double qualification, reconciling two often antagonistic walks of life, was no easy process.[153] The difficulties explain why, in one of the rare references from Germany, the ideal is expressed in negative terms, suggesting that literacy is an advantage in a monk, but no disadvantage in a knight.[154] More positive is the tone of a letter by Philip of Harvengt to Philip of Flanders, a lettered count and later patron of Chrétien de Troyes, in which count Ayulf is set up as a model, being both a valiant and a learned knight.[155] The model is also presented as a matter of principle, for we are told that chivalry does not prejudice learning, nor does knowledge of letters impede chivalry: *Non enim scientiae fortis militia vel militiae praejudicat scientia litterarum*. It is then said emphatically that the combination of both is useful and fitting in a prince (*imo in principe copula tam utilis, tam conveniens*), so that the absence of letters pulls the prince down to the level of a rustic or even a beast: *princeps quem non nobilitat scientia litteralis, non parum degenerans sit quasi rusticanus et quodammodo bestialis*. In equating the illiterate ruler with the *rusticanus*, the antithesis of what was acceptable at court, and in questioning his humanity Philip of Harvengt does more than praise one count, he confirms that the ideal of the *miles litteratus* had come to the fore simultaneously with court literature. Further examples for this connection between lay literacy and court literature have been seen in the courts of Champagne and Blois, but also in Poitou and Anjou, above all at Henry II's court at London.[156]

The literate poet Chrétien de Troyes whom the literate ruler Philip of Flanders attracted to his court went further in proclaiming this double ideal by devising for it a bold world-historical dimension in which twelfth-century France represented the climax. In the prologue to *Cligés* he maps out a cultural progress from Greece to Rome, then from Rome to the France of his day.[157] The pattern used is well known to medieval historiography (the *translatio imperii* and the *translatio studii*),[158] but Chrétien gives it a topical twist by seeing it in terms of *chevalerie et clergie*, first achieved by the Greeks, then passed on to Rome, from where it has now come to

France. (We see from this how important it was that romances with a classical theme implied that medieval knighthood continued classical antiquity, likewise the source of medieval Latinate learning, rather than the warriors of the Old Testament.)[159] Although Germany took over the French ideal of chivalry and even made the transition to written literature at the same time, the French educational explosion remained without an echo and Germans still had to go to France for their studies.[160] When soon after 1200 Chrétien's topos *chevalerie et clergie* was made the basis of the prologue to *Moriz von Craun* it was adapted to German conditions by treating only chivalry, ignoring the *translatio studii*.[161] Such a detail shows how radically Germany had been set back by the Investiture Contest. This wider context, in which Germany has lost the educational lead it once enjoyed, has to be borne in mind when considering the educational background to the rise of literacy in Germany.

(c) Vernacular literacy

We now face the question: what classes of person were involved in the production and reception of written texts in German, what were the possibilities of lay literacy? We shall not be concerned with evidence of the literate ability of individual laymen,[162] but shall confine ourselves to those walks of life where a growing preoccupation with lay literacy can be demonstrated.

We have in other words to look at those areas where the gulf was bridged between a clerical Latin written culture and a lay vernacular oral culture. The spread of vernacular literacy in this bridging operation takes three forms: the layman may himself be literate (able to read, if not to write, since we are dealing with the reception of literature) *or* he may rely on the literacy of others (depending on their ability to write in the chancery and to read out works to him which he cannot read himself)[163] *or* he may encourage written literature, even though unable to read it without assistance.[164] The bridging operation may be conducted in two directions: *either* the cleric, at home in the written culture of Latin, finds a reason to preserve a vernacular text, normally for acoustic reception, in written form for the laity *or* the layman, at home in his oral culture, acquires the skill of reading normally associated with the clergy. We shall discuss first the movement of the cleric in the direction of the vernacular world of the layman under five headings.

The first concerns the literate activity of monks. The bulk of translations into OHG was accomplished in monasteries, because at this early stage there were no other centres to which this could be entrusted if the translation into a vernacular still struggling to devise an acceptable Christian vocabulary was to be reliable. Apart from the clerics assembled at the imperial court there were in the Carolingian period no other literate centres whose Latinity would have been fit for the task, and there is only restricted evidence that the *capella regia* stands behind any OHG translations.[165] If despite the reform-movement's insistence that the provision of texts for pastoral use was no part of the monasteries' task[166] the eleventh and twelfth centuries still largely see religious literature produced by monks,[167] this is a measure of the precarious hold which literacy, confined to a restricted number of centres, still enjoyed in Germany.[168]

The monasteries were forced out of their normal sphere of written Latin into that of written texts in the vernacular meant for recital to laymen not merely under the pressure of Carolingian policy or because there were few other centres of literacy, but also because of an internal necessity. Paradoxically, there were lay elements in a monastic community of any size, whose illiteracy and restriction to the vernacular were a first call on the monks.

Our second heading is therefore the monastic *familia* in the widest sense, embracing a heterogeneous group of laymen connected with a monastery, such as benefactors, tenants, feudal vassals, peasants and serfs attached to monastic property.[169] Other contacts between monks and the laymen's world include provision for the poor, the sick, and pilgrims, the running of a *schola externa*, but also highlights in the liturgical year when processions and festivals, especially on saints' days, attracted neighbouring laymen to 'their' monastery.[170] Such occasions provided an opportunity for monastic propaganda, for attaching laymen more firmly to the local monastery. Propaganda on these occasions, meant for a large concourse of laymen, demanded sermons in the vernacular, but also saints' hymns addressed to laymen or sung by them, even if only in the refrains.[171] The *Gandersheimer Reimchronik* was composed at a collegiate foundation, but in the vernacular since it was also addressed to the (illiterate) ministerials attached to Gandersheim.[172] We do not have to accept Bédier's thesis about the genesis of the chanson de geste at monastic houses along pilgrim routes[173] to be persuaded by Ohly's suggestion that religious literature at such centres was largely destined for laymen, including pilgrims.[174] Although he makes this comment with reference to France, the observations made by Haubrichs on OHG hymns indicate that it is just as applicable to Germany. Pastoral obligations towards the variegated *familia* of monasteries could not but impel them towards vernacular literature for domestic consumption, quite apart from any external pressure.

A third heading includes another lay element within the monastic community making for the use of the vernacular in written texts: the presence of lay monks and lay brothers. On another front this opens up the same question of the area of contact between monks and laymen,[175] again in close connection with literacy if we bear in mind that monastic writings use the term *litteratus* to distinguish the choir monk from the lay brother or *conversus*.[176] With lay monks and lay brothers we move from the *familia* of the monastery (however close their ties, these laymen lived outside the monastic house) to within the convent, where their illiteracy is part of the institution itself.[177]

To Teske we owe an analysis of these two groups, distinguishing them from each other and also from choir monks.[178] The latter, known as *cantores*, are characterised by the literacy inseparable from their liturgical function and the place of the *lectio* in the daily life of the monastery. This is not the case with the lay monks, known as *conversi*, but also as *idiotae* as a mark of their illiteracy and ignorance of Latin (what little they knew was confined to simple prayers learned by heart).[179] Such *illitterati* found a place within a monastery, commonly regarded as the main refuge of literacy, because of dissatisfaction with recruitment of *oblati*, the suspicion that aristocratic families were using this as a means of getting rid of unwanted offspring.[180] This could be dealt with by recruiting adults instead, whose voluntary entry into the community was clearly preferable. However, to this religious gain there corresponded an educational disadvantage: whereas *oblati* joined the community at an age when they could be educated in the monastic school, adult *conversi* had previously undergone no education as laymen and there is no evidence that provision was made for it once they joined the community at a more advanced age.[181] As a result the monastery now consists of two groups distinguished by the fact of literacy: *cantores* (who had entered still as *oblati* or as secular clerics, therefore educated,[182] who then took monastic vows) as opposed to *conversi* (laymen who joined the community too late to acquire literacy). Literacy separates these two groups and imposes on them different functions within the *claustrum*, but what they have in common is that the *lectio* (reading aloud to listeners, as in the refectory) was intended for the whole community and had to take account of the fact that some knew no Latin. The pastoral responsibility (and hence the use of the vernacular) which the monastery showed towards the *familia* of laymen outside its walls was also shown towards the lay monks inside.

The same is true of lay brothers, also known as *conversi* or *barbati* and likewise distinguished from the *cantores* by their illiteracy. This class, founded by Wilhelm von Hirsau towards the end of the eleventh century and obviously meeting a widespread need, represents an attempt by some members of the convent's *familia* to draw closer to the monastery.[183] These lay brothers became members of the monastic community, but without being monks: they were members of an order, but did not belong to the *claustrum*.[184] Their duties lay more in the practical sphere of running the estates owned by the community, tasks which made no great claims on an educated training which the lay brothers did not have.[185] Like the *familia* from which they were drawn and like the lay monks these lay brothers had religious needs and interests which could only be satisfied by vernacular instruction which took account of their lack of any formal education.[186] They represent yet another lay element in the monastery for which orally delivered literature in German was a necessity.

We pass beyond the monastery and its immediate range of influence with the fourth category: vernacular literature composed by a member of the secular clergy whose duties involve him in the world in a way quite foreign to the monk. Whereas OHG literature had been produced by monks, the revival of vernacular literature from 1060 is marked by the first signs, alongside monastic authorship, of works composed by the secular clergy. Despite the theological simplicity of some of their products[187] it would be mistaken to see in these authors ordinary parish priests.[188] What must be taken into account is the movement towards grouping secular clerics in a non-monastic common life (canons regular),[189] as with Ezzo and the collegiate foundation in Bamberg, but this makes it difficult to draw a line in authorship between a monk in a monastery and a secular cleric in a collegiate institution.[190]

Although it may often be impossible to tell whether an author was a monk or a secular cleric, enough give their status as secular clerics explicitly[191] for it to be clear that we are dealing with a new development, contributing to the rise of works in the language of the layman.[192] Whereas earlier scholarship had been content with distinguishing ecclesiastic authors from secular ones,[193] Rupp first suggested the division of the former into monks and clerics,[194] although Meissburger, concerned with monastic authorship in the eleventh and twelfth centuries, criticised his method of simply basing his division on Ehrismann's suggestions. If we disregard Ehrismann's surmises (because he was concerned with answering a different question) and base ourselves on pointed references the anonymity of much religious literature deprives us of the author's name, but also of his ecclesiastic status. Nonetheless, there remains a number of authors who can be claimed as secular clerics: Ezzo is attested as a *canonicus* and *scholasticus*,[195] whilst others refer to themselves as *priester* or as *pfaffe*.[196] Even Meissburger is forced to admit this hard core of authors designated as secular clerics, whilst those for whom no reference to name and status is given could just as well be secular clerics as monks.[197]

Beyond this we lack clear pointers to where and under what conditions these clerics were active as authors. Ezzo could be connected with the collegiate foundation of St. Gangolf at Bamberg, but Gunther's episcopal court is equally possible.[198] For Pfaffe Lamprecht Bumke has discussed the possibility that he wrote for the archiepiscopal court at Cologne, but also at Trier (for the archbishop's court?),[199] whilst it is generally accepted that Pfaffe Konrad was employed at the court of Henry the Lion. In other words, quite apart from any other centres there is some evidence that clerics produced religious literature for laymen at court, no longer for a monastic community, a change of focus which placed greater stress on the vernacular. For a further example we may turn to Heinrich von Veldeke, regarded as a cleric (at least as one with a clerical education), who composed the legend *Servatius* in the vernacular for illiterate laymen.[200] He was prompted by Hessel, in charge of the church in Maastricht and also of the pilgrims' hostel, who had an interest in propagating the claims of this saint in the vernacular in order to appeal to the greatest number of lay pilgrims.[201]

In the last paragraph we have already crossed to the fifth category, comprising court clerics as authors,[202] including Veldeke as the author of a romance for a court patron. Medieval rulers relied on the services of such intellectuals for various reasons: they were not tied to one place like monks and if they held an ecclesiastical benefice their services were at the expense of the Church.[203] The growth of chanceries at secular courts rendered the cleric's literate skills indispensable, however much the Church criticised this diversion of his activities to the secular ends of the court.[204] They were also employed as tutors, notaries and authors.[205] The court cleric was the principal agent of change in a cultural process which combined knightly values with those of literate culture.[206] Since they were responsible for literate tasks at court it is not surprising that court clerics should be the authors of the earliest secular narrative literature in the twelfth century. This is regarded as the case with the 'Spielmannsepen', with works with a classical theme such as the *Liet von Troye* of Herbort von Fritzlar or Veldeke's *Eneide*, with the heroic theme of the *Nibelungenlied* (whose author was probably a cleric) or with the Arthurian theme of Lancelot (Ulrich von Zatzikhoven was likewise probably a cleric).[207]

Under five headings we have followed (from the Carolingian beginnings to the rise of court literature) the stages in which various types of ecclesiastic devoted their literate skills to the needs of the *illitterati*: first, monks on whom Carolingian rulers relied for the needs of their ecclesiastical policy or who had to take account of illiteracy within the monastery or its immediate surroundings, but then secular clerics whose duties confronted them more closely with the needs of laymen or whose literacy was focused on the secular ruler's court. Under each heading the movement has been from literate ecclesiastic to illiterate layman; the former had to pay heed to the latter's inability to read, so that what the cleric wrote was for recital to the layman. At this point we change our approach and consider the converse movement by which various classes of laymen penetrated the world of literacy, acquiring a clerical skill which made it possible for them to read written texts, however rare these literate laymen may have been still in the twelfth and even the thirteenth century and however long the practice of public recital persisted.

In considering the literate layman two points have to be borne in mind. The first is the wide semantic scope of *clericus* which allows us to say that the lettered layman entered the clerical realm of literacy. *Clericus* had an ecclesiastic sense (one who has taken holy orders), but also an educational one (one who is a secretary, scribe or scholar),[208] so that from the twelfth century the word no longer had only the former sense.[209] This change did not fail to worry ecclesiastics who saw in it an erosion of their educational monopoly,[210] but we must see in it a sign of disturbances to the traditional symbiosis of two cultures brought about by incipient lay literacy. The other point concerns literacy on so modest a level that some might deny it literate status altogether. What is involved here is not literacy in the sense of reading for oneself, but exposure to literacy and its standards by hearing written works recited. This is no longer identical with complete illiteracy (an acquaintance only with orality), nor with a fully fledged ability to read, it is best described as the position of a *quasi litteratus*, as with Baldwin II of Guines, a position to which Fleckenstein grants decisive importance in court literature.[211] It is a feature of medieval literacy particularly true of the layman.

The first class of layman of whom literacy could be expected was the king. He participated in ecclesiastical culture from the ceremony of his consecration and coronation, since this included him among the celebrants of the liturgy, but he also collaborated with that culture by maintaining a *capella* at his court, and with it activities in writing, thought and literature.[212] Theoderic in Italy, Visigothic kings in Spain and Charles at Aachen, by having classical works recited to them or even reading them themselves, continued the tradition of the philosopher king, in however attenuated a form.[213] An early example from German literature is Otfrid's dedication to Ludwig the German, in which the twin qualities *fortitudo* and *sapientia* are attributed to the Franks at large, but also to their ruler in particular.[214] The picture of the Frankish king as a friend of literature owes much to classical tradition and imperial support for Otfrid's work, so that there is room to doubt how far Ludwig's literacy went beyond an encouragement of monastic literature, whether he read these works himself or was dependent on a recital.[215] Even if the latter was the case, this is no different from Theoderic having written works read out to him and each is to be seen as a *quasi litteratus*.[216] However many exceptions there may be, the recurrence of the proverb *rex illiteratus est quasi asinus coronatus* in the twelfth century indicates that this requirement could now be voiced,[217] whilst the example of Henry II of England, a patron of literature in Latin and the vernacular and also able to read himself, shows that this demand need not be unrealistic, at least in the French-speaking world.[218] Where Germany stood is brought out by Bumke's observation that the princely families from which emperors were elected were regularly illiterate until a dynasty came to rule, but that they deemed it necessary to rectify this for their successors.[219]

By the twelfth century we witness something similar amongst princes as a second category of incipient lay literacy.[220] Politically the princes took on the powers of the king,[221] but were also ready to gain a foothold in the literate culture to which the king had gained access,[222] so that a twelfth-century history attributes to Fulk the Good the admission that knowledge, eloquence and letters are as appropriate for counts as for kings, a remark with greater bearing on the historian's own day than on Fulk's time.[223] The situation in Germany has been described more precisely. Until the twelfth century it was the royal court which, apart from monasteries, had been the focus of literature, a fact which remains unaltered so long as we have regard to the whole range of literature (and include Latin). However, once we focus on what is new in this century (court literature in the vernacular) the picture changes, for it is the princely courts which encourage this new type of literature.[224] These princes may remain personally illiterate[225] (although there are exceptions),[226] but in their encouragement of written literature these rulers must be classified as *quasi litterati*. The same is true of pragmatic literacy practised at these courts,[227] for changes in government, requiring written records, made the princes dependent on the services of *litterati* in their chanceries.[228] That these two developments (written literature and pragmatic literacy) were interconnected has been shown by the fact that both are attested at the same centres at approximately the same time.[229]

With our third category we move to the occasional knight who was able to read, to the *miles litteratus* discussed by Turner for twelfth- and thirteenth-century England. The literacy regarded as an advantage in kings and princes could also extend theoretically to knighthood at large,[230] as is suggested by the chronicler's report on Fulk the Good, for he finishes with the general reflection that the man endowed with a knowledge of letters and learning was regarded as the best amongst knights.[231] This betrays an awareness of a possible conflict between culture and *militia*, but also the possibility of overcoming it, as in this particular example.[232] One of the rare examples from Germany points in the same direction: in the *Historia beati Erkanberti* it is said that knowledge of letters is of great use to one about to withdraw from the world (as a monk), but does no harm to one proposing to be a knight.[233] This implies a bridging of the gap between literate clergy and illiterate knighthood which is potential (because expressed negatively), but this gap is actually closed when, with an eye to Lanzelet's ability to read, it is said in *Die Crone* that he held two offices, being both a knight and a cleric.[234] Here the word *pfaffe*, like *clericus* from the twelfth century, designates not someone in holy orders, but a *litteratus*, someone who had undergone a clerical education.[235]

This helps us to understand one way in which the new phenomenon of the *miles litteratus* could come about. Apart from cases where a young nobleman was educated by a tutor at court,[236] the possibility existed of someone enjoying clerical status (in minor orders) as a student, but then choosing a secular life, as permitted by canon law.[237] Such a person was, like Lanzelet, a *pfaffe* in the educational, not the ecclesiastic sense.[238] This possibility was welcome to feudal families, often confronted with the predicament that their dynastic plans were thwarted by the death of the elder son. This difficulty could be overcome by withdrawing a younger son from the clerical career for which he had been educated (but having prudently postponed entering major orders), so that this younger son rejoined the world as a knight, but an educated one.[239] *Die Crone* is silent about how Lanzelet became a *pfaffe*, but in Hartmann's *Gregorius*, albeit without dynastic considerations, the hero's path from knightly birth to monastic education and back to knightly status is sketched, possibly reflecting the author's own status, a ministerial, but educated for administrative service at court.[240] For a knight educated in this way literacy was more than the status of *quasi litteratus*, as Hartmann makes clear in his own case.[241]

A fourth category concerns the ability of noblewomen to read.[242] With them literacy first penetrated lay society (the first attested individual readers of German works, with Otfrid and Notker, are women), long before the nobleman was prepared to have truck with reading himself.[243] The Latinity of such women generally barred ambitious reading in that language,[244] so that their literacy focused more on German and the rise of vernacular literature is partly owing to their encouragement.[245] Our earliest evidence suggests devotional literature for these readers: the *Sachsenspiegel* includes psalters and religious books under women's possessions, but other examples underline this view,[246] just as the books held by the statues of Gepa and Gerburg at Naumburg are probably psalters as attributes of a literate noblewoman.[247] If Christ was considered of royal descent this implies an aristocratic rank for Mary, who can therefore be depicted by Otfrid as reading the psalter at the Annunciation.[248] Religious conceptions here follow social practice, but the reverse is true when the model of Mary as a reader is later used to justify women reading religious books against clerical suspicions.[249]

The evidence for court literature suggests that it was also encouraged by noblewomen, that authors wrote with an eye to them, and that they recognised the possibility that, however dominant recital to listeners still was, individual women readers were to be reckoned with.[250] At the start of court literature this was already the case. In view of the more advanced state of lay literacy in the French-speaking world we need not be surprised that Constance Fitzgilbert read a life of Henry I for herself,[251] but the more precocious state of literacy amongst noblewomen means that Germany, too, can match this already with the works of Heinrich von Veldeke. He wrote his *Servatius* at the prompting of Hessel, but also at the request of the countess Agnes of Loon.[252] It is not known whether, alongside the recital of this legend to pilgrims at Maastricht, she can be regarded as an individual reader, but such doubts are dispelled by the poet's *Eneide*, the uncompleted text of which was lent to the countess of Cleves for personal perusal.[253]

Our next category is made up of *religiosae*, sometimes called *semireligiosae* to designate their uncertain position between laity and monastic life. They emerged around 1200, about the same time as the mendicant orders, and the meeting between these two movements has been seen as a historical turning-point, dictating much of the religious life and literature north of the Alps in the thirteenth century.[254] A considerable number of béguines were noblewomen or members of a town patriciate by origin,[255] which accounts largely for their ability to read, but such communities, even before the mendicants incorporated them into their orders, resembled conventual life to the extent that they practised *lectio* in both senses: individual devotional reading and recital to assembled members.[256] Since literacy in such circles did not necessarily extend to Latin (or any advanced knowledge of Latin) there was a pressure towards providing this reading-matter in the vernacular.

The fact that such communities were generally set up in towns leads us to our sixth category of literate layman: towndwellers as potential readers. The everyday needs of merchants made for pragmatic literacy,[257] but not more so than the feudal ruler's need for literacy in his chancery. These two centres of incipient literacy can be compared in another respect for, just as the feudal lord was dependent on clerics for written administration, so too were merchants and town authorities initially before their educational policy yielded fruits in lay literacy. The scribe employed on his voyage by the merchant in *Der guote Gerhart* of Rudolf von Ems is a cleric,[258] as are many who fill literate posts in towns, such as scribes, notaries, schoolmasters, even to the extent of duties shared between cathedral school and town administration.[259] Moreover, just as some literate laymen were to be found at the secular court, so is the same increasingly true of towndwellers, first as scribal transactions move from Latin to the vernacular,[260] then as merchants, perhaps still illiterate, see the advantages of schooling for their sons.[261] Like the princely courts towndwellers depend on clerical *litterati* and also see the point of acquiring literacy for themselves. Even though he may have in mind conditions in Italy, where literacy was developed far earlier than in Germany, Thomasin von Zerclaere, when referring to the reading reception of his German work, sees these individual readers as merchants (*wuocheraere*).[262]

With the author of a written work we come to our last category. Some authors of religious literature in the twelfth century indicate that they were laymen,[263] but a layman who composed such a work must have been in close touch with a religious institution[264] and can therefore not be termed simply a layman, but at least *quasi litteratus*. As regards court literature the assumption of a layman as author was unproblematic as long as it was maintained that all important poets were knights.[265] This is now questioned and instead the educational status of these authors is felt to be decisive.[266] With this question their clerical status comes much more to the fore and Bumke has emphasised that most authors of court narrative literature belong to this category.[267] They are therefore court clerics such as we discussed above, *pfaffen* either because they had taken holy orders or because they were literate. In the latter case they may have been laymen returned to secular life after a clerical education, but unless this is indicated expressly (as when Hartmann states his ministerial status) such literate authors cannot reliably be termed laymen. Against earlier scholarship much court literature, despite its secular interests, must be seen against a background of clerical, rather than knightly literacy.[268]

How decisive this is can be seen from Bumke's list of court authors of narrative literature who were clerics, but also, outside German literature, from the clerical, highly literate standing of Chrétien himself. He betrays a Latinate education in classical literature (allusions to Virgil, Macrobius and Ovid, whom he translated) and in medieval Latin (*comediae*, Alanus ab Insulis),[269] but also including a training in poetics, rhetoric and dialectic, as well as acquaintance with the school of Chartres.[270] It is little wonder that in the prologue to *Cligés* he praises *clergie* alongside knighthood.[271] If from the beginning the Arthurian romance in France was imbued with clerical, literate learning it is fitting that its transfer to Germany was effected by Hartmann, a knight, but with a clerical education which enabled him to cope with Chrétien's *clergie*. That Hartmann is no isolated example is clear from what Gottfried says of Veldeke and Rudolf von Ems in turn of Gottfried himself (so that a conscious literary tradition is being formed in the vernacular):[272] the skills of all these authors (even though their works go back to French sources) derive from the study of Latin texts, from their clerical training in the schools.[273] This is true of all these clerical authors, whether called that because they had taken orders (Ulrich von Zatzikhoven is generally identified with a *plebanus* or secular priest attested in Thurgau)[274] or because they had had a clerical education while remaining laymen or returning to lay status (as with Hartmann).

If some of these literate authors retain their lay status despite a clerical education, there are two others (Wolfram and Ulrich von Lichtenstein) who proclaim their lay status as well as their illiteracy.[275] The importance of Wolfram, coupled with the ministerial rank of Hartmann and the knightly status of many lyric poets, doubtless led to the earlier view that all major poets of court literature were knights. If we now place greater stress on clerical authors in narrative literature these two have now become exceptions.[276] Only recently has Wolfram's statement about illiteracy been seen less as a personal confession of inability to read and more as a polemical objection to the clerical penetration of the layman's literature which we have been tracing.[277] Even apart from this, it is possible that, like Frau Ava dependent on learned help from her sons or Ulrich von Lichtenstein relying on his *schríber* in matters literate,[278] Wolfram had access to written sources through the good offices of someone else, that he was *quasi litteratus*.[279]

Lyric poetry is different from narrative literature, at least in Germany,[280] although here too the question to be asked is not about the position of a knightly 'Minnesänger' in the feudal hierarchy (there is no satisfactory way of answering this question),[281] but instead about his educational status.[282] This question reveals a difference between the love-poets of Provence and their German colleagues, already present in the contrast between the literate background of Guillaume IX of Aquitaine and the absence of such in Der Kürenberger.[283] In Provence a number of troubadours come from the world of the clergy, are *clerici* with access to the learned tradition of Latin.[284] The Provençal love-poet is therefore often a *litteratus* and there is little reason to doubt the *vidas* when they refer to him as *savis de letras* or *ben letratz* or the reality of the competition between them and *illitterati* at court, especially amongst professional entertainers.[285] In Germany the position is different because the poets of *Minnesangs Frühling* are for the most part aristocratic amateurs and laymen, even belonging to the upper reaches of the nobility[286] (expressly literate cases occur only later).[287] This means that indications of literacy are largely lacking – a reflection of the still unlettered state of the German nobility. Exceptions there are, but few. Veldeke and Hartmann belong here because, as narrative authors of whose literate status in that genre we are informed, they are also active as lyric poets, but also Morungen and Walther.[288] How these latter acquired their literacy is unknown, but this does not affect the marked difference between Germany and Provence as regards literacy, or within Germany between narrative literature, largely the preserve of literate authors, and the lyric, mainly cultivated by noblemen whose literate status escapes us.

In the last pages we have been following two complementary movements: from the literate world of the Church to the oral realm of laymen, and conversely the penetration of this literate world by various members of the laity. The spread of vernacular literacy results from a progressive breakdown of the barriers between a clerical Latin written culture and a lay vernacular oral culture.

We have, in other words, to look for common ground where the two cultures overlap, and this can be established for the various categories in the two movements. For Carolingian monasteries to provide vernacular texts for pastoral use was no part of their monastic task;[289] the monastic *familia* lived in the world, but focused on the monastery; of lay brothers the converse can be said (they lived in the monastery, but as laymen), while lay monks likewise stand at the meeting-point of lay illiteracy with monastic learning;[290] the task of the secular clergy was to provide a bridge between illiterate laymen and the religion of the book (in this sense any priest, not just a bishop, could be called a *pontifex*), whilst the court cleric, as criticism of him made clear, was neither one thing nor the other.[291] Similar remarks can be made of the classes of laymen who had contact with the world of literacy. The king was the only layman who participated by his office in ecclesiastical culture;[292] the prince could be seen as a *copula* between knighthood and letters,[293] just as the *miles litteratus* was anomalous enough to occasion comment,[294] whilst the reading ability of noblewomen was a point where the cultural barrier between the two worlds began to crumble.[295] Members of lay religious communities could be seen as quasi-religious or semireligious, because they belonged neither to the lay nor to the clerical world.[296] The clerics who provided literate services for the towns had taken minor orders only[297] and, like those at courts, enjoyed the privileges of clergy without being divorced from secular life, whilst lastly the lay author was at the least *quasi litteratus* or, if fully literate, paradoxically combined the status of *miles* or *laicus* with that of *clericus*.[298]

The two movements therefore meet on a large measure of common ground. Unlike Grundmann, who dismissed such cases as exceptional,[299] we need to stress the importance of these encounters, especially in the monastery and at court, where two cultural worlds made contact and began to penetrate one another.[300]

We have had occasion to distinguish authors and audience who could be termed *litterati* from those best described as *quasi litterati*. This leads us to the question how far literacy helped to differentiate the audience, what bearing it had on their reception of literature.[301] Since the possibility of laymen reading as well as hearing arose above all at court, I shall confine myself to court literature.

That the audience's reception of court literature could be differentiated we know from a number of indications. Allusions to other literary works in Wolfram's *Parzival* suggest that certain courts were acquainted with the works in question, but others not, so that his work was received in different ways at different courts.[302] That concerns the distinction of one court from another, whereas differences within any one court are suggested by Wolfram's description of his audience as made up of *tumbe* and *wîse*[303] or by Mohr's suggestion of two types of recipient: those who had no knowledge of Chrétien's version and those who did (and were therefore more interested in how than in what).[304] Of wider importance is the evidence that the court consisted of two parts, a smaller permanent circle and a larger changing group of transient members: whereas the latter heard no more than a few parts of a long narrative, the former alone had the chance of hearing the complete work and appreciating its overall structure.[305] From this follows the probability of two levels of appreciation of court literature. Ulrich von Lichtenstein is explicit with regard to one poem: *Diu liet vil maneger niht verstuont, / als noch die tumben ofte tuont; / swer aber was sô rehte wîs, / der si verstuont, der gabe in prîs*.[306] We have also seen that some authors had doubts about all the audience's ability to understand the novel implications of fiction: Gottfried was prepared for the literal-minded and Herrand von Wildonie had his difficulties with those uncourtly enough to demand witnesses for fictional truth.[307]

These examples are revealing, but not relevant to our concern, for none necessarily implies that the distinction between appreciating a work and failure to do so is identical with the difference between being able to read and not.[308] One way of overcoming this is to look at another manner of subdividing the court. A differentiation of the audience found in the *Roman de Thèbes* (v. 14: *clerc ou chevalier*) is not to be construed as 'everybody' (as with 'young and old' or 'men and women') since these two groups are expressly distinguished from the *vilains* excluded from the performance.[309] Elsewhere in French the ladies of the court can be added as a third group, once more excluding others.[310] This threefold division of the audience recurs in German when Hadloub refers to his aristocratic audience as *edel frouwen, hôhe pfaffen, ritter guot* or when Thomasin von Zerclaere sees the court composed of *vrume rîtr und guote vrouwen / und wîse phaffen*.[311] Likewise, historical sources refer to *milites et clerici* at court, sometimes extending this to include ladies.[312] Without regarding these three groups as rigidly cut off from each other as regards literacy (*some* knights were able to read and the occasional reader could also attend a recital), we may take these groups as representative of three possible receptions, not always mutually exclusive. We may regard the knights (certainly in Germany) as illiterate listeners, whereas the noblewomen, although present as listeners, were also readers, whilst the court clerics, likewise present at an oral performance, were readers in the full sense of Latin education. What are the differences between these groups in their reception and understanding of court literature?

If we start with the knights, representing that segment of the audience which could not read, not all were able, like Baldwin of Guines as *quasi litteratus*, to rise above the restrictions of illiteracy by exposure to literate values when hearing written works recited. This is suggested by complaints of literate authors about the inattentiveness of many listeners: although this may have become a topos, the inattentive listener had a basis in reality and was an undeniable bugbear of the baronial hall.[313] He was envisaged by Chrétien when he played a trick on latecomers to a recital of *Yvain* by incorporating a deferred prologue for those who had hoped to skip a theoretical opening and arrive in time for the narrative action.[314]

Whether they were inattentive or superficial, illiterate listeners were subjected to an episodic understanding of a work because of its oral delivery. Before Chrétien's *conjointure* (a narrative consisting of adventures whose significance lay in their interdependence) Arthurian material had been presented in the form of an isolated adventure (the lais of Marie de France or the oral sources of Chrétien's romances).[315] Episodic works called for an episodic response, which has also been shown as typical of oral literature in general: if the author is absorbed in the task of recital to the detriment of patterning and cohesiveness (open to the poet who composes in writing), his listeners are unlikely to be any more able to rise above the single episode and to correlate one with another.[316] With the written romance new demands are made of authors in structural patterning (Thomas and Gottfried seize this opportunity more readily than Béroul and Eilhart), but also of listeners. If the meaning of an episode now lay not in itself, but was to be grasped by comparison with others, the author and his audience had to abandon an episodic approach, to forgo a characteristic strength of oral poetry in favour of an attitude facilitated best by the written dimension. The illiterate listener was now at a disadvantage by comparison with the reader. This listener's less sophisticated attitude, interested in the narrative action primarily as a sequence of events, persisted after the more complex romance had made its appearance, as is suggested for the Tristan tradition in Germany after Gottfried. The continuations by Ulrich von Türheim and Heinrich von Freiberg are added to Gottfried's text in most manuscript traditions, but are capable of satisfying only a 'basic curiosity about story as event'.[317] It would be wrong to regard this merely as a later decline in taste, for the narrative outline of the Tristan story rests on a concatenation of fabliau episodes from the beginning, certainly with Eilhart and possibly the focus of interest of some of Gottfried's listeners.[318]

The author of a work intended for listeners and for readers regarded the latter as better qualified to appreciate his work and, in addressing them, he at times spoke above the heads of listeners, bringing it home to them that educationally and aesthetically they were underprivileged. On the most elementary level a work in written form means that the illiterate listener depended on the services of a literate mediator to translate it into German and then recite it.[319] By contrast, a literate member of the audience may still have needed a translator (if his reading ability was restricted to German), but could dispense with the reciter. The double formula or other indications that a work could be received in two ways must have brought it home to the illiterate listener that there were aspects of the work from which he was excluded. Instructions how the reader was to resolve an acrostic must have passed by the *illitteratus* as meaningless, excluding him from a literature which, although still meant for public recital, was accessible in its higher reaches only to the reader.[320] These higher reaches included much more than an isolated *jeu d'esprit* like the acrostic, as when the author reminds the audience of what has already been said and recommends the reader to turn back the pages and collate two passages.[321] In granting the reader the privilege of proceeding, like himself, at an independent pace, the author stresses the bond of literacy linking them both, but excluding those whose education confines them to the status of listeners.

If we regard the *frouwen* as representative of a second group within the court audience, members of the laity who were able to read, this is because, although this group may have included the odd *miles litteratus*, it was with the noblewoman that literacy first found acceptance amongst laymen. A literature whose literate artistry could best be appreciated by readers was therefore primarily addressed to noblewomen as potential readers, as in the case of Wolfram's *Parzival*: appealing to the interests of women, but also circulating in written form to be read by them.[322]

Women's interests are consulted in a different manner in the *Iwein* of Hartmann, an author who anticipated readers as well as listeners, even though he may not refer to them explicitly (or to women as readers) in this work. Mertens suggests that in his favourable depiction of Laudine Hartmann has an eye to the feminine members of his audience as much as did Wolfram.[323] We can, however, take this further. For the women in a court audience Laudine spoke *pro domo*, for like her they were often abandoned by their husbands for the sake of feudal obligations (attendance at a ruler's court, warfare).[324] By playing down Chrétien's misogynistic view of the heroine's inconstancy and showing awareness of her difficulties Hartmann has taken sides in this conflict between the sexes. The bond between literate author and women readers need not have been confined to literacy; it could embrace shared interests, putting both at a distance from male values, as is also implied by Wolfram's reservations about knighthood, expressed from the woman's point of view as its most obvious victim.[325]

This argument could also be employed by an author who was probably a cleric[326] (and therefore, by virtue of his literacy and distance from knightly values, closer to the literate noblewoman than many others at court). An example is *Der heimliche Bote*, which undercuts from the woman's point of view the man's boasting of his physical achievements in chivalry, for she, like Laudine, stands only to lose from his continuous absence.[327] Reservations about knighthood and a shared literacy could bring cleric and noblewoman into alliance at court, just as she could also feel closer to the concerns of a literate author (cleric and author at court were often one and the same person).

The appeal of court literature to the interests of women means that men amongst the listeners were exposed to a new kind of literature which they were invited to consider from the woman's point of view. Such men may be compared with the *quasi litteratus*: just as he, technically illiterate, was exposed to the standards of written literature, so were male listeners expected to consider the values of a literature meant also for the feminine reader.

We can now see how the author's recommendations which passed over the heads of his illiterate listeners were much more intelligible to the reader. For the literate noblewoman the double formula *hoeren oder lesen* had a twofold relevance: unlike the unlettered menfolk she was involved in both aspects. By contrast to the listener, instructions how to resolve an acrostic made textual sense to the literate noblewoman.[328] As a reader she enjoyed the advantage of receiving a work in a sequence chosen by herself, not by the author or reciter (as has been proposed in the case of Mechthild von Magdeburg) or of skipping a particular passage.[329] The reader could correlate different passages in the same work (and be encouraged to do this by the author), a possibility denied the listener, unable to turn back a recital.[330] This practice is attested in learned, devotional and pragmatic literature (where for various reasons it may be desirable)[331] and presupposes what monastic literature terms the *studiosus lector*,[332] but can we also expect so careful a reader in an aesthetic context? To illustrate this we may turn to the advice given by Wolfram's Gurnemanz to Parzival at the close of Book III.[333]

The episode is based on a folktale motif: the eight pieces of advice given by the older man all produce narrative situations soon afterwards in Book IV in which Parzival shows that he has taken the advice to heart. Even listeners accustomed to episodic understanding must have been able to grasp the connection between advice and execution: the time gap is minimal, the audience come fresh from a similar patterning (Herzeloyde's advice to her son is earlier tested in practice within Book III)[334] and may be assumed to have been acquainted with this folktale motif.[335] However, we are concerned with much more than a listener's ability to comprehend connections between two adjacent narrative segments, for the advice given by Gurnemanz has ramifications far beyond Book IV and with unexpected implications. Gurnemanz regarded Parzival as born to be a feudal ruler and couched his advice accordingly, so that Book IV shows the hero realising this promise at Pelrapeire. A little later, however, there are hints in Book V that, even if Gurnemanz did not realise it, his advice was better geared to Grail-kingship,[336] and these hints are finally confirmed by Trevrizent in Book IX[337] or as late as Book XVI.[338] Wolfram makes considerable demands of his audience: they have to switch imaginatively from what they expected to what they could not have foreseen, but they have also to correlate verbal allusions separated not by a few hundred, but by thousands of lines. A technique like this impels us to assume a reader who can turn back pages for confirmation, not a listener who cannot reverse a recital.

The question whether we can assume such a *studiosus lector* for court literature can be answered by two examples, already mentioned, in which authors encourage readers to act in this way. Gottfried recommends that a point be confirmed from an earlier passage (8741f. refers back to 7208ff.) which the reader is to look up.[339] The prose *Lancelot* goes further in explicitness on a similar occasion: it gives the gathering in the manuscript where the earlier passage can be found and it indicates the bold lettering by which it may be recognised, so that a reader checking back is implied.[340] In these three cases the *studiosus lector* is a hope which the author of court literature may entertain. *Lancelot* refers back, giving detailed instructions; Gottfried refers back, but gives no instructions;[341] Wolfram reckons with people who, if they are to understand him, will need to turn back.

However great these demands on the careful reader, there were limits to the literacy of laypeople whose ability to read was confined to the vernacular and whom for shorthand convenience we have equated with the educated noblewoman. These limits are defined by Latinity, not simply being able to read that language, but rather an acquaintance with its literature, poetics and rhetoric. Noblewomen, as was educational practice, still learned to read on the basis of Latin psalms, but this level of Latinity did not equip them to appreciate Latin literature and its artistry.³⁴² This suggests two levels of literacy: one equipping a person to read the vernacular, but little more, the other resting on a foundation of Latinity as well. For this reason different degrees of literacy can be defined by a range of abilities, starting with *optime litteratus*, moving through *bene* or *satis* as qualifiers, and finishing with *commode* or *modice litteratus*.³⁴³ Thomasin von Zerclaere distinguished the literacy of a cleric from that of *ein man, / der tiefe sinne niht verstên kan*, who had to content himself with reading the court romance.³⁴⁴ Making use of Thomasin's distinction we now ask how a cleric was better equipped than a literate layman as a reader.

The presence of clerics at court means that they could also be present in the audience for court literature where they constitute a second group of *litterati*. As clerics they stood especially close to the clerical authors of court literature, so that, for all the secular interests of that literature, cleric can be seen speaking to cleric at court, even if this dialogue may have been commissioned by a lay ruler for a circle which also included laymen. This relationship between clerical author and clerical members of his audience means that literacy brings about a stratification within the audience at court: not merely could the court author appeal to the literate noblewoman over the heads of her illiterate menfolk, he could also address court clerics over the heads of noblewomen.

Those clerics who formed a regular part of the court may be imagined as listeners present at the recital of literature alongside laymen, but as *litterati* they enjoyed the additional advantages listed for the noblewoman as a reader. However, these clerics enjoy a further advantage, for their Latinity conferred benefits on them closed to those whose literacy was confined to the vernacular (or to not more than an elementary acquaintance with Latin).³⁴⁵ If we regard court literature composed by clerics as the attempt to establish classical status for the vernacular by applying to it the standards of rhetoric and poetics which clerics studied in the schools, then only other clerics in their audience, similarly schooled, were able to assess how successful this attempt had been.³⁴⁶ We have seen this in the case of Rudolf von Ems: in his *Alexander* he appeals to one able to judge the quality of his work by reading its Latin sources.³⁴⁷ Such a referee must be more than literate in the simplest sense, he must also be able to read Latin and be well versed in Latin literature. A similar suggestion has been made for Rudolf's literary master, Gottfried, on the grounds that his text 'assumes a clerically trained reader conversant with classical Latin literature'.³⁴⁸ Stevens also says that Gottfried's work was composed primarily for clerics, as only they had familiarity with classical texts.³⁴⁹ This may be acceptable at the present stage of the argument, but should not exclude the lower level of literacy, confined to the vernacular, which Gottfried also had in mind.

Gottfried provides a striking example of an author's expectation of Latinate literacy amongst some of his audience. In the love-grotto scene he depicts the lovers singing together of the fate of four women crossed in love in classical antiquity (Phyllis, Canace, Biblis and Dido), to whom may be added Thisbe, referred to earlier.³⁵⁰ Gottfried's mention of these five figures is so brief and lacking in details about the nature of their fate (or their possible relevance to his story) that he must have assumed knowledge of them with some of his audience.[351] Nor can such references be dismissed as trifling, since they reverberate through Gottfried's work and were meant to contribute to its understanding.[352] Yet what members of Gottfried's audience would know about these classical figures unaided and grasp what they say about his German work?

The search for precedents in German literature, available both to listeners and to readers and providing information to enable them to understand Gottfried's purpose, does not take us very far. The story of Pyramus and Thisbe was admittedly referred to before the composition of *Tristan* in Hartmann's *Erec* and likewise the fate of Dido in Veldeke's *Eneide* (two authors to whom Gottfried refers, suggesting that they were known to his audience).[353] Beyond that the trail goes cold: there is no evidence that the other three figures were treated in vernacular literature before Gottfried. The story of Biblis is mentioned, it is true, by Albrecht von Halberstadt,[354] but there is no suggestion that Gottfried (let alone his audience) was acquainted with this work,[355] or that its influence spread to south Germany,[356] whilst its uncertain dating may make it too late to have been available to Gottfried's audience.[357] The likelihood is that only two of these five exemplary classical figures were known in Gottfried's day to anyone acquainted with German literature, whether a listener or a reader. The position becomes clearer once we take into account the possible reader of Latin literature: all five figures occur in Ovid, Biblis in the *Metamorphoses*, the others in the *Heroides*.[358] We may conclude that the members of his audience whom Gottfried expected to understand these references must have been able to read Latin literature and had undergone a clerical education. This implies clerics at court, not noblewomen (literate in the vernacular, but only on the simplest level of biblical or liturgical Latin).[359]

Vernacular literacy brought about an extensive differentiation of the audience for court literature. Although strictly speaking illiterate, the *quasi litteratus* was exposed to written literature and its standards by hearing it recited and was in a different position from an *illitteratus* who knew only orally composed or memorised literature. Written vernacular literature at the court thus produced two types of illiterate recipient, just as its authors anticipated two types of literate recipient whom we have included under the shorthand headings of *frouwen* and *pfaffen*.[360]

(d) Dating of the intermediate mode of reception

Repeatedly we have seen a written text destined both for readers and for listeners and have emphasised that this intermediate mode was summed up in the double formula *hoeren oder lesen*. Our task now is to consider the date when this formula first occurred in German, when vernacular authors first expected readers, not in place of listeners, but alongside or better: amongst them. To anticipate, we can say that from the beginnings of written German through towards the end of the twelfth century there are only scattered examples suggesting both types of reception, but that towards 1200 we observe a much greater concentration of examples, persisting through the thirteenth century (and beyond). I shall proceed by taking each of the three classes of evidence for the intermediate mode discussed in Chapter 7: first, an explicit reference by means of the double formula; secondly, works with separate pointers to both types of reception, but with no explicit link; thirdly, the weakest case in which we learn merely that a reciter read from the written text to listeners or that the audience heard the text recited to them. For each class we need to establish when the earliest examples can be dated.

With the first class (use of the double formula) we have to wait until about 1150 for our first example in the *Rede vom heiligen Glauben* of Der Arme Hartmann (95, 7ff.).[361] The use of the verb *lesen* suggests that the noun *gesiht* is employed in the sense of reading (as was regularly possible with the verb *sehen*), but since the twofold reception is expressed by a formula composed of verb + noun, rather than verb + verb or noun + noun (as in Latin) we may hesitate to call this earliest example a strict double formula.[362] Even so, it testifies that an author reckoned with two modes of reception in German by the middle of the twelfth century. For examples in the strict sense we have to wait somewhat longer: until the *Gregorius* of Hartmann von Aue in 1187–9 and then, about 1195, in a similar context in his *Armer Heinrich*.[363] These earliest examples are paralleled, around 1195, by the *Lanzelet* of Ulrich von Zatzikhoven and then, 1200–10, by Gottfried's *Tristan*.[364] There follow other cases during the course of the thirteenth century, giving a total frequency of forty-two until about 1300. From this chronological breakdown we may conclude that, apart from an isolated forerunner in the middle of the twelfth century, our examples start only from about 1187. This conclusion cannot be called into question from the other tradition which employs the double formula in German, for it occurs for the first time in charters as late as 1251–4.[365]

The position with the second class (pointers to reading alongside suggestions of hearing) is partly different, partly comparable. It is different in that the earliest examples are more frequent than the solitary case of Der Arme Hartmann and begin much earlier. Here we may include the *Heliand* and Otfrid from the ninth century, Notker around 1000, then Frau Ava and Priester Wernher in the twelfth century.[366] We may now assume a turning-point because with Priester Wernher we have reached 1172, the threshold of court literature, where the examples of the double formula really begin to take off. In tracing this second class beyond Wernher we come next, between 1170 and 1190, to Veldeke's *Eneide*,[367] but we shall see that there are reasons to doubt whether this work may be regarded as a turning-point for this class. This comes instead with the next undoubted examples, the *Lucidarius* (1190–5) and Gottfried's *Tristan* 1200–10).[368] These are followed by a sustained sequence of examples throughout the thirteenth century, giving a total, from the *Heliand* until about 1300, of seventy-one. Since only six come before the *Lucidarius* in 1190–5 we face a situation similar to that with the first class: the overwhelming majority of examples falls in the period beginning towards the end of the twelfth century.

When we come to the third class and its two subgroups we need to proceed with care. It is no longer sufficient to register the earliest example, because such examples do not in themselves indicate the fact, as distinct from the possibility of a twofold reception unless they are borne out by the first or second class in the same work, suggesting that the possibility was realised in practice.

In the first subgroup (the reciter reads from a written text to listeners) we register the following pattern. One isolated example from Otfrid (IV 25, 6: *thie wír hiar lasun fórna*)[369] must be included here, since the reference to the reciter reading to his listeners is confirmed as part of a twofold reception by the fact that Otfrid's work also belongs to the second class of evidence. However, this is not applicable to examples which follow chronologically until a much later date. The *Millstätter Genesis* uses the same formula about 1080,[370] but since this work contains references to listening, but none to reading we have no grounds for regarding 82, 11 as part of a twofold reception, as with Otfrid. The position is even less certain with the *Friedberger Christ* in 1120–30, for the example 29, 2f. is borne out neither by a listening nor by a reading reference. It is therefore unusable for our purposes. Although the next two examples belong to court literature, they cannot be accepted as clearcut evidence. This is true of the *Erec* of Hartmann (7305), because like the *Millstätter Genesis* it is supplemented only by a listening reference, not also by one to reading.[371] The same is true of the *Oberdeutscher Servatius*.[372] Only with Gottfried's *Tristan* do we encounter examples from this first subgroup[373] which are borne out by testimony from the first and second classes. Gottfried is followed by a range of similar cases in the thirteenth century, so that once again we have to wait from the ninth century until about 1200 for this type of reference to become relevant and achieve a breakthrough.

There remains the second subgroup in the third class (the type *hoeren lesen*, the audience hears the text recited to them). The first examples occur in 1170 in Veldeke's *Servatius* and in 1190 (or 1210?) with Herbort von Fritzlar,[374] but since each of these works contains further references only to listening, but not to reading, we can have no certainty that *hoeren lesen* is part of a twofold reception. It is therefore sounder to leave them out of account, which leaves us with the *Lucidarius* in 1190–5 as our earliest evidence, followed by Gottfried's *Tristan* in 1200–10,[375] for these examples are supplemented by references to listening and to reading (and in Gottfried's case by a double formula). Many similar examples follow in the thirteenth century, so that again the decisive turning-point falls just before the end of the twelfth century.

The first conclusion to be drawn from this survey concerns the priority of monastic literature. This is obviously true with the first class (the double formula), for only Der Arme Hartmann comes before court authors such as Hartmann von Aue and Ulrich von Zatzikhoven. In the second class the earliest evidence goes back further, but is still tied to the monastery (the *Heliand*, Otfrid, Notker, Frau Ava, Priester Wernher),[376] before non-monastic examples are attested. In the third class the first subgroup (the reciter reads to listeners) is exemplified first by Otfrid, followed by a small number of unusable examples in the eleventh and twelfth centuries until we reach the first clear case after Otfrid, Gottfried at the beginning of the thirteenth century. Only in the second subgroup of this third class do no monastic examples precede the earliest evidence from court literature. That monastic literature should enjoy priority is not surprising, given the early dominance of the monasteries in literary tradition and the double role played by reading in monastic life: devotional reading by the monk for himself, but also collective listening to the recital of a religious text.[377]

Secondly, in each of the three classes the works which constitute a turning-point all cluster around the same point in time and come from court literature. In the first class this point was represented by Hartmann's *Gregorius* (1187–9), in the second by the *Lucidarius* (1190–5), in the first subgroup of the third class by Gottfried's *Tristan* (1200–10) and in the second subgroup by the *Lucidarius* again. If these three classes together offer criteria for recognising a twofold reception, these dates suggest 1187–1210 as the limits for the first indications of a twofold reception of a vernacular literature for laymen. These limits would not be altered even if a suggested later dating of the *Lucidarius* prologue were to be accepted,[378] for this would simply mean that, in the second class as in the second subgroup of the third class, the *Lucidarius* would have to be replaced by Gottfried's *Tristan* as the earliest example. The timespan 1187–1210 remains unaffected.

Although we have been concerned with a twofold reception, whereas Scholz was occupied with a reading reception, our chronological conclusion corresponds to his suggestion of the decades around 1200.[379] For all that, there is a difference between us because the period 1187–1210 is true only of literature meant for the court and was preceded by examples from literature of the monastery, isolated and scattered though these may have been. Just as the double formula, the explicit indication of a new state of affairs, entered the vernacular long after it had been at home in Latin, so did suggestions of a twofold reception first occur in German monastic literature and only later in lay literature. What is new about court literature (apart from the isolated forerunner, Der Arme Hartmann) is the fact that the explicit, even demonstrative use of the double formula first grows popular here. The transition of lay literature to written form and literate values meant that a formula previously confined to Latin could now be used to assist literary self-awareness in a novel situation.[380]

However great this novelty, we must avoid exaggerating its extent. The acquisition by court literature of a twofold reception previously true of religious literature does not mean that evidence for religious works now ceases. There are pointers to such works still being read and also listened to around 1200 (e.g. Albertus von Augsburg, *Das Leben des heiligen Ulrich*),[381] but also many such works during the thirteenth century. Despite that a case can still be made for regarding the twofold reception as closely connected with court literature. The clustering of indicators of such a reception at the end of the twelfth century concerns at first works of court literature and this literature remains connected with the twofold reception throughout the following century. This is true of the court romance (whether classical or Arthurian in theme or a romance of love and adventure),[382] but also of the so-called court legend.[383] The court epic,[384] court didacticism,[385] and one work of court historiography[386] also belong here. Under these five headings (which belong together, as in the recurrence of Rudolf von Ems under three of them) court literature in this widest sense established itself as a written literature open both to listeners and to the occasional reader.

Here too we have to make two qualifications, concerning the hesitancy with which court literature with a secular theme first claimed for itself the literate dimension hitherto the prerogative of religious literature. When looking in the second class for the earliest example in secular literature we passed over the chronologically first case, Veldeke's *Eneide*, in favour of the *Lucidarius*. The reason was that, although Veldeke refers frequently to a listening reception and once to a reader,[387] this reading reference concerns the countess of Cleves, to whom as an individual reader he lent the manuscript, but then lost it.[388] The reading reception of this work is mentioned only because of the chance theft of the author's text, not as part of his reflection on the different ways in which he expected it to be received, as with later authors who expressly consider this problem. If Veldeke expected that the countess might read his work, he does not refer to this as a possibility which he had in mind while composing it.

Another kind of hesitancy was shown by Hartmann von Aue. Although he has been mentioned under the heading of his two court legends, he could not be adduced for the court romance despite his pioneer role in introducing the Arthurian theme to Germany, since neither romance contains the express indication of a twofold reception found in the legends.[389] His greater readiness to stress a reading reception (alongside listening) for his legends suggests that in this genre he felt safeguarded by the tradition of earlier religious works (most recently by Frau Ava, Der Arme Hartmann, Priester Wernher), but still hesitated to say the same of his secular works. His romances may have made the transition to written form and been addressed to two types of recipient, but Hartmann still shrank from saying this in so many words. For that, with an expressly secular theme, we have to wait until the more radical Gottfried.[390]

(e) Individual reading

In Chapter 5 we touched upon the apparent contradiction between the collective function of medieval literature (delivered orally in public) and the act of reading for oneself in isolation.[391] We now return to this question, asking what possibilities of 'privacy' existed in medieval life and what evidence there is for individual reading for oneself.

In a treatment of privacy in the Middle Ages it has been pointed out that solitude could be seen as negative. In monastic discipline separation from other monks could be imposed as a punishment or as a trial; the solitude of woodlands was the abode of robber knights and criminals, of heretics and, as in the Tristan story, of guilty lovers banished from society.[392] Küsters has stressed that being thrust into solitude was equated with being an outsider, with a *historia calamitatum* from which the victim sought release by attempting to rejoin the community, as Tristan and Isold show in their readiness to return to Marke's court.[393] This is only part of the picture, for there are suggestions that solitude could be regarded neutrally or even positively in the Middle Ages. We may consider this in the two areas for which we have evidence: the gregarious privacy of the monastery, and the conjunction of the public with the private realm in the feudal castle. In each case our concern is to determine how far incipient privacy provided a focus for literacy, making it possible to read in solitude, divorced from the collective situation of an audience listening to a recital.

That solitude had a positive role within the monastery is suggested by the description how Robert count of Flanders, a *persona publica*, temporarily abandons his political functions and enters on the *vita privata* of a Lenten retreat in a monastery, devoting himself to spiritual affairs.[394] More germane to our concern, because of its association with *lectio* in the sense of individual reading, is the evidence for niches of solitude built into the daily programme and into the architecture of monastic communities.[395] In Benedictine houses the wing of the cloister abutting the church usually faced south and enjoyed maximum sunlight, so that alcoves in this wing, containing desks or carrels, provided semi-private opportunities for study and devotional reading.[396] The stress laid by the Dominicans on study also had architectural repercussions. They instituted cells in the upper storey of the cloister, large enough for a bed and a desk for study and devotions, making it possible for the proctor to check that the monks were properly engaged on reading.[397] The Carthusians combined communal with solitary life as hermits living in separate cells and meeting only for worship. Their solution to the need for *lectio* was to build a series of separate abodes around a court (as in an Oxford or Cambridge college), in which each monk spent his time in reading, writing, prayer and contemplation.[398] In such ways the individual reading required of a monk in different orders found architectural expression in the provision of private or semi-private areas for study.[399]

The nearly solitary life of the Carthusians was surpassed by the radical eremitical ideal, for hermits lived in cells, but sought geographical seclusion and maintained only minimal contact with the rest of the world. The *vita solitaria* competed with the coenobitic ideal, especially in the spread of an eremitical movement as a reaction against the dominance of the liturgy and the common life.[400] Hermits resembled monks, however, in their preoccupation with devotional *lectio*, even with the composition of religious literature, as with Petrus Damiani or the suggestion that interpretations of the Song of Songs with regard to the individual soul, rather than the Church at large, are connected with the *vita solitaria*.[401] This equation of literacy with a place for solitude is also characteristic of the *inclusi* of either sex, often recruited from laymen, but in particular from laywomen. As with the hermits, some *inclusi* were well-known because of their writing,[402] amongst whom we may include in vernacular literature Frau Ava herself.[403] That the literacy of these *inclusi* could also embrace individual reading we shall see from the testimony of German literature.

The monastic community and those attached to it therefore found an institutional place for individual reading in its programme, but also an architectural place for the solitary reader (carrel, cell, hermitage, retreat). In the feudal castle an institutional place for literacy was found only with the spread of chanceries beyond the imperial court,[404] but how far this development had architectural consequences, what place the chancery had within the princely residence or whether anyone beyond clerical members of the chancery had access to its facilities largely escapes us. Nonetheless, there are indications that restricted areas of semi-privacy were found at court, where reading for oneself could take place.

One way of providing quasi-privacy was to erect a wooden partition within the great hall, separating the dining area, where the lord sat with his guests, from the private sleeping area.[405] A more permanent provision was to cater for separate areas: a hall for meetings and meals (the equivalent of capitulary and refectory in a monastery), but also a bedroom reserved for the lord and his wife, and a dormitory for servants and children (corresponding to the abbot's dwelling and the monks' dorter), possibly also a *loge*, a place for relaxation and private conversation.[406] This division between a public area and a potentially private one may not be sustainable in every respect,[407] but it is reinforced by the provision, in addition to the bedroom of the lord and his wife, of a separate heatable room for her and her womenfolk, meant for their protection, but also affording a degree of privacy greater than elsewhere in the castle.[408] Even when no place within the castle may be specified, there are indications that it was possible to find a secluded corner in which to enjoy a measure of privacy, as when Gottfried's Blanscheflur seeks solitude for her lament (1170ff.) or for confessing it to another woman (1202ff.).[409] Unlocated though this scene may be, it is tempting to place it in the *kemenâte*, the women's chamber where Blanscheflur could expect more secrecy than elsewhere.[410] It is also tempting to regard the *kemenâte* as the place of withdrawal for women, where they were separated spatially and emotionally from the castle at large and could devote themselves to women's affairs, amongst which the *Sachsenspiegel* included the reading of books (religious or not),[411] as when Constance Fitzgilbert retires to her chamber to read.[412] It was not merely their literacy, but also the possibility of withdrawing from the court (even if this was largely forced upon them by male society) which granted women a separate access to a court literature appealing to their interests, an access as readers in addition to the listening which they shared with court society at large.

Another opportunity for quasi-privacy was given not within the castle building, but in its terrain, namely the intimacy of a garden or orchard, sheltered by walls from the world outside[413] and cut off from the rest of the castle area by a gate which Marke, for example, was able to penetrate because of Brangaene's negligence.[414] In view of the nearly complete privacy which the enclosed castle garden offers the illicit assignations of Tristan and Isold take place here and the antisocial relationship of Mabonagrin and his mistress is located in a garden. Here, as in some corners of the castle building, occasional possibilities of solitude, secrecy and privacy existed, so that we should hesitate to generalise the criticism made of the Thuringian court by Walther von der Vogelweide (20, 3f.) and of castle life at large by Ulrich von Hutten.[415] Dominated by public din and turmoil the medieval castle may often have been, but not so much as to render the privacy required by the individual reader impossible.

To see whether such opportunities were used by the medieval reader we turn to the internal evidence of literary texts, first to the terms *heimlîche* and *heimlîchaere*. We saw that Gottfried referred to *des küneges heimlîchaere* at Marke's court, translated by Hatto as 'the King's secretary'. This association of a confidential, secret area with literacy is suggested to us by the modern term 'secretary', whereas *heimlîchaere* or *secretarius* implied confidentiality ('Privy Councillor') rather than literacy.[416] To cross the bridge from confidentiality to literacy we had to wait until Ulrich von Lichtenstein, who took his *schrîber* aside into a private room (*heinlîch*), so that he might read a written text (*büechelîn*) to him in secrecy (*verholne*).[417] This association of Ulrich's *schrîber* with a private room or *heinlîch* makes it likely that he is to be equated with the *heimlîchaere* at Marke's court,[418] but that with Ulrich he is seen in his literate function, as a scribe also employed as a reader. This association was not confined to professional literacy, for Ulrich describes how his lady withdrew to read a letter which he sent her (99, 21ff.).[419] From this we may conclude not merely that the professional *litteratus* had access to a private room at court (used as the chancery?), but also that a noblewoman could withdraw into solitude for reading, repeating for the German language area what was said of Constance Fitzgilbert in the Anglo-Norman realm. We now have to ask what other evidence there is for privacy used for the act of reading, proceeding from 'small-scale privacy' (only two or three persons are involved) to privacy proper (only one person reads).

That the conditions of medieval life could provide solitude for literacy can be shown by the counterpart to our concern, by suggestions that someone wishing to write could withdraw apart for that purpose. This is said in the *Laubacher Barlaam* of a king remaining alone in his private room in order to write (14972ff.: *in sîner kemenâte*; *er eine beleip*) and also of Josaphat in the *Barlaam und Josaphat* of Rudolf von Ems (14665ff.: *hiez sich lâzen eine*; *in sîner kamern er beleip*). Similarly, the prose *Lancelot* presents the queen requesting parchment and ink from a scribe, then withdrawing into a *camer* to write her letter (II 557, 25ff.), whilst Johann von Würzburg shows his hero demanding writing material, then requesting the provider to leave his bedroom while he writes his letter (*Wilhelm von Österreich* 6674ff.).[420] For these authors to suggest writing in private as a possibility implies that reading could equally well be done in solitude.

A sketch of family intimacy, in which entertainment is provided by one person's literacy, is given by Hartmann in his *Iwein* when he sketches a daughter reading aloud to her parents in the near privacy of a garden belonging to a castle (6455ff.; cf. 6436: *boumgarten*).[421] The number of people involved is smaller (and therefore the degree of intimacy is higher) when one person reads to only one other, as in the case of his *schrîber* reading to Ulrich von Lichtenstein in his *heinlich*. A similar situation is depicted by Wirnt von Grafenberg in *Wigalois*, where the daughter of the king of Persia is read to by a handmaiden (2711ff. – privacy is suggested by this taking place in a tent) and when Ebernand von Erfurt describes how Kunigunde is read to by her handmaiden (*Heinrich und Kunigunde* 3502ff. – privacy is implied by this taking place in the queen's bedroom).

Even though two persons may still be involved, we move one step closer to an individual reading to himself, when one no longer recites to the other, but both together read the text to themselves. We find this in Bruder Hermann's *Leben der Gräfin Iolande von Vianden* in a scene where Iolande reads her prayers (presumably from a prayer-book)[422] together with another nun in the convent (2216 – the privacy of devotional reading is brought out by *in einer stat verborgen* and by *heimelich*). A secular counterpart to this is found in the Manesse manuscript, where the illustration of the poet Waltram depicts two lovers reading together a text identified as the *Lanzelet* of Ulrich von Zatzikhoven.[423] Not merely in their choice of reading-matter, but also in their joint reading in lovers' seclusion, this pair represents a parallel to the scene of Paolo and Francesca reading the romance of Lancelot in Dante.[424]

Examples like these, no matter how restricted the circle, do not yet touch upon what concerns us, the individual reading to himself. We find examples of this with religious and secular reading.

Religious reading for one's own edification may be from a psalter, a prayer-book, a book of hours, or a religious book of unspecified nature. In each case the personal nature of devotional reading is reinforced by the solitude of the reader. The psalter is read under such conditions, for example, in *Mai und Beaflor* 22, 7ff., where seclusion (*eine* is used twice) is provided by a room (*gadem*), presumably set apart and guaranteeing the peace and quiet (*sunder kradem*) necessary for inward concentration. This last phrase suggests that in a feudal castle it was possible to find a secluded corner and escape the hubbub of which Walther complained in Thuringia. The psalter could be read with a greater promise of being undisturbed by those who had withdrawn as recluses. This is true of Sigune in Wolfram's *Parzival* who reads the psalter to herself while immured as an *inclusa* (437, 29ff.) whose *klôse* is situated in the depths of a forest (435, 2ff.). A *clusenerinne* who reads her psalter in the prose *Lancelot* (I 202, 17ff.) may not dwell in such wilds as Sigune (her *cluse* is adjacent to a church), but her only link with the outside world is a window through which she sees into the church. For all practical purposes her psalter reading is in seclusion.

A prayer-book can be the object of private reading, as in the *Passional* (III 195, 60ff.), where the secluded nature of prayer is underlined by *alleine* and *heimelichen*, or in the *Väterbuch* (417ff.), where *alleine* is again used and *mit inneclicher andaht* suggests the inwardness which solitude makes possible. The prayer-book is specified as a book of hours in Veldeke's *Servatius* (567f.): we may not be told the precise place where privacy was found, but *ane eine side* suggests that it existed.[425]

Religious reading-matter of unspecified nature may be in question with Trevrizent's life as a hermit in Wolfram's *Parzival*, for of the abode of the *einsidel* (456, 5) in the forest it is said: *dâ inne was / sîniu buoch dar an der kiusche las*.[426] If *buoch* refers to one book, it is identical with the psalter which the hermit consults (460, 25f.), but if more than one, he must have possessed other religious texts for reading in his retreat. In the *Passional* (III 223, 36f. and 226, 98f.) individual monastic *lectio* is referred to in the case of St Benedict, but in the *celle*, therefore in isolation from the community. In his *Servatius* Veldeke underlines the saint's religiosity by seeing it as devotional reading: we are not told what books he read, but it is clear that he read in solitude (913f.). Such seclusion has a further point, for it means that he deliberately isolated himself from the collective life of the court (912, 915), a rejection that gives point to the solitude of his religious reading.

This last example, although it concerns religious reading-matter, shows that it was possible for someone who should have participated in the social life of the court to find privacy for individual reading, to effect an escape from the noise and distractions which Walther implied was impossible in Thuringia. In secular literature we find this possibility in connection with reading a book, a letter or a love-letter.

Reading a book in isolation from others is something so natural as not to necessitate further comment when Konrad von Würzburg describes Wirnt von Grafenberg reading a romance to himself *in einer kemenâten* in which he spent the whole day in communion with the book (*Der Welt Lohn* 52ff.).[427] In his *Alexandreis* Ulrich von Etzenbach sketches how a *meister* (indicating his status as a *litteratus*) seized the opportunity while others were asleep of reading *an sîner kamer* (23450ff.). A room apart combines with the absence of distractions from others to assist uninterrupted reading (which is then disturbed by the rival attractions of a woman the reader notices in the garden and from whom he has to wrench his eyes back to his book). In the *Göttweiger Trojanerkrieg* Samlon *der wise* (probably another indication of literate status) read a book of astronomy (318ff.), again in the seclusion of a room apart (*an ain kemenatten*).

The same is involved when what is read is a letter, for in addition to the public reading of letters in the Middle Ages[428] there are cases where the recipient, especially if able to read himself, withdraws into privacy to learn the content of a letter. In the *Jüngerer Titurel* King Arthur reads a letter *tougen* (2480, 1),[429] whilst in the *Alexandreis* of Ulrich von Etzenbach a letter confirms the reliability of the messenger who brought it (20271ff.) when the recipient reads it for herself, but retires *an ir heimelîche* for that purpose.

We may not be surprised to encounter more examples of private letter-reading in the case of love-letters, but there is a danger of regarding these from a modern point of view, ignoring a medieval peculiarity which they contain. We know why Ulrich von Lichtenstein, receiving a letter from his lady and wishing to keep its content private, withdraws into a room apart (*heinlîch*): unable to read himself, he depends on a *litteratus* to read aloud to him,[430] which must take place out of public earshot. The position is not so clearcut with the *Meleranz* of Der Pleier. Here, too, the hero receives a letter from his lady and withdraws together with the messenger into what is put forward as a private area where they can be alone.[431] This resemblance to the situation presented by Ulrich cannot be for the same reason, for it is made clear that Meleranz read the letter himself.[432] We are left unenlightened not about why he takes the messenger into his *kamer* (to question him about his lady, 2862f., and receive an oral message, 2846ff.), but about the need for him to read the letter for himself in a private room. This question remains unanswered when ladies (about whose ability to read we need have no doubts) receive similar letters and likewise retire into privacy. This is so with the lady of Ulrich von Lichtenstein on two occasions where, after she has entered her *heinlîch*, she reads the letter herself and is not, like her correspondent, dependent on someone reading out to her.[433] The same is true of a scene in *Die Minnelehre* of Johann von Konstanz (1230ff.): here too the lady reads for herself, but only after having gone to *ain kamer klaine*.

From these examples we learn that the possibility of finding a secluded corner in a feudal castle existed and that such isolation was used for reading (and writing), but they do not tell us why the letters had to be read there. We might imagine that the need for privacy arose from the erotic content of the letter, from the recipient's wish for emotional communion with the distant beloved. That fails to account for those cases where the missive is not a love-letter and it cannot be the whole explanation of a passage to be considered. It occurs in the *Wilhelm von Österreich* of Johann von Würzburg when Agly proposed to read for herself a letter (9976ff.) and hence dismissed her ladies from the room (9983f.). The author says that this was because she wished to keep its content privy to herself and not reveal it to others (9985f.). Her action and the use of the verb *gesagen* imply that she read aloud to herself, a practice of which we are informed on another occasion (6970f.).[434] What is made explicit only here can be applied to the other examples: individual reading by a *litteratus* shares an oral dimension with the scribe reading out aloud to the illiterate Ulrich von Lichtenstein. The practice of reading aloud (to others or to oneself)[435] made withdrawal into a *kamer* necessary if a secret was to be preserved, but these examples also illustrate that the search for a private corner need not have been in vain, that the public realm was not omnipresent.

Over the last few pages we too have withdrawn from the public realm of recital before an assembled audience in favour of more intimate occasions: one person reading to two others or to one, two people reading together, one person reading alone. A last stage in the withdrawal of the individual reader is the act of silent reading, the kind of reading not practised by Agly in *Wilhelm von Österreich*. The complete internalisation which reading in silence represents need not be present in Latin terms like *sibi legere or per se scrutari*,[436] for these suggest individual reading, but leave it open whether this was silent or aloud. For that reason a prescription in the Benedictine Rule (expressed by *sibi legere* or a comparable construction in German)[437] is of no use to us, for the recommendation to read to oneself so as not to disturb others could imply reading *sotto voce*, rather than complete silence. More telling are such phrases as *tacite legere* or *legere in silentio*,[438] but the evidence for German counterparts is strikingly meagre, certainly up to 1300.

A dubious example comes from Bruder Hermann's *Leben der Gräfin Iolande von Vianden*, for the private devotional reading *à deux* attested for this work cannot be extended to silent reading by one person when brother Welter reads a letter sent him by Iolande (4964): *sy sante im einen bryf. er las / verholen und al stille / ir herze und iren wille, / irn kumber und iren swêre*). His reading is in secret (*verholen*) and in private, but there is no reason why *al stille* should not mean the same ('im stillen'), no necessity for it to imply silent reading.[439] The position is explicit with a passage in the *Passional* (the only example of silent reading mentioned in a German text before 1300). Significantly, the example concerns Augustine, to whom we owe a description of the novelty of Ambrose's silent reading and who used the same method on his conversion.[440] Augustine's reading is intensely inward (III 433, 70ff.), a concentration made possible by the silence of his reading (III 433, 86: *der gute man alstille saz / swigende ob dem buche*). Although *alstille* here could mean 'secretly', as with Bruder Hermann, the addition of *swigende* is a clear pointer to silent reading. It may be that silent reading is expressed unequivocally here because Augustine, like Ambrose, was known to have practised it, but even if we take it as an indication of medieval practice it is the only example to occur in the five centuries covered by our survey.[441]

If the practice of reading silently had spread by the fourteenth and fifteenth centuries from the library and the university lecture-room[442] to an ever larger part of the lay population, it has to be stressed that there is only one German-language piece of evidence beyond all doubt before 1300 and that the period after this awaits investigation. Whether in complete silence or not, there are indications enough that by this time the individual reader was a phenomenon to be reckoned with.[443]

CONCLUSIONS

(f) Cleric and layman, Latin and vernacular

In Chapter 2 we followed the emergence of written German from the shadow of written Latin, stressing the difficulties which it faced even with the Carolingian renaissance of writing, and we have seen that these attempts were followed by 150 years in which German gave way to Latin. Even after its re-emergence in the eleventh century written German still largely depended on Latin sources, Latin rhetoric and poetics,[444] and the services of clerics trained in Latin, a position which remained in force through the rest of the Middle Ages and beyond.[445] For the Middle Ages we must talk of bilingualism, of a cultural symbiosis between laymen and clerics, vernacular and Latin,[446] oral and written. This conjunction was not always untroubled, especially when laymen sought to make themselves independent.

The first stirrings of rivalry between laymen and clerics can be detected in the twelfth century, when laymen made their first attempt to break loose from the cultural tutelage of the clergy.[447] To this attempt the Church reacted by preaching a rejection of worldly autonomy or by emphasising the makebelieve in the laymen's attempt.[448] More radical were moves to deny the laymen any competence in intellectual matters. Der Henneberger (most probably with a clerical education)[449] maintains that the secrets of the stars and the heavens, difficult enough for a wise cleric to comprehend, cannot possibly be grasped by the foolish, uneducated layman.[450] The layman was intellectually disadvantaged because of his illiteracy and ignorance of Latin, still almost exclusively the vehicle for transmitting knowledge.[451] How far the cleric regarded the layman as debarred from literacy because of his lack of Latin we have seen in what Walter Map said of Valdes and his heretical followers, denying them literate status because of inability to read Latin.[452]

Walter Map also expresses a cleric's scorn for vernacular literature when he observes that, by contrast with Latin works like the *Aeneid* celebrating classical heroes, only the trifling of minstrels in vulgar rhymes celebrates in his day the deeds of Charles the Great and Pippin.[453] This jeering contrast was made at a time when the *Chanson de Roland* and other works were well known, and Walter, by also discounting the innovation of putting vernacular works (including the chansons de geste) into written form, has suppressed the voice of vernacular written literature by ignoring its existence,[454] by refusing it a written status as much as he denied Valdes an ability to read. Similarly, Arnold von Lübeck, writing a Latin version of Hartmann's *Gregorius*, said apologetically in his prologue that it was not his habit to read such things.[455] Arnold did not go as far as Walter and deny his German source literate status altogether, but his contempt for vernacular scribblings is clear. For reasons which go beyond professional rivalry and include the cultural pretensions of Latinity the Archipoeta expressed disgust at seeing preference given to the ravings of *mimi* rather than to his own work, the product of a learned *poeta*.[456] This sense of distance felt by those with a clerical education from vernacular literature went beyond such individual examples, however, if we accept the suggestion made by Knapp, pointing to a boycott of Arthurian themes by *clerici litterati* in their almost total refusal to adopt them in Latin form,[457] amounting to a denial of what Walter Map would have regarded as literate rank to themes predominant in the court literature of laymen.

Not merely the Arthurian theme, but also that of love in vernacular literature was an object of criticism by *clerici*, in the sense of religious scruples by ecclesiastics, and also because of its unreal utopianism. Schnell has interpreted the idealisation of love in the court lyric as betraying a need to justify its concept of love with regard to the different attitude in medieval Latin love-poetry of clerical provenance,[458] whilst Karnein has presented the *De Amore* of Andreas Capellanus as composed against the wishful thinking of vernacular love-poetry.[459] Something similar emerges from Huber's analysis of the relationship between Alanus ab Insulis and Gottfried von Strassburg.[460] Whereas the former regarded the paradoxes of love negatively as perversions, using them as the object of his criticism of the layman's culture of love, Gottfried affirmed these paradoxes as a positive ideal.[461] That the target of Alanus was the layman's culture in its literary form is clear when Natura refers to the delivery of works in the manner of a minstrel for which the learned cleric shows his contempt by likening them to pap fit only for children.[462] Alanus could only have seen Gottfried, writing in the vernacular, as one of the *ioculatores* whose works he regarded as intellectually inferior, whilst Gottfried, from the point of view of laymen, must have appeared as one who unlocked the treasures of Latin culture to those without direct access to it. Whereas one cleric, Alanus, saw these treasures tied to Latin and looked down on vernacular endeavours, the other cleric, Gottfried, employed the vernacular as a means of enriching the layman's culture by borrowings from the clerical realm.[463]

Not merely the themes of vernacular literature (Arthurian chivalry, love), but also language (vernacular as opposed to Latin) could therefore be a bone of contention between these two cultural worlds. A letter by Philip of Harvengt to count Henry of Champagne praises the count for his command of Latin on the grounds that anyone confined to the vulgar tongue is tied to the dullness of a donkey.[464] It has been suggested that this was more than a broadside against the *illitterati* at the count's court, that it was also directed at poets who composed in French (including Chrétien himself), at those who translated from Latin into French, granting the *quasi litterati* an inadequate access to the originals.[465] This passage reveals a division within the ranks of the court clerics: between those who claimed that intellectual standards demanded composition in Latin and those who saw their task as mediators, between an Archipoeta or an Andreas on the one hand and a Chrétien or a Gottfried on the other.

Against this background we may set complaints about the deficiencies of German as a vehicle of written communication. When the author of *Moriz von Craun* complains (1778) that *tiuschiu zunge diu ist arn*, he has in mind his difficulties in rendering a French rhymed source into German, but behind this there stands the view of those clerically educated that German as an intellectual instrument fell short of Latin.[466] We have seen an example of this when Otfrid complains of the unmanageability of the Frankish tongue in writing, forcing decisions on him which are *extra usum latinitatis*.[467] That he nonetheless composed a written work in that language should not tell against his consciousness of the obstacles which stood in the way of a written vernacular. The same applies to the *Pilatus* towards the end of the twelfth century, whose author may express the hope of mastering his linguistic problems with the help of the Holy Ghost,[468] but only after making it clear that his difficulties reside in the language he uses (1ff.). Since the source of this work, like Otfrid's, was Latin, the difficulty may have lain in translating from one language to another (as with *Moriz von Craun*), but a comparable complaint suggests that the shortcomings were those of German by comparison with Latin (*tiutschiu zunge ist vil armer an dehein ding ze bescheidenne denne latine*).[469] The conviction that these shortcomings were tied to the vernacular, rendering it unfit for purposes attainable in Latin, may lie behind the attacks launched by clerics against the author of *Das Passional* for making use of German, even though the nature of the Teutonic Order made works in the vernacular more desirable than in other orders.[470] That criticisms could be voiced even despite this is a measure of clerical suspicion about using the vernacular at all.

The difference in cultural and linguistic ranking accorded to the two traditions can also be seen whenever clerics point to the layman's inability to understand the quality of the Latin tradition. This can take the form of saying that laymen, restricted to their mother tongue, cannot understand literature in Latin, the *lingua clerici*.[471] The Archipoeta goes further in showing his sense of belonging to an élite versed in Latin when he dismisses laymen as uncomprehending outsiders.[472] Walter Map advises Giraldus Cambrensis to use the vernacular for his works in view of the inability of many, especially princes, to understand Latin, so that more profit was to be expected from using the vernacular which the laymen at court could understand.[473]

Even when the literature concerned might not use Latin as its medium, but was informed by a knowledge of Latin rhetoric transferred to the vernacular, it could still be claimed that only clerics were able to appreciate it. This is made clear by Hugo von Trimberg concerning the reception of the works of Konrad von Würzburg (for whom a clerical education and knowledge of Latin can be assumed).[474] Konrad followed the tradition of Latin rhetoric in his German writings,[475] but as a result of this fusion of Latin artistry with German text laymen failed to understand it and were dismissed as fools for scorning what they could not comprehend.[476] By contrast, educated clerics were capable of appreciating Konrad at his true worth.[477] This statement possesses an importance which goes far beyond this individual case and reinforces what we saw about the inability of anyone without a Latin education to appreciate the artistry of a clerically trained author.[478] Even though Hugo does not refer to the laymen in Konrad's audience as readers, no literacy in the sense of simply being able to read would have qualified them for this task.

Literate poets with a clerical background composing in the vernacular sometimes sought to redraw the dividing line between illiterate and vernacular on the one hand and literate and Latin on the other. By doing this they hoped to dissociate themselves from the minstrels scorned by Walter Map and Alanus ab Insulis and draw closer to their colleagues who composed in Latin.[479] Those Latin poets who ran the greatest danger of being associated with minstrels, the wandering scholars or *clerici vagi*, pressed their literacy and education as qualifications distinguishing them from unlettered *ioculatores*.[480] Like the Archipoeta, jealous of the preference which *mimi* could find, they criticised those who favoured minstrels over literate poets.[481] Already in the first Arthurian romance Chrétien distinguished his written work, the result of a clerical training, from the worthless oral products of itinerant minstrels.[482] A similar realignment is found in the Provençal lyric, where literate trobadors stressed the distance between themselves and *mimi*.[483] With authors who are educationally *clerici* the line between lay and clerical literature was potentially redrawn, allowing some works meant for laymen to claim the intellectual kudos granted to those destined for clerics.

The result was a differentiation among authors at court which corresponds to the growing divisions within the audience which we have already observed.[484] Amongst authors we find on the least ambitious educational level illiterate oral poets still active in genres such as heroic literature from whom the other classes of authors were at pains to keep their distance. Next came literate poets like Chrétien who, by performing orally in the vernacular, stood dangerously close to the minstrels, but who implied their clerical status by emphasising the literate nature of their works. Finally, clerical poets in Latin claimed an élite position which, by the gulf they stressed between Latin and vernacular, they were reluctant to share with their colleagues in the vernacular. Rivalry between these groups and attempts to shift the boundaries between them in favour of the group to which one belonged made the literary scene one of growing complexity, just as the audience at court came to be composed of illiterate laymen, literate laymen whose ability to read was restricted to the vernacular, and literate Latinate clerics. On both sides, amongst authors and within the audience, literacy acted as a catalyst for a variety of changes.

The growth of lay literacy (with authors writing for a lay audience and with some members of that audience) brought about an irruption of lay concerns into a literate field which had hitherto been the preserve of clerics. Laymen now come of age culturally, commence their escape from the inferior status to which illiteracy had confined them and proclaim their independence of the tutelage which the clerical monopoly of literacy had imposed upon them, so that the development we have been tracing may be seen as one of lay emancipation.[485]

The possible connection between literacy and liberty was known to the Middle Ages and earlier, since if literacy is regarded as a form of ideology through which power is constructed[486] it is indirectly linked with the liberty which power confers. Already in classical Greece written law was held to be a guardian of justice and with Euripides Theseus contrasted tyranny with a free city possessing a body of laws, saying that with written law justice was the same for weak and wealthy alike.[487] Legal freedom may have helped citizens to uphold their rights; it did not of course guarantee the establishment of freedom, although it made it possible.

This connection between freedom and literacy survived through the Middle Ages. Walter Map maintained a link between free birth (*liber*) and the literate disciplines of the *artes liberales*, arguing that only men of free birth had a right to study these arts and warning noblemen who neglected to educate their sons that men of unfree birth were availing themselves of this road to wealth and power for their sons.[488] Another argument rests on the medieval etymology which derived the word for 'book' from the liberty of the reader: *liber a libertate legencium*.[489] This depends on the same consideration as with Walter Map (*quia olim solis liberis studium legendi dabatur*), but must have appealed to medieval *litterati* for reasons which go beyond noble birth. They could now argue that reading makes a man free: for Konrad von Hirsau it liberates him from the cares of this world (*dictus autem liber est a liberando, quia qui vacat lectioni sepe solvit mentem a curis et vinculis mundi*), with an access to Prudentius it frees from error (... *quia nos liberat ab errore*).[490]

The clerical authors of such statements had clerical readers of Latin texts in mind, but Walter Map's warning to secular aristocrats to educate their sons shows that lay readers could be envisaged, whilst court literature suggests that some of these laymen could be readers of vernacular texts. For them reading brought an emancipation from the clerical domination of literate culture. This is a danger which Walter Map saw as a threat to the Church hierarchy from Valdensian laymen.[491] What he said of these heretics we may apply to educated laymen at large: their literate status enabled them to begin to rival clerics on their field of literacy and liberated them from their previous inferior position.

What we have been considering in the field of literacy is part of a much wider development in the late Middle Ages. The distinction between *clericus* and *laicus* was not merely the educational one with which we have been concerned, but also ecclesiological and political.[492] In the former sphere a pronounced clericalism argued an identification of the Church with the clergy, against which William of Ockham reacted with emphasis on laymen as well as clerics. In the latter realm the intellectual superiority claimed by the clergy led to demands for papal sovereignty even in the secular sphere, demands which were attacked by William of Ockham and by Marsilius of Padua on behalf of an autonomy of politics independent of religion. These developments resemble our problem, for all amount to a declericalisation of their respective sphere: of the conception of the Church, of politics, and of literate culture.[493]

Rivalry between the cultural worlds of the clergy and the laity presupposes contact between them, even interpenetration. The theme of the last few pages is the negative aspect of the symbiosis of these two worlds, confirming rather than disproving their coexistence and interplay throughout the Middle Ages. We have come across this coexistence under four main headings. First, amongst the historical factors in the rise of vernacular written literature we registered movements which brought the clergy and laymen into close contact, even rivalry or opposition.[494] Secondly, in considering vernacular literacy we saw that various social types exemplified contact between clerics and laymen, common ground on which they met, interacted and even fused.[495] Thirdly, the context of reception also revealed many cases where clergy and laity were in contact,[496] whilst, lastly, we saw that the concept of fiction in the Arthurian romance arose out of the meeting of the spoken with the written word.[497]

The creative effects of this prolonged coexistence can be shown with reference to three authors who may be seen as turning-points in the history of German medieval literature. Otfrid signals the beginning, producing the first book devoted to a work in German, but in many respects the two cultural worlds met in this work: it was meant to be read, but also to be heard; it was destined for clerics and for laymen, for the Latinate and for those who knew only the vernacular; it was intended for the monastic community, but also the imperial court.[498] A second turning-point is the *Ezzolied*, the first work to close the silent period of 150 years. Whether it was meant for Gunther's court or for a pilgrimage to the Holy Land, clerics and laymen were brought together on either occasion;[499] Gunther's Bamberg encouraged oral heroic tradition in German, but was also the seat of a learned Latin culture and thus brought these two traditions together again after the Carolingian period;[500] the style of the poem likewise contains elements from vernacular tradition alongside learned ones from the *ars rhetorica*.[501] Lastly, Hartmann von Aue, as the author of the first Arthurian romance in Germany, constitutes a third turning-point. He was also the first author to describe himself as a *miles* and as *litteratus*; he confronted an audience of laymen with an expressly literate work, based on knowledge of medieval rhetoric and poetics, and following the lead of the clerically educated Chrétien.[502] Even where Hartmann did not depend on Chrétien's model, in his *Klage-Büchlein*, he combined the theme of love from the vernacular literature of laymen with learned clerical features.[503]

The interplay between the two cultures persists through the Middle Ages and demonstrates its productive force at these decisive points in literary history. The problem of literacy and the reception of vernacular literature is therefore part of the overall question of the symbiosis of clergy and laity. It is not surprising that the most important of the three modes of reception was the intermediate one, the area where this symbiosis was at home and could develop its cultural influence to the full. In this sense it can be said that the most important part of the title of this book is the word 'and'.

APPENDIX

Middle High German 'lesen' = 'to narrate, recount, tell'

An ambiguity similar to that which dissatisfied John of Salisbury with Latin *legere*[1] is also to be found in medieval vernaculars. Thus, MHG *lesen* can be used of reading a text aloud to someone else, as in Gottfried's *Tristan* (230: *wan swâ man noch gehoeret lesen / ir triuwe, ir triuwen reinekeit*),[2] but can also denote an individual reading alone, as in Gottfried's work again (243: *Ein hêrre in Parmenîe was, / der jâre ein kint, als ich ez las*), so early in the narrative that Gottfried cannot refer to what he has already read out to his listeners. Instead, the context alludes to what he learned from his source (245f.) and we learn that Gottfried found this with Thomas (326ff.), who had learned it by reading his own sources. The verb *lesen* is therefore used of two complementary activities: an author reciting his text to an audience, but also the reader's reception of a text.

In addition, a third meaning has for long been recognised, summed up by Benecke, Müller and Zarncke: '*ich lise* ist nicht selten vollkommen gleichbedeutend mit unserem "ich sage, erzähle und ähnlichen wörtern" und darf daher durchaus nicht durch "lesen" übersetzt werden'.[3] Lexer therefore registers three usages for MHG *lesen*: 'lesen', 'vorlesen', 'sagen, erzählen, berichten',[4] and is followed by Scholz: 'lesen', 'vorlesen', 'sagen, erzählen'.[5] An example of this third meaning occurs in Gottfried when Isold warns Marke of the consequences of banishing Tristan, of what people will say in conversation or in gossip (14125: *sô wirt des maeres vil gelesen*).[6] In Gottfried's *Tristan* we therefore find all the three meanings attributed to MHG *lesen*. This semantic uncertainty illustrates how careful we must be in interpreting our evidence.

Our concern is with the first two meanings of the verb: whereas Scholz concentrated on the individual reader, we are equally concerned with the possible listener. In this Appendix we are not dealing with the difference between these two types of reading (aloud to others, aloud or silently to oneself), but with the distinction between them and the third meaning, for reading of either kind cannot be assumed where this is present. On those occasions where Scholz deals with *lesen* applied to the author's relationship to his audience he sees it in this third meaning: the reading which is thereby excluded is the act of the reciter reading his text aloud to an audience.

The meaning 'sagen, erzählen' is largely confined to three contexts: educational, liturgical and devotional. In each a complication is created by the possible role of memory alongside reading. In the educational context pupils learned by rote, but were also confronted with writing (book or writing tablet), just as the teacher may have had material in his memory, but also relied on a text. Within the liturgy laymen were expected to know short catechetical texts by heart, whilst the priest, even if he knew longer texts from regular use, had liturgical books as a prompt. In devotional literature shorter texts may have been known by heart, but longer ones were for reading. In discussing these contexts we shall look first at cases where writing and/or reading are explicitly involved, i.e. the possibility of either of the first two meanings given by Lexer and Scholz. We then turn to cases where writing is not mentioned, where it is uncertain that the text was read, but often equally uncertain whether the meaning of *lesen* must be 'sagen, erzählen'.

MIDDLE HIGH GERMAN 'LESEN' = 'TO NARRATE, RECOUNT, TELL'

Under the educational heading two usages are present: *lesen* can mean 'to teach, instruct', but equally 'to learn, study'. These usages are not peculiar to German, for in discussing the ambiguity of Latin John of Salisbury mentioned *docentis et discentis exercitium* as one of the usages of *lectio*, just as Hugh of St Victor distinguishes *docentis, discentis* from the individual reader.[7]

Lesen meaning 'to teach, instruct' is a specialised usage of *lesen* meaning 'to read aloud to others'. When Hugh of St Victor defines the teacher's activity as *lego librum illi* these words could be applied to a recital from a written text to listeners, as in the *lesen* + dative construction.[8] In this usage *lesen* is the equivalent of modern German 'vorlesen' and survives in academic German in 'Er liest mittelhochdeutsche Literatur', said of the lecturer.

When MHG *lesen* occurs in a context of formal instruction together with a reference to writing or literacy teaching is conceived on the basis of a text, by the teacher reading aloud from writing. Writing can be implied by *buoch*, as in *Der Busant* (89: *Dâ der schuole meister saz / und den jungen schuolern las / Ein buoch*) or Bruder Philipp's *Marienleben* (4811f.). The reference can also be to *buochstaben*, as in the *Alexander* of Rudolf von Ems (1362: *der buochstaben im vor las, / ein meister hiez Polinîcus*) or to *schrift*, as with the *Gottes Zukunft* of Heinrich von Neustadt (5118ff.) or *Alexius F* (152ff.). The teaching can be of the highly literate type of the seven liberal arts (translated by Notker as *bûohlist*),[9] as in the *Weltchronik* of Rudolf von Ems (15767: *da man sit lerte unde las / der sibin liste hohe kunst*) or of only one of these arts, as in *Das Passional* (III 418, 71: *der an schriften wise / mit meisterlichem prise / rethoricam in konde lesen*).

Christ's teaching, as reported in the gospels, can be depicted anachronistically as based on a written text, probably in view of what the Middle Ages regarded as the written tradition of the gospels which handed down that teaching. Examples are the *Barlaam und Josaphat* of Rudolf von Ems (3351: *Dô got mensche durch uns was / unt uns des vater lêre las*) and similar allusions by Heinrich von Hesler in the *Evangelium Nicodemi* (2476) or in *Die Erlösung* (4405ff.).

Lesen can also be used with the meaning 'to teach' without an immediate indication that writing or reading is involved. This need not exclude teaching by reading from something written, as Rudolf von Ems implies in his *Weltchronik* in reporting of the astronomy taught by Jonicus (1183: *die kunst er da lerte und las*). Quite apart from astronomy's place within the seven liberal arts (it is therefore a *bûohlist*), this follows a reference to the written nature of what was taught (1177f.) and when Philo in the same context is described as *ouh ein reht buoch meister* (1186) this implies the same of Jonicus. But for these references v. 1183 could have been taken to suggest teaching without reading from a book. Similar caution is necessary when *Das Passional* refers to Augustine as a teacher (III 417, 70: *wander under siner hant / genuge hete, den er las*), for the written basis of this teaching has to be supplied by what is said of his instruction in rhetoric (III 418, 71, quoted above). Such cases need to be borne in mind, without proof either way being possible, on other occasions where *lesen* is used of teaching. Examples are: *Virginal* (509, 4: *wâ sint ir ze schuole gewesen? / hât iu der tiuvel vor gelesen?*), Ottokar's *Österreichische Reimchronik* (8813ff.), the *Väterbuch* (31575f.) or the gnomic teaching referred to by Walther von der Vogelweide (122, 24: *Ein meister las*).[10] Only in this last group is it possible (but no more than possible) that *lesen* meant teaching without a written text, 'to say, tell, explain' rather than 'to read'.

The other function of *lesen* in an educational context ('to learn, study') is also a semantic specialisation, from 'to read to oneself', for the pupil with a text in front of him is in the same position as an individual reader. An academic survival of this usage is found in modern English, as in: 'He is reading Modern Languages at Cambridge.' Internal pointers suggest that, even in a period relatively short of written material, pupils could read in the act of learning, that writing in some form was available to them. Notker refers to his pupils as *lectores*, for whom the visual dimension of reading is stressed when he guides them from text to diagram for clarification.[11] If to understand the text they must switch attention from his translation to the Latin text this illustrates their activity as readers,[12] just as the *Murbacher Hymnen*, likewise for the monastery school, imply a vertical movement of the reader's eyes from Latin text to interlinear translation and back again.[13] Such testimony is later borne out in other ways: an illustration of a Paris disputation from the second half of the twelfth century shows the pupil with an open book,[14] while the picture of the Schulmeister von Esslingen in the Manesse manuscript shows pupils as well as teacher with a text in front of him.[15] It is irrelevant whether pupils always had access to the same text as their teacher (only feasible with the book revolution in university studies around 1200)[16] or had to make notes on a writing tablet: in either case the process of learning could involve reading.

Berthold von Regensburg sees the joint act of reading and learning in association with books (*Predigten* I 19, 11: . . . *zwei gróziu buoch, dâ wir an lesen unde lernen*). If the same is attributed to illiterate laymen in a metaphorical sense (I 48, 23ff.), this derives its force from the conjunction of reading, learning and a book in the literal sense. Ulrich von Zatzikhoven sees knowledge as coming from reading books (*Lanzelet* 7182ff.), where *lesen* suggests not merely reading, but even more the acquisition of knowledge.

With *lesen* meaning 'to teach' a written text could be implied without being expressly mentioned. The same applies to the meaning 'to learn', as with the *Alexander* of Rudolf von Ems with regard to the hero's education (2174: *und er ze schuole gelas*), for we have seen that Alexander's schooling was based on literacy (1352ff.). In his case to read at school amounts to learning from books, even though these may not be mentioned. Apart from such examples it is uncertain whether books are involved, whether *lesen* means more than 'to learn'. Gottfried's *Tristan* refers to the medical skills of Morholt's sister (7076: *swaz sô dîn swester Îsôt / von erzenîe hât gelesen*), but we cannot tell whether they were learned by pragmatic observation[17] or the study of books. Thomasin von Zerclaere mentions learning at school (*Der welsche Gast* 6388: *wer solt dâ von ze schuole lesen?*), but the oral (alongside the literate) aspect of schooling leaves it open whether reading must be involved here.[18] Such examples must remain undecided: although we cannot maintain that books were necessarily involved, we cannot claim that they were excluded. That they could at times be excluded, however, is suggested by the use of *lesen* in the sense 'to learn of something' ('erfahren'). For example, in *Die Gevatterinnen* (167: *ich bin dir lang untriu gewesen, / als du ze kirchen hast gelesen / von diner lieben gvaterin*) the verb is so far removed from its modern counterpart that it means learning orally, by hearsay or gossip. Despite this last example it is uncertain that reading was always excluded when *lesen* had the meaning 'to learn', but it is quite certain that the meaning 'to recount, tell' cannot have been intended here.

We start our consideration of the liturgical context of *lesen* by recalling the range of books which the medieval Church regarded as necessary for the liturgy.[19] What was to be read in them by the officiants was not merely words, but also in many cases neumes,[20] so that in the formula *singen und lesen*, used of the liturgy celebrated by priests,[21] the two verbs are not in conflict. Some parts of the liturgy were to be sung and others recited, but even the sung parts were read for their notation, so that in this formula *lesen* is used in the first two senses listed by Lexer and Scholz: the neumes were 'read' by the priest in the sung parts of the liturgy, whilst the spoken parts were 'read out' to the congregation. In both senses liturgical books were required: the Bible, adapted to the needs of the liturgy (e.g. psalter or gospel-book), but also martyrologies, prayer-books, hymn-books, sacramentaries, antiphonaries, missals, legendaries and sermons. The liturgy depended on a wide range of books, to be read in a double sense.

Lesen can therefore be used of the priest at church, for example with reference to baptism in the *Weltchronik* of Jans Enikel (24798ff.), a requiem Mass in the *Rennewart* of Ulrich von Türheim (35962f.), and the Mass itself in *Tristan als Mönch* (2135ff.). Only the last example explicitly mentions a book (a psalter as opposed to the psalms in *Rennewart*), but in view of liturgical practice, based on a rich supply of liturgical books, there is no call to doubt that *lesen* in such passages means 'to read' in either of the first two senses.

The last two examples refer to recital of psalms as part of the liturgy, but the psalms were also important in individual prayers,[22] so that we may consider examples of reading from the psalter as a bridge to the devotional context. Wherever *lesen* is used in conjunction with the psalter, with a book, the use of psalms in prayer (silently or aloud) was based on reading from a written text. Otfrid depicts Mary in the Annunciation scene preoccupied with the psalter (I 5, 10: *mit sálteru in hénti, then sáng si unz in énti*).[23] Wolfram's *Parzival* is rich in examples. Sigune's devout life, one long prayer (435, 25), is characterised by the psalter which she holds (438, 1: *si truoc ein salter in der hant*): prayer and a written text belong together as much as, in a different context, for Guinevere (644, 23: *diu künegîn zer kappeln was, / an ir venje si den salter las*), where reading is now explicit. Like Sigune, Trevrizent has withdrawn from the world to lead a life of penance and prayer (452, 15ff.) in which a psalter plays so much a part that it lies to hand when he needs it for another purpose (460, 25). In *Tandareis und Flordibel* Der Pleier says of Flordibel what Wolfram implied of Sigune (8065: *der meide kurzwîle was / daz si an der venje ir salter las / ze kirchen*), and the prose *Lancelot* depicts an *inclusa* in terms recalling Sigune (I 202, 17ff.).[24] Berthold von Regensburg equates women reading their psalter with their praying to God (I 253, 18f.).[25]

The conjunction of *lesen* with the psalter in these examples implies reading from a book, but certainty is absent whenever it is combined with the psalms instead, for here *lesen* could mean 'to say, recount, recite' (by heart). Examples are: *Sanct Brandan* (782ff.), the *Gebete und Benediktionen von Muri* (393f.) or the *Märterbuch* (21819f.). Such examples may be looser linguistic usage (the difference between reading a psalter and reading a psalm is linguistically not all that great), so that a psalter may have been involved implicitly.[26] However, given the medieval practice of memorising the psalms and reciting them by heart[27] it is equally possible that no written text was involved and therefore no reading in either of the first two senses.

This prepares us for the devotional context, where prayers could be read from a prayerbook or recited by heart. Three possibilities existed for private prayer in the Middle Ages, which Saenger sees as appropriate to different levels of society and literacy.[28]

First, the believer could read his prayer from a book. Of this Saenger says that the distinction between programmed and spontaneous prayer was only incipient, that prayer was more closely tied to a written text than now and that the request to say a prayer meant to read it.[29] Increased literacy in the fourteenth century led to prayers, meant to be read during Mass, being copied into books of hours, so that reading by worshippers was synchronised with the prayers of the celebrant.[30] Saenger uses this as testimony to the rise of silent reading, but for us it confirms that prayer by the individual could be based on a written text.

The second possibility was for the prayer to be recited without actually being read (or read in full) from a text which was available. Saenger suggests that in this case the written text served as a 'prompt script' for a prayer memorised as a result of frequent repetition.[31]

Thirdly, the prayer could be recited from memory in the absence of any book, since it had been learned by heart, especially shorter texts such as the Pater Noster, Ave Maria and Creed, as prescribed even for laymen.[32] Still in the late Middle Ages lay brothers, regularly illiterate, participated in the liturgy by reciting by heart the required number of Pater Nosters, while laymen at large, unable to understand oral Latin prayers, recited private prayers softly and from memory, especially at the elevation of the Host.[33]

For the modern Christian praying can be wholly unconnected with reading a text (especially as a result of the Reformation stress on spontaneous prayer),[34] but it would be anachronistic to assume that, apart from *illitterati*, medieval prayer was not closely associated with a text to be read or at least consulted. How essential the text was to someone who could read can be seen in a passage from a *Vie de Sainte Colette*: 'she prayed at night with the aid of candles and ... when a candle fell, burning her book, she cried not because her book was ruined but because her prayer had been rendered imperfect'.[35]

The question whether prayers were to be read can be discussed first for the prayers of canonical hours, then prayers at large. That the private devotions of canonical hours were not spontaneous and free from the guidance of a prescribed text is clear from a drama performed

APPENDIX

at Avignon in the fourteenth century: *et super scabellum erit quidam libellus paruulus pulcer, cuius folia Maria reuoluet quasi dicendo horas suas*.[36] The same is suggested by vernacular texts. In *Die Klage* Uote is shown in prayer, reading from the psalter at the canonical hours (3684f.), while for Mechthild von Magdeburg members of her order are to have two kinds of book, of the second of which she says (27, 56f.): *Usser dem minsten buoche sol er sine gezit vom jare leisten únserm herren*. In a comparable remark (*Ein botte der göttlichen miltekeit* 45, 2: *Ir zit las sú zuo einem mol unbedehtiklich*) *lesen* must be taken in the sense 'to read' in view of the following mention of *buochstaben und silben*, not recognisable as such to an *illitteratus*.[37]

More revealing are cases where those whose literacy allows them to pray from a written text are distinguished from those who cannot. The *Klarissenregel* lays down that educated members of the order may say the Pater Noster if there is good reason for not reading the prayers of canonical hours from a text, thereby exceptionally allowing them to do what is regularly granted to those who cannot read (6, 10ff.). The *Statuten des Deutschen Ordens* make a similar distinction between *brûdere phaffen unde leigen*: only the former can *singen unde lesen nâch den brevieren unde bûchen*, whilst the latter content themselves with Pater Nosters (34, 27ff.). Again, this distinction is based on whether the member is *genûge gelêret*. Berthold von Regensburg shows that the same may be true of women outside the monastic context (I 515, 11: *Daz dir der munt gar ze kurz wirt, swenne dû daz pater noster sprechen soll unde daz ave Mariâ unde den gelouben, oder swenne ir den salter lesen sult, ir frouwen, und iuwer tagezît. Ir sît gelêret oder ungelêret, so soltet ir iuwer tagezît sprechen*). The last word implies prayer aloud in either case, but the first use of *sprechen* suggests that those who are *ungelêret* recite shorter passages by heart, whilst *lesen* is reserved for those who are *gelêret* (and able to read longer texts).

There are also passages with no mention of a book where we have no certainty that the prayer was read. In *Servatius* Veldeke leaves it open whether the saint consulted a written text or not (567ff.)[38] and commits himself just as little over Ute (5936, 5939f.). *Alexius A* is just as uncertain (464f.). Although the evidence from monastic orders suggests that these prayers may have been long enough to demand reading in place of memorising, the case is not clearcut when no mention of a book is made.

The position with prayer at large agrees with this. Reading prayers from a book is made explicit in the *Trierer Floyris* (205: *sie hat al dise naht gelesen / ir gebet an den buoken*) and, even though the verb may be *sprechen*, prayer is likewise associated with a prescribed text in *Irregang und Girregar* (992: *nim dîn buoch / Und sprich dîn gebet über in*). However, there are also cases which are far from certain, as in Gottfried's *Tristan* (2648ff.),[39] the *Barlaam und Josaphat* of Rudolf von Ems (5806f.) or the *Oberdeutscher Servatius* (3271f.). The translation suggested for Gottfried's *lesen* ('hersagen, rezitieren')[40] could apply to all such cases.[41]

Finally, there are some cases where from the context it is clear that *lesen* used with prayer cannot involve reading, as with Christ's prayer at Gethsemane in *Die Erlösung* (4873: *Sin gebet der herre las*) or His prayer from the cross in the *St. Georgener Prediger* (253, 23ff.). In such passages the third meaning of *lesen* comes fully into its own.

In these three senses of *lesen* in MHG the most helpful guidance was provided in the devotional context where a distinction was made between the literacy of those who could read their prayer and the illiteracy of those who had to recite it by heart. The application of *lesen* to *litterati* suggests reading by them (to themselves or to others) whenever reference is also made to a written text or the need for literacy. Without such a reference reading may still be involved, but recital from memory is equally possible. There remain cases, few in number, where *lesen* is employed in one of these three contexts without a reference to a book or literacy and where, as with Christ in Gethsemane or on the cross, only recital by heart can be meant. Where we are given no such help *lesen*, used without a reference to writing or literacy, could indicate saying from memory, but need not. In order to argue that *lesen* means 'to narrate, recount, tell' we need an explicit pointer. Without it the case is by no means clear.[42]

MIDDLE HIGH GERMAN 'LESEN' = 'TO NARRATE, RECOUNT, TELL'

So far we have been concerned with three contexts in which this general meaning of *lesen* can be assumed only under certain conditions. *Lesen* can however mean 'to narrate, tell' outside these contexts, less frequently than has often been assumed, but even here particular conditions have to be satisfied.

Since the number of examples where *lesen* is used in this way is not large we may start by listing them chronologically, including cases for *vorlesen* and *überlesen*. The earliest example, from Gottfried's *Tristan*, has been mentioned as an example of *lesen* meaning 'to say' in conversation or gossip (14125: *sô wirt des maeres vil gelesen*). Konrad von Heimesfurt uses the verb in the sense 'to tell, recount' in conversation when two people meet again (*Urstende* 1310), with Rudolf von Ems *vorlesen* occurs in *Barlaam und Josaphat* in the sense of reporting past events (7605f.) and Ulrich von Türheim uses the same verb in *Rennewart* of a heavenly voice's personal announcement (34942f.).[43] In the *Passional vorlesen* is used of an Emperor's pronouncement (III 34, 41) and *überlesen* with the meaning 'to pronounce' (III 542, 26ff.), in the *Väterbuch vorlesen* has the sense of recounting in detail to a listener (28916f.),[44] as also in *Der Sünden Widerstreit* (1583). In the continuation of the *Österreichische Reimchronik vorlesen* has the force of 'to mention',[45] and in *Alexius A lesen* means 'to report, recount' in a personal encounter (616f.).[46]

We may sum up these examples (only nine (or ten) works, all confined to the thirteenth century) by stating what they have in common. In none is a written text or the ability to read mentioned; most make it clear that the context is personal communication in conversation or in formal announcements; in all *lesen* is confined to the semantic sphere of saying, telling, recounting, announcing or mentioning. They belong, in other words, to the third meaning of *lesen* listed by Lexer. Yet they have another feature in common, for with one exception[47] all come from works for which a twofold reception can be established.[48] This makes an argument by Schröder in analysing Gottfried's use of *lesen* relevant to the present question.[49] With regard to a phrase like *als ich e las* (referring back to an earlier passage) he makes a distinction, saying that Gottfried could imply recital from a written text as long as he saw himself as a reciter or reckoned with a recital of his work, but that for the individual reader of *Tristan* the phrase came from the narrator, not the displaced reciter. In such cases *lesen* now meant 'to say, mention', not 'to recite aloud from a text'. *Lesen* is ambivalent with Gottfried because the presence of potential readers has altered the conditions of reception. In view of Schröder's observation it is not fortuitous that our earliest example for *lesen* meaning 'to say, tell' was Gottfried's *Tristan* or that most examples came from works which, like his, were destined for a twofold reception. Even if the examples listed do not concern the reception of the author's own work, its double reception is sufficient, as Schröder has shown, to account for the semantic extension of *lesen* to 'to say, tell'. As was also the case with the devotional context, the contrast between reading and hearing has proved its relevance.

Schröder says of these phrases of Gottfried that, despite the ambivalence which now informs *lesen*, it would be wrong to conclude that it has become synonymous with *sprechen* or *jehen*.[50] Although he does not mention Benecke, Müller and Zarncke at this point, this remark could be directed against their assertion that *lesen* in a passage in *Tristan* with which Schröder is also concerned is completely synonymous with *sprechen* or *jehen*.[51] We may agree with Schröder that this is not the case: *lesen* may share semantic functions with these verbs, but its range passes beyond theirs, its use to mean 'to say, tell' is accompanied by a much more frequent employment for reading, to oneself or others. How far *lesen* still was from being simply equated with these verbs of saying in the thirteenth century is illustrated in Gottfried Hagen's *Chronik der Stadt Köln* when a messenger makes an oral announcement (5355: *sunder breif eme der bode las*), where *sunder breif* is added to show the absence of a written text, to indicate that *lesen* has nothing to do with reading. A similar need is felt in the *Livländische Reimchronik* (5290), where the message was given orally (at least, the text makes no mention of anything written). Or to take an example before the spread of literacy occasioned the expansion of the function of *lesen* registered in Gottfried: when the author of the *Friedberger*

Christ talks of the delivery of his work (29, 2: *daz ich nemac noch newil / necheineme dumben vorgele(sen) noch gesagen*) he is so far from seeing *vorgelesen* and *gesagen* as synonymous that he makes a distinction between them (*noch*).[52] The possibility of equating them arose only about 1200, but even that was far from making them synonyms.

The other way to determine that *lesen* is not employed in the sense 'to say, tell' is to do outside the three contexts what we did within them, to ask how far the conjunction of this verb with indications of a written text suggests an author reading it out rather than simply telling.

The first heading concerns the double formula, not in its normal guise (*lesen oder hoeren*), but in a fuller form (*lesen oder hoeren lesen*). Scholz discusses this briefly,[53] but without asking what concerns us: what is the force of the second *lesen* in this full formula? When the author of *Unser Vrouwen Klage* refers to his audience (62: *allen, die diz büechelîn / lesen oder hoeren lesen*) *büechelîn* suggests that *hoeren lesen* means that the audience heard the author read his text to them, not that they heard him simply tell them or narrate to them.[54] The position is not so immediately clear where no reference to a written text is made, as for example in *Das Leben Jesu* (1, 1: *Ich grueze alle die die dis lesen sülen vnd hoeren lesen*).[55] Even in such a case it is possible to settle the question in favour of hearing a written text read out. If the first part of this double formula (*lesen* by itself) refers to individual reading,[56] this presupposes the presence of a written text, of a *büechelîn* not expressed linguistically, so that *hoeren lesen* in *Das Leben Jesu*, as in the more explicit *Unser Vrouwen Klage*, refers to hearing the recital of something written. *Lesen* has the force of reading for oneself or listening to someone else read out in other cases where this fuller form of the double formula is employed.[57]

Under the second heading the written text reconstructed for *Das Leben Jesu* is made explicit, allowing us to interpret *lesen* as 'to read'. An example occurs in *Ortnit* when the author addresses his audience (2, 1: *Swer in freuden welle und kurzwîle wesen, / der lâze im von dem buoche singen unde lesen*). With this work, unlike those containing a double formula, there is no hint that a reader might be anticipated.[58] Instead, a recital situation with listeners is suggested (by the *lân* construction and *singen / lesen* + dative),[59] but the basis of this recital is not memorial transmission, but a written one (*buoch*), which includes the text and perhaps also the neumes which guide the singing. The reading performed by the reciter in this case is of a *buoch*, which is the word most commonly used in this situation,[60] but *schrîben* can provide the same kind of indication, as in *Diu vrône boteschaft* (384ff.), or even a combination of *schrift* and *buoch* (*Passional* III 319, 13ff.). To place *lesen* in the context of writing, as in these cases, makes better sense when it means not to recount, but more specifically to recite from a written text.[61]

The third heading includes examples where *lesen* is not used in close conjunction with a term of writing, but where writing may be presupposed from evidence elsewhere. What is at issue can be illustrated from the *Wilhelm von Österreich* of Johann von Würzburg, who makes a general observation in his prologue which has a bearing on the reception of his work (56: *die tugentrîchen bietent dar / ir ore, da man von tugenden list / mit tugenthafter rede*). These lines imply a recital situation and an author selling his wares by praising the ethical value of his work, but it remains uncertain how *lesen* is to be understood: does it mean 'to say, recount' (the editor glosses it with 'reden')[62] or more specifically 'to read the text out'? Little help is provided by a passage in which this self-recommendation is repeated (10848ff.), for here too *lesen* could be seen in either sense. Assistance comes much later when the author names himself (13228: *Johannes der tugend schribaer / haizz ich*) and makes it clear that his work exists in written form (13258ff.)[63] and is available for readers (13221). Only by taking these later references into account can we understand the lines in the prologue, where *lesen* can be seen to have the force not of 'reden', but of 'vorlesen'.

Passages from other works discussed in Chapter 4 point in the same direction. In *Der Borte* Dietrich von Glezze has his personified work make an opening remark (7: *man sol mich hubschen luten lesen*) where *lesen* is as uncertain as in *Wilhelm von Österreich* ('to narrate' or 'to read out'?), but the latter meaning is confirmed later when the work is shown to be a

MIDDLE HIGH GERMAN 'LESEN' = 'TO NARRATE, RECOUNT, TELL'

written text.[64] Likewise, a passing reference in the *Millstätter Genesis* to a point made earlier (82, 12: *als wir da vor lasen*) can be seen as recital from a written text by virtue of references elsewhere to this written dimension (1, 2: *vorbriefen*; 28, 1: *buoch*). These and other examples[65] demonstrate that it is often impossible to interpret *lesen* in the passage in which it occurs and that all the evidence available has to be taken into account. Where confirmatory evidence is not provided it must remain undecided whether *lesen* implies reading or 'to say, tell'.

To sum up: those works categorised in this book as meant to be read (to oneself or to others) must for safety's sake exclude cases where *lesen* is used in an educational, liturgical or devotional context and could possibly mean only 'to say, tell', although even here an exception must be made where a written text, and therefore reading from it, is made clear. Notker, although active as a teacher in a monastery school, gives instructions to the reader on how to use the text visually to the best advantage,[66] so that it is unlikely that he used *lesan* in the sense 'to learn', but more probable that he implied 'to learn in the process of reading'. Within the three contexts considered the meaning 'to say, tell' can only be assumed when there is an explicit pointer, whilst outside these contexts there are indications that the act of reading is much more likely to be meant.

Scholz has taken issue with the argument of this Appendix (advanced in earlier articles) and proposes the more general term 'erzählen' rather than the more specific 'Vortrag eines schriftlichen Textes', pleading for a greater degree of semantic elasticity.[67] We may agree, in view of the different functions performed by MHG *lesen*, that we need as much elasticity as possible in interpreting it. But where does the greater elasticity lie? To say, with Scholz, that *lesen* did not mean 'to read out loud', but instead 'to say, tell'? Or to say, with Schröder and in the course of this book, that *lesen* meant 'to read out loud' to listeners in the audience, but also 'to say, tell' to readers? To take *lesen* in this wider, double sense is to place it in the context of orality and writing and to suggest that changes within the relationship between orality and writing around 1200 influenced the semantics of this verb.

Notes

1 Orality and writing

1. Mertens, *Buchdruck*, p. 84.
2. Ong, *Orality*, pp. 2f.
3. Ong uses this term in connection with modern developments in communication, *ibid.*, p. 3. On the general point made here see Heinzle, *DU* (NS) 1 (1989), 1 29. Cf. also Grubmüller, *DU* (NS) 1 (1989), 1 41, and Miethke, *Universitäten*, p. 5.
4. Ong, *Orality*, p. 3.
5. Havelock, *Muse*, pp. 24ff. On the need to avoid technological determinism in this kind of argument see Finnegan, *Literacy*, pp. 8ff.
6. Goody, *Domestication*, p. 51.
7. Havelock, *Revolution*, pp. 83 and 315f. Cf. also Giesecke, *Abgang*, pp. 77ff.
8. Vollrath, *HZ* 233 (1981), 588. Kirchert, *ZfdA* 113 (1984), 75, sees Luther's Bible translation as marking the end of the predominant written culture of Latin in the Middle Ages.
9. I refer to Heinzle, *Geschichte* and to Liebertz-Grün, *Mündlichkeit*.
10. Cf. Schmidt, *PBB* 95 (1973), 324f.
11. Clanchy, *Looking back*, p. 7.
12. Judaism: Vermes, *Scripture*, pp. 79ff.; Gerhardsson, *Memory*. Christian gospels: Kelber, *Gospel*; Gerhardsson, *Memory*. On the formation of the canonical books of the Bible: Campenhausen, *Entstehung*.
13. Graham, *Written word*.
14. This despite the criticism made by Eisenstein, *Press*, p. xii. For an attempt to argue the importance of oral traditions for historians see Vansina, *Tradition*.
15. Vollrath, *HZ* 233 (1981), 587f.; Richter, *HZ* 222 (1976), 43ff.
16. Clanchy, *Memory*, pp. 88ff., 175ff., 202ff. In *History* 55 (1970), 165ff. he applies Goody's findings to medieval history, as transmitted orally or in writing. Schreiner, *ZHF* 11 (1984), 257ff., deals with the later Middle Ages and the Reformation in the light of lay literacy and obstacles in the way of the spread of knowledge. Other work by historians includes Stock, *Implications*, and the essays edited by McKitterick, *Uses*. Legal history has also been engaged in this problem, cf. the essays edited by Classen, *Recht*, and Vollrath's essay on Anglo-Saxon England, *HJb* 99 (1979), 28ff.
17. Bloomfield, *Language*, p. 21 (on this question see Stubbs, *Language*, pp. 23ff.); Coulmas, *Schrift*, pp. 30, 51.
18. Coulmas, *Schrift*, p. 49; Stubbs, *Language*, pp. 23, 29; Coulmas and Ehlich, *Writing*; Tannen, *Language*, and also *Coherence*.
19. Hucke, *JAMS* 33 (1980), 437ff., and *Übergang*, pp. 180ff.; Treitler, *MQ* 60 (1974), 333ff.; *Speculum* 56 (1981), 471ff.; *JAMS* 35 (1982), 237ff.; *EMH* 4 (1984), 135ff.; *Parergon* 2 (1984), 143ff. For the Anglo-Saxons see also Rankin, *ASE* 13 (1984), 97ff.
20. On word and picture see Meier and Ruberg, *Text*, p. 10; Gregory the Great, *PL* 77, 1128 (see Curschmann, *Pictura*, pp. 211ff.).

21 Camille, *AH* 8 (1985), 26ff.; Kemp, *Sermo*. The latter explicitly links works of art around 1200 with the transition from oral to written (pp. 7, 162), just as Hayum, *Altarpiece*, pp. 76, 79, relates the dialectic between word and image in Grünewald to the transition from manuscript to print.
22 Schmidt-Wiegand, *Eid*, pp. 55ff.; *Stammesrecht*, pp. 171ff.; *Leges barbarorum*, pp. 56ff.; Heck, *Übersetzungsprobleme*, especially pp. 4, 11f.
23 Geuenich, *DA* 39 (1983), 104ff.; Richter, *Sprachwissenschaft* 7 (1988), 412ff.
24 *Carolingians*, pp. 1ff. (even if by the former she means more Romance speech than German).
25 *Sprache*, pp. 1ff., 71ff., 169ff.
26 *EMH* 4 (1984), 135ff. (Otfrid: pp. 178ff., 204).
27 *PBB* 106 (1984), 256. Scholz, *Hören*, pp. 192ff., takes into account the possible relevance of illustrated manuscripts to hearing or reading, thereby taking up an early lead by Voss, *Studien*, pp. 121f., 130, on the *Millstätter Genesis*. The latter also discusses pictures in the Manesse manuscript for the light they throw on the literate status, or otherwise, of some of the poets (*Text*, pp. 59f., 61).
28 Assmann and Hardmeier, *Schrift*, p. 268.
29 *OT* 1 (1986), 398, 410, 429.
30 *PBB* 106 (1984), 218ff.
31 Finnegan, *Oral poetry* and *Literacy and orality*. Conversely, McKitterick refers to literacy alone in the title of *Uses*, but more correctly to literacy and orality in the Introduction (p. 1).
32 Lord: foreword to Renoir, *Key*, p. vii, and his essay in *Singers*, pp. 15ff.; Renoir, *Key*, pp. 60, 63, 157.
33 *GRM* 34 (1984), 369, 376.
34 Lord, *Singer*. Brief summaries of the theory are given by Finnegan, *Literacy*, pp. 88f., and Heinzle, *Dietrichepik*, p. 69.
35 *NLH* 16 (1984/5), 1. Curschmann, for all his reservations, is well aware of what we owe to the new questions raised (*MlJb* 16 (1981), 381).
36 *Singer*, pp. 198ff. In OE he was followed by Magoun, *Speculum* 28 (1953), 446ff. and 30 (1955), 49ff.
37 Foley, *Oral theory*, pp. 27, 48; Finnegan, *Literacy*, p. 88. In his critical bibliography, *Theory*, p. 64, Foley is wrong to criticise Finnegan's earlier book for doing the same thing as the Parry–Lord school (and for which he praises it). It is unjustified to criticise the deployment of a wide range of examples against the theory while using an equally wide range to demonstrate its extensive applicability.
38 Bäuml, *OT* 1 (1986), 398. An exception is the work of Heusler and Baesecke. The former, *Lied*, distinguished between the shorter lay meant for singing (*Versgeschichte* II 242f.) and the longer epic for reading, *Leseepos* (the current view sees the latter, too, as sung and hence received acoustically). Baesecke organised his literary history into a first volume for oral genres (*Vorgeschichte*) and a second one (incomplete) for written ones (*Frühgeschichte*).
39 Bäuml, *NLH* 16 (1984/5), 34; Kullmann, *GRBS* 25 (1984), 308.
40 Curschmann, *Medievalia et Humanistica* 8 (1977), 64.
41 *Poetry*, p. 6. This point has been conceded by Foley, *Oral theory*, p. 89. See also Hatto, *Anatomy*, p. 152.
42 Symptomatic is Magoun's equation of oral with formulaic, *Speculum* 28 (1953), 447.
43 *Oral poetry*, p. 18. Lord, *Singers*, p. 3, concedes that the word 'oral' is used in a specialised sense by the oral-formulaic school as opposed to the literal sense.
44 Finnegan, *Oral poetry*, pp. 20f.
45 *Ibid.*, p. 79. Jabbour, *ChR* 3 (1968), 174ff., argues for memorisation as distinct from composition-in-performance in Anglo-Saxon poetry.

46 Lord, *Memory*, p. 451; *Singers*, p. 115.
47 Quoted by Finnegan, *Literacy*, p. 105 (my italics).
48 Lord, *Memory*, p. 460. He confines such examples of fixed form to shorter poems, but leaves it uncertain where the dividing line may be.
49 Opland, *Poetry*, p. 10, reckons with improvising as well as memorising with the Anglo-Saxons; Harris, *Poetry*, pp. 211ff., accepts Lord's theory as only one model of oral poetry and sets beside it memorisation in the transmission of the *Edda*; Lönnroth, *Speculum* 46 (1971), 18, finds a place for an element of improvisation in a performance based essentially on memorisation. Cf. Reichl, *Diction*, p. 62 (on this see Lord, *Singers*, p. 236).
50 Lord, *Oral poetry*, p. 591 (quoted by Finnegan, *Oral poetry*, p. 80).
51 Hindu Veda: Graham, *Written word*, p. 72. Pacific Islands: Finnegan, *Literacy*, pp. 91ff. (in one account, p. 96, the poet goes off, like Caedmon, to a lonely spot to compose orally in advance). Finnegan, too, stresses that not all oral literature in this vast area is produced in this way and that other oral modes are practised (p. 90), again in contrast to the claim of the oral-formulaic school that their theory is true of 'all oral poetries' (Parry and Lord, *Songs*, p. 4). Smith, *Man* 12 (1977), 141ff., argues that the circularities in Lord's argument prevent its application to any oral tradition differing from the Yugoslav 'norm' (on this see Lord, *OT* 2 (1987), 65ff.).
52 Heroic lay: Heusler, *Dichtung*, p. 147; Hoffmann, *Heldendichtung*, pp. 55f.; Gschwantler, *Gattungen*, p. 120; Andersson, *Poetry*, p. 5; Hatto, *Medieval German*, p. 166. Praise-song: Heusler, *Dichtung*, p. 119. Eddic lay: Harris, *Poetry*, pp. 211ff. Skaldic verse: Lönnroth, *Speculum* 46 (1971), 1ff. (see also Wolf, *Erzählen*, p. 125). Lönnroth, p. 3, argues that the burden of proof lies with those claiming that *any* longer Norse poem was based on improvisation.
53 *Speculum* 30 (1955), 49ff.
54 *Key*, p. 70. Cf. Carruthers, *Book*, pp. 44, 167, on metaphors of eating applied to memory, with explicit reference to Caedmon, p. 165.
55 Fry, *Memory*, pp. 288ff., and *Caedmon*, pp. 41ff. In more general terms cf. Reichl, *Diction*, pp. 61f.
56 Benson, *PMLA* 81 (1966), 334ff. Cf. also Hoffmann, *Heldendichtung*, p. 56; Conlee, *NM* 71 (1970), 579; Fry, *Memory*, p. 290; Reichl, *Diction*, p. 60.
57 Cf. Curschmann, *Medievalia et Humanistica* 8 (1977), 67; Heinzle, *Dietrichepik*, p. 79. On the Homeric epic, the starting-point of oral-formulaic endeavours, Kullmann, *GRBS* 25 (1984), 318f., says: 'this epic looks back upon a long oral tradition, but was itself composed with the help of writing'.
58 Havelock, *Revolution*, p. 9, sees the alphabetisation of Homer as the beginning of a creative partnership between oral and written. O'Keeffe, *Song*, p. 12, conducts her argument against any binary opposition between 'orality' and 'literacy'; Street, *Literacy*, p. 3, concentrates on overlap and interaction, rather than a 'great divide'; Giesecke, *Buchdruck*, p. 313, sees writing not as replacing oral tradition, but as providing a second form of memory alongside it.
59 *Preface*, pp. 40ff.; *Revolution*, pp. 185ff.; pp. 112ff.; *Muse*, pp. 63ff.; p. 11 (with reference to *Preface*, pp. 91, 93).
60 *Revolution*, pp. 89ff., 233.
61 *Literacy*, pp. 28ff.
62 *Ibid.*, pp. 42ff., 55ff.; pp. 34ff., and *Logic*, p. 171; *Literacy*, pp. 11f.
63 *Literacy*, pp. 49ff.; *Domestication*, p. 151; *Interface*, pp. 125ff., 167ff., 254ff., 280ff. Against this Street, *Literacy*, p. 3, criticises him for polarising the difference between oral and literate modes of communication. Havelock also attempts to give weight to the relationship between these two poles: in the subtitle of *Muse* he gives its theme as orality and literacy, and one of his essays, *Revolution*, pp. 166ff., places Homer in this context.
64 One of the aims of the Sonderforschungsbereich 'Mündlichkeit und Schriftlichkeit', set up

in Freiburg in 1985, is to investigate this relationship comprehensively (Erzgräber, *Mündlichkeit*, p. 9, who likewise sees this, p. 8, as a shift from orality alone to its interplay with writing).
65 Havelock, *Preface*, pp. 61ff.; *Revolution*, p. 122. Giesecke, *Buchdruck*, p. 151, speaks of the Damocles sword of forgetting hanging over an oral culture.
66 Havelock, *Revolution*, pp. 60ff., 77ff.; Goody, *Literacy*, pp. 34ff.; *Interface*, pp. 1ff.
67 Impoverishment is suggested by Vollrath, *HZ* 233 (1981), 573; Ong, *Writing*, p. 31; Assmann and Hardmeier, *Schrift*, p. 271. Failure to realise its potential: Graham, *Written word*, p. 178, n. 16 (early writing helped people not to forget what they already knew, rather than told them what they did not know); unpointed writing in Semitic served a memorial, not communicative function (Graham, p. 98; Forster, *Thoughts*, p. 60). For classical Greece see Thomas, *Tradition*, p. 21, and for early musical notation Rankin, *ASE* 13 (1984), 104, 110.
68 Goody, *Literacy*, p. 1; *Domestication*, p. 78; Finnegan, *Literacy*, pp. 17ff.; Schlieben-Lange, *Schriftlichkeit*, pp. 194f.
69 Havelock, *Revolution*, p. 181; Goody, *Interface*, p. 220.
70 Havelock, *Revolution*, pp. 87f.; Goody, *Domestication*, p. 37; Assmann and Hardmeier, *Schrift*, pp. 267f.
71 Goody, *Domestication*, pp. 47, 144f.; *Literacy*, pp. 57f.; Finnegan, *Literacy*, pp. 22f.
72 For classicist criticisms of Havelock see Solmsen, *AJPh* 87 (1966), 99ff., and Harvey, *CR* 28 (1978), 130f. For a critique of Goody see Street, *Literacy*, pp. 44ff.
73 Goody, *Literacy*, p. 20. He now recognises it as an ethnocentric error to have granted absolute importance to the alphabet as opposed to a logographic system like Chinese (*Interface*, p. 56, cf. Gough, *Implications*, p. 73), to which could be added Japanese with *kanji* and two syllabaries (Coulmas, *Schrift*, pp. 18, 36, 57). Goody's association of scientific thinking with writing has been questioned by Staal, *Fidelity*, and Falk, *Goodies*.
74 Havelock, *Revolution*, pp. 77ff. Harris, *Literacy*, p. 45, avoids the problem by saying that the Greeks invented '*fully* alphabetic writing' (my italics).
75 Cf. the letter from W. L. Moran in *TLS* October 13–19 (1989), p. 1123.
76 Goody, *Literacy*, p. 4 (as well as his comment, p. 69, on Gough's argument in his volume).
77 Finnegan, *Literacy*, pp. 41, 11.
78 *Implications*, p. 84.
79 Grundmann, *AfK* 40 (1958), 1ff.; Thompson, *Literacy*.
80 Conversely, illiteracy was the hallmark of laymen, who were unable to read and write, and who knew only their vernacular. For this Grundmann gives a partial definition (p. 8), which has to be supplemented by the remark on the preceding page that the *idiotae* mentioned were laymen.
81 The clarity of Grundmann's definition is bought at the cost of ignoring various intermediate positions between the literacy of high culture and complete inability to read or write (Bäuml, *Speculum* 55 (1980), 239).
82 A point of some importance when we are concerned with the reception of medieval literature. On the justification of regarding medieval literacy in terms of reading, even with the clergy, see Wendehorst, *Mittelalter*, especially p. 23.
83 Clanchy, *Memory*, p. 183.
84 *Ibid.*, pp. 88ff. (on the 'technology of writing').
85 Schreiner, *ZHF* 11 (1984), 328, fn. 254. Cf. the case of Charles the Great, as in Einhard, *Vita Karoli* 25 (p. 30), on which see Thompson, *Literacy*, p. 29, and those laymen who say that they can read, but not write (Riché, *Ecoles*, p. 298).
86 Maas, *LiLi* 59 (1985), 58.
87 Cassiodorus: Riché, *Ecoles*, p. 235; knowing the psalms by heart: *ibid.* (on this type of literacy see Saenger, *Books*, p. 142); Caesarius: Grundmann, *AfK* 40 (1958), 45, fn. 2.
88 Turner, *AHR* 83 (1978), 928ff.; Bumke, *AfdA* 93 (1982), 118f.

89 Clanchy, *Memory*, p. 179.
90 Grundmann's readiness to ignore overlaps as exceptions is shown by his wording, *AfK* 40 (1958), 14: what he mentions in passing and dismisses as exceptional is what occupies us in this book.
91 Grundmann, *AfK* 26 (1936), 131, 141, fn. 34; 40 (1958), 3f.; *Schrifttum*, p. 118 (in negative terms).
92 Fromm, *Volkssprache*, p. 99.
93 Schreiner, *ZHF* 11 (1984), 330, quotes from a bible preface addressed to readers with no Latin (*die das latin nit verstanden grüntlich und doch lesen können teutsch*). Geiler von Kaysersberg writes his translation of Gerson's *Ars moriendi* for such readers, cf. Schreiner, *ZHF* 11 (1984), 346; *Grenzen*, p. 13; Kraume, *Gerson-Übersetzungen*, pp. 101f. Geith, *ZfdA* 119 (1990), 22, quotes to the effect that *Leben Jesu* texts, meant for recital at table and for private meditation, were rendered into German *durch mynne und liebe der vngelerten die / das latin nit verstant vnd darvme manigmol vertrosz hant vil zu lesende*.
94 Grundmann, *Schrifttum*, pp. 120f. A cartulary of the privileges of the Order in the Thuringian commandery, giving instructions on how to find a privilege with the help of a register, takes account of the same possibility, *ibid.*, pp. 123f.: *Ist der briff dücz, so lesen selbins, ist er aber latin, so wyse er ein prister odir sine schriber dar uff und laz ime den ducz uslegin*.
95 Steer, *Laie*, pp. 355, 360 (*verstanden layen* or *kluge* or *vernonftige* as opposed to *einfaltigen leigen*). In the fifteenth century Job Vener distinguishes between *subtilen leyen* and *groben leyen*, applying only to the former the double formula and implying therewith the possibility that they could read (Heimpel, *Vener* III 1345, 247ff.). Cf. Schreiner, *Volkssprache*, pp. 476f.
96 Grundmann, *Bewegungen*, p. 442.
97 92: *swie ich der buoche niene kan, / ich hân doch tiutsche gelesen*. Grundmann has observed, *AfK* 40 (1958), 4, that with Latin as the language of literacy *litteraliter loqui* or *litterate loqui* means 'to speak Latin'. Similarly MHG *buochisch* can mean 'Latin', e.g. Berthold von Regensburg I 44, 3.
98 *AfK* 40 (1958), 56f.
99 *De nugis curialium* I 31 (p. 124).
100 *AfK* 40 (1958), 57: 'eine "Illitteraten-Literatur" für Leser, die nicht Latein verstanden'.
101 *Laie*, p. 356.
102 On these changes see Schreiner, *ZHF* 11 (1984), 345, and also pp. 284ff.
103 *AfK* 40 (1958), 16f., 52ff.
104 *Ibid.*, p. 52: *qui enim istorum ignari sunt, illitterati dicuntur, etsi litteras noverint*. To John's ideal of literacy belongs a knowledge of the poets, historians, orators and mathematicians.
105 Recent scholarship has felt it necessary to coin a range of differentiated terms for various types of literacy. In place of the pejorative *illiteracy* Havelock suggests *non-literacy* or *preliteracy* for a society of primary orality (*Revolution*, pp. 4, 41f. See also Ong, *Orality*, p. 13; Bäuml and Spielmann, *Illiteracy*, p. 64). Bäuml proposes *quasi-literacy* for those who, unable to read or write, depend on the literacy of others (*Speculum* 55 (1980), 242, 246. See also Bumke, *Kultur*, pp. 608f., Baumann, *Written word*, pp. 19, 107, and for classical antiquity Harris, *Literacy*, pp. 33f.). The skills of this minority have been termed *craft literacy* or *scribal/professional literacy* (Havelock, *Revolution*, pp. 59, 188, 339; Parkes, *Literacy*, p. 555; Harris, *Literacy*, pp. 7f.). The position of a society in which writing skills are spreading without an increase in fluent reading has been defined as *semi-literacy* (Havelock, *Preface*, p. 40). Parkes distinguishes between *recreational literacy* (*Literacy*, pp. 555ff.) and *pragmatic literacy* (pp. 555, 557, 559f.), whilst Saenger differentiates between *phonetic literacy* and *comprehension literacy* (*Books*, p. 142; for an example of the former see Richter, *Sprachwissenschaft* 7 (1982), 420f.). The ability to read

alone (*receptive literacy*) may be distinguished from the ability to read and write (*receptive and communicative literacy*), whilst *mental literacy* describes someone, able to read but without a text in front of him, mentally decoding, say, an anagram (see p. 133).
106 In the Middle Ages craft literacy was largely practised by clerics in Latin, whilst quasi-literacy was true of laymen and the vernacular.
107 Scholz, *Hören*.
108 Scholz, pp. 111ff., has applied his results to the *Grundriß der romanischen Literaturen des Mittelalters*, and his criticisms have been accepted by Lebsanft, *ZfSL* 92 (1983), 58, fn. 17. Scholz's analysis also implies a criticism of Gallais, *CCM* 7 (1964), 479ff. and 13 (1970), 333ff.
109 Conceded as a positive point by Bumke, *AfdA* 93 (1982), 117.
110 Scholz, *Hören*, p. 92.
111 He gives no reason for this, which creates the impression that what came before can be disregarded.
112 The neglect of genres has also been criticised by Bumke, *AfdA* 93 (1982), 117, and Curschmann, *PBB* 106 (1984), 223.
113 *IASL* 8 (1983), 256f., 260.
114 Bumke, *Mäzene*, pp. 71f.; *AfdA* 93 (1982), 117f.
115 Grundmann, *AfK* 26 (1936), 129ff.; Bumke, *Mäzene*, pp. 231ff.; Scholz, *Hören*, pp. 205ff.
116 *Hören*, p. 91.
117 At one point, pp. 107ff., two pages are devoted to it, but the verbs are seen as two simultaneous aspects of one mode of reception (reading aloud to oneself), so that the possibility of public recital is excluded. Elsewhere, p. 122, the formula occupies one page, but in such a way that the visual element, the fact of reading, is stressed and hearing ignored.
118 We could say of Scholz what Street, *Literacy*, p. 44, says of Goody: that his polemical concern to highlight what has been ignored (*Hören*, p. x) is why he overstates his case.
119 There is no reason to consider this medieval development as an exception to what Havelock, *Revolution*, p. 167, said of the 'alphabetisation of Homer', that it set in motion 'a process of erosion of "orality", extending over centuries of the European experience'.
120 On one occasion, pp. 145ff., Scholz concedes that the *Ulrichsleben* was meant to be heard as well as read, and he explains this convincingly in terms of the monastic context of St Ulrich and Afra in Augsburg. The acceptability of this explanation must cast doubt on the occasions when Scholz fails to take a similar possibility into account (Green, *FMLS* 20 (1984), 303f.).
121 Green, *FMLS* 20 (1984), 296f., 299. In the context of religious writing and its oral aspects Graham, *Written word*, p. 153, has made a similar point.
122 For criticisms of Scholz's use of this concept see Kartschoke, *IASL* 8 (1983), 260; Green, *FMLS* 20 (1954), 294f.; Curschmann, *PBB* 106 (1984), 250, fn. 50.
123 If the oral-formulaic school could be criticised for its concentration on orality alone, the same must be said of Scholz's practice at the opposite pole. We need to reaffirm the connections between orality and reading stressed by Havelock and Goody.
124 Eisenstein, *Press*; Giesecke, *Buchdruck* (cf. also his essay, *Abgang*, pp. 77ff.).
125 This is expressed most radically by Eisenstein, p. 33, when she abandons an evolutionary approach in favour of a revolutionary one, seeing 'the age of incunabula as a major historical great divide'. Giesecke, p. 703, at least admits that his problem needs to be also tackled expressly from the medieval point of view, but this insight, coming at the end of his book, cannot be said to have affected the course of its argument beyond a few details.
126 Giesecke, *Buchdruck*, pp. 169ff., points to the converse fact that criticisms levelled against printing often parallel those earlier made of writing.
127 Cf. Schmidt, *Books*, pp. 26f.
128 Eisenstein, *Press*, pp. 216, 271f., suggests that the flood of new texts to be assimilated in

NOTES TO PAGES 13–15

the twelfth and thirteenth centuries may have caused problems in recruiting scribes or diverting their labours from other tasks.
129 Schmidt, *Books*, p. 31.
130 Ong, *Writing*, p. 31.
131 For this aspect of printing see Eisenstein, *Press*, pp. 216f.
132 The passage (274c–278b) is given in Assmann and Hardmeier, *Schrift*, pp. 7ff.
133 Ong, *Orality*, p. 79.
134 *Ibid.*, p. 80.
135 Giesecke, *Buchdruck*, p. 60, sees this process as an accumulation of more differentiated media.
136 She also plays down the 'book revolution' of the twelfth century (cf. Humphreys, *Book provisions*, p. 13), the pecia system of copying developed by the medieval universities (Destrez, *Pecia*; Febvre and Martin, *Coming*, pp. 21ff.; Pollard, *Pecia system*, pp. 145ff.), the vast increase in copying in monastic scriptoria in the decades before Gutenberg, largely resulting from changes in personal piety (Sprandel, *Gesellschaft*, p. 46) and in pragmatic literacy in the same period (Lerner, *Literacy*, p. 223. On pragmatic literacy in the late Middle Ages at large see Keller, Grubmüller and Staubach, *Schriftlichkeit*).
137 *Press*, p. 132.
138 *Looking back*, p. 8. In a narrower context Huot concludes her survey of the transition of the French lyric from performance to writing with the suggestion that 'it cannot be mere coincidence that the printing press arrived at a moment when the literary world was so perfectly ready for it' (*Song*, p. 337). In de Boor, *Geschichte* III 2, 10, Glier has made a similar point with regard to the medieval transition from parchment to paper.
139 How far he sees printing in a line with modern computer technology is brought out by Giesecke's terminology. He refers to typographical data processing, he compares the early Mainz printers to rented copying machines in a modern office, and with him a printed book is often termed a print-out.
140 *Buchdruck*, p. 414 (cf. p. 769, n. 26).
141 *Ibid.*, p. 33.
142 For the early modern period Rössing-Hager, *Rezipient*, p. 77, fn. 1, quotes an example from Eberlin von Günzburg (*laesen oder hoeren laesen*). We shall see that a specific social and educational situation lies behind the use of this formula in the Middle Ages, and Rössing-Hager, p. 77, suggests something similar for the Reformation period, which underlines strikingly the continuity between the Middle Ages and the early modern period in this respect. Scribner, *Flugblatt*, pp. 65ff., likewise modifies Eisenstein's stress on the role of printing in spreading Reformation ideas by pointing also to their oral dissemination among those who could not read.
143 *Buchdruck*, p. 569. On this passage from Isidore see p. 399, n. 18.
144 *Buchdruck*, p. 160 (quoted in the original, p. 727, n. 162).
145 See p. 178.
146 *Buchdruck*, p. 197.
147 *Ibid.*, p. 248.
148 Cf. Grundmann, *Bewegungen*, pp. 50ff., 170ff., 319ff.; Haverkamp, *Aufbruch*, pp. 49ff., 65ff., 275ff.; Ruh, *Eckhart*, pp. 97ff.
149 *Buchdruck*, p. 249; on Walter Map see p. 25.
150 Graham, *Written word*, pp. 10, 159.
151 *Ibid.*, p. 29.
152 *Ibid.*, pp. 20, 30.
153 *Ibid.*, p. 18.
154 To this conjunction of the written with the spoken word has to be added the coexistence for some period of time of literacy with memorising. On this see Riché, *Ecoles*, pp. 218f.; Lerner, *Literacy*, p. 177 ('Thus reading was actually secondary. It helped monks and

priests to "recognise" Psalms they already knew'); Goody, *Interface*, p. 120; Carruthers, *Book*, *passim*.
155 Scribner, *Simple Folk*, p. 2.
156 Nelson, *UTQ* 46 (1976/7), 117.
157 *Ibid.*, pp. 121f. (although Nelson also reminds us of later examples).
158 Schlieben-Lange, *Traditionen*, pp. 64ff.
159 At this point I confine myself to Latin examples. German is considered later, pp. 147ff.
160 Köhn, *Latein*, pp. 340ff.
161 *Ibid.*, pp. 346f. Köhn recognises (p. 344) that the evidence of German literature from about 1200, with references to letters in the vernacular, must qualify this point and that further work on this is called for.
162 *Ibid.*, pp. 344f.
163 *Ibid.*, pp. 344, 346.
164 *Ibid.*, p. 348.
165 *Ibid.*, pp. 349f. Here again the evidence of vernacular literature is against this as a general observation. Until the evidence from this literature has been assessed it is overhasty of Köhn to dismiss it as a fiction (p. 350).
166 *Ibid.*, pp. 341, 350f.
167 Cf. Herescu, *REL* 34 (1956), 132ff., especially 145f.; Ernout, *REL* 29 (1951), 155ff.; Skeat, *PBA* 42 (1956), 179ff.; Petzsch, *ZfdPh* 93 (1974), 106; Saenger, *Manières*, p. 131.
168 Clanchy, *Memory*, pp. 97, 218f. Already in OHG the loanword *tihtôn* is recorded in the meanings 'diktieren' and 'dichten, verfassen'. Cf. Schützeichel, *Wörterbuch*, p. 194.
169 As suggested for *Ruodlieb* by Haug and Vollmann, *Literatur*, p. 1308.
170 These examples are given by Balogh, *Philologus* 82 (1927), 214, 206, 215. In such cases the author did not necessarily write down his work himself, but this impression is created for want of any mention of a scribe.
171 Clanchy, *Memory*, p. 217.
172 Van der Werf, *Chansons*, p. 30.
173 Discussed by Balogh, *Philologus* 82 (1927), 85ff.
174 Cf. Balogh, *Philologus* 82 (1927), 83ff. and 202ff.; Hendrickson, *CJ* 25 (1929), 182ff. On palaeographic and physiological reasons for the dominance of reading aloud in classical antiquity see Saenger, *Separation*, pp. 198ff. See also Raible, *Entwicklung*. This stress at this point on the oral dimension of medieval reading (and writing) will have to be supplemented by the possibility of silence in these activities. See p. 309. The possibility of silent reading in antiquity, alongside Balogh's stress on reading aloud, is suggested by Knox, *GRBS* 9 (1968), 421ff.
175 See p. 304.
176 Graham, *Written word*, p. 134. Cf. also the bibliography he gives on p. 229, n. 58, and the quotation from H. Bacht (p. 230, n. 59).
177 Fromm, *Dichter*, pp. 66f.
178 In a very different field Mullett, *Writing*, p. 160, has said with regard to Byzantium that 'much the most interesting work in literacy studies is at present being done in the area of mixed modes in residually oral societies'.
179 E.g. Fromm, *Volkssprache*, p. 103, rightly draws attention to the mixed nature of the clerical audience for religious literature, consisting of both literate and illiterate members.
180 On the slowness of changes within this symbiosis see Fromm, *Volkssprache*, p. 106. For a long period of classical history Harris, *Literacy*, p. 25, discusses what he calls 'the partial emergence of a literate culture and the partial eclipse of an oral culture'. These words could be applied to the present inquiry.
181 Scholz, *Hören*, p. ix.
182 Bloomfield and Dunn, *Role*, pp. 1f. (and already Fechter, *Publikum*, p. 1). Cf. also the observation of O'Keeffe, *Song*, p. ix.

183 Bloomfield and Dunn, *Role*, p. 6.
184 Schröder, *ZfdA* 67 (1930), 216.
185 Scholz, *Hören*, p. 41.
186 Schröder, *Grenzen*, p. 4. It is one of the merits of the survey of OHG literature by Haubrichs, *Anfänge*, that he cuts across this distinction and devotes a section to oral poetry (including reconstructed examples) alongside two sections on written literature.
187 Kuhn, *Entwürfe*, p. 1. See also Schnell, *Nationsbewußtsein*, p. 255.
188 As defined by the editor in vol. I of *VfL*, p. vi.
189 Sprandel, *Gesellschaft*, p. 9. Cf. also Bumke, *Aufgabe*, pp. 21f.
190 Heinzle, *DU (NS)* 1 (1989) 133f. In his review of two volumes in Heinzle's literary history Wehrli, *Arbitrium* 7 (1989), 271, agrees with this up to a point. He adds however that, if we take with Haug the emergence of fiction in the twelfth-century romance as a turningpoint, then the distinction between fictional and functional literature becomes relevant – but only from that point.
191 In practice we shall also consider selected evidence from before 800 and from after 1300.
192 One author who is not accommodated here is Meister Eckhart (even though his work bestraddles the year 1300), mainly because, apart from the important exception of Mechthild von Magdeburg, German mysticism is characteristic of the fourteenth century. For an example of what his work could yield, including the questions of Latin and vernacular, cleric and layman, writing and orality, see Ortmann, *Lehre*, pp. 342ff.
193 Heinzle, *ZfdA* 112 (1983), 220f.
194 Cf. Haug, *Bildprogramm*, p. 56. Haug refers here to Johann von Würzburg's *Wilhelm von Osterreich* in 1314 as the last important romance. For this reason and in accord with a liberal interpretation of 1300 as a deadline it is included in this survey.
195 Cf. Thelen, *Dichtergebet*, pp. 517.
196 Bumke, *Epenhandschriften*, pp. 47, 49, and *Aufgabe*, p. 31.
197 Schweikle, *Minnesang*, pp. vii, 98.
198 *Ibid.*, pp. 1, 98.
199 Schneider, *Heldendichtung*, p. 540.
200 Janota, *Das vierzehnte Jahrhundert*, pp. 14ff.
201 The argument of this chapter appeared in different form in *Speculum* 65 (1990), 267ff.

2 The historical background

1 Cf. Wendehorst, *Mittelalter*, p. 11.
2 Bischoff, *Paläographie*, p. 71; Havelock, *Revolution*, p. 89.
3 Cato II 1 (p. 9). Quoted by Grundmann, *AfK* 40 (1958), 15.
4 Fossier, *Middle Ages* I 20. Particularly revealing is the way in which in a comedy by Caecilius Statius a barbarian is addressed as both illiterate and lawless (Ribbeck, *Fragmenta*, p. 144, lines 59f.). Quoted by Grundmann, *AfK* 40 (1958), 15. Grundmann also draws attention, *ibid.*, p. 30, to the distinction made by Cassiodorus between the literate Romans and the illiterate barbarian (Germanic) rulers of his day: *Variae* IX 21 (p. 286). This equation of barbarians with illiteracy could still be made by Bonizo of Sutri in the eleventh century, see Grundmann, *ibid.*, p. 48, fn. 39.
5 Harris, *Literacy*, pp. 175, 183, 196, 272.
6 Cf. the general statement by Grundmann, *AfK* 40 (1958), 13f. Numerous instances show that laymen were assumed to be illiterate (e.g. Berthold von Regensburg I 507, 14; *Niederrheinische Tundalusfragmente* 32ff.) and clerics to be literate (e.g. Hartmann's *Gregorius* 1463ff.; Thomasin, *Welscher Gast* 1103, 2643f.). Laymen were therefore dependent on clerics for access to what was transmitted in writing (e.g. Heinrich von Melk, *Gehugde* 25, 11f.; Hugo von Trimberg, *Renner* 11748ff.).
7 Haug, *Schriftlichkeit*, pp. 141f.; Haug and Vollmann, *Literatur*, p. 1017.

NOTES TO PAGES 20–5

8 For a similar categorisation see Kartschoke, *Geschichte*, p. 19. Cf. also Kirchert, *ZfdA* 113 (1984), 75.
9 Fromm, *Volkssprache*, p. 106.
10 Cf. Brall, *Gralsuche*, p. 78.
11 *Entwürfe*, p. 4.
12 Liut. 56ff. (cf. Patzlaff, *Otfrid*, pp. 88ff.; Schröder, *Verhältnis*, p. 432).
13 *Germania* 2, 3; *Annales* II 88.
14 The medieval references to this transmission are still best consulted in Grimm, *Heldensage*. See also Diebold, *Sagelied*.
15 Klingenberg, *Dichtung*, pp. 399ff.
16 Ibid. See also Wesche, *Wortschatz*, pp. 24ff. (*garminon*), 33ff. (*spell*), 40ff. (*galdar*), and especially 51ff. ('singen' and 'murmeln').
17 Klingenberg, *Dichtung*, p. 399; Helm, *Religionsgeschichte* II 2, 118f.
18 Klingenberg, *Dichtung*, p. 401.
19 Cf. Haubrichs, *Anfänge*, pp. 98f.
20 Klingenberg, *Dichtung*, p. 401.
21 Gschwantler, *Gattungen*, pp. 103ff.
22 Bloomfield and Dunn, *Role*, p. 148.
23 Ibid., pp. 129f. On praise-poems in the Middle Ages see Georgi, *Preisgedicht*.
24 Gschwantler, *Gattungen*, p. 109.
25 Ibid., pp. 106ff.
26 Cf. Einhard, *Vita Karoli* 29 (p. 33) and Poeta Saxo, *Annales* (PL 99, 726B; cf. also 731A).
27 Bloomfield and Dunn, *Role*, p. 122.
28 Ong, *Writing*, p. 25.
29 Assmann, *Schrift*, p. 270.
30 Coleridge, *Biographia* cap. 18 (p. 208). Quoted by Assmann, *Schrift*, p. 281, n. 8.
31 Fry, *Memory*, p. 290.
32 Gschwantler, *Gattungen*, p. 103.
33 Havelock, *Preface*, pp. 148f.; *Revolution*, pp. 115f.
34 Havelock, *Preface*, pp. 149f.
35 See pp. 67f.
36 Havelock, *Preface*, p. 150.
37 Cf. Baesecke, *Vorgeschichte*, pp. 65, 353ff.
38 Thompson, *Literacy*; Grundmann, *AfK* 40 (1958), 1ff.
39 Haubrichs, *Bildungswesen*, pp. 600f. Cf. Lerner, *Literacy*, pp. 173f. and Riché, *Education*, p. 65.
40 Riché, *Education*, p. 11.
41 Vv. 1549ff.
42 Cf. Krüger, *Krieger*, pp. 328f., and Fleckenstein, *Curialitas*, pp. 479f.
43 Procopius, *Bella Gothica* 1, 2, 16 (vol. II, p. 12). Cf. Grundmann, *AfK* 40 (1958), 29f.; Wormald, *TRHS* (5) 27 (1977), 97f.
44 Harris, *Literacy*, pp. 90ff., illustrates the hostility often shown in fifth-century Athens towards writing, and suggests that this may indicate that writing at this time was invading new functional territory.
45 *Historia ecclesiastica*, MGH SS 9, 353, 25f. Quoted by Grundmann, *AfK* 40 (1958), 48.
46 Wipo, *Tetralogus* 199f. (p. 81). Cf. Grundmann, *AfK* 26 (1936), 143, fn. 45.
47 *De imperio Romano* II 11 (p. 192).
48 *De nugis* I 10 (p. 12). Cf. Grundmann, *AfK* 40 (1958), 50 and Grubmüller, *DU (NS)* 1 (1989), I 42. For a discussion of other examples of this attitude on the part of medieval noblemen see Jones, *Oswald*, pp. 41ff.
49 *De nugis* I 10 (p. 12).
50 Ibid., I 31 (p. 126). Cf. Grundmann, *Bewegungen*, pp. 62f. and Schreiner, *Volkssprache*,

p. 485, on the late Middle Ages. Schreiner also refers (p. 487) to the fears voiced by Sebastian Brant. Whereas Walter Map saw the threat to the *clericus* as a priest in holy orders, Brant sees the *clericus* primarily as a *litteratus*, as an intellectual.
51 Goody, *Literacy*, pp. 11f. Cf. also Harris, *Literacy*, p. 37.
52 Cf. Guerreau-Jalabert, *BEC* 139 (1981), 27f.
53 Cf. Haubrichs, *Bildungswesen*, p. 601.
54 *Ibid.*, p. 604. See also Feldbusch, *Sprache*, p. 330.
55 Berthold von Regensburg, *Predigten* II 233, 6.
56 *ZHF* 11 (1984), 257ff. See also Giesecke, *Buchdruck*, pp. 162ff.
57 Hahn, *Autorschaft*, p. 136, sees Luther as a novel break in German literature, hitherto a process of give-and-take between Latin, literate, clerical on the one hand and vernacular, oral, lay on the other.
58 Rawson, *Life*, p. 50; Harris, *Literacy*, *passim*, who says (p. 196) of Roman culture that, despite obstacles to the spread of literacy, it was informed by the written word. He concedes that Rome was characterised by its written culture (p. 259).
59 Riché, *Education*, p. 3.
60 *Ibid.*, pp. 21f.; Harris, *Literacy*, pp. 34f., 166, 167ff., 207, 212f.
61 Rawson, *Life*, p. 50.
62 Kenney and Clausen, *History*, pp. 6f.
63 *Ibid.*, pp. 19f.; Rawson, *Life*, pp. 42f.
64 Rawson, *Life*, p. 44.
65 Hadas, *Ancilla*, p. 65.
66 Kenney and Clausen, *History*, pp. 23f.; Kenyon, *Books*, pp. 81f.; Harris, *Literacy*, p. 228.
67 Pinner, *World*, p. 54.
68 *Ibid.*, p. 57; Kenyon, *Books*, p. 82.
69 Kenney and Clausen, *History*, p. 10.
70 *Ibid.*
71 Rawson, *Life*, p. 45.
72 *Ibid.*, pp. 45f.
73 *Ibid.*, p. 48.
74 *Ibid.*, pp. 46ff.; Kenney and Clausen, *History*, p. 9.
75 Kenney and Clausen, *History*, pp. 17f.; Saenger, *Naissance*, p. 448.
76 *Tristia* III 1, 2 and 19; I 1, 28.
77 Persius I 126.
78 7, 88, 1ff.; 10, 1ff. and 59, 1f. On the first passage see however Harris, *Literacy*, p. 227.
79 Catullus 14, 25.
80 Palladius, *Historiae* I 42 (PL 74, 328C); Martial 4, 55, 27; Apuleius, *Metamorphoseos*, 9, 30, 1.
81 Columella 8, 17, 16.
82 Pliny the Younger, *Epistulae* 2, 3, 9.
83 *Epistulae ad M. Caes.* IV 3.
84 XI 83, 1.
85 *Divinae Institutiones* V 1, 1 (PL 6, 547).
86 On these two ways of reading in antiquity see Balogh, *Philologus* 82 (1927), 84ff. and 202ff.; Hendrickson, *CJ* 25 (1929/30), 182ff.; di Capua, *RAALBA* 28 (1953), 59ff.; Knox *GRBS* 9 (1968), 421ff.
87 McKitterick, *Carolingians*, p. 272.
88 Parallels are found in German literature. In *Die Erlösung* the verb *lesen* is used of pronouncements by prophets (1492, 1701) on the basis of what they had written (1495, 1688). The evangelists are likewise seen as writers in the *Heliand* 1ff., Der Stricker's *Die vier Evangelisten* 1ff. (*Kleindichtung* 4, 215) and *Der Kreuziger* 93ff. of Johannes von Frankenstein. On the difference between roll and codex see Curschmann, *Pictura*, p. 224.

89 Sprandel, *Gesellschaft*, pp. 31f. Cf. also such general statements as those by Wormald, *TRHS* (5) 27 (1977), 99 and Thomas, *Literacy*, p. 98. What this mass of writing consisted of, and how Christianity and the Church came to be dependent on it, has been shown by two contributors to McKitterick (ed.), *Uses*. Stevenson has shown that the Church required much written material if it was to function effectively (*Literacy*, pp. 17ff.). In the field of papal government in particular Noble, *Literacy*, pp. 82ff., has discussed various realms where literacy was necessary. He also points out how much the Church owed in this to the precedent of Roman imperial government.
90 Cf. Ackroyd, *Books*, pp. 48f.
91 *Ibid.*, p. 51; Harris, *Literacy*, pp. 83, 220f., 285.
92 Cf. Graham, *Written word*, p. 60 and Giesecke, *Buchdruck*, p. 153.
93 *Ibid.*, p. 62; Fouquet-Plümacher, *Buch/Buchwesen III*, pp. 276f. See also Harris, *Literacy*, pp. 294ff.
94 Graham, *Written word*, p. 51.
95 *Ibid.*, p. 52.
96 *Ibid.*, p. 122.
97 Joh. 5, 39; Acts 8, 28. Cf. also Harris, *Literacy*, pp. 281f., whose critical remarks concern how extensive literacy may have been in Judaea, which is not what interests us.
98 Harnack, *Gebrauch*; Hofmeister, *ÖAK* 17 (1966), 298ff. Harris, *Literacy*, pp. 304f., takes issue with von Harnack, but what he criticises is the view that private reading of the scriptures was true of all the faithful. It is enough that Harris, p. 326, concedes that Christianity 'did place the reading of the sacred tests near to the centre of the lives of both men and women who were dedicated to the cult'.
99 Cf. the examples discussed by Hofmeister, *ÖAK* 17 (1966), 300f., 355.
100 PG 12, 229. Cf. Hofmeister, *ÖAK* 17 (1966), 302.
101 *Ibid.*, p. 307.
102 *Viator* 13 (1982), 373f.
103 Cf. Harris, *Literacy*, p. 296.
104 *Epistulae* 147, 1 (p. 275); *Confessiones* x 3.
105 *Historia ecclesiastica*, pp. 5 and 6; Hrabanus, *Epistola* 52 (MGH Epp. 5, 506, 38f.).
106 *Regula*, cap. 48.
107 *Ibid.* On this see also McKitterick, *Carolingians*, p. 265. On individual reading within the Benedictine monastery see van Assche, *SE* 1 (1948), 13ff.
108 Although an oral culture has by definition to dispense with writing, a literate society conducts its communications both by writing and by word of mouth. It is therefore misleading to postulate an absolute contrast between an oral and a literate society. Harris, *Literacy*, p. 36, puts this point in another way when talking about the strong element of orality within the written culture of the Greek and Roman élites. Giesecke, *Buchdruck*, p. 31, argues similarly for a close co-operation between orality and writing in classical antiquity. Cf. also Thomas, *Tradition*, passim.
109 Cf. Crosby, *Speculum* 11 (1936), 88; Nelson, *UTQ* 46 (1976/7), 111f.; Harris, *Literacy*, p. 86.
110 Kenney and Clausen, *History*, p. 3.
111 Spartianus, *Hadrianus* 26, 4.
112 Tacitus, *Historiae* 4, 25. Cf. also Harris, *Literacy*, p. 226.
113 Pliny, *Epistulae* 1, 15, 2; Seneca, *Controversiae* 2, 1, 39.
114 Suetonius, *Claudius* 41, 2; Ovid, *Tristia* 4, 10, 43; Pliny, *Epistulae* 4, 7, 2.
115 Carcopino, *Life*, p. 197; Kenney and Clausen, *History*, p. 11.
116 Cf. Nettleship, *Lives*, p. 15, section 27; p. 16, sections 31f.
117 Horace, *Epistulae* 1, 19, 35ff.; *Ars* 419ff.
118 *Epistulae* 5, 3, 8ff. Cf. Hadas, *Ancilla*, p. 62.
119 On the practice of *recitatio* see Hadas, *Ancilla*, pp. 60ff.; Carcopino, *Life*, pp. 193ff.; Kenney and Clausen, *History*, pp. 11f.; Harris, *Literacy*, pp. 225f.

120 *Philologus* 82 (1927), 230ff. Another reason for individual reading aloud in classical antiquity (the introduction of *scriptura continua* and the physiology of reading) has been discussed by Saenger, *Separation*, pp. 198ff.
121 See above, p. 16.
122 Cf. Rawson, *Life*, p. 51; di Capua, *RAALBA* 28 (1953), 66ff.; von Harnack, *Quellen*, pp. 57ff.
123 Momigliano, *AS* 47 (1978), 196.
124 Carcopino, *Life*, p. 199.
125 See the bibliographical references given by Bertau and Stephan, *ZfdA* 87 (1956–57), 253, fn. 3. Cf. also Jammers, *Vortrag*, p. 128.
126 Page, *Metrum*, pp. 306f.
127 Cf. di Capua, *RAALBA* 28 (1953), 67; Riché, *Ecoles*, p. 29.
128 Haubrichs, *Anfänge*, pp. 374f.
129 Einhard, *Vita Karoli* 24 (p. 29).
130 PL 111, 9B. Other examples of public recital are given by Grundmann, *AfK* 40 (1958), 43, fn. 17.
131 Cf. Schaller, *MlJb* 6 (1970), 22f. He also regards *Waltharius* as a 'Vortragsdichtung' for recital in the monastery, *MlJb* 18 (1983), 76.
132 As suggested by Rädle, *Hrotsvit*, p. 89.
133 Gompf, *MlJb* 8 (1973), 31f., 34. Recital is suggested by v. 42 (cf. Trillitzsch edn., p. 110, note to v. 42, and Haug and Vollmann, *Literatur*, p. 1268, note to 302, 42) and is confirmed by allusions to the refectory, vv. 220, 583 (Trillitzsch, pp. 117, 134; Haug and Vollmann, pp. 1258, 1276).
134 Giraldus Cambrensis, *De rebus*, p. 72 (cf. Crosby, *Speculum* 11 (1936), 94f.); Gervase of Tilbury, *Otia imperialia*, p. 366 (cf. Thompson, *Literacy*, p. 95); Ordericus Vitalis, *Historia ecclesiastica* VI 3 (vol. III, p. 218); Archipoeta I 4 (cf. Ohly, *DVjs* 47 (1973), 48).
135 Frank, *Seitengestaltung*, p. 77, stresses the difference between the classical and early medieval attitudes to literacy. In antiquity an extensive ability to read was accompanied by a neglect of writing (for oneself), whilst the Middle Ages gave priority to the spoken word (in recital) because of widespread illiteracy, but converted writing from the activity of a slave into an act of devotion.
136 Graham, *Written word*, p. 64.
137 Hofmeister, *ÖAK* 17 (1966), 298f.; Schoeler, *Islam* 66 (1989), 215.
138 Harris, *Literacy*, p. 299, comments on the paucity of papyrus fragments of books of the New Testament from earlier than 200.
139 Ehlich, *Text*, p. 39.
140 *Vaterunser* 1907ff.
141 *Passional* I/II 324, 31ff. (cf. also 326, 49ff. concerning St Mark's account and St Peter).
142 Graham, *Written word*, p. 5.
143 *Ibid.*
144 Hofmeister, *ÖAK* 17 (1966), 299. See also Glaue, *Vorlesung*.
145 Graham, *Written word*, pp. 141f.
146 Hofmeister, *ÖAK* 17 (1966), 300.
147 Graham, *Written word*, pp. 123f.
148 Riché, *Ecoles*, pp. 29f.
149 *Ibid.*, p. 320.
150 *Regula* cap. 38. Cf. Ohly, *DVjs* 47 (1973), 41.
151 Cf. *Das Buch von geistlicher Lehre* 47, 45: ze remter, das man die letren horen mag, das man grossir gir hab zu den letren wan zu dem essen.
152 *Regula* cap. 42. Cf. Leclercq, *Amour*, p. 160; Küsters, *Garten*, pp. 25ff.
153 Illmer, *Totum*, pp. 430ff.
154 On these meanings of the MHG verb see the Appendix.

155 Cf. John of Salisbury, *Metalogicon* I 24 (p. 53, 24): *Sed quia legendi verbum equivocum est, tam ad docentis et discentis exercitium quam ad occupationem per se scrutantis scripturas; alterum, id est quod inter doctorem et discipulum communicatur, (ut uerbo utamur Quintiliani) dicatur prelectio, alterum quod ad scrutinium meditantis accedit, lectio simpliciter appelletur.* On this passage see p. 84 and also Jeauneau, *Lecture*, pp. 77ff.
156 The monastery, together with the episcopal court, was also involved with orality in another way, which went beyond Latin and included vernacular recitals by minstrels. From the repeated criticism of this practice (cf. Mönckeberg, *Stellung*, pp. 19ff.; Schreier-Hornung, *Spielleute*, pp. 68ff.; Felten, *Äbte*, pp. 26ff.; Haubrichs, *Anfänge*, p. 88) we may conclude that it was persistent (Mönckeberg, *Stellung*, pp. 26ff.; Schreier-Hornung, *Spielleute*, pp. 42ff.). Although with these recitals we enter the sphere of the vernacular, whereas hitherto we have been concerned with Latin, the oral dimension is the common factor.
157 On this see Gelb, *Study*; Gaur, *History*; Harris, *Origin*.
158 For various suggestions see Kuhn, *Zeugnis*, pp. 55, 66; Klingenberg, *Runenschrift*, p. 56; Elliott, *Runes*, pp. 9f. Cf. also Odenstedt, *ZfdA* 112 (1983), 153ff.
159 Klingenberg, *Runenschrift*, pp. 56, 111ff.
160 *Ibid.*, p. 56; Ebenbauer, *Buch*, p. 36.
161 Elliott, *Runes*, p. 62.
162 Cf. Dickins and Ross, *Dream*, pp. 1ff.; Kendrick, *Art*, pp. 128ff.
163 Kartschoke, *Geschichte*, p. 20. On the use of runes for magic purposes see also Nielsen, *FMS* 19 (1985), 75ff.; Düwel, *FMS* 22 (1988), 70ff.; Müller, *FMS* 22 (1988), 111ff.
164 Elliott, *Runes*, p. 1; Ebel, *Terminologie*, pp. 82f. The argument by Morris, *PBB* 107 (1985), 344ff., against equating the word rune with 'mystery' ignores the evidence for the use of runes in magic and assumes that they were adopted for the same pragmatic purposes as with Mediterranean scripts.
165 Klingenberg, *Runenschrift*, pp. 96ff., 111, 113; Rosenfeld, *RhM* 95 (1952), 194.
166 Arntz, *Handbuch*, p. 252; Elliott, *Runes*, p. 2; Klingenberg, *Runenschrift*, pp. 133, 136; Derolez, *ZfdPh* 78 (1959), 3.
167 Kartschoke, *Geschichte*, pp. 20f., bases himself on what Wehrli, *Literatur*, pp. 52ff., has written of the sacral and even magical function of the (religious) book in the Middle Ages, suggesting a continuity between pre-Christian and Christian attitudes in this respect. Beneath this continuity, however, we have to stress that Latin writing, as practised by medieval clerics, also performed a pragmatic function unknown to runic practice.
168 Arntz, *Handbuch*, p. 282; Kuhn, *Zeugnis*, p. 55; Ebel, *Terminologie*, pp. 86ff.
169 Arntz, *Handbuch*, p. 294; Kuhn, *Zeugnis*, p. 68; Ebel, *Terminologie*, pp. 73ff.
170 Arntz, *Handbuch*, p. 284; Ebel, *Terminologie*, pp. 14ff. The physical similarity between carving a rune and using a stylus on a wax-tablet means that Notker can use this verb of writing Latin letters, *De consolatione* 372, 15 (cf. also 223, 31).
171 Rosenfeld, *RhM* 95 (1952), 193ff.
172 *Ibid.*, p. 202. On the role of literacy in the Roman army see Harris, *Literacy*, pp. 212f., 253ff., 293f. (Vegetius talks of *litteratos milites*), but also pp. 18, 166f. and 202.
173 Harris, *Literacy*, p. 194.
174 Rosenfeld, *RhM* 95 (1952), 205 (OS *bōk*, as in *Heliand* 232, 235; OE *bōc*, *bōcland*; Ostrogothic *frabauhtabōka*).
175 *Ibid.*, pp. 205f.; Hüpper, *FMS* 20 (1986), 111.
176 *RhM* 95 (1952), 195f., 197.
177 Kuhn, *Zeugnis*, pp. 60f.; Ebel, *Terminologie*, pp. 95f.
178 Kuhn, *Zeugnis*, p. 63; Rosenfeld, *RhM* 95 (1952), 204.
179 Kuhn, *Zeugnis*, pp. 62f.
180 Cf. Starck and Wells, *Glossenwörterbuch*, p. 752. The word is not listed for consecutive texts by Schützeichel, *Wörterbuch*.

181 Starck and Wells, *Glossenwörterbuch*, p. 623, with variants *tabela* and *tabula*, listed also by Schützeichel, *Wörterbuch*, p. 192, for Notker (cf. above, n. 170).
182 Prinz, *Grundlagen*, pp. 331ff.
183 Hüpper, *FMS* 20 (1986), 112, suggests the eighth century for the loan of these words.
184 Starck and Wells, *Glossenwörterbuch*, p. 552; Schützeichel, *Wörterbuch*, p. 173.
185 This vocabulary of monastic writing practice forms part of the total vocabulary of monasticism which began to enter German in this period. On this see Eggers, *Sprachgeschichte* I 111ff.
186 Fossier, *Middle Ages* I 80.
187 *Ibid.*
188 As is suggested by Wormald, *Lex scripta*, p. 115.
189 *Ibid.*, pp. 125ff.
190 *Ibid.*, pp. 128f. Cf. also Haubrichs, *Actus et bella*, pp. 40f.
191 Wormald, *Lex scripta*, pp. 130ff.
192 *Ibid.*, p. 132. Cf. Nelson, *Literacy*, p. 263.
193 Cf. Lerner, *Literacy*, p. 165; Guerreau-Jalabert, *BEC* 139 (1981), 30.
194 Prinz, *Grundlagen*, p. 31.
195 Lerner, *Literacy*, pp. 175f.; Grundmann, *AfK* 40 (1958), 24.
196 Prinz, *Grundlagen*, p. 343.
197 Riché, *Education*, p. 110.
198 Prinz, *Grundlagen*, pp. 344f.; Lerner, *Literacy*, p. 176; von See, *Frühmittelalter*, p. 26.
199 Riché, *Education*, pp. 112f.; Köhn, *MM* 10 (1976), 9f.
200 Haubrichs, *Bildungswesen*, p. 599; Prinz,*Grundlagen*, p. 345.
201 Leclercq, *Amour*, p. 18; Prinz,*Grundlagen*, p. 344.
202 McKitterick, *Carolingians*, pp. 167f.
203 Haubrichs, *Anfänge*, p. 203.
204 Leclercq, *Amour*, pp. 27f.
205 Cf. Prinz, *Grundlagen*, p. 345.
206 Cf. von See, *Frühmittelalter*, p. 2.
207 Prinz, *Grundlagen*, pp. 345f.; Haubrichs, *Anfänge*, p. 208; Fossier, *Middle Ages* I 102.
208 *BEC* 139 (1981), 7ff., 23, 33.
209 Saenger, *Naissance*, pp. 448f. and *Coupure*, p. 451, stresses the lead of Ireland and Britain in abandoning *scriptura continua* in favour of division into words, making for greater ease in reading, necessary where Latin had not established itself as in Gaul.
210 Cf. Kartschoke, *Geschichte*, p. 27, on the connection between the monasteries founded by these missions and the rise of writing in the vernacular.
211 *BEC* 139 (1981), 8.
212 Haubrichs, *Anfänge*, p. 77.
213 On the monastic school see Haubrichs, *Anfänge*, pp. 201, 218; on the scriptorium pp. 210, 213; on the library p. 216.
214 Cf. von See, *Frühmittelalter*, pp. 12, 25.
215 Fontaine, *Pluralité*, pp. 768, 773f.; Uytfanghe, *RG* 16 (1976), 41.
216 Klopsch, *Latein*, pp. 324f.
217 This problem has been discussed by Wright, *Latin*, especially pp. 104ff.
218 *Ibid.*, pp. 105ff.
219 *Ibid.*, pp. 119ff. Canon 17 of the council of Tours states: *et ut easdem omelias quisque aperte transferre studeat in rusticam Romanam linguam aut Thiotiscam, quo facilius cuncti possint intellegere quae dicuntur*. Wright suggests that *transferre* means 'to transfer' from one mode of pronunciation to another, rather than 'to translate' from Latin to Romance, but this is rendered unlikely by the fact that the verb governs not merely *rusticam Romanam linguam*, but also *Thiotiscam* (*linguam*), where translation into a different language is involved.

220 Wright, *Latin*, pp. 122ff.
221 *EMH* 4 (1984), 136 (quoting from Reynolds and Wilson, *Scribes*, p. 83), 137.
222 *Ibid.*, p. 141.
223 *Carolingians*, p. 273. Cf. Nelson, *Literacy*, p. 262.
224 Nelson, *Literacy*, p. 268, also points to the advantage that Latin transcended the linguistic divide between the East and West Franks.
225 Irsigler, *Epoche*, pp. 25f.
226 Haubrichs, *Anfänge*, p. 22.
227 Reynolds and Wilson, *Scribes*, p. 83; Richter, *Sprachwissenschaft* 7 (1982), 423.
228 Fleckenstein, *Bildungsreform*, pp. 16, 25.
229 Cf. Treitler, *EMH* 4 (1984), 139; Ganz, *Viator* 18 (1987), 23ff.; Haubrichs, *Anfänge*, p. 214; Saenger, *Naissance*, pp. 447ff.
230 Treitler, *EMH* 4 (1984), 139f.
231 MGH *Poetae Latini Aevi Carolini* 1 320, carmen xciv, l. 7ff. (quoted by Treitler, *EMH* 4 (1984), 140, fn. 17). See also Ganz, *Viator* 18 (1987), 33 and Vezin, *Ponctuation*, p. 439; Parkes, *Pause*, pp. 35ff., 76ff. O'Keeffe, *Song*, p. 144, also stresses this and says of the systematic pointing of Latin texts that it 'was primarily performative rather than analytic'.
232 Cf. Classen, *Lage*, p. 21.
233 Einhard, *Vita Karoli* 29 (p. 33).
234 Matzel, *Untersuchungen*, p. 517.
235 *AfK* 40 (1958), 39f.
236 *Grammatica*, PL 101, 857D. Quoted by Matzel, *Untersuchungen*, p. 519.
237 Matzel, *Untersuchungen*, p. 521.
238 *Ibid.*, pp. 513ff. Cf. Haubrichs, *Anfänge*, pp. 310f.
239 *EMH* 4 (1984), 179.
240 *Ibid.*, pp. 194f.
241 *Ibid.*, p. 175.
242 *Ibid.*, p. 203.
243 *Ibid.*, pp. 205, 206.
244 *Ibid.*, p. 175.
245 *Ibid.*, p. 156.
246 Lerner, *Literacy*, pp. 185, 187.
247 Haubrichs, *Anfänge*, p. 192. On Carolingian capitularies see McKitterick, *Carolingians*, pp. 25ff.
248 Haubrichs, *Anfänge*, p. 193; Sonderegger, *Übersetzung*, pp. 113ff.
249 See above, pp. 15f.
250 Haubrichs, *Anfänge*, p. 225; *Actus et bella*, p. 45.
251 Vollmann-Profe, *Wiederbeginn*, p. 11.
252 Haubrichs, *Anfänge*, pp. 105ff.
253 The same point has been made by Wehrli in his review in *Arbitrium* 7 (1989), 271ff.
254 Cf. Grubmüller, *Sprache*, pp. 205ff.
255 Liut. 56ff. Cf. also the attitude of Walahfrid Strabo, quoted by Schröder, *Grenzen*, p. 55.
256 Liut. 103ff.
257 Cf. Schröder, *Grenzen*, pp. 55f.
258 Vollmann-Profe, *Wiederbeginn*, p. 12.
259 Hüpper-Dröge, *Schild*, p. 49; Rupp, *Literatur*, p. 9.
260 Hüpper-Dröge, *Schild*, p. 50.
261 *ZfdPh* 78 (1959), 19.
262 See also, with regard to a group of interlinear translations connected with the Reichenau, Haubrichs, *Studienprogramm*, pp. 244f.
263 Cf. von See, *Frühmittelalter*, pp. 55f.
264 Kuhn, *Dichtung*, p. 43.

265 Masser, *Aufgabe*, pp. 100f.
266 Gentry, *Kulturreform*, pp. 69f.
267 Sonderegger, *Latein*, p. 64.
268 Masser, *Aufgabe*, pp. 87ff.
269 *Ibid.*, p. 98.
270 On glosses and interlinear translations see Henkel, *Übersetzungen*, pp. 65ff., especially p. 66.
271 Masser, *Aufgabe*, p. 92.
272 *Ibid.*, p. 95.
273 *Ibid.*, p. 98.
274 Cf. the quotations from other scholars given by Masser, *ibid.*, p. 96.
275 *Ibid.*, p. 104f.
276 Sonderegger, *Sprache*, p. 58.
277 *Ibid.*, p. 52; *Latein*, p. 63.
278 Kartschoke, *Bibeldichtung*, p. 39. On the reasons for this exceptional position see p. 271.
279 Sonderegger, *Sprache*, pp. 61f.
280 Krause, *Runeninschriften*, pp. 278, 313ff.; Sonderegger, *Sprache*, pp. 57f., 89f.
281 Bergmann, *RhVj* 30 (1965), 66ff.; Kruse, *Überlieferung*, pp. 133ff.; Haubrichs, *Anfänge*, p. 217.
282 Bischoff, *Paläographie*, p. 26.
283 Schmidt-Wiegand, *FMS* 13 (1979), 56ff.
284 Haubrichs, *Anfänge*, pp. 191f.
285 *Ibid.*, pp. 225f.
286 Haug, *Schriftlichkeit*, pp. 142f.
287 For examples see Green, *Parergon* 2 (1984), 60.
288 Notker, ed. Piper, I ii, 861, 2.
289 Haubrichs, *Anfänge*, pp. 228ff., 280ff.
290 Feldbusch, *Sprache*, pp. 237ff.; Knoop, *AfdA* 100 (1989), 40.
291 Feldbusch, *Sprache*, pp. 237ff.
292 Haubrichs, *Anfänge*, p. 229.
293 Feldbusch, *Sprache*, pp. 243ff.
294 Haubrichs, *Anfänge*, p. 236.
295 Feldbusch, *Sprache*, pp. 246ff.
296 The educational usefulness of this type of interlinear translation means that it survives well beyond the OHG period. In the *Windberger Psalter*, for example, we can be sure that the German text is still subordinated to understanding the Latin. First, because the word-order of the German version follows that of the Latin; secondly, because names present in the Latin text are not given in the German, which is therefore not regarded as autonomous; thirdly, because the German version often gives more than one rendering of a Latin term (which would not be necessary if the German text had been independent, but was called for in the pedagogic context of understanding the Latin version). See also Henkel, *Übersetzungen*, pp. 65ff., on the need to read such translations vertically (from a Latin word to the vernacular interlinear rendering placed above it, and back again), rather than horizontally (as if the German version were to be read consecutively).
297 Feldbusch, *Sprache*, p. 248; Sonderegger, *Sprache*, pp. 60f.
298 Feldbusch, *Sprache*, p. 248. This has to be qualified, even in the case of Notker, in the light of the remark by Henkel, *Übersetzungen*, p. 85, about a suggestion made by Sonderegger. See also Näf, *Wortstellung*, and Braungart, *ZfdPh* 106 (1987), 2ff. and Hellgardt, *Textensembles*, p. 20.
299 Kartschoke, *Geschichte*, p. 110, stresses that monastery schools needed translations as an

access to the Latin texts which were their primary concern, but that: 'Wo der deutsche Wortlaut ins Zentrum der sprachlich-stilistischen Bemühungen rückte, entstand geistliche Dichtung – in Gestalt des Bibelepos und des Heiligenliedes etwa'.

300 Masser, *Aufgabe*, p. 100.; Hellgardt, *Textensembles*, pp. 21f.
301 On this see Green, *LwJb* 30 (1989), 9ff. and pp. 270f.

Introduction to Part II

1 On the failure of historical sources to refer to contemporary literature see Schnell, *Kirche*, pp. 99f.
2 Our concern with reception presents a peculiar difficulty. Whereas writing, an artefact, leaves a trace, reading does not, so evidence for reading is less common. In the oral context neither recital nor hearing leaves a trace directly which could serve as evidence.
3 A similar point has been made by Brüggen, *Kleidung*, p. 22. We may take encouragement from the historian's readiness to accept literary evidence, with whatever reservations. In her discussion of the knighting ceremony Orth, *Formen*, p. 137, describes literary depictions as 'zwar ... überhöht dargestellt ... aber nicht falsch', a judgment with which Fleckenstein, *Curialitas*, pp. 464 and 465, is in agreement. On using literary sources in reconstructing historical reality see also Bumke, *Kultur*, pp. 17ff.
4 Cf. Pörksen, *Erzähler*, p. 11; Thelen, *Dichtergebet*, pp. 12 and 492.
5 See p. 74.
6 See p. 132.
7 Other evidence in the *Gandersheimer Reimchronik* derives its force from the request for intercession (see p. 101), whilst in *Die Erlösung* the acrostic and its accompanying instructions are the only evidence for individual reading (see p. 158).
8 See p. 140, and Green, *Roman*, pp. 76f.
9 *Wessobrunner Schöpfungsgedicht* 1 and *Christus und die Samariterin* 1. On these examples (without an introductory prayer rather than a prologue) see Thelen, *Dichtergebet*, pp. 24f. On the reasons for not regarding *Lesên wir* as referring to a reading reception by the audience see pp. 115ff.
10 On the exposed position of prologues and epilogues in manuscript tradition cf. Wachinger, *Autorschaft*, p. 5.
11 See p. 208.
12 See p. 192.
13 *Mäzene*, pp. 19f.
14 See pp. 105f.
15 Priester Arnold, for example, addresses his audience in the *Loblied auf den heiligen Geist* as *tumpen leige liute*, for whom he has to translate any Latin term into German (see p. 98). It is of a piece with this that the author refers to what his audience has heard him say (26, 13, refers back to 21, 15ff.).
16 Bergmann, *Aufführungstext*, pp. 314ff.; Linke, *Versuch*, pp. 527ff.
17 Schnell, *Kirche*, pp. 75ff.
18 Mertens, *Gregorius*, pp. 24 and 37. Whether or not we classify Wolfram's *Willehalm* as a legend or as a romance (or as neither), he can presuppose with his audience knowledge of his *Parzival*. Cf. 10, 21ff. and Kiening, *Reflexion*, pp. 94ff.
19 See von Ertzdorff, *Rudolf*, pp. 49 and 112.
20 Cf. Bumke, *Mäzene*, p. 116, and *Geschichte*, p. 141.
21 Thelen, *Dichtergebet*, pp. 215f. and 413.
22 Cf. Bloomfield and Dunn, *Role*, pp. 106ff., especially p. 116.
23 Cf. Vollmann-Profe, *Wiederbeginn*, pp. 63 and 68ff.

3 Criteria for reception by hearing

1. *Interface*, p. 186.
2. Schlieben-Lange, *Traditionen*, p. 46; Ehlich, *Text*, p. 28.
3. Schlieben-Lange, *Traditionen*, p. 46; Knoop, *GL* 3/4 (1976), 32.
4. Schlieben-Lange, *Traditionen*, p. 47; Knoop, *GL* 3/4 (1976), 32; Vansina, *Tradition*, p. 34.
5. Schlieben-Lange, *Traditionen*, p. 47.
6. Ehlich, *Text*, p. 28.
7. *Ibid.*, pp. 28, 32, 33. On the role of memory and memory training in the Middle Ages see Carruthers, *Book*.
8. Ehlich, *Text*, p. 33. Cf. Elwert, *Einbettung*, pp. 246f.
9. Ehlich, *Text*, pp. 35f.
10. *Der welsche Gast* 9445ff.
11. Geoffroi de Vinsauf, *Poetria nova* 2031f. How traditional this non-auditory aspect of recital was is clear from the definition given in the *Rhetorica ad Herennium* I 2, 3: *Pronuntiatio est vocis, vultus, gestus moderatio cum venustate*. For further examples from classical and medieval rhetoric see Schubert, *Theorie*, pp. 57ff.
12. Pliny the Younger, *Epistulae* II 3, 9.
13. Green, *Recognising*, p. 12; *Irony*, p. 21. Cf. also the cases quoted by Knox, *Ironia*, pp. 55, 58ff.
14. On gestures in medieval drama see Roeder, *Gebärde*, and Simon, *PBB* 112 (1990), 150f.
15. Linke, *Versuch*, p. 542, fn. 40, quotes the revealing words of the town clerk of Solothurn on a drama performed there as late as 1543: *verba personarum quidem audire et gestus videre potuerim*.
16. Clanchy, *Memory*, p. 203; Kroeschell, *Rechtsgeschichte*, p. 58; Schmidt-Wiegand, *Gebärden*, cols. 1411ff. and *FMS* 16 (1982), 363ff.
17. 276, 32ff.
18. On the restrictions from which we suffer cf. Vansina, *Tradition*, p. 83.
19. Bumke, *Kultur*. p. 718; Peters, *Fürstenhof*, p. 9.
20. Cf. Hatto, *Anatomy*, p. 188. See also Bloch, *Literature*, p. 2, and Haupt, *Fest*, pp. 26f.
21. Cf. Wenzel, *Repräsentation*, pp. 342f. Hatto, *Anatomy*, p. 148, also stresses the public or social nature of much medieval literature. Cf. also Mertens, *Mäzenatentum*, p. 118.
22. Behr, *Literatur*, p. 16, sees the social and political function of court literature in terms of public display, hence oral delivery. Where Schröder, *ZfdA* 118 (1989), 279, criticises Behr's concentration on the political function of such literature, we may find fault with Behr's concentration on the public dimension (p. 249: 'Mittelalterliche Literatur ist öffentliche Literatur'), for whatever importance we may attach to it in the present context, Chapter 5 shows us that there was also the possibility of a non-public reception of medieval literature.
23. Cf. Haug, *Idealität*, p. 157: Chrétien's Arthurian romance, especially his *Erec*, 'sei nichts anderes als eine narrativ umgesetzte und ausgefaltete Diskussion der Idee des höfischen Festes'; Brunner, *Kultur*, p. 152. Cf. also Wenzel, *Repräsentation*, p. 197, and Haupt, *Fest*, p. 122.
24. Kleinschmidt, *AfK* 58 (1976) 44, 57, 62, fn. 126; Wenzel, *Repräsentation*, p. 338.
25. *Eneide* 13196ff. (cf. Hartmann, *Erec* 2166ff., 2196ff.) On the interplay between princely generosity and the renown which it occasions see Schreier-Hornung, *Spielleute*, pp. 95ff. and Salmen, *Spielmann*, p. 49. Hartung, *Spielleute*, p. 88, fn. 36, quotes a revealing passage from England: *Hic ad augmentum et famam sui nominis ... de regno Francorum cantores et joculatores muneribus allexerat, ut de illo canerent in plateis*.
26. *Eneide* 13159ff.
27. On the role of music (whether as an accompaniment to song or not) at medieval courts see Žak, *Musik*.
28. Žak, *ibid.*, pp. 7ff., discusses *clamor, strepitus, schal, kradem, doz* in terms of 'Recht und

29 *Melodien*, pp. 17f.
30 Mertens, *Rezeption*, p. 144. On Henry as *nepos Caroli* see Geith, *Carolus*, pp. 118f.
31 Mertens, *Rezeption*, p. 144. Cf. also Nellmann's review of Ott-Meimberg, *Kreuzzugsepos*, PBB 106 (1984), 304.
32 FMLS 22 (1986), 184ff. See also Fried, AfK 55 (1973), 312ff.
33 On these and other aspects of Henry's patronage see Bertau, DU 20 (1968), II 4ff.
34 MGH SS 16, 230. Cf. Ganz, *Heinrich*, p. 38.
35 Apollinaris, *Carmen* XII, 1ff. The passage from Priscus is most easily accessible in Naumann, *Dichterbuch*, pp. 5f.
36 The historical references are discussed by Diebold, *Sagelied*, pp. 27ff.
37 *Chronicon* VI 15 (p. 266).
38 Erdmann, ZfdA 73 (1936), 87ff.
39 Cf. Heger, *Lebenszeugnis*, especially pp. 203ff.
40 Schreier-Hornung, *Spielleute*, pp. 68f., 72, 82; Hartung, *Spielleute*, pp. 34, 50; Mönckeberg, *Stellung*, pp. 20, 28, 46.
41 *Galluslied*, prologue A, lines 2f. (p. 83).
42 Osterwalder, *Galluslied*, pp. 217ff., 232ff.
43 *Ibid.*, pp. 234ff., especially 238f. Mertens, AfdA 84 (1973), 217, quotes from the *Casus S. Galli* to the effect that laymen joined in singing the saint's praise, possibly only in refrains.
44 *Ibid.*, p. 242. Choral (or solo) singing to those who merely listen is also amply suggested by the stage-instructions given in medieval drama (*cantet, cantent*).
45 On the liturgical or paraliturgical function of some of these examples cf. Janota, *Studien*, pp. 37ff., 71f., but also Mertens, AfdA 84 (1973), 212ff., and Spechtler, ZfdPh 90 (1971), *Sonderheft*, pp. 169ff.
46 Haubrichs, *Georgslied*, pp. 196f.
47 Freytag, *Theorie*, p. 127.
48 Kolb, *Marienlied*, pp. 81f.
49 128, 77.
50 Borck, PBB 76 (1955), 311f.
51 Ehrismann, *Geschichte* I 249.
52 496, 7ff.
53 Haubrichs, *Georgslied*, pp. 176f.
54 *Ibid.*, p. 178.
55 *Galluslied* 16, 4 (p. 100), versions A, B and C; *Heinrichs Litanei* 1, 36.
56 86, 46.
57 Cf. *Herzog Ernst* D 2155ff., 2294, 3579ff. and the joint singing of the *leise* in the *Kreuzfahrt des Landgrafen Ludwig* 1895f., 2106f., 3100f., 4206.
58 On the public singing of the *Te Deum* and its function as an *acclamatio* see Žak, HJb 102 (1982), 1ff., who points out the respective functions of clergy and laity on such occasions, the former singing the *Te Deum*, the latter responding with *Kyrie* or something similar.
59 ZfdA 104 (1975), 68ff.
60 Acclamations in the sense of *laudes* addressed in public to rulers or bishops are discussed by Žak, *Musik*, pp. 175ff.
61 IV 4, 53: *Ther selbo liut guoto sank gemeinmuato / thesses liedes wunna al einêra stimma*. Cf. Žak, *Musik*, p. 185, fn. 113.
62 PL 193, 1436 A. Quoted by Freytag in his review of Vollmann-Profe, AfdA 99 (1988) 137, fn. 6. Collective singing of an old pilgrim-song occurs in the secular contexts of departure in Gottfried's *Tristan* 11536ff. (cf. Ganz edn, fn. to 11538) and of battle in *Die Böhmenschlacht* 47ff.

63 Cf. the examples given by Žak, *Musik*, p. 234, fn. 53, and by Haug and Vollmann, *Literatur*, p. 1138, note to 148, 46f. See also von See, *GRM* 55 (1976), 1ff.
64 Cf. for Old French literature Ross, *Old French*, p. 83.
65 On singing and playing a stringed instrument see Žak, *Musik*, p. 247 and fn. 24. On the numbers involved in such performances see p. 256. Cf. also Salmen, *Musiker*, p. 215 and McMahon, *Music*, p. 67.
66 Cf. Hofmann, *ZfdA* 92 (1963), 85; Jammers, *ZfdA* 94 (1965), 190.
67 Heusler, *Dichtung*, p. 37; Baesecke, *Vorgeschichte*, pp. 483, 493f.
68 Venantius Fortunatus, *Carmina* VII 8, 63 and 69; Jordanes, *De origine actibusque Getarum* V 43.
69 Alcuin, *Epistolae* 124 (p. 183); *Vita Liudgeri*, MGH SS 2, 412.
70 Wolf, *Non veni*, p. 86, has suggested that the ancient themes referred to are not those of native heroic tradition, but those of classical antiquity, but a differing view of the subject-matter of this literary tradition hardly affects the way in which it was transmitted (on the oral recital of works in Latin see above, p. 32).
71 The inclusion of heroic poems to be sung in the repertoire of wandering minstrels is suggested by Konrad von Würzburg, *Kleinere Dichtungen* III 32, 291ff., and by Der Marner, XV 14ff. See Heinzle, *Dietrichepik*, pp. 71f.
72 See Bertau and Stephan, *ZfdA* 87 (1956–57), 253ff.; Beyschlag, *ZfdA* 93 (1964), 157ff.; Bertau, *EG* 20 (1965), 1ff.; Jammers, *Schrift*, pp. 148ff.; Brunner, *Epenmelodien*, pp. 149ff.; *Strukturprobleme*, pp. 300ff.; Lipphardt, *Liedweisen*, pp. 275ff.
73 This has been particularly stressed by Schweikle, *Minnesang*, pp. 34ff. In playing down the importance of the lyric being sung and therefore received orally, in favour of a reading reception, he stands at the opposite pole to Jammers, *Melodien*, p. 16. The truth is likely to lie somewhere between the two.
74 Sayce, *Lyric*, pp. 76f.
75 Schweikle, *Minnesang*, p. 56.
76 Mehler, *Dicere*, argues that not merely this verb, but also *dicere*, can be used in stage-directions to indicate sung performance, at least of parts of the drama. In this he follows a lead given by Linke in his reviews of R. Steinbach (*AfdA* 83 (1972), 199ff.) and R. Bergmann (*AfdA* 85 (1974), 19ff.).
77 This is true of the *Benediktbeurer Passionsspiel*, the *Klosterneuburger Osterspiel*, the *Amorbacher Spiel von Mariae Himmelfahrt*, the *Wiener Passionsspiel*, and the *Trierer Osterspiel*. Details can be found in the editions concerned except that in the last case these are given by Froning, *Drama I*, p. 47.
78 On the *Trier-Alsfelder Marienklage* see A. Geering, *Nibelungenmelodie*, pp. 118ff., and Bertau and Stephan, *ZfdA* 87 (1956–57), 255. On the *Zehnjungfrauenspiel* see Bertau and Stephan, *ibid*.
79 Prologue, versions A, B and C (pp. 83f.), especially version B, lines 2f.: *ne tam dulcis melodia memorie laberetur*.
80 *Praefatio*, p. 2, line 13. On the neumes in manuscript M see Taeger, *ZfdA* 107 (1978), 184ff.
81 See p. 111.
82 *Lyric*, pp. 73f.
83 Cf. Bützler, *Untersuchungen*, pp. 15ff.
84 Schweikle, *Minnesang*, pp. 53f., attaches minimal importance to references to a musical accompaniment to the love-lyric, but against this see Sayce, *Lyric*, p. 380, fn. 2, and Welker, *Melodien*, p. 122.
85 For other examples cf. Žak, *Musik*, p. 245, fn. 14, but also the qualifications on p. 246.
86 *Words*, p. 161.
87 The linguistic evidence has been assembled by Ehrismann, *Geschichte* I 27ff.
88 *Ibid.*, pp. 30f.
89 *Lyric*, pp. 368, fn. 1, and 380.

90 Borck, *PBB* 76 (1954), 308f.
91 *Ibid.*, p. 309.
92 Ehrismann, *Geschichte* I 249. Cf. Borck, *PBB* 76 (1954), 312f.
93 *Words*, p. 164.
94 *Song*, p. 109.
95 A similar reference is given by Neidhart, *Winterlieder* 29, 4, 4ff. (cf. Mertens, *Kaiser*, p. 463).
96 See Sievers, *PBB* 56 (1932), 181ff. and Heinen, *Ulrich*, pp. 16ff.
97 Schweikle, *Minnesang*, pp. 115 and 145.
98 Sayce, *Lyric*, pp. 375f. On the background to the conceit of the poet's heart breaking in harmony with the fiddle-string in the *leiche* of Tannhäuser and Ulrich von Winterstetten (Sayce, *Lyric*, p. 377) see McMahon, *Music*, p. 64.
99 Masser, *WW* 39 (1989), 7.
100 See also Spanke, *NM* 31 (1930), 143ff. and Chailley, *Danse*, pp. 357ff.
101 *Words*, p. 160.
102 307ff., 402ff.
103 *Beowulf* 853ff. See Opland, *Horseback*, pp. 30ff.
104 *Ibid.*, p. 36.
105 Cf. also Janota, *Studien*, pp. 187ff., 220ff., 237ff.
106 *Georgslied*, p. 188.
107 *Ibid.*, pp. 189ff.
108 Žak, *Musik*, pp. 186ff. See also p. 106 for this possibility with the *Ludwigslied*.
109 *Vita Altmanni*, cap. 3, MGH SS 12, 230. Cf. Freytag, *Ezzos Gesang*, pp. 154ff. and his review of Vollmann-Profe, *AfdA* 99 (1988), 136f.
110 See above, pp. 66f.
111 Cf. Vollmann-Profe, *Wiederbeginn*, p. 35.
112 See Hübner, *Geißlerlieder*, pp. 11f. and 65ff.
113 Cf. Bumke, *Kultur*, p. 755, and Heinen, *Ulrich*, pp. 25ff.
114 Frau Ava, *Johannes* 26, 1ff.
115 Discussed by Mohr, *Feste*, pp. 37ff.
116 Cf. Mohr, *ibid.*, p. 45.
117 Bumke, *Kultur*, pp. 276ff.
118 *Chronicon Hanoniense*, pp. 155ff. (especially p. 156, lines 24f.).
119 Heger, *Lebenszeugnis*, pp. 222ff.
120 *Ibid.*, pp. 206ff.
121 Scholz, *Hören*, p. 94, quoting from Drube, *Hartmann*, p. 61, fn. 1.
122 Žak, *Musik*, pp. 169ff., discusses a *citharoedus* at the courts of Theoderic and Chlodwig, where the suggestion that the latter was attracted by the renown of the former's table (p. 169, fn. 7) reveals the context in which performance took place.
123 Salmen, *Spielmann*, p. 69.
124 *Vaterunser* 4645ff.
125 Scholz, *Hören*, pp. 97f.
126 See p. 99.
127 See Wolff's Introduction, p. xi.
128 Cf. Kartschoke, *IASL* 8 (1983), 257.
129 This criticism has been made by Lebsanft, *ZfSL* 92 (1982), 57.
130 On the close association of this work with Easter see Green, *Exodus*, pp. 22f.
131 On this ambiguity see Green, *Parergon* 2 (1984), 76, n. 42.
132 An example of the expansion of the simple adverb of place occurs in the *Basler Predigten*, 52, 4.
133 Scholz discusses this problem, pp. 167ff., but sees it more in terms of the private reader requiring pauses in his reading. The question has been considered with regard to recital

practice in the case of Hartmann by Linke, *Strukturen*, and in the case of Rudolf von Ems by Lenschen, *Gliederungsmittel*.

134 Cf. edition, p. 163, and also de Boor, *Geschichte* III 1, 142, and Heinzle, *Dietrichepik*, p. 75.
135 The parallel between this passage (with *singer*) and the others (with *leser*) is another indication that the latter refer to a recital in public.
136 Fischer, *Studien*, p. 262.
137 Scholz, *Hören*, pp. 88f.
138 *Ibid*., pp. 84f.
139 Scholz concedes this possibility in passing, p. 86, but grants it little importance in practice. That medieval authors had to cope with this situation in recital has been shown for Chrétien's *Yvain* by Hunt, *FMLS* 6 (1970), 14 and *FMLS* 8 (1972), 328. Scholz takes account of Hunt's argument, but suggests that it could equally well be applied to the situation of a reader, p. 175, fn. 697. That may be so, but it does not dismiss the possibility of a recital. See also p. 295.
140 Cf. p. 85: Berthold von Holle, *Crane* 4906ff., although Scholz cannot suppress some reservations (fn. 206).
141 See Neumann, *Schauspiel*.
142 Further examples from this work are 139, 255, 533, 642f. and 933f.
143 Ohly, *DVjs* 47 (1973), 26ff.
144 *Ibid*., p. 27.
145 *Ibid*., p. 29.
146 Schützeichel, *Memento Mori*, pp. 99ff.
147 Ohly, *DVjs* 47 (1973), 28.
148 *Ibid*.
149 Kartschoke, *Altdeutsche Bibeldichtung*, p. 23.
150 Thelen, *Dichtergebet*, pp. 108f.
151 On the force of *úzana* see Vollmann-Profe, *Kommentar*, pp. 147f.
152 Notker, *De consolatione* 34, 21, translates *mandavi stilo memorieque* by *Ih habo ... gescriben*. Cf. also Einhard (*Vita Karoli* 29, pp. 33f.) on Charles's concern for written transmission (*scripsit memoriaeque mandavit*).
153 Scholz, *Hören*, p. 73.
154 *Ibid*., p. 77. Cf. Schröder, *Anegenge*, p. 82.
155 Scholz, *Hören*, p. 78. Scholz is also criticised on this point by Kartschoke, *IASL* 8 (1983), 257.
156 Scholz, *Hören*, pp. 149f. A monastic context for Ebernand has been suggested by Heinzle, *Wandlungen*, p. 165, and by Schüppert, *VfL* 2, 291.
157 Cf. Cramer, *VfL* 5, 903, and Buschinger, *Lorengel*, pp. xivf.
158 Cf. Küsters, *Garten*, pp. 24ff. The Asbach and Admont versions use the present participle instead (151, 4; 229, 5).
159 On this construction see pp. 89f.
160 Cf. Mertens, *Wolfram-Studien* 1 (1970), 219ff., especially p. 230.
161 Scholz, *Hören*, p. 60.
162 Fischer, *Studien*, pp. 256ff.
163 *Ibid*., p. 257; Mundschau, *Sprecher*.
164 *Erec* 249ff.
165 Jaufre Rudel 2, 29. On the interpretation of *Morant und Galie* 5154 see the editors' note to v. 390 (p. 217).
166 Curschmann, *Nibelungenlied*, pp. 114f.
167 Cf. the editor's note on vv. 236f. (p. 344): 'Die Lektüre der Geschichte von Tristan und Isolde wird implizite mit dem Lesen der biblischen Texte verglichen. Dahinter steht natürlich die Eucharistieanalogie.'

168 For comparable examples from the same work cf. Green, *ZfdA* 115 (1986), 158f.
169 Another example from gnomic poetry is provided by Bruder Wernher 45, 1 and 6.
170 Hugo von Trimberg, *Der Renner* 5825f., uses *singer* and *sager* in general terms in a recital context.
171 A literal meaning of *singen* is also suggested for the *Jüngerer Titurel* whenever it is used in conjunction with a reference to musical accompaniment or to a melody (*dôn*, *wîse*), e.g. 2407, 3ff.; 2412, 4; 3205, 2ff.; 3812, 2ff.; 5986, 1ff.
172 *Metalogicon* I 24 (p. 53, 24), quoted p. 337, n. 155 and discussed by Jeauneau, *Jean de Salisbury*, pp. 77ff.
173 Jeauneau, *Jean de Salisbury*, p. 78.
174 *Regula*, cap. 38.
175 Other examples are found in the Zwiefalten version (32, 8) and the Admont version (227, 9). For feminine parallels cf. the *Breviarien von Sankt Lambrecht*, 141 (125a) and 142 (84a). For a monastic example not immediately dependent on the Rule cf. the use of *lesere* in Albertus von Augsburg, *Ulrichsleben* 1444. See also the conjunction of *leser* with *vor liset* in *Lucidarius* 40, 6.
176 P. 33, col. 2.
177 Although this Wolfenbüttel manuscript dates from the fifteenth century it demonstrates the continuity of this practice.
178 Scholz, *Hören*, pp. 36f., gives three examples, of which only one is German.
179 *Didascalicon*, III 8 (PL 176, 771): *Trimodum est lectionis genus docentis, discentis, vel per se inspicientis. Dicimus enim lego librum illi, et lego librum ab illo, et lego librum.* Referred to by Scholz, *Hören*, p. 53.
180 In addition, we shall see that the combination of *lesen* with the causative *lân* can denote having a text recited aloud.
181 On this passage see Green, *ZfdA* 115 (1986), 161.
182 Cf. Scholz, *Hören*, p. 53.
183 On this episode see Green, *MLR* 81 (1986), 367.
184 Cf. vv. 61ff.
185 Cf. pp. 405f.
186 This reading of *singen* + *vor* is reinforced by the following lines, 11, 11f.
187 Cf. above, p. 70, Bumke, *Mäzene*, p. 170, and Wiessner, *Kommentar*, pp. 5 (note to 4, 10), 83 (note to 17).
188 See Bach's edition, pp. xvii and xlix, as well as Heinzle, *Wandlungen*, p. 187.
189 This construction is reminiscent of *Diu vrône botschaft* 384ff., where *bediuten* and *vor* are used together.
190 Cf. also vv. 2345f.
191 This verb is mentioned only once and in passing by Scholz, *Hören*, p. 53.
192 *PBB* 111 (1989), 196ff., especially 204ff.
193 *Ibid.*, p. 206.
194 On the political dimension of *offenlîche* see Wenzel, *ZfdPh* 107 (1988), 340f.
195 These examples combine two pointers: *lesen* + *offenlîche*, but also *vor*. Cf. Ebernand von Erfurt, *Heinrich und Kunigunde* 2014ff., and Albrecht von Scharfenberg, *Jüngerer Titurel* 1469, 3f. (confirmed by 1505, 3).
196 Köhn, *Latein*, pp. 341, 350f. See above, p. 16.
197 *Der welsche Gast* 11183.
198 Cf. *Das Märterbuch* 18523 (*er offenleichenn las*), confirmed by 18526 (*las er uber laut*).
199 PL 111, 9B. Cf. also *facit ... recitare* in *Ruodlieb* V 228 (on this see Haug and Vollmann, *Literatur*, p. 1353, note to 444, 287).
200 On the correspondence between the Latin and the vernacular construction see Green, *Otfrid*, pp. 756f.

201 Notker, *Martianus Capella* 218, 8, combines *lesan* + *lân* with *fore* as a rendering for *recitari*.
202 Several pointers are used together by Rudolf von Ems, *Alexander* 4588f.: *lesen* + *heizen*, *offenlîche*, but also *vor* (4595).
203 Green, *Otfrid*, p. 756.
204 I have discussed this passage in *ZfdA* 115 (1986), 157f.
205 The evidence for this is listed *ibid.*, pp. 155f.
206 Other back-references in this work may be just as clear, even if they contain no verbal echo: 2029 (cf. 721), 5688 (cf. 5583ff.), 7168 (cf. 6457ff.), 11244 (cf. 10667ff.). That *lesen* in these passages is used in the sense of recital aloud has been stressed by Wenzel, *Geschichte*, pp. 28ff.
207 The earlier passages to which reference is made here are 24379ff., 24450ff., 25043ff., 25150ff., 25188ff., 25565ff.
208 *ZfdA* 104 (1975), 310.
209 Other examples from the same work are 6322 (refers back to 5890f., echo in *an des meisters stat*) and 6908 (refers back to 6800f., echo in *des liebes cranc*). The phrase can also refer to an earlier point in the narrative, even without a verbal echo, as in Heinrich von Freiberg, *Tristan* 2091 (refers back to 2059ff.) and 2331 (refers back to 2078f., 2126ff., 2329). Cf. also Heinrich von Neustadt, *Apollonius von Tyrland* 14940 (refers back to 2444f.).
210 *Benediktinerregel* 226, 10 (*si kileran* translates *recitetur*). Cf. also 243, 17 (where *lesan* is used of reading aloud) and 264, 22 (*si kileran* renders *legatur ei* and implies reading aloud). A similar usage occurs in the *Monsee-Wiener Bruchstücke* 37, 17, where *galesan uuarth* renders *recitatum*. That *lesen* can be used in this sense much later in the same context is illustrated by the Zwiefalten version of the MHG *Benediktinerregel* 34, 4, where the acoustic dimension of *lesin* is confirmed by *horare*.
211 *ZfdA* 104 (1975), 310. Cf. also Schröder, *MlJb* 18 (1983), 334: 'er erzählt, singt, schreibt, liest vor, d.h. er tut alles, was sein poetischer Schöpfer auch tat und mit seinem Roman getan wissen wollte'. That Gottfried's conjunction of verbs is no isolated feature can be seen by Salimbene's words of Frederick II: *legere, scribere et cantare sciebat* (quoted by Žak, *Musik*, p. 230, fn. 30).
212 Scholz, *Hören*, pp. 80ff.
213 *De confessione*, PL 207, 1088. See p. 108 and Green, *ZfdA* 115 (1986), 169, fn. 86.
214 E.g. *Vita S. Cunegundis* cap. 5, MGH SS 4, 823; William of Malmesbury, *Gesta regum Anglorum* V 447 (II 519).
215 This example differs from the others in that *hoeren lesen* is not accompanied by a reference to a written text. Such references, however, occur elsewhere in this work: there are indications to its having been written (e.g. 884, 1502, 3596, 12317ff.), it is called a book (e.g. 12317ff., 13266ff., 18636) and readers are presupposed (e.g. 13216ff.).
216 Green, *ZfdA* 115 (1986), 161.
217 Scholz, *Hören*, pp. 57ff. and 70ff.
218 *Ibid.*, pp. 81f.
219 See p. 108. That even a frequent formula like *muget ir nu wunder hoeren sagen* need not be conventional and devoid of any real function has been shown by Curschmann, *Nibelungenlied*, pp. 94f., in that work's opening stanza, which he interprets as illustrating oral transmission.
220 Scholz, *Hören*, pp. 83f., discusses the construction *hoeren schríben* which he is reluctant to interpret in the sense proposed by Kienast in his edition of Heinrich von Melk (p. 79, s.v. *schríben*): 'Geschriebenes (vorlesen) hören'. When Heinrich von Melk uses this phrase in *Von dem gemeinen lebene* (5, 1: *Als wir diu buoch horen scriben*) it is in a context in which *wir lesen* can also be used (see pp. 115ff.), not with regard to specific people, but as a general term meaning what is known to all Christians (whether they can individually read

or not) on the basis of written Christian tradition. On a second occasion (*Priesterleben* 4, 15: *da von hoerent si vil scriben*) particular persons are involved: priests are criticised for their secular preoccupations, including love (which they claim as their prerogative against laymen, 4, 16ff.). That such clerics should have access to erotic literature (in Latin?) need not surprise us, nor the fact that they could receive it by recital, in view of the acoustic reception of Latin literature in the Middle Ages.

Scholz confines his attention to Heinrich von Melk, but the phrase is used by others. Priester Arnold, *Loblied auf den Heiligen Geist* 6, 1ff., uses it in the general sense, comparable to the first example with Heinrich von Melk, of what is common knowledge in Christendom as a result of a written tradition transmitted orally to all Christians (even if a select few may also read it). In the *Jüngerer Titurel* the phrase is used in the specific sense (as with the second example from Heinrich von Melk), but in close conjunction with *hoeren lesen*: 3059, 2 and 6207, 4.

No matter whether *hoeren schríben* is used generally (of what is known to all Christians) or specifically (applying to a particular work), it suggests an oral transmission in conformity with Kienast's proposal.

221 Cf. also v. 3100.
222 See also v. 1080.
223 Mentioned by Scholz, *Hören*, p. 122.
224 See pp. 225f.
225 *Hören*, p. 81.
226 Kartschoke, *IASL* 8 (1983), 258.

4 Survey of reception by hearing

1 Schmidt-Wiegand, *Eid*, p. 70. For examples of oral charms see Flint, *Rise*, pp. 60, 66, 311f., 316. For chanting (OHG *galan, galdar, leodrûna*) see Wesche, *Wortschatz*, pp. 40ff., 51ff. and Helm, *Religionsgeschichte* II 1, 121f., 125, and for whispering Wesche, pp. 46f., 54f. and Helm, pp. 125f. On the spoken dimension of written blessings see Hellgardt, *Textensembles*, p. 26.
2 In Christian blessings *dicere* and vernacular equivalents occur in the instructions: *Pferdesegen* (370, 1 and 4; 371, 2, 5 and 8), *Contra uermes* (373, 2), *Ad fluxum* (383, 4), *Contra uberbein* (386, 3), *Augensegen* (386, 2), *Gegen Halsentzündung* (387, 4).
3 On such spoken contact see Kartschoke, *Geschichte*, pp. 123f. and Haupt, *Heilung*, p. 107. When medicine later came to depend on written, learned transmission its practitioner distinguished himself as an *artzt von den puchen* or *buochartzat* (Heinrich von Neustadt, *Apollonius von Tyrlant* 1945, 20600 ff.; *Gottes Zukunft* 8096). Another kind of knowledge about the natural world is conveyed by the *Millstätter Reimphysiologus*, whose use of rhymed verse has been seen as characteristic of a work addressed to laymen (de Boor, *Geschichte* I 125), unlikely to be literate in the first half of the twelfth century and therefore addressed by word of mouth (1, 4). The evidence for Volmar's *Steinbuch* consists only of two examples of *hoeren* (446, 588).
4 Grubmüller, *DU (NS)* 1 (1989), 141ff. and 48ff., and Henkel, *Übersetzungen*, p. 103. On Notker see pp. 183ff.
5 Haubrichs, *Studienprogramm*, pp. 237ff., especially 242f., 248f. (on the use of interlinear translations in the school: pp. 249ff. and Henkel, *Übersetzungen*, pp. 67ff.).
6 Haubrichs, *Anfänge*, pp. 268f. On verse mnemonics in medieval teaching see Klein, *Praxis*, p. 339.
7 II *Praef.*, p. 232. See Henkel, *Übersetzungen*, pp. 176ff.
8 The evidence for *Wernher von Elmendorf* is weak: two examples of *horen* (6, 149).
9 Henry the Lion despite Steer's argument, *DVjs* 64 (1990), 1ff.; instruction for laymen: 36, 5f.

10 Hearing, e.g. 2981ff., 3223, 3285 (applied to contemporary literature at large 762, 765, 1033, 1041f.); knightly addressees: Curschmann, *PBB* 106 (1984), 240f. The double formula is also used of works other than Thomasin's: 762, 1080.
11 See above, p. 80.
12 *Hoeren*, e.g. V 2 (p. 4), VI 1 (p. 7), IV 1 (p. 129); presence of listeners: see above, p. 74.
13 Listeners, e.g. 5386, 9745 (illustrating how a literate author mediates between a written tradition and laymen); request for silence: 2015f.; twofold reception of his Latin works: *Solsequium* 68, 27 (28, 5ff. also addresses *lector* in the sense of reciter, while *Registrum* 157 mentions *auditores*).
14 E.g. 425ff., 10348ff., 16183ff., 21629ff.
15 Cramer, *Geschichte*, pp. 213f.
16 Vollmann-Profe, *Wiederbeginn*, p. 52; Haubrichs, *Anfänge*, p. 396. Haubrichs has also assembled (*Georgslied*, pp. 190ff.; *Anfänge*, pp. 398f.) evidence for preliterary songs in praise of saints.
17 See above, p. 65; Osterwalder, *Galluslied*, p. 240; Haubrichs, *Georgslied*, p. 196.
18 Osterwalder, *Galluslied*, pp. 242ff. Ekkehard's remark confirms the oral nature of the German original, but also his assessment that a written text in Latin had a better chance of survival.
19 Haubrichs, *Georgslied*, p. 165, leaves it open whether performance was 'im rezitativen Sprechgesang... oder im Choral'. Processions on this saint's day: Haubrichs, *Georgslied*, pp. 189ff.; precentor: Jammers, *Schrift*, p. 156. Use of the vernacular for laymen would be reinforced by the possible connection of the work with the *translatio* of the saint's relics to Reichenau in 896 (Schützeichel, *Codex*, pp. 78ff.) or even with the abbey of Prüm (Haubrichs, *Kultur*, pp. 131ff.).
20 Haubrichs, *Anfänge*, p. 398.
21 Musical aspect: Ursprung, *Musikgeschichte*, pp. 246ff. and *Musikforschung* 5 (1952), 17ff.; *Tu autem*: above, p. 78; use in a procession: Lipphardt, *MuA* 12 (1959/60), 73ff. and Janota, *Studien*, pp. 219f. Here *De Heinrico* may also be included, whose hymn-like opening and political theme suggest public recital for which Haubrichs, *Anfänge*, pp. 187f., proposes a court audience acquainted with Latin and vernacular poetry, but also sung delivery by two choruses.
22 *Cantilena*: *Vita Altmanni*, cap. 3, MGH SS 12, 230. In Vorau 2, 1 *vor tuon*, like *vor tragen*, combined with a dative suggests recital before an audience.
23 See above, p. 71. A mixed audience including laymen is suggested for the pilgrimage by the *Vita Altmanni*, but also for Bamberg by Vollmann-Profe, *Wiederbeginn*, p. 35 (cf. also Rupp, *Dichtungen*, p. 80, and Urbanek, *ZfdPh* 106 (1987), 331, 338f.). Erdmann, *ZfdA* 73 (1936), 87ff., long ago connected this work with Gunther's preference for having poetry recited in his presence.
24 Freytag, *Theorie*, p. 94.
25 Refrains: Maurer, *Dichtungen* I 358; hymn: de Boor, *Geschichte* I 202; Kolb, *Marienlied*, pp. 8of.; Freytag, *Theorie*, p. 127 (choral song: Ehrismann, *Geschichte* II 1, 210); liturgical function: Kolb, pp. 81f.; Freytag, p. 114.
26 Sequence: Ehrismann, *Geschichte* II 1, 214; de Boor, *Geschichte* I 203; Freytag, *Theorie*, p. 132; Vollmann-Profe, *Wiederbeginn*, p. 144; liturgical function: Freytag, p. 131.
27 Maurer, *Dichtungen* I 453f.; Freytag, *Theorie*, pp. 134, 140; Flotzinger, *ZfdA* 119 (1990), 75ff. Recital can also be assumed for the *Cantilena de conversione Sancti Pauli*: the MS entitles it a *cantilena*; it may well have been recited on the relevant feastday (Vollmann-Profe, *Wiederbeginn*, p. 163); it has a variant of *Tu autem* (13, 4). *Vom Himmelreich* has been described as hymn-like (Vollmann-Profe, p. 146) and Freytag, *VfL* 4, 18, assumes a liturgical context.
28 Extracts from the relevant legislation are put together by Ehrismann, *Geschichte* I 291ff.
29 Haubrichs, *Anfänge*, p. 285.

30 E.g. the *Weißenburger Katechismus, St. Galler Glaube und Beichte II, Münchener Glaube und Beichte, Benediktbeurer Glaube und Beichte III, Pfälzer Beichte.* Cf. Hellgardt, *Textensembles*, p. 26.
31 Freytag, *Theorie*, pp. 94, 106.
32 Ehrismann, *Geschichte* II 1, 171. Lutz, *Rhetorica*, p. 155, also assumes possible recital.
33 Examples with *sprechen: Vatikanische Gebete* 72, 79, 89; *Benediktbeurer Ratschläge und Gebete* 77, 88, 103. Singen: *Gebete und Benediktionen von Muri* 37, 380, 406.
34 Ohly, *DVjs* 47 (1973), 26ff.
35 *Summa*, PL 210, 111f.: if it were not *manifesta* it would smack of heresy, if not *publica* it would be teaching rather than preaching.
36 Cf. Frank, *Seitengestaltung*, pp. 180f., on a Provençal sermon mediating between two worlds.
37 Honorius Augustodunensis, *Speculum ecclesiae*, PL 172, 829f. Cf. also Speicher, *Kommentar*, p. 117, and Kartschoke, *Geschichte*, p. 247.
38 Haubrichs, *Anfänge*, p. 292.
39 *Ibid.*, p. 307.
40 Vollmann-Profe, *Wiederbeginn*, p. 65; Kartschoke, *Geschichte*, p. 244.
41 On two types cf. Steer in de Boor, *Geschichte* III 2, 320, and for France Zink, *Prédication*, pp. 145f. Richter, *Überlieferung*, p. 211, points out that the purpose of the 'Musterbuch' is made clear in Latin collections of sermons.
42 Other examples from the former collection are 97, 21; 104, 34; 116, 29, and from the latter 44, 33.
43 When the *St. Pauler Predigten* refer to a particular saint's day (e.g. 28, 17) the author could not know that they would be read privately on that day, but he would realise that this sermon would be preached at that point in the church year. Likewise, a sermon can be given its fixed place within the service with a reference like 2, 24; the reading aloud of the lesson for the day presupposes a congregation (e.g. 4, 12) whose function is to listen (121, 13). When they are told to listen, even by a time-honoured epic formula (6, 8: *Nu muget ir hôren*) this conventional phrase had a specific function and must be taken literally, especially when, as in *Speculum Ecclesiae* 35, 21, the illiteracy of the congregation is made clear.
44 Ehrismann, *Geschichte* II 1, 185; Schützeichel, *Memento Mori*, pp. 116ff. (lay nobility); Kartschoke, *Geschichte*, p. 368.
45 See de Boor, *Geschichte* I 158f.; Rupp, *Dichtungen*, pp. 102, 138; Vollmann-Profe, *Wiederbeginn*, pp. 76f.
46 Kartschoke, *Geschichte*, p. 312. This suggests that an address to the audience like 10, 1 can be taken literally and that not merely this formula was borrowed from the sermon (*Audite, carissimi*), but its oral dimension. Vollmann-Profe, *Wiederbeginn*, p. 173, has also stressed the closeness of *Scopf von dem lône* to the oral 'Spielmannslied', but whether that implies oral recital is quite uncertain.
47 Kartschoke, *Geschichte*, p. 370.
48 Quotations translated: 10, 2f.; 11, 2f.; 17, 10ff. Cf. Kartschoke, *Geschichte*, p. 282. Moreover, the author refers to what he said earlier (21, 15ff.) in terms of what the audience heard him name (26, 12f.).
49 Ehrismann, *Geschichte* II 1, 115; *VfL* 1, 579; Vollmann-Profe, *Wiederbeginn*, p. 163.
50 Ehrismann, *Geschichte* II 1, 75; Vollmann-Profe, *Wiederbeginn*, p. 171.
51 Ganz, *Hochzeit*, pp. 70ff; *VfL* 4, 79; Vollmann-Profe, *Wiederbeginn*, p. 73.
52 Laymen: *Priesterleben* 17, 1; *Von dem gemeinen Leben* 1, 4f.; work recited: *Von dem gemeinen Leben* 1, 3; request to listen: *Priesterleben* 16, 4. *Vom Rechte* represents a form of sermon adapted, as the preacher was encouraged to do, to the interests of those addressed, in this case those working on the land (Ehrismann, *Geschichte* II 1, 199; Vollmann-Profe, *Wiederbeginn*, p. 42) and therefore illiterate. Neither rural background nor illiteracy is contradicted by Wells's suggestion of lay brothers, *MLR* 83 (1988), 508.

53 We need not take *tumben* (51) as meaning exclusively 'foolish, frivolous' (Neuschäfer edn, p. 269, note to v. 52), for the layman could also be implied, as in *tumbe leien* (on a lay audience cf. Rupp, *Dichtungen*, pp. 265ff.). The use of compounds (*hôren* + *an* or *zuo*, 475, 2251) is significant in view of Schröder's suggestion, *Anegenge*, p. 82, that their infrequency makes them less subject to conventional attrition than *hôren* alone.
54 *Hôren*: 107, 821, 1019; request for silence: 1ff.
55 See above, p. 86.
56 This is more telling in view of the same conclusion for his other works: *Gottes Zukunft* (see p. 103) and *Apollonius von Tyrland* (see p. 110).
57 See above, n. 53, on the verb *zu horen* (222).
58 Weak evidence is provided by *Das Buch der Rügen*, by *Sich hûb vor Gotes trône*, and by *Von den fünfzehenn zaichen vor dem ivngsten tag*. The first two use only a few *hoeren* references, the third has *hoeren sagen* once.
59 Bumke, *Geschichte*, pp. 422f.
60 Haubrichs, *Anfänge*, p. 256.
61 E.g. 2, 6f.; 2, 10f.; 31, 6f.
62 Ehrismann, *Geschichte* II 1, 171; Vollmann-Profe, *Wiederbeginn*, pp. 151f.
63 See above, p. 87.
64 *Hoeren*: 1144, 3607. 1142 refers back to 617ff. This conclusion for this work is confirmed by the author's *Sanct Franzisken Leben* (cf. p. 104).
65 *Hôren*: 1096, 2801ff., 2826ff.; appeals for silence: 1101f., 3090, 4493; suggestions to the uninterested: 2834ff., 2849ff., 3249ff. (see above, p. 74); *hie*: 931, 1097, 2859; reminder: 2169 refers back to 261ff.
66 398, 27 (cf. 404, 10); 399, 8. I leave on one side the question of authenticity.
67 Cf. also *lesen vnd horen* in the title 122, 1 (MSS L, B).
68 To listen: 9, 9 and 18. Although Scholz stresses the wide range of *vernemen*, he concedes its acoustic force when linked with *lesen* by *oder* (*Hören*, p. 67), as here in 9, 29.
69 In 587f. I take *Dew* as an error for *Den* (cf. the editor, p. xxv), which provides another example. If Könemann von Jerxheim intended his three works for the same kind of audience acoustic reception is likely for all. *Kaland*: hearing (1f., 93, 221), mixed audience (1ff., 72ff.) assembled on a special occasion (615ff.), deictic pointers (3, 13, 1160), *lesen* 'to read out loud' (15, 367, 392). His *Wurzgarten Mariens* provides support by referring to a twofold reception (6521f.). The *Reimbibel* has no pointers.
70 Schubert, *Theorie*, p. 72.
71 What Wormald, *Uses*, p. 111, says of the Anglo-Saxon king's oral pronouncement rather than the written text giving the force of law can also be applied to Germany. On the persistence of oral law, even alongside writing, see Johanek in de Boor, *Geschichte* III 2, 396f.
72 Bumke, *Geschichte*, pp. 356f.
73 On the *Weichbildrecht* see above, p. 62; *Schwabenspiegel Langform M*, p. 405 (*dicz puch ist gewizzen und weisen leuten gut vor ze lesen*); *Seifried Helbling* II 652ff. (p. 87; cf. Gottfried von Strassburg, *Tristan* 13232f.).
74 Cf. Schmidt-Wiegand, *Eid*, p. 62, on oathtaking.
75 Haubrichs, *Anfänge*, p. 191.
76 Ehrismann, *Geschichte* I 349f.; *VfL* 3, 427f.
77 Ehrismann, *Geschichte* I 352.
78 See above, p. 46.
79 Schmidt-Wiegand, *Eid*, p. 74.
80 Wunderli, *VR* 24 (1965), 54; Koller, *Volkssprachlichkeit*, pp. 832f., 835f.
81 *VR* 24 (1965), 36; Schmidt-Wiegand, *Eid*, p. 64.
82 Ehrismann, *Geschichte* I 353f.; Haubrichs, *Anfänge*, pp. 193f.
83 *VfL* 2, 575; Schmidt-Wiegand, *Eid*, pp. 84, 87.

84 Schmidt-Wiegand, *Eid*, pp. 78f.
85 *Chronica regia Coloniensis*, p. 267: *pax iuratur, vetera iura stabiliuntur, nova statuuntur et Teutonico sermone in membrana scripta omnibus publicantur*. Cf. Johanek in de Boor, *Geschichte* III 2, 399f. and Grundmann, *Wahlkönigtum*, pp. 117 (the difficulty of Latin leads to misunderstanding by laymen).
86 Grundmann, *Schrifttum*, pp. 96ff. See also below, p. 411, n. 168.
87 The *Statuten* also refer to (largely illiterate) lay brothers: 34, 27ff.; 64, 6. On the similar practice in other orders see Schreiner, *Verschriftlichung*, pp. 37ff.
88 *Stadtrecht* VI 30 (*lesen laten*) and VI 11 (*lesen* + dative). *Weichbildrecht*: *horen* 71, 49; *Glosse* 203, 21 and 54.
89 See above, p. 352, n. 73. In three other cases the evidence is much weaker, consisting only of references to hearing the work: the *Deutschenspiegel* (*Erster Landrechtsteil* 78, 11), the *Mühlhäuser Reichsrechtsbuch* (7, 1; 8, 3; 16, 1) and the *Schwabenspiegel* (253–18f, 20). More profitable is a group of legal texts of a special kind, making prescriptions like the *Statuten des Deutschen Ordens* for members of a monastic order. Various MHG versions of the Benedictine Rule all follow the original (cap. 58 and 66) in implying that the Rule was read out loud (*lesen* + dative) for the legal reason that no one can plead ignorance (cf. the editions of Selmer and Sullivan under these chapters). For a similar provision in another order cf. the *Klarissenregel* 26, 1.
90 MGH Const. 2, 241, 32ff.
91 *Weichbildrecht*, *Glosse* 329, 8: *ungewisser geschicht gloubt man nicht, sy were denne bewist mit den, die is sagen unde horten; unde was denne so offinbar ist, darumme gloubt man den gezeugen, die es sahen vnde horten*. Parallel examples in charters are 1670 (Wilhelm, *Corpus* III 7, 40) and 1738 (III 57, 25).
92 Hauck, *Heldendichtung*, pp. 118ff.; Diebold, *Sagelied*.
93 One of the merits of Vollmann-Profe, *Wiederbeginn*, is that she repeatedly stresses the presence of historical interests with the audience addressed (e.g. p. 28).
94 *Hören*: 139, 566, 647; recital situation: above, p. 74; *hir*: 1898, 1948 (above, p. 75).
95 *Hören*: 7484 (refers back to 7445ff.), 7998, 8920; request for silence: 1611f. Particularly well developed is the use of *lesen* in the sense of recital aloud (see above, p. 81): with the dative (e.g. 4310), with a temporal adverb pointing to a past stage in the narrative (e.g. 2270) or with both (e.g. 5688).
96 On the affiliations of this work with medieval historiography see Knab, *Annolied*, pp. 75ff.
97 Opposition to heroic literature: Nellmann edn, pp. 75f., note on stanza 1, and Haug and Vollmann, *Literatur*, p. 1427, note on 596, Str. 1. On sung delivery of heroic literature see p. 106, and on this possibility (but no more) for the *Annolied* see Nellmann, pp. 188f.
98 *Hören*: 3ff., 26, 15259. That heroic literature presented *lugene* (39) as history is argued elsewhere in this work. See p. 244.
99 In view of this clash of recitals *vor zellen* (25) is likely to point to recital before assembled listeners (cf. *vor sprechen* for preaching in 15530).
100 *Horen*: 85, 34; 195, 34. Kartschoke, *IASL* 8 (1983), 257, rightly questions the force of Scholz's interpretation (*Hören*, p. 73) of 58f. as meaning that the recipient hears and learns in the act of reading. If we take these lines instead as a double formula they provide further support for the literal meaning of *horen*.
101 *Hören*: 186, 8867, 21519; audience have already heard: 1891 (refers to 1045), 29920 (refers to 29077ff.); reception at royal court: *hören lesin* (21695), *lesin heizen* (21700), *lesin und hören* (21732). Cf. Green, *ZfdA* 115 (1986), 155ff.
102 *Hören*: 9604, 11177, 24116. *Vor sagen* is not used in the sense of 'to say in advance' in 2818 (because it sums up a preceding detail), but in a local sense ('to say in your presence') implying an oral situation. Cf. public announcements made in the narrative by means of this construction (8750, 9193f.).

103 658, 1335.
104 The use of *horen* in the *Braunschweigische Reimchronik* (1482, 1733, 7157) is supported to some extent by its combination with a deictic *hir* (96) and *lesen* to suggest previous recital (1215, 1418, 9332). Although Ottokar may employ *hôren* in his *Österreichische Reimchronik* to mean 'to hear' or 'to learn' (e.g. 25026), the former is implied when used with a verb of speech to refer to what is recited elsewhere (e.g. 18668f.), especially when confirmed by a back-reference (73512, refers to 69898ff.). The case of *Die Kreuzfahrt des Landgrafen Ludwig* is weak, resting merely on what has been previously recited (5568, refers to 5410ff.), where *lesen* means 'to read out from a written text' rather than simply 'to narrate' because of pointers to a written text (1738, 4651: *setzen* 'to write'). Gottfried Hagen's *Chronik der Stadt Köln* is also weak, using only *hoiren* (179, 1246, 4530). *Von dem Spitâle von Jêrusalêm* uses *hoeren* (355, 1061), combined with a request for silence (1313), but *lesen* + dative cannot reliably mean 'to recite aloud from writing' since there is no suggestion that it is a written text.
105 Kartschoke, *VB* 4 (1982), 23ff.
106 Kartschoke, *Geschichte*, p. 114; *VB* 4 (1982), 30f.; ibid., p. 27 (cf. Ehlich, *Text*, pp. 39f.).
107 Kartschoke, *Geschichte*, p. 140.
108 Cf. Haug and Vollmann, *Literatur*, p. 1065, note to 48, 1.
109 On the following prayer see above, p. 79; on *De poeta*: Kartschoke, *Bibeldichtung*, p. 154. *Tatians Evangelienharmonie* may claim acoustic reception because of its use in the oral context of medieval schooling (but is placed here in the light of Haubrichs, *Anfänge*, p. 261).
110 *Praefatio*, p. 1 (*non solum literatis, verum etiam illiteratis*); ibid., p. 2 (*iuxta idioma illius linguae* and *audientibus* and *cantilena*). Neumes: Taeger, *ZfdA* 107 (1978), 184ff.
111 Cf. Haubrichs, *Anfänge*, p. 389 (cf. *VfL* 6, 827). For such addressees recital in the vernacular would be the most likely assumption.
112 *Christus und die Samariterin*: de Boor, *Geschichte* I 81; Haubrichs, *Anfänge*, p. 378. *Psalm 138*: Haubrichs, *Anfänge*, p. 383, and *Arcana*, pp. 67ff. On the opening formula see Haug and Vollmann, *Literatur*, p. 1133, note to 142, 1f.
113 On *fure bringen* see above, p. 87. On *Nû fernemet* and *fore tuon* in this work see Esser, *Schöpfungsgeschichte*, pp. 52ff., 79ff. Lessons for Lent: Ehrismann, *Geschichte* II 1, 187; Voss, *Studien*, p. 171, fn. 171; Freytag, *Dichtung*, p. 128 (cf. however Esser, pp. 83ff.). Hennig has adduced syntactical and metrical grounds for delivery in liturgical recitation tone, *Untersuchungen*, p. 344. For possibly sung recital see Esser, pp. 80f.
114 *Tu autem*: Ohly, *ZfdA* 47 (1973), 29; reminiscences of lay poetry: Ehrismann, *Geschichte* II 1, 101; Vollmann-Profe, *Wiederbeginn*, p. 85; *VfL* 5, 879. By contrast, the *Drei Jünglinge im Feuerofen* and the *Ältere Judith* have only general pointers (they share the same ballad style and conventional formulas of the secular lay: de Boor, *Geschichte* I 156; Vollmann-Profe, *Wiederbeginn*, pp. 83f.; Haug and Vollmann, *Literatur*, p. 1491), but lack a precise indicator like *Tu autem*. If all three works belong together, however, then the suggestion that the *Lob Salomons* was meant for recital could be applied to the others.
115 Cf. above, p. 86.
116 Greinemann, *Gedichte*, whose results are summed up by Freytag, *Leben*, p. 75, as suggesting 'ein der Liturgie naher Gebrauchszweck der Dichtungen'. Stein, *Stil*, pp. 55ff., argues for recital in a monastic refectory.
117 Easter liturgy: Green, *Exodus*, pp. 22f.; 'Reimlektionen': Schröder, *ZfdA* 72 (1935), 239f. The doubts voiced by Papp, *Exodus*, p. 31, are unjustified in the light of pointers to the Easter liturgy.
118 Since these words introduce the naming of the lands they are not meant chronologically ('to name in advance'), but spatially ('to name in front of listeners'). How different the former construction is can be seen in 33, 1 and 65, 1.

119 *Horen*: 2, 10; 10, 1; deictic pointer: 8, 1. No assistance is given by the same author's *Alexanderlied*, for which the evidence is particularly weak.
120 *Horen*: 2, 6; 72, 16. The evidence of *vorbriefen* (see p. 128) suggests that *lesen* in 82, 12 implies recital from a written text (*buoch* 28, 1).
121 Küsters, *Garten*, pp. 18f., 22ff.; Ohly, *Hohelied-Studien*, pp. 277f.
122 The clash between clerical and lay literature (Kartschoke, *Geschichte*, p. 312), where the latter is transmitted orally, suggests the same for the former. Quotations translated: 4, 8; 9, 6; 30, 10.
123 Points in the liturgical year: p. 66, between lines 36 and 37; p. 100, line 810 (left margin); neumes: Kriedte, *Bibelfragmente*, pp. 19f.; Palmer, *ZfdA* 114 (1985), 95ff.
124 *Hoeren*: 103, 8 and 53; 104, 6. On the equation of *sehen* (12) with *lesen* see pp. 139f.
125 Listening: 716f., 2774, 4180; presence of audience: 11850f., 16468ff. (cf. Helm and Ziesemer, *Literatur*, p. 83; *VfL* 3, 753f.). This audience therefore hears something recited (13563).
126 Laymen: 8253f., 10029f., 11103; illiterate: 2063, 3005. An acoustic reception of this work makes it likely for two others by the same author: *Erlösung* (no internal evidence) and *Evangelium Nicodemi* (one reference to listening, 1822, but the work is addressed to *illitterati*, 2045f.).
127 *Gottes Zukunft*: *hoeren* (5651, 7020, 7340), twofold reception (8101). *Saelden Hort*: twofold reception (73ff.) and the suggestion of recital to others (29ff.: *lesen* + dative and with *vor*). In hoping for a greater appeal than court literature (4407f., 5411ff.) the author addresses an aristocratic public and meets literature meant for them on the same oral ground (the first reference may suggest individual readers, but the second implies oral recital).
128 *Hóren*: 104, 919, 5312; recital aloud: 2587ff. (the author asks for help not in reading his source, but in regard to his own work, a written text, cf. 75 and 1230, so that *lesen* in 2596 means recital from a text to listeners). For three other works the evidence is weak. *Judith* 2566: *lesen* may imply recital from a written text (cf. 30, 733, 2753ff.). In *Christi Hort* Gundacker von Judenburg uses *horen* (2098, 2242, 4046), but probably addresses laymen (1000: *leuten*, cf. *liutpriester*). Johannes von Frankenstein uses *horen* in *Der Kreuziger* (330, 1330, 10078), which may be supported by 10020, where *lesen* suggests recital at an earlier point (refers back to 10006f.).
129 Bumke, *Geschichte*, p. 390.
130 Cf. de Boor, *Geschichte* I 191; III 1, 522; Vollmann-Profe, *Wiederbeginn*, p. 199.
131 The evidence for Adelbrecht's *Johannes Baptista* rests on two assumptions, that it was addressed to laymen with a patronal festival in mind at which it was recited (Ehrismann, *Geschichte* II 1, 123; *VfL* 1, 62; Masser, *Legendenepik*, p. 69).
132 279, 2216, 5375.
133 Bumke, *Mäzene*, p. 116; Sanders, *Heinric*, pp. 10f., 21ff.
134 By contrast, the *Oberdeutscher Servatius* has only *hören* (1723, 2768, 2863), with no further support.
135 *Horen*: A228, 2492f. and especially 4839. Augsburg associations: Fromm, *Untersuchungen*, p. 152; Masser, *Legendenepik*, p. 92; Bumke, *Mäzene*, p. 135.
136 Geith, *Albert*, pp. 8f.
137 *Horen*: 326, 1215, 2551; *hórêre*: (52, see above, p. 80); appeal for silence: 4015; points previously read out: 2244 (refers to 670ff. with a verbal echo), 3224 (cf. 1123ff., 1990ff.), 3738 (cf. 3450ff., 3473f.). On 3789 see above, p. 85.
138 For this author's *Urstende* a listening reception is also likely, see p. 103.
139 *Vernemen*: 142; twofold reception: 16077. Cf. Green, *ZfdA* 97 (1986), 170ff. For the *Laubacher Barlaam* of Otto von Freising the evidence is not so strong: *hoeren* (188, 5908, 9486), once combined with a request for silence (15ff.). The word-play in which the author reveals his name (16678ff.) needs to be kept separate from acrostics (see pp. 131ff.):

whereas acrostics presuppose a reader to resolve them, this word-play could have been realised in recital by change of tone, emphasis or gesture. When mention is made (10ff.) of writing a text on parchment for recital to those who cannot read Otto possibly had his own work in mind (Kartschoke, *IASL* 8 (1983), 260).

140 *Margaretenleben: hören* (2, 86, 539), twofold reception (1054f.: what the saint prays for is to be realised on this occasion, see above, p. 94). *Sanct Franzisken Leben: hoeren* (2031, 2546, 3465); twofold reception (90). The evidence for the *Heiliger Georg* of Reinbot von Durne is not strong: *hoeren* (710, 1730, 2923) and the suggestion that contemporary literature, meant for recital, was part of court entertainment (341ff., 356ff., 1071ff.).

141 *Silvester: hoeren* (100), *hoeren sagen* (22f.), *hoeren lesen* (5186). *Alexius:* listening (56), *hoeren sagen* (53), *hoeren lesen* (1401). If the same recital situation can be assumed for Konrad's *Pantaleon* (Brandt, *Konrad*, pp. 74ff.), then isolated references to listening (13, 2150) need not be written off.

142 *Hoeren:* I/II 18, 14; 139, 81f.; III 58, 8; already heard by audience: I/II 154, 72; 267, 2; presence of audience: I/II 136, 3; sequence of church year: Cramer, *Geschichte*, p. 209. *Lesen* is also used of the audience hearing recited: III 5, 92; 319, 13. Likewise in the case of the *Märterbuch* (43: *illitterati* are to receive it by hearing) Cramer, pp. 207, 209, has suggested that its arrangement according to the saints' calendar implies recital on the particular saint's day.

143 *Horen:* 20945, 27597ff., 30941; request for silence: 158; recital situation: 132ff.; hearing text read out: 11522f., 41445ff., 41498f.

144 *Hoeren:* 122, 105; 193, 110; 217, 25; presence of listeners: 265, 5 (Hölscher's suggestion, *Öffentlichkeit*, p. 55, that *gemein* means 'öffentlich' in the late Middle Ages can be confirmed already from OHG, Starck and Wells, *Glossenwörterbuch*, p. 213); *lesen* + dative: 245, 28. Reference is also made to what has been recited earlier: 116, 71ff.; 122, 105ff.; 255, 90.

145 *Marienleben: hoeren* (4168f., 6560ff.); twofold reception (67, 16152f., 16236ff.). *Leben der heiligen Elisabeth: horen* (1715, 3012, 8629), previously recited (5696 refers back to 5385ff., 9715 to 9523ff., 9929 to 9847ff.). *Sante Margareten Marter:* the work's recital (58f.), the saint's prayer (575ff.). Four weak examples remain. *Alexius F* and the *Legende vom heiligen Nikolaus* both use *hoeren* once (456 and 345), but have nothing else. *Alexius A* uses *hoeren* more frequently (303, 417, 466) and suggests (1149ff.) that the audience, possibly nuns (*VfL* 1, 227) to whom it was recited, should pray for the authoress. In the *Leben der Gräfin Iolande von Vianden* Bruder Hermann uses *schríven* + *vor* + dative to imply recital from a written text to assembled listeners, possibly nuns (3824ff.). Cf. the *Apokalypse* of Heinrich von Hesler (p. 85).

146 Werner, *Studien*, p. 30; Heinzle, *Wandlungen*, pp. 194f. Masser, *ZfdPh* 107 (1988), 48ff., has argued for German texts around 1200.

147 Linke, *Drama*, pp. 737, 738; Heinzle, *Wandlungen*, p. 215.

148 Cf. Bergmann, *Aufführungstext*, pp. 314ff. and Linke, *Versuch*, pp. 527ff. On musical performance of the drama cf. Schuler, *Musik*.

149 Singing: 423, 45; 424, 101 and 421, 1; 422, 17. Neumes: Young, *Drama* I 421, fn. 1; Hartl, *Osterspiele*, p. 24. Audience addressed: Linke, *Drama*, p. 750.

150 Singing: 151, 19; 152, 31; 155, 31; notation: Schumann and Bischoff, *Carmina* I 3, 166, 170ff. (on *cantare* see Mehler, *Dicere*, pp. 146ff.); audience addressed: 164f.

151 V 115 (edn, p. 69, note to 116). Cf. also IV 57 (p. 69, note to 57ff.). See Bätschmann, *Weihnachtsspiel*, p. 34. Audience addressed: Ranke edn, p. 21. The text of the *Himmelgartner Passionsspiel* is in German, its Latin instructions point to singing in chorus (2^a, 2; 2^b, 8).

152 Singing: 35a, 428b, 440a. Melody: edn, p. 304; Mehler, *Dicere*, pp. 156ff. Plea for silence: 1ff.

153 *Cantare:* 1, 130a, 152a; *dicere:* 35a, 54a, 83a. Presumed singing: Mehler, *Dicere*, pp. 188, 196. Augustine: 139ff.

154 Singing: VIII 2, H 3, 1 1. Melody: edn, pp. 1f.
155 Singing: 82a, 112a, 124a and 40a, 43a, 55a. Melody: Froning, *Drama I*, 47 (cf. Traub, *PBB* 110 (1988), 78ff.). Audience addressed: 194ff.
156 Cf. Kaiser, *Heldenepik*, p. 181.
157 The cases are: *Himmlisches Jerusalem, Linzer Antichrist, Annolied, Kaiserchronik*.
158 Diebold, *Sagelied*, pp. 13ff.; Kartschoke, *Geschichte*, p. 186.
159 *Quoniam vulgo concinnatur et canitur* (Diebold, *Sagelied*, pp. 27ff., who on the basis of written allusions plots an oral transmission lasting at least 200–250 years).
160 References to *hoeren* are so frequent in heroic literature that they could theoretically be dismissed as conventional and uninformative. The boot is on the other foot and we are dealing here with traditional themes, transmitted orally over centuries, so that what needs special proof is rather the possibility of their being read.
161 External references to the delivery of heroic poems are provided, for example, by Einhard, *Vita Karoli* 29 (p. 33: *carmina, canebantur*), Poeta Saxo, *Annales* (PL 99, 726: *carmina, canunt*), the *Chronicon Quedlinburgense* (MGH SS 3, 31, 16: *cantabant rustici – rustici* in the sense of *illitterati*, cf. Heinzle, *Dietrichepik*, pp. 271ff.). Frutolf von Michelsberg, *Chronica* (MGH SS 6, 130, 35: *vulgari fabulatione et cantilenarum modulatione*) and Saxo Grammaticus, *Gesta* (p. 427: *cantor, carminis*).
162 From the rich literature on this subject cf. Bertau and Stephan, *ZfdA* 87 (1956–57), 253ff.; Jammers, *Schrift*, pp. 146ff.; Brunner, *Epenmelodien*, pp. 149ff.; *Strukturprobleme*, pp. 300ff.
163 Haug and Vollmann, *Literatur*, p. 1028, note to 10, 1.
164 See pp. 161f.
165 This work is so unique that to treat it here (or under any other heading) is partly out of embarrassment, but partly in view of Wehrli's association of it with the chanson de geste and his description of it as a 'christliches Heldenlied' (*Formen*, pp. 73ff., 82).
166 Yeandle, *Ludwigslied*, pp. 18ff.; Kemper, *Ludwigslied*, p. 15.
167 Haubrichs, *Anfänge*, p. 178, 180; Kemper, *Ludwigslied*, p. 8.
168 E.g. 581, 1; 630, 1f.; 1723, 2. That *hoeren sagen* need not be stereotyped is suggested by references to transmitting heroic themes before they found their way into writing: Lamprecht's *Alexanderlied* (S 1830) with the Hilde legend or Wolfram's *Willehalm* (384, 23) or *Nibelungenlied* C (342, 1) with the Dietrich legend.
169 Curschmann, *Nibelungenlied*, pp. 94f., sums this up: 'Wir haben in dieser Strophe die literarisch-poetische Metapher für den Akt des mündlichen Erzählens.'
170 Listening audience, e.g. 419, 2. Sung recital: Geering, *Nibelungenmelodie*, pp. 118ff.; Jammers, *Vortrag*, pp. 127f., 132f.; Brunner, *Strukturprobleme*, pp. 300f.; *VfL* 6, 956. Albrecht von Scharfenberg, *Jüngerer Titurel* 3364, 1, refers to blind (oral) singers of the Siegfried theme (cf. Heinzle, *Dietrichepik*, p. 89).
171 Cf. Heinzle, *Dietrichepik*, p. 70.
172 The various MSS of the *Nibelungenlied* throw no further light on its acoustic reception. Nor is much to be gained directly from *Die Klage* (no more than the traditional epic formula *wunder hoeren sagen*, 640 and 1450). Indirectly, as part of its narrative action, it contains a scene with a typical recital situation (3776f., cf. Curschmann, *Nibelungenlied*, pp. 114f.), suggesting a still surviving practice of oral delivery.
173 *Hoeren*: 597, 4. Melody: *Jüngeres Hildebrandslied* (Brunner, *Strukturprobleme*, p. 301).
174 One example of *hoeren*: 589, 3; Dresden MS: see above, p. 76; melody: Brunner, *Strukturprobleme*, p. 301.
175 *Hoeren*: 228, 1; 234, 2; 240, 2; melody: Brunner, *Strukturprobleme*, p. 301; minstrel's repertoire: Konrad von Würzburg, *Kleinere Dichtungen* III 32, 298ff.; Der Marner XV 14 (v. 270). On these see Heinzle, *Dietrichepik*, pp. 71ff.
176 1215ff. Hugo von Trimberg, *Renner* 10348ff., also refers to liquid refreshment in the recital of heroic themes.

177 *Hoeren*: 1978, 7055, 9632; presence of audience: 1ff. (together with a request for silence, 16ff.); already heard recited: 7462, 11188, 11830.
178 *Hoeren*: 10, 1 (*hoeren sagen*, 6, 5, is coupled with the previous oral transmission of the theme, 6, 1ff.); opening request: 1, 1ff.
179 1551 (and v. 1 in the continuation in K); Heinzle, *Dietrichepik*, pp. 85f.
180 *Hoeren*: 110, 2222, 2370; shared space: 1f.; request for silence: 9ff.; recital to be heard: 2674.
181 *Hoeren* in conjunction with request for a drink: 1097, 1ff.; melody: Brunner, *Strukturprobleme*, p. 301. Remaining cases are weaker, using *hoeren* with no further support or with the possibility of there having been a melody: *Sigenot* ('Bernerton', Brunner, p. 301), *Alpharts Tod* (melody of *Jüngeres Hildebrandslied*, Brunner, p. 301), *Rosengarten* D (melody of *Jüngeres Hildebrandslied*, Brunner, p. 301). *Kudrun* receives support for its nondescript evidence (the occasional *hoeren* or *hoeren sagen*) from the possibility of a melody, now lost (Brunner, p. 300).
182 Vollmann-Profe, *Wiederbeginn*, p. 217.
183 Bumke, *Geschichte*, p. 74; Vollmann-Profe, *Wiederbeginn*, p. 195.
184 *Horen*: 364, 661, 3888; Der Marner xv 261ff. Rother is also mentioned in the minstrel's repertoire listed in Hugo von Trimberg's *Renner* 16197.
185 Written veracity: Meves, *Studien*, pp. 93f.; Vollmann-Profe, *Wiederbeginn*, pp. 129f.; Bumke, *Geschichte*, pp. 74f. On the author's distinction between his work and others see 3491f., 4794ff. With *Salman und Morolf* only the use of *hoeren* (14, 2; 47, 2; 617, 2) and the possibility that, written in stanzas, it was composed to a melody (Brunner, *Strukturprobleme*, p. 300) can be adduced.
186 *Hoeren*: 103, 470, 1654; request for silence: 1; recital situation: 381f.; wine for reciter: see above, p. 76.
187 Request for silence: 1ff.; *hore zu*: cf. Schröder, *Anegenge*, p. 82; Scholz, *Hören*, pp. 78f. In his edition, p. lxxxvii, Baesecke says that these lines presuppose 'ein Buch zum Vorlesen'.
188 *Horen*: 13, 40, 2463; assembled audience: 379f.; wine for reciter: 2829 (cf. 1157f., 2396f., 2512f.).
189 Ehrismann, *Geschichte* II 1, 342; Meves, *Studien*, pp. 232ff.; Vollmann-Profe, *Wiederbeginn*, p. 220.
190 Herzog Ernst B: *hoeren* (1, 4f., 4273), deictic pointer (4467f.); D: *horen* (589, 843, 2454); earlier recited (3411 refers back to 3367ff.); G: *hoeren* (26, 6; 47, 1; 63, 1), singer (13, 13; 161, 9), need for wine (61, 8ff. – in a concluding request, 89, 11ff., the reciter invites anyone who knows more to continue singing instead). *Dukus Horant* uses *horen* occasionally (F 53, 1, 4; F 56, 6, 4; F 57, 5, 2) and was possibly composed to a melody (Brunner, *Strukturprobleme*, p. 300).
191 Written text: Vollmann-Profe, *Wiederbeginn*, p. 129. Oral recital: *Tu autem* (9094), *vor tragen* and *fure bringen* (9022, 9032), *hoeren sagen* (2375, 6461, 9086). Cf. also Henry the Lion's preference for listening to recitals (above, p. 64).
192 *Hoeren*: 162, 1f.; 360, 29f.; 417, 27f.; recital situation: 5, 5ff.; already recited: 400, 16 (cf. Kiening, *Reflexion*, pp. 156f.). If this work was intended for the same kind of audience as *Parzival* and *Titurel* then the evidence for these suggests acoustic reception in this case, too.
193 153, 4ff. and 26, 5ff. Cf. the parallel case of Heinrich von Hesler, p. 124.
194 *Hoeren*: 58f., 8233, 8547f.; back-reference of 6063 to 4617ff. In an opening generalisation with particular application to his own work Der Stricker also alludes to a twofold reception (7).
195 *Horen*: 125, 1048f., 2891; request for silence: 91; hear read out (55ff.: the author prays for help not in reading his source, but in recounting his own written version, 2144, 5482f., 5592).
196 *Horen*: 22, 4018, 10991; request for silence: 7145f.; *lesen* + dative: 649, 2094, 9314 (cf. also

lesen by itself: 4147, 9166, 13273); earlier heard recited: 10771 (refers to 9945ff., especially 9962ff.). Also relevant are 3863 (refers to 3380ff.) and 819 (cf. 407ff.).

197 *Hoeren*: 25702 (the glossary in the edition renders this by 'vorlesen lassen'), 30027; twofold reception: 36510. In his *Willehalm* Ulrich von dem Türlin uses *hoeren* (VI 22, X 29, XLIII 9) with no further support. Almost as weak is the only text in this group which is neither a 'Spielmannsepos' nor associated with a chanson de geste: the *Reinhart Fuchs* of Heinrich der Glichezare uses *hoeren* (253, 1597, 1661), but combined with allusions to a reward suggestive of performance before an assembled audience (854f., 1790f.).

198 Topsfield, *Chrétien*, pp. 13f., 18f.

199 Bumke, *Kultur*, pp. 609f.

200 *Ibid.*, pp. 725f.

201 Lambert of Ardres, *Historia*, p. 598.

202 *De confessione*, PL 207, 1088. In mentioning religious themes Peter sees them in terms of oral recital (*legi audias*). Here too secular and religious works meet on common acoustic ground.

203 4407ff. Although we shall see that these rival themes are reading-matter for ladies, this need not exclude the public recital implied in 5411ff.

204 20681ff.

205 The expectation of this practice can be seen as a matter of course by Ulrich von Lichtenstein, *Frauendienst* 112, 5ff., and Albrecht von Scharfenberg, *Jüngerer Titurel* 2958, 1ff. Gottfried also makes it clear (8626f.) that the written transmission of the Tristan story did not preclude its oral recital (cf. Ganz edn. I 299, note to v. 8626).

206 The Vorau version of the *Alexanderlied* lacks internal pointers, but its clerical adaptation of the theme to 'Heilsgeschichte' is in accord with the author's *Tobias* and its probable acoustic reception (if we can assume the same kind of audience for both works). The Strassburg text uses *hôren* occasionally (181, 3935, 4451) combined with requests for silence (125f., 4914f.).

207 E.g. 754, 3214, 6639f.

208 Bumke, *Mäzene*, p. 114; Masser, *Darbietung*, p. 391.

209 *Horen*: 655, 2902, 3123; Greek–Latin–French–German: 49ff., 70ff.; recital: 13670.

210 *Hoeren*: 4066, 20527, 20572; ill-wisher to depart: 20661ff.; *hoeren sagen* in the same passage (cf. also 18348, refers back to 17599ff.); *hoeren lesen*: 20656ff. Cf. Green, *ZfdA* 115 (1986), 163ff.

211 *Hoeren*: 172, 17362, 23112; assembled audience: 25041f.; hear recited: 20986ff. Two other works with the same classical theme may be added here. The *Göttweiger Trojanerkrieg* reinforces *hören* (2303, 4423, 21609) with references to the audience hearing a detail recounted or read out (3332, 6341, 7098 and 4604, 6588, 13806) and the *Trojanischer Krieg* of Konrad von Würzburg is just as weak: *hören* (286ff., 322f., 30940) is accompanied by no more than *sprechen und singen* on the part of the author (173, 177) and *hoeren sagen* for the audience (13088f.).

212 *Hoeren*: 11, 8184, 9309ff.; ill-wisher to keep away: 22f.; plea for silence: 2356f.; twofold reception: 9441.

213 *Hoeren*: 126f., 6435f., 10371; request for silence: 82ff., 6143ff.; twofold reception: 106 (where the context is not general, but the reception of Wirnt's work).

214 *Hoeren*: 59, 2496, 5161; request for silence: 19f.; presence of listeners: cf. the parallel between 8125 and 8132 (*hoeret* and *sitzet dâ bî*).

215 1754. That Der Stricker, as here, uses *sehen* in the sense of *lesen* is also clear from his *Karl der Große* 6176f., 9302f.

216 *Hoeren*: 255, 18153ff., 25016; vignettes of a recital: 651ff., 7335ff. (is Heinrich likely to have conceived the reception of his own work differently?); *vor sagen*: 22190.

217 *Hören*: I 53, 6; II 3, 2 and 15; 203, 13; earlier passages: II 88, 4; 135, 2 (not hearsay, but recital of this work). There remain some weaker cases. In *Gauriel von Muntabel* Konrad

von Stoffeln reinforces listening (350, 1294, 3336) with an isolated request for silence (2130ff.) and *Wigamur* hints at the possibility of oral recital with *hören sagen* (76, 210– refers back to 100ff., so scarcely conventional). Three works by Der Pleier yield very little. In *Meleranz* he uses *hoeren* and *hoeren sagen* (101, 1910, 6781; 2253, 3350, 9911), as in *Garel von dem Blühenden Tal* (31, 10408f., 12042; 15054, 19518), whilst *Tandareis und Flordibel* has *hoeren* alone (655, 1438, 13263).

218 Horen: 36, 1; 56, 1; 141, 3; sung recital: Bertau and Stephan, *ZfdA* 87 (1956/7), 267ff.; Jammers, *Vortrag*, p. 135; Mertens, *Wolfram-Studien* I (1970), 236ff.; Brunner, *Strukturprobleme*, p. 301; Ruh, *Epik* II 152.
219 Cf. Wolfram 1, 15f. with Albrecht 50, 1f.
220 1663, 1; 6077, 4. On the genuineness of 6327, 4 see Schröder, *ZfdA* 111 (1982), 129.
221 Melody: Bertau and Stephan, *ZfdA* 87 (1956/7), 262f.; Mertens, *Wolfram-Studien* I (1970), 219ff.; *VfL* 1, 169; Brunner, *Strukturprobleme*, p. 301. See also Krüger, *Studien*, pp. 239ff.
222 Hoeren: 411, 805, 1087; *hoerer*: 4267, 4970; melody: Brunner, *Strukturprobleme*, p. 301; Buschinger, *Lorengel*, pp. xivf.
223 Hôren: 354, 1594, 1692; presence of audience: 1f.; appeal to assist in telling: 3304; shared space: 2, 33; appeals for silence: 26ff., 31. Recital is also confirmed by the likelihood that the work was composed if not for Henry the Lion, then at least for the court at which he had encouraged such recitals (Bumke, *Mäzene*, p. 113; Mertens, *Eilhart*, pp. 262ff.; *Rezeption*, pp. 147f.).
224 This would be confirmed by the twofold reception of Ulrich's *Rennewart*, p. 108. Hoeren in his *Tristan*: 680, 1700, 3671.
225 Hoeren: 2056f., 3768; *lesen*: 2330ff. refers back to 2078f., 2126ff. Cf. also 296 (refers to 246ff.) and 2091 (refers to 2059ff.). Reading from a written text rather than simple recounting is suggested by Heinrich stressing his work as a book (40, 110, 650): it is this which grants an opportunity to the individual reader (2644) as well as to the public reciter. Contrast this with *Tristan als Mönch*: although the author refers to what was previously said (2325 refers back to 2220f.), the lack of any hint that the work was conceived as a written text makes it uncertain whether *lesen* can be understood as 'to recite' instead of 'to recount'.
226 1500, 1586, 2567; 7979.
227 78; 5980ff., 6395ff.; 6840. Cf. Green, *ZfdA* 115 (1986), 177ff.
228 4043, 7558, 9756; 17ff. (see above, pp. 75f.); 9798ff.; 8364; 2358 (refers back to 1287ff.), 8345 (refers to 819ff.). Cf. Green, *ZfdA* 115 (1986), 174ff.
229 2220, 5139, 7538; 2ff.; 158ff.; 16368 (refers back to 12933ff.). The reference to Konrad's work as a book (199) suggests that *las* in 16368 means 'to read out', not 'to narrate'.
230 194ff.; 182ff.; 6482.
231 379, 2956, 4456; 12692ff., 20580ff.; 19655 (two lines earlier the audience refers to the reciter: *als wir in hoeren jehen*).
232 This case rests entirely on *lesen* meaning 'to recite aloud'. In MS W (fifteenth century) the *lezer* is recommended a drink for his services in a recital now concluded (after 1488: *dat bok is nu vtghelesen / me scal dem lezer drincken gheuen*. Cf. also before 597, 953, 1234, 1401). Apart from this late MS the narrative thread is resumed after a digression with *lesen* (263f.): since it was the author as reciter (rather than as reader of his source) who dropped the thread, he resumes it now in reciting afresh.
233 724, 10588, 11904; 5834 (refers back to 3916ff.), 13576 (refers to 13531ff.), 17573 (refers to 485ff.). The twofold reception of this author's *Gottes Zukunft* (8101) and his use of *lesen hoern* for the *Visio Philiberti* (589) suggest that *Apollonius*, too, was meant for recital.
234 80, 975, 2801; 3930ff., 15360ff., 16504f.; 12661ff., 13602, 16224; 19502ff., 10849f. (on these last two examples see pp. 87 and 92). The *Demantin* of Berthold von Holle refers occasionally to listening (8564, 11759) and supports this once with hearing the work recited (9577ff.). The same is true of his *Crane* (2067, 4911), whilst *Darifant* contains no

NOTES TO PAGES 110–11

pointers, but may be associated with the others by analogy, for what that is worth. The *Wilhelm von Wenden* of Ulrich von Etzenbach has inconclusively only a few cases of *hoeren* (1051, 1879, 2282), but may be meant for recital like his *Alexandreis*. Rather more persuasive are the *Frauendienst* and *Frauenbuch* of Ulrich von Lichtenstein. Both use *hoeren* (28, 15f.; 113, 12; 595, 22), strengthened by combination with a request for silence (476, 1) and the suggestion that this book was read out to listeners (592, 6; 595, 15f.).

235 Included here because initially at least this genre was meant for a court audience (Fischer, *Studien*; Schirmer, *Versnovelle*, and for France Nykrog, *Fabliau*).
236 Fischer, *Studien*, pp. 267f., and Mundschau, *Sprecher*, p. 78.
237 Bumke, *Geschichte*, p. 291.
238 Fischer, *Studien*, pp. 250f.
239 Ibid., pp. 262ff.
240 Fischer, *Studien*, p. 270; Mundschau, *Sprecher*, pp. 76f.
241 Fischer, *Studien*, pp. 265f., 268f. *Meier Helmbrecht*: Kolb, *ZfdPh* 81 (1962), 1ff.
242 E.g. *Die Heidin* IV 160; *Der Schüler zu Paris* C 34ff.
243 E.g. *Meier Helmbrecht* 1929; Dietrich von Glezze, *Der Borte* 7; *Frauentreue* 354. In each case *lesen* means 'to recite aloud' (from a written text). In *Meier Helmbrecht* a distinction is made between reciter (1929: Swer iu ... lese) and author (1931: tihtaere), so that *lesen* does not mean 'narrate' (the author's task), but 'recite'. With Dietrich von Glezze the work is speaking in the first person and is later presented as a written text (558, cf. 20, 491). *Frauentreue* is also put forward as a written work (390).
244 Cf. *Zwei Kaufmänner und die treue Hausfrau* 19; *Die Frau als Reitpferd* 6.
245 Before this, the erotic content of *Hirsch und Hinde* seems clear (Haubrichs, *Anfänge*, p. 95), but equally its oral recital (musical notation: Ehrismann, *Geschichte* I 243; Schwab, *Lied*, pp. 90ff., who suggests performance for dancing). With the *Tanzlied von Kölbigk* song and dance combine to suggest a public setting for delivery (see above, pp. 66 and 69). On orally transmitted love-poetry before *Minnesangs Frühling* see Sayce, *Lyric*, p. 79, and Schweikle, *Minnesang*, p. 81.
246 Kuhn, *Liebe*, p. 97 ('die schon immer schrift-nähere Epik'); Bumke, *Kultur*, pp. 751f. On regarding this literature as songs meant for performance, rather than as poems see Ranawake, *PBB* 107 (1985), 137. McMahon, *Music*, p. 73, talks in similar terms of the transmission of these songs.
247 Bumke, *Kultur*, p. 758. McMahon, *Music*, p. 12, terms 'Minnesang' an oral art: even if some texts were written down soon after composition their melodies were handed down orally and written only much later. Even if we reckon with an earlier (but lost) MS transmission, writing played a smaller part in the spread of this genre: the first attested example is Ulrich von Lichtenstein about the middle of the thirteenth century (Bumke, *Geschichte*, p. 113), but even his lyrics are contained within a longer narrative work. A subordinate role of writing has also been suggested by McMahon, *Music*, p. 77, in the case of MSS with staffless neumes.
248 Bumke, *Kultur*, pp. 769f. (cf. de Boor, *Geschichte* II 233).
249 Schweikle, *Minnesang*, p. 24, may question this and stress the early use of writing, but even he postulates this only for the transmission of texts outside the context of recital, which is for him still oral delivery.
250 Gottfried, *Tristan* 17214f.; Der Stricker, *Daniel von dem Blühenden Tal* 8163ff.; Rudolf von Ems, *Der guote Gerhard* 5980ff. Cf. also the examples given above, p. 68.
251 Walther's gift of *wort ... unde wîse* (26, 4) can hardly be dismissed as a mere formula in a song for which the melody has been preserved (Bützler, *Untersuchungen*, pp. 15ff.; McMahon, *Music*, pp. 93ff.). The same applies to those songs whose delivery is referred to as *sanc* or *singen* and for which a melody can be postulated, e.g. Rudolf von Fenis II 1, 1ff. (cf. Aarburg, *Melodien*, pp. 397f., no. 25); III 1, 1ff. (pp. 407ff., no. 34); VII 1, 4 (p. 399, no. 26).

252 Someone else sings: Kaiser Heinrich III 1, 5ff.; Heinrich von Morungen VIa 2, 5f.; Ulrich von Lichtenstein KDL 46, 1, 1ff. (cf. Bumke, *Kultur*, p. 755; Kartschoke, *Ulrich*, pp. 107f.; McMahon, *Music*, p. 67). Duet singing: Burkart von Hohenfels XV, 1ff. (cf. *Kommentarband*, p. 48, with Veldeke 60, 13 as a parallel). Collective singing: Neidhart, *Winterlieder* 30, 7, 1ff.; von Stadegge 2, 1, 1; Ulrich von Lichtenstein KDL 52, 1, 1f. (see above, p. 67). Public function: Kleinschmidt, *AfK* 58 (1976), 35ff.; Ortmann and Ragotzky, *Minnesang*, pp. 227ff. On composition and recital by rulers as a display of authority cf. Mertens, *Kaiser*, pp. 462f.

253 Schweikle, *Minnesang*, pp. 34ff. Cf. also the use of *canciones, cantare, canere* for various lyric genres in the sermon codex 176 (*ZfdA* 46 (1902), 93). Schweikle's attempt to play down this evidence for public recital cannot be taken so far as to deny it altogether. Musical instruments: Tannhäuser IV 141ff.; V 116ff.; Neidhart, *Winterlieder* 4, 2, 6ff.; Otto von Botenlouben XI 118f. (cf. Sayce, *Lyric*, p. 180, fn. 2). Manesse MS: Welker, *Melodien*, pp. 121ff.

254 See above, pp. 70 and 87. Thematically at least we may conclude with a mention of the *Minnelehre* of Johann von Konstanz: he uses *hoeren* occasionally (608, 834, 881), but also a request for silence (1ff.) with *hoeren sagen* for listening to a recital.

255 *Minnesang*, p. 56.

256 Bumke, *Geschichte*, p. 317; Pickerodt-Uthleb, *Liederhandschrift*. Terms like *sanc* or *singen* may be taken literally more readily in the gnomic lyric with its far greater range of recorded melodies.

257 Kasten, *Frauendienst*, pp. 234ff.; Bumke, *Geschichte*, pp. 43, 88, 314.

258 Bäuml and Rouse, *PBB* 105 (1983), 192ff., 317ff.; Bumke, *Kultur*, pp. 774f. Manesse MS: Walther, *Codex*, plate 112, p. 229.

259 Cf. Bäuml and Rouse, *PBB* 105 (1983), 323, who draw attention (p. 329, fn. 85) to a much earlier example with Notker Balbulus, whose sequences were transferred to writing on rolls to assist singing (*Liber Ymnorum, Prooemium* 9).

260 Cf. Lomnitzer, *Erhellung*, pp. 138f., 143f.

261 Moser, *Lied*, pp. 196f.; Lomnitzer, *Erhellung*, p. 143; Schweikle, *ZfdA* 93 (1964), 99ff.

262 To this total must be added eight works belonging to the intermediate mode (see p. 392, n. 61) for which there is no separate evidence of an acoustic reception to warrant inclusion in this chapter.

263 For example, German charters of the thirteenth century (Wilhelm, *Corpus*) refer to reception by hearing and by reading as often as 641 times (and to these must be added the examples where *hoeren* is used outside the double formula).

5 Criteria for reception by reading

1 Cf. Schlieben-Lange, *Traditionen*, p. 46; Knoop, *GL* 3/4 (1976), 27.
2 Schlieben-Lange, *Traditionen*, p. 46.
3 *Ibid.*, p. 47.
4 Quoted and discussed by Schlieben-Lange, *Traditionen*, pp. 52f. See also Gadamer, *Unterwegs*, p. 14.
5 Knoop, *GL* 3/4 (1976), 29.
6 Schlieben-Lange, *Traditionen*, p. 47; Goody, *Interface*, p. xiii.
7 Ehlich, *Text*, p. 38.
8 *Ibid*.
9 *Ibid.*, p. 37.
10 Goody, *Interface*, p. xii.
11 The classic example is Augustine's description of Ambrose reading silently to himself, *Confessiones* VI 3. Ambrose was engrossed in his reading, which he did silently so as not to

be interrupted by anyone who, overhearing him, might force questions upon him. Cf. Balogh, *Philologus* 82 (1927), 85f.
12 Cramer, *Geschichte*, p. 11. See also Cramer, *Repräsentation*, pp. 259ff.
13 Hölscher, *Öffentlichkeit*, p. 13. Cf. also Wenzel, *Repräsentation*, p. 188.
14 Wenzel, *ZfdPh* 107 (1988), 350.
15 *Öffentlichkeit*, p. 130.
16 Wenzel, *ZfdPh* 107 (1988), 359; Gottfried von Strassburg, *Tristan* 8589 (Hatto, *Gottfried*, p. 154).
17 Hölscher, *Öffentlichkeit*, p. 130; Ulrich von Lichtenstein, *Frauendienst* 60, 17: *In der zît mîn schrîber quam, / den ich in eine heinlîch nam: / ez muoste vil verholne sîn. / ich bat in lesen daz büechelîn.*
18 See pp. 303ff.
19 *Regula*, cap. 48.
20 The same criticism has been made by Lebsanft, *ZfSL* 92 (1982), 58.
21 Scholz, *Hören*, pp. 37f.
22 *Ibid.*, p. 37.
23 Cf. Kartschoke, *IASL* 8 (1983), 256.
24 Cf. also the reference by Walther von Rheinau, *Marienleben* 12291f., to books of the Old Testament *diu man list / In allen kilchen überlût*.
25 Cf. also Brun von Schönebeck, *Hohes Lied* 5891f.
26 Green, *Exodus*, pp. 19ff.
27 *Der welsche Gast* 9234.
28 Kartschoke, *IASL* 8 (1983), 256.
29 Scholz, *Hören*, pp. 114f.; Konrad Fleck, *Flore und Blanscheflur* 96.
30 Scholz, *Hören*, pp. 36f.
31 *Ibid.*, p. 114.
32 See p. 154.
33 See above, p. 104.
34 *Judith* 671; Brun von Schönebeck, *Hohes Lied* 6359 and 10258. On the twofold reception of these works see pp. 206 and 198ff.
35 Scholz, *Hören*, p. 116.
36 See p. 158.
37 Scholz, *Hören*, p. 116.
38 592, 20.
39 Scholz, *Hören*, pp. 78f.
40 E.g., 10, 1ff.; 11, 1ff.; 12, 4f.; 13, 1ff.; 17, 10ff.
41 Other examples from Notker's *Psalter* are 219, 9 and 239, 13.
42 Rudolf von Ems, *Weltchronik* 2587; Lamprecht von Regensburg, *Sanct Franzisken Leben* 368 (on the twofold reception of these works see pp. 206 and 207). Other examples are Frau Ava, *Leben Jesu* 32, 6, and *Die Erlösung* 1230, 1437.
43 Scholz, *Hören*, p. 115.
44 *Ibid.*, p. 116.
45 Cf. also Herbort von Fritzlar, *Liet von Troye* 12720ff.; Otte, *Eraclius* A 5471; *Unser Vrouwen Klage* 100ff.
46 Other examples: *Millstätter Reimphysiologus* 24, 1f.; Reinbot von Durne, *Der heilige Georg* 2665; Hugo von Trimberg, *Der Renner* 5889f., 14275f., 20311f., 20459f.
47 See pp. 179ff. Scholz refers to Otfrid on p. 115.
48 See pp. 183ff.
49 See p. 207.
50 Cicero, *De oratore* II lxxv 303 (p. 428); Ovid, *Tristia* II 263 (p. 74).
51 Scholz, *Hören*, pp. 123f. Other examples from Otfrid are given p. 180.
52 Cf. also v 15, 19 and 33 and Scholz, *Hören*, p. 124.

53 In what follows I leave out of account German texts which use this phrase simply as the vernacular equivalent of what their Latin source had. Examples are: *Weißenburger Katechismus* 32, 85; *Bruchstücke der Lex Salica* 56, 20; *Benediktinerregel* (OHG) 218, 21; 219, 3, etc.; *Benediktinerregel* (MHG), Zwiefalten version 22, 2; 22, 3, etc. (similar examples occur in the Hohenfurt, Engelberg, Asbach, Munich and Admont versions).
54 V. 18448.
55 V. 5592.
56 See above, pp. 107f.
57 Scholz, *Hören*, p. 124.
58 *Ibid.*
59 I have discussed the different implications of two such phrases in *Parergon* 2 (1984), 64f. and *Otfrid*, pp. 744f.
60 Scholz, *Hören*, p. 124, who (fn. 422) corrects my mistaken reading of these lines (in Green, *Oral poetry*, p. 214).
61 On the reception of Gottfried's work see pp. 194ff.
62 *Parzival*, Bartsch and Marti edn III 160 and 163.
63 Likewise in connection with literacy and illiteracy, Harris, *Literacy*, p. 87, draws attention to the recognition by Greek (and Elizabethan) dramatists that some of their best points would pass over the heads of most of their audience.
64 This is a reference back to II 673, 17f. which, as the editorial footnote makes clear, is indeed characterised by 'fettere Schrift der gleichen Hand'.
65 Frank, *Seitengestaltung*, pp. 89ff., discusses 'non-linear reading' (looking up certain passages in a work) in the context of the page lay-out of scholastic works.
66 Cf. 85, 21ff. and 28ff.
67 Refers back to I 22, 1ff.
68 Cf. 9847ff.
69 On the twofold reception of these last two works see pp. 207 and 206.
70 Discussed briefly by Scholz, *Hören*, p. 138.
71 As we saw above, for example p. 64, in the case of Henry the Lion, where the *Annales Stederburgenses* make it clear that he had written works collected to hear them recited.
72 Scholz, *Hören*, p. 139.
73 A 2560ff.. On the reception of this work, see p. 207. A similar reference to copying is made in *Judith* (2753ff.), a work for which individual readers, but possibly also listeners were anticipated (see p. 206).
74 Cf. Green, *ZfdA* 115 (1986), 155f. An interesting recommendation by Augustine to the reader of his *De doctrina christiana* is quoted by Palmer, FMS 23 (1989), 52. Augustine expects readers and listeners (*legenti vel audienti*, cf. Palmer, *ibid.*, p. 58, fn. 28), but it is to the reader that he suggests the possibility of reading only parts of the work (*Cui autem longus est, per partes eum legat qui habere vult cognitum*).
75 I have excluded from consideration examples with the construction *wir* or *man* because they need not mean that the persons addressed were actually meant to do the reading. Cf. the *Schwarzwälder Prediger* (*Erste Abtheilung*) 2 (28). Further examples are Priester Wernher's *Maria* A 4134ff.; Brun von Schönebeck, *Hohes Lied* 3126f.; *Das Rheinische Marienlob* 3157f.; *Wigamur* 1ff.
76 For further examples from Otfrid and Notker see pp. 180 and 184.
77 Cf. Kartschoke, *Geschichte*, p. 271.
78 *Herzog Ernst* B 4466ff. and *Herzog Ernst* D 3623ff.
79 *PBB* 111 (1989), 198.
80 Cf. 2, 6f.; 2, 10f.; 2, 14f., etc.
81 Other examples are Jans Enikel, *Weltchronik* 11416ff., and Brun von Schönebeck, *Hohes Lied* 6708f.
82 Scholz, *Hören*, pp. 192ff.

83 *Epistola* IX ii 105, PL 77, 1027f.
84 A well-known example is provided by the Exultet rolls: as the parchment was unrolled by the cantor in the pulpit, the fact that the illustrations were reversed with respect to the text means that the congregation could look at the pictures while the text was read out.
85 Henkel, *Bildtexte*, pp. 1ff., discusses the banderols in the pictures of the Berlin MS of Veldeke's *Eneide* as possible links between pictures and text, but unfortunately excludes the question whether or not an individual reader was presupposed. On the whole question see Duggan, *Word and Image* 5 (1989), 227ff. and Curschmann, *Pictura*, pp. 211ff., and Neumüllers-Klauser, *Inschriften*, p. 180, on the need for the text to be read out aloud.
86 *Speculum* 55 (1980), 246. See also p. 328, n. 105.
87 Camille, *AH* 8 (1985), 32.
88 *Ibid.*, p. 33. Some earlier (Carolingian) examples are given by McKitterick, *Text*, pp. 308f., 314. Cf. also Schröder's comment on illustrations in a MS of Wolfram's *Willehalm*, *Euphorion* 70 (1976), 279.
89 Wenzel, *Partizipation*, p. 193. Cf. also the early remark in the *Libri Carolini* by Theodulf of Orléans on the need of an inscription for the accurate understanding of a picture, PL 98, 1229f. On this cf. Nelson, *Literacy*, p. 265.
90 *AH* 8 (1985), 42. Cf. also Schröder, *ZfdA* 116 (1987), 266. Something similar is implied for Grünewald's Isenheim altarpiece by Hayum, *Altarpiece*, p. 87.
91 These passages from Notker are discussed p. 185.
92 Green, *Parergon* 2 (1984), 68; Specht, *Geschichte*, p. 92.
93 These lines refer back to 5817ff. and 5869ff.
94 The MSS are listed by von Kries, *Thomasin*, IV 119 (under 'Bild Nr. 87', which is reproduced on p. 33).
95 On the two classes of recipient for Thomasin's work see p. 204.
96 *Hören*, pp. 195f.
97 Scholz, *ibid.*, p. 196, points out that the *Wiener Physiologus* has a similar remark (x, 1f.), but that the space for the picture has been left blank.
98 Scholz, *Hören*, p. 196.
99 Voss, *Studien*, p. 121.
100 *Ibid.*, pp. 121f.
101 *Ibid.*, pp. 42f.
102 See above, pp. 87f. Diemer, *Genesis*, p. 260, in the glossary to his edition translates *vorbrieven* by 'niederschreiben', as if it were identical with *verbrieven*. This is unlikely since his glossary shows a regular differentiation between the prefixes *vor-* and *ver-*.
103 *Studien*, p. 130.
104 Scholz, *Hören*, pp. 126f.
105 In what follows I leave out of account three cases, mentioned by Scholz, pp. 131f., because lack of confirmatory evidence makes them uncertain: Freidank, *Bescheidenheit* 1, 1ff.; *Das Buch der Rügen* 1f. (pointers to a reception by readers or listeners occur in the preface to the Latin source, *Praefatio in sermones nulli parcentes*, p. 15, but not in the vernacular text); *Tugendspiegel* 1f.
106 Scholz, *Hören*, p. 130.
107 The work entitles itself in v. 5: *ich haisse der minne fürgedank*.
108 Scholz, *Hören*, p. 132.
109 *Ibid.*, p. 133.
110 *Ibid.*, pp. 131f.
111 See p. 154.
112 Heinzle, *Wandlungen*, p. 187.
113 2346, 4373. See above, p. 87.
114 Green, *ZfdA* 115 (1986), 174ff.
115 Scholz, *Hören*, pp. 133f.

116 See p. 208.
117 See above, p. 74.
118 See p. 157.
119 1324ff.
120 On physical contact with a book (holding it in one's hand) as a pointer to individual reading see pp. 134f. That this is meant by Bruder Philipp is suggested by the parallel between 10094f. (*al . . . / den ditz buoch ze handen kumt*) and 10116f. (*alle die an disem buoche / lesent*).
121 Cf. also 165ff.
122 *Marienleben* 16140ff. Cf. also the close conjunction of reading with correction in 16110ff. and 16124ff.
123 Cf. Scholz, *Hören*, p. 137.
124 On the appeal to readers how to solve an acrostic see the next section.
125 On *setzen* in the context of writing see Lamprecht's *Alexanderlied*, Vorau version 173; Der Wilde Mann, *Von christlicher Lehre* 3, 1; *Kreuzfahrt des Landgrafen Ludwig* 1737ff., 4651, 5050.
126 Scholz discusses these devices, *Hören*, pp. 142ff.
127 *Ibid.*, p. 165, quoting Wehowsky, *Schmuckformen*, p. 49.
128 Bertau, *Literaturgeschichte*, p. 129.
129 *Ibid.*, p. 130.
130 Scholz, *Hören*, pp. 142 and 165.
131 Discussed by Scholz, *ibid.*, p. 145.
132 *Ibid.*, pp. 145f.
133 *Ibid.*, pp. 143f.
134 On the twofold reception of these works see Chapter 8.
135 These works (with references to Scholz if he discusses them) are: Otfrid, *Evangelienbuch* (cf. Ernst, *Liber*, pp. 206ff.); Gottfried, *Tristan* (Scholz, pp. 151f.); Heinrich von dem Türlin, *Die Crone* (Scholz, p. 161); Rudolf von Ems, *Barlaam und Josaphat* (Scholz, p. 162); *Alexander* (Scholz, p. 162); *Willehalm von Orlens* (Scholz, pp. 151f., 162); *Weltchronik* (Scholz, p. 162); Konrad von Heimesfurt, *Urstende* (Scholz, pp. 159f.); Brun von Schönebeck, *Hohes Lied* 3379ff.; *Lohengrin* (Cramer, *VfL* 5, 899); *Rheinisches Marienlob* (Scholz, p. 158). On the twofold reception of these works see Chapters 7 and 8.
136 Green, *Otfrid*, pp. 746f.
137 On the reception of the *Margaretenlegende* see p. 159.
138 Scholz makes no reference to *Von dem englischen Gruoß ein leich*, where the stanzas are arranged in groups according to the Latin wording of the angelic greeting so that the first letter of each stanza forms part of an acrostic (stanza 1 therefore begins with A, stanza 2 with V, stanza 3 with E, and so on throughout the poem). This is a written device intended for the reader, even though no instructions are given. That a phonetic realisation of the acrostic was not possible in recital is clear from stanzas 27ff., forming the acrostic TECUM, for stanza 29 begins not with *c*, but with *ch* (*Chünegin*), and stanza 30 not with *u*, but with *v* (*Von*). In agreement with this the work contains no pointer to being recited.
139 Scholz, *Hören*, p. 153. Cf. Huot, *Song*, p. 164, on the employment of similar devices in French literature.
140 Cf. Ranke, *Tristan*, p. 202.
141 Lord, *Singer*, p. 25.
142 Havelock, *Revolution*, p. 289.
143 *Ibid.*, pp. 67ff.
144 Coulmas, *Schrift*, p. 32. Cf. also Goody, *Domestication*, p. 115. Scholes and Willis, *Linguists*, pp. 215ff., have conducted linguistic tests on literates and illiterates, reaching the conclusions: 'In short, we know about phonemes because we know about letters'

(p. 220) and with regard to morphemes: 'As with segmental phonemes, access to these constructs appears to be gained through literacy' (p. 222). It does not follow from this that literacy necessarily leads to an awareness of words as separate entities. On difficulties in antiquity in this respect see Saenger, *Naissance*, p. 447.

145 Cf. von Kraus, *ZfdA* 51 (1909), 374ff.; Scholz, *Hören*, p. 153.
146 See Bumke, *Mäzene*, p. 26; Scholz, *Hören*, pp. 154f.
147 On this see p. 157.
148 Seelbach, *Kommentar*, p. 11, has suggested the possibility of anagrams in the *Meier Helmbrecht* of Wernher der Gartenaere. If we accept this it would be the only case in a vernacular work for which, while it may have been recited, we have no evidence that it was also meant for readers.
149 Scholz, *Hören*, p. 120.
150 On the author's greater concern with the reactions of his readers than with those of the reciter see pp. 145f.
151 Vollmann-Profe, *Kommentar*, p. 199, interprets the verb *singan* as meaning 'to chant' ('psallieren') and in *Otfrid*, p. 57, she accordingly translates it by 'singen'. Nonetheless, on both occasions she sees Mary's activity as a form of 'Psalterlesen' (*Kommentar, ibid.*; *Otfrid*, p. 230). The essential point for us is that until Gabriel's appearance Mary is alone and reads to herself, not to others. Cf. also Schreiner, *Rheinischer Merkur* 44/1 (1990), 83 and *FMS* 24 (1990), 322f.
152 On the conjunction of two such verbs see pp. 139ff.
153 Cf. Scholz, *Hûsvrouwe*, p. 249.
154 On the twofold reception of this work see p. 205.
155 On the two types of reception envisaged by the author, including therefore the individual readers whom he hoped to wean away from secular themes, see p. 206.
156 Cf. also 21307.
157 The privacy of this reading (to oneself) is suggested by 311f.
158 On the use of verbs of seeing to denote reading see pp. 139ff. At a date later than the deadline we have set ourselves the *Legatus divinae pietatis* of Gertrud von Helfta was translated into German. In this vernacular version Christ is imagined sitting on a reader's lap to point out an especially important passage (*Ein botte der götlichen milteheit* 3, 38).
159 See above, p. 91.
160 See above, p. 84.
161 See above, p. 85.
162 For Latin see above, pp. 16f., and for German see p. 148.
163 On the twofold reception of these works see pp. 190ff. and 205.
164 See above, p. 85.
165 *Regula*, cap. 48.
166 Cf. also the Zwiefalten version 36, 7.
167 See as well the Munich version 192, 7.
168 Cf. also III 14, 65; IV 15, 59.
169 Cf. III 13, 44.
170 The conjunction of *selbe* with reflexive in the context of private reading within the monastery is also to be found in the MHG version of the '*Epistola ad fratres de Monte Dei*' des Wilhelm von Saint-Thierry 83, 1 and 120, 1.
171 A similar contrast is made in a similar way in the *Oberaltaicher Predigten* 40, 3.
172 *Gesta regum Anglorum* V 447 (II 519).
173 If the aristocrat recited at court, it was in the aristocratic genre of the love-lyric. On this see Mertens, *Kaiser*, pp. 455ff. and Kasten, *Frauendienst*, pp. 234ff.
174 See p. 347, n. 179.
175 See p. 337, n. 155.
176 That we must be careful in interpreting *lesen* + *selber* is suggested elsewhere in the same

work when Ulrich stresses that it was Alexander, and no one else, who read out a letter to an assembled company (1856ff.). Here the context makes it clear that *lesen* + *vor* takes priority over *lesen* + *selber* (in the sense with which we are concerned).

177 Cf. also III 19, 16.
178 *Schriften*, p. 193, fn. 54.
179 Bumke, *Mäzene*, p. 114 (said of Veldeke going to the Thuringian court, but equally applicable to his going to Cleves).
180 See p. 193.
181 1837ff.
182 Cf. Scholz, *Hören*, p. 122.
183 A similar alternation between *lesen* and *sehen* occurs when Hugo von Trimberg twice refers to his knowledge of Freidank's work: *Der Renner* 5176f. (*als ich gelesen hân*) and 20110f. (*als ich in sînem getihte sach*).
184 Personal reading is implied when the letter is handed over to Alexander, 5509f.
185 Cf. 14692ff.
186 Cf. *Vita* 9, 10 (quoted in the footnotes to the edition of Veldeke's work, p. 49).
187 *Vita* 33, 1 (p. 149).
188 However, Hatto, *Parzival*, p. 220, translates this as 'I am telling you just as Kyot told it', a rendering which is admittedly just as possible. Cf. also the alternation between *Parzival* 484, 9 (*sus lâsen wir am grâle*) and 483, 20 (*dar an gesâh wir zeinem mâl / geschriben* ...).
189 See p. 192.
190 See p. 226.
191 See above, pp. 93f.
192 See above, pp. 27f., 29, 31.
193 *IASL* 8 (1983), 258.
194 *Ibid.*, p. 257.
195 See above, p. 74.
196 Admittedly, this text may date from the fifteenth century, but we are not so much concerned with its date as with the implications of its wording. Moreover, if *verlesen*, by contrast with *lesen*, were enough to convey reading aloud it is difficult to see why this has to be underlined by *offenlich*.
197 As a first example: Könemann von Jerxheim employs the double formula in his *Wurzgarten Mariens* 5082, but varies the wording in a triple formula 6521ff. The equation of *seen* with *lesen* in these passages suggests that the latter refers to individual reading, not recital.
198 Cf. Scholz, *Hûsvrouwe*, p. 266: 'Hier werden also ... der Lektüre-Ersatz durch Bilder und der Ersatz von "wârheit"-Lektüre durch das Lesen von Aventiuren gleichgesetzt'.
199 Gottfried is here concerned with the reader of his own work, not of other versions of the story. Cf. Schröder, *ZfdA* 104 9175), 322.
200 Cf. Patzlaff, *Otfrid*, p. 50, on Liut. 70 and 82.
201 *Ibid.*
202 Kartschoke, *Bibeldichtung*, p. 223. Kartschoke admittedly sees the monastic reciter included here, but we meet on common ground as regards the individual reader.
203 When Notker, *Martianus Capella* 220, 6, refers to the *lector* understanding his work he is more likely to have the reader in mind than the reciter.
204 Williram, *Hohes Lied*, Prologus 24 and 37. The *studiosus lector* (in the sense of one who *liset mit andacht*, 66, 17) is also implied in *Die heilige Regel für ein vollkommenes Leben* 66, 13ff.: *alle di ... gerne lesent und studerent an der heiligen scrifte.*
205 Cf. the edition, p. 66, below: *sicut lector in suis locis plenius scriptum inuenire poterit.*
206 See pp. 198ff., 152, 155.
207 Other examples: Heinrich von Freiberg, *Tristan* 2644; Könemann von Jerxheim, *Der Wurzgarten Mariens* 386f., 3641f., 6557; *Mariengrüße* 791, 821.
208 See p. 290.

209 Other examples are: Der Arme Hartmann, *Rede vom heiligen Glauben* 95, 9; Ulrich von Türheim, *Rennewart* 156 (referring to Wolfram's *Willehalm*); Heinrich von dem Türlin, *Die Crone* 140f.; Walther von Rheinau, *Marienleben* 16140. We shall see that there is further evidence in these works for reception by readers.
210 *IASL* 8 (1983), 256.
211 See pp. 158.
212 Further examples are: *Judith* 2725ff.; Heinrich von Hesler, *Apokalypse* 1319f.; *Rheinisches Marienlob* 1528f.; Bruder Philipp, *Marienleben* 10116f. For these works, too, the argument will suggest other pointers to readers.
213 Scholz, *Hören*, pp. 126f.
214 As expressed by Hugo von Trimberg, *Renner* 1590ff., 24520ff., and Heinrich von Hesler, *Apokalypse* 1349ff. Cf. also Stackmann, *Texte*, p. 252.
215 I know of only one case where a prayer is made for the reciter (*Frauentreue*, p. 25, in MSS H and C: ... *Der evch daz bvchel hat gelesen*), although this could apply to the author in his function as reciter.
216 On monastic (and aristocratic) recipients for *Das Leben der heiligen Elisabeth* see *VfL* 5, 635.
217 When Heinrich von dem Türlin appeals to those who may condescend to read him (*Die Crone* 141) he has in mind those sitting above, not below the salt. Other examples of an appeal to potential readers are: *Judith* 2525; Mechthild von Magdeburg, *Fließendes Licht der Gottheit* 206, 163f.; *Die Lilie* 24, 11; Walther von Rheinau, *Marienleben* 16110ff.
218 See also above, pp. 130f. There our concern was to distinguish the possible reader in the audience from the listener, but here the question is to determine the reader as opposed to the reciter.
219 Cf. also Notker's letter to Hugo von Sitten (Piper, *Schriften* I ii, 861, 2): *et preualebitis ad legendum*. That a critical reading can also turn out negatively is admitted by Berthold von Holle, *Darifant* 72f.
220 See above, p. 144.
221 Cf. above, pp. 143f., for examples from the *Heliand Praefatio* and from Otfrid's letter to Liutbert.
222 Scholz, *Hören*, p. 45. Ovid, *Tristia* I, 1, 35; III, 1, 2; IV, 10, 132; *Vita S. Wandregiseli*, MGH SS r.M. 5, 13.
223 Other examples in this work are 28164f., 39909ff., 64353ff., 68714, 73560, 93607, 95589.
224 Cf. also 2390, 2561ff.
225 See pp. 157, 158.
226 See above, pp. 89f.
227 Further examples: *Braunschweigische Reimchronik* 2557ff. (see p. 157); Jans Enikel, *Weltchronik* 13979 (cf. 13827); *Reinfried von Braunschweig* 22814ff. (cf. 20989ff.).
228 Green, *ZfdA* 115 (1986), 172f.
229 Cf. also *Lohengrin* 7623ff. in the light of 7621f.
230 See above, pp. 16f.
231 An earlier step can be included if we accept the argument of Mertens, *Mäzenatentum*, p. 132. Basing himself on the prologue of *Die gute Frau* he suggests that the expensive process of commissioning a German version of a French (or Latin) original may have been initiated by a court cleric recommending the theme to the potential patron, and that this first move was by oral means. Only after this would the author be engaged with his source in detail, reading it in preparation for adapting it to German.
232 In the case of Wolfram's access to theological knowledge Schröder, *Euphorion* 67 (1973), 222f., points to oral possibilities like the sermon and the liturgy, as well as the oral recital of MHG clerical literature.
233 On this device in 'Mären' see Fischer, *Studien*, p. 222.
234 See Fry, *Memory*, p. 289.

235 Cf. also 238, 86ff.
236 Kartschoke, *Geschichte*, p. 348; *Der Wilde Mann*, p. 91.
237 Ruh, *Epik* I 105.
238 Reproduced in Walther, *Codex*, plates 58, 112, 124. See also Frühmorgen-Voss, *Bildtypen*, p. 188. On an earlier depiction of Rudolf von Ems dictating to a scribe see Wachinger, *Autorschaft*, p. 9.
239 Jans Enikel, *Fürstenbuch* 13ff., uses *heizen schríben* to the same effect.
240 He also names and praises him 13266ff. (cf. Bumke, *Mäzene*, p. 451, n. 234).
241 Examples of the latter are Hugo von Trimberg, *Renner* 18916ff., Johannes Rothe (Honemann, *Rothe*, p. 85), Johann von Soest (*VfL* 4, 746), Michel Beheim and Hans Folz (Wachinger, *Autorschaft*, p. 16).
242 See above, p. 16.
243 *Ibid*.

6 Survey of reception by reading

1 Murdoch, *Approaches*, p. 146; Flint, *Rise*, pp. 240ff.
2 Kieckhefer, *Magic*, pp. 57f.
3 Boudriot, *Religion*, pp. 64f. (see also Murdoch, *Approaches*, p. 158, fn. 69). Many examples of the association of priests or monks with magic are given by Flint, *Rise*, e.g. pp. 67, 207, 245f., 363f.
4 Haubrichs, *Anfänge*, pp. 419ff. (cf. also Flint, *Rise*, p. 314). Haubrichs also stresses, pp. 413f., the grey zone between magic incantations and Christian blessings.
5 Stuart and Walla, *ZfdA* 116 (1987), 79, also suggest the possibility of antiquarian interests on the part of a scribe.
6 Runes: Arntz, *Handbuch*, pp. 273ff.; Elliott, *Runes*, pp. 66ff. Amulets: Boudriot, *Religion*, pp. 64ff.; Düwel, *FMS* 22 (1988), 92ff. On the OHG evidence for this practice see Wesche, *Wortschatz*, pp. 56ff., who interprets *runstaba* as amulets with writing. For examples of written magic see Flint, *Rise*, pp. 53, 245, 246, 247, 316, 320. *Zoubargescrip*: Wesche, *Wortschatz*, pp. 57f.; Helm, *Religionsgeschichte* II 2, 126.
7 *Münchener Wundsegen* 22: *Sprich den segen dristunt und also manigen pater noster und tuo nith mer, wan als hie gescriben si*; *Wurmsegen* B (MSD II 281); *Zwei deutsche Arzneibücher* 139, 3 and 154, 17; Erhart Hesel, *Arzneibuch*, p. 45; *Mittelniederdeutsches Arzneibuch*, pp. 122, 149.
8 *Roßarzneibuch* 15 (2): *Der da wil haben roß arczney, der lezz ditz puech*. The editor (p. 1) suggests that the text was written in German because it was meant for practical, not scholarly use (cf. also Heinzle, *Wandlungen*, p. 206).
9 Examples of a diagram: 3, 19 and 31; 10, 15; 11, 9 (on the uncertainty of such evidence see p. 126). Mnemonic verses: 18, 7ff. (on the analytic view of language for the reader: p. 133).
10 Cf. Haug, *Schriftlichkeit*, pp. 142f. On the interlinear gloss as a hallmark of school instruction see Wieland, *ASE* 14 (1985), 153ff.
11 Haubrichs, *Anfänge*, pp. 243f., 253, 248f. and *Studienprogramm*, pp. 243, 250, 249f. On the *Murbacher Hymnen* see also Henkel, *Übersetzungen*, pp. 67ff., who in analysing the relationship between Latin word and vernacular gloss (p. 208) reconstructs the movements of the reader's eyes. In his *Flore und Blanscheflur* Konrad Fleck shows that pupils used writing tablets (820), so that the use of *lesen* meaning 'to learn' (see pp. 317f.) suggests reading and writing in the course of instruction. See also p. 158 on reading the *Windberger Psalter* in monastic schooling.
12 Haubrichs, *Anfänge*, p. 269.
13 *Ibid*., p. 99.
14 *Ibid*., pp. 100ff.
15 72, 9: ... *Die diß puch gern lesend* (with no parallel in the Latin text).

16 Vollmann-Profe, *Wiederbeginn*, pp. 128f.; Bennewitz, *Literatur*, pp. 334; de Boor, *Geschichte* III 2, 347.
17 Edn, pp. xviii and xxxiv (together with plate 1).
18 1, 15 and 22.
19 10675, 11969ff. On the latter see Scholz, *Hûsvrouwe*, p. 259, and on its uncertainty p. 127.
20 14693f. On other visual aspects of the reception of this work see Scholz, *Hûsvrouwe*, p. 249.
21 1 and 6 (a general observation which bears on this example); 14705ff. Whoever the *wuocheraere* (7101ff. – see p. 291) may be, Thomasin had in mind a group of recipients of whom he used the word *lesen* (cf. Scholz, *Hûsvrouwe*, p. 252).
22 Curschmann, *PBB* 106 (1984), 239; Düwel, *Fabula* 32 (1991), 67ff.
23 3, 22 (no Latin equivalent); 4, 34 (*Ich pit euch leser und leserinne*).
24 11819f., 14793f., 15828ff. These references are not quite so precise as one suggesting a reader in Otfrid (Green, *Otfrid*, p. 752), but they are of the same type. On something similar with Notker cf. Green, *Parergon* 2 (1984), 63f.
25 24606ff. (on the *wîse man* cf. above, p. 131); reader of an earlier work: 24602.
26 Participation of laymen: Haubrichs, *Georgslied*, pp. 188ff. (on the *Ezzolied*, see p. 350, n. 23). The situation of catechetical literature is best summed up when Priester Arnold refers to his audience as *die vil tumpen leigen*, who listen to what he has to teach them (*Loblied auf den heiligen Geist* 59a, 4; 21, 1). Beyond the limits of our inquiry the spread of literacy meant that catechetical texts and interpretation could later serve as devotional reading-matter (Adam, *Vaterunserauslegungen*).
27 See above, p. 98.
28 Devotional reading of French sermons alongside public delivery: Zink, *Prédication*, pp. 139ff. and Frank, *Seitengestaltung*, pp. 172f. Meant for reading: Ruh, *VB* 3 (1981), 14.
29 The majority of sermons were transmitted in Latin because this made them universally applicable. They presuppose a cleric who could read Latin, even if he gave the sermon in a vernacular.
30 Zink, *Prédication*, p. 162.
31 Richter, *Überlieferung*, p. 214.
32 Zink, *Prédication*, p. 162 ('aux lisières du monde clérical').
33 Richter, *Überlieferung*, pp. 158, 160, 217.
34 Vollmann-Profe, *Wiederbeginn*, p. 65 (cf. however the reservation of Kartschoke, *Geschichte*, p. 244).
35 Haubrichs, *Anfänge*, p. 307. With these last two works it is surmise that they were read as well as heard, so that, unlike Notker, they cannot be included in the intermediate mode.
36 Grundmann, *Bewegungen*, p. 462.
37 *Ibid.*, p. 463.
38 Richter, *Überlieferung*, p. 221f.
39 95, 7f. (see above, p. 140).
40 In 75, 18 and 77, 21 (cf. edn, p. xvii) the recipient is referred to the Rule so precisely that a reader, expected to consult it, may be implied. More telling is the comment on the spiritual reward for those who read and study the scriptures (66, 13) in an act of devotional communion (66, 17).
41 Grundmann, *Bewegungen*, p. 457ff.
42 Haubrichs, *Anfänge*, pp. 255f. Since for both works this is no more than a surmise they cannot safely be included under the intermediate mode.
43 Acrostics: between vv. 21 and 64. Potential readers: 1528f., 4699 (on the reasons for not regarding *leser* as a reciter in this kind of context see above, p. 144).
44 A reader is also implied if we accept the same kind of audience as for the author's *Sanct Franziken Leben*, where readers as well as listeners are made clear. See p. 207.
45 4883, 4009. Heinzle, *Wandlungen*, p. 182, draws attention to 4635ff. (the author is obliged as a cleric to recount to laymen in the vernacular what *Die wîsen in latîne* have said).

NOTES TO PAGES 154-5

Coupled with the evidence for readers, this suggests that some of these laymen may have been able to read only in German. Scholz, *Hören*, pp. 97f., dismisses any oral dimension of delivery as 'fingiert', but I see it as anticipated in the act of written composition, so that Heinrich reckoned with listeners as well as readers.

46 2, 41; 4, 5. Cf. Neumann, *Beiträge*, pp. 182f.
47 79, 175; 206, 123. Even if it may not go back to Mechthild, but to the Dominican responsible for the written version, the division of her work into chapters and their systematic listing under titles (pp. 3f.) presuppose an early respect for the reader's wish to use the work without being a prisoner to the sequence of the text (cf. Palmer, *FMS* 23 (1989), 77f.).
48 Listening and reading: see p. 205; the reader: *Schlußvers* 10, p. 450 (*Swer ditze bvch lesen welle*). This evidence removes some of the doubt whether a reader must be involved when the (monastic) audience is told what they may find elsewhere if they look for it (80, 39).
49 Find on one folio: 24, 11; general theme: 19, 35f.
50 158, 30ff.
51 Invitation: 6528ff.; readers: 386, 3641, 6557.
52 See above, p. 135. In calling his book a *speculum animae* at this point the author stresses the visual dimension: the recipient is to look into the book (read it) as into a mirror.
53 821.
54 *Sieben Tagzeiten* MS M, 1-18. On the *leich* see p. 366, n. 138.
55 See above, p. 39, and de Boor, *Geschichte* III 2, 396.
56 Written law in German up to 1300 falls into two periods. An early one culminates in the twelfth century (examples are few, are recorded in writing by chance as isolated, once-only records, and are brief). The second period starts in 1235, shows a greater frequency of texts (especially charters), greater length and interconnections (amounting to the start of a written tradition), and parallels between Germany and elsewhere (de Boor, *Geschichte* III 2, 397; Schnell, *Verhältnis*, p. 60, fn. 32).
57 See above, pp. 99f.
58 Cf. Heinzle, *Wandlungen*, p. 20. The vernacular was called for, as was said in the fourteenth century, *quia Latinitatis difficultas errores et dubia maxima pariebat et laycos decipiebat* (Kirchhoff, *AfD* 3 (1957), 294, fn. 17; cf. also Heinzle, p. 209).
59 Herkommer, *NdJb* 100 (1977), 29f.; Heinzle, *Wandlungen*, p. 101; de Boor, *Geschichte* III 2, 413.
60 The last example is the first instance of a German text (as well as Latin) used to record the (German) proceedings of an imperial diet (1235). Together with the dating of the other monuments (and the absence of charters in German before 1235) this justifies regarding this year as a turning-point.
61 Written Mosaic law: *Urschwabenspiegel, Königebuch*, pp. 227 (15b, l. 9ff.), 228 (15b, l. 3); Roman imperial law in writing: *Urschwabenspiegel, Kaiserchronik*, pp. 270 (19, 27ff.), 287 (37, 1ff.), 289 (39, 1ff.).
62 Germanic legislation: see above, p. 39. Charles: *Urschwabenspiegel, Landrecht*, pp. 312 (44a, 30), 314 (44b, 14), 319 (44i, 12); Ludwig: pp. 321 (45a, 7), 329 (49, 24).
63 Ambiguous: the audience are told that they can find something in the text or that it is given *ut supra or alzo vor geschreben ist* (*Glosse* 188, 54; *Weichbildrecht* 73, 41; *Glosse* 228, 31; 234, 7). Twofold reception: *Glosse* 181, 8.
64 It is quite uncertain when the recipient is told that something may be found in the Bible, e.g. in the *Königebuch* 7b (p. 95). More suggestive cross-references: *Lehnrecht* 84 (p. 370), *Zweiter Landrechtsteil* 146 (p. 217), *Königebuch* 116 (p. 109). Reading for practical purposes is to be expected for legal literature and is confirmed by Schmidt-Wiegand, *FMS* 26 (1988), 371 from *Sachsenspiegel* MSS of a later period. It also lies behind the frequent stress on the need for scribes and written records in law (e.g. *Mainzer Reichslandfrieden* 262, 18ff.; *Bayrischer Landfrieden* 599, 27; *Österreichisches Landrecht* 73, 18ff.).
65 *Königebuch* 20, p. 131.

66 Uncertain: references to what can be found in the Bible (10, 1; 12, 8 and 11), even when such consultation is seen as reading (5, 6). Wrong type of reader: 79, 22f.
67 Cross-reference: 1 (24); 2 (32); 6 (2). More precisely defined: 4 (9); 187 (12); 217 (7).
68 Despite its stress on the historical tradition of written law the *Schwabenspiegel* implies an individual reader only in references to what may be found elsewhere, sometimes with the verb *lesen*, e.g.: *Urschwabenspiegel, Königebuch* 11b (p. 207); *Landrecht* 174b (p. 460); 220 (p. 488). *Lesen: Königebuch* 14a (p. 212); 18h (p. 257); *Kaiserchronik* 15 (p. 267).
69 To the approximately 3,500 German charters (1235–1300) in Wilhelm's *Corpus* there corresponds what he estimates to be a total of about half a million in Latin (Wilhelm, *Geschichte*, p. 20).
70 Bumke, *Kultur*, p. 637, fn. 70, quotes an interesting example from 1275.
71 Sprandel, *Gesellschaft*, p. 113.
72 Cf. above, n. 58 and also the remark by Konrad von Mure quoted by Kirchhoff, *AfD* 3 (1957), 293f.
73 For example, the transactions of count Konrad I of Freiburg with monastic orders and churches are recorded in Latin charters, whilst those with laymen are in German. Cf. Stolzenberg, *AfD* 7 (1961), 232ff.; 8 (1962), 247ff.
74 Cf. Vancsa, *Auftreten*, p. 46.
75 In drawing attention to the parallel between the development of charters in the Upper Rhine region in the second half of the thirteenth century and the encouragement of literature Schmitt, *PBB* 66 (1942), 213f., also points to close links between landed nobility and town patriciates. Cf. also Bumke, *Ministerialität*, p. 69, and Schnell, *Verhältnis*, pp. 48ff.
76 Schmidt-Wiegand, *Eid*, p. 89.
77 Latin examples are quoted by Kirchhoff, *AfD* 3 (1957), 318: Zürich 1219 and Cologne 1238, while the German example comes from Wilhelm, *Corpus* I 20, 44 (no. 6).
78 Kirchhoff, *AfD* 3 (1957), 318 (Kloster Renn 1173 and Bredelar ca. 1210. Kirchhoff's source for the former, Hirsch, *MÖIG* 52 (1938), 229, gives it as Kloster Reun). For the German example see Wilhelm, *Corpus* I 25, 20 (no. 14).
79 If we ignore the *Kaiserchronik* (for which there is no evidence of a reader) the first German examples are the *Sächsische Weltchronik* and the *Weltchronik* of Rudolf von Ems, considerably later than the Latin chronicles of Frutolf von Michelsberg and Otto von Freising.
80 Cf. Schnell, *Prosaauflösung*, pp. 214ff.
81 Cf. the *Sächsische Weltchronik* on Dietrich von Bern, a bone of contention on this point: 134, 37 (see also Knape, *Typik*, p. 22). Heroic literature may still survive in oral form, but undergoes trivialisation in the later Middle Ages because it lacked the literary opportunities opened up by the *Nibelungenlied* in written form (Wolf, *Heldensagen*, p. 319) and because of the attrition of its earlier historical function.
82 Heinzle, *Wandlungen*, pp. 212, 214; *VfL* I, 1089f.; Herkommer, *NdJb* 100 (1977), 7ff.
83 Wenzel, *Geschichte*, p. 118, quotes Schmid, *Selbstverständnis*, p. 398, to the effect that, whereas oral transmission of history was characteristic of a dynasty in its earliest stages, only written transmission later provided a secure base for political success.
84 267, 33 indicates no more than a written text, not its reader, and recommendations to consult other works are similarly dubious (e.g. 79, 1; 83, 17; 134, 37). Those who read or write: 226, 14; general allusion to reading (58: *horet gerne guote lere / unde leset in den buoken*). Scholz, *Hören*, p. 73, interprets *horen* as a function of *lesen* (the addressee is to hear or learn by reading), an interpretation criticised by Kartschoke, *IASL* 8 (1983), 257, as arbitrary. Our doubts about Scholz's dismissal of a hearing reception of this work (see p. 353, n. 100) do not undermine the case for reading.
85 Acrostics: 1ff., 867ff., 3794ff., 8798ff., 21518ff.; *paragraf*: 2390ff. (the editor regards it as an interpolation, p. 32, commentary on 2249–2395, so that at least its author expected readers). On Heinrich von Neustadt see above, pp. 74f.
86 *Korônik*: 11416ff.; read elsewhere: 13979 (refers back to 13827), 25758.

87 291.
88 Consulting a chronicle: 1302, 2019; anagram: 53ff.; recipients see: 2560f. (*blick* in this passage is rendered by 'Stelle' in the glossary).
89 Said above: 1019, 1038ff.; reading at various points: 39910f. (refers back to 11591ff.), 73560 (refers to 69121f.); reception from the reader: 41f.
90 The place of vernacular biblical literature within the Latin tradition (Otfrid mentions Juvencus, Arator and Prudentius) has been treated by Kartschoke, *Bibeldichtung*. On the Latin tradition see Herzog, *Bibelepik*.
91 Haubrichs, *Praefatio*, pp. 400ff.; Vollmann-Profe, *Kommentar*, pp. 4f. and *Otfrid*, pp. 204ff.; Rexroth, *Volkssprache*, p. 294. *Christus und die Samariterin* may begin with *Lesen wir* but, as with the oral formula *Ik gihorta ðat seggen* of which it is a literate variant (Haug and Vollmann, *Literatur*, pp. 1128f., note to 138, 1), there are no grounds for relating it to the audience rather than the author.
92 Masser, *Bibelepik*, pp. 38f.
93 Vollmann-Profe, *Wiederbeginn*, p. 86. Another factor is the presence of 'Heilsgeschichte' in biblical literature (the Bible or a biblical book could be termed *historia*, see Knape, *Historie*, pp. 134ff.), so that the clergy's criticism of the layman's oral history (see p. 244) meant stressing the written accuracy of its own history, incorporated in biblical literature.
94 Knape, *Historie*, pp. 102ff., 134ff., 168f.
95 Masser, *Legendenepik*, p. 72. The statutes of the Order refer to Moses, Joshua and David as *Gotes rittere* (Perlbach, *Statuten* 25, 4ff.), like the knights of the Order, and a papal bull describes them as *novi sub tempore gratiae Machabei* (Helm and Ziesemer, *Literatur*, p. 97).
96 Grundmann, *Schrifttum*, pp. 96ff.; Wenzel, *Geschichte*, pp. 28ff.
97 The earliest example, the OHG *Tatian*, is weak: it rests on the assumption that it was meant for use in the monastic school, with instruction both orally and by reading (cf. Haubrichs, *Anfänge*, p. 361).
98 Kartschoke concedes that this *lector* might conceivably be a reciter, but prefers to see in him the attentive reader (*Bibeldichtung*, p. 331). Comparing these *capitula* with a parallel in Hrabanus Maurus, Haubrichs describes them, *Praefatio*, p. 428, as a 'Lesehilfe' (for the individual reader). This concern for the reader would thus be an early example of what was done more ambitiously by the Dominican redactor of the text of Mechthild von Magdeburg (see p. 372, n. 47) or by Vincent of Beauvais with his *Speculum* (cf. Parkes, *Influence*, p. 133).
99 49, 1.
100 24, 37, 42, 40. The arrangement of the work in three columns to be considered together and the use of Latin in two of them and of a mixture of German and Latin in the third suggest learned addressees. Cf. Ohly, *Hohelied-Studien*, p. 277.
101 *Jüngstes Gericht* 35, 5: *swer dize buoch lese*.
102 P. 178: *Ir sult merchen in den salmen sus so ir leset, also an disem salmen*. Various considerations suggest that the German interlinear text was subordinate to understanding the Latin. The German word-order follows that of Latin. Names in the Latin text are not given in the German (e.g. 55, 1). The German text sometimes gives more than one word in translation (e.g. 55, 3), a practice unnecessary if it had been autonomous, but called for in the educational context of understanding the Latin.
103 Margins too narrow: 13ff. (Scholz, *Hören*, p. 137); acrostics: Scholz, pp. 158f.; *VfL* 5, 199.
104 Copied correctly: 2753ff.; recipient has read already: 2390 (*als du da vor gelesen has*), 2535, 2561ff.; frequent reading: 2324ff., 2725ff. (cf. Kartschoke, *IASL* 8 (1983), 256).
105 8875ff. (whereas more general references like 1308ff., 1331ff. may simply asseverate the truth of the German text).
106 1324ff. (cf. 1319: *die diz buch / lesen*). When Heinrich recommends Germany to *Diz buch tigere schouwen an* (1296) he is hoping for attentive readers.

107 Corrections from other poets: XVIII 72ff.; readers in general: XVIII 62.
108 363: *alle, die diz buch lesen.*
109 63ff.
110 4407ff. (see above, p. 135).
111 1771ff., 1834ff. (see above, p. 132).
112 7790 (refers back to 6849ff.), 11 (*swer nû wil daz büechel lesen*).
113 1, 9 and edn, pp. 69f. No internal pointers to a reader occur in the *Reimbibel* of Könemann von Jerxheim (III 111ff. is not persuasive by itself). However, the expectation of readers for the same author's *Wurzgarten Mariens* (see above, p. 154) makes them likely here, too.
114 Court authors in both genres: Heinrich von Veldeke, Hartmann von Aue, Rudolf von Ems, Konrad von Würzburg, Heinrich von Freiberg. On the courts: Heinzle, *Wandlungen*, p. 173.
115 Ambiguous: a *schrîben* + dative construction (A 171ff., where I am more sceptical than Scholz, *Hören*, pp. 114f.) and a remark about sending copies of the work elsewhere (A 256off.). Those who read the work: A 137ff.
116 A 2505ff., 2539ff.
117 Invitation to correct: 1578ff.; literate instructions: 1570ff.; acrostic: 1ff.
118 1206: *fuore baz wirt daz dem lesêre kunt* (cf. the *Vita*, edn, p. 66).
119 Acrostics: edn, pp. ivf.; Scholz, *Hören*, pp. 145f.; above, p. 132; instructions: 4451ff. That this *leser* must be an individual reader (cf. also 3490), rather than reciter, is clear from the impossibility of realising acrostics acoustically over sixty-one chapters.
120 Reader: 157; reading reception of his works: Green, *ZfdA* 97 (1986), 151ff.; acrostic: 16151ff.
121 1382f. Konrad's *Silvester* may be included here in view of an opening recommendation (14f.), but only if we take *lesen* as individual reading (as opposed to recital, 5186). This possibility will also be seen for his *Engelhard*, where a similar phrase is perhaps borrowed from Gottfried, who uses it in the sense of personal reading. The argument for *Silvester* is therefore very circumstantial.
122 III 310, 6f. (refers back to III 118, 15ff.).
123 292, 73.
124 1496: the possible reference to two aspects of recital (preparing a written version which is then read out) is undermined by 1497, where the variation of *lesen* by *vernemen* points to a recipient, not a reciter. Easing of childbirth: 1545f.
125 47ff.
126 Calculating a date: 9926ff.; recipients see: 2464f.; opening recommendation: 22f.
127 Leave to erase: 10094ff.; prayers of readers: 10116f.
128 16152ff.
129 Corrections and literacy: 165, 12317, 16140. Two other invitations imply literacy by mentioning erasing (2808ff., 16124ff.), possible only for a reader. Request to read the whole work: 16116 (on the verb *überlesen* see Scholz, *Hören*, pp. 54f.).
130 Cf. Werner, *Studien*; Heinzle, *Wandlungen*, pp. 194ff.
131 Mary's lament: 248ff.; Longinus: 275ff.; Mary Magdalene: 35ff., 70ff., 136ff., 158ff. This last figure may provide another reason for the rise of German dramas. Werner, *Studien*, p. 35, basing himself on Saxer, *Culte*, points out that the cult of this sinner saint reached its peak in Germany in the thirteenth century. See also Aus der Fünten, *Magdalena*, p. 206.
132 Which is not to say that the play was exclusively in German and that, in its complete form as distinct from a souffleur's roll, it did not also contain Latin. See Bergmann, *IASL* 9 (1984), 1ff.
133 VII 25ff., 54ff.; VIII 5ff., 30ff., 64ff. Cf. Werner, *Studien*, p. 118. On parallels with the new piety see Heinzle, *Wandlungen*, p. 202: Mary Magdalene, like Longinus, stands for a

spectacular conversion of a type known in the thirteenth century (St Francis, Elisabeth of Thuringia).
134 As Werner, *Studien*, p. 39, suggests for the *Benediktbeurer Passionsspiel*.
135 164f. Linke (see above, p. 105) sees the drama as performing the task of the sermon by other means.
136 E.g. 19, 23, 47.
137 Ranke edn, p. 18. The caveat voiced by Bergmann, *IASL* 9 (1984), 20, concerns knighthood, but leaves the courtly dimension untouched. Here we may suspect the depiction of the world in courtly colours to be deliberate.
138 *Benediktbeurer Passionsspiel* 41ff.; *Osterspiel von Muri* III 51ff. (edn, pp. 18f.; Heinzle, *Wandlungen*, p. 203).
139 For Klosterneuburg see Hartl, *Osterspiele*, pp. 29f., 31; for Amorbach cf. the stage instruction, edn, p. 44, with its mention of a *monasterium* (cf. Völker, *Überlegungen*, p. 261 and fn. 24; Heinzle, *Wandlungen*, pp. 203, 204).
140 Klosterneuburg: Young, *Drama* I 431; Amorbach: edn, pp. 29, 49, 53, 56 (Heinzle, *Wandlungen*, p. 205).
141 Neumann, *Schauspiel* I 305.
142 These are: rivalry with court secularism, the appeal of the new religious movements to the layman by means additional to the sermon, the religious importance of the figure of Mary Magdalene.
143 The case of the *Osterspiel von Muri*, preserved in a souffleur's roll, is a special one, not to be confused with individual reading by a member of the audience.
144 Bergmann, *Aufführungstexte*, pp. 314ff.; Linke, *Versuch*, pp. 527ff.
145 Heinzle, *Wandlungen*, p. 199.
146 Whether these were meant for this drama in its present transmission context or as part of an earlier collection of plays is quite uncertain (Linke, private letter 12 June 1989).
147 See p. 357, n. 172.
148 Cf. Bertau, *Literatur*, p. 745.
149 Cf. Kartschoke, *PBB* 111 (1989), 197f. and especially 199f. The contexts where we have seen an interplay between vernacular and Latin accompanying the shift between oral and written include legal literature, charters, and vernacular sermons delivered on the basis of a Latin text. On the similar practice with medieval letter-writing see pp. 15f.
150 Wolf, *Nibelungensage*, pp. 227ff.; *Nibelungenlied*, pp. 171ff.; *Heldensagen*, pp. 305ff.; *Mönchskultur*, pp. 157ff.; *Traditions*, pp. 67ff.
151 Problematic light: *Hildebrandslied* (cf. also Neuser, *Hildebrandslied*, pp. 1ff.), the *Finnsburgh* episode, and especially *Waltharius*. Substance not questioned: *Finnsburgh Lay*, *Chanson de Roland*.
152 Cf. also Haubrichs, *Heldenliedersammlung*, pp. 38ff. (and Fichtenau, *MIÖG* 61 (1953), 271ff.) on Einhard's report on this collection.
153 Curschmann, *PBB* 111 (1989), 384, says of these: 'Schriftlichkeit nur in technischem Sinn und jederzeit wieder auflösbar'.
154 In considering influence from the chanson de geste Wolf suggests two stages, the first oral and the second concerning the genesis of the written form of the *Nibelungenlied*. With regard to the romance he suggests that details in this epic commonly regarded as a courtly dressing go back to literary contact between two narrative genres. Where Bumke, *Geschichte*, p. 200, sees the unity of the *Nibelungenlied* as the probable work of the author of its written form, made possible by written composition, Wolf goes further, seeing a parallel between this ambitious task and the *mout bel conjointure* of Chrétien de Troyes (Wolf, *Nibelungenlied*, pp. 178f., 180). What counts is that an overall conception was attempted, not that it was everywhere successful (cf. Nagel, *Widersprüche*, pp. 367ff.).
155 Whether they actually used written sources is neither here nor there, it is their claim to belong to a literate tradition which is decisive.

156 Audience hears author dependent on a book: *Rabenschlacht* 339, 3f.; author has heard a book say or has heard from a book: *Biterolf und Dietleib* 124f., 179; *Wolfdietrich D* 5, 128, 2; the book recites a detail or informs us: *Dietrichs Flucht* 1924; *Rosengarten D* 319, 1; *Kudrun* 505, 1; *Wolfdietrich B* 3, 2; *Wolfdietrich D* 4, 50, 4; it has been read in a book: *Dietrichs Flucht* 6644; tale handed down in writing: *Biterolf und Dietleib* 2005, 10664; to be confirmed from writing or by those who can read: *Eckenlied* 1, 7ff.; *Laurin D* 1ff.

157 'This book': *Alpharts Tod* 467, 4; *Rosengarten A* 382, 4 and *D* 447, 3; *Wolfdietrich D* 5, 189, 2; 'the book here': *Alpharts Tod* 55, 5; 'this German book': *Alpharts Tod* 45, 1.

158 At the beginning: *Ortnit* 2, 1f.; *Wolfdietrich C* 2, 1f.; 4, 1; at the conclusion: *Dietrichs Flucht* 10128f.; *Rosengarten D* 633, 4; *Virginal* 1097, 10; *Laurin D* 2817.

159 See above, p. 76.

160 The *Nibelungenlied C* (1161, 1ff.; 1164, 2ff.) claims historical veracity by linking Uote and Siegfried with Lorsch.

161 *Kudrun* 916, 1ff.; *Wolfdietrich C* 4, 1ff. and *D* 10, 128, 1f.

162 Examples for St Denis are given by Lofmark, *Authority*, p. 27.

163 Curschmann, *PBB* 111 (1989), 410, has pointed to another respect in which heroic literature in written form remains exposed to orality.

164 The isolated evidence from the *Lied vom Hürnen Seyfried* (title: *Und wenn jr das leßt recht und eben*) is too late to be safely applicable to our period.

165 On the satisfactory functioning of this oral tradition see Bumke, *Geschichte*, p. 39.

166 To the extent that the main class of lay readers was made up of women it may also be the case, if we can generalise what Wolfram implies about women as the primary victims of knightly violence (see p. 192), that a genre which gave so much scope to this attracted them as readers much less than the romance.

167 On the transposition of oral themes into written form by clerical authors of 'Spielmannsepen' see Salmen's review of Schreier-Hornung, *Spielleute*, *ZfdPh* 102 (1983), 456.

168 The source is a book: *Münchener Oswald* 6; *König Rother* 4713; *Orendel* 157; *Herzog Ernst D* 3899; writing: *Orendel* 154; transferred to writing: *Herzog Ernst B* 6004; in Latin: *Herzog Ernst B* 4466f.; *D* 2049ff.

169 'This book': *Salman und Morolf E* 146, 2; 783a; *Herzog Ernst D* 53, 78, 1941; 'the book': *Wiener Oswald* 1954; *König Rother*, Berlin fragment IIa, 11; *Münchener Oswald* 3564; *Orendel* 3934; written: *Wiener Oswald* 5; a text to be recited: *Orendel* 2829; *Münchener Oswald* (MS I, p. 33, col. 2).

170 Bamberg: *Herzog Ernst B* 4466ff. and *D* 3623ff.; Trier (in the case of *Orendel*): see p. 107.

171 Here we do not have to base the argument on the surmise that each work was meant for the same type of audience. Wolfram wrote his *Willehalm* for the Thuringian court (3, 8f.), where he composed Book VI of *Parzival* (Bumke, *Wolfram*, p. 5) which, as we shall see, concludes with a pointer to a reading reception (by women).

172 118, 10255ff. (*swer* is not unspecific here; it ties up with *iuch* and *iu* in the two lines before). A reference to the reading reception of Wolfram's *Willehalm*, 156f., corroborates what we have just seen.

173 VII–VIII.

174 On this see p. 275.

175 Cf. Bumke, *Mäzene*, pp. 70ff. and *Kultur*, pp. 682ff.

176 These authors have therefore to be seen as court clerics, see p. 287.

177 Grundmann, *AfK* 26 (1936), 129ff.; Bumke, *Mäzene*, pp. 231ff.; Scholz, *Hören*, pp. 205ff.

178 The best statement of this is by Bumke, *Liebe*, pp. 39f.

179 On women as readers see p. 290.

180 Haug, *Literaturtheorie*, p. 103.

181 On the rivalry between literate and oral poets see pp. 310ff.

182 Bumke, *Kultur*, pp. 609f.

183 Wernher specifies the written transmission of his material from Hebrew to Latin and

thence to German (A 83ff., 123ff., 136ff.). Clerical transmission, involving authoritative mediators like Matthew and Jerome, is naturally in writing, even in the last stage, where a vernacular is involved.

184 49ff., 57ff., 74ff.
185 *Eneide* 354ff., 13505ff.; *Lancelot* II 115, 24ff.
186 *Tristan* 1ff. Important consequences result from this establishment of a written tradition in the vernacular, especially in the romance (on a similar development in legal literature, see p. 155). It can be said as a matter of course that vernacular romances circulate in book form (e.g. Hugo von Trimberg, *Renner* 21637ff.), that literature is now composed in writing and meant for readers, both in Latin and in German (*ibid.*, 17837ff.) and that the truth of a work is maintained by reference not merely to a Latin, but also to a written German source (e.g. Ulrich von Etzenbach, *Alexandreis* 25100ff., which I take as a reference to *Herzog Ernst D*, not to a Latin version). In all this German literature in written form moves on to ground hitherto occupied by Latin.
187 Wolf, *Gottfried*, pp. 8ff., 21ff. and Béroul, *Tristran* 1265ff. Henkel, *UR* 17 (1990), 92f., interprets the Béroul passage (especially 1268: *Berox l'a mex en sen memoire*) to imply that even with a written version Béroul depends on his memory. This need not follow if we recall Einhard's words about Charles the Great committing oral tradition to writing (*scripsit memoriaeque mandavit*) and Isidore of Seville, *Etymologiae* I 3: *Vsus litterarum repertus propter memoriam rerum* (cf. O'Keeffe, *Song*, pp. 51f.). With Béroul we are dealing with two types of memory, one oral and the other in writing.
188 Wolf, *Gottfried*, pp. 57f.
189 *Ibid.*, pp. 66, 69, 76, 81f., 84.
190 Lord, *Singer*, pp. 94f., sees the oral performer's episodic concentration as accounting for Homer's nods, whilst Havelock, *Revolution*, pp. 174f., 178 and especially 181f., contrasts this with the possibilities of patterning provided by writing.
191 See p. 196.
192 *Der welsche Gast* 1026ff. Cf. Düwel, *Fabula* 32 (1991), 67ff.
193 See p. 158.
194 *Der Welt Lohn* 52ff. Examples of works by named authors described as meant for readers include Hartmann's *Erec* (referred to by Heinrich von dem Türlin, *Crone* 2348ff.) and *Iwein* (Der Pleier, *Garel* 32), Wolfram's *Parzival* (cf. *Von dem übeln wîbe* 408f. and *Reinfried von Braunschweig* 16680f.) and *Willehalm* (Ulrich von dem Türlin, *Willehalm* XLVI 17ff.), and Gottfried's *Tristan* (Rudolf von Ems, *Alexander* 3159; Heinrich von Freiberg, *Tristan* 40ff., 108ff.; Ulrich von Türheim, *Tristan* 1ff.).
195 See p. 140.
196 Acrostics: edn, II 754; reading and readers: 8069ff., 2209f., 12960. See also Green *ZfdA* 97 (1986), 163ff. In a request for prayer from readers of the *Trojanischer Krieg* of Konrad von Würzburg (49837f.) the evidence is not quite so strong, since this is added by the scribe, but presumably one aware of the likely reception of the MS on which he worked.
197 Hartmann's *Erec* and *Iwein* will be considered later under the intermediate mode.
198 Scholz, *Hören*, pp. 125ff. This bookish prologue must have been highly novel since most MSS omit it, presumably because it ran counter to conventional recital practice (Scholz, p. 127).
199 Acrostic: 182ff. (cf. also Kratz, *ZfdPh* 108 (1989), 402ff.); reader: 140f.
200 Said above: II 683, 24; 384, 6 (the latter said not by the narrator, but by a character in the narrative, see p. 180 for an example from Otfrid). More precise reference: II 689, 20 (refers back to II 673, 17, where the passage is in bolder letters, see commentary of ed. on 17f.).
201 II 115, 14. All the evidence for *Lancelot* comes from vol. II of Kluge's edition, so that it may not even date from the thirteenth century.
202 4074.

203 Acrostic: 7621ff.; reading: 7622f. By contrast, a recommendation to seek confirmation in other books (1980) is unconvincing. Wolfram's *Parzival* is discussed in the next chapter.
204 Ulrich von Türheim: 3658; Heinrich von Freiberg: 2644. Gottfried's version is discussed as an example of twofold reception.
205 Bumke, *Geschichte*, pp. 244f., discusses this work under 'Legendarische Stoffe' which he sees (p. 243) as hardly separable from romances of love and adventure. Rudolf refers to it as a written work in *Willehalm von Orlens* 15630ff. On the possibility of readers: Green, *ZfdA* 97 (1986), 177f.
206 Bumke, *Geschichte*, p. 236.
207 Personification of book addresses reader: 2143, 2162f. (cf. Scholz, *Hören*, pp. 133ff.); acrostics: 1ff., 2143ff., 5595ff., 9735ff., 12205ff.; visual dimension: 5646ff. This expectation of readers makes it understandable that Rudolf should also recommend reading the (lost) *Cligés* of Ulrich von Türheim, 4390ff.
208 *Darifant* 72f. Berthold can reckon with the understanding of his audience when he refers to *Demantin* in his *Crane*, 2138ff.
209 *Engelhard* 1; *Silvester* 14; Gottfried, *Tristan* 172.
210 22816 (refers back to 20989ff.).
211 20622f.
212 13221. In the double problem presented by Ulrich von Lichtenstein (the reception of his lyrics, discussed by Kartschoke, *Ulrich*, pp. 103ff., and the reception of the narrative in which they were incorporated) only the latter concerns us in this section. Kartschoke, pp. 111, 129, recognises that the text could be read in two ways (aloud to others or by an individual to himself), the first of which we have already considered (p. 361, n. 234). If Ulrich suggests that his lyrics can also be read (Kartschoke, pp. 112f.), can the same be said of his narrative? Of his audience's literary awareness there is no doubt (he can recommend an owner of a copy to add lyrics as they appear, *Frauendienst* 592, 19ff.), but was this owner *litteratus* (and read the copy himself) or *quasi litteratus* (and had it read out)? Only on the probable assumption that the *Frauenbuch* and *Frauendienst* were meant for the same kind of audience can this question be answered in favour of individual readers, for these are explicitly foreseen for the former work (660, 28), again as women.
213 On an initially court audience see p. 361, n. 235, on clerical authorship Tiemann, *RF* 72 (1960), 406ff. for France and Schirmer, *Versnovelle*, pp. 299ff. for Germany.
214 Fischer, *Studien*, pp. 274f.
215 Mundschau, *Sprecher*, pp. 88f.: *Janne Bot den segger, want hi ene sproke gemaect hadde ende in ghescrift over gav.*
216 Book: *Der Busant* 760; *Zwei Kaufmänner und die treue Hausfrau* 19; *Der Frauen Trost* 639; *Die Heidin IV* 1900; written: *Der Junker und der treue Heinrich* 803, 1880; on parchment: *Dulciflorie* 388; read out: *Frauentreue* 353; *Zwei Kaufmänner* 19. In both these last cases the conjunction of *lesen* with *buochelîn* (cf. *Frauentreue* 390) suggests reading aloud from a written text.
217 *Studien*, p. 275.
218 36.
219 See p. 110.
220 The possibility of anagrams suggested by Seelbach, *Kommentar*, p. 11, I do not find convincing. A solitary anticipation of a reader occurs in the *Kleinreden der Wiener Handschrift* 8, 1: *Leset vnt merchet dise schrift*.
221 Bumke, *Kultur*, pp. 752, 758; Kuhn, *Voraussetzungen*, p. 99.
222 On the chansonniers cf. Jammers, *Liederbuch*, p. 121 and Gruber, *LiLi* 15 (1985), 47. On oral and written transmission of the French lyric see van der Werf, *Chansons*, pp. 26ff.
223 *Voraussetzungen*, pp. 96ff.
224 Towns: on the connection of A with Strassburg see Kuhn, *Voraussetzungen*, pp. 99f.; *VfL* 3; 578; for B and Konstanz: Sayce, *Lyric*, pp. 53f.; for C and Zürich: Kuhn, pp. 100ff.;

Sayce, pp. 55f.; *VfL* 3, 586f. Episcopal courts: for Strassburg see Kuhn, *Voraussetzungen*, p. 99; *VfL* 3, 573; Voetz, *Überlieferungsformen*, p. 233 (sceptical); Konstanz: Sayce, *Lyric*, p. 54; Voetz, p. 235 (sceptical); Zürich: Kuhn, p. 100; Sayce, p. 54; Peters, *Literatur*, pp. 102ff.

225 A is dated in the 1270s, possibly in connection with Konrad von Lichtenberg, bishop of Strassburg (*VfL* 3, 582; Sayce, *Lyric*, p. 52; Bumke, *Kultur*, pp. 766f.). B: about 1300, in connection with Heinrich von Klingenberg, bishop of Konstanz and earlier canon at Zürich. C: about 1300, intended for a patrician family at Zürich, to whose literary circle Heinrich von Klingenberg belonged as well as members of the secular and ecclesiastic nobility. On the dating of the hypothetical manuscript collections around 1250: for *AC see *VfL* 3, 578f., 583; Kuhn, *Voraussetzungen*, p. 94; *BC: *VfL* 3, 592f., 594; Bumke, *Kultur*, pp. 764, 768f.; *EC: Kuhn, p. 88. On the bilingual nature of the *Carmina Burana*, presupposing a circle of mixed culture, see Wachinger, *Liebeslieder*, pp. 275ff., and indeed on its plurilingualism Sayce, *Plurilingualism*. The collection was associated with the bishop of Seckau by Bischoff (*Carmina* I 3, xff.; *Carmina, Faksimile-Ausgabe*, pp. 13ff.), which is questioned by Steer, *ZfdA* 112 (1983), 1ff. (cf. also Vollmann edn, pp. 900f.).

226 Schweikle, *Minnesang*, p. 25; Bumke, *Kultur*, pp. 772f., 774f. The miniature of Waltram (Walther, *Codex*, plate 103, under the name Alram von Gresten) captures a Dante-like scene of intimate literacy: under the sign Amor a couple read the *Lanzelet* of Ulrich von Zatzikhoven (Salowsky, *HJbb* 19 (1975), 40ff.). On various forms of writing depicted in these miniatures see Curschmann, *Pictura*, pp. 221ff.

227 Der Taler 3, 6 (in MS C Hartwig von Raute is also depicted entrusting a written poem to a messenger, Walther, *Codex*, plate 79). Ulrich von Lichtenstein sends a messenger with writing (e.g. *Frauendienst* 318, 13ff.), but instructs him to recite the written poem (20, 21f.; 125, 9ff.).

228 His lady reads: 394, 12ff. (for a later parallel see Hadloub 1, 29ff.); readers of his 'Leich': 426, 4f. Furthermore, if the *Frauendienst* was read by individuals, their reading must have included the lyrics in it.

229 For example, the omission of most musical notation in the transmission of the lyric has been explained by a transition from performance to reading (Schweikle, *Minnesang*, p. 51 and tentatively Welker, *Melodien*, p. 113; cf. also Schlosser, *LiLi* 3 (1973), H. 11, pp. 87f.), but it has also been argued that the melodies were too well known to need recording (Bumke, *Kultur*, p. 779; Müller-Blattau, *ZfdPh* 90 (1971), *Sonderheft*, pp. 155ff.).

230 Later codification: *VfL* 3, 591; anonymous transmission in a Latin text, as with *MF* I, v 1ff.; *Ubermuot diu alte*: Voetz, *Überlieferungsformen*, pp. 237, 241; no purposeful collection: Voetz, p. 237.

231 Voetz, *Überlieferungsformen*, p. 240.

232 *Ibid.*, pp. 241f. Reproduced in Mittler and Werner, *Codex*, plate G 6, p. 550.

233 See p. 415, n. 280.

234 Reading a written source: Der Meißner XII 1, 8; reference to a written source: Der Meißner XVIII 1, 16 (cf. Objartel, *Meißner*, pp. 316f.); Der Kanzler I 1, 1ff.; Boppe VI 2, 4; Hermann der Damen I 6, 5; III 2, 15f.; own work written: Reinmar von Zweter 188, 9; not understood by laymen: Reinmar von Zweter, 188, 5; Der Wilde Alexander VI 1, 1ff.; Der Kanzler II 9, 4ff.

235 Roll fragments of Reinmar: Bäuml and Rouse, *PBB* 105 (1983), 192ff., 317ff. The picture of the poet in MS C is reproduced in Walther, *Codex*, plate 112. Meant for the reciter in performance: Bäuml and Rouse, p. 323. Other rolls: Bumke, *Kultur*, p. 774.

7 Criteria for the intermediate mode of reception

1 Lord, *Singer*, p. 129.
2 Finnegan, *Literacy*, p. 144.

3 Scholz, *Hören*, p. 91.
4 Finnegan, *Literacy*, p. 141.
5 Cf. Green, *Mündlichkeit*, p. 12.
6 Finnegan, *Literacy*, p. 141, who also quotes Goody, *Literacy*, pp. 4f.
7 *Ibid.*, p. 142.
8 See above, pp. 35ff.
9 Harris, *Literacy*, p. 125, argues in the context of Hellenistic Greece against contrasting the written culture of the élite with the oral culture of the masses on the grounds that such a dichotomy is too sharp. On republican Rome he suggests, p. 157, that 'oral and written procedures were intermingled'.
10 Lüdtke, VR 23 (1964), 7.
11 Wunderli, VR 24 (1965), 60.
12 *Ibid.*, pp. 60 and 63.
13 *Ibid.*, pp. 61f.
14 Schlieben-Lange, *Traditionen*, p. 48.
15 Cf. Lüdtke's description of the role of the literate clerics, VR 23 (1964), 12.
16 See above, p. 85.
17 Cf. Schröder in his review of Scholz, MlJb 18 (1983), 334.
18 Cf. Green, *Irony*, pp. 368ff.
19 See above, pp. 11f.
20 Scholz, *Hören*, pp. 107ff.
21 Balogh, *Philologus* 82 (1927), 207, fn. 47. Quoted by Scholz, *Hören*, p. 107.
22 See p. 226, and also Green, *Hören*, pp. 43f.
23 Scholz concedes this, *Hören*, p. 109.
24 See above, p. 142.
25 See above, pp. 142ff.
26 Vv. 65ff., 16152ff., 16236ff. See p. 174.
27 Something similar is true of Bruder Philipp's *Marienleben*. Those who criticise the work and erase passages (10094ff.) must be readers, rather than simply the reciter. This suggests that the phrase 10116f. (*alle die an disem buoche / lesent*) and the double (even triple) formula 10083ff. refer to the reader.
28 Cf. Green, *ZfdA* 115 (1986), 161f.
29 The same is suggested by two other strands of evidence (legal and historical) which I have discussed in *Hören*, pp. 42f.
30 See pp. 179ff.
31 Kartschoke, IASL 8 (1983), 257.
32 *Ibid.*, p. 255.
33 On the context of such phrases in the *Weltchronik* see Green, *ZfdA* 115 (1986), 156ff.
34 See above, p. 90.
35 Schröder, *ZfdA* 104 (1975), 310f.
36 Cf. also v. 22645.
37 Vv. 51f.
38 Examples of the double formula in the works listed above are: Hugo von Trimberg, *Der Renner* 19; *Unser Vrouwen Klage* 62; *Passional* III 330, 57; *Väterbuch* 41484f.
39 Examples can be found in a wide range of genres. Cf. Gottfried's *Tristan* (discussed pp. 194ff.), but also, treated in Chapter 8, the *Rennewart* of Ulrich von Türheim, *Der welsche Gast* of Thomasin von Zerclaere, *Der Renner* of Hugo von Trimberg, the *Urstende* of Konrad von Heimesfurt.
40 See above, p. 140.
41 See p. 192.
42 Cf. 1, 1 (on *vorbrieven* see above, p. 128); 28, 1.

43 Herbort refers to his work as a book (18448) and as written (4081, 9384). He also refers to an earlier point by *obene* (18276).
44 This remains valid despite the uncertainty of dating Herbort's work between 1190 and 1210 (cf. *VfL* 3, 1028).
45 *Epistulae* 2, 3, 9. See above, p. 27.
46 *Epistulae* 5, 3, 8ff. See also above, p. 31.
47 PG 12, 229. See above, p. 29.
48 PL 39, 2325.
49 *Annales, Praefatio*, 267, 16.
50 PL 106, 124.
51 *Carmina*, p. 912.
52 *Historia* XVI, 2 (pp. 705f.); XIX, 2 (pp. 884f.).
53 PL 39, 2325.
54 PL 106, 124.
55 See above, p. 27.
56 *Ibid.* and *De civitate Dei* XXII, cap. 30 (PL 41, 801).
57 Thegan, *Vita*, cap. 19 (p. 594).
58 *Vita S. Cunegundis*, cap. 5 (p. 823). A similar phrase (*aut ipsi legere, aut legentes possitis audire*) is used by William of Malmesbury of Robert Earl of Gloucester, *Gesta* V 447 (II 519).
59 *Policraticus*, I *Prologus* (PL 199, 387 and 388).
60 Philip of Harvengt, *Epistolae*, 16 (PL 203, 149). Quite apart from the double formula de Gaiffier, *Etudes*, p. 475ff., argues that the Latin legend was meant for oral recital and devotional reading.
61 This division into three areas is not meant absolutely. Otfrid wrote for the monastery, but dedicated his work to a secular ruler, while Gottfried, whose *Tristan* is inconceivable without the background of the court, was connected with the patriciate of Strassburg (Tomasek, *Utopie*, pp. 248ff.; Krohn, *Gottfried* III, 215ff.).
62 I have discussed the reception of this author's work in *Otfrid*, pp. 737ff.
63 Examples of *scríban* in this function are Lud. 10; I 1, 113; I 2, 11 and 17; I 3, 47; I 19, 26f.; II 2, 6; II 4, 103; III 1, 7f.; IV 1, 5; V 12, 4; V 24, 4; V 25, 10. For *scribere* and *conscribere* see Liut. 9, 22, 28, 55.
64 Cf. also II 4, 103; V 12, 4; V 24, 4. For *scribere* cf. Liut. 99.
65 *Volumen*: 37; *liber*: 1, 28, 100, 122; *lectio*: 10, 51, 55, 76, 86, 87; *scriptio*: 74.
66 *Liber*: 37.
67 *Buah*: Lud. 87, 91; Sal. 5, 23; I 3, 1; III 1, 11; *giscrib*: V 25, 45; *livol*: III 1, 2; *lekza*: Sal. 5; V 12, 1.
68 For example, *scríban* in I 3, 47 is translated by Erdmann in his edition as 'erzählen' in his commentary on I 3, 45–50 (pp. 349f.).
69 On Lud. 91, for example, cf. Vollmann-Profe, *Kommentar*, p. 22.
70 Cf. Haug and Vollmann, *Literatur*, p. 1089.
71 V 25, 37f., 42 and 49.
72 Scholz, *Hören*, pp. 135ff.
73 Cf. Liut. 99; I 1, 57f.; II 4, 103; II 9, 1; V 12, 4.
74 V 15, 19 and 33.
75 The phrase *hiar forna* also belongs here only when its spatial meaning (as distinct from a temporal one) is made clear by conjunction with a verb of reading or writing. Cf. II 2, 6; II 3, 29f.; IV 25, 5f.; V 24, 4.
76 Cf. Ernst, *Liber*, p. 206.
77 See above, pp. 130f.
78 Other examples are II 23, 18; III 14, 65; IV 15, 59; Hart. 125.
79 In this example *selbo* underlines the reader's independence: the author makes a statement

(44a) which the reader may confirm for himself. Other examples with *selbo* are II 7, 75; II 9, 71; II 24, 2; III 14, 4; V 13, 3; Hart. 38.
80 Cf. also III 13, 44; IV 28, 18.
81 Liut. 85. Cf. Patzlaff, *Otfrid*, p. 50; Haug and Vollmann, *Literatur*, p. 1096, note to 80, 99f.
82 Vollmann-Profe, *Kommentar*, pp. 4f., discusses the literary and political reasons for Ludwig the German's interest in Otfrid's work, whilst on p. 87 she refers to the secular audience for the work.
83 On this see Schützeichel, *Codex*, pp. 48ff.
84 I have discussed these passages in *Otfrid*, pp. 751ff.
85 Discussed by McKenzie, *Otfrid*, pp. 68ff.
86 Moreover, the majority of these additions occur in the authoritative MS V which Otfrid is thought to have corrected himself.
87 Cf. Kartschoke, *Bibeldichtung*, pp. 330f.
88 Patzlaff, *Otfrid*, p. 50.
89 Ohly, *DVjs* 47 (1973), 26ff. The two texts are given in Steinmeyer, *Sprachdenkmäler*, p. 102.
90 Ernst, *Liber*, p. 342, observes that the lector for the week was required to pray Psalm 50, 17 before each recital, the wording of which is recognisable in vernacular form at the start of Otfrid's work (I 2, 3ff.).
91 Since *legentes* (70) and *legentibus* (82) are used in the context of synaloephe with regard to oral delivery, they probably stand for the reciter. Cf. Patzlaff, *Otfrid*, p. 50.
92 See above, pp. 88f.
93 This is a reference back to IV 22, 20–2, 33f. (cf. also 23, 6 and 8).
94 Nor can Otfrid's remark IV 25, 6 be equated with *wir lesen* in the sense of what Christendom knows at large as a result of written transmission (see above, pp. 115ff). Whereas this is used only in the present, Otfrid employs the past tense and by adding *hiar forna* points to a specific text recently read out. See also p. 418, n. 369.
95 Liut. 5ff.
96 Otfrid refers to this poetry as 'song' (*laicorum cantus*), by which he means not simply 'poetry', but specifically 'sung poetry' because of his allusion to its sound (*sonus, vocum*) impinging upon the ears (*aures*). That he should see vernacular poetry in this negative light is not surprising in view of his dismissal of the unlettered culture of laymen (Liut. 103).
97 Cf. *partem evangeliorum* and *conscriberem* in Liut. 9f.
98 See Ernst, *Liber*, pp. 141f.
99 A similar situation is presupposed by Alcuin's letter about the Lindisfarne monks' preference for heroic poetry over Christian literature (MGH Epp. 4, 1, no. 124, p. 183). The contrast is between pagan lays sung to musical accompaniment and Christian literature in written form, yet both meet on the common ground of oral recital. See Green, *Otfrid*, p. 759.
100 Cf. Petzsch, *Cantus*, p. 224.
101 On the sung delivery of Otfrid's work see Jammers, *Epos*, pp. 114ff.; Petzsch, *Cantus*, pp. 219ff.; Stephan, *Dichtung*, pp. 141ff.; Bertau, EG 20 (1960), 1ff.; Ernst, *Liber*, pp. 332ff.; Engel, *Bezeichnungen*, pp. 90ff. and 147ff.
102 Green, *Otfrid*, pp. 762f. (with further literature).
103 *Ibid.*, p. 763.
104 *Ibid.*, pp. 763f.
105 *Ibid.*, pp. 765f. Cf. Thelen, *Dichtergebet*, pp. 168f.
106 Green, *Otfrid*, p. 766 (I 1, 121f.; I 6, 15ff.). Cf. Thelen, *Dichtergebet*, p. 159.
107 McKenzie, *Otfrid*, p. 16 (cf. Kartschoke, *Bibeldichtung*, p. 328).
108 McKenzie, *Otfrid*, pp. 22 and 75; Kartschoke, *Bibeldichtung*, p. 331.
109 In Liut. 24 Otfrid talks of the difficulties of Latin for a Frankish audience, but in I 1, 119ff. they are dependent on a Frankish version because they can understand no other language.

110 Ernst, *Liber*, p. 333. Cf. also von Ertzdorff, *Hochzeit*, p. 262. Ernst draws attention to the fact that Alcuin composed a more easily understandable prose version of the *Vita Willibrordi* for general recital in the church, but reserved a more difficult verse version for the monk's cell (*Vita Willibrordi, prologus*, p. 113). Cf. Ernst, *Liber*, p. 397 and Ohly, *DVjs* 47 (1973), 60.
111 Ernst, *Liber*, p. 335.
112 Ohly, *DVjs* 47 (1973), 59, fn. 86; Ernst, *Liber*, p. 344. Schröder, *AfdA* 89 (1978), 101, reads Otfrid's distinction between chapters which give the gospel account *literaliter* or *historice* and those which interpret it *mystice* or *spiritaliter* as implying that the *lector* could omit the latter when faced with *parvuli* incapable of understanding such exegesis. This distinction is not expressly made between *illitterati* and *litterati*, but is reconcilable with it.
113 Ohly, *DVjs* 47 (1973), 62; Jammers, *Epos*, p. 181; Ernst, *Liber*, p. 344.
114 Ernst, *Liber*, p. 164; von Ertzdorff, *Hochzeit*, pp. 263f.
115 Vollmann-Profe, *Kommentar*, pp. 4f. In *GRM* 59 (1978), 479, she stresses this lay aspect of the audience.
116 For a fuller treatment of this author see Green, *Notker*, pp. 57ff.
117 Cf. de Boor, *Geschichte* I 107.
118 Kelle, *Geschichte* I 394, 10.
119 In what follows we may hope to glimpse Notker's teaching methods by focusing on his additions to his Latin sources, instead of what he may have taken over from them. For this reason the solitary double formula (*Psalter* 862, 10) must be seen as characteristic of his source (quoted in the edition, p. 861).
120 The words do not occur in the Latin original of Boethius's *De consolatione*.
121 Piper, *Schriften* I ii, 859ff.
122 Kelle, *Geschichte* I 394, 16. Cf. Schützeichel, *Studien*, pp. 56f.
123 *De interpretatione* 510, 13.
124 Cf. also *Psalter* 370, 13.
125 Cf. also *Martianus Capella* 220, 6; *Categorien* 465, 17. Devotional reading of Notker's psalms by the individual reader (outside the context of the monastic school) is also suggested by the gloss of Ekkehard IV (Kelle, *Geschichte* I 394, 15f.).
126 Other examples are: *Categorien* 371, 19; 372, 4; *De interpretatione* 510, 13.
127 By this phrasing I hope to avoid the error of the converse suggestion that a knowledge of reading was confined to those with Latin.
128 The author of the *Loblied auf den heiligen Geist*, for example, addresses laymen (cf. 38, 1f.) and therefore translates any Latin phrase into the vernacular for them (e.g. 10, 1ff.; 11, 1ff.).
129 E.g. *Psalter* 1050, 14.
130 Other examples are: *Psalter* 592, 6; 593, 1; 767, 6; 979, 6; 1003, 16; *Ymnus Zachariae* 1104, 16; *Fides Sancti Athanasii* 1107, 16; 1110, 9. In some cases the explanatory Latin phrase is to be found in the Latin source, but Notker's decision to retain them suggests that he could expect his monastic audience to be acquainted with them.
131 Cf. also *De consolatione* 116, 4; *Martianus Capella* 2, 6; *De interpretatione* 511, 24; *Psalter* 558, 8; 685, 8.
132 See above, p. 184.
133 Cf. *De consolatione* 235, 2; *Categorien* 402, 7; *De interpretatione* 520, 12; 522, 13; 543, 21; 566, 16; 567, 11 and 18; 573, 26.
134 The use of *târuore* in the last example opens up another possibility of determining a visual reception of Notker's works. By itself the word is ambiguous, since it could be meant spatially (something said at an earlier point in a book) or temporally (applicable to a reading and to a hearing reception). A reference to an earlier written passage is implied when *târuore* is used with spatial pointers like *gescriben ist* (*Psalter* 52, 15) or *stât* (*De consolatione* 129, 24; 267, 12; *Psalter* 58, 17; 539, 9; 547, 7; 786, 1;, 805, 30). The presence

of someone who reads this earlier passage is implied when *târuore* is used with a visual verb such as *sehan* (*De interpretatione* 522, 13) or *lesan* (*Psalter* 712, 2, with *dâr* instead of *târuore*). I have discussed this usage in *Notker*, pp. 64ff.
135 I list such terms in *Notker*, p. 67.
136 Cf. Specht, *Geschichte*, p. 92.
137 *Geschichte* I 105.
138 Ibid., p. 111.
139 The relevant verbs, applied to those addressed, are: *gehôren* (*De consolatione* 134, 9; *Psalter* 801, 22), *fernemen* (*Categorien* 383, 4; *De interpretatione* 499, 22; *Psalter* 91, 21), *losen* (*Categorien* 413, 19; *Psalter* 242, 19).
140 The intermediate position of these additions by Notker tells us why they have been ignored in scholarship: for the Latinist interested in the original text of Boethius they are meaningless excrescences, whilst for the Germanist they were unimportant as Latin terms with no vernacular counterparts.
141 Other passages: *De consolatione* 96, 8ff. (*Depositio* not included); 163, 18ff.; *Martianus Capella* 105, 10 (*Et hic* missing); 106, 21ff.; 109, 12ff.; 110, 10ff.; 151, 16ff. (*Depositio* comes as late as 153, 9); 178, 4ff.; 192, 12ff.; 209, 21ff.
142 Quintilian, *Institutio oratoria* IV 11, 3, 46 (p. 266).
143 *Categorien* 439, 13 (followed by 439, 16 *Et hic suspende* and 439, 18 *Hic depone*); 440, 23 (followed by 440, 26 *taz ist interposita ratio*).
144 *De consolatione* 127, 5ff.; 135, 11ff.; 300, 7ff.; 337, 19ff. (*Depositio* not included); *Martianus Capella* 8, 6ff. (*Depositio* comes as late as 11, 5); 55, 9ff.; 61, 11ff. (*Et hic* missing); 74, 20ff.; *De interpretatione* 535, 17ff.; 550, 20ff.; 554, 17ff.; 558, 7ff.; 559, 19ff.
145 Cf. Schwarz, *PBB* 99 (1977), 33, on one of the functions of a gloss: 'Sie signalisierte dem Lehrer ... wo ein Exkurs einzuleiten ist'.
146 This example differs from the others in coming not at the close of a Latin sentence, but after its German counterpart.
147 The phrase *interposita ratio* is also used in the passages beginning at *Martianus Capella* 178, 4 (cf. 178, 16 *interposita ratio* and 179, 1 *Et hic interpositio*) and *Categorien* 440, 23 (cf. 440, 26 *taz ist interposita ratio*).
148 This group finishes with the variant *Hic clausula*. Cf. also *Martianus Capella* 179, 21 to conclude the passage beginning 178, 4. *Clausula*, meaning conclusion of a period, performs the same function as *depositio*.
149 *Geschichte* I 111.
150 There are other OHG texts which must be kept distinct from Notker's works, even though some of them may have been likewise intended for the monastery school: the *Benediktinerregel* (cf. Haubrichs, *Anfänge*, p. 243; *Studienprogramm*, p. 243), *Carmen ad Deum* (Haubrichs, *Anfänge*, p. 269), *Altalemannische Psalmenübersetzung* (Haubrichs, *Anfänge*, p. 253; *Studienprogramm*, p. 250), *Tatian* (Haubrichs, *Anfänge*, p. 261), the *Murbacher Hymnen* (Haubrichs, *Anfänge*, pp. 248f.; *Studienprogramm*, pp. 249f.). It is likewise true of the texts thought to have been meant for nunneries: the *Predigtsammlung A, B, C* (Vollmann-Profe, *Wiederbeginn*, p. 65), the *Rheinfränkische Psalmenübersetzung* (Haubrichs, *Anfänge*, p. 255), and the *Altsächsischer Psalmenkommentar* (Haubrichs, *Anfänge*, p. 256).
    These differ from Notker in that only he refers to his works being heard and read. With these other texts, although they contain no reference to it, reading is a (probable) hypothesis and could embrace reading out to the community and also individual reading. However, as this twofold reception is not explicitly indicated it is safer not to classify them under the intermediate mode.
151 I have discussed the reception of Hartmann's works in *MLR* 81 (1986), 357ff.
152 Mertens, *Überlegungen*, pp. 1ff.
153 *Iwein* 2791ff.

154 Mertens, *Gregorius*, pp. 103f. (also pp. 76 and 92).
155 Wapnewski, *Hartmann*, p. 104. If he regards this conjunction as naïve, this may be because he takes *geléret* in the sense of modern German 'gelehrt'. However, we have seen that *geléret* can be used in the sense of 'literate, able to read' (cf. Heinrich von Freiberg, *Tristan* 5539, see above, p. 133; *Rolandslied* 2114, see above, p. 138). If we read Hartmann's statement in this light it is anything but naïve, especially when applied to a German layman before 1200.
156 The opening lines of this work lead up to a preoccupation with written sources: 6f., 16f., 29.
157 Scholz, *Hören*, p. 49.
158 Another confirmation is provided by Rudolf von Ems. At the beginning of *Barlaam und Josaphat* he says: *und bite, swer diz maere lese / daz er sich bezzernde wese* (157f.), where at issue is the moral improvement which his work is to bring his audience (as opposed to a reciter). When at the conclusion of his work the author takes up the same idea, but uses the double formula (16077: ... *swer ez hoere oder lese, / daz er sich bezzernde wese*), we may take it that, like Hartmann, he is anticipating two modes of reception.
159 *Gregorius* 722, 3143.
160 Mertens, *Gregorius*, p. 80, also discusses the last lines of the prologue (vv. 171ff.) in the light of a possible twofold reception. He regards these lines naming the author as superfluous where the author recited his work, but as called for when the work spread beyond the court for which it was first commissioned. Mertens raises the possibility that the occasion for *Gregorius* finding its way onto parchment, including these lines, may have been the spread to other courts. His assumption of two modes of reception on the basis of such a passage can be paralleled by the prologue to the *Wigalois* of Wirnt von Grafenberg (Scholz, *Hören*, p. 127).
161 Vv. 9019, 9723. Both details occur in Chrétien's text (5899 and 6248), but have not previously been mentioned in Hartmann's, who must therefore refer to what he has read in his French source, not to what he recited earlier to his audience.
162 Mentioned by name in the Wolfenbüttel fragment 4629[12].
163 Chrétien's description of the horse may include the same detail (5323ff.), but Hartmann cannot be referring to him. When a medieval author consults his source he does this alone and keeps the audience at bay.
164 Cramer, *Erec*, pp. 319, 321.
165 If *lesen* in 7305 implies a reciter delivering his work and listeners before him, this helps us in interpreting references which would otherwise be ambiguous. These include an allusion to the audience hearing the story (396), to their hearing it recounted (2079; cf. 2239; 7179; refers back to 7148; 7268, refers back to 6709ff.; 9746, refers back to 9573ff.) and to the author as reciter recounting it to them (6821; cf. 7226, 8461). By themselves these references are unreliable, but appear in a different light in conjunction with 7303ff.
166 From the fact that Hartmann adds that the daughter could read French it might be concluded that this sketch illustrates court life in France, without regard to Germany. This could be true of the family intimacy of this scene (lay literacy in Germany was not so advanced as in France, so that what Hartmann describes may have had little bearing on Germany, even though it may have been meant to stimulate imitation of France). Nonetheless, it cannot be said to be true of reading aloud to others, as is brought home by Hartmann's use of the double formula in his legends.
167 If we accept this conclusion about recital it throws light on otherwise ambiguous references to an oral situation, as when the audience's reception is seen in terms of hearing (26, 7728). More suggestive is the recital situation conjured up as Kalogreant is on the brink of telling his story to Arthur's court (249ff.), especially if we regard this scene with Hartmann, as suggested with Chrétien, as a 'deferred prologue', transposed to this point in the narrative to catch those members of the real audience who paid little attention to the

authorial prologue or even turned up too late for it, but in time for the beginning of the story. On this see Hunt, *FMLS* 6 (1970), 14 and *FMLS* 8 (1972), 328; Green, *Oral poetry*, pp. 172f.; Scholz, *Hören*, p. 175, fn. 697.
168 Kartschoke, *IASL* 8 (1983), 256.
169 Schwietering, *Schriften*, p. 148.
170 For earlier treatments of this see Green, *Oral poetry*, pp. 163ff., and *Wolfram*, pp. 271ff.
171 Horacek, *Buochstap*, pp. 129ff.; Grundmann, *AfK* 40 (1958), 1ff.; Eggers, *Litteraturam*, pp. 533ff.; Ohly, *Gebet*, pp. 455ff.; Grundmann, *AfK* 49 (1967), 391ff. Grundmann sought to render the idea of Wolfram as a literate poet ridiculous by his title 'Dichtete Wolfram von Eschenbach am Schreibtisch?' That this was not unthinkable has been shown by Wachinger from an illustration in a *Willehalm* MS and by the title he has chosen for his article in *Wolfram-Studien* 12 (1992), 9ff.
172 Curschmann, *PBB* 106 (1984), 218ff.; Brall, *Gralsuche*, pp. 70ff. The present consensus seems to be that 115, 27 is no autobiographical confession, but an affirmation by Wolfram, in which he sets himself apart from Hartmann and Gottfried, that as a lay author he belongs to the cultural world of medieval laymen. Cf. Brall, *Gralsuche*, pp. 82ff.; Bumke, *Geschichte*, p. 162; Grubmüller, *DU (NS)* 1 (1989), 1 44.
173 Horacek, *Buochstap*, p. 136. Cf. also Nellmann, *Erzähltechnik*, pp. 53f.
174 Horacek, *Buochstap*, p. 137; Nellmann, *Erzähltechnik*, pp. 26 and 35ff.
175 *Erzähltechnik*, p. 26.
176 *Ibid.*, pp. 1f.
177 In discussing 213, 13 *hie ze Wildenbere* (on deictic pointers to an oral recital see p. 75) Neumann, *ZfdA* 100 (1971), 94, suggests that it refers to the first recital, whether by the author or by a literate *clericus*.
178 For examples see Green, *ZfdA* 115 (1986), 163f., 171f., 174f.
179 Examples of Wolfram's usage are: 416, 28ff.; 562, 18ff.; 827, 12ff.
180 Curschmann, *DVjs* 45 (1971), 650.
181 Curschmann, *PBB* 106 (1984), 233.
182 See Grundmann, *AfK* 26 (1936), 129ff.; Bumke *Mäzene*, pp. 231ff.; Scholz, *Hören*, pp. 205ff.; Bumke, *Kultur*, pp. 704ff.
183 337, 28ff.; 827, 29f.
184 These are listed by Nellmann, *Erzähltechnik*, p. 3, fn. 14.
185 Sieverding, *Kampf*, pp. 167f. Cf. also Brackert, *Parzival*, pp. 143ff.
186 E.g. by Hatto, *Parzival*, p. 175.
187 *Erzähltechnik*, p. 4, fn. 16.
188 See above, pp. 140f.
189 One might ask whether the women are described as intelligent (337, 1: *sinnec*) because the author is addressing them and knows that he can expect greater insight into his concerns from their point of view. Or because he knows that they can read and therefore subject his work to a closer scrutiny? Or both?
190 *Hören*, p. 124.
191 786, 3ff.; 788, 14ff. See above, p. 122.
192 Curschmann, *PBB* 106 (1984), 237.
193 Cf. Gottfried, *Tristan*, Ganz edn 1 172, fn. to v. 4684.
194 Scholz, *Hören*, p. 109.
195 On the visual dimension of oral recital see above, pp. 61f. This dimension has been stressed with Wolfram by Wynn, *Witz*, p. 125, who says that the author addresses listeners and spectators in his audience, and by Curschmann, *PBB* 106 (1984), 238, who describes his performance as a 'Vollzug in Lesung, Musik und gemeinsamem Anschauen'.
196 Cf. Schröder, *ZfdA* 104 (1975), 318f.; Gottfried, *Tristan*, Ganz edn 1 xxivff.; Huber, *Tristan*, p. 23; Bumke, *Geschichte*, p. 189. See also Glendinning, *DVjs* 61 (1987), 617ff.
197 Vv. 155ff.

198 On the classical elements in Gottfried's education see Stevens, *Renewal*, pp. 67ff., and Wisbey, *Living*, pp. 257ff.
199 Vv. 150ff.
200 Wolf, *Gottfried*, p. 57.
201 See the note on v. 8270 in Ganz edn I 352 and also xxxvi.
202 See the fn. on v. 19436, *ibid.*, II 298, but also the introduction, I xxxiiif.
203 See the note on v. 17900, *ibid.*, II 330.
204 Wolf, *Gottfried*, p. 57.
205 Hatto, *Gottfried*, p. 43.
206 Schröder, *ZfdA* 104 (1975), 312.
207 After giving his explanation of Tristan's name Gottfried adds: *diz maere, der daz ie gelas, / der erkennet sich wol, daz der nam / dem lebene was gehellesam* (2016ff.). Since this explanation was probably also in Thomas's version it seems likely that the reading was by those acquainted with the Tristan story at large, not just from Gottfried's version.
208 Mentioned in v. 170.
209 Hatto, *Gottfried*, p. 43; Schröder, *ZfdA* 104 (1975), 313.
210 Refers back to vv. 1789ff.
211 Cf. the note on vv. 236f. in Ganz edn I 344.
212 Here I differ from Speckenbach, *Studien*, p. 54, who sees the *edele herzen* as Gottfried's listeners. I see them as listeners, too, but primarily (from Gottfried's point of view) as readers.
213 Refers back to vv. 7208ff.
214 See above, pp. 131f., but also Schirok, *ZfdA* 113 (1984), 188ff., and Bonath, *ZfdA* 115 (1986), 101ff.
215 Cf. Stein on Gottfried's prologue, *Euphorion* 69 (1975), 375, fn. 23.
216 They are mentioned in v. 233.
217 The relevance of this recital practice to the literary situation in Gottfried's day is suggested by the manner in which he illustrates it at two points. In v. 8059 the entertainment provided at the Irish court by Isold is summed up: *si sanc, si schreip und si las*, which Hatto, *Gottfried*, p. 147, translates as 'she sang, she wrote, and she read for them'. At a later point (19192f.) a similar sketch is presented of entertainment given by Tristan: *er seite ir schoeniu maere, / er sanc, er schreib ir unde las*. Schröder, *ZfdA* 104 (1975), 310 translates this passage in a manner close to Hatto's rendering of the first ('er erzählte schöne Geschichten, sang ihr Lieder vor, schrieb selber etwas und las es ihr vor'). Elsewhere, *MlJb* 18 (1983), 334, Schröder says of Tristan's activity: 'er erzählt, singt, schreibt, liest vor, d.h. er tut alles, was sein poetischer Schöpfer auch tat und mit seinem Roman getan wissen wollte'.
218 Cf. also vv. 16932 (with *iezuo dâ*), 17576, 18605.
219 The pointers are as follows: 7155 (cf. 7188ff.), 16493 (16479ff.), 16932 (16707ff.), 17421 (17331ff.), 17576 (17351ff.), 18605 (18447ff.).
220 Bertau, *Literaturgeschichte*, p. 131.
221 Cf. also 3824, 6977.
222 Cf. *VfL* I, 1057.
223 *Magdeburger Schöppenchronik*, pp. 168f.
224 See pp. 278f.
225 *Magdeburger Schöppenchronik*, pp. 168f.
226 See above, pp. 117f.
227 Cf. above, p. 125.
228 This example is doubtful, since the use of *man* and *wir* is reminiscent of the constructions *wir lesen* and *man liset* (see above, pp. 115f.).
229 See above, pp. 119f.
230 See above, pp. 140f.

231 *Ibid.*
232 E.g. 778, 1016f., 1048ff.
233 Hagenlocher, *ZfdA* 118 (1989), 131ff.
234 *Ibid.*, p. 132.
235 *Ibid.*, p. 133.
236 *Ibid.*, p. 135.
237 *Ibid.*, p. 147.
238 *Ibid.*
239 *Ibid.*, p. 158.
240 See p. 278.
241 Rörig, *WaG* 13 (1953), 29ff.
242 Examples of the double formula from the fifteenth century include Job Vener (Heimpel, *Vener* III 1345, 248), the *Margaretalegende nach Cod. Helmstedt. 1231 (Wolfenbüttel)* 349f., in extended form a plenary from Lübeck (Kämpfer, *Studien*, p. 240), and the *Kölnische Chronik* (see p. 14). This last example repeats in the context of printing the argument used in the sixth century by Caesarius of Arles in the context of writing. Together they establish the continuity of this formula throughout the Middle Ages.

Behind this continuity the same situation, listeners and readers, is to be found. Schreiner, *Volkssprache*, p. 479, fn. 45, points out that translators of religious books in the fifteenth century met the accusation that such books for laymen undermined the authority of the Church by stressing that reading at home did not dispense from hearing the word of God in church. They thereby repeat an argument used by Origen (see above, p. 178). Dietrich Kolde recommends recipients of his *Christenspiegel* to read it for themselves, but also to others who cannot read (Schreiner, *Volkssprache*, p. 482). Stephan von Landskron suggests that laymen hear the word of God preached, but also read it themselves if they are able to, leaving it to others better equipped to read it to them if they cannot read (Weidenhiller, *Untersuchungen*, p. 181). The use of a *peichtpuchel* is recommended as preparation for confession, but if the layman is illiterate he is to seek advice from a priest or have the book read out to him (*ibid.*, pp. 481f.).

On the continuation of the double formula and the practice behind it into the Reformation period see the references to Rössing-Hager and Scribner, p. 330, n. 142.
243 Goody, *Interface*, pp. 118f.
244 *Ibid.*, p. 118.
245 Cf. Schlieben-Lange, *Traditionen*, pp. 52f.
246 On this problem, especially in the late Middle Ages and the Reformation period, see Schreiner, *ZHF* 11 (1984), 257ff.; *Volkssprache*, pp. 468ff.

8 Survey of the intermediate mode of reception

1 See above, pp. 170ff.
2 Cf. Green, *Parergon* 2 (1984), 58 and 68. (Notker's use of a Latin double formula within a German text, *Psalter* 862, 8, cannot be applied to this work, for he is following Augustine, cf. edn p. 861). Miethke, *Universitäten*, has discussed the role of the spoken word alongside books in the teaching practice of medieval universities, but his questions need also to be asked of teaching in the monastery. A beginning has been made by Grubmüller, *DU (NS)* 1 (1989), 141ff.
3 To avoid encumbering this chapter with more notes I refrain from indicating earlier passages where the evidence for hearing and for reading was given in Chapters 4 and 6. Reference is made easier by the arrangement of genres in this chapter (from section a to section j) in the same way as earlier. Thus *Wernher von Elmendorf* is discussed in section a in this chapter, but also in the corresponding section in Chapters 4 and 6.
4 7: *swer guotiu maere hoert ode list* (a general remark with a particular application to his

Welscher Gast). In mentioning that other works could be heard and read (762, 1079) Thomasin suggests that this is how he regards the reception of contemporary literature at large.
5 42, 4. If this were dismissed as deriving from the Latin text, it could still be rescued as summing up what was said in the German prologue independently of any Latin source.
6 19 (with regard to his *büechelin*, 15).
7 *Solsequium* 68, 27: *omnium legencium, audiencium scireque volencium*.
8 Cf. Schmidtke, *PBB* 92 (1970), 289, on the twofold public for such collections.
9 95, 7f.
10 This depends on extrapolating from Heinrich's other works, *Apollonius von Tyrland* and *Gottes Zukunft*, for both of which reading was implied. If we can accept the reader for the *Visio* he existed alongside the listener (589).
11 Lamprecht also refers to reading out his text to listeners, 1142.
12 This author was included in Chapter 4, but not 6, because although there are (weak) pointers to hearing, there is none to reading – other than what the double formula implies.
13 At one point in a title in MSS L and B (122, 1) and in two references (25, 17 and 31) which I take to apply also to the reception of this work.
14 9, 29. The conjunction of *lesen* with *vernemen* by means of 'or' suggests that the latter has the force of *hoeren* (Scholz, *Hören*, p. 66).
15 6521ff. (*Horen oder lesen / Eder scriven*), varied by 5082 (*horen unde seen*). A twofold reception would also be probable for the *Kaland* and *Reimbibel* if they were meant for a similar audience.
16 61ff., 1636ff. These formulas, together with the suggestion that the audience hears the work recited (76), make up for the uncertainty of *hoeren* references (121, 135, 237) too weak for inclusion in Chapter 4.
17 *Büchlein von der Himmelfahrt Mariae* 563f.; *Buch von geistlicher Lehre* 3, 3ff. (general, but with particular import); *Der Seele Rat* 6538ff.; *Pariser Tagezeiten* 4062: The second of these works refers to recital (47, 45) in the refectory and to the *collatio*, but does not make it clear that it was meant for such a context, although this is likely (cf. 97, 44ff.). For the third work a solitary reference to *horen*, even if reinforced by *zu horen* (220ff.), is hardly enough to demonstrate reception by listeners.
18 *Glosse* 181, 8.
19 *Königebuch* 20, p. 131.
20 See p. 229.
21 In an earlier article, *Hören*, p. 32, I gave this total as 339. This is now corrected.
22 58f. (see also p. 353, n. 100). The literal function of *horen* is borne out by a reference like 285, 22: ... *als ir davor habet gehort lesen*. If so, 58f. must be seen as a double formula, summing up the two dimensions for which there was independent evidence.
23 21731f.
24 *Horen lesin* of the work's reception (21695), *lesin* in the sense of recital in conjunction with *horin* (21700ff.), and frequently of a point previously recited to listeners of which they need to be reminded. Cf. Green, *ZfdA* 115 (1986), 155ff.
25 IV 25, 6. See p. 418, n. 369.
26 10ff. That *sehen* could stand in for *lesen*, as here, is nothing new to us, so that we may agree when Scholz, *Hören*, pp. 159f., registers this as a double formula.
27 Hear the book recited: 1126, 12508; recited earlier: 5744 (refers to 2709ff.). Cf. also 11317.
28 6102 (here, as in 5351, *schouwen* stands for *lesen*), 12542 (*ir horer und ir lesere*).
29 *Gottes Zukunft* 8101; *Saelden Hort* 73ff., 3983f. (the preoccupation with religious literature at large is seen similarly: 127f., 5445).
30 96f. It is uncertain whether this can also be applied to Konrad's work. At the least, it suggests how he conceived the reception of religious literature in his day.
31 Albertus suggests the recital situation by mentioning those *die ez iemer gehoren lesen*

(1546), whilst Ebernand lays more stress on what he recited to his audience (2244 refers back to 670ff., 3224 refers to 1123ff., 1990ff.).

32 1054: *wer von mir gerne höret lesen / oder selber liset*. Wetzel may be assumed to have referred to these two possibilities in the light of his own work's reception.
33 90, 375. These two examples illustrate the interchangeability of *lesen* and *sehen*.
34 In both works this includes the construction *hoeren lesen*: *Silvester* 5186, *Alexius* 1401.
35 Fols. 1r., 25 and 14r., 10.
36 *Passional* I/II 114, 41; III 330, 57 (again with a parallel between *sehen* and *lesen*); *Väterbuch* 41484f. Both works use the *horen lesen* construction (*Passional* III 5, 92; 319, 13; *Väterbuch* 11523, 41448, 41499) and the *Passional* also refers to what was earlier recited to the audience (III 332, 2).
37 The former is underlined by references to what has already been recited. See p. 356, n. 144.
38 53f. (the inclusion of *horn* and *lesenn* signifies a twofold reception).
39 See p. 356, n. 145.
40 10083f. Here I take *hoeren* and *lesen* to belong together, as in a double formula, so that *heizen* governs only *schríben* ('to order copies to be made'), not *lesen* in the sense of arranging for the work to be recited. If so, religious merit accrues both to the twofold audience (listeners and readers) and to the person who ensures that other audiences are made acquainted with the work.
41 Once in the prologue (67) and twice as part of a triple formula. In one of these (16237f.) *sehen* and *lesen* reinforce the visual dimension of reading, whilst the other (16152ff.) sketches a situation similar to what we found with Bruder Philipp.
42 6: *daz man wol hoeret oder siht*. That *sehen* can be equated with *lesen* is confirmed by the author's use of the same verb in *Daniel von dem Blühenden Tal* (see below n. 50), but more particularly from other passages in *Karl der Große* (6175ff., 9302f.). We may therefore classify v. 6 as a double formula.
43 Even if this concerns a possibility not foreseen by the author it is evidence for reading on one occasion and deserves inclusion as much as the attentive reader of *Wernher von Elmendorf*.
44 That the latter need not exclude the former is suggested by the *hoeren lesen* construction in the sketch of a recital situation (20656) and by references to what has earlier been recited to the audience (6548 refers back to 2764ff., 13065f. to 10815ff., 17621f. to 7613ff.).
45 At least the continuator refers to a point recited earlier, 44904.
46 Combined (in the case of *Erec*) with a reference to previous recital, 7305.
47 Cf. Mertens, *Gregorius*, pp. 24 and 37. That readers were found for *Erec* within little more than a generation is confirmed by what Heinrich von dem Türlin says of Arthur's retinue, as he had learned of it from Hartmann's work (*Crone* 2348ff.).
48 9441.
49 106.
50 1754: *ir mohtet hoeren unde sehen*. This reference back to 1264ff. implies an audience composed of those who could have heard and read this earlier point.
51 If we could accept a twofold reception for this romance it would probably also be applicable to the others by this author (*Meleranz* and *Garel von dem Blühenden Tal* contained pointers to hearing just as uncertain as with *Tandareis* and no indications of reading at all). The case for these two is thus even weaker than for *Tandareis*.
52 The uniqueness of Wolfram's position is not that he was a knight who had nothing to do with books (that was still the norm for German knights), but that as such he was the author of a court romance. On the literate status of most authors of court narrative literature see p. 291.
53 Written dimension: 2524, 1ff.; 5960, 4; 5988, 2; 5990, 1; 6327, 1. Double formula: 1663, 1 and 6077, 4.
54 Double formula: 177, 4685. Pointers to listeners include a *hoeren lesen* construction (230) and references to reciting to them at an earlier stage (see p. 197).

55 Like Gottfried, Heinrich refers to what has been previously recited: 296 refers to 246ff., 2091 to 2059ff., 2330ff. to 2078f., 2126ff., 2329.
56 On the assumption of the same kind of audience for Rudolf's works see Green, *ZfdA* 115 (1986), 152.
57 7100ff.
58 Heinrich von Neustadt underlines the recital situation by references to earlier recital (p. 360, n. 233). Johann von Würzburg achieves the same with a *hoeren lesen* construction, 10849.
59 *Frauendienst* 426, 4: *Der leich vil guot ze singen was: / manc schoene vrowe in gerne las.*
60 On Romance parallels see Peters, *Frauendienst*, pp. 161ff.
61 The comparative figures in this paragraph are affected only slightly by one consideration. In some works the only evidence for hearing or reading was the use of a double formula, so that to complete our earlier surveys these cases must now be added to the totals in Chapters 4 and 6.

To Chapter 4 eight works now have to be added: five to devotional literature (Könemann von Jerxheim, *Wurzgarten Mariens*; *Unser Vrouwen Klage*; *Büchlein von der Himmelfahrt Mariae*; Heinrich von Burgeis, *Der Seele Rat*; *Pariser Tagezeiten*), one to legal literature (*Schwabenspiegel Langform M*), one to biblical literature (*Leben Jesu*) and one to legends (Bruder Philipp, *Marienleben*).

Fourteen examples have to be added to Chapter 6, under devotional literature (David von Augsburg; *Büchlein von der Himmelfahrt Mariae*; *Der Seele Rat* of Heinrich von Burgeis; *Pariser Tagezeiten*); legends (Konrad von Fussesbrunnen, *Kindheit Jesu*; Wetzel von Bernau, *Margaretenleben*; Lamprecht von Regensburg, *Sanct Franzisken Leben*; *Väterbuch*; *Sante Margareten Marter*); court epic (Der Stricker, *Karl der Große*); romance (Ulrich von Zatzikhoven, *Lanzelet*; Konrad Fleck, *Flore und Blanscheflur*; Der Stricker, *Daniel von dem Blühenden Tal*; Albrecht von Scharfenberg, *Der Jüngere Titurel*).
62 On the 'Gebrauchskontext' of early Romance texts which may have occasioned their being put into written form, thereby making them available for readers as well as listeners, see Frank, *Seitengestaltung*, pp. 102ff.
63 I have discussed these contexts before, but only with regard to works with a double formula (Green, *Hören*, pp. 35ff.). Now the survey is widened to include all works for which a twofold reception is likely, on whatever grounds.
64 On the difficulties in this see Peters, *Erfahrung*, pp. 53ff., but also the comments of Küsters and Langer, *Arbitrium* 9 (1991), pp. 38f.
65 Kokott, *Literatur*, pp. 152ff.; Bumke, *Mäzene*, pp. 71, 136.
66 Bumke, *Mäzene*, pp. 63f., 66, 136f.; Ganz, *Heinrich*, p. 39.
67 *VfL* 3, 761.
68 Cf. von Ertzdorff, *Rudolf*, pp. 101ff.; Brackert, *Rudolf*, pp. 83ff.
69 *VfL* 1, 1007f.; Wenzel, *Geschichte*, pp. 119ff.; Bumke, *Geschichte*, p. 351.
70 *VfL* 1, 1213; Bumke, *Mäzene*, p. 216.
71 Bumke, *Mäzene*, p. 274; Cramer, *Geschichte*, p. 142.
72 *Die Erlösung*: *VfL* 2, 601f. *Der Saelden Hort*: Bumke, *Geschichte*, p. 389.
73 *Gregorius*: Mertens, *Gregorius*, pp. 16ff., especially 23f.; Cormeau and Störmer, *Hartmann*, pp. 139ff.; Zäck, *Sündaere*, pp. 431f. *Armer Heinrich*: Mertens, p. 24; Cormeau and Störmer, p. 159.
74 *VfL* 5, 174; Bumke, *Geschichte*, p. 381.
75 See von Ertzdorff, *Rudolf*, pp. 80ff.; Brackert, *Rudolf*, pp. 27f.
76 Rudolf von Ems mentions him and his work in a list of court poets in *Alexander* 3259ff.
77 Bumke, *Mäzene*, pp. 240f.
78 *Ibid.*, pp. 16, 27. Cf. also Reinbot von Durne, *Der heilige Georg* 34ff.
79 Cf. von der Burg, *Stricker*, pp. 178ff.
80 Bumke, *Mäzene*, pp. 251f., 274, 286f.; *Geschichte*, p. 259.

81 Bumke, *Mäzene*, pp. 19, 25, 200f.; *Geschichte*, p. 260; Behr, *Literatur*, pp. 125ff.
82 Bumke, *Mäzene*, pp. 18, 24, 113ff.; *Geschichte*, p. 139.
83 *Erec*: Ruh, *Epik* I 108; Mertens, *Gregorius*, pp. 24, 32ff.; Bumke, *Mäzene*, pp. 172; *Geschichte*, p. 147. *Iwein*: Mertens, *Gregorius*, p. 24; Cormeau and Störmer, *Hartmann*, pp. 224f. Cf. also Thum, *Probleme*, pp. 47ff. and Mertens, *Mäzenatentum*, pp. 117ff.
84 Bumke, *Mäzene*, p. 153.
85 Bumke, *Wolfram*, p. 5; *Mäzene*, pp. 28, 164f.; *Geschichte*, p. 163.
86 Bumke, *Mäzene*, pp. 27, 174.
87 Reisel, *Aspekte*, pp. 61ff.
88 Cf. von Ertzdorff, *Rudolf*, pp. 67ff.; Brackert, *Rudolf*, p. 27.
89 *VfL* 3, 894 (against this cf. Bumke, *Mäzene*, pp. 174, 386f.). Knapp, *Heinrich*, pp. 147ff., suggests instead another court, Andechs-Meranien.
90 Ulrich's *Tristan*: Bumke, *Mäzene*, pp. 251, 276; *Geschichte*, p. 194. Rudolf's *Alexander*: von Ertzdorff, *Rudolf*, pp. 98ff.; Bumke, *Geschichte*, p. 251.
91 Cf. von Ertzdorff, *Rudolf*, pp. 89ff.; Brackert, *Rudolf*, p. 26; Bumke, *Mäzene*, pp. 251f., 268, 276.
92 Heinzle, *Stellung*, pp. 108f.
93 Cf. Grubmüller, *Minne*, pp. 45f.; Bumke, *Mäzene*, pp. 202f.; *Geschichte*, p. 274.
94 Brandt, *Konrad*, p. 79; Kokott, *Konrad*, pp. 67f.
95 Bumke, *Mäzene*, p. 222; *Geschichte*, p. 238.
96 Bumke, *Mäzene*, pp. 14ff., 196; *Geschichte*, p. 228.
97 *VfL* 7, 729; Bumke, *Mäzene*, p. 33.
98 Cramer in his edition, p. 179; Bumke, *Mäzene*, p. 196.
99 Bumke, *Mäzene*, p. 277; *Geschichte*, p. 195; Behr, *Literatur*, pp. 220f.
100 Bumke, *Mäzene*, p. 267; Cramer, *Geschichte*, p. 27.
101 On this see Grundmann, *AfK* 40 (1958), 50f. On the (restricted) evidence for literacy amongst secular noblemen in Germany see p. 289.
102 See above, pp. 63f.
103 *Gregorius*, p. 18.
104 On the threefold grouping of the court audience which this presupposes see pp. 293ff. Cf. also Henkel, *Litteratus*, pp. 334ff. In the particular case of Hartmann's *Gregorius* Ernst, *Euphorion* 73 (1979), 82f., has stressed the dependence of aristocratic families on clerical commemoration of their dead members and located its audience 'in den Berührungszonen zwischen Laienadel und Monasterium'. In such a zone of contact between two cultural worlds two different modes of reception are understandable.
105 *Kultur*, p. 617. For qualifications of Bumke's argument see the reviews by Fried, *AfK* 64 (1982), 227ff. and Johanek, *GRM* 36 (1986), 209ff.
106 *Kultur*, pp. 624ff.
107 Cf. Schreiner, *Hof*, pp. 88f.
108 Bumke, *Kultur*, p. 630.
109 *Ibid.*, p. 701.
110 Cf. edn, pp. 50f. See also Schreiner, *Hof*, p. 71.
111 From his analysis of the restricted number of permanent members of the court, as opposed to those who attended for only a short period, Bumke, *Kultur*, pp. 703f., draws the conclusion that only relatively few would have been present as an audience for the lengthier works of narrative literature.
112 Cf. Grundmann, *AfK* 26 (1936), 129ff.; Bumke, *Mäzene*, pp. 231ff.; Scholz, *Hören*, pp. 205ff.
113 Bumke, *Mäzene*, p. 244; *Liebe*, pp. 39f.
114 *Frauendienst* 593, 11.
115 *Crone* 29990ff.
116 140f.

117 Bumke, *Kultur*, p. 706.
118 On this differentiation see pp. 296ff. Haupt, *Fest*, p. 159, stresses the role of the court as a point of contact between humanist *litterati* and feudal *illitterati*.
119 Schnell, *Kirche*, pp. 75ff.
120 Haubrichs, *Anfänge*, pp. 270ff.
121 *VfL* 4, 1; Bumke, *Geschichte*, p. 368.
122 *VfL* 1, 451; Kartschoke, *Geschichte*, p. 280.
123 Heinzle, *Wandlungen*, p. 187; Bumke, *Geschichte*, p. 377.
124 *VfL* 5, 520f.; Bumke, *Geschichte*, p. 411.
125 Bumke, *Geschichte*, p. 379.
126 This work contains no pointers to the context of its reception and no suggestions are given in the secondary literature. However, the use of the first person singular in the final prayer (544ff.) and the reference to reading (563ff.) suggest that it may conceivably have been meant for monastic devotions.
127 *VfL* 1, 1085f.; Bumke, *Geschichte*, p. 419.
128 Herkommer, *NdJb* 100 (1977), 30; Heinzle, *Wandlungen*, pp. 101f.; de Boor, *Geschichte* III 2, 416; Bumke, *Geschichte*, p. 359.
129 Herkommer, *NdJb* 100 (1977), 30; Heinzle, *Wandlungen*, pp. 101f.; de Boor, *Geschichte* III 2, 416; Bumke, *Geschichte*, p. 360.
130 The case for this work rests on the possible parallel with the other two.
131 Cf. de Boor, *Geschichte* III 2, 420.
132 Herkommer, *NdJb* 100 (1977), 27ff., 32; Heinzle, *Wandlungen*, p. 214; de Boor, *Geschichte* III 1, 190.
133 *VfL* 3, 909; Haubrichs, *Anfänge*, p. 339.
134 *VfL* 7, 173ff.; Haubrichs, *Notizen*, pp. 7ff.
135 Masser, *Legendenepik*, pp. 63f.; Vollmann-Profe, *Wiederbeginn*, p. 100; Kartschoke, *Geschichte*, pp. 302f.
136 Cramer, *Geschichte*, p. 205, although doubts are voiced by Masser, *Legendenepik*, pp. 122f.
137 *VfL* 4, 596; Cramer, *Geschichte*, p. 205.
138 *VfL* 2, 648; Heinzle, *Wandlungen*, p. 222.
139 Priester Wernher: Fromm, *Untersuchungen*, p. 152; Masser, *Legendenepik*, pp. 91f.; Kartschoke, *Geschichte*, pp. 328, 332. Albertus von Augsburg: *VfL* 1, 114; Geith in his edition, p. 9; Bumke, *Geschichte*, pp. 392f.
140 Masser, *Legendenepik*, p. 178; Heinzle, *Wandlungen*, p. 165; Bumke, *Mäzene*, pp. 285f.; *Geschichte*, p. 395.
141 *VfL* 5, 520; Bumke, *Geschichte*, p. 397.
142 *VfL* 5, 635.
143 *Passional*: *VfL* 7, 334; Masser, *Legendenepik*, pp. 187f.; Bumke, *Geschichte*, p. 401. *Väterbuch*: Masser, *Legendenepik*, pp. 187f.; Bumke, *Geschichte*, p. 402. On both the *Passional* and the *Väterbuch* see also Richert, *Wege*, pp. 158ff. and 305. Hugo von Langenstein: *VfL* 4, 234ff.; Masser, *Legendenepik*, p. 186; Bumke, *Geschichte*, pp. 400f. Bruder Philipp: *VfL* 7, 588f.; Masser, *Legendenepik*, pp. 108f.; Bumke, *Geschichte*, p. 211.
144 Whereas Bumke regards such a work as part of court literature, Fried, *AfK* 64 (1982), 230, registers it as monastic literature. See also Johanek, *GRM* 36 (1986), 213.
145 Cf. Frank, *Seitengestaltung*, p. 208, on the position in Romania.
146 See above, p. 30.
147 Leclercq, *Amour*.
148 Cf. Wendehorst, *MIÖG* 71 (1963), 67ff.
149 Henkel, *Übersetzungen*, pp. 67ff.
150 I leave on one side the point made by Stein, *Stil*, p. 11: 'Fragwürdig ist allerdings auch methodisch bereits hier die Behauptung, daß jemand, der lesen konnte, nur lateinische Werke las bzw. nur in Ausnahmefällen deutsche.'

151 See above, p. 34.
152 On the connections between monasteries and laymen see p. 285.
153 See pp. 285f.
154 Leyser, *Hermits*, pp. 45ff.
155 The many layers of monastic life have been brought out well in the case of nunneries by Elm, *Stellung*, p. 14.
156 Schützeichel, *Memento*, p. 101 (with further literature).
157 *Ibid.*, pp. 106f.
158 Cf. Haubrichs, *Anfänge*, p. 316.
159 Ekkehard IV, *Casus* cap. 135 (p. 429). Mentioned by Haubrichs, *Anfänge*, p. 209.
160 Cf. Schreiner, *Hof*, p. 72, fn. 13.
161 MGH Cap. 1, 168 (number 75). Quoted by Nelson, *Literacy*, p. 278. On the involvement of the clergy at large in warfare see Prinz, *Klerus*.
162 Cf. Schreiner, *Hof*, p. 73.
163 See above, pp. 74 and 101.
164 *Wandlungen*, p. 168.
165 See above, p. 160.
166 Cf. Willmes, *Adventus*, p. 67, fn. 220, and p. 70, fn. 237.
167 Haubrichs, *Anfänge*, pp. 209 and 316.
168 *Ibid.*, pp. 316 and 396.
169 Grundmann, *Schrifttum*, pp. 96ff.
170 *Ibid.*, pp. 115ff.
171 *Ibid.*, pp. 120f.
172 *Ibid.*, pp. 113f.
173 *VfL* 4, 270, 273; de Boor, *Geschichte* III 1, 380, 382; Bumke, *Mäzene*, p. 71; Cramer, *Geschichte*, pp. 112f.
174 *VfL* 3, 838; Cramer, *Geschichte*, pp. 301, 302.
175 Cf. de Boor, *Geschichte* III 2, 108; Bumke, *Geschichte*, pp. 383, 384.
176 *VfL* 3, 706f.
177 Cf. de Boor, *Geschichte* III 2, 410.
178 *VfL* 2, 565; de Boor, *Geschichte* III 1, 192; Heinzle, *Wandlungen*, pp. 75, 76; Bumke, *Geschichte*, p. 350.
179 *VfL* 1, 1056f., 1060; de Boor, *Geschichte* III 1, 497f.; Heinzle, *Wandlungen*, p. 185; Bumke, *Geschichte*, p. 383.
180 Leipold, *Auftraggeber*, pp. 64f.; Brandt, *Konrad*, pp. 72f.; Bumke, *Mäzene*, pp. 262f., 289.
181 Leipold, *Auftraggeber*, pp. 69ff.; Brandt, *Konrad*, p. 73; Bumke, *Mäzene*, pp. 262, 288.
182 Cf. de Boor, *Geschichte* III 2, 147; Bumke, *Geschichte*, p. 381.
183 Bertau, *Literatur*, pp. 961ff.; Krohn, *Gottfried* 3, 215ff.; Tomasek, *Utopie*, pp. 248ff.
184 Cf. de Boor, *Geschichte* II 173.
185 *Ibid.*, III 1, 93 (cf. also *VfL*¹ 3, 1047).
186 Schnell, *Verhältnis*, pp. 48ff.
187 *Ibid.*, p. 52.
188 Outside the context of literature Dilcher, *Oralität*, pp. 9ff., has discussed the interplay between orality and writing in the pragmatic sphere of town laws.
189 *Literatur*, pp. 961ff.
190 Of this group Bertau, p. 962, says that they are a 'Klerus, den man sich nicht zu "klerikal" vorstellen darf'.
191 *Utopie*, pp. 248ff.
192 *Ibid.*, p. 253, fn. 180.
193 Krohn, *Gottfried* III 225f.
194 Unlike Wolfram, Gottfried makes no reference to women in his audience, but it is difficult not to imagine them present, especially as potential readers.

195 *Studien*, pp. 96ff.
196 *Ibid.*, p. 109.
197 *Mäzene*, pp. 288f.
198 2, 1ff.; 5, 1ff.; 8, 1ff. For a detailed discussion see Renk, *Manessekreis*.
199 Cf. Peters, *Literatur*, p. 104.
200 *VfL* 2, 47; Ruh, *Schriften* II 58; Heinzle, *Wandlungen*, pp. 98f.
201 *VfL* 1, 644; Ruh, *Schriften* II 56, 58; Heinzle, *Wandlungen*, pp. 99f; Bumke, *Geschichte*, p. 416.
202 *VfL* 5, 828f.; de Boor, *Geschichte* III 2, 106; Bumke, *Geschichte*, p. 418.
203 Waetzold edn, p. 14; Schmitz, *Dichtungen*, pp. 191f.; de Boor, *Geschichte* III 2, 122.
204 Grundmann, *Bewegungen*, pp. 199ff.
205 *Ibid.*, pp. 225, 457ff., 471.
206 Cf. Elm, *Stellung*, p. 8, who describes the paradox of this phrase as defining 'ihren Ort auf der Grenze zwischen Kloster und Welt, Ordensleben und Laienstand'.
207 Heinzle, *Wandlungen*, p. 98.
208 Grundmann, *Bewegungen*, pp. 338f.
209 *VfL*¹ 4, 467; Teske, *Thomasin*, pp. 13ff.; Bumke, *Mäzene*, pp. 71, 257; *Geschichte*, p. 330.
210 Bumke, *Geschichte*, p. 382.
211 Edn., pp. xif.
212 Bumke, *Mäzene*, pp. 263, 289f.; Brandt, *Konrad*, p. 71f.
213 Cf. Jaeger, *Origins*, and Bumke, *Mäzene*, pp. 256ff.
214 Erdmann, *ZfdA* 73 (1936), 87ff.; Ploss, *JbfrL* 19 (1959), 288ff.
215 Vollmann-Profe, *Wiederbeginn*, p. 34.
216 That the role played by bishops in the Carolingian imperial church system involved them in military obligations has been shown by Prinz, *Klerus*. See also Oexle, *Deutungsschemata*, pp. 96f., for episcopal militias in a later period.
217 Bumke, *Mäzene*, p. 158.
218 Schreiner, *Hof*, pp. 80ff.
219 *Ibid.*, p. 83.
220 Buoncompagno: Teske, *Thomasin*, pp. 34ff.; Heger, *Lebenszeugnis*, pp. 239ff. Eilbert: *VfL* 2, 410; Teske, *Thomasin*, pp. 26ff.; Heger, *Lebenszeugnis*, pp. 238f.
221 Thomasin: Teske, *Thomasin*, pp. 13ff. Walther: Heger, *Lebenszeugnis*, passim. Nibelungenlied: Münz, *Euphorion* 65 (1971), 345ff.; Meves, *Bischof*, pp. 246ff.
222 I have discussed this formula in *Hören*, pp. 23f.
223 There is only one German example (the *Rede vom heiligen Glauben*) which corresponds, imperfectly, to the construction with two verbal abstracts (*auditus et visus*).
224 See above, p. 27.
225 *Policraticus*, PL 199, 387 and 388.
226 Scholz, *Hören*, p. 107; Balogh, *Philologus* 82 (1927), 207, fn. 47.
227 The works (in the sequence in which they were discussed above) are: *Der Saelden Hort*; Hartmann von Aue, *Gregorius* and *Der Arme Heinrich*; Konrad von Fussesbrunnen, *Kindheit Jesu*; Rudolf von Ems, *Barlaam und Josaphat*; Wetzel von Bernau, *Margaretenleben*; Der Stricker, *Karl der Große*; Ulrich von Türheim, *Rennewart*; Ulrich von Zatzikhoven, *Lanzelet*; Wirnt von Grafenberg, *Wigalois*; Albrecht von Scharfenberg, *Jüngerer Titurel*; *Unser Vrouwen Klage*; *Büchlein von der Himmelfahrt Mariae*; Lamprecht von Regensburg, *Sanct Franzisken Leben*; *Das Passional*; *Väterbuch*; Hugo von Trimberg, *Der Renner*; Könemann von Jerxheim, *Wurzgarten Mariens*; Heinrich von Burgeis, *Der Seele Rat*; Heinrich von Neustadt, *Gottes Zukunft*; *Sante Margareten Marter*; Walther von Rheinau, *Marienleben*; Gottfried von Strassburg, *Tristan*; Konrad Fleck, *Flore und Blanscheflur*; David von Augsburg; *Geistlicher Herzen Bavngart*; *Die Lilie*; *Pariser Tagezeiten*; Thomasin von Zerclaere, *Der welsche Gast*. Whereas in *Hören*, p. 25, fn. 10, I included

Rudolf von Ems, *Willehalm von Orlens*, as using a double formula with *oder*, I now omit it because it refers to a work other than Rudolf's.
228 The works are: Rudolf von Ems, *Weltchronik*; *Der Saelden Hort*; *Märterbuch*; Wolfram von Eschenbach, *Parzival*; Der Stricker, *Daniel von dem Blühenden Tal*; Der Arme Hartmann, *Rede vom heiligen Glauben*; *Schwabenspiegel Langform M*; *Sächsische Weltchronik*; *Leben Jesu*; Lamprecht von Regensburg, *Sanct Franzisken Leben*; *Das Passional*; Bruder Philipp, *Marienleben*; *Sächsisches Weichbildrecht*; Brun von Schönebeck, *Hohes Lied*; Gottfried von Strassburg, *Tristan*; *Geistlicher Herzen Bavngart*; Thomasin von Zerclaere, *Der welsche Gast*; Konrad von Heimesfurt, *Urstende*. Neither in this note nor in the preceding one have I been able to list the *Secretum Secretorum* of Hiltgart von Hürnheim, who uses the double formula without *oder* or *und*.
229 Discussed by Scholz, *Hören*, p. 122.
230 Cf. Boehm, *Ort*, pp. 672ff.; Seifert, *AfB* 21 (1977), 226ff.
231 *Etymologiae* I 41. See p. 237.
232 *Ibid.* See p. 238. Isidore terms historical accounts *monumenta* (written texts) which transmit a record of the past. On this written dimension of Roman historiography see Boehm, *Ort*, pp. 674f., and above, p. 20.
233 *Dialogus*, p. 17. See p. 238.
234 *De scripturis* cap. 3, PL 175, 12: *apud veteres nulli licebat scribere res gestas, nisi a se visas.*
235 *Sententie* I 1, 6 (p. 171): *Mos enim hic aput antiquos erat, ut nullus rem gestam que historia proprie appellatur scribere presumeret, nisi eam geri vidisset.*
236 *Gesta Friderici* 2, 41.
237 The evidence is as follows: *Sanct Brandan* 814ff., 841ff.; *Herzog Ernst* 6003ff., 4466ff.; Herbort von Fritzlar, *Liet von Troye* 49ff.; *Moriz von Craun* 37ff.; *Die Klage* 3464ff., 4295ff., 4307ff.; Der Stricker, *Karl der Große* 8233ff.; prose *Lancelot* I 482, 5ff.; II 26, 26ff.; 109, 25ff.; 328, 15ff.; 434, 5ff.; 434, 11ff.; 436, 3ff.; 437, 2ff.; 793, 12ff.; III 383, 15; 388, 5ff.; Rudolf von Ems, *Barlaam und Josaphat* 16022ff., 16036ff.; Rudolf von Ems, *Der guote Gerhart* 6801ff.; Konrad von Würzburg, *Trojanischer Krieg* 296ff., 13080ff.; *Väterbuch* 3438ff., 11275ff., 11499ff., 30529ff.; *Passional* III 100, 52ff.; *Kreuzfahrt des Landgrafen Ludwigs des Frommen von Thüringen* 5404ff. (cf. 3713ff.), 5973ff.; Gundacker von Judenburg, *Christi Hort* 3593ff.
238 The other examples of the formula in the *Väterbuch* are 3441, 11275, 11503.
239 On the historical implications of the German prose *Lancelot* see Heinzle, *Stellung*, pp. 104ff.
240 Cf. Knape, *Historie*, pp. 165ff.
241 See p. 207.
242 Cf. Schmidt-Wiegand, *FMS* 16 (1982), 363ff., especially p. 369.
243 Heuwieser edn, p. 36.
244 MGH Leg. Germ. 5, 2 (p. 407, 4).
245 Bitterauf edn, p. 61.
246 Edn., p. 20, 15.
247 Examples are taken from Kirchhoff, *AfD* 3 (1957), 318, where bibliographical details are given.
248 Wilhelm, *Corpus* I 25, 20 (number 14); 102, 2 (number 65); 132, 15 (number 91).
249 *Ibid.*, 104, 13 (number 68).
250 Clanchy, *Memory*, p. 203; Stock, *Implications*, p. 47.
251 Clanchy, *Memory*, p. 204.
252 E.g. Wilhelm, *Corpus* I 25, 41 (number 16); 68, 7 (number 38); 101, 31 (number 64); 131, 9 (number 89).
253 *Ibid.*, 78, 11 (number 50); 85, 30 (number 52); 124, 35 (number 82); 161, 8 (number 119).
254 *Ibid.*, 104, 13 (number 68); 149, 2 (number 98); 192, 10 (number 165); 221, 12 (number 219).

255 *Ibid.* (for the shorter formula), 102, 2 (number 65); 286, 43 (number 287); 299, 21 (number 309); 312, 2 (number 325); and (for the triple formula) 132, 23 (number 92); 148, 25 (number 97); 157, 10 (number 113); 164, 2 (number 122).
256 When the historical reliability of oral heroic literature comes under clerical attack these works begin to stress their written status as well as their derivation from written sources (see above, p. 162). As regards the romance Haug, *Literaturtheorie*, p. 123, when talking of the prologue to Hartmann's *Iwein*, refers to a 'dichterische(s) Selbstverständnis..., das seine Legitimation aus der Gelehrtheit, aus dem Zugang zur schriftlichen Überlieferung zieht'.

Conclusions for Part II

1 These genres are hymns and catechetical literature, drama, heroic literature, the 'Spielmannsepen', 'Mären' and gnomic poetry.
2 Meister Albrant, *Roßarzneibuch*; *Zwei deutsche Arzneibücher*; Erhart Hesel, *Arzneibuch*; *Mittelniederdeutsches Arzneibuch*.
3 Similar cross-references occur in another legal text, the *Schwabenspiegel Langform M*.
4 *Die heilige Regel für ein vollkommenes Leben*; Mechthild von Magdeburg, *Fließendes Licht*; *Rede von den fünfzehn Graden*; Hartwig von dem Hage, *Sieben Tagzeiten*; *Mariengrüße*; *Von dem englischen Gruoß ein leich*.
5 See above, p. 206.
6 See pp. 375, n. 121, and 165.
7 Street, *Literacy*, pp. 19ff
8 *Ibid.*, pp. 42 and 45.
9 *Ibid.*, pp. 111 and 120. Cf. Clanchy, *Memory*, pp. 219 and 230.
10 *Literacy*, p. 1.
11 *Ibid.*, p. 97.
12 Schreiner, *ZHF* 11 (1984), 257ff., and *Volkssprache*, pp. 468ff.
13 Goody, *Literacy*, pp. 52ff., 44ff., 67f.; Street, *Literacy*, pp. 47ff.
14 Street, *Literacy*, pp. 54f.
15 *Ibid.*, pp. 62f.

9 Literacy, history and fiction

1 Isidore of Seville, *Etymologiae* I 40.
2 *DVjs* 54 (1980), 581ff.
3 E.g. *Rhetorica ad Herennium* I, 8, 13 (*Historia est res gesta ... Argumentum est ficta res*).
4 Cf. von Moos, *PBB* 98 (1976), 93ff.
5 Haug, *Literaturtheorie*, passim.
6 On this subject see Boehm, *Ort*, pp. 663ff., and Seifert, *AfB* 21 (1977), 226ff.
7 *Etymologiae* I 44. Cf. Boehm, *Ort*, p. 678, and Seifert, *AfB* 21 (1977), 229.
8 See above, p. 226. The classical conception of history soon found its way into Christian tradition: the best known example is Luc. 1, 1ff., but it can also be illustrated from other evangelists. Cf. Werner vom Niederrhein, *Die vier Sciven* 17, 8ff. (on the medieval view of the evangelists as writers see above, p. 28).
9 See above, p. 227.
10 Robert of Melun, *Sententie* III 171; Konrad von Hirsau, *Dialogus*, p. 17; Vincent of Beauvais (cf. Seifert, *AfB* 21 (1977), 239, fn. 60); Remigius of Auxerre, *Commentum* II 107.
11 10, 22.
12 *Etymologiae* I 41.
13 1, 8, 13.
14 *Etymologiae* I 41 (cf. above, p. 238).

15 *Ibid.*
16 Cf. Boehm, *Ort*, pp. 674f.
17 *Roman de Troie* 45ff. Homer was a *clers merveillos / E sages e escientos* (45f.), but did not witness the events at Troy (56). Darius too was a *clerc merveillos / E des set arz escientos* (99f.), but wrote about what he had personally seen (105ff.).
18 *Etymologiae* I 41. This reliance on the evidence of one's eyes later finds its way into German vernacular literature. Hugo von Langenstein, in the context of seeing and hearing (*Martina* 48, 100), says: *Swaz man hie mit den ougen siht / Daz weiz man wol vnd zwivilt niht* (48, 103f.). The author of *Sanct Brandan* uses the same trust in what is seen (44ff.) to aid his own case: he implies a parallel between Brandan's actual disbelief and the potential disbelief of his audience, whose doubts are to be allayed by what Brandan witnesses on his voyage.
19 *Dialogus*, p. 17.
20 See above, p. 20.
21 *Pro L. Murena* 7, 16. Cf. Grundmann, *AfK* 40 (1958), 17.
22 *Germania* 2, 3; *Annales* II 88.
23 Einhard, *Vita Karoli* 29 (p. 33).
24 Cf. Much, *Germania*, p. 21.
25 *Ibid.*, p. 27.
26 *Getica*, paragraph 28 (p. 61).
27 See above, p. 333, n. 12.
28 Vollmann-Profe, *Kommentar*, p. 67.
29 Cf. Haug and Vollmann, *Literatur*, p. 1097, note to 80, 119–122.
30 *Gesta*, p. 3.
31 Cf. Hauck, *Heldendichtung*, pp. 118ff.
32 Höfler, *Anonymität*, p. 387; Grundmann, *Geschichtsschreibung*, pp. 7ff.
33 Höfler, *Anonymität*, p. 387; Wenskus, *ZfbLg* 36 ii (1973), 393ff.; Störmer, *Nibelungentradition*, pp. 1ff.
34 Cf. Clanchy, *History* 55 (1970), 172.
35 *Ibid.*, p. 165.
36 *Ibid.*, p. 168. At the conclusion of his essay (p. 176) Clanchy remarks that writing has given us true history, but robbed us of the immediate relevance of history to society.
37 *Revolution*, p. 23; *Preface*, pp. 121f.
38 *Tradition*, p. 24.
39 *Ibid.*, p. 120.
40 *HZ* 233 (1981), 576.
41 *Ibid.*, p. 580.
42 *Literacy*, pp. 32ff.
43 *Ibid.*, p. 33.
44 *Ibid.*, p. 32.
45 Cf. Frappier, *Chansons, passim*; Heinzle, *Dietrichepik*, pp. 223ff.
46 Haubrichs, *Anfänge*, pp. 136f.
47 Cf. Kolb, *Heldendichtung*, p. 448.
48 Haubrichs, *Heldensage*, p. 199; Vollrath, *HZ* 233 (1981), 575.
49 See also Wolf, *Traditions*, pp. 69ff.
50 Marold, *Darstellung*, pp. 167f.
51 *Ibid.*, pp. 172, 174.
52 Arguing with a different end in view (the 'neotraditionalist' view of the oral prehistory of the *Chanson de Roland*) Menéndez Pidal, *Chanson*, p. 274, has made a similar point.
53 In the following our concern will not be whether a particular work actually presents the historical truth in an objective sense, but rather with the kinds of argument put forward by medieval authors to suggest their historical reliability.

54 Cf. Simon, *AfD* 5/6 (1959/60), 90.
55 *Ibid.*, p. 91.
56 *Getica*, paragraph 38 (pp. 63f.). Discussed by Wagner, *Getica*, pp. 60ff.
57 *Chronica*, MGH SS 6, 130. Discussed by Gschwantler, *Heldensage*, pp. 219ff.; Hauck, *Heldendichtung*, p. 124; Ploss, *JbfrL* 19 (1959), 285ff.
58 *Chronica*, MGH SS 6, 130.
59 *Ibid.*
60 *Chronicon*, p. 232. Discussed by Gschwantler, *Heldensage*, pp. 232ff.
61 *Chronicon*, p. 232.
62 *Chronik*, pp. 376f. This chronicle is discussed by Gschwantler, *Heldensage*, pp. 266ff.
63 Heinzle, *Dietrichepik*, pp. 271ff. (despite Bräuer, *Literatur*, p. 779, n. 43).
64 *Chronik*, p. 380.
65 *Ibid.*
66 14164ff.
67 14176ff. Discussed by Gschwantler, *Heldensage*, pp. 239f., and *Zeugnisse*, pp. 45ff.
68 14187.
69 Gschwantler, *Zeugnisse*, p. 55, concludes his discussion of two possible interpretations of 14176ff. by saying: 'in jedem Fall wird mit Nachdruck der Vorrang des Buches gegenüber der mündlichen Überlieferung postuliert'.
70 *Einladung*, p. 230.
71 *Literacy*, pp. 53f.
72 *Tradition*, pp. 121f. It is true that Goody himself talks of a 'homeostatic tendency' in oral society (*Literacy*, p. 33), but this sits unhappily with the categorical statement in the same sentence that 'the annals of a literate society *cannot but enforce* a more objective recognition of the distinction between what was and what is' (my italics).
73 See above, p. 8.
74 Cf. Sowinski, *Herzog Ernst*, p. 406.
75 Vollmann-Profe, *Wiederbeginn*, p. 37.
76 Ebenbauer, *Stoffe*, pp. 271, 274; Bumke, *Geschichte*, p. 64.
77 Ott-Meimberg, *Karl*, pp. 81, 83; Vollmann-Profe, *Wiederbeginn*, pp. 134f. Of Henry the Lion's commission of a German version it is said (9034): dâ ist daz rîche wol mit gêret.
78 Röcke, *Abenteuerromane*, p. 404; Vollmann-Profe, *Wiederbeginn*, pp. 228f.
79 Herkommer, *DVjs* 50 (1976), 44ff.; Vollmann-Profe, *Wiederbeginn*, pp. 230f.; Bumke, *Geschichte*, pp. 76f.
80 Knab, *Annolied*, pp. 75ff.; Vollmann-Profe, *Wiederbeginn*, p. 37; Kartschoke, *Geschichte*, p. 338.
81 *Alexanderlied* 4; *Rolandslied* 9079.
82 Bumke, *Mäzene*, p. 83; Vollmann-Profe, *Wiederbeginn*, pp. 44, 46.
83 *VfL* 5, 88f.; Meves, *Studien*, p. 98; Bumke, *Geschichte*, p. 75.
84 Sowinski, *Herzog Ernst*, p. 421; Vollmann-Profe, *Wiederbeginn*, p. 231.
85 *Annolied* 20, 4; 26, 5 (cf. Vollmann-Profe, *Wiederbeginn*, p. 107; Kartschoke, *Geschichte*, p. 337; Haug and Vollmann, *Literatur*, p. 1440, note to 620, 26, 10); *Alexanderlied* (S) 18, 1714, 1959ff. (cf. Bumke, *Mäzene*, p. 105; *Geschichte*, p. 61); *Kaiserchronik* 15ff., 186 (cf. Bumke, *Mäzene*, p. 83); *Rolandslied* 16, 3762, 9020ff., 9079ff. (cf. Kartschoke, *PBB* 111 (1989), 196ff.); *König Rother* 16, 3480; *Herzog Ernst* 2244f., 4466ff. (cf. Sowinski, *Herzog Ernst*, p. 421).
86 *Kaiserchronik* 16534.
87 *Rolandslied* 8.
88 *König Rother*, Berlin fragment IIa, 11ff. (cf. Meves, *Studien*, p. 97; Vollmann-Profe, *Wiederbeginn*, pp. 130f.).
89 See above, p. 101.
90 Cf. Shaw, *Epos*, p. 291.

91 With the exception of the *Annolied* (for which lay patronage is unlikely) cf. Bumke, *Mäzene*, pp. 75ff., on the patrons for these works.
92 Cf. Schirmer and Broich, *Studien*, pp. 43ff.; Bezzola, *Origines* III 2, 149ff., 269ff.
93 Cf. Metzner, *Geschichtsdichtung*, pp. 623ff.
94 4467ff.: whoever doubts the truth of this story is recommended to consult the text written in Latin at Bamberg to be persuaded of the truth (4475f.). We have seen (p. 125) that the author is far from expecting anyone to do what he recommends, but this in no way weakens the case he makes for historical veracity. It is further strengthened in this passage by the placing in the imperial crown of the jewel brought back from the East by Ernst (4464ff.), for that, too, confirms the truth of the story (4466). Cf. Sowinski, *Herzog Ernst*, p. 390, but also p. 421. On concrete (non-written) objects as surviving testimony to what is reported of the past see below, n. 101.
95 3479ff., 4784ff., and the Berlin fragment IIa, 5ff. On these passages see Schnell, *PBB* 104 (1982), 345ff.
96 *Historia ecclesiastica*, MGH SS 9, 355, 54. Cf. Wenzel, *Geschichte*, p. 70, and Schnell, *PBB* 104 (1982), 347f.
97 Cf. also 4299: *in latînischen buochstaben*.
98 Cf. Curschmann, *Nibelungenlied*, p. 107; Kartschoke, *PBB* 111 (1989), 197f., 199f.
99 A historical importance, going far beyond the *Klage*, can be claimed for this passage if we connect it with the transfer of heroic epics to writing in the thirteenth century, starting with the *Nibelungenlied* (see above, pp. 161f.).
100 Discussed by Szklenar, *Poetica* 9 (1977), 51f.
101 Physical testimony which can still be seen is sometimes adduced as confirmation of the truth of a work. This we have seen in the case of the 'Waise' jewel in the imperial crown in *Herzog Ernst* 4464ff., but it is also true of the physical presence of a grave to support the reliability of a legend (*Väterbuch* 10074ff.). Cf. also the 'Märe' *Constantin* (96ff.) and the reference to the spring in the Odenwald where Siegfried met his end in *Nibelungenlied* C (1013, 1ff.).
102 XIII 78ff. (p. 17).
103 On the medieval view of the legend as *historia* see Knape, *Historie*, pp. 168ff.
104 Cf. also 1322ff. for the relevance of St John's account of doubting Thomas (1330: *er ensêhe selber sîne wunde*).
105 2443ff.
106 *Böhmenschlacht* 172 (*Vnd das mine ougen namen war*, cf. also 58f.); *Schlacht bei Göllheim* 60 (*Mir sagete ein ritter, der it sach*, cf. also 242f.).
107 7759ff., 53864ff. A negative example is provided by 33956ff.
108 II 1ff. The author then proceeds to tell the *wârheit* (9) on the authority of Ulrich von Lichtenstein, whose ethical standing (13, 18) is such that he can be equated with those eyewitnesses trusted by historians because they are *veraces* (see above, pp. 242f.).
109 Two examples from 'Mären' where the author claims to have witnessed himself what he recounts are *Der weiße Rosendorn* 1ff. and *Meier Helmbrecht* 7f.
110 Cf. also 321ff. The other examples are Wetzel von Bernau, *Margaretenleben* 1171ff., and Hartwig von dem Hage, *Margaretenlegende* 83ff.
111 Cf. 4ff., 63ff., 2147ff.
112 1104f., 4003, 4081, but also the presence of acrostics (see above, p. 132).
113 *Passional* I/II 324, 31ff.; 326, 49ff. and III 100, 52ff.; *Väterbuch* 3438ff., 11275ff., 30529ff.; *Alexius* A 696ff. (with reference to Alexius himself); *Leben der heiligen Elisabeth* 9756ff.
114 On the Bible as *historia* see Knape, *Historie*, pp. 134ff.
115 Werner vom Niederrhein, *Die vier Sciven* 17, 3ff. (where the evangelist is also described as *ein harde warhaftir man*, cf. the *veraces* above, pp. 242f.); *Passional* I/II 324, 31ff.; 326, 49ff.
116 1309ff., 3593ff.
117 *Evangelium Nicodemi* 679ff.

118 Walther von Rheinau, *Marienleben* 14012ff.; Heinrich von Neustadt, *Gottes Zukunft* 1255ff.
119 *Moriz von Craun* 33ff.; Herbort von Fritzlar, *Liet von Troye* 52ff.; Konrad von Würzburg, *Trojanischer Krieg* 296ff., 13080ff.
120 Rudolf von Ems, *Alexander* 2202ff.; Ottokar, *Österreichische Reimchronik* 19461ff.; *Kreuzfahrt des Landgrafen Ludwigs des Frommen von Thüringen* 5404ff., 3713ff., also 5973ff. (the author says that he will name some who took part in accordance with what he has learned from a knight who saw and heard what happened, whilst elsewhere he describes how the Emperor instructed a monk Walther to write down the exploits of the eponymous hero).
121 8233ff. The need for an omniscient angel arises from the possible objection that, if all the rearguard fell at Roncesvalles, how can the author know of their exploits in such detail (cf. Menéndez Pidal, *Chanson*, p. 283). This is an objection which Hartmann von Aue meets on the plane of fiction (see p. 256), whereas Der Stricker deals with it in terms of the historicity of a legend. On Der Stricker's argument see also Kartschoke, *PBB* 111 (1989), 198.
122 244, 5ff. and 246, 2f.
123 An example also occurs in Rudolf von Ems, *Der guote Gerhart* 6801ff. (said of the Emperor personally involved in the events narrated). For this work Brackert, *Rudolf*, pp. 205f., has made the case that it was meant to be regarded as *historia*. One example is known to me from 'Mären': *Das Rädlein* 5ff., whose author claims to owe his written account to an eyewitness.
124 *Legendar aus dem Anfang des 12. Jahrhunderts* 329; Hugo von Langenstein, *Martina* 231, 47ff.; *Märterbuch* 19387ff. (cf. also 19813ff., 23879ff.).
125 *Passional* I/II 365, 91ff.; *Leben der heiligen Elisabeth* 307ff. (cf. 3461ff.); *Alexius A* 731ff. (cf. *Alexius F* 1315ff.). Cf. also Alber's *Tnugdalus* 27ff.
126 965ff.
127 Also to be grouped here are four works which Ebenbauer, *Dilemma*, pp. 52ff., classifies as 'historisierende Romane': *Die gute Frau* 3019ff., 3033ff.; Rudolf von Ems, *Willehalm von Orlens* 15582ff.; *Flos unde Blankeflos* 1471ff.; Konrad Fleck, *Flore und Blanscheflur* 7862ff. Of these Ebenbauer says (p. 53) that they testify the 'Zunahme des "Historischen" im Roman des 13. Jahrhunderts'.
128 *Legendar aus dem Anfang des 12. Jahrhunderts* 329ff.; Alber's *Tnugdalus* 27ff. (cf. also the *Niederrheinische Tundalusfragmente* 50ff.); Ebernand von Erfurt, *Heinrich und Kunigunde* 151ff. Cf. also Reinbot von Durne, *Der heilige Georg* 381ff.; *Passional* I/II 330, 24ff. and III 116, 79ff.; *Leben der heiligen Elisabeth* 325ff., 3461ff., 9921ff.
129 *Livländische Reimchronik* 8495ff.; Ottokar's *Österreichische Reimchronik* 223ff., 965ff., 53860ff.
130 The three examples known to me from French literature belong to the same range of historical genres attested for Germany: the *Roman de Troie* of Benoît de Sainte-Maure (87ff.) concerns the history of classical antiquity, the prologue to the prose translation of the *Historia Karoli Magni et Rotholandi* (Mölk, *Literarästhetik*, pp. 100ff.) falls under the heading of medieval history, whilst the *Vie de saint Thomas* by Guernes de Pont-Sainte-Maxence (146ff.) is a saint's legend. All three French examples take up a position as regards the problem of orality or writing: Benoît in his contrast between Homer and Darius concerning written tradition (see above, p. 238), the prologue to the *Historia* by granting second place to *oïr dire* (11, 27), the legend by its conjunction of hearing with lying (146).
131 I have presented the above argument in compressed form in *RPL* 10 (1987), 159ff.
132 On Geoffrey as a cleric see Parry and Caldwell, *Geoffrey*, pp. 73f.
133 See the edition by Griscom, p. 219.
134 Schirmer, *Darstellungen*, pp. 8, 17ff. (and fn. 54–6).

135 *Ibid.*, p. 12, fn. 18, and p. 29.
136 Cf. Knape, *Historie*, pp. 80f.
137 See Mertens, *Artus*, pp. 291f.
138 *Ibid.*, p. 292; Johanek, *FMS* 21 (1987), 351f.
139 Schirmer, *Darstellungen*, pp. 16f., 31; Johanek, *FMS* 21 (1987), 354, 361, 366.
140 Johanek, *FMS* 21 (1987), 354.
141 *Ibid.*, p. 366.
142 Cf. Loomis, *Diffusion*, pp. 52ff.; Parry and Caldwell, *Geoffrey*, pp. 83ff.
143 Johanek, *FMS* 21 (1987), 350.
144 John Hardyng, *Chronicle*, p. 131. Cf. Johanek, *FMS* 21 (1987), 357.
145 Schirmer, *Darstellungen*, p. 18.
146 *Gesta* I 11.
147 *Historia* I 11, 12, 18.
148 *Ibid.*, p. 13. Cf. Johanek, *FMS* 21 (1987), 377.
149 *Historia* I 17.
150 See above, p. 244.
151 *Descriptio* VI 179 and 208.
152 *De speculo* II 51 (p. 90). Cf. Curschmann, *GRM* 69 (1988), 348.
153 See above, p. 108.
154 Cf. Johanek, *FMS* 21 (1987), 378.
155 Schwietering, *Typologisches*, pp. 40f. Marichal, *Naissance*, discusses the use of *romanz* for vernacular as opposed to Latin texts, applied first to French narratives with a classical theme.
156 See above, p. 238.
157 *Brut* 1ff. Cf. Marichal, *Naissance*, p. 453.
158 Köhler, *Selbstauffassung*, p. 12; Ruh, *Epik* I 100f.; Mertens, *Artus*, p. 295; Haug, *Literaturtheorie*, p. 92. Klopsch, *Name*, pp. 147ff., has also argued that the author of *Ruodlieb* made use of heroic material because this tied his hands less in fashioning a non-historical, fictional narrative. This raises the question how far the development of fiction in the vernacular may have had precedents in Latin.
159 *Origines* III 1, 66f.
160 *Ibid.*, p. 67. That these classical themes were also regarded as historical in their German adaptations is clear from the placing of the *Alexanderlied* in the context of 'Heilsgeschichte' (Vollmann-Profe, *Wiederbeginn*, p. 207) and has been suggested for Veldeke's *Eneide* by Thomas, *ZfdPh* 108 (1989), *Sonderheft*, pp. 65ff. (cf. also Kartschoke, *Eneasroman*, pp. 869ff.)
161 Schmolke-Hasselmann, *Versroman*, p. 147.
162 Haug, *Literaturtheorie*, p. 121.
163 Cf. Tomasek, *Utopie*; Mohr, *Fabula* I (1958), 201ff.; Völker, *Elemente*; Niessen, *Märchenmotive*; Mauritz, *Ritter*; Nolting-Hauff, *Poetica* 6 (1974), 129ff.; Cormeau, *Wolfram-Studien* 5 (1979), 63ff.; Green, *FMS* 14 (1980), 352ff.
164 See above, p. 244.
165 Schirmer, *Darstellungen*, p. 45.
166 *Roman de Brut* 1211f.
167 *Ibid.*, 1247ff.
168 Cf. Zink, *CCM* 24 (1981), 19.
169 Köhler, *Selbstauffassung*, p. 13; Knapp, *DVjs* 54 (1980), 599.
170 *Roman de Rou* 6396.
171 *Ibid.*, 6410.
172 *Ibid.*, 6415ff.
173 *Etymologiae* I 44.
174 *Literaturtheorie*, p. 90.

175 *Erec* 23ff. Cf. Zink, CCM 24 (1981), 20.
176 *Perceval* 7f. Cf. Zink, CCM 24 (1981), 21.
177 See *Sprachkunst* 2 (1971), 15ff., and *Löwenritter*, pp. 214ff. Cf. also Haug, *Land*, pp. 65f.
178 Vv. 171ff.
179 As in Chrétien's *Erec* and in German literature in the case of the *Annolied* and the *Kaiserchronik* (see above, p. 101).
180 See above, p. 251. Cf. Wace's use of *fable* (*Roman de Brut* 1212) and *fabler* (*Roman de Rou* 6396).
181 Vv. 176f. That *avantures* and *merveilles* are closely related for Calogrenant is suggested by 362ff. and by the *mervoille* which he finds at the spring (432).
182 Vv. 174.
183 Vv. 577f.
184 Wolf, *Sprachkunst* 2 (1971), 17f.
185 *Ibid.*, p. 18.
186 Cf. Ollier, YFS 51 (1974), 28f.
187 Vv. 9ff., especially 19ff.
188 Haug, *Literaturtheorie*, p. 103.
189 *Ibid.*, p. 102, fn. 17, for further literature, to which may be added Uitti, *Vernacularization*, p. 96, who suggests a link with John of Salisbury.
190 Köhler, *Selbstauffassung*, p. 13; Ruh, *Epik* I 98ff., especially 101.
191 See above, p. 245. Cf. also Wolf, *Kultur*, *passim*, who stresses this aspect of German literature with regard to topical history, imperial history and a clerical view of 'Heilsgeschichte'.
192 Cf. Ruh, *Epik* I 108. The same point is made frequently by Wolf, *Kultur*, and also by Illmer in that same volume in connection with the educational consequences of the Investiture Contest (pp. 149ff.).
193 Vv. 1032ff. Cf. also 1035: *sît ez nieman sach*.
194 Cf. Knopf, *Frühzeit*, pp. 1f.
195 Christ, *Rhetorik*, p. 317.
196 *Ibid.*
197 Vv. 2443ff. (see above, p. 247).
198 Vv. 8946ff.
199 *Shape*, pp. 164f.
200 *Ibid.*, p. 165.
201 Arndt, *Erzähler*, p. 157.
202 Vv. 7620f., 7630f.
203 Vv. 7485f.
204 In the lines (7487ff.) immediately following the two just quoted Hartmann illustrates his position with regard to Isidore's argument. He says that if he himself never witnessed the horse's saddle he at least writes in full conformity with his source, which he specifies as a written one (7491). The lack of a witness makes it all the more important to stress the other dimension of Isidore's definition.
205 Vv. 7278ff.
206 Vv. 7459f.
207 The presence of this fictional world later explains the narrator's unreadiness to believe in the (factual) truth of his own construction, 9209f.
208 FMS 19 (1985), 26f.
209 The first suggestion was made by Sawicki, *Gottfried*, p. 158, whilst the qualification came from Knapp, *DVjs* 54 (1980), 600. On the relationship between history and fiction in Gottfried's work see Chinca, *History*.
210 Vv. 155ff.
211 Brackert, *Rudolf*, pp. 151ff.

212 *Ibid.*, pp. 152f.
213 *Istôrje*: 448, 5884, 15919, 18696 (cf. Knape, *Historie*, pp. 112ff.). *Geste*: 8946 (cf. Green, *Oral poetry*, p. 215).
214 Knape, *Historie*, p. 114.
215 Vv. 18467ff.
216 Vv. 17104.
217 Vv. 17140ff.
218 See the note to v. 17142 in Ganz's edition, II 330. Further bibliographical references are given by Okken, *Kommentar* II 80 (n. 1621).
219 Vv. 10074ff.
220 On the timeless dimension of the grotto see Tomasek, *Utopie*, p. 153.
221 Christ, *Rhetorik*, pp. 313f. In what follows I owe much to Christ, pp. 291ff.
222 Christ, *Rhetorik*, p. 314.
223 Vv. 8605ff. Cf. Christ, *Rhetorik*, pp. 296f.
224 Vv. 8626f.
225 Christ, *Rhetorik*, p. 297.
226 *Literatur*, p. 921.
227 Vv. 6878ff. Cf. Christ, *Rhetorik*, pp. 302ff.
228 Vv. 6897f., 6901.
229 Vv. 16811ff. Cf. Christ, *Rhetorik*, pp. 310ff.
230 Vv. 16906ff., 16920ff.
231 Christ, *Rhetorik*, pp. 305ff.
232 Vv. 4557ff.
233 Vv. 4589ff.
234 Hatto, *Tristan*, p. 104, translates *maere* in v. 4557 by 'source', but in v. 4594 by 'story'.
235 Vv. 4963ff.
236 Vv. 4976f.
237 Cf. Christ, *Rhetorik*, p. 322.
238 *WW* 20 (1970), 289ff. Cf. also Christ, *Rhetorik*, pp. 323ff.
239 That Tristan, just as much as the narrator, is concerned with this is made clear by 3120: *nu habt ir al mîn dinc vernomen. / i'ne weiz, wie'z iu gevalle.*
240 Cf. Green, *Advice*, pp. 64ff.
241 504,1ff.
242 See above, p. 257.
243 15, 11ff. and 381, 28ff.
244 397, 7f.
245 XIII 78ff. (p. 17). See above, p. 247.
246 *MLR* 67 (1972), 820ff.
247 Cf. Green, *Aventiure*, pp. 110ff.
248 The two passages mentioned above where the source has to stand in for a witness belong here: 15, 11ff. (discussed in *Aventiure*, pp. 112f.) and 381, 28ff. (*ibid.*, p. 117).
249 *MLR* 67 (1972), 826.
250 *Aufsätze*, pp. 90f.
251 Cf. Schultz, *Shape*, p. 162.
252 74, 10ff.; 737, 25; 827, 17.
253 216, 9ff.
254 Schultz, *Shape*, p. 163.
255 14, 12ff.; 263, 30.
256 59, 26f.
257 271, 14f.
258 327, 26.
259 349, 28; 353, 1.

260 778, 26.
261 238, 8ff.
262 *Yvain* 149ff.
263 Gallais, *CCM* 7 (1964), 491.
264 Hunt, *FMLS* 6 (1970), 14; *FMLS* 8 (1972), 328; Green, *Oral poetry*, pp. 172f.
265 *Hören*, p. 175, fn. 697.
266 The closest approach is the reference by Giraldus Cambrensis to *Arturi nostri famosi, ne dicam fabulosi* (see above p. 251), but even this may apply more to what is reported about him than to the historical person himself.
267 Ott, *Kompilation*, p. 134.
268 Ott, *Chronistik*, pp. 182f., 198f., and *Kompilation*, pp. 123f.
269 Cf. Heinzle, *Wandlungen*, p. 135.
270 Heinzle, *Stellung*, p. 109; Metzner, *Geschichtsdichtung*, pp. 623ff.
271 See above, pp. 255f.
272 Bumke, *Geschichte*, p. 207, where the necessary qualifications are made.
273 *Ibid.*, pp. 208, 211. Cf. Cramer, *Geschichte*, pp. 16f., on the fourteenth century.
274 Cramer, *Geschichte*, p. 18; Schnell, *Verhältnis*, passim.
275 Schnell, *Prosaauflösung*, p. 231.
276 Cf. Ebenbauer, *Dilemma*, p. 53.
277 Heinzle, *Stellung*, p. 108. See Knapp, *DVjs* 54 (1980), 583f., for a discussion of Jean Bodel's equation of the truth of the chansons de geste with their historical reliability (*res gesta* as opposed to the *res ficta* of the Arthurian romance – on this contrast see Schmolke-Hasselmann, *Versroman*, pp. 246f.).
278 See Haug, *DVjs* 54 (1980), 204f.
279 As established in detail by Brackert, *Rudolf*.
280 *Ibid.*, p. 239.
281 Cf. von Ertzdorff, *Rudolf*, pp. 269ff. (Petrus Comestor and Godfrey of Viterbo).
282 *Ibid.*, pp. 101ff; Wehrli, *Geschichte*, p. 489.
283 V. 6814. Cf. Brackert, *Rudolf*, pp. 200ff., 208.
284 *Ibid.*, p. 207.
285 *Literaturtheorie*, p. 246.
286 *Prosaauflösung*, p. 230.
287 *PBB* 112 (1990), 76f.
288 *Stellung*, pp. 104ff.
289 *Ibid.*, p. 108.
290 On this interpretation of the Arthurian world see Freytag, *Mundus*, pp. 134ff.
291 These references are discussed by Knape, *Historie*, pp. 213ff.
292 Only some references are discussed by Knape, *Historie*, p. 235. These need to be supplemented by Speckenbach, *Endzeiterwartung*, p. 210, fn. 1.
293 I 482, 5f.
294 III 383, 15: *Da sie hetten geeßen in dem hoff, der konig Artus det her vor kuommen die schriber, die da pflagen zu beschriben die abenture der ritter von dem hoff des koniges Artus. Und da Bohort hett erzalt die abenture von dem heyligen gral, in der wise als er es gesehen hett, und die wurden beschriben und behalten in der abtey von Salaberis.*
295 The reference II 689, 20ff. to an earlier passage distinguished by its script and giving a date is to 673, 17f., where the date given is 226 (cf. also the fn. to 670, 25). Cf. however Ruh, *Literatur*, p. 131, where the different dating does not alter the fact that a date is after all given.
296 Heinzle, *Stellung*, pp. 109f.; Ruh, *Wolfram-Studien* 1 (1970), 260ff.
297 Cf. Kolb, *Munsalvaesche*, pp. 51ff.; Ragotzky, *Studien*, pp. 110f.; Mohr, *Aufsätze*, p. 188.
298 Cf. Ragotzky, *Studien*, p. 110; Haug, *Literaturtheorie*, p. 356.
299 As is suggested by Ebenbauer, *ZfdA* 108 (1979), 398ff.

300 *Ibid.*, pp. 398f.
301 *Ibid.*, pp. 401f.
302 *Ibid.*, pp. 402f.
303 Discussed by Thornton, *Weltgeschichte*.
304 Cf. Cramer's edition of *Lohengrin*, pp. 130ff.
305 *Ibid.*, pp. 163ff. The survey of the Saxon dynasty begins with stanza 731.
306 Heinzle, *Stellung*, p. 110.
307 Cf. Heinzle, *Stellung*, p. 109; Ebenbauer, *Dilemma*, pp. 68f.; Ott, *Kompilation*, pp. 133f. This is in full agreement with the argument of Schnell, *Verhältnis*.
308 See Riley, *Theory*, especially pp. 163ff.; Williamson, *House*.
309 The second half of this chapter appeared in abbreviated form in *Fiction*, pp. 95ff.
310 The correlation of romance, fiction and literacy underlies Haug's *Literaturtheorie*, but questions about fiction have been raised by Heinzle, *PBB* 112 (1990), 55ff. Romance and fiction are discussed by Jauss, *Genese*, pp. 423ff., but questioned by Gumbrecht, *Fiktional*, pp. 433ff.
311 Rösler, *Poetica* 12 (1980), 283ff., and *Schriftkultur*, pp. 109ff.
312 Cf. Haug, *Literaturtheorie*, p. 105; Rösler, *Poetica* 12 (1980), 309f. The decisive argument was made by Aristotle in his *Poetics*, Chapter 9 (Potts, *Aristotle*, p. 29).
313 The freedom of manoeuvre which this made possible has been described by Pérennec, *Recherches* I 295. The conjunction of orality, writing and fiction in the case of Chrétien has also been stressed by Curschmann in his review of Haug, *Literaturtheorie*, *GRM* 69 (1988), 349.
314 *Wiederbeginn*, pp. 195f.

10 Recital and reading in their historical context

1 For a first sketch of this section see Green, *LwJb* 30 (1989), 9ff.
2 The definition of OHG literature by Sonderegger, *Literatur*, p. 189, is acceptable as a factual statement, but by failing to substantiate what is meant by 'in verschiedenartiger Dichte' it leaves unmentioned this gap in time.
3 Ehrismann, *Geschichte* I 364ff. This Latin literature was written for a different audience, under different conditions and on a different level than German, so that disparate phenomena are being equated. Moreover, to discuss Latin literature in the tenth and eleventh centuries should have meant also taking it into account in the preceding and following periods. Ehrismann's procedure has been criticised by Schröder, *Grenzen*, pp. 20f., and Rupp, *GRM* 8 (1950), 19f. See also Geuenich, *DA* 39 (1983), 109 (quoting from Langosch).
4 Stammler, *Schriften*, p. 9.
5 Meissburger, *Grundlagen*, pp. 268ff., especially 268, 275. This approach has been criticised by Schröder, *ZfdA* 100 (1971), 195ff.
6 As is done more logically by Baesecke in treating oral genres in the first volume of his literary history, expressly entitled *Vorgeschichte des deutschen Schrifttums*.
7 Klopsch, *Latein*, p. 330; Guerreau-Jalabert, *BEC* 139 (1981), 26, fn. 4; Wright, *Latin*, pp. 144, 148.
8 Cf. Schröder, *Grenzen*.
9 For this the best short survey is still Baesecke, *Schriften*, pp. 102f.
10 Kartschoke, *Geschichte*, pp. 64f.
11 Wolf, *Kultur*, pp. 33f.
12 Haubrichs, *Anfänge*, pp. 281, 307f.
13 Ullmann, *Principles*, pp. 117ff., argues that the theocratic king, by deriving his authority from God (*rex Dei gratia*), had emancipated himself from the people, the earlier source of the king's power.
14 Ehrismann, *Geschichte* I 290ff., lists the evidence for this.

15 Riché, *Ecoles*, p. 70. That the Roman Empire was similarly dependent on writing has been shown by Harris, *Literacy*, pp. 154f., 206, 232, 332f.
16 McKitterick, *Church*, pp. 45ff.; Feldbusch, *Sprache*, pp. 222ff.
17 Rupp, *Dichtungen*, p. 308.
18 Riché, *Ecoles*, pp. 316f.
19 For the *Heliand* see Haubrichs, *Praefatio*, pp. 400ff. For Otfrid see Vollmann-Profe, *Kommentar*, pp. 4f., and *Otfrid*, pp. 204ff.
20 Geuenich, *DA* 39 (1983), 112, 121f., 129f.
21 Vollmann-Profe, *Kommentar*, p. 5; Mohr and Haug, *Muspilli*, pp. 74ff. On Otfrid see Haug and Vollmann, *Literatur*, p. 1098, note to 84, 1–92, 126.
22 There was resistance to Charles's policy even in his own day (Illmer in Wolf, *Kultur*, pp. 143f.).
23 Cf. Haubrichs, *Bildungswesen*, p. 604; *Anfänge*, p. 329.
24 Uytfanghe, *Francia* 11 (1983), 603, also draws attention to Ludwig's aloofness from the German language.
25 Feldbusch, *Sprache*, pp. 328ff.; McKitterick, *Carolingians*, pp. 220f.
26 Feldbusch, *Sprache*, pp. 327f. Cf. also Schützeichel, *Bezeichnung*, p. 31, and Jacobsen, *Literatur*, pp. 437ff.
27 An example of intellectual isolation in the geographical sense has been given by Schröder, *ZfdA* 100 (1971), 205, in the case of Candidus.
28 On the discontinuity of even the vocabulary of OHG cf. Günther, *PBB* 112 (1990), 352.
29 Liut. 74ff.
30 *Ibid.*, 12ff. Cf. Schröder, *ZfdA* 100 (1971), 196.
31 Piper edn I 860, 32ff. Cf. Schröder, *ZfdA* 100 (1971), 196, 204.
32 Kelle, *Geschichte* I 394, 10: *primus barbaricam scribens faciensque saporam*.
33 Sonderegger, *Sprache*, p. 104; Geuenich, *DA* 39 (1983), 127.
34 Thelen, *Dichtergebet*, p. 213, makes the same point from a more restricted point of view.
35 Schröder, *Verhältnis*, p. 430; Kartschoke, *Geschichte*, p. 154; Haug and Vollmann, *Literatur*, p. 1225, note to 262, 16f.
36 Schröder, *Verhältnis*, p. 437.
37 *Ibid.*, and *ZfdA* 100 (1971), 208.
38 Kartschoke, *Geschichte*, pp. 53f., 269f., and especially Haug and Vollmann, *Literatur*, p. 1407. Hellgardt, *Textensembles*, p. 19, stresses that the MS tradition of these works starts only in the twelfth century.
39 Although Williram's *Hohes Lied* conservatively belongs to the OHG tradition now coming to an end (Haubrichs, *Geschichte*, pp. 276ff.), it also belongs to this new context: not just because of its dating around 1060, but because, like these other works, it enjoyed a further (much richer) manuscript tradition and was the basis for a later work, the *St. Trudperter Hohes Lied* (Sonderegger, *Sprache*, p. 113).
40 This point is placed in a wider context by Grubmüller, *Gegebenheiten*, p. 217.
41 Erdmann, *Entstehung*, p. 66.
42 *Ibid.*
43 Cf. Flori, *Idéologie*, pp. 121ff.; *Essor*, pp. 164ff.
44 Haug, *Schriftlichkeit*, p. 146.
45 See still Mirbt, *Publizistik*. Cf. Althoff, *Geschichtsschreibung*, p. 97, fn. 10.
46 Cf. Leclercq, *Monks*, pp. 9f.
47 Cf. von See, *Frühmittelalter*, p. 30.
48 On the distinction between these two see pp. 285f.
49 Kartschoke, *Geschichte*, p. 214.
50 Grundmann, *Bewegungen*, pp. 492, 503ff.
51 *Ibid.*, pp. 507f.
52 *Ibid.*, p. 509.

53 *Ibid.*, p. 524.
54 *Ibid.*, p. 510. Cf. Haverkamp. *Aufbruch*, p. 170.
55 *Cur ipse, qui monachus ac mundo mortuus erat, viventibus praedicaret?* (Grundmann, *Bewegungen*, p. 511). Cf. Johanek, *Klosterstudien*, pp. 42f.
56 Ullmann, *Denken*, p. 22.
57 Schützeichel, *Memento Mori*, p. 80.
58 *Ibid.*, pp. 80ff., and *LwJb* 5 (1964), 1ff.
59 Schützeichel, *Memento Mori*, pp. 99ff.
60 Henkel, *Übersetzungen*, p. 15.
61 Baldwin, *Masters*, pp. 138ff.
62 Eisenstein, *Press*, p. 12.
63 On this see Miethke, *Universitäten*, pp. 8f. and fn. 12 for further literature.
64 Le Goff, *Intellectuels*, pp. 95ff.; Baldwin, *Culture*, p. 56; Karnein, *Renaissance*, pp. 119ff.
65 These new devices made it possible to consult a book for a particular point instead of having to read it through as a whole. Cf. Parkes, *Influence*, pp. 115ff.; Rouse, *Naissance*, pp. 77ff.
66 Bumke, *Geschichte*, pp. 23, 25.
67 Bumke, *Kultur*, pp. 596ff. See also Zotz, *Urbanitas*, pp. 408ff., for examples associating *urbanus* or *curialis* with literacy and a knowledge of letters.
68 Bumke, *Kultur*, pp. 601ff.
69 Seebold, *Sprachen*, p. 231. What Schreiner, *ZHF* 11 (1984), 310f., likewise says of the later Middle Ages is applicable to the first beginnings of the tendency which he traces.
70 Cf. Duby, *Culture*, p. 250.
71 Bumke, *Geschichte*, pp. 137f., has observed how soon after their composition the manuscript tradition is attested for a number of narrative works in court literature.
72 Sprandel, *Gesellschaft*, p. 127.
73 For a historical survey see Jaeger, *Origins*.
74 On the prestige which could attach to literacy see Lord, *Singers*, p. 24.
75 Cramer has used these two aspects as organising principles of his essay *Roman*, pp. 323ff.
76 Köhn, *MM* 12/1 (1979), 254f.
77 Schröder, *ZfdA* 91 (1961), 38ff.; Green, *GLL* 28 (1975), 246ff.
78 Haug, *Schriftlichkeit*, pp. 151f.; *Literaturtheorie*, pp. 80ff.
79 Worstbrock, *ZfdA* 92 (1963), 248ff.; Schäfer-Maulbetsch, *Studien*, pp. 83ff., 195ff., 527ff.; Lengenfelder, *Liet*, pp. 35ff.
80 Cramer, *Roman*, p. 324.
81 Jaeger, *Origins*, p. 227.
82 Cf. Flori, *Essor*, pp. 191ff.
83 Green, *Exodus*, pp. 188ff.
84 On this as one of the purposes of romances with a classical theme, especially in French, see Köhler, *Ideal*, pp. 44ff., and Bezzola, *Origines* II 2, 517ff.
85 Green, *Oral poetry*, pp. 193, fn. 4, and 198, fn. 1.
86 *Ibid.*, pp. 194ff., 211, 215f.
87 *Ibid.*, pp. 193, fn. 5, 197f., 216.
88 Cf. Huot, *Song*, pp. 84f.
89 Bumke, *Geschichte*, pp. 211f.
90 Bumke, *Kultur*, pp. 37f.
91 *Ibid.*, pp. 624f.
92 Assmann and Hardmeier, *Schrift*, pp. 64, 275.
93 Heinzle, *Wandlungen*, pp. 19f.
94 Herkommer, *NdJb* 100 (1977), 7ff.
95 Cf. Haverkamp, *Aufbruch*, p. 285; Karnein, *Renaissance*, p. 122.
96 Ehlers, *Schulen*, p. 60; Baldwin, *Culture*, p. 39.

97 Skrzypczak, *Stadt, passim* and Keller, *Veränderung*, pp. 21ff.
98 Assmann and Hardmeier, *Schrift*, pp. 53, 109.
99 Skrzypczak, *Stadt*, p. 3, gives historical priority to the town in this process, but gives no comparative evidence for this.
100 1187f. On this see Skrzypczak, *Stadt*, p. 29.
101 Schmitt, *PBB* 66 (1942), 200f.; Skrzypczak, *Stadt*, pp. 32ff.
102 Skrzypczak, *Stadt*, pp. 40f.
103 *Ibid.*, pp. 42ff. See also Sprandel, *Gesellschaft*, pp. 186ff.; Lerner, *Literacy*, pp. 212ff.; Haverkamp, *Aufbruch*, p. 283; Köhn, *Schulbildung*, pp. 218ff.
104 Sprandel, *Gesellschaft*, pp. 187f., 189.
105 Schmitt, *PBB* 66 (1942), 209, 212ff.; Skrzypczak, *Stadt*, pp. 70ff.
106 Schmitt, *PBB* 66 (1942), 211; Skrzypczak, *Stadt*, pp. 84ff.
107 On Konrad von Würzburg in this capacity see Peters, *Literatur*, pp. 97ff., and on Jans Enikel cf. Liebertz-Grün, *Mittelalter*, pp. 71ff.
108 On their literary importance in the thirteenth century see Heinzle, *Wandlungen*, pp. 81ff.
109 Elm, *Mendikantenstudium*, pp. 588f.; Köhn, *MM* 10 (1976), 30f.; Bumke, *Geschichte*, pp. 370f.
110 Grundmann, *Bewegungen*, p. 524.
111 Baldwin, *Culture*, p. 33; Bumke, *Geschichte*, pp. 369f.
112 Grundmann, *Bewegungen*, pp. 452ff.
113 *Ibid.*, p. 458.
114 *Ibid.*, pp. 452ff., 459ff.
115 *Ibid.*, pp. 461f.
116 For an earlier version of this section see Green, *Renaissance*, pp. 17ff.
117 Köhn, *MM* 10 (1976), 10.
118 Fleckenstein, *Bildungsreform*, pp. 23, 25f.
119 Jaeger, *DVjs* 61 (1987), 574.
120 On Heito see *VfL* 3, 939ff., and Haubrichs, *Anfänge*, pp. 242f., 244, 248, 281f.
121 See above, pp. 271f.
122 *MGH Cap.* 1, 346, 34: *Ut scola in monasterio non habeatur, nisi eorum qui oblati sunt.*
123 Köhn, *MM* 10 (1976), 13; Prinz, *Grundlagen*, p. 354.
124 Baldwin, *Culture*, p. 4.
125 This has been shown in detail by Jaeger, *Origins*, in the case of Otto the Great and his brother Brun, archbishop of Cologne.
126 Jaeger, *DVjs* 61 (1987), 572ff.
127 *Ibid.*, p. 595; *Origins*, p. 5.
128 Jaeger, *Origins*, pp. 31ff.
129 Jaeger, *DVjs* 61 (1987), 571f.
130 Southern, *Schools*, p. 118.
131 Guibert de Nogent, *Gesta Dei per Francos*, PL 156, 680: *Et villas video, urbes et oppida studiis fervere grammaticae.* Quoted by Vàrvaro, *SMV* 10 (1962), 300.
132 Cf. Johanek, *Klosterstudien*, pp. 41, 62.
133 Cf. Classen, *AfK* 48 (1966), 160; Karnein, *Renaissance*, p. 105.
134 Köhn, *MM* 10 (1976), 17.
135 Mansi, *Conciliorum* 20, 509. Cf. also Baldwin, *Culture*, p. 39.
136 Jaeger, *DVjs* 61 (1987), 608.
137 Cf. Bumke, *Mäzene*, pp. 256ff.
138 See above, p. 275.
139 Classen, *AfK* 48 (1966), 165; Schnell, *Kirche*, p. 96.
140 See pp. 287, 291f.
141 Classen, *AfK* 48 (1966), 165f.
142 Jaeger, *DVjs* 61 (1987), 610f.

143 On this see Eifler, *Tugendsystem*.
144 Schirmer and Broich, *Studien*.
145 On the attitude of the Church to court clerics see Köhn, *MM* 12/1 (1979), 227ff.
146 Jaeger, *Origins*, p. 224.
147 Ernst, *Liber*, pp. 156ff.
148 Jaeger, *Origins*, p. 224. See also the contribution of Illmer in Wolf, *Kultur*, pp. 143ff.
149 In this sense court literature had an educational role to play. Cf. Jaeger, *Origins*, p. 209.
150 It is one of the merits of Wolf, *Kultur*, that he sees German developments in connection with French and gives due regard to cultural ascendancy passing to France.
151 Cf. Bumke's review of Scholz, *Hören*, *AfdA* 93 (1982), 118f.
152 Discussed by Vàrvaro, *SMV* 10 (1962), 299ff.
153 *Ibid.*, p. 314.
154 *Et dicebat, litterarum peritia nemini militaturo obesse, seculum relicturo plurimum prodesse.* Quoted by Thompson, *Literacy*, p. 110, n. 102.
155 *PL* 203, 149. Discussed by Vàrvaro, *SMV* 10 (1962), 315, and Jaeger, *Origins*, p. 225.
156 Bumke, *Kultur*, pp. 596ff.; Schirmer and Broich, *Studien*, pp. 27ff.
157 Vv. 28ff.
158 Bertau has used the medieval *translatio* idea as an organising principle of his literary history, *Literatur*, pp. 123ff., 227ff.
159 See above, p. 277.
160 Ehlers, *Scholaren*, pp. 97ff.; Karnein, *Renaissance*, p. 134.
161 Vv. 6ff. Cf. Mertens, *Rezeption*, p. 135.
162 The work of Grundmann, *AfK* 40 (1958), 1ff. and Thompson, *Literacy*, needs to be brought up to date, especially for Germany.
163 On access to the literacy of others see Bäuml, *Speculum* 55 (1980), 239, 246. On the close connection between reading for oneself and listening to others read out loud cf. the remark made by William of Malmesbury about Robert of Gloucester, *Gesta* II 519: *Litteras ita fovetis, ut cum sitis tantarum occupationum mole districti, horas tamen aliquas vobis surripiatis, quibus aut ipsi legere, aut legentes possitis audire.*
164 The most renowned example of this is count Baldwin II of Guines who had works translated from Latin and recited aloud (cf. Lambert of Ardres, *Historia*, p. 598: *transferre sibi et sepius ante se legere fecit*). On Baldwin's encouragement of literature see Vàrvaro, *SMV* 10 (1960), 322, and Fleckenstein, *Miles*, pp. 320f.
165 The major exception is the *Isidor* translations (cf. *VfL* 1, 300f.; Matzel, *Die Sprache* 12 (1966), 144ff., *Untersuchungen*, and *Problem*, pp. 15ff.; Kartschoke, *Geschichte*, pp. 108f.), although Kartschoke concedes (p. 79) that we lack certainty on this.
166 Boehm, *Bildungswesen*, p. 169.
167 Meissburger, *Grundlagen*, p. 182.
168 Pressure on monasteries towards recital in the vernacular also occurred in the particular case of the knightly orders. Grundmann, *Schrifttum*, pp. 96ff., has investigated the example of the Teutonic Knights. The position will have been no different with those secular knights who joined this order or the Templars only temporarily, as *familiares* and *halpbrûdere* (Kolb, *ZfdA* 116 (1987), 274f., 276f.).
169 Cf. Teske, *FMS* 10 (1976), 257f.; Haubrichs, *Kultur*, pp. 135ff.; *Anfänge*, pp. 207, 316.
170 Haubrichs, *Anfänge*, p. 316.
171 See above, p. 96.
172 Vv. 82f. (cf. *VfL* 2, 279).
173 Bédier, *Légendes*.
174 *DVjs* 47 (1973), 26ff.
175 Teske, *FMS* 10 (1976), 249.
176 Turner, *AHR* 83 (1978), 931, quotes from Du Cange, *Glossarium*, to this effect. See also Leclercq, *Frères*, pp. 156f.

177 Teske, *FMS* 10 (1976), 278.
178 *FMS* 10 (1976), 248ff. and 11 (1977), 288ff.
179 *FMS* 10 (1976), 256f., 289, 316f.
180 See above, p. 273, and Teske, *FMS* 10 (1976), 282 (an invasion of the monasteries by *semihomines*!).
181 *FMS* 10 (1976), 316.
182 *Ibid.*, p. 289.
183 Cf. Schützeichel, *Memento Mori*, p. 101.
184 *FMS* 11 (1977), 299f.
185 *Ibid.*, p. 300.
186 Vollmann-Profe, *Wiederbeginn*, p. 32.
187 On vernacular works by comparison with Latin ones of the same period see Naumann, *Dichter*.
188 Vollmann-Profe, *Wiederbeginn*, p. 31.
189 *Ibid.*, p. 32.
190 Meissburger, *Grundlagen*, p. 183.
191 Lists have been given by Meissburger, *Grundlagen*, p. 183, fn. 18, and Esser, *Schöpfungsgeschichte*, p. 66. To these names must be added Priester Wernher (given by Rupp, *Dichtungen*, p. 296).
192 Rupp, *Dichtungen*, p. 308.
193 Cf. the comment of Esser, *Schöpfungsgeschichte*, p. 62, on Scherer's view (1875) of the authorship of the *Wiener Genesis*. That Ehrismann's approach was similar has been shown by Meissburger, *Grundlagen*, p. 183, with regard to Heinrich, the author of *Die Litanei*.
194 *Dichtungen*, pp. 295ff.
195 *Vita Altmanni*, MGH SS 12, 230, 10ff.
196 The term *priester* is used of themselves by Arnold (*Loblied auf den heiligen Geist* 50, 4), who also refers to himself as *ewart* in *Juliana* 1, 4 (if these works are by the same author), by Alber (*Tnugdalus* 2184) and by Adelbrecht (*Johannes Baptista* 18, 4). *Pfaffe* is used by Lamprecht (*Tobias* 7, *Alexanderlied* 1, 2), Werner vom Niederrhein (*Die vier Sciven* 32, 12) and Konrad (*Rolandslied* 9079). In his *Maria* Wernher is referred to as *priester* in MS A (1136) and as *pfaffe* in MS D (1242).
197 *Grundlagen*, p. 183, fn. 18.
198 Bumke, *Mäzene*, p. 256.
199 *Ibid.*, p. 76.
200 V. 180. On Veldeke as a cleric see Bumke, *Mäzene*, p. 116.
201 Sanders, *Heinric*, pp. 10, 23.
202 Suggested by Esser, *Schöpfungsgeschichte*, p. 66, and Bumke, *Mäzene*, p. 64.
203 Turner, *AHR* 83 (1978), 932. Fleckenstein, *Miles*, pp. 306ff., has stressed that it was thanks to their literacy that the position of clerics at court grew so much more important.
204 Köhn, *MM* 12/1 (1979), 227ff. On the functions of the court cleric see Baldwin, *Masters, princes*, pp. 175ff.
205 Bumke, *Geschichte*, p. 32. Peters, *Hofkleriker*, pp. 31ff., has sketched a broad spectrum of four different types of court cleric, with different functions, to which she adds clerical authors of whose non-literary duties nothing is known, but whom she includes as court clerics in a wider sense.
206 Fleckenstein, *Miles*, pp. 302ff.
207 On Albrecht von Scharfenberg see Fromm, *Titurel*, pp. 16ff. Bumke, *Mäzene*, pp. 71f., stresses not merely these isolated examples, but argues that most court narrative literature in Germany was the work of court clerics, at least in the beginning. On their role in French literature see Karnein, *Renaissance*, p. 124, and Kasten, *Minnesang*, p. 167.
208 Turner, *AHR* 83 (1978), 930.

209 Oexle, *Deutungsschemata*, p. 108.
210 Clanchy, *Memory*, p. 178, quotes the complaint by Philip of Harvengt about the contemporary practice of calling anyone who is literate, even a layman, a *clericus*.
211 Bäuml's proposal (*Speculum* 55 (1980) 242, 246 – see p. 328, n. 105) is therefore much more than a terminological point. Quasi-literacy of this kind is present when a German author uses *lesen* of learning a detail from his French source, even though, despite his literacy in Latin, his ignorance of French made him dependent on an interpreter's oral translation of his source. Examples are Konrad von Würzburg, *Partonopier und Meliur* 1138f., 2673, 4519 (cf. 208ff.) and Ulrich von Etzenbach, *Wilhelm von Wenden* 2176, 5792ff. (cf. 233 and de Boor, *Geschichte* III 1, 106).
212 Duby, *Culture*, p. 253.
213 Riché, *Ecoles*, pp. 14, 28f., 73.
214 Ernst, *Liber*, pp. 155ff.
215 Cf. Thompson, *Literacy*, p. 31; Green, *Otfrid*, p. 748.
216 Cassiodorus, *Variae* IX 24 (p. 290).
217 Grundmann, *AfK* 40 (1958), 50ff. This argument finds its way into German in the *Buch der Könige alter ê und niuwer ê (Kaiserchronik)*, p. 277. Cf. Hugo von Trimberg, *Renner* 1245ff.
218 Schirmer and Broich, *Studien*, pp. 28ff., 200ff.
219 Bumke, *Kultur*, pp. 603ff. A similar consideration is voiced by Konrad von Würzburg in *Partonopier und Meliur*, where the motive of Meliur's father in having him educated in literacy (8068f.) is clearly voiced, 8072ff. Cf. the *Sächsische Weltchronik* 152, 4ff.; *Alexius F* 100ff. The more a *litteratus* pressed the need for writing at court, the more he suggested his own indispensability. Cf. Thomasin von Zerclaere, *Welscher Gast* 9251ff.
220 Duby, *Culture*, pp. 253f., 255; *Ordres*, p. 312.
221 Bumke, *Mäzene*, p. 61.
222 Duby, *Culture*, p. 254.
223 *Gesta consulum Andegavorum*, p. 140. Cf. Duby, *Culture*, p. 254; Vàrvaro, *SMV* 10 (1962), 313.
224 Bumke, *Mäzene*, p. 42.
225 Bumke, *Kultur*, pp. 604f.
226 Cf. Fleckenstein, *Miles*, p. 319.
227 Turner, *AHR* 83 (1978), 934, 945.
228 Bumke, *Kultur*, pp. 624ff.
229 *Ibid.*, pp. 630f.
230 In the fourteenth century Johannes Rothe not merely sees literacy as a qualification fitting in a knight (*Der Ritterspiegel* 2605ff.), he also transfers the argument about the *asinus coronatus* from the ruler to the knight (1465ff.). Cf. Schreiner, *BuW* 9 (1975), 232.
231 *Gesta consulum Andegavorum*, p. 140.
232 Vàrvaro, *SMV* 10 (1962), 314.
233 Quoted p. 411, n. 154. Cf. Grundmann, *AfK* 26 (1936), 144; Vàrvaro, *SMV* 10 (1962), 314.
234 Vv. 2075f.
235 Hugo von Trimberg refers in his Latin *Solsequium* to a *Miles quidam litteratus* (56, 32). This character plays no essential part in what follows, which suggests that, as with Lanzelet, the literate knight was by now a not unknown phenomenon. Cf. also Konrad von Würzburg, *Partonopier und Meliur* 19620ff., 19852; Ottokar's *Österreichische Reimchronik* 20951ff.; prose *Lancelot* I 165, 29. In each case the educational and literate status of one called a knight is expressly stated.
236 Turner, *AHR* 83 (1978), 941f. Peters, *Fürstenhof*, pp. 16ff., discusses the implications of Hermann of Thuringia sending his sons to the French court for their education.
237 This has been discussed by Dunbabin, *Clerk*, pp. 26ff. Cf. also Bumke, *Mäzene*, pp. 55f.; Sprandel, *Gesellschaft*, pp. 109f.

238 Konrad von Würzburg sketches how this could come about, *Partonopier und Meliur* 19622ff.
239 For examples see Mertens, *Gregorius*, pp. 64ff.
240 *Gregorius* 1181ff. Cf. Mertens, *Gregorius*, pp. 163f. Ernst, *Euphorion* 72 (1978), 164, 166f., interprets the young Gregorius as a *puer oblatus*.
241 What calls for comment in Hartmann's case is not his ability to read, but the fact that he was able to consult written sources (French and Latin) with understanding (Scholz, *Hören*, p. 213). Cf. Turner, *AHR* 83 (1978), 931: 'A *miles literatus*, a "learned knight", was rare enough to arouse comment by a chronicler, but not a knight who was merely literate in today's sense.'
242 See Grundmann, *AfK* 26 (1936), 129ff.; Bumke, *Mäzene*, pp. 231ff.; Scholz, *Hören*, pp. 205ff.; Schreiner, *FMS* 24 (1990), 314ff.; McKitterick, *Frauen*, pp. 65ff. A concise picture of a court cleric acting as tutor to a noblewoman is given by Gottfried in *Tristan* 7712ff., where the literate nature of Isold's education is made clear (7730f., 8059ff., 8143ff.).
243 Kartschoke, *Geschichte*, p. 18. On women readers for Otfrid and Notker, see above, pp. 180 and 184.
244 Cf. Bumke, *Mäzene*, p. 243; Schreiner, *FMS* 24 (1990), 333 ('Anfangsgründe'). On the possibility of using the psalter as a text for learning Latin cf. Kirchert, *ZfdA* 113 (1984), 72.
245 Bumke, *Mäzene*, pp. 231ff.
246 *Sachsenspiegel* 91, 7ff. Cf. also *Buch der Könige alter ê und niuwer ê* (*Landrecht*) 371 (26, 12); *Magdeburger Schöffenrecht*, p. 129; *Schwabenspiegel Langform M* (*Erster Landrechtsteil*), p. 154. Berthold von Regensburg can also assume as a matter of course that women read the psalter (*Predigten* I 49, 31).
247 Pinder, *Wesen* I, plates 410, 411.
248 *Evangelienbuch* I 5, 5ff. On Mary as a reader in this scene see above, p. 134. and Schreiner, *FMS* 24 (1990), 322f.
249 *FMS* 24 (1990), 339f.
250 Bumke, *Mäzene*, pp. 236ff.; Grundmann, *AfK* 26 (1936), 146f.; Bumke, *Kultur*, p. 705. The attraction of court literature for noblewomen means probably that they played a more important part in encouraging it than is suggested by direct references.
251 Geoffrey Gaimar, *Lestorie des Engles* 6496f. Cf. Auerbach, *Literatursprache*, p. 221.
252 *Servatius* 6177. Cf. Bumke, *Mäzene*, p. 238; Sanders, *Heinric*, p. 10.
253 *Eneide* 13445ff. See above, p. 140, and Bumke, *Mäzene*, p. 113; Sanders, *Heinric*, pp. 11f.
254 Ruh, *Eckhart*, pp. 98f.
255 *Ibid.*, p. 98.
256 Grundmann, *Bewegungen*, p. 225, reports this for example of a community in Nürnberg: 'Sie wählen eine Subpriorin; sie lesen, so gut sie es verstehen, die Stundengebete; die Meisterin hält die Tischlesung in deutscher Sprache.'
257 Boehm, *Bildungswesen*, pp. 161f.; Keller, *Veränderung*, pp. 21ff.
258 Cf. 1189f., 1882ff.
259 Sprandel, *Gesellschaft*, pp. 193f., 219. For examples from the fourteenth century see von Brandt, *ZVLGA* 38 (1958), 164ff.
260 Sprandel, *Gesellschaft*, p. 194.
261 *Ibid.*, pp. 194f.
262 *Der welsche Gast* 7101ff. Cf. Curschmann, *PBB* 106 (1984), 241.
263 Kartschoke, *Geschichte*, p. 217.
264 As is made clear when Frau Ava says that she received assistance from her (clerical?) sons, *Jüngstes Gericht* 35, 1ff. Cf. Küsters, *Garten*, p. 174.
265 As suggested by de Boor, *Geschichte* II 6.
266 Cf. Bumke, *Mäzene*, p. 70.
267 *Ibid.*, pp. 71f.
268 Schnell, *Verhältnis*, p. 112.

269 Virgil: Ziltener, *Chrétien* (even with all the qualifications necessary); Macrobius: Hunt, *CetM* 33 (1981/82), 211ff.; Ovid: Guyer, *RR* 12 (1921), 97ff., 216ff.; Laurie, *Studies*. On *comediae* see Hunt, *MSt* 40 (1978), 120ff., and on Alanus cf. Luttrell, *Creation*, and Hunt, *BBSIA* 30 (1978), 209ff.
270 Poetics and rhetoric: Hunt, *FMLS* 6 (1970), 1ff. and 8 (1972), 320ff.; dialectic: Hunt, *Viator* 10 (1979), 95ff.; *MLR* 72 (1977), 285ff.; Chartres: Wetherbee, *Platonism*, pp. 220ff.
271 Vv. 25ff.
272 Stevens, *Renewal*, pp. 67ff.; *Literaturbegriff*, pp. 19ff.
273 Stevens, *Renewal*, p. 77.
274 *VfL*^{1} 4, 621.
275 In his discussion of such cases Scholz, *Hören*, pp. 211ff., also includes Wirnt von Grafenberg (pp. 217f.). I exclude him because of doubts whether he must be regarded as illiterate (cf. Ruh, *Epik* I 105).
276 On Wolfram's exceptional position see Fromm, *Titurel*, p. 18.
277 Brall, *Gralsuche*, pp. 71f., 82, 84.
278 On Ulrich von Lichtenstein and literacy see Kartschoke, *WA* 16 (1981), 103ff.; Heinen, *JEGPh* 83 (1984), 159ff.
279 Cf. Bumke, *Geschichte*, p. 162.
280 In this paragraph I deal only with the authors of the love-lyric. By contrast, gnomic poets were essentially professionals and often literate, even expressly so. Cf. Bumke, *Mäzene*, pp. 69f.; *Kultur*, pp. 691ff.; Franz, *Studien*, pp. 28ff.
281 Bumke, *Ministerialität*.
282 Cf. Wolf, *WA* 24 (1983), 202, fn. 5.
283 Discussed by Wolf, *WA* 24 (1983), 197ff.
284 Cf. Schnell, *Verhältnis*, pp. 103f.; Wolf, *WA* 24 (1983), 202; Kasten, *Frauendienst*, pp. 88ff.
285 Kasten, *Frauendienst*, pp. 112f., 114, 130.
286 Bumke, *Kultur*, pp. 685ff.
287 Examples from the Manesse manuscript are Rost, Kirchherr zu Sarnen, der Schulmeister von Esslingen, Der Tugendhafte Schreiber, Rudolf der Schreiber, Der Kanzler.
288 Bumke, *Kultur*, p. 690; *Walther*, p. 193; Kasten, *Frauendienst*, pp. 330, 343; Knapp, *Waltherus*, pp. 45ff.
289 Rupp, *Dichtungen*, p. 293. The knightly orders are even more anomalous, combining monasticism with knighthood (Rousset, *Histoire*, p. 100; Oexle, *Deutungsschemata*, p. 85) and, in the case of the Templars, causing St Bernard to wonder whether they are to be called monks or knights (PL 182, 927; cf. Green, *Exodus*, p. 394).
290 Teske, *FMS* 10 (1976), 321, and 11 (1977), 319, stresses the exceptional position of these two classes: members of a monastic order who are characterised by lay illiteracy and occupy middle ground between the monastic *familia* and the choir monks. On the lay brothers cf. Leclercq, *Frères*, p. 153.
291 Köhn, *MM* 12/1 (1979), 234; Duby, *Ordres*, p. 312; Fleckenstein, *Miles*, p. 323, says that these clerics at court 'die Kluft zwischen der unschriftlichen heimischen und der schriftlichen christlichen und antiken Kultur überbrückten'.
292 Duby, *Ordres*, pp. 74, 177; Ullmann, *Denken*, pp. 20, 24 (the king as a *persona ecclesiastica*, as a 'Zwitterding'); Kantorowicz, *King*, pp. 10, 43, 44f., 193, 320 (the king as a *persona mixta*, temporal and spiritual).
293 Cf. Philip of Harvengt, PL 203, 149: *Non enim scientiae fortis militia vel militiae prejudicat scientia litterarum, imo in principe copula tam utilis, tam conveniens est duarum.* Quoted by Vàrvaro, *SMV* 10 (1962), 315. Cf. Duby, *Culture*, p. 250.
294 Cf. Matthew Paris on a royal officer of Henry III: *quidam miles literatus sive clericus militaris* (*Chronica majora* 5, 242). Cf. Turner, *AHR* 83 (1978), 931; Clanchy, *Memory*, p. 179.
295 Grundmann, *AfK* 24 (1936), 139, says that 'die Frauen die Bildungsgrenze zwischen Klerus

und Laientum überschneiden und verwischen'. Cf. Fleckenstein, *Miles*, pp. 323f. ('Zwischenstellung').

296 Grundmann, *Bewegungen*, pp. 321, 338 ('Zwischenform', 'Zwitterstellung'); Zink, *Destinataires*, pp. 71 ('un public féminin intermédiaire entre le monde du cloître et le monde tout court'), 74; *Prédication*, p. 162 ('Un public qui n'appartient entièrement ni au monde clérical ni au monde laïque'). Elm, *Stellung*, p. 8, locates the life of St Elisabeth and her followers (*vita sororum in seculo*) in the middle ground between the monastery and the world (cf. also p. 14) and hence sees it as a *via media* (p. 17).

297 Skrzypczak, *Stadt*, pp. 160ff. Even when the town clerk can be a layman (*ibid.*, p. 132: *laicus litteratus*) this is still as anomalous as the *miles litteratus*, a bridge between two hitherto largely separate worlds.

298 Curschmann, *PBB* 106 (1984), 231: 'Wer sich in dieser Zeit als gebildeter Ritter, als *miles litteratus* ausgibt, widerspricht sich nachgerade selbst.' Cf. the similar terms of Bumke, *Mäzene*, p. 71, on Hartmann: 'Ritter und Gelehrter, *miles* und *clericus*, sind gegensätzliche Begriffe; ihr Zusammenfall ist fast ein Paradox.'

299 See p. 328, n. 90.

300 The first part of this section appeared originally in abbreviated form in *RPL* 9 (1986), 143ff.

301 With this question we return to the aesthetic implications of literacy considered in Chapter 9 in regard to fiction. On the importance of education for the rise of court literature see also Henkel, *Litteratus*, 334ff.

302 Schirok, *Parzivalrezeption*, pp. 18ff.

303 Gottfried's distinction between *edele herzen* and *ir aller werlt* within his audience is also relevant here. Wessel, *Metaphorik*, pp. 195ff., has shown that Gottfried suggests a parallel between those in his audience who fail to grasp the significance of his metaphors and the world of Marke.

304 Mohr, *Wolfram*, pp. 90f.

305 Bumke, *Kultur*, pp. 703f., 723, 724f.; Ganz, *Heinrich*, p. 31; Rösener, *Frau*, p. 197; Fleckenstein, *Miles*, pp. 312f.

306 *Frauendienst* 444, 8ff. Cf. Kartschoke, *WA* 16 (1981), 109f.

307 See above, pp. 247 and 260.

308 Wolfram, in addition to appealing to the *wîsen*, also addressed women as potential readers and Gottfried's *edele herzen* may have included the literate members of his audience, but there is no explicit evidence that these select groups are made up only of *litterati*. Nor may we assume that the ability to understand the virtuosity of Ulrich von Lichtenstein was confined to readers if we recall the complexity of skaldic verse, meant for listeners.

309 Vv. 15ff.

310 *Yder* 6764ff. Cf. Gallais, *CCM* 13 (1970), 337.

311 Hadloub 2, 52; *Der welsche Gast* 14695f. (Boppe VI 3, 1ff. also refers to his audience as composed of *hohe pfaffen*, of *werde leijen* and of *vrouwen*). Hadloub makes his aristocratic audience clear by the terms he chooses (*edel, hôh, ritter*), confirmed by the historical evidence we have for them (cf. Renk, *Manessekreis*). Thomasin's ties with the patriarchal court of Aquileia suggest something similar of his audience (on them see Rocher, *Thomasin*, pp. 850ff.).

312 For examples of *clerici* alongside *milites* at court see Fenske, *Knappe*, pp. 60, 62, 75, 90; Fleckenstein, *Miles*, p. 314; Szabó, *Hof*, p. 360. On the additional presence of women cf. Rösener, *Frau*, p. 207; Zotz, *Urbanitas*, p. 414; Fleckenstein, *Curialitas*, p. 477 (*Nachwort*).

313 Cf. above, pp. 77f.

314 See above, pp. 263f.

315 Cf. the comments on Ott and Walliczek, *Bildprogramm*, by Mertens, *PBB* 105 (1983), 443.

Brogsitter, *Held*, pp. 16ff., also suggests the existence of a simpler narrative scheme for some Arthurian material alongside the more complex model devised by Chrétien.
316 See above, p. 164.
317 Stevens, *Renewal*, p. 68.
318 Cf. Gillespie, *Siegfriedliebe*, pp. 161, 165, 169.
319 This point is made by Benoît de Sainte-Maure at the start of the romance tradition in French with reference to his Latin source, *Roman de Troie* 37ff. See Marichal, *Naissance*, p. 450.
320 For examples see above, pp. 132, 197.
321 See above, pp. 122 and 132.
322 See above, p. 192. See also Bumke, *Mäzene*, pp. 243f., and *Liebe*, pp. 39f., for the attractions which court literature had for the women in the audience.
323 *Laudine*, p. 12.
324 Bräuer, *Geschichte*, pp. 223f.
325 Gottfried may resemble Hartmann in making a special appeal to women by his suggestion that Isold was a more exemplary lover than Tristan (see Hahn, *Raum*, pp. 11ff.; Wessel, *Metaphorik*, pp. 444ff.; Wisbey, *Living*, pp. 268f.).
326 On the possible clerical status of the author of *Der heimliche Bote* see Wenzel, *Frauendienst*, pp. 128f.; *VfL* 3, 647.
327 Vv. 11ff. Cf. Wenzel, *Frauendienst*, pp. 126ff.
328 As in *Die Erlösung* 1837ff. (see above, p. 132).
329 On Mechthild see p. 372, n. 47, and on the possibility of skipping p. 157.
330 Cf. Zink, *CCM* 24 (1981), 6. See also above, p. 123.
331 For examples see above, pp. 123 (Williram, *Hohes Lied*), 155 (*Schwabenspiegel Langform M*), 158 (Heinrich von Hesler, *Apokalypse*).
332 See above, p. 158 (*Praefatio* to the *Heliand* and Williram, *Hohes Lied*).
333 I have discussed this example in greater detail in *Advice*, pp. 46ff.
334 Cf. Green, *Advice*, pp. 38ff.
335 *Ibid.*, pp. 34, 75, n. 10.
336 In Book V it is suggested that Gurnemanz's surmise that Parzival is of high birth (170, 23) might have a more precise bearing on his being born into the Grail dynasty (333, 30: *ganerbe*), that his recommendation to show compassion (170, 25), to relieve suffering (170, 26) and to bring assistance (171, 2) might refer not simply to Pelrapeire, but more tellingly to Munsalvaesche (255, 17ff.), and that *der kumberhafte werde man* might be Anfortas.
337 From Trevrizent at this stage Parzival learns of the vacancy in the line of succession to Grail kingship, so that Gurnemanz's realisation that the young boy was born to be a *volkes hêrre* (170, 22) gives way to his qualification as *grâles hêrre* (477, 21). Only now is *ganerbe* specified more closely: Parzival alone comes into question.
338 In Book XVI it is made finally clear that Gurnemanz's recommendation of *diemuot* (170, 28) is the quality to be shown by Parzival as Grail king (798, 30) and in Book XV that the *gotes gruoz* (171, 4) held out by Gurnemanz as the reward for following his advice is to be seen more precisely in terms of his being called to Munsalvaesche (781, 4: *got wil genâde an dir nu tuon*).
339 See above, pp. 122, 141, 196. By using the verb *sehen* Gottfried suggests that he has a reader in mind.
340 See above, pp. 164f.
341 Of Gottfried's acrostic Stevens, *Renewal*, p. 82, says: 'the expectation is that this implied reader will not be content simply to scan the manuscript consecutively and establish its literal sense, but will peruse it backwards and forwards to discover hidden links'.
342 Cf. Saenger, *Books*, p. 142 (especially if we take into account the uncertain Latinity even of nuns, cf. Haug and Vollmann, *Literatur*, p. 1378, note to 506, 23). Grundmann, *AfK* 40

(1958), 46, quotes from Ekkehard von Aura to the effect that a Latin work could be composed in a simpler style for the benefit of literate laymen.
343 Fleckenstein, *Miles*, p. 320.
344 *Der welsche Gast* 1103ff. Cf. Scholz, *Hûsvrouwe*, p. 266. Elsewhere (9315ff.) Thomasin implies a differentiation within literacy, arguing that an ability to read is not the same as an ability to understand and that this criticism can be made of some clerics. In making this distinction (*waenestu, swer wol lesen kan, / daz er sî ein gelêrter man?*) Thomasin is no longer using *gelêrt* in the simple sense of 'literate', but has made a first move towards the meaning of the modern 'gelehrt'.
345 Vàrvaro, *SMV* 10 (1962), 309f., quotes examples from classical and medieval Latin to the effect that a knowledge of *grammatica* involved acquaintance with the Latin poets.
346 This is the argument of Stevens, *Renewal*, pp. 67ff.
347 See above, p. 141. Heinrich von Neustadt, *Gottes Zukunft* 63ff., likewise expects his critical reader to be Latinate if he is to be capable of judging the quality of his work by comparison with its Latin source.
348 Stevens, *Renewal*, p. 82.
349 Ibid., p. 86.
350 Vv. 17186ff., 3612ff.
351 Cf. Gottfried, *Tristan*, Ganz edn, note on vv. 17191f.; Ganz, *Tristan*, p. 398; Krohn, *Gottfried* III 168 (note on vv. 17184ff.); *VfL* 7, 265; Stevens and Wisbey, *Gottfried*, p. xiii.
352 Ganz, *Tristan*, pp. 397ff.; Krohn, *Gottfried* III 169 (note on v. 17184ff.); Wisbey, *Living*, pp. 259, 267, 270.
353 *Erec* 7705ff.; *Eneide* 287ff. Stackmann, *Arcadia* I (1966), 252f., has interpreted Hartmann's episode (together with that of Chrétien) as a contrafacture of Ovid.
354 XXI 10ff.
355 Bartsch edn, p. cxxix.
356 Ibid., p. cxxx; *VfL* 7, 264.
357 Neumann, *PBB* 76 (1954), 321ff.; *VfL* 1, 188; Stackmann, *Arcadia* I (1966), 238.
358 Ganz, *Tristan*, p. 398.
359 Bezzola, *Origines* III 1, 148f., Marichal, *Naissance*, pp. 465f., 467, and Zink, *CCM* 24 (1981), 13f., have shown, by comparing the *Alexandreis* of Walter of Chatillon and the *De bello Troiano* of Joseph of Exeter with the French vernacular romances on these subjects, that many classical allusions present in the Latin versions have been excised from the vernacular works. They see in this the difference between works meant for a clerical audience, who would understand these points, and works for laymen, who would not.
360 The argument of the last few pages resumes some points made elsewhere, in *Rîtr*, pp. 1ff.
361 See also Scholz, *Hören*, p. 122.
362 Cf. above, p. 226.
363 *Gregorius* 3995; *Armer Heinrich* 22f. See above, pp. 187, 188.
364 *Lanzelet* 9441; *Tristan* 177. See above, pp. 208 and 196f. From this list of the earliest examples I have omitted Konrad von Fussesbrunnen, *Kindheit Jesu* 91f. (*swer ie gehôrt oder hât gelesen / von unser frouwen ein liet*), on the grounds that, although it betrays knowledge of the twofold reception, it does not apply to this work itself (see above, p. 207). Even to include it in our list (it is commonly dated 1190-1200) would not affect the dating proposed.
365 Wilhelm, *Corpus* I 102, 2 (number 65): *allin die disen brief lesent alde hoerent*. See above, p. 229.
366 See above, pp. 206 (*Heliand*, Otfrid, Frau Ava), 183ff. (Notker), 207 (Priester Wernher).
367 See above, 208.
368 See above, pp. 204 (*Lucidarius*), 194ff. (*Tristan*).
369 I have discussed this formula in *Otfrid*, pp. 745f., 757. We saw above, p. 181, that it does

not refer to what Otfrid read in his source, but recalls what he had previously told his audience by reading aloud to them. Scholz doubts this second point (personal letter 18 September 1990), sees *wir lasun* in conjunction with *unsih* and *uns* in the preceding line, and reads the phrase with regard to Otfrid's readers. For him, therefore, *lesan* here means 'to read', not 'to recite'. There are reasons for questioning this. We have seen, pp. 115ff., that there are grounds for scepticism with constructions like *wir lesen* or *man liset* (they can refer to Christian written tradition at large, not necessarily to particular readers). When Otfrid recommends his reader to consult a passage elsewhere he uses the present tense, implying the future (as in II 3, 29f.), but when he refers to what he has said elsewhere he employs the past tense (II 2, 6; V 24, 4), as in this passage. Finally, if Otfrid uses *wir* of himself as author/reciter in IV 25, 6 (*wír hiar lasun fórna*), this is no more than an authorial plural, such as occurs in V 24, 4 (*wír hiar scríbun fórna*). Cf. also the parallel between *unsu smahu nídiri* (Lud. 26) and *mea parva humilitas* (Liut. 130f.). For these reasons I refer *wir lasun* to Otfrid's role as author and reciter, not to the community of his readers.

370 82, 11 (refers back to 81, 25ff.).
371 If we regard Hartmann's romances as meant for a twofold reception, like his legends, this is because of the explicit pointers in the legends and on the assumption that he composed both genres for the same kind of audience. The absence of an explicit pointer makes *Erec* 7305 unusable for our present purpose.
372 V. 1757 (refers back to 1553ff.). The use of *wir* must make us even more doubtful.
373 Cf. 7155, 16493, 16932, 17421, 17565, 18605. See above, p. 197.
374 *Servatius* 6210f.; *Liet von Troye* 13670.
375 *Lucidarius* 36, 23; *Tristan* 230.
376 On the monastic background of these authors (and of Der Arme Hartmann) see above, pp.215f.
377 See above, pp. 217ff.
378 Steer, *DVjs* 64 (1990), 1ff.
379 *Hören*, p. 92.
380 Haug, *Literaturtheorie*, p. 91, has made a similar point about the self-awareness of court literature with regard to its fictional nature.
381 See above, p. 207.
382 Examples under this heading are the *Lanzelet* of Ulrich von Zatzikhoven, Gottfried's *Tristan*, Wolfram's *Parzival*, the *Wigalois* of Wirnt von Grafenberg, Konrad Fleck's *Flore und Blanscheflur*, Der Stricker's *Daniel*, *Die Crone* of Heinrich von dem Türlin, the *Alexander* of Rudolf von Ems, and also his *Willehalm von Orlens*, the *Partonopier und Meliur* and the *Engelhard* of Konrad von Würzburg, the *Jüngerer Titurel*, *Lohengrin*, *Reinfried von Braunschweig*, the *Wilhelm von Österreich* of Johann von Würzburg, and possibly also the work of Ulrich von Lichtenstein. The case for a twofold reception of all these works is discussed above, pp. 208ff.
383 To this genre belong Hartmann's *Gregorius* and *Armer Heinrich*, the *Barlaam und Josaphat* of Rudolf von Ems, as well as the *Silvester* and *Alexius* of Konrad von Würzburg. See above, p. 207.
384 Two examples belong here: Der Stricker's *Karl der Große* and the *Rennewart* of Ulrich von Türheim. See above, p. 208.
385 Two examples are provided by the *Lucidarius* and by Thomasin's *Welscher Gast*. See above, p. 204.
386 Rudolf von Ems, *Weltchronik*. See above, p. 206.
387 See above, p. 208.
388 See above, p. 140.
389 See above, pp. 186ff.
390 For a slightly different version of this section see Green, *Roman*, pp. 67ff.

391 See above, p. 114.
392 Duby, *History*, pp. 55, 511.
393 *Garten*, p. 244.
394 Cf. Duby, *History*, pp. 5f., 7.
395 The monk's cell as the place for his solitary *lectio* is referred to in the *Passional* III 223, 36f.; 226, 98f. and the *Buch von geistlicher Lehre* 42, 28 (for writing, but presumably also for reading). Cf. also the passage from Alcuin referred to p. 384, n. 110 (*cubile*).
396 See Dickinson, *Life*, p. 29, on evidence from England.
397 *Ibid.*, p. 48; Duby, *History*, p. 487.
398 Dickinson, *Life*, p. 49; Duby, *History*, pp. 482f.
399 Küsters, *Garten*, pp. 286f., also points to criticism of the predominance of the liturgy, at the cost of meditation and *lectio*, voiced by monastic reform-movements and the effects which this change in attitude had on monastic furnishings.
400 *Ibid.*, pp. 118, 253.
401 *Ibid.*, pp. 253f.
402 *Ibid.*, pp. 138f.
403 The author of the poems in question is commonly identified with the *Ava inclusa* whose death is reported in the Melk annals for 1127 (*VfL* 1, 560).
404 Cf. Klewitz, *DA* 4 (1941), 224ff.; Fleckenstein, *Hofkapelle*; Bumke, *Mäzene*, pp. 58ff.; *Kultur*, pp. 624ff.
405 Duby, *History*, p. 420.
406 *Ibid.*, pp. 61f., 323.
407 *Ibid.*, pp. 323ff.
408 Cf. Rösener, *Frau*, pp. 216f.; Duby, *History*, pp. 344f. Such a room, not always restricted to women, but often expressly associated with literacy, can be termed a *kemenate* (e.g. Jans Enikel, *Weltchronik* 22421ff.; Otto von Freising, *Laubacher Barlaam* 14972ff.) or a *kamer* (e.g. prose *Lancelot* II 557, 25; Rudolf von Ems, *Barlaam und Josaphat* 368, 5ff.). Quite apart from the context of literacy *kemenate* can also be seen as a place for private musings, as in *Karl und Galie* 8454ff. (cf. *alleyne*, but also *ungemeyne*), or for confidential advice, as in the same work 10463ff. (cf. *alleyne* and its contrast with *gemeyne*). On *gemeine* to denote the public context see Hölscher, *Öffentlichkeit*, p. 55.
409 Cf. Küsters, *Klagefiguren*, pp. 37, 48, 67.
410 Cf. Haug and Vollmann, *Literatur*, p. 1547, note to 868, 6642: 'Wenn man in die Kemenate bestellt wird, so heißt das, daß es um eine nicht öffentliche Angelegenheit geht.'
411 See above, p. 290.
412 *Ibid.*
413 Duby, *History*, pp. 63, 322.
414 Gottfried von Strassburg, *Tristan* 18182ff.
415 Cf. Orth, *Ritter*, pp. 70ff. (especially p. 71, fn. 225).
416 In *Ruodlieb* XIII 35f. *secretum* (reinforced by *conclave*) is used as the equivalent of *heimliche* (cf. Haug and Vollmann, *Literatur*, p. 1382, note to 518, 35).
417 *Frauendienst* 60, 17ff. Cf. also 60, 1ff. (where the function of the *schríber* as scribe is also mentioned) and 101, 9ff. (that the letter had to be read out is made clear in 101, 23). In his *Weltchronik* 32077ff. Rudolf von Ems uses *heimliche* in the sense of 'confidential matters' in conjunction with the reading and writing performed by a scribe.
418 Wenzel, *ZfdPh* 107 (1988), 359, fn. 58.
419 Cf. also *Frauendienst* 57, 17ff.
420 From Johann's description of writing a letter in 6980ff. it is clear that there is an oral dimension to this activity (*munt* alongside *hant*). This makes it necessary for Wilhelm to write his letter alone in his room.
421 See above, p. 86.
422 On the use of *lesen* with prayers and prayer-books see the Appendix, pp. 319f.

423 Walther, *Codex*, plate 103 (under Alram von Gresten); Salowsky, *HJbb* 19 (1975), 40ff.
424 *Inferno* V 127ff.
425 Cf. also Brandan reading his book *an einer ecken* (*Lohengrin* 126).
426 459, 21f.
427 See above, p. 164.
428 Köhn, *Latein*, pp. 340ff. See above, p. 16.
429 Cf. also *tougenlîche* to describe the writing of a letter in *Reinfried von Braunschweig* 8124ff.
430 Implied by *Frauendienst* 60, 1ff. (Ulrich has to await the return of his scribe before he can learn the content of a letter he has received). Cf. Kartschoke, *WA* 16 (1981), 111f. and 140, n. 16.
431 Cf. 2814, 2821, 2829, 2837f.
432 2877f.
433 *Frauendienst* 57, 20ff.; 99, 23f.
434 That reading is presented as taking place orally is of a piece with writing orally, which the same work also illustrates (see above, n. 420).
435 On the practice of reading aloud to oneself in Latin and in the vernacular see above, pp. 16f. and 148. Hendrickson, *CJ* 25 (1929/30), 192, concedes that reading silently in classical antiquity was not impossible, but stresses that it was unusual and for a special purpose.
436 *Sibi legere*: as in the Benedictine Rule, quoted above, pp. 136f. *Sibi lectitare* is used by Bertholdus Augiensis, quoted above, p. 178. An example of *per se scrutari* from John of Salisbury is quoted p. 337, n. 155 (cf. also. p. 138). Although Raible, *Entwicklung*, p. 9, takes such phrases to indicate silent reading, I am rather more sceptical (cf. in the case of the Benedictine Rule Chaytor, *Script*, p. 14).
437 See above, pp. 136f.
438 *Tacite legere*: Chirius Fortunatianus, *Ars rhetorica*, p. 130; Augustine, *Confessiones* VI 3 (on Ambrose). On this phrase see di Capua, *RAALBA* 28 (1953), 64ff. *Legere in silentio*: Augustine, *Confessiones* VIII 29.
439 That *stille* used by itself could contrast with 'in public' as much as with 'aloud' is suggested by Veldeke, *Eneide* 13260; Albrecht von Scharfenberg, *Jüngerer Titurel* 2416, 1f.; Brun von Schönebeck, *Hohes Lied* 7309f.
440 See Balogh, *Philologus* 82 (1927), 85f., 88f. and Scholz, *Hören*, pp. 103f.
441 This should not surprise us if we take into account the contributions of Saenger on reading practice in the Middle Ages, including reading aloud or silently (*Manières*, pp. 131ff.; *Viator* 13 (1982), 367ff.; *Books*, pp. 141ff.; *Separation*, pp. 198ff.). His conclusion is that silent reading became feasible as a widespread practice only with the abandonment of *scriptura continua* in the British Isles in the seventh and eighth centuries (cf. Saenger, *Naissance*, pp. 447ff., and *Coupure*, pp. 451ff.), but that the possibility of silent reading was realised in practice for Latin texts only in the thirteenth century, and for French in the fourteenth. Raible, *Entwicklung*, pp. 27, 30, connects silent reading with the development of scholasticism. These findings confirm our suspicion that the solitary example of *Das Passional* owes more to Augustine's reading practice than to habits current in Germany towards the end of the thirteenth century.
442 Saenger, *Manières*, pp. 131ff., and *Viator* 13 (1982), 367ff. For silent reading in libraries he points to the evidence of college libraries in Paris, Oxford and Cambridge, and in the case of the lecture-room (where the explosion of book-production at university centres meant that students as well as the lecturer had texts in front of them) he adduces the need for students to follow silently in their copies what the lecturer read out to them from his. This practice was initially confined to Latin and to university centres, two further reasons for us not to be surprised at the lack of German-language evidence before 1300.
443 The argument of this section was put forward in a different form and context in Green, *Individual*, pp. 291ff.

444 On the similar position in France see Martin, *RFHL* 46 (1977), 597.
445 Wehrli, *Literatur*, p. 34, says that the dependence of the German language on Latin in the Middle Ages means that there is no 'autonome deutsche Sprachgeschichte'. He extends this judgment to literature as well (p. 43) and sees this obtaining as far as the eighteenth century at least. Similarly, Binns, *Culture*, has argued for the intellectual and cultural pre-eminence of Latin in Elizabethan and Jacobean England, even in view of Shakespeare, Marlowe and Sidney.
446 For the late Middle Ages Palmer, *PBB* 113 (1991), 247, talks of an 'Einbettung der deutschen Schriftkultur in ein übergeordnetes lateinisches Schriftwesen'.
447 We may term this the first occasion, as distinct from Otfrid's criticism of the oral poetry of laymen which was far from amounting to serious competition for clerical literature. See Vollmann-Profe, *Wiederbeginn*, p. 27.
448 Ibid., pp. 119, 199. Cf. also Kartschoke, *Geschichte*, p. 387, and Bumke, *Geschichte*, pp. 89f.
449 *VfL* 3, 1007.
450 Der Henneberger 7, 1ff.
451 The readiness of clerics to push laymen intellectually into an inferior category did not fail to call forth a critical reaction from the latter. A striking example is given by Heinrich von dem Türlin in his rejection of the logic-chopping of the dialecticians (*Die Crone* 10807ff.). On this passage see Jillings, *Crone*, pp. 213f.; Knapp, *Heinrich*, pp. 158f.; Schnell, *Recht*, pp. 222 and 228, fn. 17.
452 See above, p. 10.
453 *De nugis* IV 1 (p. 404).
454 Clanchy, *Memory*, p. 158.
455 Arnold von Lübeck, *Gesta*, prefacio 6 (p. 67). Cf. also Ganz, *Dienstmann*, p. 253, and Zäck, *Sündaere*, p. 343.
456 Archipoeta IV 25, 2ff.
457 *DVjs* 54 (1980), 627f.
458 Schnell, *Causa*, pp. 137ff., 151ff.
459 Karnein, *De Amore*.
460 Huber, *Aufnahme*, pp. 79ff.
461 Ibid., pp. 96ff. The difference between vernacular and clerical Latin love-poetry has been stressed by Wolf, *Anfänge*, p. 242.
462 Alanus, *De planctu* 2, 845, 17ff. Quoted and discussed by Huber, *Aufnahme*, p. 101.
463 Both these clerical authors are literate and highly Latinate, but address different types of audience: Alanus an exclusively clerical and Latin-speaking one, Gottfried one which comprised laymen and clerics.
464 PL 203, 154.
465 Krüger, *Krieger*, p. 336. Cf. also Jaeger, *Origins*, pp. 225f.
466 Cf. Tomasek, *ZfdA* 115 (1986), 260. The difficulty of translation may well lie behind the remark made in *Das Anegenge* 386ff., but here too the point is made in terms of the deficiency of the German language.
467 See above, p. 48.
468 *Pilatus* 31ff. Cf. Haug, *Literaturtheorie*, pp. 71f.
469 Cf. Weinhold, *ZfdPh* 8 (1877), 255; Haug, *Literaturtheorie*, p. 73.
470 Cf. Richert, *Wege*, pp. 320ff. On the need for works in the vernacular in the Teutonic Order see p. 411, n. 168.
471 Cf. *Tanto viro locuturi*, stanza 1* (p. 14). Quoted by Schüppert, *Kirchenkritik*, p. 33.
472 Archipoeta IV 20, 1ff.
473 Giraldus Cambrensis, *Expugnatio Hibernica*, pp. 410f. Cf. Türk, *Nugae*, p. 101; Clanchy, *Memory*, p. 214; Kasten, *Frauendienst*, p. 98.
474 Brandt, *Konrad*, p. 66.

475 Hugo von Trimberg, *Der Renner* 1202ff.
476 *Ibid.*, 1205, 1213f.
477 *Ibid.*, 1215f.
478 See above, pp. 298f.
479 Gnomic poets, the literacy of many of whom placed them in a position of rivalry with clerics (e.g. Fegfeuer I 3, 7ff.; cf. Wangenheim edn, p. 168), seek to keep their distance at all costs from singers who are not educated (*ibid.*, p. 248, fn. 2).
480 Cf. Schüppert, *Kirchenkritik*, p. 33, fn. 1.
481 *Sapiens hoc carmen audit*, stanza 10 (p. 364). Quoted by Schüppert, as in the last n.
482 *Erec* 19ff. Cf. Haug, *Literaturtheorie*, p. 103.
483 Cf. Kasten, *Frauendienst*, pp. 90, 112f., 114f.
484 See above, pp. 293ff.
485 On the contribution of writing and literacy to establishing autonomy cf. Johanek, *Schreiber*, p. 196.
486 Cf. Nelson, *Literacy*, p. 258.
487 Harris, *Literacy*, pp. 76, 334.
488 See above, p. 24.
489 Cf. Grubmüller, *Liber*, pp. 95ff.
490 Konrad von Hirsau, *Dialogus*, lines 104f.; Huygens, *Accessus*, p. 14.
491 See above, p. 25.
492 On this see Imbach, *Laien*, pp. 16ff.
493 The argument of the last few pages has been put forward in a different form in Green, *Humanism*, pp. 89ff.
494 See above, pp. 270ff.
495 See above, pp. 284ff.
496 See above, pp. 210ff.
497 See above, p. 269.
498 See above, pp. 179ff.
499 See pp. 71 and 350, n. 23.
500 Cf. Vollmann-Profe, *Wiederbeginn*, p. 34.
501 Urbanek, *ZfdPh* 106 (1987), 321ff.; 107 (1988), 26ff.
502 See above, pp. 186ff.
503 Cf. Mertens, *Überlegungen*, pp. 1ff.

Appendix: Middle High German 'lesen' = 'to narrate, recount, tell'

1 See above, p. 84.
2 Translated by Hatto, *Gottfried*, p. 44, as 'one hears the recital of their devotion' and by Ganz edn, fn. to v. 230, as 'wo man auch später noch vortragen hören wird'.
3 *Wörterbuch* I 1007b.
4 *Handwörterbuch* I 1889.
5 *Hören*, p. 41.
6 Ganz edn, fn. to v. 14125, suggests 'sagen, reden' for *maere lesen*. Schröder, *ZfdA* 104 (1975), 310, translates 'dann wird es überall heißen', and adds: 'Sofern da eher an Gerede als an eine offizielle Verlautbarung gedacht ist, wäre die Bedeutung "sprechen" hier erreicht.'
7 See above, p. 337, n. 155, and p. 347, n. 179.
8 See above, p. 85.
9 *De consolatione* 73, 22 (see above, p. 183).
10 Other examples from *Das Passional* differ in implying the meaning 'to teach' without suggesting the presence of writing. Cf. III 43, 19; 95, 9f.; 364, 86f.; 396, 36ff.
11 See above, p. 185.

12 Cf. Braungart, *ZfdPh* 106 (1987), 11.
13 Henkel, *Übersetzungen*, pp. 67ff.
14 Johanek, *Klosterstudien*, p. 52.
15 Walther, *Codex*, plate 96.
16 Cf. above, p. 275.
17 On this type of learning for laymen, bypassing the need for books, cf. p. 349, n. 3.
18 Other examples: Rudolf von Ems, *Weltchronik* 2852f.; Hugo von Langenstein, *Martina* 17, 93f.; *Passional* III 192, 26f.; Konrad Fleck, *Flore und Blanscheflur* 1025; *Der Busant* 74f.; *Das Märterbuch* 4836, 24658.
19 Cf. Sprandel, *Gesellschaft*, pp. 52f. In Martin and Vezin, *Mise*, p. 105, it is pointed out that every member of the clergy who took part in the liturgy had his own book, proper to his function, and Giesecke, *Buchdruck*, p. 243, reminds us of choral books, large enough to be read from a distance during the liturgy. Hugo von Trimberg, *Der Renner* 22382ff., makes it clear that a priest needs to be literate to read the books required for the liturgy.
20 A non-liturgical example is provided by the neumes in Otfrid's *Evangelienbuch* (Heidelberg MS), placed at a point where they would be visible to the reciter for two full pages of text. See Jammers, *Epos*, p. 150; Stephan, *Dichtung*, p. 147; Bertau and Stephan, review of Jammers, *Epos*, p. 199.
21 Cf. Schwietering, *Schriften*, pp. 32ff.
22 Cf. Ochsenbein, *Latein*, p. 49.
23 On this see Schreiner, *FMS* 24 (1990), 314ff.
24 Cf. also I 16, 21.
25 Cf. also I 49, 31ff. This passage illustrates the intermediate position of literate laywomen: they read the psalter in the literal sense (like clerics), but their metaphorical reading of the heavens is the only reading which Berthold associates with laymen (cf. I 19, 9ff. and 48, 23ff.).
26 As suggested by the way in which Veldeke in his *Servatius* varies between *salme lesen* (5919) and *saltere lesen* (329).
27 Carruthers, *Book*, pp. 82, 88; Haug and Vollmann, *Literatur*, p. 1378, note to 506, 23.
28 Saenger, *Books*, p. 150. Saenger is talking of the fifteenth century, but his differentiation is applicable to earlier periods.
29 *Ibid.*, p. 143.
30 *Ibid.*, p. 153 (cf. also p. 154, Paris BN, MS fr. 190).
31 *Ibid.*, p. 149.
32 Learning shorter catechetical texts by heart was prescribed for laymen in the Carolingian period (examples are listed by Ehrismann, *Geschichte* I 290ff.). In view of this practice it is probable that *lesen* means 'to recite' by memory, not from a written text, in the *Geistlicher Herzen Bavngart* 95, 2.
33 Saenger, *Books*, p. 153.
34 *Ibid.*, pp. 143, 156.
35 *Ibid.*, p. 144.
36 Young, *Drama* II 241. On the written dimension of late medieval personal piety see Johanek, *Schreiber*, p. 205.
37 On the literate ability to recognise what is meant by letters and syllables (let alone to read them) see above p. 133.
38 That the religious devotions of Servatius were normally by means of reading might however be deduced from 913f. See above p. 307.
39 Cf. Schröder, *ZfdA* 104 (1975), 310 on these lines: 'Die Pilger ... lasen sicher nicht vor, sie sagten Gelesenes und Gelerntes auswendig her.'
40 Ganz edn, fn. to v. 2650.
41 Other examples where *lesen* occurs in the context of prayer without reference to a written

text include *Trost in Verzweiflung* 14, 3; Herbort von Fritzlar, *Liet von Troye* 15775; Hugo von Langenstein, *Martina* 221, 12f.

42 The argument of this Appendix up to this point has appeared in a slightly different form in *Lesen*, pp. 85ff.

43 Cf. also 31613ff.

44 In 5892 and 5940 recital aloud is meant, with no suggestion of a written text.

45 V. 55118. In 81392 *vorlesen* has the force 'to recite, narrate', but in 83031 it remains unclear whether the messenger reads from a letter or gives an oral report.

46 To this list *Von dem Spitâle von Jêrusalêm* 590 (*Davon ich iuch unz har las*) could perhaps be added with the meaning 'to narrate, tell', on the grounds that this work contains no references to a written text and therefore no suggestion that *lesen* might mean 'to recite from writing'. The same applies to the *Jungfrau, Frau und Witwe* 120, 21 (*Als ich do vor han gelesen*), for this 'Märe' likewise contains no internal reference to its written status. I leave on one side *Sanct Brandan* 1328 (*wie er ez dicke hôrte lesen*) on the grounds that this wording does not express the way in which Thomas heard that Christ had risen from the dead, but reflects anachronistically the way in which this was transmitted in Christian tradition. Finally, it might be possible to add Heinrich von Neustadt, *Gottes Zukunft* 4689 (the editor glosses *lesen* here by 'erzählen'), but this work, like those listed above, was meant for a twofold reception.

47 *Alexius* A.

48 See Chapter 8.

49 See above, p. 175.

50 *ZfdA* 104 (1975), 311.

51 *Wörterbuch* I 1008a. Schröder refers to this later in his article, p. 312, where he makes his rejection clear.

52 Although the author of the *Friedberger Christ* implies two modes of delivery (*vorgelesen* or *gesagen*) his words cannot be transferred to his audience to suggest two modes of reception, since there is no other reference to the written status of his work or to the possibility that it was meant for readers as well.

53 *Hören*, pp. 81f.

54 Cf. also 1636ff.

55 Cf. also 1, 9ff.

56 Against this Kartschoke, *IASL* 8 (1983), 258, has made the hypothetical suggestion that *lesen* in the double formula could refer to the reciter, not the individual reader. On reasons for doubting this see above, pp. 142ff.

57 Further examples: *Väterbuch* 41484f.; *Schwabenspiegel Langform M, Königebuch* 20 (p. 131); Wetzel von Bernau, *Margaretenleben* 1054f.; Hugo von Trimberg, *Der Renner* 19; *Sante Margareten Marter* 575f.

58 On the absence of references to a reading reception of heroic literature see above, pp. 162f.

59 On these two constructions see above, pp. 85 and 88f.

60 Other examples are: *Zwei Kaufmänner und die treue Hausfrau* 19; Ulrich von Lichtenstein, *Frauendienst* 592, 6; *Lucidarius* 36, 23ff.; *Schwabenspiegel Langform M, Lehnrecht*, p. 405; *Hamburgisches Stadtrecht* (1270) VI 11 and 30; Konrad von Würzburg, *Engelhard* 6482.

61 When Ulrich von Etzenbach, *Alexandreis* 4732, says *als mir die âventiure las* we may take *lesen* to mean not simply 'to tell', but specifically 'to tell in written form' in view of the alternative construction with *schrîben* (3120: *die âventiure hât von in geschriben*) and the phrasing in 22380f. Similarly, the two variants used by Brun von Schönebeck (*Hohes Lied* 5744: *also ich uch e vore las* and 6359: *also ich uch schreib da bevorne*) suggest that *lesen* means 'to read out from a written text'. In the *Lübecker Stadtrecht* (p. 170, Beilage E: ... *allen dhen, de dese scrift anset unde horet lesen*) the combination of *scrift* (the legal document to be pronounced publicly) with *lesen* makes it clear that *lesen* means 'to read out from a fixed text in written form'.

62 See edn, p. 317.
63 Cf. Bumke, *Mäzene*, p. 451, n. 234.
64 558 (cf. 20, 491).
65 Other examples: *Kreuzfahrt des Landgrafen Ludwigs des Frommen von Thüringen* 5568; *Morant und Galie* 55ff.; *Flos und Blankeflos* 263f.; *Frauentreue* 354.
66 See above, p. 185.
67 Personal letter, 18 September 1990.

Bibliographical index

Primary sources

Works are listed here under the name of the author, where this is known, or under the name of the work itself. Otherwise, entries are to be found under the name of the editor. Occasionally, where they are referred to in the course of the argument, more than one edition is cited. Numbers in bold print refer to pages in this book where the work in question is mentioned.

Latin works

Admonitio generalis, MGH Leg. Cap. 1, 53ff. **44**
Aelred of Rievaulx, *De speculo caritatis*, ed. A. Hoste and C. H. Talbot, Turnhout 1971, pp. 3ff. **251, 403**
Alanus ab Insulis, *De planctu naturae*, ed. N. M. Häring, in: *Studi Medievali* ser. III 19 (1978), 2, 797ff. **311, 422**
  Summa de arte praedicatoria, PL 210, 111ff. **351**
Alcuin, *Carmina*, MGH Poetae Latini Aevi Carolini 1, 169ff. **45, 339**
  Epistolae, MGH Epp. 4, 1, 18ff. **68, 344, 383**
  Grammatica, PL 101, 849ff. **45, 339**
  Vita Willibrordi, MGH SS r.M. 7, 113ff. **384, 420**
Annales Stederburgenses, MGH SS 16, 199ff. **64, 78, 364**
Annales Xantenses, ed. B. von Simson, Hanover 1909 **228**
Apollinaris Sidonius, *Carmina*, MGH AA 8, 173ff. **65, 343**
Apuleius, *Metamorphoseos*, ed. J. van der Vliet, Leipzig 1897 **334**
Archipoeta, ed. H. Krefeld and H. Westphal, Heidelberg 1958 **32, 310, 312, 336, 422**
Arnold von Lübeck, *Gesta Gregorii Peccatoris*, ed. J. Schilling, Göttingen 1986 **310, 422**
Augustine, *De civitate Dei*, PL 41, 13ff. **32, 179, 382**
  Confessiones, ed. W. H. D. Rouse, Cambridge, Mass., 1968 **29, 335, 362, 421**
  Epistulae, ed. A. Goldbacher, Part 3, Vienna 1904 (CSEL 44) **29, 335**
Bede, *Historia ecclesiastica*, ed. C. Plummer, Oxford 1975 **29, 250, 335**
Benedict, *Regula Monachorum*, ed. J. McCann, London 1952 **30, 34, 40, 84, 136f., 274, 309, 335, 336, 363, 367, 421**
Bertholdus Augiensis, *Annales*, MGH SS 5, 267ff. **178, 382, 421**
Caesarius of Arles, *Sermo CCCIII*, PL 39, 2324ff. **14, 178, 327, 382**
Carmina Burana, ed. A. Hilka, C. Schumann, B. Bischoff, Heidelberg 1930, 1941, 1961, 1970
  Faksimile-Ausgabe, ed. B. Bischoff, Munich 1967
  Carmina Burana. Texte und Übersetzungen, ed. B. K. Vollmann, Frankfurt 1987 **167, 178, 380, 382**
Cassiodorus, *Variae*, MGH AA 12, 3ff. **9, 40, 327, 332, 413**
Cato, *M. Catonis quae extant*, ed. H. Jordan, Leipzig 1860 **20, 238, 239**
Catullus, ed. G. P. Goold, Cambridge, Mass., 1988 **27, 334**

BIBLIOGRAPHICAL INDEX

Chirius Fortunatianus, *Ars rhetorica*, ed. K. Halm, *Rhetores latini minores*, Leipzig 1863, pp. 81ff.   421
Chronica regia Coloniensis, ed. G. Waitz, Hanover 1880   353
Chronicon Hanoniense, ed. L. Vanderkindere, *La chronique de Gislebert de Mons*, Brussels 1904   72, 345
Chronicon Quedlinburgense, MGH SS 3, 22ff.   357
Cicero, *De oratore*, ed. E. W. Sutton and H. Rackham, Cambridge, Mass., 1967   363
   Pro L. Murena, ed. H. Kasten, Leipzig 1961   238f., 242, 399
Columella, ed. E. S. Forster and E. H. Heffner, Cambridge, Mass., 1968   334
Ecbasis cuiusdam captivi per tropologiam, ed. W. Trillitzsch, Leipzig 1964   32, 336
Einhard, *Vita Karoli*, ed. O. Holder-Egger, MGH Scriptores rerum Germanicarum in usum scholarum, Hanover 1922   39, 45, 46, 49, 162, 239, 333, 336, 339, 346, 357, 378, 399
Ekkehard IV, *Casus Sancti Galli*, ed. G. Meyer von Knonau, St. Gallen 1877   218, 343, 395
Fronto, *Epistulae ad M. Caes.*, ed. M. P. J. van den Hout, Leiden 1954   27, 178f., 225, 334
Frutolf von Michelsberg, *Chronica* (ed. as part of Ekkehard von Aura, *Chronicon Urspergense*), MGH SS 6, 33ff.   243, 357, 373, 400
Geoffrey of Monmouth, *Historia regum Britanniae*, ed. A. Griscom, London 1929   249f., 252, 253, 264, 268
Geoffroi de Vinsauf, *Poetria nova*, ed. E. Faral, *Les arts poétiques du XIIe et du XIIIe siècle*, Paris 1924, pp. 197ff.   62, 342
Gerhoch von Reichersberg, *Commentarius in psalmos*, PL 193, 623ff.   66f., 71, 343
Gervase of Tilbury, *Otia imperialia*, MGH SS 27, 363ff.   32, 336
Gesta consulum Andegavorum, ed. L. Halphen and R. Poupardin, Paris 1913   289, 413
Gildas, *De excidio et conquestu Britanniae*, MGH AA 13 (Chronica minora saec. IV-VII, vol. III), pp. 3ff.   250
Giraldus Cambrensis, *De rebus a se gestis*, ed. J. S. Brewer, *Giraldus Cambrensis, Opera*, London 1861, vol. I   336
   Descriptio Kambriae, ed. J. S. Brewer, *Giraldus Cambrensis, Opera*, London 1868, vol. VI   251, 252, 403, 406
   Expugnatio Hibernica, ed. J. F. Dimock, London 1867, pp. 207ff.   422
Gregory the Great, *Epistolae*, PL 77, 442ff.   126, 365
Historia Britonum, MGH AA 13 (Chronica minora saec. IV-VII, vol. III), pp. 113ff.   250
Honorius Augustodunensis, *Speculum ecclesiae*, PL 172, 807ff.   351
Horace, *Ars poetica*, ed. H. R. Fairclough, Cambridge, Mass., 1978   30, 335
   Epistulae, ed. H. R. Fairclough, Cambridge, Mass., 1978   30, 335
Hrabanus Maurus, *De universo*, PL 111, 9ff.   32, 88, 89, 181, 336
   Epistulae, MGH Epp. 5, 381ff.   29, 335
Hugh of St. Victor, *De scripturis*, PL 175, 9ff.   227, 237, 397
   Didascalicon, PL 176, 741ff.   85, 136, 138, 317, 347
Hugo of Fleury, *Historia ecclesiastica*, MGH SS 9, 349ff.   24, 246, 248, 249, 252, 267, 268, 333, 401
Hugo von Trimberg, *Registrum multorum auctorum*, ed. K. Langosch, Berlin 1942   350
   Solsequium, ed. E. Seemann, Munich 1914   350, 390, 413
Huygens, R. B. C. (ed.), *Accessus ad auctores*, Brussels 1954   423
Isidore of Seville, *Etymologiae*, ed. W. M. Lindsay, Oxford 1910   226f., 237f., 242, 247, 248, 249, 255, 256, 258, 266, 267, 330, 378, 397, 398, 399, 403, 404
John of Salisbury, *Metalogicon*, ed. C. C. I. Webb, Oxford 1929   84, 86, 136, 138, 316, 317, 337, 347, 421
   Policraticus, PL 199, 385ff.   179, 225, 382
Jonas of Orléans, *De institutione laicorum*, PL 106, 121ff.   178, 382
Jordanes, *Getica*, MGH AA 5, 53ff.   67, 239, 243, 344, 399, 400
Konrad von Hirsau, *Dialogus super auctores*, ed. R. B. C. Huygens, Berchem 1955   227, 237, 238, 314, 397, 398, 399, 423

Lactantius, *Divinae institutiones*, PL 6, 111ff.   27f., 179, 334
Lambert of Ardres, *Historia comitum Ghisnensium*, MGH SS 24, 557ff.   108, 359, 411
Lex Baiwariorum, MGH Leg. 1, 5, 2, 267ff.   228, 397
Mainzer Reichslandfriede, MGH Const. 2, 250ff. (No. 196a)   100, 101, 155, 353, 372
Mansi, J. D., *Sacrorum conciliorum nova et amplissima collectio*, Florence 1759ff., Venice 1769ff., Paris 1901ff.   410
Map, Walter, *De nugis curialium*, ed. M. R. James, C. N. L. Brooke, R. A. B. Mynors, Oxford 1983   10, 14, 24f., 310, 312, 313f., 328, 333, 334, 422
Martial, ed. W. M. Lindsay, Oxford 1965   27, 179, 225, 334
Modus qui et Carelmanninc, ed. W. Bulst, *Carmina Cantabrigiensia*, Heidelberg 1950, pp. 13ff.   106
Nettleship, H., *Ancient lives of Virgil*, Oxford 1879   30, 335
Notker Balbulus, *Liber Ymnorum*, ed. W. von den Steinen, Bern 1948   362
Ordericus Vitalis, *Historia ecclesiastica*, ed. M. Chibnall, Oxford 1969ff.   32, 336
Origen, *In Genesim homiliae*, PG 12, 146ff.   178, 382
Otto von Freising, *Chronicon*, ed. A. Hofmeister, Hanover 1912   65, 243, 251, 373, 400
  Gesta Friderici, ed. G. Waitz, Hanover 1912   227, 397
Ovid, *Tristia*, ed. G. P. Goold, Cambridge, Mass., 1988   27, 334, 335, 363, 369
Palladius, *Historiae monachorum*, PL 74, 250ff.   27, 334
Paris, Matthew, *Chronica majora*, ed. H. R. Luard, London 1872ff.   9, 415
Persius, ed. O. Scheel, Munich 1950   27, 334
Peter of Blois, *De confessione*, PL 207, 1078ff.   92, 108, 251, 348, 359
Petrus von Andlau, *De imperio Romano*, ed. J. Hürbin, ZfRG (GA) 13 (1892), 163ff.   24, 333
Philip of Harvengt, *Epistolae*, PL 203, 1ff.   179, 283, 311, 382, 411, 415
Pliny the Younger, *Epistulae*, ed. R. A. B. Mynors, Oxford 1963   27, 31, 62, 177, 334, 335, 342, 382
Procopius, *Bella Gothica*, ed. J. Haury, *Opera omnia* II, Leipzig 1963   333
Quintilian, *Institutio oratoria*, ed. H. E. Butler, London 1966ff.   385
Ratpert, *Galluslied*, ed. P. Osterwalder, Berlin 1982   65, 66, 69, 96, 343, 344, 350
Remigius of Auxerre, *Commentum in Martianum Capellam*, ed. C. E. Lutz, Leiden 1962 and 1965   237, 398
Rhetorica ad Herennium, ed. H. Caplan, London 1964   238, 258, 342, 398
Ribbeck, O. (ed.), *Scaenicae Romanorum poesis fragmenta. 2: Comicorum fragmenta*, Leipzig 1873   332
Robert of Melun, *Sententie*, ed. R. M. Martin, *Oeuvres de Robert de Melun* 3, 3ff., Louvain 1947   227, 237, 397, 398
Ruodlieb, ed. F. P. Knapp, Stuttgart 1977   331, 347, 420
Sapiens hoc carmen audit, ed. G. M. Dreves, C. Blume, H. M. Bannister, *Analecta hymnica medii aevi* 46, 363f. (No. 320), Leipzig 1905   312, 423
Saxo Grammaticus, *Gesta Danorum*, ed. A. Holder, Strassburg 1886   239, 357, 399
Saxo, Poeta, *Annales de gestis B. Caroli Magni*, PL 99, 683ff.   357
Spartianus, *Hadrianus*, ed. H. Peter, *Scriptores historiae Augustae*, Leipzig 1884   335
Suetonius, *Claudius*, ed. J. C. Rolfe, Cambridge, Mass., 1979   335
Tacitus, *Annales*, ed. E. Koestermann, Leipzig 1952   21, 22, 239, 333, 399
  Germania, ed. J. G. C. Anderson, Oxford 1938   21, 22, 239, 333, 399
  Historiae, ed. C. H. Moore, Cambridge, Mass., 1962   335
Tanto viro locuturi, ed. K. Strecker, *Moralisch-satirische Gedichte Walters von Chatillon*, Heidelberg 1929, pp. 1ff.   312, 422
Thegan, *Vita Hludowici imperatoris*, MGH SS 2, 590ff.   179, 382
Theodulf of Orléans, *Libri Carolini*, PL 98, 999ff.   32, 365
Traditiones Frisingenses, ed. T. Bitterauf, Munich 1905   228, 397
Traditiones Patavienses, ed. M. Heuwieser, Munich 1930   228, 397
Venantius Fortunatus, *Carmina*, MGH AA 4, 7ff.   67, 344

BIBLIOGRAPHICAL INDEX

Vita Altmanni, MGH SS 12, 228ff. 71, 345, 350
Vita S. Cunegundis, MGH SS 4, 821ff. 179, 348, 382
Vita Liudgeri, MGH SS 2, 404ff. 68, 344
Vita S. Wandregiseli, MGH SS r.M. 5, 13ff. 369
William of Malmesbury, *Gesta regum Anglorum*, ed. W. Stubbs, London 1887ff. 138, 251, 253, 348, 367, 382, 403, 411
William of Newburgh, *Historia rerum Anglicarum*, ed. R. Howlett, London 1884 251, 403
William of Tyre, *Historia rerum in partibus transmarinis gestarum*, in: *Recueil des historiens des croisades. Historiens occidentaux*, vol. 1, parts 1 and 2, Paris 1844 178, 382
Wipo, *Tetralogus*, ed. H. Bresslau, Hanover 1977 24, 333

Vernacular works

Abecedarium Nordmannicum, MSD, pp. 19f. 21f., 151, 231
Adelbrecht, *Johannes Baptista*, ed. F. Maurer, *Religiöse Dichtungen* II 328ff. 355, 412
Ad equum errehet, ed. E. von Steinmeyer, *Sprachdenkmäler*, p. 373 95
Ad fluxum sanguinis narium, ed. E. von Steinmeyer, *Sprachdenkmäler*, pp. 379f. 349
Ältere Judith, ed. F. Maurer, *Religiöse Dichtungen* I 398ff. 354
Alber, *Tnugdalus*, ed. A. Wagner, Erlangen 1882, pp. 119ff. 98, 148, 248, 249, 352, 401, 402, 412
Albertus von Augsburg, *Leben des heiligen Ulrich*, ed. K.-E. Geith, Berlin 1971 80, 81, 104, 131, 132, 144, 159, 207, 216, 302, 347, 368, 375, 390, 394
Albrant, Meister, *Roßarzneibuch*, ed. G. Eis, Konstanz 1960 151, 370, 398
Albrecht von Halberstadt, *Ovidübersetzung*, ed. K. Bartsch, Quedlinburg 1861 72, 299, 418
Albrecht von Scharfenberg, *Der Jüngere Titurel*, ed. W. Wolf, Berlin 1955ff. 81, 89, 93, 109, 142, 209, 213, 268, 308, 347, 349, 359, 360, 391, 392, 396, 407, 412, 419, 421
Alemannische Tochter Syon, ed. J. F. L. T. Merzdorf, *Der Mönch von Heilbronn*, Berlin 1870 99, 352
Alexius, ed. H. F. Massmann, Quedlinburg 1843 (A: pp. 45ff., F: pp. 118ff.) 89, 248, 317, 320, 321, 356, 401, 402, 413, 425
Alpharts Tod, ed. E. Martin, *Deutsches Heldenbuch* II 3ff., Berlin 1866 358, 377
Altalemannische Psalmenübersetzung, ed. E. von Steinmeyer, *Sprachdenkmäler*, pp. 293ff. 95, 151, 204, 385
Altdeutsche Exodus, ed. E. Papp, Munich 1968
Altsächsischer Psalmenkommentar, MSD, pp. 233ff. Also E. Wadstein, *Kleinere altsächsische Sprachdenkmäler*, Leipzig 1899, pp. 4ff. 99, 153f., 385
Amorbacher Spiel von Mariae Himmelfahrt, ed. R. Heym, *ZfdA* 52 (1910), 1ff. 105, 160, 344, 357, 376
Anegenge, ed. D. Neuschäfer, Munich 1966 80, 98, 116, 352, 422
Annolied, ed. F. Maurer, *Religiöse Dichtungen* II 3ff. Also E. Nellmann, Stuttgart 1986 68, 92f., 101, 104, 244, 245, 272, 353, 357, 400, 401, 404
Armer Hartmann, *Die Rede vom heiligen Glauben*, ed. F. Maurer, *Religiöse Dichtungen* II 567ff. 81, 93, 98, 115, 140, 141, 153, 204, 216, 226, 230, 300, 301, 302, 369, 396, 397, 419
Arnold, Priester, *Legende von der heiligen Juliana*, ed. F. Maurer, *Religiöse Dichtungen* III 7ff. 412
    Loblied auf den Heiligen Geist, ed. F. Maurer, *Religiöse Dichtungen* III 57ff. 98, 118f., 341, 349, 351, 363, 371, 412
Arnsteiner Mariengebet, ed. F. Maurer, *Religiöse Dichtungen* I 433ff. 97
Athis und Prophilias, ed. C. von Kraus, *Mittelhochdeutsches Übungsbuch*, Heidelberg 1926, pp. 63ff. 67
Augensegen, ed. E. von Steinmeyer, *Sprachdenkmäler*, pp. 386f. 349
Ava, Frau, *Johannes*, ed. F. Maurer, *Religiöse Dichtungen* II 382ff. 72, 115, 216, 345

BIBLIOGRAPHICAL INDEX

Jüngstes Gericht, ed. F. Maurer, *Religiöse Dichtungen* II 498ff.   158, 216, 374, 414
Leben Jesu, ed. F. Maurer, *Religiöse Dichtungen* II 398ff.   103, 216, 363
Basler Predigten, ed. W. Wackernagel, *Altdeutsche Predigten und Gebete aus Handschriften*, Basel 1876, pp. 43ff. (nos. XXVII-XXXV)   345
Benediktbeurer Gebet zum Meßopfer, ed. F. Maurer, *Religiöse Dichtungen* II 316ff.   99
Benediktbeurer Glaube und Beichte III, ed. E. von Steinmeyer, *Sprachdenkmäler*, pp. 357ff.   351
Benediktbeurer Passionsspiel, ed. O. Schumann and B. Bischoff, *Carmina Burana* I 3, Heidelberg 1970, pp. 149ff.   62, 105, 160, 161, 344, 356, 375, 376
Benediktinerregel (Middle High German versions), ed. C. Selmer, *Middle High German translations of the Regula Sancti Benedicti*, Cambridge, Mass., 1933 (Admont: pp. 206ff., Asbach: pp. 129ff., Engelberg: pp. 89ff., Hohenfurth: pp. 48ff., Munich: pp. 167ff., Zwiefalten: pp. 13ff.). Also M. C. Sullivan (ed.), *Middle High German Benedictine Rule*, Hildesheim 1976   80, 84f., 137, 346, 347, 348, 353, 364, 367
Benediktinerregel (Old High German version), ed. E. von Steinmeyer, *Sprachdenkmäler*, pp. 190ff.   38, 49, 53, 91, 95, 151, 204, 364, 385
Benoît de Sainte-Maure, *Roman de Troie*, ed. L. Constans, Paris 1904ff.   238, 248, 251f., 399, 402, 417
Beowulf, ed. F. Klaeber, New York 1941   70, 345
Béroul, *Tristran*, ed. A. Ewert, Oxford 1967 and 1970   164, 194, 378
Berthold von Holle, *Crane*, ed. K. Bartsch, Nürnberg 1858, pp. 19ff.   165, 209, 213, 346, 360, 379
Darifant, ed. K. Bartsch, Nürnberg 1858, pp. 191ff.   165, 209, 213, 360f., 369, 379
Demantin, ed. K. Bartsch, Stuttgart 1875   165, 209, 213, 360, 379
Berthold von Regensburg, *Predigten*, ed. F. Pfeiffer, Berlin 1965   25, 66, 75, 153, 318, 319, 320, 328, 332, 334, 414, 424
Biterolf und Dietleib, ed. O. Jänicke, *Deutsches Heldenbuch* I 1ff., Berlin 1866   106, 358, 377
Böhmenschlacht, ed. A. Bach, *Die Werke des Verfassers der Schlacht bei Göllheim*, Bonn 1930, pp. 210ff.   247, 401
Boppe, ed. F. H. von der Hagen, *Minnesinger* II 377ff. and III 405ff.   87, 380, 416
Braunschweigische Reimchronik, MGH Deutsche Chroniken 2   130, 134, 157, 206, 211, 265, 354, 369, 374
Breviarien von Sankt Lambrecht, ed. A. E. Schönbach, *ZfdA* 20 (1876), 129ff.   347
Bruchstücke der Lex Salica, ed. E. von Steinmeyer, *Sprachdenkmäler*, pp. 55ff.   46, 47, 100, 364
Brun von Schönebeck, *Ave Maria*, ed. W. Norlind, *NdJb* 53 (1927), 59ff.   198, 207, 220, 391
Hohes Lied, ed. A. Fischer, Tübingen 1893   80, 87, 92, 103, 144, 158, 198–201, 206, 220, 363, 364, 366, 388–389, 390, 397, 421, 425
Buch der Könige alter ê und niuwer ê, ed. K. A. Eckhardt, Aalen 1975   156, 265, 413, 414
Buch der Rügen, ed. T. von Karajan, *ZfdA* 2 (1842), 6ff.   352, 365
Buch von geistlicher Lehre, ed. A. Wielander, *Ein Tiroler Christenspiegel des 14. Jahrhunderts*, diss. Fribourg 1959   205, 216, 237, 336, 390, 420
Büchlein von der Himmelfahrt Mariae, ed. J. Klapper, *ZfdA* 50 (1908), 172ff.   70, 205, 216, 390, 392, 394, 396
Burkart von Hohenfels, KDL, pp. 33ff.   362
Busant, ed. F. H. von der Hagen, *Gesamtabenteuer* I 331ff., Darmstadt 1961   327, 379, 424
Cantilena de conversione Sancti Pauli, ed. F. Maurer, *Religiöse Dichtungen* I 261ff.   350
Carmen ad Deum, ed. E. von Steinmeyer, *Sprachdenkmäler*, pp. 290ff.   95, 151, 385
Cato, Rumpfüberlieferung, ed. F. Zarncke, *Der deutsche Cato*, Leipzig 1852, pp. 27ff.   96
Cato Z, ed. L. Zatočil, *Cato a Facetus*, Brünn 1952, pp. 29ff. (Cato Z^1: pp. 51ff.)   95f., 151, 231, 349, 370
Chrétien de Troyes, *Cligés*, ed. A. Micha, Paris 1957   283f., 292

Erec, ed. W. Foerster, Halle 1934   254, 255, 262, 313, 342, 386, 404, 423
Perceval, ed. A. Hilka, *Li contes del Graal*, Halle 1932   254, 262, 263, 404
Yvain, ed. W. Foerster, Halle 1926   254f., 256, 263f., 269, 295, 296, 346, 406
Christherre-Chronik, ed. H. F. Massmann, *Der keiser und der kunige buoch*, Quedlinburg 1854, pp. 118ff.   102, 157, 206, 212
Christus und die Samariterin, ed. E. von Steinmeyer, *Sprachdenkmäler*, pp. 89ff.   102, 341, 354, 374
Coleridge, S. T., *Biographia litteraria*, ed. G. Watson, London 1960   333
Constantin, ed. F. H. von der Hagen, *Gesamtabenteuer* II 575ff., Darmstadt 1961   401
Contra uermes pecus edentes, ed. E. von Steinmeyer, *Sprachdenkmäler*, pp. 373f.   349
Corpus der altdeutschen Originalurkunden bis zum Jahre 1300, ed. F. Wilhelm, R. Newald, H. de Boor, D. Haacke, Lahr 1932ff.   101, 155f., 205, 229f., 300, 353, 362, 373, 397f., 418
Dante Alighieri, *Divine Comedy*, ed. C. S. Singleton, London 1970   306
David von Augsburg, ed. F. Pfeiffer, *Deutsche Mystiker des 14. Jahrhunderts* I 310ff., Leipzig 1845   99, 205, 222, 223, 352, 392, 396
De Heinrico, ed. E. von Steinmeyer, *Sprachdenkmäler*, pp. 110ff.   350
Deutschenspiegel, ed. K. A. Eckhardt and A. Hübner, Hanover 1933   155, 156, 205, 216, 231, 353, 373
Deutung der Meßgebräuche, ed. F. Maurer, *Religiöse Dichtungen* II 290ff.   98
Dietrich und Wenezlan, ed. J. Zupitza, *Deutsches Heldenbuch* V 267ff., Berlin 1870   176f.
Dietrich von Glezze, *Der Borte*, ed. O. R. Meyer, Heidelberg 1915   86, 129, 322, 361
Dietrichs Flucht, ed. E. Martin, *Deutsches Heldenbuch* II 57ff., Berlin 1866   83, 93, 377
Dream of the Rood, ed. B. Dickins and A. S. C. Ross, London 1945   35, 337
Drei Jünglinge im Feuerofen, ed. F. Maurer, *Religiöse Dichtungen* I 402ff.   354
Drei listige Frauen II, ed. H. Niewöhner, *Neues Gesamtabenteuer*, Dublin 1967, pp. 140ff.   83
Dukus Horant, ed. P. F. Ganz, F. Norman, W. Schwarz, Tübingen 1964   358
Dulciflorie, ed. H. Niewöhner, *Der Sperber*, Berlin 1913, pp. 95ff.   379
Eberhard, Priester, *Gandersheimer Reimchronik*, ed. L. Wolff, Halle 1927   57, 74, 75, 101, 109, 125, 130, 131, 142, 218, 265, 285, 341, 353
Ebernand von Erfurt, *Heinrich und Kunigunde*, ed. R. Bechstein, Quedlinburg 1860   80, 85, 104, 120, 132, 144, 159, 207, 216, 248, 249, 306, 346, 347, 355, 375, 391, 401, 402
Eckenlied, ed. M. Wierschin, Tübingen 1974   106, 357, 377
Eilhart von Oberge, *Tristrant*, ed. F. Lichtenstein, Strassburg 1877   76, 109, 164, 194, 360
Die 'Epistola ad fratres de Monte Dei' des Wilhelm von Saint-Thierry, ed. V. Honemann, Munich 1978   367
Erfurter Judeneid, MSD, pp. 320f.   100
Die Erlösung, ed. F. Maurer, Leipzig 1934   57, 103, 132, 140, 158, 206, 212, 317, 320, 334, 341, 355, 363, 392, 417
Esther, ed. K. Schröder, *Germanistische Studien* I (1872), 247ff.   89
Exhortatio ad plebem christianam, ed. E. von Steinmeyer, *Sprachdenkmäler*, pp. 49ff.   79, 97
Ezzolied, ed. F. Maurer, *Religiöse Dichtungen* I 269ff.   66, 69, 71, 96, 270, 272, 286, 287, 314f., 350, 371
Fegfeuer, ed. W. Wangenheim, *Das Basler Fragment einer mitteldeutsch-niederdeutschen Liederhandschrift und sein Spruchdichter-Repertoire (Kelin, Fegfeuer)*, Bern 1972   84, 423
Fleck, Konrad, *Flore und Blanscheflur*, ed. E. Sommer, Quedlinburg 1846   110, 117, 209, 220, 360, 363, 370, 392, 396, 402, 419, 424
Flos und Blankeflos, ed. O. Decker, Rostock 1913   85, 110, 118, 347, 360, 402, 426
Die Frau als Reitpferd, ed. H. Niewöhner, *Neues Gesamtabenteuer*, Dublin 1967, pp. 36ff.   361
Frauentreue, ed. K. Burchardt, *Das mittelhochdeutsche Gedicht von der Frauentreue*, diss. Berlin 1910   166, 361, 369, 379, 426

Der Frauen Trost, ed. F. H. von der Hagen, *Gesamtabenteuer* III 429ff., Darmstadt 1961   379
Freidank, *Bescheidenheit*, ed. H. E. Bezzenberger, Halle 1872   365
Friedberger Christ, ed. F. Maurer, *Religiöse Dichtungen* II 103ff.   103, 176, 301, 321f., 425
Gaimar, Geoffrey, *Lestorie des Engles*, ed. T. D. Hardy and C. T. Martin, London 1888   246, 250, 290, 414
Ganz, P. (ed.), *Tristan*, Wiesbaden 1978
Gebet einer Frau, ed. F. Maurer, *Religiöse Dichtungen* III 621ff.   97
Gebete und Benediktionen von Muri, ed. F. Wilhelm, *Denkmäler deutscher Prosa des 11. und 12. Jahrhunderts*, Munich 1960, pp. 73ff.   97, 319, 351
Gegen Halsentzündung, ed. E. von Steinmeyer, *Sprachdenkmäler*, pp. 387ff.   349
Geistlicher Herzen Bavngart, ed. H. Unger, Munich 1969   99, 148, 154, 205, 222, 352, 372, 390, 396, 397, 424
Georgslied, ed. W. Haubrichs, *Georgslied und Georgslegende im frühen Mittelalter*, Königstein 1979   53, 65, 71, 96, 345, 350
Gertrud von Helfta, *Ein botte der göttlichen miltekeit*, ed. O. Wieland, Ottobeuren 1973   320, 367
Die Gevatterinnen, ed. H. Niewöhner, *Neues Gesamtabenteuer*, Dublin 1967, pp. 40ff.   318
Der Göttweiger Trojanerkrieg, ed. A. Koppitz, Berlin 1926   135, 266, 308, 359
Gottfried von Strassburg, *Tristan*, ed. P. Ganz, Wiesbaden 1978   58, 67, 69, 83, 91, 109, 114, 116f., 120, 122, 123, 124f., 131f., 133, 134, 141, 143, 164, 165, 171, 175, 187, 191, 193, 194–197, 199, 201, 209, 220, 221, 224, 257–261, 292, 294, 297, 298f., 300, 301, 302, 303, 305, 311, 316, 318, 320, 321, 343, 346, 348, 352, 359, 361, 363, 366, 368, 378, 381, 382, 387, 391, 395, 396, 397, 404f., 414, 416, 417, 418, 419, 423, 424
Guernes de Pont-Sainte-Maxence, *Vie de saint Thomas*, ed. E. Walberg, Paris 1936   402
Gundacker von Judenburg, *Christi Hort*, ed. J. Jaksche, Berlin 1910   228, 248, 355, 397
Die gute Frau, ed. E. Sommer, *ZfdA* 2 (1842), 392ff.   148, 369, 402
Hagen, F. H. von der, *Minnesinger. Deutsche Liederdichter des zwölften, dreizehnten und vierzehnten Jahrhunderts*, Leipzig 1838
Hagen, Gottfried, *Chronik der Stadt Köln*, ed. H. Cardauns, Leipzig 1875   88, 265, 321, 354
Hamburgisches Stadtrecht vom Jahre 1270, ed. J. M. Lappenberg, *Die ältesten Stadt-, Schiff- und Landrechte Hamburgs*, Aalen 1966, pp. 1ff.   89, 100, 353, 425
Hammelburger Markbeschreibung, ed. E. von Steinmeyer, *Sprachdenkmäler*, pp. 62f.   100
Hardyng, John, *Chronicle*, ed. H. Ellis, London 1812   250, 267, 403
Hartmann von Aue, *Armer Heinrich*, ed. H. Paul, Halle 1930   187f., 189, 207, 212, 300, 386, 392, 396, 418, 419
    Erec, ed. A. Leitzmann, Tübingen 1963   58, 72, 82, 83, 109, 187, 188f., 208, 212, 256f., 261, 299, 301, 342, 378, 386, 393, 404, 418
    Gregorius, ed. F. Neumann, Wiesbaden 1958   24, 92, 134, 139, 187, 188, 207, 212, 214, 225, 290, 300, 302, 310, 332, 386, 392, 393, 396, 414, 418, 419
    Iwein, ed. G. F. Benecke, K. Lachmann, L. Wolff, Berlin 1968   83, 86, 109, 187, 189f., 208, 212, 256, 258, 267, 296, 306, 378, 385, 386, 387–388, 393, 404
    Klage-Büchlein, ed. H. Zutt, Berlin 1968   186f., 315
Hartwig von dem Hage, *Margaretenlegende*, ed. W. Schmitz, Göppingen 1976, pp. 260ff.   133, 159, 232, 366, 375, 401
Die sieben Tagzeiten, ed. W. Schmitz, Göppingen 1976, pp. 307ff.   132f., 154, 372, 398
Die Heidin, ed. L. Pfannmüller, Berlin 1911   139
Die Heidin IV, ed. R. Kienast, E. Henschel, U. Pretzel, Leipzig 1957   361, 379
Die heilige Regel für ein vollkommenes Leben, ed. R. Priebsch, Berlin 1909   153, 368, 371, 398
Der heimliche Bote, ed. H. Meyer-Benfey, *Mittelhochdeutsche Übungsstücke*, Halle 1920, pp. 30ff. (under the title *Lehren für Frauen und Männer*)   129, 296, 417
Heinrich der Glichezare, *Reinhart Fuchs*, ed. G. Baesecke, Halle 1925   359
Heinrich von Burgeis, *Der Seele Rat*, ed. H.-F. Rosenfeld, Berlin 1932   99, 205, 220, 390, 392, 396

Heinrich von Freiberg, *Tristan*, ed. A. Bernt, Halle 1906, pp. 1ff.   109f., 133, 138, 165, 209, 213, 348, 360, 368, 378, 379, 386, 392
Heinrich von Hesler, *Apokalypse*, ed. K. Helm, Berlin 1907   74, 85, 103, 123, 124, 130, 145, 157, 158, 206, 216, 355, 356, 369, 374, 417
  Erlösung, ed. O. von Heinemann, *ZfdA* 32 (1888), 111ff. and 446ff.   158, 206, 216, 231, 355, 375
  Evangelium Nicodemi, ed. K. Helm, Tübingen 1902   158, 206, 216, 248, 317, 355, 375, 401
Heinrich von Kröllwitz, *Vaterunser*, ed. G. C. F. Lisch, Quedlinburg 1839   33, 74, 99, 131, 154, 205, 211, 345, 352, 371
Heinrich von Melk, ed. R. Kienast, Heidelberg 1946   98
  Von dem gemeinen lebene, ed. F. Maurer, *Religiöse Dichtung* III 302ff.   120, 348f., 351
  Das Priesterleben, ed. F. Maurer, *Religiöse Dichtung* III 258ff.   349, 351
  Von des todes gehugde, ed. F. Maurer, *Religiöse Dichtung* III 328ff.   68, 332
Heinrich von Morungen, ed. H. Moser and H. Tervooren, *Minnesangs Frühling. I: Texte*, Stuttgart 1977, pp. 236ff.   362
Heinrich von Neustadt, *Apollonius von Tyrland*, ed. S. Singer, Berlin 1906, pp. 3ff.   67, 71, 110, 165, 209, 220, 348, 349, 352, 360, 390, 392
  Gottes Zukunft, ed. S. Singer, Berlin 1906, pp. 331ff.   103, 158, 206, 220, 248, 317, 349, 352, 355, 390, 396, 402, 418, 425
  Visio Philiberti, ed. S. Singer, Berlin 1906, pp. 455ff.   99, 204, 220, 352, 390
Heinrich von dem Türlin, *Die Crone*, ed. G. H. F. Scholl, Amsterdam 1966   69, 109, 164, 209, 212, 215, 289f., 359, 366, 369, 378, 391, 393, 419, 422
Heinrich von Veldeke, *Eneide*, ed. G. Schieb and T. Frings, Berlin 1964   58, 59, 63f., 72, 108, 120, 124, 134, 139, 140, 164, 176, 199, 208, 212, 287, 290, 299, 300, 303, 342, 391, 403, 414, 418, 421
  Servatius, ed. T. Frings and G. Schieb, Halle 1956   59, 85, 91, 92, 104, 140, 141, 287, 290, 301, 307, 320, 355, 414, 419, 424
Heinrichs Litanei, ed. F. Maurer, *Religiöse Dichtung* III 124ff.   66, 97, 343, 412
Heliand, ed. O. Behaghel, Halle 1933   49, 50, 69, 102, 144, 157, 158, 181, 206, 216, 271, 300, 301, 334, 337, 344, 354, 368, 369, 374, 408, 417, 418
Der Henneberger, ed. F. H. von der Hagen, *Minnesinger* III 39ff.   310, 422
Herbort von Fritzlar, *Liet von Troye*, ed. G. K. Frommann, Quedlinburg 1837   108f., 121, 164, 177, 228, 248, 276, 287, 301, 359, 363, 381, 397, 402, 419, 425
Hermann, Bruder, *Leben der Gräfin Iolande von Vianden*, ed. J. Meier, Breslau 1889   86, 306, 309, 356
Hermann der Damen, ed. F. H. von der Hagen, *Minnesinger* III 160ff.   380
Herrand von Wildonie, *Vier Erzählungen*, ed. H. Fischer and P. Sappler, Tübingen 1969   147, 247, 260, 294, 401
Herzog Ernst B, ed. K. Bartsch, Vienna 1869, pp. 15ff. (*D*: ed. F. H. von der Hagen and J. G. Büsching, *Deutsche Gedichte des Mittelalters* I 1ff., Berlin 1808; *G*: ed. K. Bartsch, Vienna 1869, pp. 189ff.)   72, 77, 84, 86f., 107, 125, 137, 227, 228, 245, 246, 247, 248, 343, 358, 364, 377, 378, 397, 400, 401
Hesel, Erhart, *Das Arzneibuch*, ed. B. D. Haage, Göppingen 1972   151, 370, 398
Hildebrandslied, ed. E. von Steinmeyer, *Sprachdenkmäler*, pp. 1ff.   22, 50, 105, 106, 162, 241
Hiltgart von Hürnheim, *Secretum Secretorum*, ed. R. Möller, Berlin 1963   80, 96, 144, 152, 204, 214, 215f., 371, 390, 397
Himmelgartner Passionsspiel, ed. E. Sievers, *ZfdPh* 21 (1889), 385ff.   356
Hirsch und Hinde, ed. E. von Steinmeyer, *Sprachdenkmäler*, p. 399   361
Die Hochzeit, ed. F. Maurer, *Religiöse Dichtung* II 179ff.   98, 351
Homilie Bedas, ed. E. Wadstein, *Kleinere altsächsische Sprachdenkmäler*, Leipzig 1899, p. 18   97f., 153
Hürnen Seyfrid, ed. K. C. King, Manchester 1958   377

Hugo von Langenstein, *Martina*, ed. A. von Keller, Stuttgart 1856   104, 147, 159, 207, 217, 248, 356, 394, 399, 402, 424, 425

Hugo von Trimberg, *Der Renner*, ed. G. Ehrismann, Berlin 1970   68, 96, 108, 109, 117, 131, 152, 175, 204, 219f., 312, 332, 347, 350, 357, 358, 363, 368, 369, 370, 371, 378, 381, 390, 396, 413, 423, 424, 425

Irregang und Girregar, ed. F. H. von der Hagen, *Gesamtabenteuer* III 43ff., Darmstadt 1961   320

Isidor, ed. H. Eggers, Tübingen 1964   45, 53, 272, 411

Jans Enikel, *Fürstenbuch*, MGH Deutsche Chroniken 3, 599ff.   70, 87, 102, 139, 265, 370
  Weltchronik, MGH Deutsche Chroniken 3, 1   102, 157, 206, 220, 265, 318, 353, 364, 369, 373, 420

Jaufre Rudel, ed A. Jeanroy, Paris 1915   82, 346

Johann von Konstanz, *Minnelehre*, ed. F. E. Sweet, Paris 1934   308, 362

Johann von Würzburg, *Wilhelm von Österreich*, ed. E. Regel, Berlin 1906   87, 92, 110, 148, 165, 209, 213, 306, 308f., 322, 332, 360, 370, 392, 419, 420

Johannes von Frankenstein, *Der Kreuziger*, ed. F. Khull, Stuttgart 1882   131, 158, 207, 216, 334, 355, 375

Judith, ed. R. Palgen, Halle 1924   145, 146, 158, 206, 216, 355, 363, 364, 369, 374

Jüngere Judith, ed. F. Maurer, *Religiöse Dichtungen* II 225ff.   103, 354

Jungfrau, Frau und Witwe, ed. A. von Keller, *Erzählungen aus altdeutschen Handschriften*, Stuttgart 1855, pp. 120ff.   425

Der Junker und der treue Heinrich, ed. F. H. von der Hagen, *Gesamtabenteuer* III 187ff., Darmstadt 1961   379

Kaiser Heinrich, ed. H. Moser and H. Tervooren, *Minnesangs Frühling. I: Texte*, Stuttgart 1977, pp. 70ff.   87, 362

Kaiserchronik, MGH Deutsche Chroniken 1, 1   66, 67, 101, 104, 119, 120, 156, 244, 245, 246, 248f., 265, 272, 357, 373, 400, 404

Der Kanzler, KDL, pp. 185ff.   380

Karl der Große – Liebeszauber, ed. F. H. von der Hagen, *Gesamtabenteuer* I 617ff., Darmstadt 1961   166

Karl und Galie, ed. D. Helm, Berlin 1986   108, 358f., 420

Die Klage, ed. K. Bartsch, Leipzig 1875   83, 86, 143, 161, 162, 227, 228, 247, 248, 250, 320, 357, 397, 401

Klarissenregel, ed. D. Brett-Evans, *Euphorion* 54 (1960), 135ff.   320, 353

Kleinreden der Wiener Handschrift, ed. A. Mihm, *PBB (T)* 87 (1965), 406ff.   379

Klosterneuburger Osterspiel, ed. K. Young, *Drama of the medieval church* I 421ff., Oxford 1951   105, 160, 219, 344, 356, 376

Könemann von Jerxheim, *Der Kaland*, ed. L. Wolff, Neumünster 1953, pp. 71ff.   75, 220, 352, 390
  Reimbibel, ed. L. Wolff, Neumünster 1953, pp. 309ff.   352, 375, 390
  Wurzgarten Mariens, ed. L. Wolff, Neumünster 1953, pp. 126ff.   131, 154, 205, 220, 352, 368, 375, 390, 392, 396

König Rother, ed. J. de Vries, Heidelberg 1922   63, 107, 245, 246, 248, 276, 358, 377, 400, 401

Konrad, Pfaffe, *Rolandslied*, ed. F. Maurer, Leipzig 1940   64, 66, 67, 72, 78, 87, 92, 107, 138, 245, 287, 358, 386, 400, 412

Konrad, Priester, *Predigten*, ed. A. E. Schönbach, *Altdeutsche Predigten* III 3ff., Darmstadt 1964   98

Konrad von Fussesbrunnen, *Kindheit Jesu*, ed. H. Fromm and K. Grubmüller, Berlin 1973   104, 207, 212, 247, 256, 390, 392, 396, 418

Konrad von Heimesfurt, *Unser vrouwen hinvart*, ed. K. Gärtner and W. J. Hoffmann, Tübingen 1989, pp. 1ff.   67, 104
  Diu Urstende, ed. K. Gärtner and W. J. Hoffmann, Tübingen 1989, pp. 53ff.   103, 131, 139, 158, 206, 223, 321, 355, 366, 374, 381, 390, 397

BIBLIOGRAPHICAL INDEX

Konrad von Stoffeln, *Gauriel von Montabel*, ed. F. Khull, Graz 1885   359f.
Konrad von Würzburg, *Alexius*, ed. P. Gereke, Halle 1926   104, 159, 207, 220, 356, 391, 419
  Engelhard, ed. P. Gereke, Tübingen 1963   74, 91, 110, 165, 209, 213, 231, 360, 375, 379, 419, 425
  Kleinere Dichtungen, ed. E. Schröder, Berlin 1959   344, 357
  Pantaleon, ed. P. Gereke, Halle 1927   356
  Partonopier und Meliur, ed. K. Bartsch, Vienna 1871   110, 138, 147f., 360, 413, 414, 419
  Silvester, ed. P. Gereke, Halle 1925   104, 165, 207, 220, 231, 356, 375, 379, 391, 419
  Trojanischer Krieg, ed. A. von Keller, Stuttgart 1858   208, 223, 228, 248, 266, 359, 378, 397, 402
  Der Welt Lohn, ed. E. Schröder, *Konrad von Würzburg, Kleinere Dichtungen* I 1ff., Berlin 1959   134f., 143, 164, 307, 378
Kraus, C. von, *Deutsche Liederdichter des 13. Jahrhunderts*, Tübingen 1951ff.
Kreuzfahrt des Landgrafen Ludwigs des Frommen von Thüringen, MGH Deutsche Chroniken 4, 2   228, 248, 343, 354, 366, 397, 402, 426
Kudrun, ed. B. Symons and B. Boesch, Tübingen 1954   162, 358, 377
Lamprecht, Pfaffe, *Alexanderlied* (Vorau and Strassburg versions), ed. K. Kinzel, Halle 1884   116, 137, 244, 245, 276, 287, 354, 357, 359, 366, 400, 403, 412
  Tobias, ed. F. Maurer, *Religiöse Dichtungen* II 522ff.   103, 287, 354, 359, 412
Lamprecht von Regensburg, *Sanct Franzisken Leben*, ed. K. Weinhold, Paderborn 1880, pp. 43ff.   104, 119, 121f., 207, 216, 352, 356, 363, 371, 391, 392, 396, 397
  Tochter Syon, ed. K. Weinhold, Paderborn 1880, pp. 261ff.   99, 147, 154, 205, 216, 352, 371, 390
Lancelot, prose, ed. R. Kluge, Berlin 1948ff.   88, 109, 123, 126f., 164f., 209, 212, 228, 248, 249, 267, 297, 306, 307, 359, 364, 378, 397, 406, 413, 420
Laubacher Barlaam, ed. A. Perdisch, Tübingen 1913   306
Laurin, ed. O. Jänicke, *Deutsches Heldenbuch* I 201ff., Berlin 1866 (A: ed. G. Holz, *Laurin und der kleine Rosengarten*, Halle 1897, pp. 1ff.; D: *ibid.*, pp. 96ff.)   72, 74, 77, 82, 84, 85, 106, 357, 377
Leben der heiligen Elisabeth, ed. M. Rieger, Stuttgart 1868   105, 123, 145, 159, 207, 216, 248, 356, 369, 375
Leben Jesu, ed. C. Gerhardt, Leiden 1970   158, 207, 216, 322, 375, 392, 397
Legendar aus dem Anfang des 12. Jahrhunderts, ed. H. Busch, ZfdPh 10 (1879), 129ff., 390ff.; 11 (1880), 12ff.   248, 249, 402
Legende vom heiligen Nikolaus, ed. K. Bartsch, *Konrad von Würzburg, Partonopier und Meliur*, Vienna 1871, pp. 333ff.   356
Die Lilie, ed. P. Wüst, Berlin 1909   99, 154, 205, 222, 352, 369, 372, 390, 396
Linzer Antichrist, ed. F. Maurer, *Religiöse Dichtungen* III 361ff.   103, 355, 357
Livländische Reimchronik, ed. L. Meyer, Paderborn 1876   81, 90, 91, 101, 249, 321, 348, 353, 402
Lob Salomons, ed. F. Maurer, *Religiöse Dichtungen* I 317ff.   103, 354
Loblied auf den heiligen Geist, ed. F. Maurer, *Religiöse Dichtungen* III 53ff.   384
Lohengrin, ed. T. Cramer, Munich 1971   80, 109, 165, 209, 213, 268, 360, 366, 369, 379, 407, 419, 421
Lucidarius, ed. F. Heidlauf, Berlin 1915   96, 146, 152, 211, 266, 300, 302, 303, 347, 371, 418, 419, 425
Ludwigslied, ed. E. von Steinmeyer, *Sprachdenkmäler*, pp. 85ff.   22, 66, 106, 345, 357
Lübecker Stadtrecht, ed. J. F. Hack, *Das alte lübische Recht*, Lübeck 1839   425
Das Märterbuch, ed. E. Gierach, Berlin 1928   159, 207, 212, 248, 319, 356, 391, 397, 402, 424
Magdeburger Schöffenrecht, ed. P. Laband, *Magdeburger Rechtsquellen*, Aalen 1967, pp. 70ff.   414
Magdeburger Schöppenchronik, ed. K. Janicke, Leipzig 1869   388

BIBLIOGRAPHICAL INDEX

Mai und Beaflor, ed. A. J. Vollmer, Leipzig 1848   89, 147, 307
Mainauer Naturlehre, ed. W. Wackernagel, Stuttgart 1851   151, 231, 370
Mainzer Reichslandfriede, MGH Const. 2, 250ff. (No. 196a)   100, 101, 155, 353, 372
Margaretenlegende nach Cod. Helmstedt. 1231 (Wolfenbüttel), ed. G. G. van den Andel, *Die Margaretalegende in ihren mittelalterlichen Versionen. Eine vergleichende Studie*, Groningen 1933, pp. 109ff.   389
Mariengrüße, ed. F. Pfeiffer, ZfdA 8 (1851), 274ff.   79, 82, 154, 368, 398
Mariensequenz aus Muri, ed. F. Maurer, *Religiöse Dichtungen* I 453ff.   97, 350
Mariensequenz aus Seckau, ed. F. Maurer, *Religiöse Dichtungen* I 462ff.   97, 350
Der Marner, ed. P. Strauch, Strassburg 1876   107, 344, 357, 358
Maurer, F., *Die religiösen Dichtungen des 11. und 12. Jahrhunderts. Nach ihren Formen besprochen und herausgegeben*, Tübingen 1964ff.
Mechthild von Magdeburg, *Das fließende Licht der Gottheit*, ed. H. Neumann, Munich 1990   70, 117, 154, 211, 297, 320, 332, 369, 372, 374, 398, 417
Der Meissner, ed. G. Objartel, Berlin 1977   380
Melker Marienlied, ed. F. Maurer, *Religiöse Dichtungen* I 357ff.   65f., 96f., 350
Memento Mori, ed. F. Maurer, *Religiöse Dichtungen* I 249ff. Also R. Schützeichel, *Das alemannische Memento mori*, Tübingen 1962, pp. 126ff.   78, 98, 274, 351, 409
Millstätter Exodus, ed. E. Papp, Munich 1968   75, 103, 116, 354
Millstätter Genesis, ed. J. Diemer, Vienna 1862   103, 127f., 177, 301, 323, 325, 355, 381
Millstätter Reimphysiologus, ed. F. Maurer, *Religiöse Dichtungen* I 169ff.   117, 127, 349, 363
Der Minne Frigedanc, ed. B. J. Docen, *Miscellaneen zur Geschichte der teutschen Literatur* II 171ff., Munich 1807   129, 365
Minnesangs Frühling, ed. H. Moser and H. Tervooren, Stuttgart 1977
Mittelniederdeutsches Arzneibuch, ed. J. H. Gallée, NdJb 15 (1889), 105ff.   151, 370, 398
Monsee-Wiener Bruchstücke, ed. G. A. Hench, Strassburg 1890   45, 53, 348
Morant und Galie, ed. T. Frings and E. Linke, Berlin 1976   68, 82, 92, 107f., 121, 346, 358, 426
Moriz von Craun, ed. U. Pretzel, Tübingen 1956   228, 248, 284, 311, 312, 397, 402
Mühlhäuser Reichsrechtsbuch, ed. H. Meyer, Leipzig 1969   155, 353
Münchener Glaube und Beichte, ed. E. von Steinmeyer, *Sprachdenkmäler*, pp. 345ff.   73, 351
Münchener Oswald, ed. M. Curschmann, Tübingen 1974   76, 85, 107, 358, 377
Münchener Wundsegen, ed. F. Wilhelm, *Denkmäler deutscher Prosa des 11. und 12. Jahrhunderts*, Munich 1960, p. 52   151, 370
Murbacher Hymnen, ed. E. Sievers, Halle 1874   49, 53, 95, 151, 204, 217, 318, 370, 385
Muspilli, ed. E. von Steinmeyer, *Sprachdenkmäler*, pp. 66ff.   50, 102
Neidhart von Reuental, ed. E. Wiessner, Tübingen 1955   67, 70, 87, 345, 362
Nibelungenlied, ed. H. de Boor, Wiesbaden 1961. Also M. S. Batts, *Das Nibelungenlied. Paralleldruck der Handschriften A, B und C nebst Lesarten der übrigen Handschriften*, Tübingen 1971. C: ed. U. Hennig, Tübingen 1977   69, 105, 106, 161, 162, 224, 247, 287, 348, 357, 373, 377, 396, 401
Niederrheinische Tundalusfragmente, ed. A. Wagner, Erlangen 1882, pp. 111ff.   332, 402
Notker, ed. P. Piper, *Die Schriften Notkers und seiner Schule*, Freiburg 1882–3   51, 127, 183–186, 204, 215, 217, 272, 290, 300, 301, 323, 340, 365, 369, 384–385, 408, 414, 418
Boethius, Bearbeitung von Aristoteles' Schrift de interpretatione, ed. Piper I 2, 499ff.   120, 125, 184, 185, 186, 384, 385
Canticum Ezechie Regis, ed. E. H. Sehrt and T. Starck, *Notkers des Deutschen Werke* III 1059ff., Halle 1955   184
Boethius, Commentar zu den Categorien des Aristoteles, ed. Piper I 2, 367ff.   186, 384, 385
Boethius de Consolatione Philosophiae, ed. E. H. Sehrt and T. Starck, Halle 1933–4   125, 183, 184, 185, 327, 337, 346, 384, 385, 423
Fides Sancti Athanasii Episcopi, ed. E. H. Sehrt and T. Starck, *Notkers des Deutschen Werke* III 1107ff., Halle 1955   384

BIBLIOGRAPHICAL INDEX

Martianus Capella de Nuptiis Philologiae et Mercurii, ed. E. H. Sehrt and T. Starck, Halle 1935   185, 186, 348, 368, 384, 385
Psalter, ed. E. H. Sehrt and T. Starck, Halle 1952ff.   119, 125, 137, 139, 144, 184, 185, 363, 384, 385, 389
Ymnus Zachariae, ed. E. H. Sehrt and T. Starck, *Notkers des Deutschen Werke* III 1103f., Halle 1955   384
Oberaltaicher Predigten, ed. A. E. Schönbach, *Altdeutsche Predigten* II 3ff., Darmstadt 1964   98, 367
Oberdeutscher Servatius, ed. F. Wilhelm, Munich 1910   301, 320, 355, 372
Orendel, ed. H. Steinger, Halle 1935   76f., 85, 107, 358, 377
Ortnit, ed. A. Amelung, *Deutsches Heldenbuch* III 3ff., Berlin 1871   85, 106, 322, 357, 377
Osterspiel von Muri, ed. F. Ranke, Aarau 1944   105, 111, 160, 161, 356, 375f.
Otfrid von Weissenburg, *Evangelienbuch*, ed. O. Erdmann, Halle 1882   5, 21, 48, 49, 50, 53, 66, 79, 89, 102, 120, 121, 122, 123, 125, 130, 132, 134, 137, 138f., 143, 157, 158, 179–183, 206, 216, 239, 242, 270, 271, 272, 288, 290, 300, 301, 311, 312, 314, 319, 333, 343, 346, 363, 364, 366, 367, 368, 369, 382–384, 390, 408, 414, 418f., 422, 424
Otte, *Eraclius*, ed. W. Frey, Göppingen 1983   131, 363
Otto von Botenlouben, KDL, pp. 307ff.   362
Otto von Freising, *Laubacher Barlaam*, ed. A. Perdisch, Tübingen 1913   134, 355f., 420
Ottokar von Steiermark, *Österreichische Reimchronik*, MGH Deutsche Chroniken 5, 1/2   66, 71, 143, 146, 157, 206, 212, 247, 248, 249, 317, 321, 354, 369, 374, 401, 402, 413, 425
Pariser Tagezeiten, ed. S. Waetzoldt, Hamburg 1880   136, 205, 222, 390, 392, 396
Passional I and II, ed. K. A. Hahn, Frankfurt 1845; III, ed. F. K. Köpke, Quedlinburg 1852   33, 71, 86, 89, 104, 159, 175, 207, 217, 227, 228, 248, 249, 307, 312, 317, 321, 322, 356, 381, 391, 394, 396, 397, 401, 402, 420, 423, 424
Petruslied, ed. E. von Steinmeyer, *Sprachdenkmäler*, pp. 103f.   66, 71, 78, 96, 350
Pfälzer Beichte, ed. E. von Steinmeyer, *Sprachdenkmäler*, pp. 331f.   351
Der Pfaffe mit der Schnur, ed. H. Niewöhner, *Neues Gesamtabenteuer*, Dublin 1967, pp. 140ff.   83
Pferdesegen, ed. E. von Steinmeyer, *Sprachdenkmäler*, pp. 370f.   349
Philipp, Bruder, *Marienleben*, ed. H. Rückert, Quedlinburg 1853   70, 81, 130, 135, 146, 148, 159, 207, 217, 317, 366, 369, 375, 381, 391, 392, 394, 397
Pilatus, ed. K. Weinhold, ZfdPh 8 (1877), 253ff.   311f., 422
Der Pleier, *Garel von dem Blühenden Tal*, ed. W. Herles, Vienna 1981   165, 213, 360, 378, 391
   Meleranz, ed. K. Bartsch, Stuttgart 1861   165, 213, 308, 360, 391, 421
   Tandareis und Floribel, ed. F. Khull, Graz 1885   165, 209, 213, 319, 360, 391
Predigtsammlung A, B, C, ed. E. von Steinmeyer, *Sprachdenkmäler*, pp. 156ff., 168ff., 173ff.   98, 153, 385
Priestereid, ed. E. von Steinmeyer, *Sprachdenkmäler*, pp. 64f.   100
Psalm 138, ed. E. von Steinmeyer, *Sprachdenkmäler*, pp. 105ff.   102
Rabenschlacht, ed. E. Martin, *Deutsches Heldenbuch* II 219ff., Berlin 1866   377
Das Rädlein, ed. F. H. von der Hagen, *Gesamtabenteuer* III 105ff., Darmstadt 1961   402
Rede von den fünfzehn Graden, ed. W. Dolfel, *Germania* 6 (1861), 144ff.   130, 154, 398
Reinbot von Durne, *Der heilige Georg*, ed. C. von Kraus, Heidelberg 1907   249, 356, 363, 402
Reinfried von Braunschweig, ed. K. Bartsch, Stuttgart 1871   110, 119, 120, 135, 165, 209, 220, 360, 369, 378, 419, 421
Reinmar von Zweter, ed. G. Roethe, Leipzig 1887   167, 380
Rheinfränkische Psalmenübersetzung, ed. E. von Steinmeyer, *Sprachdenkmäler*, pp. 301ff.   153f., 385
Rheinisches Marienlob, ed. A. Bach, Leipzig 1934   87, 99, 129, 144, 145, 146, 154, 205, 216, 364, 365, 366, 369, 371

BIBLIOGRAPHICAL INDEX

Der Ritter unterm Zuber, ed. F. H. von der Hagen, *Gesamtabenteuer* II 297ff., Darmstadt 1961   147
Roman de Thèbes, ed. G. Raynaud de Lage, Paris 1966 and 1968   294
Rosengarten, ed. G. Holz, Halle 1893   358, 377
Rothe, Johannes, *Ritterspiegel*, ed. H. Neumann, Halle 1936   413
Die Rothsche Sammlung, ed. K. Roth, *Deutsche Predigten des 12. und 13. Jahrhunderts*, Quedlinburg 1839   75
Rudolf von Ems, *Alexander*, ed. V. Junk, Leipzig 1928/9   86, 88, 92, 108, 109, 141, 143, 164, 208, 212, 248, 258, 266, 298, 317, 318, 348, 359, 366, 378, 391, 393, 402, 419
Barlaam und Josaphat, ed. F. Pfeiffer, Berlin 1965   93, 104, 146, 159, 207, 212, 227, 228, 248, 266, 306, 317, 320, 321, 355, 366, 375, 386, 396, 397, 419, 420
Der guote Gerhart, ed. J. A. Asher, Tübingen 1971   110, 165, 209, 212, 228, 266, 278, 291, 360, 361, 379, 397, 402
Weltchronik, ed. G. Ehrismann, Berlin 1915   82, 83, 85, 90, 92, 101f., 119, 124, 157, 173, 175, 206, 211, 225, 265, 266, 317, 353, 363, 366, 373, 381, 390, 397, 419, 420, 424
Willehalm von Orlens, ed. V. Junk, Berlin 1905   75f., 110, 129f., 143, 165, 209, 212, 360, 366, 379, 397, 402, 419
Rumelant von Sachsen, ed. F. H. von der Hagen, *Minnesinger* II 367ff., III 49 and 52ff.   87
Sachsenspiegel, ed. K. A. Eckhardt, Göttingen 1955   155, 156, 277, 305, 414
Sächsische Weltchronik, MGH Deutsche Chroniken 2   101, 121, 123, 156f., 205f., 216, 265, 268, 353, 364, 373, 390, 397, 413
Sächsisches Taufgelöbnis, ed. E. von Steinmeyer, *Sprachdenkmäler*, pp. 20ff.   97
Sächsisches Weichbildrecht, ed. A. von Daniels and F. von Gruben, Berlin 1858   62, 79, 80, 99, 100, 101, 144, 145, 155, 205, 220, 352, 353, 372, 390, 397
Der Saelden Hort, ed. H. Adrian, Berlin 1927   103, 108, 109, 135, 158, 164, 206, 212, 225, 355, 359, 367, 390, 392, 397
Salman und Morolf, ed. F. Vogt, Halle 1880   358, 377
Sanct Brandan, ed. C. Schröder, Erlangen 1871   143, 247, 248, 319, 397, 399, 401, 425
St. Galler Glaube und Beichte II, ed. E. von Steinmeyer, *Sprachdenkmäler*, pp. 341ff.   73, 351
St. Galler Passionsspiel, ed. E. Hartl, Halle 1952   78, 105, 356
St. Georgener Prediger, ed. K. Rieder, Berlin 1908   320
St. Pauler Predigten, ed. A. Jeitteles, Innsbruck 1878   75, 116, 351
St. Trudperter Hohes Lied, ed. H. Menhardt, Halle 1933   103, 408
Sante Margareten Marter, ed. K. Bartsch, *Germania* 4 (1859), 440ff.   105, 207, 220, 247, 356, 392, 396, 425
Die Schlacht bei Göllheim, ed. A. Bach, Bonn 1930, pp. 193ff.   247, 401
Der Schüler zu Paris C, ed. H.-F. Rosenfeld, *Mittelhochdeutsche Novellenstudien*, Leipzig 1927, pp. 207ff.   361
Schwabenspiegel Langform M, ed. K. A. Eckhardt, Aalen 1971   86, 89, 99f., 100, 155, 205, 216, 352, 390, 392, 397, 398, 414, 417, 425
Schwäbische Trauformel, MSD, pp. 319f.   100
Schwarzwälder Prediger, ed. F. R. Grieshaber, *Deutsche Predigten des XIII. Jahrhunderts*, Stuttgart 1844 and 1846   364
Scopf von dem lône, ed. F. Maurer, *Religiöse Dichtungen* II 260ff.   351
Seifried Helbling, ed. J. Seemüller, Halle 1886   74, 96, 247, 261f., 350, 352, 401
Der Sêle Cranz, ed. G. Milchsack, PBB 5 (1878), 548ff.   99
Sich hûb vor Gotes trône, ed. K. Bartsch, *Die Erlösung*, Quedlinburg 1858, pp. viiiff.   352
Sigenot, ed. J. Zupitza, *Deutsches Heldenbuch* V 207ff., Berlin 1870   358
Speculum Ecclesiae, ed. G. Mellbourn, Lund 1944   73, 75, 88, 98, 116, 351
Von Stadegge, KDL, pp. 415f.   362
Stadtbuch von Augsburg, ed. C. Meyer, Augsburg 1872   142, 155, 231, 368, 373

BIBLIOGRAPHICAL INDEX

Von Stamhein, KDL, pp. 417ff. 87
Statuten des Deutschen Ordens, ed. M. Perlbach, Halle 1890 100, 320, 353, 374
Steinmeyer, E. von, *Die kleineren althochdeutschen Sprachdenkmäler*, Berlin 1916
Straßburger Eide, ed. E. von Steinmeyer, *Sprachdenkmäler*, pp. 82ff. 47, 100
Der Stricker, *Daniel von dem Blühenden Tal*, ed. M. Resler, Tübingen 1983 68, 74, 84, 109, 208f., 212, 359, 361, 391, 392, 397, 419
   Karl der Große, ed. K. Bartsch, Quedlinburg 1857 107, 138, 208, 212, 228, 248, 266, 358, 359, 391, 392, 396, 397, 402
   Kleindichtung, ed. W. W. Moelleken, Göppingen 1973ff. 334
Der Sünden Widerstreit, ed. V. Zeidler, Graz 1892 321
Summa Theologiae, ed. F. Maurer, *Religiöse Dichtungen* I 304ff. 98, 351
Der Taler, ed. K. Bartsch, *Die Schweizer Minnesänger*, Darmstadt 1964, pp. 66ff. 167, 380
Tannhäuser, ed. J. Siebert, Halle 1934 70, 345, 362
Tanzlied von Kölbigk, ed. E. E. Metzner, *Zur frühesten Geschichte der europäischen Balladendichtung: der Tanz in Kölbigk*, Frankfurt 1972, pp. 43ff. ('Theodericus Bericht') 66, 69, 361
Tatian, *Evangelienharmonie*, ed. E. Sievers, Paderborn 1872 49, 354, 374, 385
Thomas, *Tristan*, ed. B. H. Wind, Geneva 1960 164, 194, 195, 258
Thomasin von Zerclaere, *Der welsche Gast*, ed. H. Rückert, Quedlinburg 1852. Also F. W. von Kries, Göppingen 1984/5 62, 88, 93, 96, 114, 116, 126, 127, 135, 141, 143, 152, 164, 204, 223, 224, 291, 294, 298, 318, 332, 342, 350, 363, 371, 378, 381, 389f., 396, 397, 413, 414, 416, 418, 419
Trierer Capitulare, ed. E. von Steinmeyer, *Sprachdenkmäler*, pp. 305ff. 100
Trierer Floyris, ed. E. von Steinmeyer, *ZfdA* 21 (1877), 307ff. 320
Trierer Osterspiel, ed. E. Hartl, *Das Drama des Mittelalters. Osterspiele*, Leipzig 1937, pp. 45ff. 75, 105, 344, 357
Trierer Silvester, MGH Deutsche Chroniken 1, 2 87, 104
Tristan als Mönch, ed. B. C. Bushey, Göppingen 1974 318
Trost in Verzweiflung, ed. F. Maurer, *Religiöse Dichtungen* II 342ff. 425
Tugendspiegel, ed. G. Rosenhagen, *Kleinere mhd. Erzählungen, Fabeln und Lehrgedichte. III: Die Heidelberger Hs. Cod. pal. germ. 341*, Dublin 1970, pp. 21ff. 365
Twinger von Königshofen, Jakob, *Deutsche Chronik*, ed. in: *Die Chroniken der oberrheinischen Städte, Straßburg* I *(Die Chroniken der deutschen Städte vom 14. bis ins 16. Jahrhundert, 8)*, Leipzig 1870 243f.
Ulrich von dem Türlin, *Willehalm*, ed. S. Singer, Prague 1893 133, 163, 208, 359, 378
Ulrich von Etzenbach, *Alexandreis*, ed. W. Toischer, Tübingen 1888 109, 138, 139f., 141, 266, 307f., 359, 361, 368, 378, 425
   Wilhelm von Wenden, ed. H.-F. Rosenfeld, Berlin 1957 361, 413
Ulrich von Lichtenstein, *Frauenbuch*, ed. K. Lachmann, Berlin 1841, pp. 594ff. 59, 145, 209, 212, 361, 379, 419
   Frauendienst, ed. K. Lachmann, Berlin 1841, pp. 1ff. 59, 70, 71, 84, 85, 89, 93, 115, 118, 119, 120, 167, 209, 210, 212, 215, 294, 305f., 308, 309, 359, 361, 363, 379, 380, 392, 393, 419, 420, 421, 425
   Lyric poems, KDL, pp. 428ff. 67, 70, 71, 167, 210, 294, 345, 361, 362, 379, 380
Ulrich von Türheim, *Rennewart*, ed. A. Hübner, Berlin 1964 81, 108, 163, 208, 212, 215, 318, 321, 359, 360, 369, 381, 396
   Tristan, ed. H. F. Massmann, Leipzig 1843 109, 144, 164, 165, 209, 212, 360, 378, 379, 393
Ulrich von Winterstetten, KDL, pp. 495ff. 67, 345
Ulrich von Zatzikhoven, *Lanzelet*, ed. K. A. Hahn, Frankfurt 1845 58, 77f., 93, 109, 172, 208, 212, 287, 300, 301, 306, 318, 359, 380, 392, 396, 418, 419
Unser Vrouwen Klage, ed. G. Milchsack, *PBB* 5 (1878), 193ff. 94, 135, 154, 175, 205, 216, 322, 363, 372, 381, 390, 392, 396

BIBLIOGRAPHICAL INDEX

Urschwabenspiegel, ed. K. A. Eckhardt, *Buch der Könige alter ê und niuwer ê (Studia Iuris Suevici I: Urschwabenspiegel)*, Aalen 1975   155, 156, 205, 216, 278, 353, 372, 373
Väterbuch, ed. K. Reissenberger, Berlin 1914   88, 104, 175, 207, 217, 228, 248, 258, 307, 317, 321, 356, 381, 392, 394, 396, 397, 401, 425
Vatikanische Gebete, ed. F. Wilhelm, *Denkmäler deutscher Prosa des 11. und 12. Jahrhunderts*, Munich 1960, pp. 69ff.   351
Virginal, ed. J. Zupitza, *Deutsches Heldenbuch* v 1ff., Berlin 1870   67, 71, 73f., 76, 106, 248, 317, 358, 377, 402
Volmar, *Steinbuch*, ed. H. Lambel, Heilbronn 1877   349
Vom Himmelreich, ed. F. Maurer, *Religiöse Dichtungen* I 365ff.   350
Vom Himmlischen Jerusalem, ed. F. Maurer, *Religiöse Dichtungen* II 140ff.   68, 98, 351, 357
Vom Rechte, ed. F. Maurer, *Religiöse Dichtungen* II 156ff.   351
Von dem englischen Gruoß ein leich, ed. P. Wackernagel, *Das deutsche Kirchenlied von der ältesten Zeit bis zu Anfang des XVII. Jahrhunderts*, II No. 344, Leipzig 1867   154, 366, 398
Von dem Spitâle von Jêrusalêm, ed. A. Küster, Wiesbaden 1897   354, 425
Von dem übeln wîbe, ed. K. Helm, Tübingen 1955   10, 328, 378
Von den fünfzehenn zaichen vor dem ivngsten tag, ed. H. Eggers, *PBB* 74 (1952), 355ff.   352
Von der Babylonischen Gefangenschaft, ed. F. Maurer, *Religiöse Dichtungen* I 418ff.   98
Vorauer Marienlob, ed. F. Maurer, *Religiöse Dichtungen* I 352ff.   96
Diu vrône botschaft ze der christenheit, ed. R. Priebsch, Graz 1895   86, 88, 98f., 124, 322, 347
Wace, *Roman de Brut*, ed. I. Arnold, Paris 1938, 1940. Quotations from I. D. O. Arnold and M. M. Pelan (ed.), *La partie Arthurienne du Roman de Brut*, Paris 1962   252f., 264, 403, 404
Roman de Rou, ed. H. Andressen, Heilbronn 1877, 1879   253, 254f., 259, 404
Die Wahrheit, ed. F. Maurer, *Religiöse Dichtungen* I 426ff.   98
Walberan, ed. O. Jänicke, *Deutsches Heldenbuch* I 238ff., Berlin 1866   84, 106, 357
Walther von der Vogelweide, ed. F. Maurer, Tübingen 1955/6 (I have retained Lachmann's conventional numbering for easier reference)   69, 70, 72, 73, 224, 305, 307, 317, 361, 396
Walther von Rheinau, *Marienleben*, ed. E. Perjus, Åbo 1950   104f., 124, 131, 145, 160, 173, 174f., 207, 220, 248, 356, 363, 369, 375, 381, 391, 396, 402
Wartburgkrieg, ed. T. A. Rompelman, Amsterdam 1939   75
Der weiße Rosendorn, ed. F. H. von der Hagen, *Gesamtabenteuer* III 17ff., Darmstadt 1961   401
Weißenburger Katechismus, ed. E. von Steinmeyer, *Sprachdenkmäler*, pp. 29ff.   351, 364
Werner vom Niederrhein, *Die vier Schiven*, ed. F. Maurer, *Religiöse Dichtungen* III 435ff.   99, 125f., 248, 364, 398, 401, 412
Wernher, Bruder, ed. A. E. Schönbach, *Beiträge zur Erklärung altdeutscher Dichtwerke III, IV: Die Sprüche des Bruder Wernher I. II*, Sitzungsberichte der Wiener Akademie der Wissenschaften 148, 7 (Vienna 1904) and 150, 1 (1905)   84, 347
Wernher, Priester, *Maria*, ed. C. Wesle, Halle 1927   104, 117f., 124, 140, 159, 164, 207, 211, 216, 300, 301, 303, 355, 364, 375, 377f., 394, 412, 418
Wernher der Gartenaere, *Meier Helmbrecht*, ed. C. E. Gough, Oxford 1942. Also H. Brackert, W. Frey, D. Seitz, Frankfurt 1972   85f., 110, 166, 361, 367, 379, 401
Wernher von Elmendorf, ed. J. Bumke, Tübingen 1974   152, 204, 211, 349, 371, 389, 391
Wessobrunner Gebet, ed. E. von Steinmeyer, *Sprachdenkmäler*, p. 16 (lines 10–14)   79
Wessobrunner Schöpfungsgedicht, ed. E. von Steinmeyer, *Sprachdenkmäler*, p. 16 (lines 1–9)   79, 102, 341
Wetzel von Bernau, *Margaretenleben*, ed. G. G. van den Andel, *Die Margaretalegende in ihren mittelalterlichen Versionen. Eine vergleichende Studie*, Groningen 1933, pp. 125ff.   94, 104, 137, 138, 207, 212, 356, 391, 392, 396, 401, 425
Wiener Genesis, ed. K. Smits, Berlin 1972   102f., 128, 272, 354, 365, 412

BIBLIOGRAPHICAL INDEX

Wiener Oswald, ed. G. Baesecke, Heidelberg 1912   107, 118, 358, 377
Wiener Passionsspiel, ed. R. Froning, *Das Drama des Mittelalters*. I: *Die lateinischen Osterfeiern und ihre Entwicklung in Deutschland. Osterspiele, Passionsspiele*, Stuttgart 1891, pp. 302ff.   62, 78, 105, 344, 356
Wiener Physiologus, ed. F. Maurer, *Religiöse Dichtungen* I 174ff.   365
Wiener Predigten, ed. H. Hoffmann von Fallersleben, *Fundgruben* I 66ff., Breslau 1830   73, 86
Wien-Münchener Evangelienübersetzung, ed. H. Kriedte, *Deutsche Bibelfragmente in Prosa des XII. Jahrhunderts*, Kattowitz 1930, pp. 64ff.   103, 355
Wigamur, ed. F. H. von der Hagen and J. G. Büsching, *Deutsche Gedichte des Mittelalters*, Berlin 1808, 1 1ff. (paginated separately as the third item in the volume)   360
Der Wilde Alexander, KDL, pp. 1ff.   380
Der Wilde Mann, *Vespasian*, ed. F. Maurer, *Religiöse Dichtungen* III 532ff.   126
Von christlicher Lehre, ed. F. Maurer, *Religiöse Dichtungen* III 578ff.   366
Williram von Ebersberg, *Hohes Lied*, ed. J. Seemüller, Strassburg 1878   53, 118, 123, 131, 144, 158, 165, 368, 374, 408, 417
Windberger Psalter, ed. K. Kirchert, Zürich 1979   158, 340, 370, 374
Wirnt von Grafenberg, *Wigalois*, ed. J. M. N. Kapteyn, Bonn 1926   86, 109, 128, 130, 145, 148, 164, 208, 212, 306, 359, 378, 386, 396, 415, 419
Wolfdietrich A, ed. H. Schneider, Halle 1931. *B*: O. Jänicke, *Deutsches Heldenbuch* III 167ff., Berlin 1871; *C*: O. Jänicke, *Deutsches Heldenbuch* IV 13ff., Berlin 1873; *D*: O. Jänicke, *Deutsches Heldenbuch* IV 16ff., Berlin 1873   76, 86, 106, 141, 162, 163, 357, 377
Wolfram von Eschenbach, ed. K. Bartsch and M. Marti, Leipzig 1929ff.
   Parzival, ed. K. Lachmann, Berlin 1926   58, 109, 122, 134, 136, 139, 141, 165, 171, 176, 177, 190–194, 209, 212, 215, 247, 261–263, 268, 292, 294, 296, 297, 307, 319, 358, 368, 377, 378, 387, 397, 405f., 416, 417, 419
   Titurel, ed. J. Heinzle, *Stellenkommentar zu Wolframs Titurel. Beiträge zum Verständnis des überlieferten Textes*, Tübingen 1972   109, 358, 360
   Willehalm, ed. K. Lachmann, Berlin 1926   87, 107, 163, 208, 212, 358, 377, 378
Würzburger Markbeschreibungen, ed. E. von Steinmeyer, *Sprachdenkmäler*, pp. 115ff.   51, 100
Yder, ed. H. Gelzer, Dresden 1913   416
Züricher Arzneibuch, ed. F. Wilhelm, *Denkmäler deutscher Prosa des 11. und 12. Jahrhunderts*, Munich 1960, pp. 53ff.   95
Zwei deutsche Arzneibücher aus dem 12. und 13. Jahrhundert, ed. F. Pfeiffer, Sitzungsberichte der Wiener Akademie der Wissenschaften 42 (1863), 110ff.   151, 370, 398
Zwei Kaufmänner und die treue Hausfrau, ed. F. H. von der Hagen, *Gesamtabenteuer* III 357ff., Darmstadt 1961   361, 379, 425

Secondary literature

Endnote references in the text of this book give a keyword which enables the entry in the bibliography to be recognised.

Aarburg, U., 'Melodien zum frühen deutschen Minnesang. Eine kritische Bestandsaufnahme', in: H. Fromm (ed.), *Der deutsche Minnesang. Aufsätze zu seiner Erforschung*, Darmstadt 1961, pp. 378ff.
Ackroyd, P. R., 'Books in the ancient world. 3: Books in the ancient Near East and in the Old Testament', in: P. R. Ackroyd and C. F. Evans (ed.), *The Cambridge History of the Bible*. I: *From the beginnings to Jerome*, Cambridge 1970, pp. 30ff.
Adam, B., *Katechetische Vaterunserauslegungen. Texte und Untersuchungen zu deutschsprachigen Auslegungen des 14. und 15. Jahrhunderts*, Munich 1976

Althoff, G., 'Pragmatische Geschichtsschreibung und Krisen. 1. Zur Funktion von Brunos Buch vom Sachsenkrieg', in: H. Keller *et al.* (ed.), *Pragmatische Schriftlichkeit*, pp. 95ff.
Andersson, T. M., 'Die oral-formulaic poetry im Germanischen', in: H. Beck (ed.), *Heldensage und Heldendichtung im Germanischen*, Berlin 1988, pp. 1ff.
Arndt, P. H., *Der Erzähler bei Hartmann von Aue. Formen und Funktionen seines Hervortretens und seine Äußerungen*, Göppingen 1980
Arntz, H., *Handbuch der Runenkunde*, Halle 1944
Ashcroft, J., 'Konrad's Rolandslied, Henry the Lion, and the northern crusade', *FMLS* 22 (1986), 184ff.
Assche, M. van, '"Divinae vacare lectioni". De "ratio studiorum" van Sint Benedictus', *SE* 1 (1948), 13ff.
Assmann, A. and J., and Hardmeier, C. (ed.), *Schrift und Gedächtnis. Beiträge zur Archäologie der literarischen Kommunikation*, Munich 1983
Auerbach, E., *Literatursprache und Publikum in der lateinischen Spätantike und im Mittelalter*, Bern 1958
Baesecke, G., *Vor- und Frühgeschichte des deutschen Schrifttums. I: Vorgeschichte*, Halle 1940; *II: Frühgeschichte*, Halle 1950, 1953 (two fascicles only)
Kleinere Schriften zur althochdeutschen Sprache und Literatur (ed. W. Schröder), Bern 1966
Bätschmann, E., *Das St. Galler Weihnachtsspiel*, Bern 1977
Bäuml, F. H., 'Der Übergang mündlicher zur artes-bestimmten Literatur des Mittelalters. Gedanken und Bedenken', in: N. Voorwinden and M. de Haan, *Oral poetry. Das Problem der Mündlichkeit mittelalterlicher epischer Dichtung*, Darmstadt 1979, pp. 238ff.
'Varieties and consequences of medieval literacy and illiteracy', *Speculum* 55 (1980), 237ff.
'Medieval texts and the two theories of oral-formulaic composition: a proposal for a third theory', *NLH* 16 (1984–5), 31ff.
'The oral tradition and Middle High German literature', *OT* 1 (1986), 398ff.
Bäuml, F. H., and Rouse, R. H., 'Roll and codex: a new manuscript fragment of Reinmar von Zweter', *PBB* 105 (1983), 192ff. and 317ff.
Bäuml, F. H., and Spielmann, E., 'From illiteracy to literacy: prolegomena to a study of the Nibelungenlied', in: J. J. Duggan (ed.), *Oral literature*, Edinburgh 1975, pp. 62ff.
Baldwin, J. W., *Masters, princes and merchants. The social views of Peter the Chanter and his circle*, Princeton 1970
The scholastic culture of the Middle Ages, 1000–1300, Lexington, Mass., 1971
'Masters at Paris from 1179 to 1215. A social perspective', in: R. L. Benson and G. Constable (ed.), *Renaissance and renewal in the twelfth century*, Oxford 1982, pp. 138ff.
Balogh, J., '"Voces paginarum". Beiträge zur Geschichte des lauten Lesens und Schreibens', *Philologus* 82 (1927), 84ff. and 202ff.
Baugh, A. C., 'The Middle English romance. Some questions of creation, presentation, and preservation', *Speculum* 42 (1967), 1ff.
Baumann, G. (ed.), *The written word. Literacy in transition*, Oxford 1986
Bédier, J., *Les légendes épiques. Recherches sur la fonction des chansons de geste*, Paris 1926ff.
Behr, H.-J., *Literatur als Machtlegitimation. Studien zur Funktion der deutschsprachigen Dichtung am böhmischen Königshof im 13. Jahrhundert*, Munich 1989
Bender, K.-H., *König und Vasall. Untersuchungen zur Chanson de Geste des XII. Jahrhunderts*, Heidelberg 1967
Benecke, G. F., Müller, W., Zarncke, F., *Mittelhochdeutsches Wörterbuch*, Leipzig 1854ff.
Bennewitz, I., 'Moraldidaktische Literatur', in: U. Liebertz-Grün (ed.), *Aus der Mündlichkeit in die Schriftlichkeit*, pp. 33ff.
Benson, L. D., 'The literary character of Anglo-Saxon formulaic poetry', *PMLA* 81 (1966), 334ff.
Bergmann, R., 'Zu der althochdeutschen Inschrift aus Köln', *RhVj* 30 (1965) 66ff.

'Überlieferung, Interpretation und literaturgeschichtliche Stellung des Osterspiels von Muri', *IASL* 9 (1984), 1ff.
'Aufführungstext und Lesetext. Zur Funktion der Überlieferung des mittelalterlichen geistlichen deutschen Dramas', in: H. Broet, J. Nowé, G. Tournoy (ed.), *The theatre in the Middle Ages*, Louvain 1985, pp. 314ff.
Bertau, K., 'Epenrezitation im deutschen Mittelalter', *EG* 20 (1965), 1ff.
'Das deutsche Rolandslied und die Repräsentationskunst Heinrichs des Löwen', *DU* 20 (1968), H. 2, pp. 4ff.
Deutsche Literatur im europäischen Mittelalter, Munich 1972
Über Literaturgeschichte. Literarischer Kunstcharakter und Geschichte in der höfischen Epik um 1200, Munich 1983
Bertau, K. H., and Stephan, R., 'Zum sanglichen Vortrag mhd. strophischer Epen', *ZfdA* 87 (1956/57), 253ff.
Review of E. Jammers, *Epos*, in: W. Kleiber (ed.), *Otfrid von Weißenburg*, Darmstadt 1978, pp. 193ff.
Beyschlag, S., 'Langzeilen-Melodien', *ZfdA* 93 (1964), 187ff.
Bezzola, R. R., *Les origines et la formation de la littérature courtoise en Occident (500–1200)*, Paris 1958ff.
Binns, J. W., *Intellectual culture of Elizabethan and Jacobean England: the Latin writings of the age*, Leeds 1990
Bischoff, B., *Paläographie des römischen Altertums und des abendländischen Mittelalters*, Berlin 1979
Bloch, R. H., *Medieval French literature and law*, Berkeley 1977
Bloomfield, L., *Language*, New York 1933
Bloomfield, M. W., and Dunn, C. W., *The role of the poet in early societies*, Cambridge 1989
Boehm, L., 'Der wissenschaftstheoretische Ort der historia im frühen Mittelalter', in: FS for J. Spörl, Munich 1965, pp. 663ff.
'Das mittelalterliche Erziehungs- und Bildungswesen', in: E. Wischer (ed.), *Propyläen Geschichte der Literatur. Literatur und Gesellschaft in der westlichen Welt. II: Die mittelalterliche Welt, 600–1400*, Berlin 1982, pp. 143ff.
Bonath, G., 'Nachtrag zu den Akrosticha in Gottfrieds "Tristan"', *ZfdA* 115 (1986), 101ff.
Boor, H. de, *Geschichte der deutschen Literatur von den Anfängen bis zur Gegenwart*, Munich 1949 (I), 1953 (II), 1962 (III 1), 1987 (III 2)
'Die Schreiber der Nibelungenhandschrift B', *PBB* 94 (1972), 81ff.
Borck, K.-H., 'Der Tanz zu Kölbigk', *PBB* 76 (1954), 241ff.
Boudriot, W., *Die altgermanische Religion in der amtlichen kirchlichen Literatur des Abendlandes vom 5. bis 11. Jahrhundert*, Darmstadt 1964
Brackert, H., *Rudolf von Ems. Dichtung und Geschichte*, Heidelberg 1968
'"der lac an riterschefte tôt". Parzival und das Leid der Frauen', in: FS for G. Schweikle, Stuttgart 1989, pp. 143ff.
Bräuer, R. (ed.), *Geschichte der deutschen Literatur. Mitte des 12. bis Mitte des 13. Jahrhunderts*, Berlin 1990 (*Geschichte der deutschen Literatur von den Anfängen bis zur Gegenwart*, II)
Brall, H., *Gralsuche und Adelsheil. Studien zu Wolframs Parzival*, Heidelberg 1984
Brandt, A. von, 'Geistliche als kaufmännisches Schreiberpersonal im Mittelalter', *ZVLGA* 38 (1958), 164ff.
Brandt, R., *Konrad von Würzburg*, Darmstadt 1987
Braungart, G., 'Notker der Deutsche als Bearbeiter eines lateinischen Schultextes: Boethius De Consolatione Philosophiae', *ZfdPh* 106 (1987), 2ff.
Brewer, D. S., 'Orality and literacy in Chaucer', in: W. Erzgräber and S. Volk (ed.), *Mündlichkeit und Schriftlichkeit im englischen Mittelalter*, Tübingen 1988, pp. 85ff.
Brogsitter, K. O., 'Der Held im Zwiespalt und der Held als strahlender Musterritter', in: F.

Wolfzettel (ed.), *Artusrittertum im späten Mittelalter. Ethos und Ideologie*, Giessen 1984, pp. 16ff.
Brüggen, E., *Kleidung und Mode in der höfischen Epik des 12. und 13. Jahrhunderts*, Heidelberg 1989
Brunner, H., 'Epenmelodien', in: FS for S. Beyschlag, Göppingen 1970, pp. 149ff.
'Strukturprobleme der Epenmelodien', in: E. Kühebacher (ed.), *Deutsche Heldenepik in Tirol. König Laurin und Dietrich von Bern in der Dichtung des Mittelalters*, Bozen 1979, pp. 300ff.
Brunner, O., 'Die ritterlich-höfische Kultur', in: A. Borst (ed.), *Das Rittertum im Mittelalter*, Darmstadt 1976, pp. 142ff.
Bützler, C., *Untersuchungen zu den Melodien Walthers von der Vogelweide*, Jena 1940
Bumke, J., *Wolfram von Eschenbach*, Stuttgart 1964
Ministerialität und Ritterdichtung. Umrisse der Forschung, Munich 1976
Mäzene im Mittelalter. Die Gönner und Auftraggeber der höfischen Literatur in Deutschland 1150–1300, Munich 1979
Review of M. G. Scholz, *Hören und Lesen*, AfdA 93 (1982), 116ff.
'Liebe und Ehebruch in der höfischen Gesellschaft', in: R. Krohn (ed.), *Liebe als Literatur. Aufsätze zur erotischen Dichtung in Deutschland*, Munich 1983, pp. 25ff.
Höfische Kultur. Literatur und Gesellschaft im hohen Mittelalter, Munich 1986
'Epenhandschriften. Vorüberlegungen und Informationen zur Überlieferungsgeschichte der höfischen Epik im 12. und 13. Jahrhundert', in: FS for K. Stackmann, Göttingen 1987, pp. 45ff.
'Walther von der Vogelweide', in: U. Liebertz-Grün (ed.), *Aus der Mündlichkeit in die Schriftlichkeit*, pp. 193ff.
Geschichte der deutschen Literatur im hohen Mittelalter, Munich 1990
Geschichte der mittelalterlichen Literatur als Aufgabe, Opladen 1991
'Untersuchungen zur Überlieferungsgeschichte der höfischen Epik im 13. Jahrhundert. Die Herbort-Fragmente aus Skokloster. Mit einem Ezkurs zur Textkritik der höfischen Romane', ZfdA 120 (1991), 257ff.
Burg, U. von der, *Strickers Karl der Große als Bearbeitung des Rolandsliedes. Studien zu Form und Inhalt*, Göppingen 1974
Burke, P., *Popular culture in early modern Europe*, London 1988
Buschinger, D., *Lorengel*, Göppingen 1979
Caliebe, M., *Dukus Horant. Studien zu seiner literarischen Tradition*, Berlin 1975
Calin, W. C., *The Old French epic of revolt: Raoul de Cambrai, Renaud de Montauban, Gormond et Isembard*, Geneva 1962
Camille, M., 'Seeing and reading: some visual implications of medieval literacy and illiteracy', AH 8 (1985), 26ff.
Campenhausen, H. von, *Die Entstehung der christlichen Bibel*, Tübingen 1968
Capua, F. di, 'Osservazioni sulla lettura e sulla preghiera ad alta voce presso gli antichi', RAALBA 28 (1953), 59ff.
Carcopino, J., *Daily life in ancient Rome*, London 1973
Carruthers, M. J., *The book of memory. A study of memory in medieval culture*, Cambridge 1990
Chailley, J., 'La danse religieuse au moyen âge', in: *Arts libéraux et philosophie au moyen âge. Actes du quatrième congrès international de philosophie médiévale, Montréal 1967*, Montréal 1969, pp. 357ff.
Chaytor, H. J., *From script to print. An introduction to medieval vernacular literature*, Cambridge 1950
Chinca, M. G., *History, fiction, verisimilitude. Studies in the poetics of Gottfried's 'Tristan'*, London 1993
Christ, W., *Rhetorik und Roman. Untersuchungen zu Gottfrieds von Straßburg 'Tristan und Isold'*, Meisenheim 1977

Clanchy, M. T., 'Remembering the past and the good old law', *History* 55 (1970), 165ff.
From memory to written record. England 1066–1307, London 1979
'Looking back from the invention of printing', in: D. P. Resnick (ed.), *Literacy in historical perspective*, Washington D.C. 1983, pp. 7ff.
Classen, P., 'Die hohen Schulen und die Gesellschaft im 12. Jahrhundert', *AfK* 48 (1966), 155ff.
'Die geistesgeschichtliche Lage. Anstöße und Möglichkeiten', in: P. Weimar (ed.), *Die Renaissance der Wissenschaften im 12. Jahrhundert*, Zürich 1981, pp. 11ff.
Classen, P. (ed.), *Recht und Schrift im Mittelalter*, Sigmaringen 1977
Congar, Y., *Laie*, in: H. Fries (ed.), *Handbuch theologischer Grundbegriffe* II 7ff., Munich 1963
Conlee, J. W., 'A note on verse composition in the *Meters of Boethius*', *NM* 71 (1970), 576ff.
Cormeau, C., 'Artusroman und Märchen. Beschreibung und Genese der Struktur des höfischen Romans', *Wolfram-Studien* 5 (1979), 63ff.
Cormeau, C., and Störmer, W., *Hartmann von Aue. Epoche – Werk – Wirkung*, Munich 1985
Coulmas, F., *Über Schrift*, Frankfurt 1981
Coulmas, F., and Ehlich, K. (ed.), *Writing in focus*, Berlin 1983
Cramer, T., *Hartmann von Aue. Erec*, Frankfurt 1972
'Der deutsche höfische Roman und seine Vorläufer', in: H. Krauss (ed.), *Europäisches Hochmittelalter*, Wiesbaden 1981, pp. 323ff.
Geschichte der deutschen Literatur im späten Mittelalter, Munich 1990
'Brangend und brogend. Repräsentation, Feste und Literatur in der höfischen Kultur des späten Mittelalters', in: H. Ragotzky and H. Wenzel (ed.), *Höfische Repräsentation. Das Zeremoniell und die Zeichen*, Tübingen 1990, pp. 259ff.
Crosby, R., 'Oral delivery in the Middle Ages', *Speculum* 11 (1936), 88ff.
Curschmann, M., '*Spielmannsepik*'. *Wege und Ergebnisse der Forschungen von 1907–1965*, Stuttgart 1968
'Das Abenteuer des Erzählens. Über den Erzähler in Wolframs *Parzival*', *DVjs* 45 (1971), 627ff.
'The concept of the oral formula as an impediment to our understanding of medieval oral poetry', *Medievalia et Humanistica* 8 (1977), 63ff.
'"Nibelungenlied" und "Nibelungenklage". Über Mündlichkeit und Schriftlichkeit im Prozeß der Episierung', in: C. Cormeau (ed.), *Deutsche Literatur im Mittelalter. Kontakte und Perspektiven. Hugo Kuhn zum Gedenken*, Stuttgart 1979, pp. 85ff.
'Hören – Lesen – Sehen. Buch und Schriftlichkeit im Selbstverständnis der volkssprachlichen literarischen Kultur Deutschlands um 1200', *PBB* 106 (1984), 218ff.
Review of W. Haug, *Literaturtheorie*, *GRM* 69 (1988), 348ff.
Review of R. Schmidt-Wiegand, *Text*, *PBB* 110 (1988), 267ff.
'Zur Wechselwirkung von Literatur und Sage. Das "Buch von Kriemhild" und Dietrich von Bern', *PBB* 111 (1989), 380ff.
'*Pictura laicorum litteratura*? Überlegungen zum Verhältnis von Bild und volkssprachlicher Schriftlichkeit im Hoch- und Spätmittelalter bis zum Codex Manesse', in: H. Keller *et al.* (ed.), *Pragmatische Schriftlichkeit*, pp. 211ff.
Davis, N. Z., 'Les conteurs de Montaillou', *Annales ESC* 34 (1979), 61ff.
Derolez, R., 'Die "Hrabanischen Runen"', *ZfdPh* 78 (1959), 1ff.
Dickinson, J. C., *Monastic life in medieval England*, London 1961
Diebold, M., *Das Sagelied. Die aktuelle deutsche Heldendichtung der Nachvölkerwanderungszeit*, Bern 1974
Diemer, J., *Genesis und Exodus nach der Milstäter Handschrift*, Vienna 1862
Dilcher, G., 'Oralität, Verschriftlichung und Wandlungen der Normstruktur in den Stadtrechten des 12. und 13. Jahrhunderts', in: H. Keller *et al.* (ed.), *Pragmatische Schriftlichkeit*, pp. 9ff.
Drube, H., *Hartmann und Chrétien*, Münster 1931
Duby, G., *Les trois ordres ou l'imagination du féodalisme*, Paris 1978

'The culture of the knightly class. Audience and patronage', in: R. L. Benson and G. Constable (ed.), *Renaissance and renewal in the twelfth century*, Oxford 1982, pp. 248ff.
Duby, G. (ed.), *A history of private life. II: Revelations of the medieval world*, Cambridge, Mass., 1988
Düwel, K., 'Buchstabenmagie und Alphabetzauber. Zu den Inschriften der Goldbrakteaten und ihrer Funktion als Amulette', *FMS* 22 (1988), 70ff.
'Lesestoff für junge Adlige. Lektüreempfehlungen in einer Tugendlehre des 13. Jahrhunderts', *Fabula* 32 (1991), 67ff.
Dunbabin, J., 'From clerk to knight: changing orders', in: C. Harper-Bill and R. Harvey (ed.), *The ideals and practice of medieval knighthood II*, Woodbridge 1988, pp. 26ff.
Ebel, E., *Die Terminologie der Runentechnik*, diss. Göttingen 1963
Ebenbauer, A., 'Tschionatulander und Artus. Zur Gattungsstruktur und zur Interpretation des Tschionatulanderlebens im "Jüngeren Titurel"', *ZfdA* 108 (1979), 374ff.
'Buch', in: *Reallexikon der germanischen Altertumskunde* IV 34ff., Berlin 1981
'Antike Stoffe', in: V. Mertens and U. Müller (ed.), *Epische Stoffe des Mittelalters*, Stuttgart 1984, pp. 247ff.
'Das Dilemma mit der Wahrheit. Gedanken zum "historisierenden Roman" des 13. Jahrhunderts', in: C. Gerhardt, N. F. Palmer, B. Wachinger (ed.), *Geschichtsbewußtsein in der deutschen Literatur des Mittelalters*, Tübingen 1985, pp. 52ff.
Eggers, H., *Deutsche Sprachgeschichte I. Das Althochdeutsche*, Reinbek 1963
'Non cognovi litteraturam (zu "Parzival" 115, 27)', in: H. Rupp (ed.), *Wolfram von Eschenbach*, Darmstadt 1966, pp. 533ff.
Ehlers, J., 'Die hohen Schulen', in: P. Weimar (ed.), *Die Renaissance der Wissenschaften im 12. Jahrhundert*, Zürich 1981, pp. 57ff.
'Deutsche Scholaren in Frankreich während des 12. Jahrhunderts', in: J. Fried (ed.), *Schulen und Studium im sozialen Wandel des hohen und späten Mittelalters*, Sigmaringen 1986, pp. 97ff.
Ehlich, K., 'Text und sprachliches Handeln. Die Entstehung von Texten aus dem Bedürfnis nach Überlieferung', in: A. and J. Assmann (ed.), *Schrift*, pp. 24ff.
Ehrismann, G., *Geschichte der deutschen Literatur bis zum Ausgang des Mittelalters*, Munich 1932 (I), 1922 (II 1), 1927 (II 2), 1935 (III)
Eifler, G. (ed.), *Ritterliches Tugendsystem*, Darmstadt 1970
Eisenstein, E. L., *The printing press as an agent of change. Communications and cultural transformations in early-modern Europe*, Cambridge 1980
Elliott, R. W. V., *Runes. An introduction*, Manchester 1959
Elm, K., 'Die Stellung der Frau in Ordenswesen, Semireligiosentum und Häresie zur Zeit der heiligen Elisabeth', in: *Sankt Elisabeth, Fürstin – Dienerin – Heilige*, Sigmaringen 1981, pp. 7ff.
'Mendikantentum, Laienbildung und Klerikerschulung im spätmittelalterlichen Westfalen', in: B. Moeller, H. Patze, K. Stackmann (ed.), *Studien zum städtischen Bildungswesen des späten Mittelalters und der frühen Neuzeit*, Abhandlungen der Akademie der Wissenschaften in Göttingen, Philologisch-historische Klasse, Dritte Folge, Nr. 137, Göttingen 1983, pp. 586ff.
Elwert, G., 'Die gesellschaftliche Einbettung von Schriftgebrauch', in: FS for N. Luhmann, Frankfurt 1987, pp. 238ff.
Engel, W., *Die dichtungstheoretischen Bezeichnungen im 'Liber evangeliorum' Otfrids von Weißenburg*, diss. Frankfurt 1969
Erdmann, C., *Die Entstehung des Kreuzzugsgedankens*, Stuttgart 1935
'Fabulae curiales. Neues zum Spielmannsgesang und zum Ezzo-Liede', *ZfdA* 73 (1936), 87ff.
Ernout, A., 'Dictāre "dicter", allem. *dichten*', *REL* 29 (1951), 155ff.
Ernst, U., *Der Liber Evangeliorum Otfrids von Weißenburg. Literarästhetik und Verstechnik im Lichte der Tradition*, Cologne 1975

'Der Antagonismus von *vita carnalis* und *vita spiritualis* im *Gregorius* Hartmanns von Aue. Versuch einer Werkdeutung im Horizont der patristischen und monastischen Tradition', *Euphorion* 72 (1978), 16off. and 73 (1979), 1ff.

Ertzdorff, X. von, *Rudolf von Ems. Untersuchungen zum höfischen Roman im 13. Jahrhundert*, Munich 1967

'Die Hochzeit zu Kana. Zur Bibelauslegung Otfrids von Weißenburg', in: W. Kleiber (ed.), *Otfrid von Weißenburg*, Darmstadt 1978, pp. 251ff.

Erzgräber, W., and Volk, S. (ed.), *Mündlichkeit und Schriftlichkeit im englischen Mittelalter*, Tübingen 1988

Esser, J., *Die Schöpfungsgeschichte in der 'Altdeutschen Genesis' (Wiener Genesis V. 1–231). Kommentar und Interpretation*, Göppingen 1987

Falk, H., 'Goodies for India – literacy, orality, and Vedic culture', in: W. Raible (ed.), *Erscheinungsformen kultureller Prozesse*, Tübingen 1990, pp. 103ff.

Febvre, L., and Martin, H.-J., *The coming of the book. The impact of printing 1450–1800*, London 1979

Fechter, W., *Das Publikum der mittelhochdeutschen Dichtung*, Frankfurt 1935

Feldbusch, E., *Geschriebene Sprache. Untersuchungen zu ihrer Herausbildung und Grundlegung ihrer Theorie*, Berlin 1985

Felten, F. J., *Äbte und Laienäbte im Frankenreich*, Stuttgart 1980

Fenske, L., 'Der Knappe: Erziehung und Funktion', in: J. Fleckenstein (ed.), *Curialitas*, pp. 55ff.

Fichtenau, H., 'Karl der Große und das Kaisertum', *MIÖG* 61 (1953), 271ff.

Finnegan, R., *Oral poetry. Its nature, significance and social context*, Cambridge 1977

Literacy and orality. Studies in the technology of communication, Oxford 1988

Fischer, H., *Studien zur deutschen Märendichtung*, Tübingen 1968

Fleckenstein, J., *Die Bildungsreform Karls des Großen als Verwirklichung der Norma Rectitudinis*, Bigge-Ruhr 1953

Die Hofkapelle der deutschen Könige, Stuttgart 1959 and 1966

'Miles und clericus am Königs- und Fürstenhof. Bemerkungen zu den Voraussetzungen zur Entstehung und zur Trägerschaft der höfisch-ritterlichen Kultur', in: *Curialitas*, pp. 302ff.

Fleckenstein, J. (ed.), *Curialitas. Studien zu Grundfragen der höfisch-ritterlichen Kultur*, Göttingen 1990

Flint, V. I. J., *The rise of magic in early medieval Europe*, Oxford 1991

Flori, J., *L'idéologie du glaive. Préhistoire de la chevalerie*, Geneva 1983

L'essor de la chevalerie XIe–XIIe siècles, Geneva 1986

Foley, J. M., 'The oral theory in context', in: FS for A. B. Lord, Columbus, Ohio, 1980, pp. 27ff.

Oral-formulaic theory and research. An introduction and annotated bibliography, New York 1985

Fontaine, J., 'De la pluralité à l'unité dans le "latin carolingien"?', in: *Settimane di Studio del Centro di Studi sull'alto medioevo XXVII: Nascita dell'Europa ed Europa Carolingia: un'equazione da verificare*, Spoleto 1981, pp. 765ff.

Forster, L., 'Thoughts on the mnemonic function of early systems of writing', in: FS for K. von See, Odense 1988, pp. 59ff.

Fossier, R. (ed.), *The Cambridge illustrated history of the Middle Ages. I: 350–950*, Cambridge 1989

Fouquet-Plümacher, D., *Buch/Buchwesen III. Die Entwicklung von der Antike bis zur Neuzeit*, in: *Theologische Realenzyklopädie* VII 275ff., Berlin 1981

Fouracre, P., 'Using the background to the *Ludwigslied*: some methodological problems', in: J. L. Flood and D. N. Yeandle (ed.), *'Mit regulu bithuungan'. Neue Arbeiten zur althochdeutschen Poesie und Sprache*, Göppingen 1989, pp. 80ff.

Frank, B., *Seitengestaltung mittelalterlicher Handschriften im Kontext von Mündlichkeit und Schriftlichkeit. Zur Verschriftlichung der romanischen Sprachen*, diss. Freiburg 1991
Franz, K., *Studien zur Soziologie des Spruchdichters in Deutschland im späten 13. Jahrhundert*, Göppingen 1974
Frappier, J., *Les chansons de geste du cycle de Guillaume d'Orange*, Paris 1955, 1965, 1983
Freytag, H., *Die Theorie der allegorischen Schriftdeutung und die Allegorie in deutschen Texten besonders des 11. und 12. Jahrhunderts*, Bern 1982
'Ezzos Gesang. Text und Funktion', in: K. Grubmüller, R. Schmidt-Wiegand, K. Speckenbach (ed.), *Geistliche Denkformen in der Literatur des Mittelalters*, Munich 1984, pp. 154ff.
'Die frühmittelhochdeutsche geistliche Dichtung in Österreich', in: H. Zeman (ed.), *Die österreichische Literatur. Ihr Profil von den Anfängen im Mittelalter bis ins 18. Jahrhundert (1050–1750)*, Graz 1986, pp. 119ff.
Review of G. Vollmann-Profe, *Wiederbeginn*, *AfdA* 99 (1988), 132ff.
Freytag, W., '*Mundus fallax*, Affekt und Recht oder exemplarisches Erzählen im Prosa-Lanzelot', *Wolfram-Studien* 9 (1986), 134ff.
'Geistliches Leben und christliche Bildung. Hrotsvit und andere Autorinnen des frühen Mittelalters', in: G. Brinker-Gabler (ed.), *Deutsche Literatur von Frauen* I 65ff., Munich 1988
Fried, J., 'Königsgedanken Heinrichs des Löwen', *AfK* 55 (1973), 312ff.
Review of J. Bumke, *Mäzene*, *AfK* 64 (1982), 227ff.
Fromm, H., *Untersuchungen zum Marienleben des Priesters Wernher*, Turku 1955
'Der oder die Dichter des Nibelungenliedes?', in: *Colloquio italo-germanico sul tema: I Nibelunghi*, Rome 1974 (Accademia Nazionale dei Lincei, Atti dei Convegni Lincei 1), pp. 63ff.
'Die Erzählkunst des "Rother"-Epikers', in: W. J. Schröder (ed.), *Spielmannsepik*, Darmstadt 1977, pp. 351ff.
'Der "Jüngere Titurel". Das Werk und sein Dichter', *Wolfram-Studien* 8 (1984), 11ff.
'Volkssprache und Schriftkultur', in: P. Ganz (ed.), *The role of the book in medieval culture*, Turnhout 1986, pp. 99ff.
Froning, R., *Das Drama des Mittelalters. I: Die lateinischen Osterfeiern und ihre Entwicklung in Deutschland. Osterspiele, Passionsspiele*, Stuttgart 1891
Frühmorgen-Voss, H., 'Bildtypen in der Manessischen Liederhandschrift', in: I. Glier, G. Hahn, W. Haug, B. Wachinger (ed.), *Werk – Typ – Situation. Studien zu poetologischen Bedingungen in der älteren deutschen Literatur*, Stuttgart 1969, pp. 184ff.
Text und Illustration im Mittelalter. Aufsätze zu den Wechselbeziehungen zwischen Literatur und bildender Kunst, Munich 1975
Frühwald, W., *Der St. Georgener Prediger. Studien zur Wandlung des geistlichen Gehaltes*, Berlin 1963
Fry, D. K., 'Caedmon as a formulaic poet', in: J. J. Duggan (ed.), *Oral literature*, Edinburgh 1975, pp. 41ff.
'The memory of Caedmon', in: FS for A. B. Lord, Columbus, Ohio, 1980, pp. 282ff.
Fünten, W. aus der, *Maria Magdalena in der Lyrik des Mittelalters*, Düsseldorf 1966
Fuhrmann, H., *Einladung ins Mittelalter*, Munich 1988
Gadamer, H.-G., 'Unterwegs zur Schrift?', in: A. and J. Assmann (ed.), *Schrift*, pp. 10ff.
Gaiffier, B. de, *Etudes critiques d'hagiographie et d'iconologie*, Brussels 1967
Gallais, P., 'Recherches sur la mentalité des romanciers français du moyen âge', *CCM* 7 (1964), 479ff. and 13 (1970), 333ff.
Ganz, D., 'The preconditions for Caroline minuscule', *Viator* 18 (1987), 23ff.
Ganz, P. F., Review of I. Ochs, '*Willehalm*'-Eingang', *PBB* 91 (1969), 412ff.
'Tristan, Isolde und Ovid. Zu Gottfrieds "Tristan" Z. 17182ff.', in: FS for H. de Boor, Munich 1971, pp. 397ff.

'Dienstmann und Abt. "Gregorius Peccator" bei Hartmann von Aue und Arnold von Lübeck', in: FS for W. Schröder, Berlin 1974, pp. 250ff.
'"Die Hochzeit": *fabula* und *significatio*', in: L. P. Johnson, H.-H. Steinhoff, R. A. Wisbey (ed.), *Studien zur frühmittelhochdeutschen Literatur*, Berlin 1974, pp. 58ff.
'"Nur eine schöne Kunstfigur". Zur "Goldenen Schmiede" Konrads von Würzburg', *GRM* 60 (1979), 27ff.
'Heinrich der Löwe und sein Hof in Braunschweig', in: D. Kötzsche (ed.), *Das Evangeliar Heinrichs des Löwen. Kommentar zum Faksimile*, Frankfurt 1989, pp. 28ff.
Gaur, A., *A history of writing*, London 1984
Geering, A., 'Die Nibelungenmelodie in der Trierer Marienklage', in: *Internationale Gesellschaft für Musikwissenschaft. 4. Kongreß Basel 1949, Kongreßbericht*, Basel 1951, pp. 118ff.
Geith, K.-E., *Albert von Augsburg: das Leben des Heiligen Ulrich*, Berlin 1971
Carolus Magnus. Studien zur Darstellung Karls des Großen in der deutschen Literatur des 12. und 13. Jahrhunderts, Munich 1977
'Die Leben-Jesu-Übersetzung der Schwester Regula aus Lichtenthal', *ZfdA* 119 (1990), 22ff.
Gelb, I. J., *A study of writing*, Chicago 1963
Gentry, F. G., 'Von der karolingischen Kulturreform bis zur Rezeption der höfischen Literatur Frankreichs', in: U. Liebertz-Grün (ed.), *Aus der Mündlichkeit in die Schriftlichkeit*, pp. 46ff.
Georgi, A., *Das lateinische und deutsche Preisgedicht des Mittelalters in der Nachfolge des Genus demonstrativum*, Berlin 1969
Gerhardsson, B., *Memory and manuscript. Oral tradition and written transmission in rabbinic Judaism and early Christianity*, Uppsala 1961
Geuenich, D., 'Die volkssprachige Überlieferung der Karolingerzeit aus der Sicht eines Historikers', *DA* 39 (1983), 104ff.
Giesecke, M., *Der Buchdruck in der frühen Neuzeit. Eine historische Fallstudie über die Durchsetzung neuer Informations- und Kommunikationstechnologien*, Frankfurt 1991
'Der "abgang der erkantnusz" und die Renaissance "wahren Wissens". Frühneuzeitliche Kritik an den mittelalterlichen Formen handschriftlicher Informationsverarbeitung', in: H. Keller et al. (ed.), *Pragmatische Schriftlichkeit*, pp. 77ff.
Gillespie, G., '"Tristan- und Siegfriedliebe": a comparative study of Gottfried's Tristan and the Nibelungenlied', in: A. Stevens and R. Wisbey (ed.), *Gottfried von Strassburg and the medieval Tristan legend*, Cambridge 1990, pp. 155ff.
Glaue, P., *Die Vorlesung heiliger Schriften im Gottesdienste. I. Teil: Bis zur Entstehung der altkatholischen Kirche*, Berlin 1907
Glendinning, R., 'Gottfried von Straßburg and the school tradition', *DVjs* 61 (1987), 617ff.
Gompf, L., 'Die "Ecbasis cuiusdam captivi" und ihr Publikum', *MlJb* 8 (1973), 30ff.
Goody, J. (ed.), *Literacy in traditional societies*, Cambridge 1981
The domestication of the savage mind, Cambridge 1984
The logic of writing and the organization of society, Cambridge 1986
The interface between the written and the oral, Cambridge 1989
Gough, K., 'Implications of literacy in traditional China and India', in: J. Goody, *Literacy*, pp. 69ff.
Graham, W. A., *Beyond the written word. Oral aspects of scripture in the history of religion*, Cambridge 1987
Green, D. H., *The Millstätter Exodus. A crusading epic*, Cambridge 1966
'The Alexanderlied and the emergence of the romance', *GLL* 28 (1975), 246ff.
'On recognising medieval irony', in: A. P. Foulkes (ed.), *The uses of criticism*, Bern 1976, pp. 11ff.
'The concept âventiure in Parzival', in: D. H. Green and L. P. Johnson, *Approaches to Wolfram von Eschenbach. Five essays*, Bern 1978, pp. 83ff.

'Oral poetry and written composition. (An aspect of the feud between Gottfried and Wolfram)', in: Green and Johnson, *Approaches*, pp. 163ff.
Irony in the medieval romance, Cambridge 1979
'Parzival's departure – folktale and romance', *FMS* 14 (1980), 352ff.
'Advice and narrative action. Parzival, Herzeloyde and Gurnemanz', in: FS for L. Forster, Baden-Baden 1982, pp. 33ff.
'On the primary reception of narrative literature in medieval Germany', *FMLS* 20 (1984), 289ff.
'The primary reception of the works of Notker the German', *Parergon* 2 (1984), 57ff.
'The reception of Hartmann's works: listening, reading, or both?', *MLR* 81 (1986), 357ff.
'On the primary reception of the works of Rudolf von Ems', *ZfdA* 115 (1986), 151ff.
'The spread of literacy. An aspect of the twelfth-century renaissance in Germany', *RPL* 9 (1986), 143ff.
'Literacy and history in German literature of the Middle Ages', *RPL* 10 (1987), 159ff.
'Zur primären Rezeption von Otfrids Evangelienbuch', in: R. Bergmann, H. Tiefenbach, L. Voetz (ed.), *Althochdeutsch*, Heidelberg 1987, pp. 737ff.
'Über Mündlichkeit und Schriftlichkeit in der deutschen Literatur des Mittelalters. Drei Rezeptionsweisen und ihre Erfassung', in: FS for K. Stackmann, Göttingen 1987, pp. 1ff.
'Die Schriftlichkeit und die Geschichte der deutschen Literatur im Mittelalter', *LwJb* 30 (1989), 9ff.
'Zur primären Rezeption von Wolframs 'Parzival'', in: FS for W. Schröder, Tübingen 1989, pp. 271ff.
'Orality and reading. The state of research in medieval studies', *Speculum* 65 (1990), 267ff.
'Hören und Lesen: zur Geschichte einer mittelalterlichen Formel', in: W. Raible (ed.), *Erscheinungsformen kultureller Prozesse*, Tübingen 1990, pp. 23ff.
'Mündlichkeit und Schriftlichkeit im höfischen Roman des 13. Jahrhunderts', in: P. Schulze-Belli and M. Dallapiazza (ed.), *Liebe und Aventiure im Artusroman des Mittelalters*, Göppingen 1990, pp. 67ff.
'Individual and society: the evidence of writing and orality in late medieval Germany', in: G. Tarugi (ed.), *Homo sapiens, Homo humanus. II: Litteratura, arte e scienza nella seconda metà del quattrocento*, Florence 1990, pp. 291ff.
'History and fiction in German literature of the late Middle Ages', in: G. Tarugi (ed.), *Homo sapiens, Homo humanus. II: Litteratura, arte e scienze nella seconda metà del quattrocento*, Florence 1990, pp. 95ff.
'The spread of humanism: a view from the German Middle Ages', in: S. Troiani and A. Grilli (ed.), *Studi Umanistici Piceni* 12, Fano 1992, pp. 89ff.
'Renaissance and education in the Middle Ages', in: L. R. Secchi Tarugi (ed.), *L'educazione e la formazione intellettuale nell' età dell'umanesimo*, Milan 1992, pp. 17ff.
'Middle High German *lesen* = "sagen, erzählen"?', in: J. Flood, P. Salmon, O. Sayce, C. J. Wells (ed.), *'Das unsichtbare Band der Sprache'. Studies in German language and linguistic history in memory of Leslie Seiffert*, Stuttgart 1993, pp. 85ff.
'*Vrume rîtr und guote vrouwen / und wîse phaffen*. Court literature and its audience', in: FS for R. Wisbey, Tübingen 1994, pp. 1ff.
Greinemann, E., *Die Gedichte der Frau Ava. Untersuchungen zur Quellenfrage*, diss. Freiburg 1968
Grimm, W., *Die deutsche Heldensage*, Gütersloh 1889
Grosse, S., '"Vremdiu maere" – Tristans Herkunftsberichte', *WW* 20 (1970), 289ff.
Gruber, J., 'Singen und Schreiben, Hören und Lesen als Parameter der (Re-)Produktion und Rezeption des Occitanischen Minnesangs des 12. Jahrhunderts', *LiLi* 15 (1985), 35ff.
Grubmüller, K., 'Sprache und ihre Verschriftlichung in der Geschichte des Deutschen', in: W. Besch, O. Reichmann, S. Sonderegger (ed.), *Sprachgeschichte. Ein Handbuch zur Geschichte der deutschen Sprache und ihrer Erforschung*, Berlin 1984, pp. 205ff.

'Gegebenheiten deutschsprachiger Textüberlieferung bis zum Ausgang des Mittelalters', in: W. Besch, O. Reichmann, S. Sonderegger (ed.), *Sprachgeschichte. Ein Handbuch zur Geschichte der deutschen Sprache und ihrer Erforschung*, Berlin 1984, pp. 214ff.
'Minne und Geschichtserfahrung. Zum "Frauendienst" Ulrichs von Lichtenstein', in: C. Gerhardt, N. F. Palmer, B. Wachinger (ed.), *Geschichtsbewußtsein in der deutschen Literatur des Mittelalters*, Tübingen 1985, pp. 37ff.
'Liber a libertate legencium. Vokabularien als Instrumente von Kontinuität und Wandel', in: P. Ganz (ed.), *The role of the book in medieval culture* II 95ff., Turnhout 1986
'Mündlichkeit, Schriftlichkeit und Unterricht. Zur Erforschung ihrer Interferenzen in der Kultur des Mittelalters', *DU (NS)* 1 (1989), 1 41ff.
Grundmann, H., 'Die Frauen und die Literatur im Mittelalter. Ein Beitrag zur Frage nach der Entstehung des Schrifttums in der Volkssprache', *AfK* 26 (1936), 129ff.
'Litteratus – illitteratus. Der Wandel einer Bildungsnorm vom Altertum zum Mittelalter', *AfK* 40 (1958), 1ff.
Religiöse Bewegungen im Mittelalter. Untersuchungen über die geschichtlichen Zusammenhänge zwischen der Ketzerei, den Bettelorden und der religiösen Frauenbewegung im 12. und 13. Jahrhundert und über die geschichtlichen Grundlagen der deutschen Mystik, Darmstadt 1961
Geschichtsschreibung im Mittelalter. Gattungen – Epochen – Eigenart, Göttingen 1965
'Dichtete Wolfram von Eschenbach am Schreibtisch?', *AfK* 49 (1967), 391ff.
'Deutsches Schrifttum im Deutschen Orden', in: H. Grundmann, *Ausgewählte Aufsätze. 3: Bildung und Sprache*, Stuttgart 1978, pp. 96ff.
Wahlkönigtum, Territorialpolitik und Ostbewegung im 13. und 14. Jahrhundert, 1198–1378 (Gebhardt Handbuch der deutschen Geschichte 5, ninth edition dtv), Munich 1979
Gschwantler, O., *Heldensage in der Historiographie des Mittelalters*, Habilitationsschrift Vienna 1971
'Älteste Gattungen germanischer Dichtung', in: K. von See (ed.), *Europäisches Frühmittelalter*, Wiesbaden 1985, pp. 91ff.
'Zeugnisse zur Dietrichsage in der Historiographie von 1100 bis gegen 1350', in: H. Beck (ed.), *Heldensage und Heldendichtung im Germanischen*, Berlin 1988, pp. 35ff.
Günther, H., 'Zur neueren Schriftlichkeitsforschung', *PBB* 112 (1990), 349ff.
Guerreau-Jalabert, A., 'La "renaissance carolingienne": modèles culturels, usages linguistiques et structures sociales', *BEC* 139 (1981), 5ff.
Gumbrecht, H. U., 'Wie fiktional war der höfische Roman?', in: D. Henrich and W. Iser (ed.), *Funktionen des Fiktiven*, Munich 1983, pp. 433ff.
Gurevich, A. J., 'Oral and written culture of the Middle Ages: two "peasant visions" of the late twelfth–early thirteenth centuries', *NLH* 16 (1984/5), 51ff.
Gurjewitsch, A. J., *Mittelalterliche Volkskultur*, Munich 1987
Guyer, F. E., 'The influence of Ovid on Crestien de Troyes', *RR* 12 (1921), 97ff., 216ff.
Hadas, M., *Ancilla to classical reading*, New York 1954
Hagenlocher, A., 'Littera Meretrix. Brun von Schönebeck und die Autorität der Schrift im Mittelalter', *ZfdA* 118 (1989), 131ff.
Hahn, G., *Walther von der Vogelweide. Eine Einführung*, Munich 1986
'"Res sine verbis Lutherus". Konturen der Autorschaft Martin Luthers', in: W. Haug and B. Wachinger (ed.), *Autorentypen*, Tübingen 1991, pp. 130ff.
Hahn, I., *Raum und Landschaft in Gottfrieds Tristan. Ein Beitrag zur Werkdeutung*, Munich 1963
Harnack, A. von, *Die Quellen der sogenannten apostolischen Kirchenordnung nebst einer Untersuchung über den Ursprung des Lectorats und der anderen niederen Weihen*, Leipzig 1886
Über den privaten Gebrauch der heiligen Schriften in der alten Kirche, Leipzig 1912
Harris, J., 'Eddic poetry as oral poetry: the evidence of parallel passages in the Helgi poems for

questions of composition and performance', in: R. J. Glendinning and H. Bessason (ed.), *Edda. A collection of essays*, Manitoba, pp. 210ff.
Harris, R., *The origin of writing*, London 1986
Harris, W. V., *Ancient literacy*, Cambridge, Mass., 1989
Hartl, E., *Das Drama des Mittelalters. Osterspiele*, Darmstadt 1964
Hartung, W., *Die Spielleute. Eine Randgruppe in der Gesellschaft des Mittelalters*, Wiesbaden 1982
Harvey, F. D., Review of E. A. Havelock, *Origins of Western literacy*, Toronto 1976, CR 28 (1978), 130f.
Hatto, A. T., *Gottfried von Strassburg. Tristan*, Harmondsworth 1960
'Medieval German', in: A. T. Hatto (ed.), *Traditions of heroic and epic poetry* I 165ff., London 1980
Parzival. Wolfram von Eschenbach, Harmondsworth 1980
'Towards an anatomy of heroic epic poetry', in: J. B. Hainsworth (ed.), *Traditions of heroic and epic poetry* II 145ff., London 1989
Haubrichs, W., 'Die Praefatio des Heliand. Ein Zeugnis der Religions- und Bildungspolitik Ludwigs des Deutschen', in: J. Eichhoff and I. Rausch (ed.), *Der Heliand*, Darmstadt 1973, pp. 400ff.
'Bildungswesen (5.-10. Jh.)', in: *Reallexikon der germanischen Altertumskunde* II 598ff., Berlin 1976
Georgslied und Georgslegende im frühen Mittelalter. Text und Rekonstruktion, Königstein 1979
Die Kultur der Abtei Prüm zur Karolingerzeit. Studien zur Heimat des althochdeutschen Georgsliedes, Bonn 1979
'Nekrologische Notizen zu Otfrid von Weißenburg. Prosopographische Studien zum sozialen Umfeld und zur Rezeption des Evangelienbuches', in: H. Wenzel (ed.), *Adelsherrschaft und Literatur*, Bern 1980, pp. 7ff.
'Altsächsische Literatur', in: K. von See (ed.), *Europäisches Frühmittelalter*, Wiesbaden 1985, pp. 217ff.
Die Anfänge: Versuche volkssprachiger Schriftlichkeit im frühen Mittelalter (ca. 700–1050/60), Frankfurt 1988 (vol. 1, part 1 of J. Heinzle, *Geschichte der deutschen Literatur von den Anfängen bis zum Beginn der Neuzeit*)
'Heldensage und Heldengeschichte. Das Konzept der Vorzeit in den Quedlinburger Annalen', in: FS for H. Kolb, Bern 1989, pp. 171ff.
'Veterum regum actus et bella – Zur sog. Heldenliedersammlung Karls des Großen', in: FS for H.-F. Rosenfeld, Göppingen 1989, pp. 17ff.
'Das monastische Studienprogramm der "Statuta Murbacensia" und die altalamannischen Interlinearversionen', in: FS for W. Kleiber, Stuttgart 1989, pp. 237ff.
'Arcana regum. Der althochdeutsche hundertachtunddreißigste Psalm und die Synode zu Tribur (895)', in: FS for J. Rathofer, Cologne 1990, pp. 67ff.
Hauck, K., 'Heldendichtung und Heldensage als Geschichtsbewußtsein', in: FS for O. Brunner, Göttingen 1963, pp. 118ff.
Haug, W., '*Das Land, von welchem niemand wiederkehrt*'. *Mythos, Fiktion und Wahrheit in Chrétiens 'Chevalier de la Charrete', im 'Lanzelet' Ulrichs von Zatzikhoven und im 'Lancelot'-Prosaroman*, Tübingen 1978
'Paradigmatische Poesie. Der spätere deutsche Artusroman auf dem Wege zu einer "nachklassischen" Ästhetik', *DVjs* 54 (1980), 204ff.
'Das Bildprogramm im Sommerhaus von Runkelstein', in: W. Haug, J. Heinzle, D. Huschenbett, N. H. Ott (ed.), *Runkelstein. Die Wandmalereien des Sommerhauses*, Wiesbaden 1982, pp. 15ff.
'Schriftlichkeit und Reflexion. Zur Entstehung und Entwicklung eines deutschsprachigen Schrifttums im Mittelalter', in: A. and J. Assmann (ed.), *Schrift*, pp. 141ff.

BIBLIOGRAPHICAL INDEX

Literaturtheorie im deutschen Mittelalter. Von den Anfängen bis zum Ende des 13. Jahrhunderts. Eine Einführung, Darmstadt 1985
'Von der Idealität des arthurischen Festes zur apokalyptischen Orgie in Wittenwilers *Ring*', in: W. Haug and R. Warning (ed.), *Das Fest*, Munich 1989, pp. 157ff.
Haug, W., and Vollmann, B. K., *Frühe deutsche Literatur und lateinische Literatur in Deutschland 800–1150*, Frankfurt 1991
Haupt, B., *Das Fest in der Dichtung. Untersuchungen zur historischen Semantik eines literarischen Motivs in der mittelhochdeutschen Epik*, Düsseldorf 1989
'Heilung von Wunden', in: G. Kaiser (ed.), *An den Grenzen höfischer Kultur. Anfechtungen der Lebensordnung in der deutschen Erzähldichtung des hohen Mittelalters*, Munich 1991, pp. 77ff.
Havelock, E. A., *The literate revolution in Greece and its cultural consequences*, Princeton 1982
Preface to Plato, Cambridge, Mass., 1982
The Muse learns to write. Reflexions on orality and literacy from antiquity to the present, New Haven 1986
Haverkamp, A., *Aufbruch und Gestaltung. Deutschland 1056–1273*, Munich 1984
Haymes, E. R., 'Formulaic density and Bishop Njegoš', *CL* 32 (1980), 390ff.
'Chevalerie und alte maeren. Zum Gattungshorizont des "Nibelungenliedes"', *GRM* 34 (1984), 369ff.
Hayum, A., *The Isenheim altarpiece. God's medicine and the painter's vision*, Princeton 1989
Heck, P., *Übersetzungsprobleme im frühen Mittelalter*, Tübingen 1931
Heger, H., *Das Lebenszeugnis Walthers von der Vogelweide. Die Reiserechnungen des Passauer Bischofs Wolfger von Erla*, Vienna 1970
Heimpel, H., *Die Vener von Gmünd und Straßburg 1162–1447. Studien und Texte zur Geschichte einer Familie sowie des gelehrten Beamtentums in der Zeit der abendländischen Kirchenspaltung und der Konzilien von Pisa, Konstanz und Basel*, Göttingen 1982
Heinen, H., 'Ulrich von Lichtenstein: *homo (il)litteratus* or poet/performer', *JEGPh* 83 (1984), 159ff.
'Ulrich von Lichtenstein's sense of genre', in: H. Heinen and I. Henderson (ed.), *Genres in medieval German literature*, Göppingen 1986, pp. 16ff.
Heinzle, J., *Mittelhochdeutsche Dietrichepik. Untersuchungen zur Tradierungsweise, Überlieferungskritik und Gattungsgeschichte später Heldendichtung*, Zürich 1978
'Wann beginnt das Spätmittelalter?', *ZfdA* 112 (1983), 207ff.
Wandlungen und Neuansätze im 13. Jahrhundert (1220/30–1280/90), Königstein 1984 (vol. II, part II of J. Heinzle (ed.), *Geschichte der deutschen Literatur von den Anfängen bis zum Beginn der Neuzeit*)
'Die Stellung des Prosa-Lancelot in der deutschen Literatur des 13. Jahrhunderts', in: F. Wolfzettel (ed.), *Artusrittertum im späten Mittelalter. Ethos und Ideologie*, Giessen 1984, pp. 104ff.
Das Nibelungenlied. Eine Einführung, Munich 1987
'Wie schreibt man eine Geschichte der deutschen Literatur des Mittelalters?', *DU* (NS) 1 (1989) 127ff.
'Die Entdeckung der Fiktionalität. Zu Walter Haugs "Literaturtheorie im deutschen Mittelalter"', *PBB* 112 (1990), 55ff.
Hellgardt, E., 'Lateinisch-deutsche Textensembles in Handschriften des 12. Jahrhunderts', in: N. Henkel and N. F. Palmer (ed.), *Latein und Volkssprache*, pp. 10ff.
Helm, K., *Altgermanische Religionsgeschichte. II: Die nachrömische Zeit. 2: Die Westgermanen*, Heidelberg 1953
Helm, K., and Ziesemer, W., *Die Literatur des deutschen Ritterordens*, Giessen 1951
Hendrickson, G. L., 'Ancient reading', *CJ* 25 (1929), 182ff.

Henkel, N., *Deutsche Übersetzungen lateinischer Schultexte. Ihre Verbreitung und Funktion im Mittelalter und in der frühen Neuzeit*, Munich 1988

'Bildtexte. Die Spruchbänder in der Berliner Handschrift von Heinrichs von Veldeke Eneasroman', in: FS for D. Wuttke, Baden-Baden 1989, pp. 1ff.

'Die Geschichte von Tristan und Isolde im deutschen Mittelalter', *UR* 17 (1990), 71ff.

'Litteratus – illitteratus. Bildungsgeschichtliche Grundvoraussetzungen bei der Entstehung der höfischen Epik in Deutschland', in: E. Iwasaki (ed.), *Akten des VIII. Internationalen Germanistenkongresses Tokyo 1990. Begegnung mit dem 'Fremden'. Grenzen – Traditionen – Vergleiche* IX 334ff., Munich 1991

Henkel, N., and Palmer, N. F. (ed.), *Latein und Volkssprache im deutschen Mittelalter 1100–1500*, Tübingen 1992

Hennig, U., *Untersuchungen zur frühmittelhochdeutschen Metrik am Beispiel der 'Wiener Genesis'*, Tübingen 1968

Herescu, N. I., 'Le mode de composition des écrivains ("dictare")', *REL* 34 (1956), 132ff.

Herkommer, H., 'Der Waise, *aller fürsten leitesterne*. Ein Beispiel mittelalterlicher Bedeutungslehre aus dem Bereich der Staatssymbolik, zugleich ein Beitrag zur Nachwirkung des Orients in der Literatur des Mittelalters', *DVjs* 50 (1976), 44ff.

'Eike von Repgows "Sachsenspiegel" und die "Sächsische Weltchronik". Prolegomena zur Bestimmung des Sächsischen Weltchronisten', *NdJb* 100 (1977), 7ff.

Herzog, R., *Die Bibelepik der lateinischen Spätantike. Formgeschichte einer erbaulichen Gattung*, Munich 1975

Heusler, A., *Lied und Epos in germanischer Sagendichtung*, Dortmund 1905

Die altgermanische Dichtung, Potsdam n.d. [1923]

Deutsche Versgeschichte, vol. II, Berlin 1956

Hirsch, H., 'Zur Frage des Auftretens der deutschen Sprache in den Urkunden und der Ausgabe deutscher Urkundentexte', *MÖIG* 52 (1938), 227ff.

Höfler, O., 'Die Anonymität des Nibelungenliedes', in: K. Hauck (ed.), *Zur germanisch-deutschen Heldensage*, Darmstadt 1961, pp. 330ff.

Hölscher, L., *Öffentlichkeit und Geheimnis. Eine begriffsgeschichtliche Untersuchung zur Entstehung der Öffentlichkeit in der frühen Neuzeit*, Stuttgart 1979

Hoffmann, W., *Mittelhochdeutsche Heldendichtung*, Berlin 1974

Hofmann, D., 'Die Frage des musikalischen Vortrags der altgermanischen Stabreimdichtung in philologischer Sicht', *ZfdA* 92 (1963), 83ff.

Hofmeister, P., 'Bibellesen und Bibelverbot', *ÖAK* 17 (1966), 298ff.

Honemann, V., 'Johannes Rothe in Eisenach. Literarisches Schaffen und Lebenswelt eines Autors um 1400', in: W. Haug and B. Wachinger (ed.), *Autorentypen*, Tübingen 1991, pp. 69ff.

Horacek, B., 'Ichne kan deheinen buochstap', in: FS for D. Kralik, Horn 1954, pp. 129ff.

Huber, C., 'Wort-Ding-Entsprechungen. Zur Sprach- und Stiltheorie Gottfrieds von Straßburg', in: FS for H. Fromm, Tübingen 1979, pp. 268ff.

Gottfried von Straßburg. Tristan und Isolde. Eine Einführung, Munich 1986

Die Aufnahme und Verarbeitung des Alanus ab Insulis in mittelhochdeutschen Dichtungen. Untersuchungen zu Thomasin von Zerklaere, Gottfried von Straßburg, Frauenlob, Heinrich von Neustadt, Heinrich von St. Gallen, Heinrich von Mügeln und Johannes von Tepl, Munich 1988

Hucke, H., 'Toward a new historical view of Gregorian chant', *JAMS* 33 (1980), 437ff.

'Der Übergang von mündlicher zu schriftlicher Musiküberlieferung im Mittelalter', in: *International Musicological Society. Report of the 13th Congress, Berkeley 1977*, Kassel 1981, pp. 180ff.

Hübner, A., *Die deutschen Geißlerlieder. Studien zum geistlichen Volksliede des Mittelalters*, Berlin 1931

Hüpper, D., 'Buoh und scrift. Gattungen und Textsorten in frühmittelalterlichen volkssprachigen Schriftzeugnissen: Zur Ausbildung einer Begrifflichkeit', FMS 20 (1986), 93ff.
Hüpper-Dröge, D., Schild und Speer. Waffen und ihre Bezeichnungen im frühen Mittelalter, Frankfurt 1983
Humphreys, K. W., The book provisions of the medieval friars 1215–1400, Amsterdam 1964
Hunt, T., 'The rhetorical background to the Arthurian prologue. Tradition and the Old French vernacular prologues', FMLS 6 (1970), 1ff.
'Tradition and originality in the prologues of Chrestien de Troyes', FMLS 8 (1972), 320ff.
'The dialectic of "Yvain"', MLR 72 (1977), 285ff.
'Chrestien and the comediae', MSt 40 (1978), 120ff.
'Redating Chrestien de Troyes', BBSIA 30 (1978), 209ff.
'Aristotle, dialectic and courtly literature', Viator 10 (1979), 95ff.
'Chrestien and Macrobius', CetM 33 (1981/82), 211ff.
Hunter, I. M. L., 'Lengthy verbatim recall: the role of text', in: A. W. Ellis (ed.), Progress in the psychology of language, vol. 1, London 1985, pp. 207ff.
Huot, S., From song to book. The poetics of writing in Old French lyric and lyrical narrative poetry, Ithaca 1987
Illmer, D., 'Totum namque in sola experientia usque consistit. Eine Studie zur monastischen Erziehung und Sprache', in: F. Prinz (ed.), Mönchtum und Gesellschaft im Frühmittelalter, Darmstadt 1976, pp. 430ff.
'Neue Einflüsse auf Erziehung, Ausbildung und Wissenschaft', in: A. Wolf, Deutsche Kultur im Hochmittelalter 1150–1250, Essen 1986, pp. 143ff.
Imbach, R., Laien in der Philosophie des Mittelalters. Hinweise und Anregungen zu einem vernachlässigten Thema, Amsterdam 1989
Irsigler, F., 'Epoche – sozialgeschichtlicher Abriß', in: U. Liebertz-Grün (ed.), Aus der Mündlichkeit in die Schriftlichkeit, pp. 12ff.
Jabbour, A., 'Memorial transmission in Old English poetry', ChR 3 (1968), 174ff.
Jacobsen, P. C., 'Die lateinische Literatur der ottonischen und frühsalischen Zeit', in: K. von See (ed.), Europäisches Frühmittelalter, Wiesbaden 1985, pp. 437ff.
Jaeger, C. S., The origins of courtliness. Civilizing trends and the formation of courtly ideals 939–1210, Philadelphia 1985
'Cathedral schools and humanist learning, 950–1150', DVjs 61 (1987), 569ff.
Jammers, E., Ausgewählte Melodien des Minnesangs. Einführung, Erläuterungen und Übertragung, Tübingen 1963
'Zur Frage des Vortrags der altgermanischen Stabreimdichtung', ZfdA 94 (1965), 189ff.
Schrift Ordnung Gestalt. Gesammelte Aufsätze zur älteren Musikgeschichte, Bern 1969
'Das mittelalterliche deutsche Epos und die Musik', in: W. Kleiber (ed.), Otfrid von Weißenburg, Darmstadt 1978, pp. 114ff.
'Der musikalische Vortrag des altdeutschen Epos', in: N. Voorwinden and M. de Haan (ed.), Oral poetry. Das Problem der Mündlichkeit mittelalterlicher epischer Dichtung, Darmstadt 1979, pp. 127ff.
Janota, J., Studien zu Funktion und Typus des deutschen geistlichen Liedes im Mittelalter, Munich 1968
'Das vierzehnte Jahrhundert – ein eigener literarhistorischer Zeitabschnitt?', in: W. Haug, T. R. Jackson, J. Janota (ed.), Zur deutschen Literatur und Sprache des 14. Jahrhunderts, Heidelberg 1983, pp. 9ff.
Jauss, H. R., 'Zur historischen Genese der Scheidung von Fiktion und Realität', in: D. Henrich and W. Iser (ed.), Funktionen des Fiktiven, Munich 1983, pp. 423ff.
Jeauneau, E., 'Jean de Salisbury et la lecture des philosophes', in: M. Wilks (ed.), The world of John of Salisbury, Oxford 1984, pp. 77ff.
Jillings, L., Diu Crone of Heinrich von dem Türlin: the attempted emancipation of secular narrative, Göppingen 1980

Johanek, P., 'Klosterstudien im 12. Jahrhundert', in: J. Fried (ed.), *Schulen im sozialen Wandel des hohen und späten Mittelalters*, Sigmaringen 1986, pp. 35ff.
Review of J. Bumke, *Mäzene*, *GRM* 36 (1986), 209ff.
'König Arthur und die Plantagenets. Über den Zusammenhang von Historiographie und höfischer Epik in mittelalterlicher Propaganda', *FMS* 21 (1987), 346ff.
'Der Schreiber und die Vergangenheit. Zur Entfaltung einer dynastischen Geschichtsschreibung an den Fürstenhöfen des 15. Jahrhunderts', in: H. Keller *et al.* (ed.), *Pragmatische Schriftlichkeit*, pp. 195ff.
Jones, G. F., 'Konnte Oswald von Wolkenstein lesen und schreiben?', in: H.-D. Mück and U. Müller (ed.), *Gesammelte Vorträge der 600-Jahrfeier Oswalds von Wolkenstein*, Göppingen 1978, pp. 39ff.
Kämpfer, W., *Studien zu den gedruckten mittelniederdeutschen Plenarien. Ein Beitrag zur Entstehungsgeschichte spätmittelalterlicher Erbauungsliteratur*, Münster 1954
Kaiser, G., 'Deutsche Heldenepik', in: H. Krauss (ed.), *Europäisches Hochmittelalter*, Wiesbaden 1981, pp. 181ff.
Kantorowicz, E. H., *The king's two bodies. A study in medieval political theology*, Princeton 1957
Karnein, A., *De Amore in volkssprachlicher Literatur. Untersuchungen zur Andreas-Capellanus-Rezeption in Mittelalter und Renaissance*, Heidelberg 1985
'Renaissance und höfische Kultur des 12. Jahrhunderts in Frankreich', in: U. Liebertz-Grün (ed.), *Aus der Mündlichkeit in die Schriftlichkeit*, pp. 104ff.
Kartschoke, D., *Altdeutsche Bibeldichtung*, Stuttgart 1975
Bibeldichtung. Studien zur Geschichte der epischen Bibelparaphrase von Juvencus bis Otfrid von Weißenburg, Munich 1975
'Ulrich von Liechtenstein und die Laienkultur des deutschen Südostens im Übergang zur Schriftlichkeit', in: H. Birkhan (ed.), *Die mittelalterliche Literatur in Kärnten*, Vienna 1981, pp. 103ff.
'Biblia versificata. Bibeldichtung als Übersetzungsliteratur betrachtet', *VB* 2 (1982), 23ff.
Review of M. G. Scholz, *Hören*, *IASL* 8 (1983), 253ff.
Heinrich von Veldeke: Eneasroman, Stuttgart 1986
'Kleinepik', in: U. Liebertz-Grün (ed.), *Aus der Mündlichkeit in die Schriftlichkeit*, pp. 290ff.
'*In die latine bedwungin*. Kommunikationsprobleme im Mittelalter und die Übersetzung der "Chanson de Roland" durch den Pfaffen Konrad', *PBB* 111 (1989), 196ff.
'Der Wilde Mann und die religiösen Bewegungen im 12. Jahrhundert', in: FS for H.-F. Rosenfeld, Göppingen 1989, pp. 69ff.
Geschichte der deutschen Literatur im frühen Mittelalter, Munich 1990
Kasten, I., *Frauendienst bei Trobadors und Minnesängern im 12. Jahrhundert. Zur Entwicklung und Adaption eines literarischen Konzepts*, Heidelberg 1986
Kelber, W., *The oral and the written gospel*, Philadelphia 1983
Kelle, J., *Geschichte der deutschen Literatur. I: Von der ältesten Zeit bis zur Mitte des 11. Jahrhunderts*, Berlin 1892
Keller, H., 'Die Veränderung gesellschaftlichen Handelns und die Verschriftlichung der Administration in den italienischen Stadtkommunen', in: H. Keller *et al.* (ed.), *Pragmatische Schriftlichkeit*, pp. 21ff.
Keller, H., Grubmüller, K., Staubach, N. (ed.), *Pragmatische Schriftlichkeit im Mittelalter. Erscheinungsformen und Entwicklungsstufen*, Munich 1992.
Kelly, S., 'Anglo-Saxon lay society and the written word', in: R. McKitterick (ed.), *Uses*, pp. 36ff.
Kemp, W., *Sermo corporeus. Die Erzählung der mittelalterlichen Glasfenster*, Munich 1987
Kemper, R., 'Das *Ludwigslied* und die liturgischen Rechtstitel des westfränkischen Königtums', in: J. L. Flood and D. N. Yeandle (ed.), '*Mit regulu bithuungan*'. *Neue Arbeiten zur althochdeutschen Poesie und Sprache*, Göppingen 1989, pp. 1ff.

Kendrick, T. D., *Anglo-Saxon art to A.D. 900*, London 1972
Kenney, E. J., and Clausen, W. V. (ed.), *The Cambridge history of classical literature. II 1: The early republic*, Cambridge 1982
Kenyon, F. G., *Books and readers in ancient Greece and Rome*, Oxford 1951
Kieckhefer, R., *Magic in the Middle Ages*, Cambridge 1990
Kienast, R., *Der sogenannte Heinrich von Melk*, Heidelberg 1946
Kiening, C., *Reflexion – Narration. Wege zum 'Willehalm' Wolframs von Eschenbach*, Tübingen 1991
Kirchert, K., 'Grundsätzliches zur Bibelverdeutschung im Mittelalter', *ZfdA* 113 (1984), 61ff.
Kirchhoff, H. G., 'Zur deutschsprachigen Urkunde des 13. Jahrhunderts', *AfD* 3 (1957), 287ff.
Klein, D., 'Zur Praxis des Lateinunterrichts: *Versus memoriales* in lateinisch-deutschen Vokabularien des späten Mittelalters', in: N. Henkel and N. F. Palmer (ed.), *Latein und Volkssprache*, pp. 337ff.
Klein, T., 'Heinrich von Veldeke und die mitteldeutschen Literatursprachen. Untersuchungen zum Veldeke-Problem', in: T. Klein and C. Minis, *Zwei Studien zu Veldeke und zum Straßburger Alexander*, Amsterdam 1985, pp. 1ff.
Kleinschmidt, E., 'Minnesang als höfisches Zeremonialhandeln', *AfK* 58 (1976), 35ff.
Klewitz, H.-W., 'Kanzleischule und Hofkapelle', *DA* 4 (1941), 224ff.
Klingenberg, H., *Runenschrift – Schriftdenken. Runeninschriften*, Heidelberg 1973
'Dichtung', in: *Reallexikon der germanischen Altertumskunde* V 394ff., Berlin 1984
Klopsch, P., 'Latein als Literatursprache', in: E. Wischer (ed.), *Propyläen Geschichte der Literatur. Literatur und Gesellschaft der westlichen Welt. II: Die mittelalterliche Welt, 600–1400*, Berlin 1982, pp. 310ff.
Knab, D., *Das Annolied. Probleme seiner literarischen Einordnung*, Tübingen 1962
Knape, J., *Historie in Mittelalter und früher Neuzeit. Begriffs- und gattungsgeschichtliche Untersuchungen im interdisziplinären Kontext*, Baden-Baden 1984
'Zur Typik historischer Personen-Erinnerungen in der mittelhochdeutschen Weltchronistik des 12. und 13. Jahrhunderts', in: C. Gerhardt, N. F. Palmer, B. Wachinger (ed.), *Geschichtsbewußtsein in der deutschen Literatur des Mittelalters*, Tübingen 1985, pp. 17ff.
Knapp, F. P., 'Literatur und Publikum im österreichischen Hochmittelalter', in: M. Weltin (ed.), *Babenberger Forschungen*, Vienna 1976, pp. 160ff.
'Historische Wahrheit und poetische Lüge. Die Gattungen weltlicher Epik und ihre theoretische Rechtfertigung im Hochmittelalter', *DVjs* 54 (1980), 581ff.
'Heinrich von dem Türlin. Literarische Beziehungen und mögliche Auftraggeber, dichterische Selbsteinschätzung und Zielsetzung', in: P. Krämer and A. Cella (ed.), *Die mittelalterliche Literatur in Kärnten*, Vienna 1981, pp. 145ff.
'*Waltherus de Vogelweide vagus*. Der zwischenständische Sänger und die lateinische Literatur in 'Österreich'', in: H.-D. Mück (ed.), *Walther von der Vogelweide. Beiträge zu Leben und Werk*, Stuttgart 1989, pp. 45ff.
Knoop, U., 'Die Differenz von Dialekt und Schriftlichkeit – ein vorläufiger Überblick', *GL* 3/4 (1976), 22ff.
Knopf, J., *Frühzeit des Bürgers. Erfahrene und verleugnete Realität in den Romanen Wickrams, Grimmelshausens, Schnabels*, Stuttgart 1978
Knox, B. M. W., 'Silent reading in antiquity', *GRBS* 9 (1968), 421ff.
Köhler, E., *Ideal und Wirklichkeit in der höfischen Epik. Studien zur Form der frühen Artus- und Graldichtung*, Tübingen 1956
'Zur Selbstauffassung des höfischen Dichters', in: E Köhler, *Trobadorlyrik und höfischer Roman. Aufsätze zur französischen und provenzalischen Literatur des Mittelalters*, Berlin 1962, pp. 9ff.
Köhn, R., 'Monastisches Bildungsideal und weltgeistliches Wissenschaftsdenken. Zur Vorgeschichte des Mendikantenstreites an der Universität Paris', *MM* 10 (1976), 1ff.

'"Militia curialis". Die Kritik am geistlichen Hofdienst bei Peter von Blois und in der lateinischen Literatur des 9.–12. Jahrhunderts', *MM* 12/1 (1979), 227ff.

'Latein und Volkssprache, Schriftlichkeit und Mündlichkeit in der Korrespondenz des lateinischen Mittelalters', in: J. O. Fichte *et al.* (ed.), *Zusammenhänge, Einflüsse, Wirkungen. Kongreßakten zum 1. Symposium des Mediävistenverbandes in Tübingen, 1984*, Berlin 1986, pp. 340ff.

'Schulbildung und Trivium im lateinischen Hochmittelalter und ihr möglicher praktischer Nutzen', in: J. Fried (ed.), *Schulen und Studium im sozialen Wandel des hohen und späten Mittelalters*, Sigmaringen 1986, pp. 203ff.

Kokott, H., *Literatur und Herrschaftsbewußtsein. Wertstrukturen der vor- und frühhöfischen Literatur. Vorstudien zur Interpretation mittelhochdeutscher Texte*, Frankfurt 1978

Konrad von Würzburg. Ein Autor zwischen Auftrag und Autonomie, Stuttgart 1989

Kolb, H., 'Der *Meier Helmbrecht* zwischen Epos und Drama', *ZfdPh* 81 (1962), 1ff.

Munsalvaesche. Studien zum Kyotproblem, Munich 1963

'Das Melker Marienlied', in: G. Jungbluth (ed.), *Interpretationen mittelhochdeutscher Lyrik*, Bad Homburg v.d.H. 1969

'Mittelalterliche Heldendichtung', in: E. Wischer (ed.), *Propyläen Geschichte der Literatur. Literatur und Gesellschaft der westlichen Welt. II: Die mittelalterliche Welt, 600–1400*, Berlin 1982, pp. 446ff.

'Ein Kreuz mit drei Enden. Zu Wolframs "Willehalm" 406, 1–407, 7', *ZfdA* 116 (1987), 268ff.

Koller, E., 'Zur Volkssprachlichkeit der Straßburger Eide und ihrer Überlieferung', in: R. Bergmann, H. Tiefenbach, L. Voetz (ed.), *Althochdeutsch*, Heidelberg 1987, pp. 828ff.

Kratz, B., 'Ein zweites Akrostichon in der "Crône" Heinrichs von dem Türlin', *ZfdPh* 108 (1989), 402ff.

Kraume, H., *Die Gerson-Übersetzungen Geilers von Kaysersberg. Studien zur deutschsprachigen Gerson-Rezeption*, Munich 1980

Kraus, C. von, 'Wort und Vers in Gottfrieds Tristan', *ZfdA* 51 (1909), 301ff.

Krause, W., *Die Runeninschriften im älteren Futhark*, Göttingen 1966

Kriedte, H., *Deutsche Bibelfragmente in Prosa des XII. Jahrhunderts*, Kattowitz 1930

Kries, F. W. von, *Thomasin von Zerclaere. Der Welsche Gast*, Göppingen 1984, 1985

Kroeschell, K., *Deutsche Rechtsgeschichte I (bis 1250)*, Reinbek 1979

Krohn, R., *Gottfried von Straßburg. Tristan. III: Kommentar, Nachwort und Register*, Stuttgart 1981

Krüger, R., *Studien zur Rezeption des sogenannten Jüngeren Titurel*, Stuttgart 1986

Krüger, S., '"Verhöflichter Krieger" und miles illitteratus', in: J. Fleckenstein (ed.), *Curialitas*, pp. 326ff.

Kruse, N., *Die Kölner volkssprachige Überlieferung des 9. Jahrhunderts*, Bonn 1976

Küsters, U., *Der verschlossene Garten. Volkssprachliche Hohelied-Auslegung und monastische Lebensform im 12. Jahrhundert*, Düsseldorf 1985

Kuhn, Hans, 'Das Zeugnis der Sprache über Alter und Ursprung der Runenschrift', in: FS for G. Neckel, Leipzig 1938, pp. 54ff.

Kuhn, Hugo, *Minnesangs Wende*, Tübingen 1952

Dichtung und Welt im Mittelalter, Stuttgart 1969

'Eine Stiftungsnotiz für ein deutsches Lied', in: H. Kuhn, *Text und Theorie*, Stuttgart 1969, pp. 158ff.

Entwürfe zu einer Literatursystematik des Spätmittelalters, Tübingen 1980

Liebe und Gesellschaft (ed. W. Walliczek), Stuttgart 1980

'Die Voraussetzungen für die Entstehung der Manessischen Handschrift und ihre überlieferungsgeschichtliche Bedeutung', in: H. Kuhn, *Liebe und Gesellschaft*, pp. 86ff.

Kullmann, W., 'Oral poetry theory and neoanalysis in Homeric research', *GRBS* 25 (1984), 307ff.

Laurie, H. C. R., *Two studies in Chrétien de Troyes*, Geneva 1972
Lebsanft, F., 'Hören und Lesen im Mittelalter', *ZfSL* 92 (1982), 52ff.
Leclercq, J., *L'amour des lettres et le désir de Dieu*, Paris 1957
'Comment vivaient les frères convers', in: *I laici nella 'societas christiana' dei secoli XI e XII (Miscellanea del Centro di Studi Medioevali, 5)*, Milan 1968, pp. 152ff.
Monks and love in twelfth-century France. Psycho-historical studies, Oxford 1979
Le Goff, J., *Les intellectuels au moyen âge*, Paris 1957
Time, work, and culture in the Middle Ages, Chicago 1980
Leipold, I., *Die Auftraggeber und Gönner Konrads von Würzburg. Versuch einer Theorie der 'Literatur als soziales Handeln'*, Göppingen 1976
Lengenfelder, H., *Das Liet von Troye Herborts von Fritzlar. Untersuchungen zur epischen Struktur und geschichts-moralischen Perspektive*, Bern 1975
Lenschen, W., *Gliederungsmittel und ihre erzählerischen Funktionen im 'Willehalm von Orlens' des Rudolf von Ems*, Göttingen 1967
Le Roy Ladurie, E., *Montaillou: village occitan de 1294 à 1324*, Paris 1978
Lerner, R. E., 'Literacy and learning', in: R. L. De Molen (ed.), *One thousand years. Western Europe in the Middle Ages*, Boston 1974, pp. 165ff.
Lexer, M., *Mittelhochdeutsches Handwörterbuch*, Leipzig 1872ff.
Leyser, H., *Hermits and the new monasticism. A study of religious communities in Western Europe 1000–1150*, London 1984
Liebertz-Grün, U., *Das andere Mittelalter. Erzählte Geschichte und Geschichtsbewußtsein um 1300. Studien zu Ottokar von Steiermark, Jans Enikel, Seifried Helbling*, Munich 1984
Liebertz-Grün, U. (ed.), *Aus der Mündlichkeit in die Schriftlichkeit: höfische und andere Literatur. 750–1320*, Reinbek 1988
Linke, H., *Epische Strukturen in der Dichtung Hartmanns von Aue. Untersuchungen zur Formkritik, Werkstruktur und Vortragsgliederung*, Munich 1968
Review of R. Steinbach, *Oster- und Passionsspiele*, *AfdA* 83 (1972), 199ff.
Review of R. Bergmann, *Entstehung und Geschichte*, *AfdA* 85 (1974), 19ff.
'Versuch über deutsche Handschriften mittelalterlicher Spiele', in: V. Honemann and N. F. Palmer (ed.), *Deutsche Handschriften 1100–1400*, Tübingen 1988, pp. 527ff.
Lipphardt, W., 'Die Anfänge des deutschen Kirchenliedes in althochdeutscher Zeit', *MuA* 12 (1959/60), 73ff.
'Epische Liedweisen des Mittelalters in schriftlicher Überlieferung', in: E. Kühebacher (ed.), *Deutsche Heldenepik in Tirol. König Laurin und Dietrich von Bern in der Dichtung des Mittelalters*, Bozen 1979, pp. 275ff.
Lönnroth, L., 'Hjálmar's Death-song and the delivery of Eddic poetry', *Speculum* 46 (1971), 1ff.
Lofmark, C., 'Wolfram's source references in *Parzival*', *MLR* 67 (1972), 820ff.
The authority of the source in Middle High German narrative poetry, London 1981
Lomnitzer, H., 'Zur wechselseitigen Erhellung von Text- und Melodiekritik mittelalterlicher deutscher Lyrik', in: P. F. Ganz and W. Schröder (ed.), *Probleme mittelalterlicher Überlieferung und Textkritik*, Berlin 1968, pp. 118ff.
Lord, A. B., *The singer of tales*, New York 1965
'Oral poetry', in: A. Preminger (ed.), *Encyclopedia of poetry and poetics*, Princeton 1965
'Memory, fixity, and genre in oral traditional poetries', in: FS for A. B. Lord, Columbus, Ohio, 1980, pp. 451ff.
'Characteristics of orality', *OT* 2 (1987), 54ff.
Epic singers and oral tradition, Ithaca 1991
Lüdtke, H., 'Die Entstehung romanischer Schriftsprachen', *VR* 23 (1964), 3ff.
Luttrell, C., *The creation of the first Arthurian romance. A quest*, London 1974
Lutz, E. C., *Rhetorica divina. Mittelhochdeutsche Prologgebete und die rhetorische Kultur des Mittelalters*, Berlin 1984

Maas, U., 'Lesen – Schreiben – Schrift. Die Demotisierung eines professionellen Arkanums im Spätmittelalter und in der frühen Neuzeit', *LiLi* 59 (1985), 55ff.
Magoun, F. P., 'Oral-formulaic character of Anglo-Saxon narrative poetry', *Speculum* 28 (1953), 446ff.
'Bede's story of Caedman: the case history of an Anglo-Saxon oral singer', *Speculum* 30 (1955), 49ff.
Marichal, R., 'Naissance du roman', in: M. de Gandillac and E. Jeauneau (ed.), *Entretiens sur la renaissance du 12e siècle*, Paris 1968, pp. 449ff.
Marold, E., 'Wandel und Konstanz in der Darstellung der Figur des Dietrich von Bern', in: H. Beck (ed.), *Heldensage und Heldendichtung im Germanischen*, Berlin 1988, pp. 149ff.
Martin, H.-J., 'Pour une histoire de la lecture', *RFHL* 46 (1977), 583ff.
Martin, H.-J., and Vezin, J. (ed.), *Mise en page et mise en texte du livre manuscrit*, Paris 1990
Masser, A., *Bibel- und Legendenepik des deutschen Mittelalters*, Berlin 1976
'Wege der Darbietung und der zeitgenössischen Rezeption höfischer Literatur', in: E. Kühebacher (ed.), *Deutsche Heldenepik in Tirol. König Laurin und Dietrich von Bern in der Dichtung des Mittelalters*, Bozen 1979, pp. 382ff.
'Das Evangelium Nicodemi und das mittelalterliche Spiel', *ZfdPh* 107 (1988), 48ff.
'Aufgabe und Leistung der frühen volkssprachigen Literatur', in: A. Masser and A. Wolf (ed.), *Geistesleben um den Bodensee im frühen Mittelalter*, Freiburg 1989, pp. 87ff.
'Zu den sogenannten "Mädchenliedern" Walthers von der Vogelweide', *WW* 39 (1989), 3ff.
Matzel, K., *Untersuchungen zur Verfasserschaft, Sprache und Herkunft der althochdeutschen Übersetzungen der Isidor-Sippe*, Bonn 1970
'Das Problem der "karlingischen Hofsprache"', in: FS for H. de Boor, Munich 1971, pp. 15ff.
Mauritz, H.-D., *Der Ritter im magischen Reich. Märchenelemente im französischen Abenteuerroman des 12. und 13. Jahrhunderts*, Bern 1974
McKenzie, D. A., *Otfrid von Weissenburg: narrator or commentator? A comparative study*, Stanford 1946
McKitterick, R., *The Frankish church and the Carolingian reforms, 789–895*, London 1977
The Carolingians and the written word, Cambridge 1989
'Text and image in the Carolingian world', in: R. McKitterick (ed.), *Uses*, pp. 296ff.
'Frauen und Schriftlichkeit im Frühmittelalter', in: H.-W. Goetz (ed.), *Weibliche Lebensgestaltung im frühen Mittelalter*, Cologne 1991, pp. 65ff.
McKitterick, R. (ed.), *The uses of literacy in early mediaeval Europe*, Cambridge 1990
McMahon, J. V., *The music of early Minnesang*, Columbia, S.C., 1990
Mehler, U., *Dicere und cantare. Zur musikalischen Terminologie und Aufführungspraxis des mittelalterlichen geistlichen Dramas in Deutschland*, Regensburg 1981
Meier, C., and Ruberg, U. (ed.), *Text und Bild. Aspekte des Zusammenwirkens zweier Künste in Mittelalter und früher Neuzeit*, Wiesbaden 1980
Meisenburg, T., 'Die großen Buchstaben und was sie bewirken können: Zur Geschichte der Majuskel im Französischen und im Deutschen', in: W. Raible (ed.), *Erscheinungsformen kultureller Prozesse*, Tübingen 1990, pp. 281ff.
Meissburger, G., *Grundlagen zum Verständnis der deutschen Mönchsdichtung im 11. und im 12. Jahrhundert*, Munich 1970
Menéndez Pidal, R., *La Chanson de Roland et la tradition épique des Francs*, Paris 1960
Mertens, D., 'Früher Buchdruck und Historiographie. Zur Rezeption historiographischer Literatur im Bürgertum des deutschen Spätmittelalters beim Übergang vom Schreiben zum Drucken', in: B. Moeller, H. Patze, K. Stackmann (ed.), *Studien zum städtischen Bildungswesen des späten Mittelalters und der frühen Neuzeit*, Göttingen 1983, pp. 83ff.
Mertens, V., 'Zu Text und Melodie der Titurelstrophe: *Iamer ist mir entsprungen*', *Wolfram-Studien* 1 (1970), 219ff.
Review of J. Janota, *Studien*, *AfdA* 84 (1973), 212ff.

'Der Ruf – eine Gattung des deutschen geistlichen Liedes im Mittelalter?', ZfdA 104 (1975), 68ff.

Gregorius Eremita. Eine Lebensform des Adels bei Hartmann von Aue in ihrer Problematik und ihrer Wandlung in der Rezeption, Zürich 1978

Laudine. Soziale Problematik im 'Iwein' Hartmanns von Aue, Berlin 1978

Review of N. H. Ott and W. Walliczek, 'Bildprogramm', PBB 105 (1983), 434ff.

'Artus', in: V. Mertens and U. Müller (ed.), Epische Stoffe des Mittelalters, Stuttgart 1984, pp. 290ff.

'Kaiser und Spielmann. Vortragsrollen in der höfischen Lyrik', in: G. Kaiser and J.-D. Müller (ed.), Höfische Literatur, Hofgesellschaft, höfische Lebensformen um 1200, Düsseldorf 1986, pp. 455ff.

'Das literarische Mäzenatentum der Zähringer', in: K. Schmid (ed.), Die Zähringer. Eine Tradition und ihre Erforschung, Sigmaringen 1986, pp. 117ff.

'Eilhart, der Herzog und der Truchseß. Der "Tristrant" am Welfenhof', in: D. Buschinger (ed.), Tristan et Iseut, mythe européen et mondial, Göppingen 1987, pp. 262ff.

'"Factus est per clericum miles cythereus". Überlegungen zu Entstehungs- und Wirkungsbedingungen von Hartmanns Klage-Büchlein', in: T. McFarland and S. Ranawake (ed.), Hartmann von Aue. Changing perspectives, Göppingen 1988, pp. 1ff.

'Rezeption der französischen Adelsliteratur', in: U. Liebertz-Grün (ed.), Aus der Mündlichkeit in die Schriftlichkeit, pp. 135ff.

Metzner, E. E., 'Die deutschsprachige chronikalische Geschichtsdichtung im Rahmen der europäischen Entwicklung', in: W. Erzgräber (ed.), Europäisches Spätmittelalter, Wiesbaden 1978, pp. 623ff.

Meves, U., Studien zu 'König Rother', 'Herzog Ernst' und 'Grauer Rock' ('Orendel'), Frankfurt 1976

'Bischof Wolfger von Passau, sîn schrîber, meister Kuonrât und die Nibelungenüberlieferung', in: Hohenemser Studien zum Nibelungenlied, Dornbirn 1981, pp. 246ff.

Miethke, J., Die mittelalterlichen Universitäten und das gesprochene Wort, Munich 1990

Mirbt, C., Die Publizistik im Zeitalter Gregors VII., Leipzig 1894

Mölk, U., Französische Literarästhetik des 12. und 13. Jahrhunderts, Prologe – Exkurse – Epiloge, Tübingen 1969

Mönckeberg, A., Die Stellung der Spielleute im Mittelalter. I: Spielleute und Kirche im Mittelalter, Berlin 1910

Mohr, W., 'Parzival und die Ritter. Von einfacher Form zum Ritterepos', Fabula 1 (1958), 201ff.

'Minnesang als Gesellschaftskunst', in: H. Fromm (ed.), Der deutsche Minnesang. Aufsätze zu seiner Erforschung, Darmstadt 1961, pp. 197ff.

'Mittelalterliche Feste und ihre Dichtung', in: FS for K. Ziegler, Tübingen 1969, pp. 37ff.

'Tristan und Isolde', GRM 55 (1976), 54ff.

Wolfram von Eschenbach. Aufsätze, Göppingen 1979

Mohr, W., and Haug, W., Zweimal 'Muspilli', Tübingen 1977

Momigliano, A., 'The historians of the classical world and their audiences', AS 47 (1978), 193ff.

Moos, P. von, 'Poeta und historicus im Mittelalter. Zum Mimesis-Problem am Beispiel einiger Urteile über Lucan', PBB 98 (1976), 93ff.

Morris, R. L., 'Northwest-Germanic rūn- "Rune". A case of homonymy with Gothic rūna "mystery"', PBB 107 (1985), 344ff.

Moser, H., '"Lied" und "Spruch" in der hochmittelalterlichen deutschen Dichtung', in: H. Moser (ed.), Mittelhochdeutsche Spruchdichtung, Darmstadt 1972, pp. 180ff.

Much, R., Die Germania des Tacitus, Heidelberg 1937

Müller, G., 'Von der Buchstabenmagie zur Namenmagie in den Brakteateninschriften', FMS 22 (1988), 111ff.

Müller-Blattau, W., 'Versuche zur musikalischen Gestaltung des mittelalterlichen Liedes', *ZfdPh* 90 (1971), *Sonderheft: Neue Arbeiten zum mittelalterlichen Lied*, pp. 153ff.
Münz, W., 'Zu den Passauer Strophen und der Verfasserfrage des Nibelungenliedes', *Euphorion* 65 (1971), 345ff.
Mullett, M., 'Writing in early mediaeval Byzantium', in: R. McKitterick (ed.), *Uses*, pp. 156ff.
Mundschau, H., *Sprecher als Träger der 'tradition vivante' in der Gattung 'Märe'*, Göppingen 1972
Murdoch, B., 'Peri Hieres Nousou: approaches to Old High German medical charms', in: J. L. Flood and D. N. Yeandle (ed.), *'Mit regulu bithuungan'. Neue Arbeiten zur althochdeutschen Poesie und Sprache*, Göppingen 1989, pp. 142ff.
Näf, A., *Die Wortstellung in Notkers Consolatio*, Berlin 1979
Nagel, B., 'Widersprüche im Nibelungenlied', in: H. Rupp (ed.), *Nibelungenlied und Kudrun*, Darmstadt 1976, pp. 367ff.
Naumann, B., *Dichter und Publikum in deutscher und lateinischer Bibelepik des frühen 12. Jahrhunderts. Untersuchungen zu frühmittelhochdeutschen und mittellateinischen Dichtungen über die kleineren Bücher des Alten Testaments*, Nürnberg 1968
Naumann, H., *Frühgermanisches Dichterbuch*, Berlin 1931
Nellmann, E., *Wolframs Erzähltechnik. Untersuchungen zur Funktion des Erzählers*, Wiesbaden 1973
    Review of M. Ott-Meimberg, *Kreuzzugsepos*, *PBB* 106 (1984), 297ff.
Nelson, J. L., 'Literacy in Carolingian government', in: R. McKitterick (ed.), *Uses*, pp. 258ff.
Nelson, W., 'From "Listen, lordings" to "Dear reader"', *UTQ* 46 (1976/7), 110ff.
Neumann, B., *Geistliches Schauspiel im Zeugnis der Zeit. Zur Aufführung mittelalterlicher religiöser Dramen im deutschen Sprachgebiet*, Munich 1987
Neumann, F., 'Meister Albrechts und Jörg Wickrams Ovid auf Deutsch', *PBB* 76 (1954), 321ff.
    'Wolfram von Eschenbach auf dem Wildenberg', *ZfdA* 100 (1971), 94ff.
Neumann, H., 'Beiträge zur Textgeschichte des "Fließenden Lichts der Gottheit" und zur Lebensgeschichte Mechthilds von Magdeburg', in: K. Ruh (ed.), *Altdeutsche und altniederländische Mystik*, Darmstadt 1964, pp. 175ff.
Neumüllers-Klauser, R., 'Frühe deutschsprachige Inschriften', in: N. Henkel and N.F. Palmer (ed.), *Latein und Volkssprache*, Tübingen 1992, pp. 178ff.
Neuschäfer, D., *Das Anegenge. Textkritische Studien, diplomatischer Abdruck, kritische Ausgabe, Anmerkungen zum Text*, Munich 1966
Neuser, P.-E., 'Das karolingische "Hildebrandslied". Kodikologische und rezeptionsgeschichtliche Aspekte des 2° Ms. theol. 54 aus Fulda', in: FS for J. Rathofer, Cologne 1990, pp. 1ff.
Nielsen, K. M., 'Runen und Magie. Ein forschungsgeschichtlicher Überblick', *FMS* 19 (1985), 75ff.
Niessen, M., *Märchenmotive und ihre Funktion für den Aufbau des höfischen Romans, dargestellt am 'Iwein' Hartmanns von Aue*, diss. Münster 1973
Noble, T. F. X., 'Literacy and the papal government in late antiquity and the early middle ages', in: R, McKitterick (ed.), *Uses*, pp. 82ff.
Nolting-Hauff, I., 'Märchen und Märchenroman. Die Beziehung zwischen einfacher Form und narrativer Großform in der Literatur', *Poetica* 6 (1974), 129ff.
Nykrog, P., *Les fabliaux. Nouvelle édition*, Geneva 1973
Objartel, G., *Der Meißner der Jenaer Liederhandschrift. Untersuchungen, Ausgabe, Kommentar*, Berlin 1977
Ochsenbein, P., 'Latein und Deutsch im Alltag oberrheinischer Dominikanerinnenklöster des Spätmittelalters', in: N. Henkel and N. F. Palmer (ed.), *Latein und Volkssprache*, pp. 42ff.
Odenstedt, B., 'The inscription on the Meldorf fibula', *ZfdA* 112 (1983), 153ff.
Oexle, O. G., 'Deutungsschemata der sozialen Wirklichkeit im frühen und hohen Mittelalter. Ein Beitrag zur Geschichte des Wissens', in: F. Graus (ed.), *Mentalitäten im Mittelalter. Methodische und inhaltliche Probleme*, Sigmaringen 1987, pp. 65ff.

Ohly, F., *Hohelied-Studien. Grundzüge einer Geschichte der Hoheliedauslegung des Abendlandes bis um 1200*, Wiesbaden 1958
'Wolframs Gebet an den Heiligen Geist im Eingang des "Willehalm"', in: H. Rupp (ed.), *Wolfram von Eschenbach*, Darmstadt 1966, pp. 455ff.
'Zum Dichtungsschluß Tu autem, domine, miserere nobis', *DVjs* 47 (1973), 26ff.
O'Keeffe, K. O'B., *Visible song. Traditional literacy in Old English verse*, Cambridge 1990
Okken, L., *Kommentar zum Tristan-Roman Gottfrieds von Straßburg*, Amsterdam 1984, 1985, 1988
Ollier, M.-L., 'The author in the text: the prologues of Chrétien de Troyes', *YFS* 51 (1974), 26ff.
Ong, W. J., *Orality and literacy. The technologizing of the word*, London 1982
'Orality, literacy, and medieval textualization', *NLH* 16 (1984/5), 1ff.
'Writing is a technology that restructures thought', in: G. Baumann (ed.), *Word*, pp. 23ff.
Opland, J., *Anglo-Saxon oral poetry. A study of the traditions*, New Haven 1980
'From horseback to monastic cell: the impact on English literature of the introduction of writing', in: J. D. Niles (ed.), *Old English literature in context*, Cambridge 1980, pp. 30ff.
Orth, E., 'Ritter und Burg', in: J. Fleckenstein (ed.), *Das ritterliche Turnier im Mittelalter. Beiträge zu einer vergleichenden Formen- und Verhaltensgeschichte des Rittertums*, Göttingen 1985, pp. 19ff.
'Formen und Funktionen der höfischen Rittererhebung', in: J. Fleckenstein (ed.), *Curialitas*, pp. 128ff.
Ortmann, C., 'Eckharts Lehre für die Ungelehrten. Zum Verhältnis von Deutsch und Latein in der deutschen Predigt', in: *FS for H. Fromm*, Tübingen 1979, pp. 342ff.
Ortmann, C., and Ragotzky, H., 'Minnesang als "Vollzugskunst". Zur spezifischen Struktur literarischen Zeremonialhandelns im Kontext höfischer Repräsentation', in: H. Ragotzky and H. Wenzel (ed.), *Höfische Repräsentation. Das Zeremoniell und die Zeichen*, Tübingen 1990, pp. 227ff.
Osterwalder, P., *Das althochdeutsche Galluslied Ratperts und seine lateinischen Übersetzungen durch Ekkehart IV. Einordnung und kritische Edition*, Berlin 1982
Ott, N. H., 'Chronistik, Geschichtsepik, historische Dichtung', in: V. Mertens and U. Müller (ed.), *Epische Stoffe des Mittelalters*, Stuttgart 1984, pp. 182ff.
'Kompilation und Zitat in Weltchronik und Kathedralikonographie. Zum Wahrheitsanspruch (pseudo-)historischer Gattungen', in: C. Gerhardt, N. F. Palmer, B. Wachinger (ed.), *Geschichtsbewußtsein in der deutschen Literatur des Mittelalters*, Tübingen 1985, pp. 119ff.
Ott, N. H., and Walliczek, W., 'Bildprogramm und Textstruktur. Anmerkungen zu den "Iwein"-Zyklen auf Hoheneck und in Schmalkalden', in: C. Cormeau (ed.), *Deutsche Literatur im Mittelalter. Kontakte und Perspektiven. Hugo Kuhn zum Gedenken*, Stuttgart 1979, pp. 473ff.
Ott-Meimberg, M., 'Karl, Roland, Guillaume', in: V. Mertens and U. Müller (ed.), *Epische Stoffe des Mittelalters*, Stuttgart 1984, pp. 81ff.
Page, C., 'The Boethian metrum "Bella bis quinis": a new song from Saxon Canterbury', in: M. Gibson (ed.), *Boethius. His life, thought and influence*, Oxford 1981, pp. 306ff.
Palmer, N. F., 'Zur Vortragsweise der Wien-Münchener Evangelienübersetzung', *ZfdA* 114 (1985), 95ff.
'Kapitel und Buch. Zu den Gliederungsprinzipien mittelalterlicher Bücher', *FMS* 23 (1989), 43ff.
'Von der Paläographie zur Literaturwissenschaft', *PBB* 113 (1991), 212ff.
Papp, E., *Die altdeutsche Exodus*, Munich 1968
Parkes, M. B., 'The literacy of the laity', in: D. Daiches and A. Thorlby (ed.), *The medieval world*, London 1973, pp. 555ff.

'The influence of the concepts of *ordinatio* and *compilatio* on the development of the book', in: FS for R. W. Hunt, Oxford 1976, pp. 115ff.
Pause and effect. An introduction to the history of punctuation in the West, Aldershot 1992
Parry, A. (ed.), *The making of Homeric verse. The collected papers of Milman Parry*, Oxford 1971
Parry, J. J., and Caldwell, R. A., 'Geoffrey of Monmouth', in: R. S. Loomis (ed.), *Arthurian literature in the Middle Ages. A collaborative history*, Oxford 1959, pp. 72ff.
Parry, M., and Lord, A. B., *Serbocroatian heroic songs*, vol. 1, Cambridge, Mass., 1954
Patzlaff, R., *Otfrid von Weißenburg und die mittelalterliche versus-Tradition. Untersuchungen zur formgeschichtlichen Stellung der Otfridstrophe*, Tübingen 1975
Pérennec, R., *Recherches sur le roman Arthurien en vers en Allemagne aux XIIe et XIIIe siècles*, Göppingen 1984
Perlbach, M., *Die Statuten des Deutschen Ordens*, Halle 1890
Peters, U., *Frauendienst. Untersuchungen zu Ulrich von Lichtenstein und zum Wirklichkeitsgehalt der Minnedichtung*, Göppingen 1971
Fürstenhof und höfische Dichtung. Der Hof Hermanns von Thüringen als literarisches Zentrum, Konstanz 1981
Literatur in der Stadt. Studien zu den sozialen Voraussetzungen und kulturellen Organisationsformen städtischer Literatur im 13. und 14. Jahrhundert, Tübingen 1983
Religiöse Erfahrung als literarisches Faktum. Zur Vorgeschichte und Genese frauenmystischer Texte des 13. und 14. Jahrhunderts, Tübingen 1988
'Hofkleriker – Stadtschreiber – Mystikerin. Zum literarhistorischen Status dreier Autorentypen', in: W. Haug and B. Wachinger (ed.), *Autorentypen*, Tübingen 1991, pp. 69ff.
Petzsch, C., 'Die Rubriken der Kolmarer Liederhandschrift', ZfdPh 93 (1974), 88ff.
'Otfrids "cantus lectionis"', in: W. Kleiber (ed.), *Otfrid von Weißenburg*, Darmstadt 1978, pp. 219ff.
Pickerodt-Uthleb, E., *Die Jenaer Liederhandschrift. Metrische und musikalische Untersuchungen*, Göppingen 1975
Pinder, W., *Die Kunst der deutschen Kaiserzeit bis zum Ende der staufischen Klassik*, Frankfurt 1952
Pinner, H. L., *The world of books in classical antiquity*, Leiden 1958
Ploss, E., 'Bamberg und die deutsche Literatur des 11. und 12. Jahrhunderts', JbfrL 19 (1959), 275ff.
Pörksen, U., *Der Erzähler im mittelhochdeutschen Epos. Formen seines Hervortretens bei Lamprecht, Konrad, Hartmann, in Wolframs Willehalm und in den 'Spielmannsepen'*, Berlin 1971
Pollard, G., 'The *pecia* system in the medieval universities', in: FS for N. R. Ker, London 1978, pp. 145ff.
Potts, L. J., *Aristotle on the art of fiction*, Cambridge 1968
Prinz, F., *Klerus und Krieg im früheren Mittelalter. Untersuchungen zur Rolle der Kirche beim Aufbau der Königsherrschaft*, Stuttgart 1971
Grundlagen und Anfänge. Deutschland bis 1056, Munich 1985
Rädle, F., 'Hrotsvit von Gandersheim', in: U. Liebertz-Grün (ed.), *Aus der Mündlichkeit in die Schriftlichkeit*, pp. 84ff.
Ragotzky, H., *Studien zur Wolfram-Rezeption. Die Entstehung und Verwandlung der Wolfram-Rolle in der deutschen Literatur des 13. Jahrhunderts*, Stuttgart 1971
Raible, W., 'Vom Text und seinen vielen Vätern oder: Hermeneutik als Korrelat der Schriftliteratur', in: A. and J. Assmann (ed.), *Schrift*, pp. 20ff.
'Zur Entwicklung von Alphabetschrift-Systemen. Is fecit cui prodest', Sitzungsberichte der Heidelberger Akademie der Wissenschaften, Philosophisch-historische Klasse, Jahrgang 1991, Bericht 1, Heidelberg 1991, pp. 5ff.

Ranawake, S., Review of O. Sayce, *Lyric*, *PBB* 107 (1985), 135ff.
Ranke, F., *Tristan und Isold*, Munich 1925
Ranke, F. (ed.), *Das Osterspiel von Muri*, Aarau 1944
Rankin, S., 'From memory to record: musical notations in manuscripts from Exeter', *ASE* 13 (1984), 97ff.
Rawson, E., *Intellectual life in the late Roman republic*, London 1985
Reichl, K., 'Formulaic diction in Old English epic poetry', in: J. B. Hainsworth (ed.), *Traditions of heroic and epic poetry* II 42ff., London 1989
Reisel, J., *Zeitgeschichtliche und theologisch-scholastische Aspekte im 'Daniel von dem blühenden Tal' des Stricker*, Göppingen 1986
Renk, H.-E., *Der Manessekreis, seine Dichter und die Manessische Handschrift*, Stuttgart 1974
Renoir, A., *A key to old poems. The oral-formulaic approach to the interpretation of West-Germanic verse*, University Park 1988
Rexroth, K. H., 'Volkssprache und werdendes Volksbewußtsein im ostfränkischen Reich', in: H. Beumann and W. Schröder (ed.), *Aspekte der Nationenbildung im Mittelalter*, Sigmaringen 1978, pp. 275ff.
Reynolds, L. D., and Wilson, N. G., *Scribes and scholars: a guide to the transmission of Greek and Latin literature*, Oxford 1974
Riché, P., *Education and culture in the barbarian West from the sixth through the eighth century*, Columbia, S.C., 1976
Les écoles et l'enseignement dans l'occident chrétien de la fin du Ve siècle au milieu du XIe siècle, Paris 1979
Richert, H.-G., *Wege und Formen der Passionalüberlieferung*, Tübingen 1978
Richter, D., *Die deutsche Überlieferung der Predigten Bertholds von Regensburg. Untersuchungen zur geistlichen Literatur des Spätmittelalters*, Munich 1969
Richter, M., 'Kommunikationsprobleme im lateinischen Mittelalter', *HZ* 222 (1976), 43ff.
'Die Sprachpolitik Karls des Großen', *Sprachwissenschaft* 7 (1982), 412ff.
Riley, E. C., *Cervantes's theory of the novel*, Oxford 1962
Rocher, D., *Thomasin von Zerklaere: Der wälsche Gast, 1215–16*, Lille 1977
Röcke, W., 'Höfische und unhöfische Minne- und Abenteuerromane', in: V. Mertens and U. Müller (ed.), *Epische Stoffe des Mittelalters*, Stuttgart 1984, pp. 395ff.
Roeder, A., *Die Gebärde im Drama des Mittelalters. Osterfeiern – Osterspiele*, Munich 1974
Rörig, F., 'Mittelalter und Schriftlichkeit', *WaG* 13 (1953), 29ff.
Rösener, W., 'Die höfische Frau im Mittelalter', in: J. Fleckenstein (ed.), *Curialitas*, pp. 171ff.
Rösler, W., 'Die Entdeckung der Fiktionalität in der Antike', *Poetica* 12 (1980), 283ff.
'Schriftkultur und Fiktionalität. Zum Funktionswandel der griechischen Literatur von Homer bis Aristoteles', in: A. and J. Assmann (ed.), *Schrift*, pp. 109ff.
Rössing-Hager, M., 'Wie stark findet der nicht-lesekundige Rezipient Berücksichtigung in den Flugschriften?', in: H.-J. Köhler (ed.), *Flugschriften als Massenmedium der Reformationszeit*, Tübingen 1981, pp. 77ff.
Roloff, V., 'Intertextualität und Problematik des Autors (am Beispiel des *Tristan* von Béroul)', in: F. Wolfzettel (ed.), *Artusroman und Intertextualität*, Giessen 1990, pp. 107ff.
Rosenfeld, H., 'Buch, Schrift und lateinische Sprachkenntnis bei den Germanen vor der christlichen Mission', *RhM* 95 (1952), 193ff.
Ross, D. J. A., 'Old French', in: A. T. Hatto (ed.), *Traditions of heroic and epic poetry* I 79ff., London 1980
Rouse, M. A. and R. H., 'La naissance des Index', in: H.-J. Martin, R. Chartier, J.-P. Vivet (ed.), *Histoire de l'édition française. I: Le livre conquérant du moyen âge*, Paris 1982, pp. 77ff.
Rousset, P., *Histoire d'une idéologie: la croisade*, Lausanne 1983
Ruh, K., *Höfische Epik des deutschen Mittelalters*, Berlin 1967 and 1980
'Der Gralsheld in der 'Queste del Saint Graal'', *Wolfram-Studien* 1 (1970), 240ff.

'Epische Literatur des deutschen Spätmittelalters', in: W. Erzgräber (ed.), *Europäisches Spätmittelalter*, Wiesbaden 1978, pp. 117ff.
'Deutsche Predigtbücher des Mittelalters', *VB* 3 (1981), 11ff.
Kleine Schriften II, Berlin 1984
Meister Eckhart. Theologe, Prediger, Mystiker, Munich 1985
Rupp, H., *Deutsche religiöse Dichtungen des 11. und 12. Jahrhunderts. Untersuchungen und Interpretationen*, Freiburg 1958
'Über das Verhältnis von deutscher und lateinischer Dichtung im 9. bis 12. Jahrhundert', *GRM* 8 (1958), 19ff.
'Die Literatur der Karolingerzeit', in: B. Boesch (ed.), *Deutsche Literaturgeschichte in Grundzügen. Die Epochen deutscher Dichtung*, Berlin 1961, pp. 9ff.
Rychner, J., *Contributions à l'étude des fabliaux I*, Geneva 1960
Saenger, P., 'Manières de lire médiévales', in: H.-J. Martin, R. Chartier, J.-P. Vivet (ed.), *Histoire de l'édition française I: Le livre conquérant du moyen âge*, Paris 1982, pp. 131ff.
'Silent reading: its impact on late medieval script and society', *Viator* 13 (1982), 367ff.
'Books of hours and the reading habits of the later Middle Ages', in: R. Chartier (ed.), *The culture of print. Power and the uses of print in early modern Europe*, Cambridge 1989, pp. 141ff.
'La naissance de la coupure et de la séparation des mots', in: H.-J. Martin and J. Vezin (ed.), *Mise*, pp. 447ff.
'Coupure et séparation des mots sur le continent au moyen âge', in: H.-J. Martin and J. Vezin (ed.), *Mise*, pp. 451ff.
'The separation of words and the physiology of reading', in: D. R. Olson and N. Torrance (ed.), *Literacy and orality*, Cambridge 1991, pp. 198ff.
Salmen, W., *Der fahrende Musiker im europäischen Mittelalter*, Kassel 1960
Der Spielmann im Mittelalter, Innsbruck 1983
Review of A. Schreier-Hornung, *Spielleute*, *ZfdPh* 102 (1983), 455f.
Salowsky, H., 'Ein Hinweis auf das Lanzelet-Epos Ulrichs von Zatzikhoven in der Manessischen Liederhandschrift', *HJbb* 19 (1975), 40ff.
Sanders, W., *Heinric van Veldeken. Porträt eines maasländischen Dichters des 12. Jahrhunderts*, Bonn 1976
Sawicki, S., *Gottfried von Straßburg und die Poetik des Mittelalters*, Berlin 1932
Saxer, V., *Le culte de Marie Madeleine en occident*, Paris 1959
Sayce, O., *The medieval German lyric 1150–1300. The development of its themes and forms in their European context*, Oxford 1982
Plurilingualism in the Carmina Burana. A study of the linguistic and literary influences on the codex, Göppingen 1992
Schäfer-Maulbetsch, R. B., *Studien zur Entwicklung des mittelhochdeutschen Epos. Die Kampfschilderung in 'Kaiserchronik', 'Rolandslied', 'Alexanderlied', 'Eneide', 'Liet von Troye' und 'Willehalm'*, Göppingen 1972
Schaller, D., 'Vortrags- und Zirkulardichtung am Hof Karls des Großen', *MlJb* 6 (1970), 14ff.
'Ist der "Waltharius" frühkarolingisch?', *MlJb* 18 (1983), 63ff.
Schirmer, K.-H., *Stil- und Motivuntersuchungen zur mittelhochdeutschen Versnovelle*, Tübingen 1969
Schirmer, W. F., *Die frühen Darstellungen des Arthurstoffes*, Cologne 1958
Schirmer, W. F., and Broich, U., *Studien zum literarischen Patronat im England des 12. Jahrhunderts*, Cologne 1962
Schirok, B., *Parzivalrezeption im Mittelalter*, Darmstadt 1982
'Zu den Akrosticha in Gottfrieds "Tristan". Versuch einer kritischen und weiterführenden Bestandsaufnahme', *ZfdA* 113 (1984), 188ff.
Schlieben-Lange, B., 'Schriftlichkeit und Mündlichkeit in der französischen Revolution', in: A. and J. Assmann (ed.), *Schrift*, pp. 194ff.

Traditionen des Sprechens. Elemente einer pragmatischen Sprachgeschichtsschreibung, Stuttgart 1983
Schlosser, H. D., 'Historischer Text und Kommunikation. Das Beispiel Minnesang', *LiLi* 3 (1973), H. 11, pp. 81ff.
Schmid, K., 'Welfisches Selbstverständnis', in: FS for G. Tellenbach, Freiburg 1968, pp. 389ff.
Schmid-Calabert, C., *Der Ortnit AW als Brautwerbungsdichtung. Ein Beitrag zum Verständnis mittelhochdeutscher Schemaliteratur*, Bern 1985
Schmidt, W., 'Vom Lesen und Schreiben im späten Mittelalter', *PBB* 95 (1973), 309ff.
Books – their evolution and development (Season's greetings to our authors and friends 1988/89, de Gruyter, Berlin)
Schmidt-Wiegand, R., 'Gebärden', in: A. Erler and E. Kaufmann (ed.), *Handwörterbuch zur deutschen Rechtsgeschichte* 1 1411ff., Berlin 1971
'Eid und Gelöbnis, Formel und Formular im mittelalterlichen Recht', in: P. Classen (ed.), *Recht und Schrift im Mittelalter*, Sigmaringen 1977, pp. 55ff.
'Stammesrecht und Volkssprache in karolingischer Zeit', in: H. Beumann and W. Schröder (ed.), *Aspekte der Nationenbildung im Mittelalter*, Sigmaringen 1978, pp. 171ff.
'Die volkssprachlichen Wörter der Leges barbarorum', *FMS* 13 (1979), 56ff.
'Gebärdensprache im mittelalterlichen Recht', *FMS* 16 (1982), 363ff.
'Die Bilderhandschriften des Sachsenspiegels als Zeugen pragmatischer Schriftlichkeit', *FMS* 22 (1988), 357ff.
Schmidt-Wiegand, R. (ed.), *Text – Bild – Interpretation. Untersuchungen zu den Bilderhandschriften des Sachsenspiegels*, Munich 1986
Schmitt, L. E., 'Die sprachschöpferische Leistung der deutschen Stadt im Mittelalter', *PBB* 66 (1942), 196ff.
Schmitz, W., *Die Dichtungen des Hartwig von dem Hage. Untersuchungen und Edition*, Göppingen 1976
Schmolke-Hasselmann, B., *Der arthurische Versroman von Chrestien bis Froissart. Zur Geschichte einer Gattung*, Tübingen 1980
Schneider, H., *Heldendichtung, Geistlichendichtung, Ritterdichtung*, Heidelberg 1943
Schnell, R., *Zum Verhältnis von hoch- und spätmittelalterlicher Literatur. Versuch einer Kritik*, Berlin 1978
'Recht und Dichtung. Zum gerichtlichen Zweikampf in der "Crône" Heinrichs von dem Türlin', in: P. Krämer and A. Cella (ed.), *Die mittelalterliche Literatur in Kärnten*, Vienna 1981, pp. 217ff.
'Zur Karls-Rezeption im "König Rother" und in Ottes "Eraclius"', *PBB* 104 (1982), 345ff.
'Prosaauflösung und Geschichtsschreibung im deutschen Spätmittelalter. Zum Entstehen des Prosaromans', in: L. Grenzmann and K. Stackmann (ed.), *Literatur und Laienbildung im Spätmittelalter und in der Reformationszeit*, Stuttgart 1984, pp. 214ff.
Causa amoris. Liebeskonzeption und Liebesdarstellung in der mittelalterlichen Literatur, Bern 1985
'Kirche, Hof und Liebe. Zum Freiraum mittelalterlicher Dichtung', in: E. Ruhe (ed.), *Mittelalterbilder aus neuer Perspektive*, Munich 1985, pp. 75ff.
'Deutsche Literatur und deutsches Nationalbewußtsein in Spätmittelalter und früher Neuzeit', in: J. Ehlers (ed.), *Ansätze und Diskontinuität deutscher Nationsbildung im Mittelalter*, Sigmaringen 1989, pp. 247ff.
Schoeler, G., 'Die Frage der schriftlichen oder mündlichen Überlieferung der Wissenschaften im frühen Islam', *Der Islam* 62 (1985), 201ff.
'Mündliche Thora und Hadīt: Überlieferung, Schreibverbot, Redaktion', *Der Islam* 66 (1989), 213ff.
Schönbach, A. E., 'Zur Geschichte der mittelhochdeutschen Lyrik', *ZfdA* 46 (1902), 93ff.
Scholes, R. J., and Willis, B. J., 'Linguists, literacy, and the intensionality of Marshall

McLuhan's Western man', in: D. R. Olson and N. Torrance (ed.), *Literacy and orality*, Cambridge 1991, pp. 215ff.
Scholz, M. G., 'Die "hûsvrouwe" und ihr Gast. Zu Thomasin von Zerclaere und seinem Publikum', in: FS for K. H. Halbach, Göppingen 1972, pp. 247ff.
Hören und Lesen. Studien zur primären Rezeption der Literatur im 12. und 13. Jahrhundert, Wiesbaden 1980
Schreier-Hornung, A., *Spielleute, Fahrende, Außenseiter: Künstler der mittelalterlichen Welt*, Göppingen 1981
Schreiner, K., 'Bücher, Bibliotheken und 'Gemeiner Nutzen' im Spätmittelalter und in der Frühneuzeit. Geistes- und sozialgeschichtliche Beiträge zur Frage nach der "utilitas librorum"', *BuW* 9 (1975), 202ff.
'Grenzen literarischer Kommunikation. Bemerkungen zur religiösen und sozialen Dialektik der Laienbildung im Spätmittelalter und in der Reformation', in: L. Grenzmann and K. Stackmann (ed.), *Literatur und Laienbildung im Spätmittelalter und in der Reformationszeit*, Stuttgart 1984, pp. 1ff.
'Laienbildung als Herausforderung für Kirche und Gesellschaft. Religiöse Vorbehalte und soziale Widerstände gegen die Verbreitung von Wissen im späten Mittelalter und in der Reformation', *ZHF* 11 (1984), 257ff.
'"Hof" (curia) und "höfische Lebensführung" (vita curialis) als Herausforderung an die christliche Theologie und Frömmigkeit', in: G. Kaiser and J.-D. Müller (ed.), *Höfische Literatur, Hofgesellschaft, Höfische Lebensformen um 1200*, Düsseldorf 1986, pp. 67ff.
'Volkssprache als Element gesellschaftlicher Integration und Ursache sozialer Konflikte. Formen und Funktionen volkssprachlicher Wissensverbreitung um 1500', in: F. Seibt and W. Eberhard (ed.), *Europa 1500. Integrationsprozesse im Widerstreit: Staaten, Regionen, Personenverbände, Christenheit*, Stuttgart 1987, pp. 468ff.
'Konnte Maria lesen? Von der Magd des Herrn zur Symbolgestalt mittelalterlicher Frauenbildung', *Rheinischer Merkur* 44, 1 (1990), 82ff.
'Marienverehrung, Lesekultur, Schriftlichkeit. Bildungs- und frömmigkeitsgeschichtliche Studien zur Auslegung und Darstellung von "Mariä Verkündigung"', *FMS* 24 (1990), 314ff.
'Verschriftlichung als Faktor monastischer Reform. Funktionen von Schriftlichkeit im Ordenswesen des hohen und späten Mittelalters', in: H. Keller et al. (ed.), *Pragmatische Schriftlichkeit*, pp. 37ff.
Schröder, E., *Das Anegenge. Eine literarhistorische Untersuchung*, Strassburg 1881
'Studien zu Konrad von Würzburg IV. V', Nachrichten von der königlichen Gesellschaft der Wissenschaften zu Göttingen, Philologisch-historische Klasse 1917, pp. 96ff.
'Rudolf von Ems und sein Literaturkreis', *ZfdA* 67 (1930), 209ff.
'Zur "Exodus": Termin und Publicum', *ZfdA* 72 (1935), 239f.
Schröder, W., 'Grenzen und Möglichkeiten einer althochdeutschen Literaturgeschichte', Berichte über die Verhandlungen der sächsischen Akademie der Wissenschaften zu Leipzig, Philologisch-historische Klasse 105, 2, Berlin 1959
'Zum Vanitas-Gedanken im deutschen Alexanderlied', *ZfdA* 91 (1961), 38ff.
'Kontinuität oder Diskontinuität in der Frühgeschichte der deutschen Literatur? Zu Gerhard Meißburger, Grundlagen zum Verständnis der deutschen Mönchsdichtung im 11. und 12. Jahrhundert', *ZfdA* 100 (1971), 195ff.
'*kunst* und *sin* bei Wolfram von Eschenbach', *Euphorion* 67 (1973), 219ff.
'*Die von Tristande hant gelesen*. Quellenhinweise und Quellenkritik im "Tristan" Gottfrieds von Straßburg', *ZfdA* 104 (1975), 307ff.
'Wolfram-Rezeption und Wolfram-Verständnis im 14. Jahrhundert. Zur Faksimile-Ausgabe der älteren Wiener *Willehalm*-Handschrift (Cod. Vindob. 2670)', *Euphorion* 70 (1976), 258ff.

'Zum Verhältnis von Lateinisch und Deutsch um das Jahr 1000', in: H. Beumann and W. Schröder (ed.), *Aspekte der Nationenbildung im Mittelalter*, Sigmaringen 1978, pp. 425ff.
Review of R. Hartmann, *Allegorisches Wörterbuch*, *AfdA* 89 (1978), 101ff.
'Der Schluß des "Jüngeren Titurel"', *ZfdA* 111 (1982), 103ff.
Review of M. G. Scholz, *Hören*, *MlJb* 18 (1983), 333ff.
'Text und Bild in der "Großen Bilderhandschrift" von Wolframs "Willehalm"', *ZfdA* 116 (1987), 239ff.
'Die Rolle der Mäzene und der wahre Patron des Ulrich von Etzenbach', *ZfdA* 118 (1989), 243ff.
Schubert, M. J., *Zur Theorie des Gebarens im Mittelalter. Analyse von nichtsprachlicher Äußerung in mittelhochdeutscher Epik. Rolandslied, Eneasroman, Tristan*, Cologne 1991
Schüppert, H., *Kirchenkritik in der lateinischen Lyrik des 12. und 13. Jahrhunderts*, Munich 1972
Schützeichel, R., *Das alemannische Memento Mori. Das Gedicht und der geistig-historische Hintergrund*, Tübingen 1962
'Justitiam vendere', *LwJb* 5 (1964), 1ff.
Althochdeutsches Wörterbuch, Tübingen 1969
'Zur Bezeichnung "cluniazensisch" und zur Methode der Interpretation mittelalterlicher religiöser Dichtung', in: L. P. Johnson, H.-H. Steinhoff, R. A. Wisbey (ed.), *Studien zur frühmittelhochdeutschen Literatur*, Berlin 1974, pp. 28ff.
Codex Pal. lat. 52. Studien zur Heidelberger Otfridhandschrift, zum Kicila-Vers und zum Georgslied, Abhandlungen der Akademie der Wissenschaften in Göttingen, Philologisch-historische Klasse 130, Göttingen 1982
Schuler, E. A., *Die Musik der Osterfeiern, Osterspiele und Passionen des Mittelalters*, Kassel 1951
Schultz, J. A., *The shape of the Round Table. Structures of Middle High German Arthurian romance*, Toronto 1983
Schumann, O., and Bischoff, B. (ed.), *Carmina Burana. I: Text, 3: Die Trink- und Spielerlieder – Die geistlichen Dramen*, Heidelberg 1970
Schwab, U., 'Das althochdeutsche Lied "Hirsch und Hinde" in seiner lateinischen Umgebung', in: N. Henkel and N. F. Palmer (ed.), *Latein und Volkssprache*, pp. 74ff.
Schwarz, A., 'Glossen als Texte', *PBB* 99 (1977), 25ff.
Schweikle, G., 'Textkritik und Interpretation', *ZfdA* 93 (1964), 99ff.
Minnesang, Stuttgart 1989
Schwietering, J., *Philologische Schriften* (ed. F. Ohly and M. Wehrli), Munich 1969
'Die Demutsformel mittelhochdeutscher Dichter', in: *Philologische Schriften*, pp. 140ff.
'Typologisches in mittelalterlicher Dichtung', in: *Philologische Schriften*, pp. 269ff.
Scribner, R. W., 'Flugblatt und Analphabetentum. Wie kam der gemeine Mann zu reformatorischen Ideen?', in: H.-J. Köhler (ed.), *Flugschriften als Massenmedium der Reformationszeit*, Tübingen 1981, pp. 65ff.
For the sake of simple folk: popular propaganda for the German Reformation, Cambridge 1981
See, K. von, 'Hastings, Stiklastaðir und Langemarck. Zur Überlieferung vom Vortrag heroischer Lieder auf dem Schlachtfelde', *GRM* 55 (1976), 1ff.
'Das Frühmittelalter als Epoche der europäischen Literaturgeschichte', in: K. von See (ed.), *Europäisches Frühmittelalter*, Wiesbaden 1985, pp. 5ff.
Seebold, E., 'Die kontinentalgermanischen Sprachen und Literaturen', in: F. Wischer (ed.), *Propyläen Geschichte der Literatur. Literatur und Gesellschaft in der westlichen Welt. II: Die mittelalterliche Welt, 600–1400*, Berlin 1982, pp. 221ff.
Seelbach, U., *Kommentar zum 'Helmbrecht' von Wernher dem Gartenaere*, Göppingen 1987
Seifert, A., 'Historia im Mittelalter', *AfB* 21 (1977), 226ff.
Shaw, F., 'Das historische Epos als Literaturgattung in frühmittelhochdeutscher Zeit', in: L. P.

Johnson, H.-H. Steinhoff, R. A. Wisbey (ed.), *Studien zur frühmittelhochdeutschen Literatur*, Berlin 1974, pp. 275ff.
Sieverding, N., *Der ritterliche Kampf bei Hartmann und Wolfram. Seine Bedeutung im 'Erec' und 'Iwein' und in den Gahmuret- und Gawan-Büchern des 'Parzival'*, Heidelberg 1985
Sievers, E., 'Zur Klangstruktur der mhd. Tanzdichtung', PBB 56 (1932), 181ff.
Simon, E., Review of B. Neumann, *Schauspiel*, PBB 112 (1990), 150ff.
Simon, G., 'Untersuchungen zur Topik der Widmungsbriefe mittelalterlicher Geschichtsschreiber bis zum Ende des 12. Jahrhunderts', AfD 5/6 (1959/60), 73ff.
Skrzypczak, H., *Stadt und Schriftlichkeit im deutschen Mittelalter*, diss. Berlin (Freie Universität) 1956
Smith, A., 'On audio and visual technologies: a future for the written word?', in: G. Baumann (ed.), *Word*, pp. 171ff.
Smith, J. D., 'The singer or the song? A reassessment of Lord's "Oral Theory"', *Man* 12 (1977), 141ff.
Smits, K., *Die frühmittelhochdeutsche Wiener Genesis. Kritische Ausgabe mit einem einleitenden Kommentar zur Überlieferung*, Berlin 1972
Solmsen, F., Review of E. A. Havelock, *Preface*, AJPh 87 (1966), 99ff.
Sonderegger, S., 'Die althochdeutsche Lex Salica-Übersetzung', in: FS for W. Jungandreas, Trier 1964, pp. 113ff.
Althochdeutsche Sprache und Literatur. Eine Einführung in das älteste Deutsch: Darstellung und Grammatik, Berlin 1974
'Die althochdeutsche Literatur', in: K. von See (ed.), *Europäisches Frühmittelalter*, Wiesbaden 1985, pp. 189ff.
'Latein und Althochdeutsch. Grundsätzliche Überlegungen zu ihrem Verhältnis', in: FS for H. F. Haefele, Sigmaringen 1985, pp. 59ff.
Southern, R. W., 'The schools of Paris and the school of Chartres', in: R. L. Benson and G. Constable (ed.), *Renaissance and renewal in the twelfth century*, Oxford 1982, pp. 113ff.
Sowinski, B., *Herzog Ernst. Ein mittelalterliches Abenteuerbuch*, Stuttgart 1979
Spanke, H., 'Tanzmusik in der Kirche des Mittelalters', NM 31 (1930), 143ff.
Specht, F. A., *Geschichte des Unterrichtswesens in Deutschland von den ältesten Zeiten bis zur Mitte des dreizehnten Jahrhunderts*, Stuttgart 1885
Spechtler, F. V., 'Beiträge zum deutschen geistlichen Lied des Mittelalters', ZfdPh 90 (1971), *Sonderheft: Neue Arbeiten zum mittelalterlichen Lied*, pp. 169ff.
Speckenbach, K., *Studien zum Begriff 'edelez herze' im Tristan Gottfrieds von Straßburg*, Munich 1965
'Endzeiterwartung im "Lancelot-Gral-Zyklus". Zur Problematik des Joachitischen Einflusses auf den Prosaroman', in: K. Grubmüller, R. Schmidt-Wiegand, K. Speckenbach (ed.), *Geistliche Denkformen in der Literatur des Mittelalters*, Munich 1984, pp. 210ff.
Speicher, S., *'Vom Rechte'. Ein Kommentar im Rahmen der zeitgenössischen Literaturtradition*, Göppingen 1986
Sprandel, R., *Gesellschaft und Literatur im Mittelalter*, Paderborn 1982
Staal, F., 'The fidelity of oral tradition and the origins of science', Mededelingen der Koninklijke Nederlandse Akademie van Wetenschappen, Afd. Letterkunde 49, 8, Amsterdam 1986, pp. 251ff.
Stackmann, K., 'Mittelalterliche Texte als Aufgabe', in: FS for J. Trier, Cologne 1964, pp. 240ff.
'Ovid im deutschen Mittelalter', *Arcadia* 1 (1966), 231ff.
Stammler, W., *Kleine Schriften zur Literaturgeschichte des Mittelalters*, Berlin 1953
Starck, T., and Wells, J. C., *Althochdeutsches Glossenwörterbuch (mit Stellennachweis zu sämtlichen gedruckten althochdeutschen und verwandten Glossen)*, Heidelberg 1972ff.
Steer, G., 'Carmina Burana in Südtirol. Zur Herkunft des clm 4660', ZfdA 112 (1983), 1ff.
'Der Laie als Anreger und Adressat deutscher Prosaliteratur im 14. Jahrhundert', in:

W. Haug, T. R. Jackson, J. Janota (ed.), *Zur deutschen Literatur und Sprache des 14. Jahrhunderts*, Heidelberg 1983, pp. 354ff.
'Der deutsche *Lucidarius*: ein Auftragswerk Heinrichs des Löwen?', *DVjs* 64 (1990), 1ff.
Stein, P. K., 'Formaler Schmuck und Aussage im "strophischen" Prolog zu Gottfrieds von Straßburg "Tristan"', *Euphorion* 69 (1975), 371ff.
'Stil, Struktur, historischer Ort und Funktion. Literarhistorische Beobachtungen und methodologische Überlegungen zu den Dichtungen der Frau Ava', in: FS for A. Schmidt, Stuttgart 1976, pp. 5ff.
Stephan, R., 'Über sangbare Dichtung in althochdeutscher Zeit', in: U. Ernst and P.-E. Neuser (ed.), *Die Genese der europäischen Endreimdichtung*, Darmstadt 1977, pp. 141ff.
Stevens, A., 'Zum Literaturbegriff bei Rudolf von Ems', in: D. McLintock, A. Stevens, F. Wagner (ed.), *Geistliche und weltliche Epik des Mittelalters in Österreich*, Göppingen 1987, pp. 19ff.
'The renewal of the classic: aspects of rhetorical and dialectical composition in Gottfried's *Tristan*', in: A. Stevens and R. Wisbey (ed.), *Gottfried von Strassburg and the medieval Tristan legend*, Cambridge 1990, pp. 67ff.
Stevens, J., *Words and music in the Middle Ages. Song, narrative, dance and drama, 1050–1350*, Cambridge 1986
Stevenson, J., 'Literacy in Ireland: the evidence of the Patrick dossier in the Book of Armagh', in: R. McKitterick (ed.), *Uses*, pp. 11ff.
Stock, B., *The implications of literacy. Written language and models of interpretation in the eleventh and twelfth centuries*, Princeton 1983
Störmer, W., 'Nibelungentradition als Hausüberlieferung in frühmittelalterlichen Adelsfamilien? Beobachtungen zu Nibelungennamen im 8./9. Jahrhundert vornehmlich in Bayern', in: F. P. Knapp (ed.), *Nibelungenlied und Klage. Sage und Geschichte, Struktur und Gattung*, Heidelberg 1987, pp. 1ff.
Stolzenberg, I., 'Urkundsparteien und Urkundensprache. Ein Beitrag zur Frage des Aufkommens der deutschsprachigen Urkunde am Oberrhein', *AfD* 7 (1961), 214ff. and 8 (1962), 147ff.
Street, B. V., *Literacy in theory and practice*, Cambridge 1984
Stuart, H., and Walla, F., 'Die Überlieferung der mittelalterlichen Segen', *ZfdA* 116 (1987), 53ff.
Stubbs, M., *Language and literacy. The sociolinguistics of reading and writing*, London 1980
Szabó, T., 'Der mittelalterliche Hof zwischen Kritik und Idealisierung', in: J. Fleckenstein (ed.), *Curialitas*, pp. 350ff.
Szklenar, H., 'Die literarische Gattung der *Nibelungenklage* und das Ende "alter maere"', *Poetica* 9 (1977), 41ff.
Taeger, B., 'Ein vergessener handschriftlicher Befund: die Neumen im Münchener "Heliand"', *ZfdA* 107 (1978), 184ff.
Tannen, D. (ed.), *Coherence in spoken and written discourse*, London 1983
Spoken and written language. Exploring orality and literacy, London 1983
Teske, H., *Thomasin von Zerclaere. Der Mann und sein Werk*, Heidelberg 1933
Teske, W., 'Laien, Laienmönche und Laienbrüder in der Abtei Cluny. Ein Beitrag zum "Konversen-Problem"', *FMS* 10 (1976), 248ff. and 11 (1977), 288ff.
Thelen, C., *Das Dichtergebet in der deutschen Literatur des Mittelalters*, Berlin 1989
Thomas, H., 'Matière de Rome – Matière de Bretagne. Zu den politischen Implikationen von Veldekes "Eneide" und Hartmanns "Erec"', *ZfdPh* 108 (1989), *Sonderheft 'Literatur und Sprache im rheinisch-maasländischen Raum zwischen 1150 und 1450'*, pp. 65ff.
Thomas, K., 'The meaning of literacy in early modern England', in: G. Baumann (ed.), *Word*, pp. 97ff.
Thomas, R., *Oral tradition and written record in classical Athens*, Cambridge 1989
Thompson, J. W., *The literacy of the laity in the Middle Ages*, New York 1960

Thornton, A. G., *Weltgeschichte und Heilsgeschichte in Albrechts von Scharfenberg Jüngerem Titurel*, Göppingen 1977
Thum, B., 'Politische Probleme der Stauferzeit im Werk Hartmanns von Aue: Landesherrschaft im "Erec" und 'Iwein"', in: R. Krohn, B. Thum, P. Wapnewski (ed.), *Stauferzeit: Geschichte, Literatur, Kunst*, Stuttgart 1978, pp. 47ff.
Tiemann, R., 'Bemerkungen zur Entstehungsgeschichte der Fabliaux', *RF* 72 (1960), 406ff.
Tomasek, T., *Die Utopie im 'Tristan' Gotfrids von Straßburg*, Tübingen 1985
'Die mittelhochdeutsche Verserzählung "Moriz von Craûn". Eine Werkdeutung mit Blick auf die Vor-Geschichte', *ZfdA* 115 (1986), 254ff.
Topsfield, L. T., *Chrétien de Troyes. A study of the Arthurian romances*, Cambridge 1981
Traub, A., 'Zur Musik der Trierer Marienklage und des Trierer Osterspiels', *PBB* 110 (1988), 78ff.
Treitler, L., 'Homer and Gregory: the transmission of epic poetry and plainchant', *MQ* 60 (1974), 333ff.
'Oral, written, and literate process in the transmission of medieval music', *Speculum* 56 (1981), 471ff.
'The early history of music writing in the West', *JAMS* 35 (1982), 237ff.
'Orality and literacy in the music of the Middle Ages', *Parergon* 2 (1984), 143ff.
'Reading and singing: on the genesis of Occidental music-writing', *EMH* 4 (1984), 135ff.
Türk, E., *Nugae Curialium. Le règne d'Henri II Plantagenêt (1145–1189) et l'éthique politique*, Geneva 1977
Turner, R. V., 'The *miles literatus* in twelfth- and thirteenth-century England: how rare a phenomenon?', *AHR* 83 (1978), 928ff.
Uitti, K. D., 'Vernacularization and Old French romance mythopoesis with emphasis on Chrétien's *Erec et Enide*', in: R. T. Pickens (ed.), *The sower and his seed. Essays on Chrétien de Troyes*, Lexington, Kentucky, 1983, pp. 81ff.
Ullmann, W., *Principles of government and politics in the Middle Ages*, London 1961
'Politisches Denken und politische Organisation', in: E. Wischer (ed.), *Propyläen Geschichte der Literatur. Literatur und Gesellschaft in der westlichen Welt. II: Die mittelalterliche Welt, 600–1400*, Berlin 1982, pp. 11ff.
Urbanek, F., 'Das Ezzolied in den Traditionen von *Ars rhetorica* und germanisch-heimischer Redekunst', *ZfdPh* 106 (1987), 321ff. and 107 (1988), 26ff.
Ursprung, O., 'Freisings mittelalterliche Musikgeschichte', in: J. Schlecht (ed.), *Wissenschaftliche Festgabe zum zwölfhundertjährigen Jubiläum des heiligen Korbinian*, Munich 1924, pp. 246ff.
'Das Freisinger Petrus-Lied', *Die Musikforschung* 5 (1952), 17ff.
Uytfanghe, M. van, 'Le latin des hagiographes mérovingiens et la protohistoire du français. Etat de question. Première partie: à quelle époque a-t-on cessé de parler latin?', *RG* 16 (1976), 5ff.
'Histoire du latin, protohistoire des langues romanes et histoire de la communication', *Francia* 11 (1983), 579ff.
Vancsa, M., *Das erste Auftreten der deutschen Sprache in den Urkunden*, Leipzig 1895
Vansina, J., *Oral tradition as history*, London 1985
Vàrvaro, A., 'Scuola e cultura in Francia nel XII secolo', *SMV* 10 (1962), 299ff.
Vermes, G., 'Scripture and tradition in Judaism. Written and oral Torah', in: G. Baumann, *Word*, pp. 79ff.
Vezin, J., 'La ponctuation du VIIIe au XIIe siècle', in: H.-J. Martin and J. Vezin (ed.), *Mise*, pp. 439ff.
Violante, C., *Laici nella 'societas christiana' del secolo XI e XII*, Milan 1968
Völker, P.-G., 'Überlegungen zur Geschichte des geistlichen Spiels im Mittelalter', in: I. Glier, G. Hahn, W. Haug, B. Wachinger (ed.), *Werk – Typ – Situation. Studien zu poetologischen Bedingungen in der älteren deutschen Literatur*, Stuttgart 1969, pp. 252ff.

Völker, W., *Märchenhafte Elemente bei Chrétien de Troyes*, Bonn 1972
Voetz, L., 'Überlieferungsformen mittelhochdeutscher Lyrik', in: E. Mittler and W. Werner (ed.), *Codex Manesse. Katalog zur Ausstellung vom 12. Juni bis 2. Oktober 1988 Universitätsbibliothek Heidelberg*, Heidelberg 1988, pp. 224ff.
Vollmann-Profe, G., *Kommentar zu Otfrids Evangelienbuch. I: Widmungen, Buch I, 1–11*, Bonn 1976
Review of D. Kartschoke, *Bibeldichtung*, GRM 59 (1978), 477ff.
Wiederbeginn volkssprachiger Schriftlichkeit im hohen Mittelalter (1050/60–1160/70), Königstein 1986 (vol. I, part II of J. Heinzle (ed.), *Geschichte der deutschen Literatur von den Anfängen bis zum Beginn der Neuzeit*)
Otfrid von Weißenburg. Evangelienbuch, Stuttgart 1987
Vollrath, H., 'Gesetzgebung und Schriftlichkeit. Das Beispiel der angelsächsischen Gesetze', HJb 99 (1979), 28ff.
'Das Mittelalter in der Typik oraler Gesellschaften', HZ 233 (1981), 571ff.
Voss, H., *Studien zur illustrierten Millstätter Genesis*, Munich 1962
Wachinger, B., 'Deutsche und lateinische Liebeslieder. Zu den deutschen Strophen der Carmina Burana', in: H. Fromm (ed.), *Der deutsche Minnesang. Aufsätze zu seiner Erforschung* II 275ff., Darmstadt 1985
'Autorschaft und Überlieferung', in: W. Haug and B. Wachinger (ed.), *Autorentypen*, Tübingen 1991, pp. 1ff.
'Wolfram von Eschenbach am Schreibpult', *Wolfram-Studien* 12 (1992), 9ff.
Wagner, N., *Getica. Untersuchungen zum Leben des Jordanes und zur frühen Geschichte der Goten*, Berlin 1967
Wailes, S. L., *Studien zur Kleindichtung des Stricker*, Berlin 1981
Walther, I. E., *Codex Manesse. Die Miniaturen der Großen Heidelberger Liederhandschrift*, Frankfurt 1988
Wapnewski, P., *Hartmann von Aue*, Stuttgart 1976
Wehowsky, G., *Schmuckformen und Formbruch in der deutschen Reimpaardichtung des Mittelalters*, diss. Breslau 1936
Wehrli, M., *Formen mittelalterlicher Erzählung. Aufsätze*, Zürich 1969
Geschichte der deutschen Literatur vom frühen Mittelalter bis zum Ende des 16. Jahrhunderts, Stuttgart 1980
Literatur im deutschen Mittelalter. Eine poetologische Einführung, Stuttgart 1984
Review of W. Haubrichs, *Anfänge*, and of G. Vollmann-Profe, *Wiederbeginn*, Arbitrium 7 (1989), 271ff.
Weidenhiller, P. E., *Untersuchungen zur deutschsprachigen katechetischen Literatur des späten Mittelalters. Nach den Handschriften der Bayerischen Staatsbibliothek*, Munich 1965
Weinhold, K., 'Zu dem deutschen Pilatusgedicht. Text, Sprache und Heimat', ZfdPh 8 (1877), 253ff.
Welker, L., 'Melodien und Instrumente', in: E. Mittler and W. Werner (ed.), *Codex Manesse. Katalog zur Ausstellung vom 12. Juni bis 2. Oktober 1988 Universitätsbibliothek Heidelberg*, Heidelberg 1988, pp. 113ff.
Wells, D. A., Review of S. Speicher, 'Vom Rechte', MLR 83 (1988), 505ff.
Wendehorst, A., 'Monachus scribere nesciens', MIÖG 71 (1963), 67ff.
'Wer konnte im Mittelalter lesen und schreiben?', in: J. Fried (ed.), *Schulen und Studium im sozialen Wandel des hohen und späten Mittelalters*, Sigmaringen 1986, pp. 9ff.
Wenskus, R., 'Wie die Nibelungen-Überlieferung nach Bayern kam', ZfbLg 36 ii (1973), 393ff.
Wenzel, H., *Frauendienst und Gottesdienst. Studien zur Minne-Ideologie*, Berlin 1974
'Zur Repräsentation von Herrschaft in mittelalterlichen Texten. Plädoyer für eine Literaturgeschichte der Herrschaftsbereiche und ihrer Institutionen', in: J. Bumke, T. Cramer, G. Kaiser, H. Wenzel (ed.), *Adelsherrschaft und Literatur*, Bern 1980, pp. 339ff.

Höfische Geschichte. Literarische Tradition und Gegenwartsdeutung in den volkssprachigen Chroniken des hohen und späten Mittelalters, Bern 1980
'Öffentlichkeit und Heimlichkeit in Gottfrieds "Tristan"', *ZfdPh* 107 (1988), 335ff.
'Partizipation und Mimesis. Die Lesbarkeit der Körper am Hof und in der höfischen Literatur', in: H. U. Gumbrecht and K. L. Pfeiffer (ed.), *Materialität der Kommunikation*, Frankfurt 1988, pp. 178ff.
'Repräsentation und schöner Schein am Hof und in der höfischen Literatur', in: H. Ragotzky and H. Wenzel (ed.), *Höfische Repräsentation. Das Zeremoniell und die Zeichen*, Tübingen 1990, pp. 171ff.
Werf, H. van der, *The chansons of the troubadours and trouvères. A study of the melodies and their relation to the poems*, Utrecht 1972
Werner, W., *Studien zu den Passions- und Osterspielen des deutschen Mittelalters in ihrem Übergang vom Latein zur Volkssprache*, Berlin 1965
Wesche, H., *Der althochdeutsche Wortschatz im Gebiete des Zaubers und der Weissagung*, Halle 1940
Wessel, F., *Probleme der Metaphorik und die Minnemetaphorik in Gottfrieds von Straßburg 'Tristan und Isolde'*, Munich 1984
Wetherbee, W., *Platonism and poetry in the twelfth centuy. The literary influence of the school of Chartres*, Princeton 1972
Wieland, G. R., 'The glossed manuscript: classbook or library book?', *ASE* 14 (1985), 153ff.
Wiessner, E., *Kommentar zu Neidharts Liedern*, Leipzig 1954
Wilhelm, F., *Zur Geschichte des Schrifttums in Deutschland bis zum Ausgang des 13. Jahrhunderts*, Munich 1920
Wilhelm, F., (ed.), *Corpus der altdeutschen Originalurkunden bis zum Jahre 1300*, Lahr 1932ff.
Williamson, E., *The half-way house of fiction. Don Quixote and Arthurian romance*, Oxford 1985
Willmes, P., *Der Herrscher-'Adventus' im Kloster des Frühmittelalters*, Munich 1976
Wisbey, R., 'Living in the presence of the past: exemplary perspectives in Gottfried's *Tristan*', in: A. Stevens and R. Wisbey (ed.), *Gottfried von Strassburg and the medieval Tristan legend*, Cambridge 1990, pp. 257ff.
Wolf, A., 'Erzählkunst und verborgener Schriftsinn. Zur Diskussion um Chrétiens "Yvain" und Hartmanns "Iwein"', *Sprachkunst* 2 (1971), 1ff.
'Mittelalterliche Heldensagen zwischen Vergil, Prudentius und raffinierter Klosterliteratur. Beobachtungen zum "Waltharius"', *Sprachkunst* 7 (1976), 180ff.
'Die Verschriftlichung der Nibelungensage und die französisch-deutschen Literaturbeziehungen im Mittelalter', in: *Hohenemser Studien zum Nibelungenlied*, Dornbirn 1981, pp. 227ff.
'Die Anfänge des Minnesangs und die Troubadourdichtung', *WA* 24 (1983), 197ff.
Deutsche Kultur im Hochmittelalter 1150–1250, Essen 1986
'Nibelungenlied – chanson de geste – höfischer Roman. Zur Problematik der Verschriftlichung der deutschen Nibelungensagen', in: F. P. Knapp (ed.), *Nibelungenlied und Klage. Sage und Geschichte, Struktur und Gattung*, Heidelberg 1987, pp. 171ff.
'Die Verschriftlichung von europäischen Heldensagen als mittelalterliches Kulturproblem', in: H. Beck (ed.), *Heldensage und Heldendichtung im Germanischen*, Berlin 1988, pp. 305ff.
Gottfried von Straßburg und die Mythe von Tristan und Isolde, Darmstadt 1989
'"Non veni solvere sed adimplere"', in: F. Link (ed.), *Paradeigmata. Literarische Typologie des Alten Testaments. I: Von den Anfängen bis zum 19. Jahrhundert*, Berlin 1989, pp. 85ff.
'Volkssprachliche Heldensagen und lateinische Mönchskultur. Grundsätzliche Überlegungen zum "Waltharius"', in: A. Masser and A. Wolf (ed.), *Geistesleben um den Bodensee im frühen Mittelalter*, Freiburg 1989, pp. 157ff.

'Frühmittelalterliches Erzählen im Spannungsfeld von Vers, Abschnitt und Strophe: Versuch einer Bestandsaufnahme', in: H. L. C. Tristram (ed.), *Metrik und Medienwechsel. Metrics and media*, Tübingen 1991, pp. 107ff.

'*Fol i allai – fol m'en revinc!* Der Roman vom Löwenritter zwischen *mançonge* und *maere*', in: FS for W. Hoffmann, Göppingen 1991, pp. 205ff.

'Medieval heroic traditions and their transitions from orality to literacy', in: A. N. Doane and C. B. Pasternack (ed.), *Vox intexta. Orality and textuality in the Middle Ages*, Madison 1991, pp. 67ff.

Wormald, C. P., 'The uses of literacy in Anglo-Saxon England and its neighbours', *TRHS* (5) 27 (1977), 95ff.

'*Lex scripta* and *verbum regis*: legislation and Germanic kingship, from Euric to Cnut', in: P. H. Sawyer and I. N. Wood (ed.), *Early medieval kingship*, Leeds 1977, pp. 105ff.

Worstbrock, F. J., 'Zur Tradition des Trojastoffes und seiner Gestaltung bei Herbort von Fritzlar', *ZfdA* 92 (1963), 248ff.

'Dilatatio materiae. Zur Poetik des *Erec* Hartmanns von Aue', *FMS* 19 (1985), 1ff.

Wright, R., *Late Latin and early Romance in Spain and Carolingian France*, Liverpool 1982

Wunderli, P., 'Die ältesten romanischen Texte unter dem Gesichtspunkt von Protokoll und Vorlesen', *VR* 24 (1965), 44ff.

Wynn, M., 'Der Witz in der Tragik. Das erste Buch von Wolframs "Willehalm" und sein Schluß', *Wolfram-Studien* 7 (1982), 117ff.

Yeandle, D. N., 'The *Ludwigslied*: king, Church, and context', in: J. L. Flood and D. N. Yeandle (ed.), '*Mit regulu bithuungan*'. *Neue Arbeiten zur althochdeutschen Poesie und Sprache*, Göppingen 1989, pp. 18ff.

Young, K., *The drama of the medieval church*, Oxford 1951

Zäck, R., *Der Guote Sündaere und der Peccator Precipuus. Eine Untersuchung zu den Deutungsmodellen des 'Gregorius' Hartmanns von Aue und der 'Gesta Gregorii Peccatoris' Arnolds von Lübeck ausgehend von den Prologen*, Göppingen 1989

Żak, S., *Musik als 'Ehr und Zier' im mittelalterlichen Reich. Studien zur Musik im höfischen Leben, Recht und Zeremoniell*, Neuss 1979

'Das Tedeum als Huldigungsgesang', *HJb* 102 (1982), 1ff.

Zeumer, K., 'Studien zu den Reichsgesetzen des XIII. Jahrhunderts', *ZRG (GA)* 23 (1902), 61ff.

Ziltener, W., *Chrétien und die Aeneis. Eine Untersuchung des Einflusses von Vergil auf Chrétien von Troyes*, Graz 1957

Zink, M., *La prédication en langue romane avant 1300*, Paris 1976

'Les destinataires des recueils de sermons en langue vulgaire au xiie et au xiiie siècle. Prédication effective et prédication dans un fauteuil', in: *La piété populaire au moyen âge (Actes du 99e Congrès National des Sociétés Savantes, Besançon 1974, 1)*, Paris 1977, pp. 59ff.

'Une mutation de la conscience littéraire: Le langage romanesque à travers des exemples français du xiie siècle', *CCM* 24 (1981), 3ff.

Zotz, T., 'Urbanitas. Zur Bedeutung und Funktion einer antiken Wertvorstellung innerhalb der höfischen Kultur des hohen Mittelalters', in: J. Fleckenstein (ed.), *Curialitas*, pp. 392ff.

Zumthor, P., *Introduction à la poésie orale*, Paris 1983

La poésie et la voix dans la civilisation médiévale, Paris 1984

'The text and the voice', *NLH* 16 (1984/5), 67ff.

'*Litteratus/illitteratus*. Remarques sur le contexte vocal de l'écriture médiévale', *Romania* 106 (1985), 1ff.

Index of names

This index is confined to the authors of secondary literature referred to in the text. The titles of primary works, together with the names of their authors and editors, are to be found in the bibliographical index.

Aarburg, U., 361
Ackroyd, P. R., 335
Adam, B., 371
Althoff, G., 408
Andersson, T. M., 326
Arndt, P. H., 404
Arntz, H., 337, 370
Ashcroft, J., 64
Assche, M. van, 335
Assmann, A. and J., 325, 327, 330, 333, 409, 410
Auerbach, E., 414

Baesecke, G., 47, 271, 272, 325, 333, 344, 358, 407
Bätschmann, E., 356
Bäuml, F. H., 5, 325, 327, 328, 362, 380, 411, 413
Baldwin, J. W., 409, 410, 412
Balogh, J., 31, 226, 331, 334, 363, 381, 396, 421
Baumann, G., 328
Bédier, J., 285, 411
Behr, H.-J., 342, 393
Benecke, G. F., 316, 321
Bennewitz, I., 371
Benson, L. D., 326
Bergmann, R., 340, 341, 356, 375, 376
Bertau, K., 131, 197, 221, 259, 336, 343, 344, 357, 360, 366, 376, 383, 388, 395, 411, 414
Beyschlag, S., 344
Bezzola, R. R., 252, 401, 403, 409, 418
Binns, J. W., 422
Bischoff, B., 332, 340, 356, 380
Bloch, R. H., 342
Bloomfield, L., 4, 324
Bloomfield, M. W., 22, 331, 332, 333, 341
Boehm, L., 397, 398, 399, 411, 414
Bonath, G., 388

Boor, H. de, 186, 330, 346, 349, 350, 351, 354, 355, 361, 372, 384, 385, 394, 395, 396, 414
Borck, K.-H., 343, 345
Boudriot, W., 370
Brackert, H., 387, 392, 393, 402, 404, 406
Bräuer, R., 400, 417
Brall, H., 333, 387, 415
Brandt, A. von, 414
Brandt, R., 356, 393, 395, 396, 422
Braungart, G., 340, 424
Brogsitter, K. O., 417
Broich, U., 401, 411, 413
Brüggen, E., 341
Brunner, H., 344, 357, 358, 360
Brunner, O., 342
Bützler, C., 344, 361
Bumke, J., 17, 19, 63, 222, 274, 287, 291, 327, 328, 329, 332, 341, 342, 345, 347, 352, 355, 358, 359, 360, 361, 362, 367, 368, 370, 373, 376, 377, 379, 380, 387, 392, 393, 394, 395, 396, 400, 401, 406, 409, 410, 411, 412, 413, 414, 415, 416, 417, 420, 422, 426
Burg, U. von der, 392
Buschinger, D., 346, 360

Caldwell, R. A., 402, 403
Camille, M., 4, 126, 127, 325, 365
Campenhausen, H. von, 324
Capua, F. di, 334, 336, 421
Carcopino, J., 325, 336
Carruthers, M. J., 326, 331, 342, 424
Chailley, J., 345
Chinca, M. G., 404
Christ, W., 259, 404, 405
Clanchy, M. T., 3, 13, 16, 232, 240, 324, 327, 328, 331, 342, 397, 398, 399, 413, 415, 422
Classen, P., 324, 339, 410

INDEX OF NAMES

Clausen, W. V., 334, 335
Conlee, J. W., 326
Cormeau, C., 392, 393, 403
Coulmas, F., 133, 324, 327, 366
Cramer, T., 114, 189, 350, 356, 363, 366, 392, 393, 394, 395, 406, 407, 409
Crosby, R., 335, 336
Curschmann, M., 5, 106, 193, 324, 325, 326, 329, 334, 346, 348, 350, 357, 365, 371, 376, 377, 380, 387, 401, 403, 407, 414, 416

Derolez, R., 337
Dickinson, J. C., 420
Diebold, M., 333, 343, 353, 357
Diemer, J., 365
Dilcher, G., 395
Drube, H., 73, 345
Duby, G., 409, 413, 415, 420
Düwel, K., 337, 370, 371, 378
Dunbabin, J., 413
Dunn, C. W., 22, 331, 332, 333, 341

Ebel, E., 37, 337
Ebenbauer, A., 400, 406, 407
Eggers, H., 338, 387
Ehlers, J., 409, 411
Ehlich, K., 324, 336, 342, 354, 362
Ehrismann, G., 69, 270, 287, 343, 344, 345, 350, 351, 352, 354, 355, 358, 361, 407, 424
Eifler, G., 411
Eisenstein, E. L., 12, 13, 324, 329, 330, 409
Elliott, R. W. V., 337, 370
Elm, K., 395, 396, 410, 416
Elwert, G., 342
Engel, W., 383
Erdmann, C., 343, 350, 396, 408
Ernout, A., 331
Ernst, U., 366, 382, 383, 384, 393, 411, 413, 414
Ertzdorff, X. von, 341, 384, 392, 393, 406
Erzgräber, W., 327
Esser, J., 354, 412

Falk, H., 327
Febvre, L., 350
Fechter, W., 331
Feldbusch, E., 4, 52, 53, 334, 340, 408
Felten, F. J., 337
Fenske, L., 416
Fichtenau, H., 376
Finnegan, R., 5, 6, 8, 169, 324, 325, 326, 327, 380, 381
Fischer, H., 82, 166, 346, 361, 369, 379

Fleckenstein, J., 339, 341, 410, 411, 412, 413, 415, 416, 418, 420
Flint, V. I. J., 349, 370
Flori, J., 408, 409
Foley, J. M., 5, 325
Fontaine, J., 338
Forster, L., 327
Fossier, R., 332, 338
Fouquet-Plümacher, D., 335
Frank, B., 336, 351, 364, 371, 392, 394
Franz, K., 415
Frappier, J., 399
Freytag, H., 71, 343, 345, 350, 351, 354
Freytag, W., 354, 406
Fried, J., 343, 393, 394
Fromm, H., 17, 328, 331, 333, 355, 394, 412, 415
Froning, R., 344, 357
Frühmorgen-Voss, H., 370
Fry, D. K., 7, 23, 326, 333, 369
Fünten, W. aus der, 375
Fuhrmann, H., 244

Gadamer, H.-G., 362
Gaiffier, B. de, 382
Gallais, P., 329, 406, 416
Ganz, D., 339
Ganz, P. F., 343, 351, 387, 388, 392, 416, 418, 422, 423, 424
Gaur, A., 337
Geering, A., 344, 357
Geith, K.-E., 328, 343, 355, 394
Gelb, I. J., 337
Gentry, F. G., 340
Georgi, A., 333
Gerhardsson, B., 324
Geuenich, D., 4, 325, 408
Giesecke, M., 12, 14, 324, 326, 327, 329, 330, 334, 335, 424
Gillespie, G., 417
Glaue, P., 336
Glendinning, R., 387
Gompf, L., 336
Goody, J., 3, 7, 8, 22, 25, 61, 62, 114, 202, 232, 233, 240, 241, 244, 324, 327, 329, 331, 334, 362, 366, 381, 389, 398, 400
Gough, K., 8, 327
Graham, W. A., 4, 15, 17, 33, 324, 326, 327, 329, 330, 331, 335, 336
Green, D. H., 329, 332, 340, 341, 342, 345, 347, 348, 353, 354, 355, 359, 360, 363, 364, 365, 366, 369, 371, 375, 378, 379, 381, 382, 383,

478

INDEX OF NAMES

384, 385, 387, 389, 390, 392, 396, 402, 403,
  405, 406, 407, 409, 410, 413, 415, 416, 417,
  418, 419, 421, 423, 425
Greinemann, E., 354
Grimm, W., 333
Grosse, S., 260
Gruber, J., 379
Grubmüller, K., 324, 330, 333, 339, 349, 387,
  389
Grundmann, H., 8, 9, 10, 14, 20, 23, 219, 274,
  293, 327, 328, 329, 330, 332, 333, 336, 338,
  353, 371, 374, 377, 387, 393, 395, 396, 399,
  408, 409, 410, 411, 413, 414, 415, 416, 417
Gschwantler, O., 23, 326, 333, 393, 400
Günther, H., 408
Guerreau-Jalabert, A., 41, 334, 338, 407
Gumbrecht, H. U., 407
Guyer, F. E., 415

Hadas, M., 335
Hagenlocher, A., 200, 201, 389
Hahn, G., 334
Hahn, I., 417
Harnack, A. von, 335, 336
Harris, J., 326
Harris, R., 337
Harris, W. V., 327, 328, 331, 332, 333, 334, 335,
  336, 364, 381, 408, 423
Hartl, E., 376
Hartung, W., 342, 343
Harvey, F. D., 327
Hatto, A. T., 115, 195, 305, 325, 326, 342, 363,
  368, 387, 388, 405, 423
Haubrichs, W., 19, 22, 23, 47, 66, 70, 241, 285,
  332, 333, 334, 336, 337, 338, 339, 340, 343,
  349, 350, 351, 352, 354, 357, 361, 370, 371,
  374, 376, 385, 394, 395, 399, 407, 408, 410,
  411
Hauck, K., 353, 399, 400
Haug, W., 20, 21, 237, 252, 254, 331, 332, 336,
  340, 342, 344, 347, 353, 354, 357, 370, 374,
  377, 382, 383, 398, 399, 400, 403, 404, 406,
  407, 408, 409, 417, 419, 420, 422, 423, 424
Haupt, B., 342, 349, 394
Havelock, E. A., 3, 7, 8, 21, 23, 133, 240, 324,
  326, 327, 328, 329, 332, 333, 366, 378
Haverkamp, A., 409, 410
Haymes, E. R., 5
Hayum, A., 325, 365
Heck, P., 4, 325
Heger, H., 343, 345, 396
Heimpel, H., 328, 389

Heinen, H., 345, 415
Heinzle, J., 19, 212, 266, 267, 277, 324, 325,
  326, 332, 344, 346, 347, 356, 357, 358, 365,
  370, 371, 372, 373, 375, 376, 393, 394, 395,
  396, 397, 399, 400, 406, 407, 409, 410
Hellgardt, E., 341, 351, 408
Helm, K., 333, 349, 355, 370, 374
Hendrickson, G. L., 331, 334, 421
Henkel, N., 340, 349, 365, 370, 378, 393, 394,
  409, 416, 424
Hennig, U., 354
Herescu, N. I., 331
Herkommer, H., 372, 373, 394, 400, 409
Herzog, R., 374
Heusler, A., 67, 68, 325, 326, 344
Hirsch, H., 373
Höfler, O., 399
Hölscher, L., 114, 115, 356, 363, 420
Hoffmann, W., 326
Hofmann, D., 344
Hofmeister, P., 335, 336
Honemann, V., 370
Horacek, B., 190, 191, 387
Huber, C., 311, 387, 422
Hucke, H., 4, 324
Hübner, A., 345
Hüpper, D., 337, 338
Hüpper-Dröge, D., 339
Humphreys, K. W., 330
Hunt, T., 346, 387, 406, 415
Huot, S., 69, 330, 366, 409

Illmer, D., 336, 404, 408, 411
Imbach, R., 423
Irsigler, F., 339

Jabbour, A., 325
Jacobsen, P. C., 408
Jaeger, C. S., 282, 396, 409, 410, 411, 422
Jammers, E., 336, 344, 350, 357, 360, 379, 383,
  384, 424
Janota, J., 19, 332, 343, 345, 350
Jauss, H. R., 407
Jeauneau, E., 337, 347
Jillings, L., 422
Johanek, P., 352, 353, 393, 394, 403, 409, 410,
  423, 424
Jones, G. F., 333

Kämpfer, W., 389
Kaiser, G., 357
Kantorowicz, E. H., 415

INDEX OF NAMES

Karnein, A., 311, 409, 410, 411, 412, 422
Kartschoke, D., 11, 79, 87, 142, 144, 146, 149, 173, 174, 329, 333, 337, 338, 340, 345, 346, 349, 351, 353, 354, 355, 356, 357, 362, 363, 364, 368, 369, 370, 371, 373, 374, 376, 379, 381, 383, 387, 394, 400, 401, 402, 403, 407, 408, 411, 414, 415, 416, 421, 422, 425
Kasten, I., 362, 367, 412, 415, 422, 423
Kelber, W., 324
Kelle, J., 384, 408
Keller, H., 330, 410, 414
Kemp, W., 4, 325
Kemper, R., 357
Kendrick, T. D., 337
Kenney, E. J., 334, 335
Kenyon, F. G., 334
Kieckhefer, R., 370
Kienast, R., 348
Kiening, C., 341, 358
Kirchert, K., 324, 333, 414
Kirchhoff, H. G., 372, 397
Klein, D., 349
Kleinschmidt, E., 342, 362
Klewitz, H.-W., 420
Klingenberg, H., 21, 22, 333, 337
Klopsch, P., 338, 403, 407
Knab, D., 353, 400
Knape, J., 373, 374, 397, 401, 403, 405, 406
Knapp, F. P., 237, 310, 393, 403, 404, 406, 415, 422
Knoop, U., 52, 342, 362
Knopf, J., 404
Knox, B. M. W., 331, 334
Knox, D., 342
Köhler, E., 403, 404, 409
Köhn, R., 15, 16, 88, 331, 347, 409, 410, 411, 412, 413, 421
Kokott, H., 392, 393
Kolb, H., 343, 350, 361, 399, 406, 411
Koller, E., 352
Kratz, B., 378
Kraume, H., 328
Kraus, C. von, 134, 367
Krause, W., 340
Kriedte, H., 355
Kries, F. W. von, 365
Kroeschell, K., 342
Krohn, R., 221, 282, 395, 418
Krüger, R., 360
Krüger, S., 333, 422
Kruse, N., 340
Küsters, U., 303, 336, 346, 355, 414, 420

Kuhn, Hans, 37, 337
Kuhn, Hugo, 18, 21, 49, 166, 332, 339, 361, 379, 380
Kullmann, W., 325, 326

Laurie, H. C. R., 415
Lebsanft, F., 329, 345, 363
Leclereq, J., 336, 394, 408, 415
Le Goff, J., 409
Leipold, I., 395
Lengenfelder, H., 409
Lenschen, W., 346
Lerner, R. E., 330, 333, 338, 339, 410
Lexer, M., 316, 321
Leyser, H., 395
Liebertz-Grün, U., 324, 410
Linke, H., 341, 342, 344, 346, 356, 376
Lipphardt, W., 344, 350
Lönnroth, L., 326
Lofmark, C., 262, 377, 405
Lomnitzer, H., 362
Lord, A. B., 5, 6, 7, 10, 17, 18, 133, 169, 325, 326, 366, 378, 380, 409
Lüdtke, H., 170, 381
Luttrell, C., 415
Lutz, E. C., 351

Maas, U., 327
Magoun, F. P., 6, 7, 325
Marichal, R., 403, 417, 418
Marold, E., 399
Martin, H.-J., 330, 422, 424
Masser, A., 49, 50, 340, 341, 345, 355, 356, 359, 374, 394
Matzel, K., 45, 339, 411
Mauritz, H.-D., 403
McKenzie, D. A., 182, 383
McKitterick, R., 4, 43, 324, 325, 334, 335, 339, 365, 408, 414
McMahon, J. V., 344, 345, 361, 362
Mehler, U., 344, 356
Meier, C., 324
Meissburger, G., 270, 287, 407, 411, 412
Menéndez Pidal, R., 399, 402
Mertens, D., 324
Mertens, V., 64, 66, 186, 214, 296, 341, 342, 343, 345, 346, 360, 362, 367, 369, 385, 386, 391, 392, 393, 403, 411, 414, 416, 417, 423
Metzner, E. E., 401, 406
Meves, U., 358, 396, 400
Miethke, J., 324, 389, 409
Mirbt, C., 408

INDEX OF NAMES

Mölk, U., 402
Mönckeberg, A., 337, 343
Mohr, W., 294, 345, 406, 408, 416
Momigliano, A., 336
Moos, P. von, 237, 398
Morris, R. L., 337
Moser, H., 362
Much, R., 399
Müller, G., 337
Müller, W., 316, 321
Müller-Blattau, W., 380
Münz, W., 396
Mullett, M., 331
Mundschau, H., 82, 346, 361, 379
Murdoch, B., 370

Näf, A., 340
Nagel, B., 376
Naumann, B., 412
Naumann, H., 343
Nellmann, E., 191, 343, 353, 387
Nelson, J. L., 338, 339, 365, 395, 423
Nelson, W., 15, 331, 335
Neumann, B., 346, 376
Neumann, F., 387, 418
Neumann, H., 372
Neumüllers-Klauser, R., 365
Neuser, P.-E., 376
Nielsen, K. M., 337
Niessen, M., 403
Noble, T. F. X., 335
Nolting-Hauff, I., 403
Nykrog, F., 361

Objartel, G., 380
Ochsenbein, P., 424
Odenstedt, B., 337
Oexle, O. G., 396, 413, 415
Ohly, F., 78, 181, 183, 285, 336, 346, 351, 354, 355, 374, 384, 387
O'Keeffe, K. O'B., 326, 331, 339, 378
Okken, L., 405
Ollier, M.-L., 404
Ong, W. J., 3, 5, 324, 327, 328, 330, 333
Opland, J., 6, 326, 345
Orth, E., 341, 420
Ortmann, C., 332, 362
Osterwalder, P., 65, 343, 350
Ott, N. H., 406, 407
Ott-Meimberg, M., 400

Page, C., 336

Palmer, N. F., 355, 364, 372, 422
Papp, E., 354
Parkes, M. B., 328, 339, 374, 409
Parry, J. J., 402, 403
Parry, M., 5, 6, 7, 17, 18, 326
Patzlaff, R., 143, 144, 181, 333, 368, 383
Pérennec, R., 407
Perlbach, M., 374
Peters, U., 342, 380, 392, 396, 410, 412, 413
Petzsch, C., 331, 383
Pickerodt-Uthleb, E., 363
Pinder, W., 414
Pinner, H. L., 334
Ploss, E., 396, 400
Pörksen, U., 341
Pollard, G., 330
Potts, L. J., 407
Prinz, F., 338, 395, 396, 410

Rädle, F., 336
Ragotzky, H., 362, 406
Raible, W., 331, 421
Ranawake, S., 361
Ranke, F., 356, 366, 376
Rankin, S., 327
Rawson, E., 334, 336
Reichl, K., 326
Reisel, J., 393
Renk, H.-E., 222, 396, 416
Renoir, A., 5, 325
Rexroth, K. H., 374
Reynolds, L. D., 339
Riché, P., 327, 330, 333, 334, 336, 338, 408, 413
Richert, H.-G., 394, 422
Richter, D., 351, 371
Richter, M., 4, 324, 325, 328, 339
Riley, E. C., 407
Rocher, D., 416
Röcke, W., 400
Roeder, A., 342
Rörig, F., 201, 389
Rösener, W., 416, 420
Rösler, W., 407
Rössing-Hager, M., 330, 389
Rosenfeld, H., 36, 37, 337
Ross, D. J. A., 344
Rouse, M. A. and R. H., 362, 380, 409
Rousset, P., 415
Ruberg, U., 324
Ruh, K., 330, 370, 371, 393, 396, 403, 404, 406, 414, 415

481

INDEX OF NAMES

Rupp, H., 287, 339, 350, 351, 352, 407, 408, 412, 415

Saenger, P., 29, 319, 327, 328, 331, 334, 336, 338, 339, 417, 421, 424
Salmen, W., 344, 345, 377
Salowsky, H., 380, 421
Sanders, W., 355, 412, 414
Sawicki, S., 404
Saxer, V., 375
Sayce, O., 69, 344, 345, 361, 379, 380
Schäfer-Maulbetsch, R. B., 409
Schaller, D., 336
Schirmer, K.-H., 361, 379
Schirmer, W. F., 401, 402, 403, 411, 413
Schirok, B., 388, 416
Schlieben-Lange, B., 15, 327, 331, 342, 362, 381, 389
Schlosser, H. D., 380
Schmid, K., 373
Schmidt, W., 3, 324, 329, 330
Schmidt-Wiegand, R., 4, 325, 340, 342, 349, 352, 353, 372, 373, 397
Schmitt, L. E., 373, 410
Schmitz, W., 396
Schmolke-Hasselmann, B., 403, 406
Schneider, H., 19, 332
Schnell, R., 265, 311, 332, 341, 372, 373, 394, 395, 401, 406, 407, 410, 414, 415, 422
Schoeler, G., 336
Scholes, R. J., 366
Scholz, M. G., 10, 11, 12, 13, 17, 18, 19, 63, 72, 73, 74, 75, 77, 78, 79, 80, 82, 91, 92, 93, 115, 117, 118, 119, 120, 121, 122, 126, 127, 128, 129, 130, 131, 132, 133, 134, 142, 146, 149, 169, 173, 174, 187, 188, 191, 226, 263, 264, 316, 322, 323, 325, 329, 331, 332, 345, 346, 347, 348, 349, 352, 353, 358, 363, 364, 365, 366, 367, 368, 369, 371, 372, 373, 374, 375, 378, 379, 380, 381, 382, 384, 386, 390, 393, 396, 397, 414, 415, 418, 419, 425
Schreier-Hornung, A., 337, 342, 343
Schreiner, K., 324, 327, 328, 333, 334, 353, 367, 389, 393, 395, 396, 398, 409, 413, 414, 424
Schröder, E., 18, 221, 332, 346, 352, 354, 358
Schröder, W., 18, 91, 175, 195, 321, 323, 332, 333, 339, 342, 348, 360, 365, 368, 369, 381, 384, 387, 388, 407, 408, 409, 423, 424, 425
Schubert, M. J., 342, 352
Schüppert, H., 422, 423
Schützeichel, R., 331, 337, 338, 346, 350, 351, 383, 384, 395, 408, 409, 412

Schuler, E. A., 356
Schultz, J. A., 257, 405
Schumann, O., 356
Schwab, U., 361
Schwarz, A., 385
Schweikle, G., 19, 68, 332, 344, 345, 361, 362, 380
Schwietering, J., 368, 387, 403, 424
Scribner, R. W., 15, 330, 331, 389
See, K. von, 338, 339, 344, 408
Seebold, E., 409
Seelbach, U., 367, 370
Seifert, A., 397, 398
Shaw, F., 400
Sieverding, N., 387
Sievers, E., 345
Simon, G., 400
Skrzypczak, H., 410, 416
Smith, J. D., 326
Solmsen, F., 327
Sonderegger, S., 49, 50, 53, 339, 340, 407, 408
Southern, R. W., 410
Sowinski, B., 400, 401
Spanke, H., 345
Specht, F. A., 365, 385
Spechtler, F. V., 343
Speckenbach, K., 388, 406
Speicher, S., 351
Spielmann, E., 328
Sprandel, R., 18, 330, 332, 335, 373, 409, 410, 413, 414, 424
Staal, F., 327
Stackmann, K., 369, 418
Stammler, W., 270, 407
Starck, T., 337, 338, 356
Steer, G., 9, 10, 328, 349, 351, 380, 419
Stein, P. K., 354, 388, 394
Stephan, R., 336, 344, 357, 360, 383, 424
Stevens, A., 388, 415, 417, 418
Stevens, J., 69
Stevenson, J., 335
Stock, B., 324, 397
Störmer, W., 392, 393, 399
Stolzenberg, I., 373
Street, B. V., 232, 233, 244, 326, 327, 329, 398
Stuart, H., 370
Stubbs, M., 324
Szabó, T., 416
Szklenar, H., 401

Taeger, B., 344, 354
Tannen, D., 324

482

INDEX OF NAMES

Teske, H., 396
Teske, W., 285, 411, 412, 415
Thelen, C., 79, 332, 341, 346, 383, 408
Thomas, H., 403
Thomas, R., 327, 335
Thompson, J. W., 23, 327, 333, 411, 413
Thornton, A. G., 407
Thum, B., 393
Tiemann, R., 379
Tomasek, T., 221, 382, 395, 403, 405, 422
Topsfield, L. T., 359
Traub, A., 357
Treitler, L., 4, 43, 45, 324, 339
Türk, E., 422
Turner, R. V., 289, 327, 411, 412, 413, 414, 415

Uitti, K. D., 404
Ullmann, W., 407, 409, 415
Urbanek, F., 350, 423
Ursprung, O., 350
Uytfanghe, M. van, 408

Vancsa, M., 373
Vansina, J., 240, 244, 324, 342
Vàrvaro, A., 410, 411, 413, 415, 418
Vermes, G., 324
Vezin, J., 339, 424
Völker, P.-G., 376
Völker, W., 403
Voetz, L., 380
Vollmann, B. K., 178, 331, 332, 336, 344, 347, 353, 354, 357, 374, 380, 382, 383, 399, 400, 408, 417, 420, 424
Vollmann-Profe, G., 47, 71, 239, 269, 339, 341, 345, 346, 350, 351, 352, 353, 354, 355, 358, 367, 371, 374, 382, 383, 384, 394, 396, 399, 400, 403, 407, 408, 412, 422, 423
Vollrath, H., 4, 240, 241, 324, 327, 399
Voss, H., 128, 325, 354, 365

Wachinger, B., 341, 370, 380, 387
Wagner, N., 400
Walla, F., 370
Walther, I. E., 362, 370, 380, 421, 424

Wapnewski, P., 187, 386
Wehowsky, G., 366
Wehrli, M., 332, 337, 339, 357, 406, 422
Weidenhiller, P. E., 389
Weinhold, K., 422
Welker, L., 344, 362, 380
Wells, D. A., 351
Wells, J. C., 337, 338, 356
Wendehorst, A., 327, 332, 394
Wenskus, R., 399
Wenzel, H., 114, 126, 342, 347, 348, 363, 365, 373, 374, 392, 401, 417, 420
Werf, H. van der, 331, 379
Werner, W., 356, 375, 376
Wesche, H., 333, 349, 370
Wessel, F., 416, 417
Wetherbee, W., 415
Wieland, G. R., 370
Wiessner, E., 347
Wilhelm, F., 205, 373, 418
Williamson, E., 407
Willis, B. J., 366
Willmes, P., 395
Wilson, N. G., 339
Wisbey, R., 388, 417, 418
Wolf, A., 161, 162, 194, 195, 254, 255, 326, 344, 373, 376, 378, 388, 399, 404, 407, 411, 415, 422
Wormald, C. P., 39, 333, 335, 338, 352
Worstbrock, F. J., 257, 409
Wright, R., 338, 339, 407
Wunderli, P., 170, 352, 381
Wynn, M., 387

Yeandle, D. N., 357
Young, K., 356, 376, 424

Zäck, R., 422
Žak, S., 342, 343, 344, 345, 348
Zarncke, F., 316, 321
Ziesemer, W., 355, 374
Ziltener, W., 415
Zink, M., 351, 371, 403, 404, 416, 417, 418
Zotz, T., 409, 416